Pardon and Amnesty under Lincoln and Johnson

The Restoration of the Confederates to Their Rights and Privileges, 1861-1898

By
JONATHAN TRUMAN DORRIS

INTRODUCTION BY
J. G. RANDALL

GREENWOOD PRESS, PUBLISHERS
WESTPORT, CONNECTICUT

67127

Library of Congress Cataloging in Publication Data

Dorris, Jonathan Truman, 1883-1972.
   Pardon and amnesty under Lincoln and Johnson.

   Reprint of the 1953 ed. published by University of
North Carolina Press, Chapel Hill.
   Bibliography: p.
   Includes index.
   1. Pardon--United States. 2. Amnesty--United States.
3. Reconstruction--United States. 4. Political crimes
and offenses--Southern States. I. Title.
[KF7221.D6 1977]   343'.73'012   77-5940
ISBN 0-8371-9646-9

Originally published in 1953 by University of North Carolina
Press, Chapel Hill

Reprinted with the permission of University of North Carolina
Press

Reprinted in 1977 by Greenwood Press, Inc.

Library of Congress catalog card number 77-5940

ISBN 0-8371-9646-9

Printed in the United States of America

PARDON AND AMNESTY
UNDER LINCOLN
AND JOHNSON

TO THE MEMORY OF
LIEUT. DONALD HUGH DORRIS, USNR, who wrote in his *Log of the Vincennes* on Christmas Day, 1941, while patrolling the Atlantic, before the ship went to its fate in the Pacific: "Peace on Earth and Good Will toward all Men may sometime reign over this Globe, and I hope that I may be able to make some small Contribution to its Attainment."

ACKNOWLEDGMENTS

MAJOR SOURCES of unpublished documentary information were the Departments of Justice, State, War, Navy, the Library of Congress, and the National Archives, at Washington; the State Department of Archives and History, Raleigh, North Carolina; and Federal Court records at Louisville and Frankfort, Kentucky. Much material was obtained in the libraries of the University of Illinois, University of North Carolina (manuscript), Duke University (manuscript), University of Kentucky, Eastern Kentucky State College, and the Widener Library of Harvard University (manuscript). Other places also made contributions.

The merits of the volume are largely due to several persons who read from one to all of the chapters of the manuscript. I am indebted therefore to James G. Randall of the University of Illinois, Frank L. Owsley of the University of Alabama, A. J. Hanna of Rollins College, William B. Hesseltine of the University of Wisconsin, Robert McElroy of Princeton University, William A. Russ, Jr., of Susquehanna University, Ottis C. Skipper of Mississippi College for Women, Douglas Southall Freeman, Edwin C. Mims of Vanderbilt University, William Baringer of the University of Florida, and Horace W. Raper, William E. Keene, and Richard A. Edwards of Eastern Kentucky State College.

My wife, Maud Weaver Dorris, encouraged from the beginning the preparation of the study for publication. Finally, I acknowledge the efficiency of my student secretary, Miss Catherine Hume, who for more than two years typed revisions of the manuscript. I assume responsibility for historical errors and other imperfections in the contents of the book.

J. T. D.
State College
Richmond, Kentucky

CONTENTS

		PAGE
INTRODUCTION *by* J. G. RANDALL		xiii

I PUNISHMENT FOR REBELLION   3

II CLEMENCY BEFORE DECEMBER, 1863   9
Political Prisoners, 9 • *Prisoners of War,* 17 • *The Military Oath and Persons Taking It,* 20 • *Administering the Oath,* 26 •

III A PLAN OF AMNESTY   29
Its Development, 29 • *Amnesty and Reconstruction,* 34 • *Southern Opposition,* 38 • *Northern Criticism,* 42

IV APPLICATION OF THE AMNESTY   48
Administering the Oath, 48 • *Determining the Scope of Pardon,* 53 • *Prisoners of War,* 57 • *Efforts to Prevent Fraud,* 64 • *Evaluating the Amnesty,* 67 •

V PRESIDENT LINCOLN'S CLEMENCY   74
"An Incident of Friendship," 74 • *Denials of Clemency,* 75 • *Partiality toward Kentuckians,* 80 • *Leniency toward Confederates,* 86 •

VI AMNESTY AFTER THE WAR   95
An Avenging President, 95 • *Questions of Treason and Amnesty,* 102 • *President Johnson's First Amnesty,* 108 • *The Plight of the Southerners,* 115 •

VII GENERAL ROBERT E. LEE AND AMNESTY   119
An Application for Pardon, 119 • *The Oath Omitted,* 124 • *An Evaluation,* 131 •

VIII PARDON SEEKERS AND BROKERS   135
The Amnesty Papers, 135 • *The Magnitude of the Task,* 138 • *Pardon Attorneys,* 144 • *Pardon Brokeresses,* 146 • *Charges for Pardon,* 151 •

ix

PAGE

IX OATHS, RELEASES, PAROLES, AND PARDONS   153
The Rank and File, 153 • General and Mrs. Richard S.
Ewell, 161 • General Howell Cobb, 167 • Other
Generals, 171 • Admiral Raphael Semmes, 178 •

X PARDONING NORTH CAROLINIANS   187
The Favored State, 187 • Rules and Regulations, 189
• Pardon Seekers and Pardons, 191 • Holden's Partial-
ity, 194 • Gilmer, Turner, and Graham, 196 • For-
mer Governor Vance's Petition, 201 • Holden versus
Vance, 204 • The Convention and Election, 208 •
The Advertised Pardons; Other Petitions, 212 • The
Last Pardons, 215 •

XI PARDONING THE PROPERTIED CLASS   221
The Thirteenth Exception, 221 • The Freedmen's Bu-
reau, 227 • Examples of Restoration, 234 • Other
Details, 238 •

XII PARDONING CIVIL LEADERS   244
The Desire for Pardon, 244 • Reagan and Stephens,
245 • John Archibald Campbell, 250 • Memminger
and Trenholm, 255 • Mallory, Yulee, and Allison, 257
• Clement C. Clay, 263 • Seddon and Breckinridge,
271 •

XIII PARDONING JEFFERSON DAVIS   278
Johnson versus Davis, 278 • Demands for Punishment,
281 • Pleas for Clemency, 284 • Arguments for and
against Clemency, 290 • Indictment for Treason, 294
• Varina Howell Davis, 296 • Later Views on Punishment, 299 • Refusal to Ask for Pardon, 302 • Release from Prison and Pardon, 305 •

XIV EFFORTS TO CURTAIL PRESIDENTIAL AMNESTY   313
Johnson's Increasing Clemency, 313 • Effects of Pardon
and Amnesty, 316 • The Fourteenth Amendment, 319
• Repeal of the Amnesty Clause in the Confiscation Act,
325 • Denial of the Political Benefits of Pardon, 330 •
Pardon and Amnesty, 333 •

PAGE

XV OTHER PRESIDENTIAL AMNESTIES   339
Another Amnesty Desired, 339 • *Drafting the Procla-*
mation, 342 • *Criticism of the Proclamation,* 344 •
Effects of the Second Amnesty, 348 • *Threats of Im-*
peachment, 350 • *The Third Proclamation of Amnesty,*
352 • *The Last Presidential Amnesty,* 356 •

XVI CONGRESSIONAL AMNESTY   362
Clemency and Politics, 362 • *Early Removals,* 367 •
General and Universal Amnesty Bills, 370 • *The Gen-*
eral Amnesty Law of 1872, 375 • *The Amnesty Bill of*
1876, 379 • *Jury, Official, and Military Disabilities,* 383
• *The Last Removals and Universal Amnesty,* 386 •

XVII PARDON AND AMNESTY IN THE COURTS   393
Early Decisions, 393 • *The Ironclad Test Oath,* 396 •
The Restoration of Property, 398 • *Failure to Restrict*
Amnesty, 402 • *The Effect of Johnson's Last Amnesty,*
407 • *The Personal Aspect of Pardon and Amnesty,* 411
• *Failures of Pardon to Restore Property,* 413 • *Effect*
of Pardon on Claims to Realty, 418 • *Conclusion,* 421

BIBLIOGRAPHY   425

INDEX   441

INTRODUCTION

IN TREATING amnesty and pardon in the turbulent administrations of Lincoln and Johnson, Dr. Dorris is not only covering a subject for which no adequate monograph has previously been presented; he is also probing into topics that are fundamental, that go back to first causes, and that involve some of the most challenging problems which statesmen have faced. When two broad sections are pitted in combat for four deadly years with each side drawing upon war-engendered emotion and assailing the opponent with weapons of propaganda and legalism, with each contender fiercely distrustful of its foe, and finally with one side victorious in arms while uncertainly divided as to a program of peace, the questions of individual or collective guilt are not subject to easy solution.

Part of the problem has to do with the basic cycle or sequence of war and peace. What is the purpose of war? It is, ultimately, to produce peace. It is common to speak of "war aims," but the true purposes of a nation at war have no meaning except as "peace aims" —that is, for the attainment of objectives that are to hold good in time of peace. The business of war itself is to kill, to annihilate, and to force a decision at arms. One may well ask: what is accomplished when war goes on indefinitely? What if peace cannot be made, or what if, being made, it excludes the very essentials of peacetime living and of satisfactory relationships? What if, in the blundering generation of the 1860's, the warring parties could do nothing better than to perpetuate a postwar condition of hateful sectionalism and punitive vindictiveness at the conclusion of a struggle whose avowed purpose, from the national standpoint, was to restore the Union?

What in the legal sense is war? And what is the status of the individual citizen in time of war? Is the individual, whether citizen or soldier, to be held guilty and punished because of great forces beyond his control which have plunged the nation into a holocaust of bloodshed and violence? Even if a great sweeping wrong has been committed, is wholesale retribution the legal answer, the ethical answer, or even the practically possible answer? As Burke said, "I do not know the method of drawing up an indictment against a whole people." And what of the practical problem, not only of indictment, but of arrest and prosecution, of verdict and sentence, and of executing the sentence?

In connection with these broad problems—only partially envisaged in these introductory remarks—there were, in the United States of the 1860's, two far-reaching factors that the historian must recognize: the attitude of Lincoln toward the South and toward civil rights; and the obvious distinction between governmental or legal pronouncements of abstract principle and practical performance in terms of what an army, a general, or a government finds to be a workable policy in the actual conduct of affairs.

As to Lincoln's attitude toward Southerners, it is well known that his own background (in Kentucky, southern Indiana, and even in Illinois where many of his associates were of Southern origin) was that of sympathetic understanding toward the South in general and individual Southerners—such as Joshua F. Speed of Kentucky and Alexander H. Stephens of Georgia—in particular. Of this general attitude he gave full evidence in his devotion to the Whig party, his support of Harrison, Clay, and Taylor, his Cooper Union speech of February, 1860, and his poignantly conciliatory inaugural address of 1861. No one who has studied Lincoln's views and background could characterize that inaugural speech as deceitful, as "double talk," or as provocative. While upholding the Union, Lincoln believed in and hoped for the avoidance of war. One of the tragedies of that frenzied period is that this distinguished speech, so eloquent and appealing as read today, was not adequately received and understood in the South. Then also, as to civil rights, Lincoln believed firmly in all the safeguards of impartial treatment, of fair trial, and of correct court procedures. There were thousands of political prisoners under Lincoln, and one cannot brush aside the abuses that arose in that connection, but there were offsetting factors. The emergency was alarming, and Lincoln's aim was preventive as to the public safety rather than punitive as to persons. No lasting stigma was attached to those arrested; for the most part they were released without trial after short periods of detention. In the case of Clement L. Vallandigham (arrested for making an anti-Lincoln speech) Lincoln was more lenient than the military authorities, and this was typical; often he sought to prevent measures of provost-marshals or generals which he considered unnecessarily harsh or inappropriate to the military function. In commenting upon methods dealing with disloyalty, Lincoln announced his belief that accused persons ought "not to be punished without regular trials in our duly constituted courts under the forms and all the substantial provisions of law and of the Constitution." (Nicolay and Hay, *Lincoln, Works*, VII, 281.) He did not favor an indiscriminate drive against the allegedly disloyal which would result in arresting innocent persons, and on this point he declared: "On principle I dislike an oath which requires a man to swear he has not done wrong. It rejects the Christian principle of forgiveness on terms of repentance. I think it is enough if the man does no wrong hereafter." (*Ibid.*, IX, 303.)

Attention must now be given to the distinction, which is not always sufficiently held in view, between legal or statutory pronouncements and actual performance. There were strict declarations on paper which put those who adhered to the Confederacy, if only because of Southern residence, into the category of "rebels" and traitors, just as there were Southern declarations that Northerners were alien enemies. There was also the refusal of the government at Washington to "recognize" the Confederacy as a lawful government or a permanent entity. Yet this is to be regarded as a stiff principle or a governmental talking point rather than a guide to effective procedure. In other words, Southerners were not actually treated as traitors or rebels. The Supreme Court of the United States held (in the Prize Cases and in *Miller* vs. *United States*) that the conflict was a *war* though recognizing that it was also an *insurrection*. Whatever the theory, Confederates were *in practice* treated as rightful belligerents. The laws of war, embodied in the Lieber code promulgated to the Union armies, were observed. That is to say, for the obvious avoidance of unjustifiable cruelty, the rights and customs belonging to those regularly engaging in recognized war were "conceded" to the Confederacy. Thus as a matter of practical wartime policy Confederate officers and soldiers were relieved from individual responsibility for acts which, if performed outside the pattern of war, would have been criminal. There was talk of retaliation, and mention of it on paper; but if once launched it would have produced an impossible situation. Lincoln

opposed it—for instance, in the Fort Pillow affair—and on the broad
subject he said: "Blood can not restore blood, and government
should not act for revenge." The idea of "anything to win" or "no
holds barred" was not Lincoln's concept.

Lincoln's amnesty plan, embodied in his proclamation of December 8, 1863, was an essential link in the whole chain of his policy
which embraced reconstruction of the Union, restoration of normal
government in the states, preservation of state individuality and
boundaries, and emancipation. He did not favor carpetbag government or needlessly suppressive measures in the South. His plan was
broad and simple; his manner of announcing it was not that of
arrogant command but of reason and persuasion. The pardon which
he announced was general without being universal—it involved
exceptions—but it was generous in the restoration of rights (except
as to slaves), and it was made available to any citizen in a seceded
state who would sincerely take a simple oath to support the Constitution of the United States "and the union of the States thereunder." There was also a pledge to support all acts, congressional
and presidential, relating to slaves, unless modified or voided by the
Supreme Court.

In linking oath-and-pardon with reconstruction as essential parts
of a whole, Lincoln had in mind the obvious unwisdom of launching new regimes in Southern commonwealths without assurance
that they were to be promoted and supported by the loyal element.
As he said, he would "build only from the sound." He had to have
a trustworthy foundation for the governments he was seeking to
erect in Louisiana, Arkansas, Tennessee, and elsewhere. He did not
make annoying or complicated demands, but he did insist upon the
indispensable requirement of allegiance.

Thus began the wartime program of broad amnesty so far as it
applied to men within the Confederacy. As months passed, a number of problems arose which made the program appear less simple
than at first. Who would administer the oath? How could abuses
be avoided? Should loyal men, as well as those considered disloyal,
be required to swear? Would loyalists refuse the oath on the ground
that it was unfair and unnecessary for them? Would not this kind
of question be a considerable factor in loyal Tennessee? What
about prisoners of war, or those under sentence of military courts,

or those under Federal indictment for some war-connected offense? If handbills announcing Lincoln's amnesty were distributed among Southern soldiers, how would this type of psychological warfare be regarded, and would it possibly backfire? Should easy release— something like a jail clearance—be made possible to prisoners by reason of the President's edict? And what if Confederate officers should take the oath with a view to free access behind Union lines for purposes of espionage and mischief? Since the President would be besieged with requests for special pardons, could he give sufficient attention to these demands? If he should be moved to order a discharge, as from Johnson's Island, on a plea that seemed hard to refuse, how could he be assured that such a release would not become an embarrassing precedent? These and other problems show how difficult and elaborate the pardon program became, even though conceived on simplest lines and announced in most direct terms.

Lincoln was a pardoning President, both in general scope and in the particular instance. (Incidentally, as a kind of working definition, the word "pardon" is commonly applied to a release or act of forgiveness given to an individual; the word "parole" is used in the case of a released soldier; while "amnesty" is the appropriate term for a general pardon or a broad governmental policy of oblivion covering great numbers of persons designated in a sweeping category.) When a personal case was brought up to Lincoln, perhaps with a mother's or wife's tearful appeal (often with a good deal of reason) in behalf of the prisoner or condemned man, Lincoln found it hard to refuse clemency. He did, however, refuse it in some instances, as in the case of John Yates Beall, sentenced by court-martial for would-be murder and outlawry on Lake Erie. Though the question of Beall's Confederate commission created a complication, he was held guilty of murderous attempts while in civilian dress. After careful study, the President rejected numerous appeals for clemency and allowed the sentence of hanging to be enforced. If, therefore, Lincoln was in general lenient, as he undoubtedly was, his attitude was not due to weakness or lack of firm backbone. That his adherence to a policy of nonvindictiveness toward the South extended to the end of his life was shown by his leniency in the Hampton Roads conference of February, 1865, and by the Cabinet meeting on the last day of his life when he clearly showed his objection to punishing Confederate leaders.

What happened after the war, despite contrary factors, was substantially a continuation under President Johnson of the program of his predecessor. This was true in spite of the fact that Johnson at first seemed so vindictive that, for a brief time, he was praised by the Radicals. This phase, however, soon passed, and after the new President had lived through the hysterical sequel of the assassination and had matured his policy, he showed his independence, refused to cater to the Radicals, and carried forward a plan of reconstruction which, by the testimony of Secretary Seward, "grew during the administration of Mr. Lincoln." (*House Report No.* 7, 40 Cong., 1 sess., 78-79 [first pagination], 401 [second pagination].) It is true that both Lincoln and Johnson encountered vigorous opposition and obstruction in the field of reconstruction, so that the Radicals in Congress defeated Lincoln's plan of practical and generous restoration as well as Johnson's, which was conceived along the same lines. In spite of this, however, the war President and his successor were able to keep the function of pardon in their own hands. It was the executive power which set the pattern in this field. A vastly different result would have followed if Ben Wade or Thad Stevens had set the pattern as to clemency.

In regarding Johnson's plan in the matter of pardon and amnesty as essentially similar to Lincoln's, one needs to take account of certain deviations. Johnson excluded from general amnesty those whose taxable property exceeded twenty thousand dollars, and he seems never to have thrown off his vengeful feeling toward Jefferson Davis, though Lincoln's idea as to the Confederate President was to look the other way: if he escaped, all the better. The point is that these were exceptions. As to his general program, Johnson pursued a fairly lenient course. Beginning with May 29, 1865, he issued a series of amnesty proclamations. Certain classes were excepted, but the men thus excluded were eligible for special pardon on application to the President if they complied with the oath requirement. One of the familiar factors in the Johnson administration was the granting of pardons to thousands who availed themselves of the privilege. Johnson's own statement was that clemency would be "liberally extended."

An important factor in Lincoln's planning was his reliance upon a rather considerable element of Unionism in the South. He was thinking not merely of Union status as shown by an oath, but also of the question as to how newly qualified Unionists would use their influence and their vote. The oath was set up as a condition of participation in the forming of reconstructed governments in the states, but the other side of the question was that no one was coerced into taking the oath, and, if a sufficient number of oath-takers had not been forthcoming, Lincoln's whole plan could not have been expected to get very far. The war President was thinking of normal times. He looked forward to the withdrawal of Federal forces and the freedom of the Southern people to take over their own regimes. One notes an air of confidence as he labored for these objectives, but he could hardly have proceeded with such assurance if he did not believe that, at least in the foreseeable future, Union-minded Southerners would be in the majority. His belief along this line was of a piece with his basic political philosophy, involving self-rule by the people.

It is not to be supposed that Lincoln's sense of assurance was merely a matter of wishful thinking. This is a large subject on which a good deal of further research is needed, but from material now available there is ample reason to emphasize the strength of Union-mindedness in the South. One need not specify all the factors belonging to this situation, but historians are familiar with the war-weariness of the time, the discontent with conscription, the many desertions, the depreciation of the currency, and in general the painful wish of large masses of the people to have the wretched war brought to a close. There had been in the South from the very outset a lively resentment against secession and an uneasy feeling that the people had been misguided by precipitate leaders who had plunged them into a needless war. The case of Alexander H. H. Stuart of Virginia comes to mind in this connection. Having regarded secession as inexpedient, he was ready when hostilities ceased to promote measures of reunion. John Minor Botts, another Virginian, regretted his state's secession; his conduct after the war showed his steadfastness in Union loyalty. Alexander H. Stephens, one of the most distinguished leaders of Georgia, was opposed to the secession of his state. On June 8, 1865, he wrote from Fort Warren to President Johnson indicating that the war had been inaugurated against his judgment and that he accepted its results. If one studies the records of the United States Court of Claims in the postwar years one finds the statements of a large number of Southerners who presented to the court evidence of their wartime Unionism. Another voluminous body of evidence in the same field is found in the archives of the Southern Claims Commission. As the researches of Frank Wysor Klingberg have demonstrated, numerous Southerners whose records were probed by the commission gave evidence to support their claims based upon loyalty to the United States. Such factors as these show that Lincoln was not indulging in idle speculation when he seriously relied upon renewed Southern allegiance.

In the treatment of Confederate leaders the basic American quality of reasonableness came to the fore. There were a few short imprisonments of Confederate officials—such as Alexander H. Stephens and John H. Reagan—but these men were soon released and allowed to go unmolested. The government enforced no imprisonment or punishment upon Robert E. Lee. His officers and men, with Lee himself, were allowed to go free under parole by Grant's easy and generous terms of surrender, in which, as one knows by a careful study of the sources, Lincoln had a prior hand. (The seizure of "Arlington" was a separate affair—an invalid and irregular one as the United States Supreme Court later decided. It was unrelated to the main problem of clemency. Title to "Arlington" was ultimately cleared by purchase from the Lee heirs on an appropriation of $150,000 by Congress.) What has been called the "flight into oblivion" of Confederate leaders to avoid some nameless fate was, after all, a needless escape. Had these men remained in their homes there would probably have been no greater severity than brief detention of a selected few in some Federal fort.

The one great exception, of course, was the case of Jefferson Davis. He was arrested in May of 1865, held at Fortress Monroe for two years (a serious hardship), indicted for treason in the United States Circuit Court at Richmond, set free from Fortress Monroe on *habeas corpus* in 1867, and released by the circuit court on bond while still under indictment. Here was one of the most baffling questions of the postwar period. Always the government was unready to go forward with the trial of Davis, and after repeated delays in prosecution there came on Christmas Day of 1868 the unconditional and universal amnesty proclamation of President Johnson. After that complete and general pardon the indictment at Richmond was dismissed, and a somewhat technical proceeding on the docket of the United States Supreme Court was also dropped. The high court by that time was presided over by Chief Justice Salmon P. Chase, who, though liable to circuit duty at Richmond, had shown a notable reluctance to participate in the treason prosecution against Davis. The harshness toward the Confederate President, in the two years of his imprisonment and in the menace of the indictment at Richmond, was not typical; it was quite exceptional. Even in his case, however, ultimate complete release was the policy adopted.

These and many other matters are treated by Dr. Dorris with extensive use of sources and with significant contributions to some of the slightly understood problems of the "late unpleasantness." The reader will recognize that the author has explored a complicated field and has grappled with a challenging and difficult task. It is a broad subject which the "history books" do not cover, nor the "law books" either. Looking over the whole problem, and contrasting the Lincoln and Johnson policy with recent totalitarian regimes, the reader will recognize that these two Presidents, though in time of war, kept in view the principles of civilized society. If the struggle of that day had the inscrutable and unnatural quality of a "brothers' war," and if the "road to reunion" had many detours and obstructions, it was nevertheless true that military peace-making was quickly accomplished, while for the look ahead a sense of humanity won out in the amnesty policy of the Union.

J. G. RANDALL

Urbana, Illinois
November, 1952

PARDON AND AMNESTY
UNDER LINCOLN
AND JOHNSON

CHAPTER ONE

PUNISHMENT FOR REBELLION

———◆———

IF THE Confederate States of America existed today, the events of their struggle for independence and the years following would have been very different. In reality, there would have been no Civil War and no Reconstruction as these terms are now understood in American history. There would have been a second American Revolution with its concomitant and consequent results. But such is not the record of those years. Instead, the government of the United States experienced the acid test of a great military conflict, which determined the character of the Union, and the result made the struggle a civil war and not a revolution.

It should be noted, however, that the social and economic changes in the slave states resulting from the war were decidedly revolutionary in character. One might also truthfully state that the basis on which political institutions were established in ten Southern states during the period of congressional reconstruction was likewise revolutionary. Nevertheless, the Union emerged from the experiences of the 1860's stronger and "more perfect" than ever; but unfortunately the gain was achieved at enormous costs, not the least of which was the proscription by the government of those who had been arrayed against it. A people endeavoring to establish an independent nation were given, in their effort, the odious appellations of "rebels" and "traitors," and, in their failure, found themselves at the mercy of those from whom they desired to be entirely separated.

The hundreds of thousands who supported the Confederacy were regarded by the authorities at Washington, at the outset, as having placed themselves in a criminal status with respect to their relationship to the government of the United States.[1] Just what was this criminal status? Furthermore, what punishment should be meted out to those guilty of rebellion? These were questions which confronted the Federal authorities throughout the conflict and even after the close of the war.

In the language of the Constitution, "Treason against the United States, shall consist only in levying War against them, or in adhering to their Enemies, giving them Aid and Comfort." After stating the conditions necessary to convict one of the offense, this basic law also specifies that "the Congress shall have power to declare the Punishment of Treason, but no Attainder of Treason shall work Corruption of Blood, or Forfeiture except during the Life of the Person attainted."[2] As early as 1790 death was made the penalty for such conduct.[3] This law remained unmodified until the Civil War, when the general prevalence and variety of offenses against the government, occasioned by the organization of the Confederacy, called for special punitive measures to meet emergencies. Not every offense could be regarded as treason, as that term was commonly understood, and consequently the penalty of death was too severe to apply in every condition. Congress, therefore, on July 31, 1861, passed a law which provided that anyone found guilty of conspiracy to overthrow the United States Government or to interfere with the operation of its laws "shall be guilty of a high crime, and upon conviction thereof . . . shall be punished by a fine not less than five hundred dollars and not more than five thousand dollars; or by imprisonment" for not more than six years, "or by both such fine and imprisonment."[4] Other laws, passed a few days later, provided that "property used for insurrectionary purposes" was liable to confiscation, that any person using slave labor "shall forfeit the claim to such labor," and that anyone found guilty of "recruiting soldiers and sailors to serve against the United States" should be fined and imprisoned.[5]

1. If the entire population of the Confederate States may be regarded as having supported the rebellion, the number of offenders should be given as millions instead of hundreds of thousands.
2. Art. III, sec. 3.
3. *U. S. Stat. at Large*, I, 112.
4. *Ibid.*, XII, 284.
5. *Ibid.*, 317, 319.

Thus it appears that the authorities at Washington took the practical position very early that the rebellion was something more than, or different from, an act whose perpetrators were guilty of treason and should suffer the penalty of death. A more lenient policy, therefore, was adopted than the law of 1790 provided. And, as Judge John C. Underwood of the Federal Circuit Court for the district of Virginia stated in May, 1867, when considering the case of Jefferson Davis, "It is a little remarkable that in the midst of a gigantic civil war, the congress of the United States changed the punishment of an offense from death, to fine and imprisonment; but under the circumstances," the Judge continued, "it was very honorable to the government of the United States, and exhibited clemency and moderation." It is likely, however, that the jurist had in mind a more stringent law enacted a year later and described hereinafter.[6]

As might be expected, there was some dissatisfaction with the uncertainty of the application of the punitive measures mentioned above. Some people believed the laws permitted too much leniency in dealing with offenders. They regarded the participants in the rebellion as traitors and insisted that the penalty of death should be applied to them. Senator Lyman Trumbull voiced this sentiment when he declared: "If an individual should be convicted of treason against this government, I would execute him. . . . I do not believe that this is the time to mitigate the punishment for treason."[7]

Men like Trumbull, however, were not to determine the treatment of persons engaged in the rebellion. The prevailing opinion continued to be favorable to a differentiation in the classification of offenders as to the nature of their offenses against the government and as to a corresponding degree of punishment. For about a year, indictments were made on the basis of the existing laws, but it should be noted that convictions were rare. The usual procedure of the authorities was to arrest and detain those suspected, liberating them on bond for good behavior when advisable.[8] Finally, the desire for a more satisfactory delineation of the punishment for treason and rebellion caused Congress, in the summer of 1862, to pass laws

6. Dunbar Rowland (ed.), *Jefferson Davis, Constitutionalist*, VII, 173, cited hereafter as Dunbar Rowland, *Davis.*
7. *Cong. Globe*, 37 Cong., 1 Sess., 2170.
8. See Ch. II.

somewhat more satisfactory than earlier punitive measures. Punishment for rebellion was to be more severe. On July 2 a measure was enacted providing that all elective and appointive officers of the Federal government, before entering upon their duties, should swear that they had "never voluntarily borne arms against the United States, or aided their enemies," and that they would defend the United States at all times.[9] On January 24, 1865, Congress required the oath of attorneys applying for the privilege of practicing in the United States courts.[10] This test oath was to become a serious hindrance to qualification for office during reconstruction.[11]

On July 17, 1862, a much more definitive punitive law was enacted. Its first section concerned punishment for treason and provided: "That every person who shall hereafter commit the crime of treason against the United States, and shall be adjudged guilty thereof, shall suffer death . . . ; or, at the discretion of the court, he shall be imprisoned for not less than five years, and fined not less than ten thousand dollars." The next section recognized offenses somewhat different from the crime of treason and more in keeping with the exigencies of the time. Offenders could be apprehended and punished without reference to the more drastic penalties for treason. Any person who should thereafter "incite . . . assist, or engage in any rebellion or insurrection against the authority of the United States," on conviction therefor, was to "be punished by imprisonment for a period not exceeding ten years, or by a fine not exceeding ten thousand dollars, and by liberation of all his slaves, if any he have; or by both of said punishments, at the discretion of the court."[12]

Those convicted were to be disqualified to hold office in the United States forever. Furthermore, "to insure the speedy termination" of the war the President was authorized to seize all property and effects of those engaged in the rebellion and "to apply the same and use the proceeds thereof for the support of the army and the navy of the United States." The process of confiscation was to

9. *U. S. Stat. at Large*, XII, 502.
10. *Ibid.*, XIII, 424.
11. See the case of *Ex parte Garland*, Ch. XVII.
12. *U. S. Stat. at Large*, XII, 589.

affect all civil, military, and naval officers of the Confederacy and each of its member states, and all citizens who aided or gave comfort to the rebellion. Nevertheless, in the passage of this law, a message from the President, indicating his displeasure with its severity, caused Congress to pass a joint resolution declaring that "no proceedings under said act shall be so construed as to work a forfeiture of the real estate of the offender beyond his natural life." In effect this action meant that the heirs of persons who might be convicted under the law would retain an interest in any property belonging to such persons, a condition which the Supreme Court later sustained.[13] Thus the constitutional guarantee against injury by a bill of attainder was recognized in the measure.

But the most mitigating feature of this Confiscation Act, as the measure was called, was the clement nature of the thirteenth section. This clause deserves special mention, since it bears directly upon the general subject under consideration. It provided that: "The President is hereby authorized at any time hereafter, by proclamation to extend to any persons who may have participated in the existing rebellion in any state or part thereof, pardon and amnesty, with such exceptions and at such time and on such conditions as he may deem expedient for the public welfare." It will be shown later that the President already had this power under the Constitution, but it should be observed here that the inclusion of this section in the law suggested to those engaged in rebellion the possibility of returning to their former allegiance to the United States with impunity. It also expressed the scope of the mitigating policy which both Lincoln and Johnson were later to apply in dealing with the Confederates—a policy of clemency which was ultimately to become a bitter issue between the executive and Congress.[14]

In February, the following year (1863), Congress endeavored to define, or enlarge, the scope of the President's power to pardon. A law was enacted providing that, where the person convicted was sentenced to both pecuniary and corporal punishment, "the President shall have full discretionary powers to pardon or remit, in

13. See Ch. XVII.
14. See the controversy over the repeal of this section in Ch. XIV.

whole or in part, either one of the two kinds of punishment, without in any manner impairing the legal validity of the other kind."[15] In this manner the President was authorized to vary the degree of an individual's pardon, if he desired to do so. The pardon, therefore, might be full or incomplete, or it might permit only a part of the penalty imposed to operate.

The next month (March 3) Congress arranged for the disposition of abandoned and captured property within the seceded area or otherwise liable to confiscation. The law enacted applied to miscellaneous property that the Federals found in localities from which the Confederates had been driven. Its provisions also covered any property "whose owner shall be voluntarily absent and engaged in aiding or encouraging the rebellion." The measure further provided that such properties should be sold to the highest bidder and the proceeds deposited in the Treasury of the United States. Furthermore, any claimant of property thus disposed of might "within two years after the suppression of the rebellion prefer his claim to the proceeds thereof in the court of claims," and on proof of his loyalty to the Union receive the money.[16]

The above measures show the extent of the punishment to which persons engaged in the rebellion against the United States were to be subjected. By such legislation the authorities at Washington manifested their determination not to recognize the independence of the Confederate States, but instead to resort to such means as they saw fit to put down the rebellion and preserve the Union. Moreover, the laws indicate the range to which the remedial policy of pardon and amnesty was later to be applied during the war and the period of reconstruction. As the narrative progresses other legislation and conditions which further affected the functioning of pardon and amnesty will also be given.[17]

15. *U. S. Stat. at Large*, XII, 656-57.
16. *Ibid.*, 820. For cases involving pardon and this law see Ch. XVII. An interesting case involving Richard L. Cox of the District of Columbia is in Ch. XI.
17. See Chs. XIV and XVII for laws to restrict the benefits of amnesty.

CHAPTER TWO

CLEMENCY BEFORE DECEMBER, 1863

————◆————

POLITICAL PRISONERS

D URING the excitement and confusion attending the early days
of the war, numerous arrests, indictments, and imprisonments
were made by the civil and military authorities.[1] In those dark days
the Federal government often found it difficult to differentiate between its enemies and friends. The supporters of disunion appeared
to be everywhere—in legislative halls, in judicial tribunals, in executive councils, and in the army and navy. Furthermore, the military
reverses of 1861 weakened the general morale of the North, and
the uncertainty of foreign action further augmented the national
embarrassment.[2]

By February, 1862, however, the general upheaval had subsided
sufficiently to permit a correct estimate of the situation. The line
separating the loyal and disloyal areas was pretty clearly drawn,
and the general attitude of the North was recognized as favorable
to the administration's policy of coercing the seceded states and
saving the Union. Moreover, the Federal government was seen to
be firmly established and fearlessly functioning in the loyal states,

1. See *War of the Rebellion: . . . Official Records of the Union and
Confederate Armies*, 2 Ser., I, II, *passim*, cited hereafter as *Offic. Rec.*
2. Edward McPherson (ed.), *The Political History of the United States
of America during the Great Rebellion . . .* , 152-62, cited hereafter as
McPherson, *Rebellion*; James F. Rhodes, *History of the United States from
the Compromise of 1850*, III, 552-58, cited hereafter as Rhodes, *History of
the United States; Offic. Rec.*, 2 Ser., II, 98-99.

at least above the Mason and Dixon Line. As an executive order expressed it: "Meantime a favorable change of public opinion has occurred. The line between loyalty and disloyalty is plainly defined. The whole structure of the Government is firm and stable. Apprehension of public danger and facilities for treasonable practices have diminished with the passions which prompted heedless persons to adopt them. The insurrection is believed to have culminated and to be declining."[3]

Even though the administration was considerably mistaken in its conclusion that the rebellion was declining, it was right in concluding that a more lenient course should be pursued in dealing with the large number of persons detained as political prisoners. It was evident that there were those among them who were innocent of any offense against the government, and there were others who had repented of their imprudent acts and were ready to declare their loyalty to the Union, or at least agree not to render assistance to the Confederacy.

In reality, the authorities had deemed it advisable for months earlier to extend clemency to certain political prisoners, and many had already been given their liberty on taking the oath of allegiance to the United States or on giving their parole of honor not to aid the rebellion. Now the President believed it prudent to release a large number of prisoners forthwith. Thereupon, on February 14, through Secretary of War Stanton, he directed the release of all political prisoners and other persons held in military custody "on their subscribing to a parole engaging themselves to render no aid or comfort to the enemies of the United States." The order also stated that such persons who kept their parole should be granted "an amnesty for any past offenses of treason or disloyalty which they may have committed."[4] It should be noted, however, that the President's order did not permit the release of all state prisoners. The Secretary of War was directed to "except . . . any persons de-

3. J. D. Richardson (ed.), *Messages and Papers of the Presidents, 1789-1897*, VI, 102-4, cited hereafter as Richardson, *Messages . . . of the Presidents.* (The later edition is cited as Richardson, *Messages . . . of the Presidents* [1913 ed.]).
4. *Offic. Rec.,* 2 Ser., II, *passim,* especially 221-23; Richardson, *Messages . . . of the Presidents,* VI, 102-4.

tained as spies . . . or others whose release at the present moment may be deemed incompatible with the public safety."[5]

Pursuant to this order scores of prisoners were released on taking the following oath of allegiance: "I do solemnly swear (or affirm) that I will support, protect, and defend the Constitution and Government of the United States against all enemies, whether domestic or foreign, and that I will bear true faith, allegiance and loyalty to the same, any ordinance, resolution or law of any State convention, or legislature to the contrary, not withstanding; and further, that I do this with a full determination, pledge, and purpose, without any mental reservation or evasion whatsoever. So help me God."

The oath often contained other stipulations, such as requiring the prisoner to pledge himself never to enter any of the states of the Confederacy or to "hold any correspondence whatever with persons in those states without permission from the Secretary of States." He might also be required to swear that he had not paid and would "not pay to any person . . . anything of value as a condition for interceding for his liberation."[6] Indeed prisoners were warned that to pay attorneys to intercede in their behalf would be an additional reason for continuing their confinement. They were instructed to communicate only with the Department of State in seeking relief.[7] Yet attorneys seemed necessary, and were often engaged by persons needing counsel.

Where indictments for treason existed, a person thus embarrassed might take the oath and receive a pardon, which he would offer in court with a plea that the indictment be dismissed and the case dropped. This procedure appears to have been common in a border state like Kentucky. The case of William N. Stephens of Shelby County illustrates such action. Stephens had been indicted for treason, his case docketed in the United States Circuit Court at Louisville, and the law firm of Caldwell and Caldwell engaged to defend him. Sometime thereafter (June 5, 1863) he took the oath of allegiance and, on being recommended to the President for clem-

5. An excellent account of the status of state prisoners in 1861 and 1862 is given in Frederic Bancroft's *Life of William H. Seward*, II, Ch. 34.

6. *Offic. Rec.*, 2 Ser., III, 52; II, 895-96.

7. *Ibid.*, 2 Ser., I, 614. See forms of oath, *ibid.*, 711-33.

ency by "many loyal citizens of Kentucky," received a pardon on September 2. His attorneys forthwith presented the pardon in court with a plea to have the indictment dismissed and the defendant discharged. The attorney for the government, Joshua Tevis, admitted the plea, and, on October 12, Judge Bland Ballard ordered the accused discharged.[8]

In another instance the accused, William Murray Brown of Shelby County, was charged with robbing the mail. Before his indictment he had resigned his commission as captain in the Confederate army, taken the oath of allegiance, and had henceforth conducted himself as a law-abiding citizen. Consequently, being petitioned by "many other loyal citizens of Kentucky," Lincoln pardoned him, on December 26, 1863, and Judge Ballard dismissed his case about two months later.[9] No bond was executed in this case, but in that of Paul King of Floyd County conditions were different. King was indicted for treason (with hundreds of others in the Frankfort, Kentucky, area) and gave bond for twenty thousand dollars for his appearance in court. The case remained on the docket with some attention until January 5, 1864, when the accused man gave bond for five thousand dollars to keep the peace.[10] Pardon, of course, was not a determining factor in this case.

As time passed, the contents of oaths were often made to include the penalty one might receive if convicted of violating his parole. By August, 1862, Provost Marshal D. R. Howlett of Paducah, Kentucky, was requiring persons to swear, in addition to the oath above, that they would "well and faithfully perform all the duties which" might be required of them by the United States, "with a full and clear understanding that death, or other punishment by the judgment of a Military Commission," would be the "penalty for the violation" of their solemn oaths and paroles of honor. These words, of course, were expected to cause the oath-taker to observe his obligation more faithfully.

The records of the United States Circuit Court for Kentucky give some idea of the magnitude and nature of this paroling business

8. Order Book A, United States Circuit Court, Louisville, Kentucky, Case No. 337.

9. *Ibid.*, Book B, Case No. 469.

10. Order Book B, U. S. Circuit Court records, Frankfort, Kentucky, 223, 234, 265, 318, 319, 414.

ın the border states. The five volumes of "Bonds and Custody for Good Behavior" in the Federal Building in Louisville contain the names of hundreds of persons thus released. The amount of bond required ranged from five hundred to twenty thousand dollars, with principals and their sureties usually sharing equal amounts.

It should be noted that a principal and his surety were not required to deposit money with the court to satisfy the bond. They agreed instead that the amount fixed should "be levied and made of" their "respective lands and tenements, goods and chattels," and rendered to the use of the government of the United States if the parole were violated. If the principal kept "the peace" and was "of good behavior towards the Government," and otherwise conducted himself as "a loyal citizen during the present rebellion," the bond became void.

Occasionally special stipulations were made part of a bond for good behavior. Dr. John Orr of Campbell County was arrested on charges of disloyalty and taken to Camp Chase, near Columbus, Ohio, but was soon released on taking the oath of allegiance and giving bond for five thousand dollars (June 24, 1862). He also agreed to give immediate information to the nearest officer in command "of any hostile movement, gathering, or conspiracy" knowledge of which he might obtain, and to notify the authorities of any person attempting to enlist recruits for, or encouraging others to join, "the so-called Confederate army or to give aid or comfort thereto." If he did not do this, the nearest post commander might "seize and sell or otherwise dispose of any and all" of his and his sureties' properties, "without having recourse to any proceedings of law."[11]

The records in Louisville contain peace bonds for many Kentucky counties. Such obligations were usually attested by the county judges. Sometimes the justices of the peace and city judges attended to the business. The names of many citizens in the state, therefore, are thus recorded as court officials, principals, and sureties. In Madison County, County Judge James N. Embry ad-

11. *Ibid.* There is a great quantity of records in the Washington archives relating to the subject of arrests, indictments, oaths, and bonds for good behavior, but the accounts from the Kentucky area are sufficient for this study.

ministered the oaths and determined the bonds for some accused persons, while Justices Peter T. Phelps and John W. Brown officiated when others took the oath and gave bond. In Jefferson County most of the business was done by Judge Bland Ballard, though some bonds were acknowledged before the judge of the city court, George W. Johnson.

A few prisoners who desired to be discharged objected to taking the oath of allegiance or even to giving their parole of honor not to aid the rebellion. Such persons were either incensed at being arrested and detained, often denying any act which warranted their imprisonment, or they feared that taking the oath of allegiance would jeopardize property which they owned within the seceded area. The Assistant Adjutant General reported on December 9, 1862, that there were "in the Old Capitol Prison . . . a great many prisoners of state whose only objection to taking the oath of allegiance . . . was apparently that their property and families were beyond the lines of the United States forces, and that such a course on their part would only subject them to arrest and incarceration by the Confederate authority and their property by the existing laws of the Confederate government to confiscation."[12]

The interesting case of Michael Berry will not only illustrate this last objection but it will also indicate the nature of the charges often preferred against many of the prisoners of state and the factors which frequently produced their release.

Berry, captain and part owner of a merchant ship plying between Charleston and New York, was captured on October 7, 1861, and charged with openly expressing sympathy for the cause of the secessionists and with flying the Confederate flag into and out of the port of Charleston after the secession of South Carolina. The Federal agent who investigated the case reported at first favorably to the prisoner's early release. He recommended that Berry be discharged on taking the oath of allegiance, since he acted for a distinguished shipping house of New York. The freight was theirs, and though it was contraband of war no one, not even the Federal officials, had ever questioned the company's transactions. The mem-

12. *Offic. Rec.*, 2 Ser., I, 564-748; V, 56. See also the cases of Charles J. Faulkner of Virginia and Charles Morehead of Kentucky, *ibid.*, 2 Ser., II, 472-76, 819.

bers of the firm, therefore, were the principals in the treasonable business, and Berry, the agent. "While they are at large and respected and cherished he ought not to be in durance unless the public safety demands it." Berry objected to taking the oath of allegiance, fearing that if he did the Confederates would confiscate property which he owned in Charleston. In the meantime, the Federal agent had become apprehensive of the prisoner's future conduct and concluded that he should be detained. The prisoner had caused the official to suspect him of planning to become a blockade runner if he regained his liberty.[13]

Finally, on December 3, 1861, Berry wrote the Secretary of State, declaring his loyalty and protesting against his incarceration. He reminded Seward of his past excellent record of forty-five years as a seaman plying between New York and Charleston, of his many distinguished passengers, of his having flown the Palmetto flag of South Carolina from his ship even when Daniel Webster and William H. Seward were his passengers, and of his always using this flag as a racing emblem. He explained that the enemy flag which he was charged with flying was this same Palmetto flag, flown as of old with the Stars and Stripes, on one of his accustomed trips from New York in March, 1861, while racing with another merchant ship in a trial of speed over the same distance. He stated that he had taken an oath of allegiance to the United States when he was admitted to citizenship as an Irish immigrant, and he believed that this oath should suffice. Furthermore, he complained of having already "lost $30,000 in vessels . . . confiscated by the United States Government in consequence of their being in part owned by citizens of the South." He declined, therefore, to take the oath of allegiance again, fearing that, in his present predicament, other property in Charleston, valued at $25,000, would be confiscated by the Confederates if they learned of his oath. He offered instead "to give such parole as under the circumstances would be safe" for him to make and "reasonable and just" for Seward to ask.

It was not until May 7, 1862, however, that Berry's request was granted. The parole which he signed indicates the obligation generally required in such cases. It was: "I, Michael Berry, of Charleston, S. C., do hereby give my parole of honor that I will render no

13. *Offic. Rec.*, 2 Ser., II, 933-37.

aid or comfort to the enemies in hostility to the Government of the United States, and that I will not go into any of the states in armed insurrection against the authority of the Government of the United States; and further that I will not hold any correspondence with persons residing in those states without permission from the Secretary of War."

It should be noted that Berry addressed his petition for release to the Secretary of State but gave his parole of honor to the Secretary of War. In the interval (December, 1861, to May, 1862) the President had transferred the custody of all state prisoners to the War Department. The order making this transfer further provided: "That a special commission of two persons, one of military rank and the other in civil life, be appointed to examine the cases of the state prisoners . . . and to determine whether in view of the public safety and the existing rebellion they should be discharged or remain in military custody or be remitted to the civil tribunals for trial."[14] It was on the recommendation of this commission that Berry was discharged.

General John A. Dix and Judge Edwards Pierrepont were appointed to the commission. These men, therefore, were authorized to investigate the cases and determine the immediate disposition of prisoners of state. General Dix had been assisting the Department of State in disposing of such prisoners, and so the commission under the War Department had the advantage of his earlier experience.

Hundreds of cases involving political prisoners were reviewed by Dix and Pierrepont during the next few months, and in most instances the prisoners were released on their oaths, or paroles, and any property taken from them during their incarceration was restored. It appears, however, that the commission did very little after the early summer of 1862. In fact, General Dix was placed in command at Fortress Monroe in June of that year.[15] It might also be stated that, although the Federal authorities had thousands of state prisoners during the remainder of the war (Rhodes says 13,535), the big problem of that nature was the disposition of prisoners of war. For that purpose there existed a commissary-general of prisoners

14. *Ibid.*, 249.
15. *Ibid.*, II, 261, 277, 285, 1267 ff.; III, 618.

who also came to exercise general supervision over the disposition of political prisoners.

Others (Rhodes, Bancroft, Randall) have discussed at length the abuses and excesses of the power exercised by the government in its efforts to anticipate and prevent acts which, if allowed, would have aided the enemy. Perhaps John A. Marshall's *American Bastile* contains the most virulent denunciation of the government's treatment of political prisoners; but another contemporary, Samuel S. Cox (*Three Decades of Federal Legislation*), is more temperate in his criticism of the treatment of state prisoners. The ultimate objective of the Federal authorities, however, was commendable; and if one innocent person suffered, hundreds of others who were guilty escaped and rendered aid to the Confederacy. If undue caution was taken, the error was committed on the side of right, admitting, of course, that the cause of the Union was just.

Prisoners of War

The above discussion concerns political, or state, prisoners and not prisoners of war. At this point, consideration will be given to the clemency allowed the latter class, especially during the years 1861-1863. The number of persons in the second class, of course, far exceeded that in the first class.

As soon as the Confederate armies began to retreat before the Federal advance, many people, in the border states especially, who had earlier espoused the cause of the Confederacy, began to show signs of desiring to renew their loyalty to the Union. There were those who had entered the Southern service under compulsion, and there were others who had willingly joined the secession movement but who had become discouraged at the first indications of defeat. Both classes gave evidence of willingness to declare their loyalty to the United States. They all preferred liberty, of course, to being prisoners of war, and some even offered to enlist in the Union army, if they might do so.[16] In this connection it is interesting to know that the great African explorer, Henry M. Stanley, fought first on the Southern and later on the Northern side. His earlier service was in the Confederate army, but, after being captured, he volunteered

16. *Ibid.*, III, 335-457; V, 19, 21, 32.

in the United States navy and served the Union until the close of the war.

Not every change, however, was from the Southern to the Northern side. There are instances where the transfers of sympathy were just the reverse. One such case in Kentucky is of special interest because the young man involved, James Bennett McCreary, born in 1838, later served eighteen years in Congress (six in the Senate) and two terms (eight years) as Governor of Kentucky. An account of his action may properly be given here. It appears certain that McCreary, of Richmond, Madison County, was not opposed to maintaining the Union before E. Kirby Smith's and Braxton Bragg's invasions of Kentucky in the late summer of 1862. Had he been in favor of disunion, he surely would not have waited for nearly a year and a half before entering the Confederate service. There is also evidence that he was sympathetic for a time with the activities for the Union of Curtis F. Burnam, a prominent citizen of Richmond and a friend of Lincoln.[17] Furthermore, it appears certain that McCreary offered to serve on the staff of Cassius M. Clay when that gentleman was commissioned a major general in the Union army on his return from Russia in June, 1862. General Clay never took the field, as originally planned, and McCreary remained at home until after Smith's veterans overwhelmingly defeated General William Nelson's raw troops in the sanguinary Battle of Richmond on August 30, 1862.[18]

Soon after this battle the Eleventh Kentucky Cavalry, C.S.A., was organized in Madison County, with David Waller Chenault as colonel and McCreary as major. The regiment was attached to General John Hunt Morgan's brigade in November, and McCreary, who later became its lieutenant colonel, remained faithful to the Confederacy to the end of the war. It might be said, however, that he and many others of the more than eight hundred troopers of this valiant "Chenault Regiment," temporarily organized at Richmond on September 10, 1862, would probably never have fought against the Union if the battle in Madison County had resulted in a de-

17. See "What I Remember," the reminiscences of the late Lucia Burnam, daughter of Curtis F. Burnam, the Richmond, Kentucky, *Daily Register* in March issues, 1938.

18. Cassius M. Clay, *The Life of Cassius Marcellus Clay, Memoirs, Writings, and Speeches*, Ch. XVI.

cisive victory for the Federals, as the Battle of Perryville (October 8, 1862) did. Thus the fortunes of war, and not any long-standing decision or purpose, often determined the subsequent recruiting for both Confederate and Federal armies. Consequently, a desire to return to their former allegiance to the Union was to be expected of many who had embraced the Confederate cause under such influences. It appears, however, that McCreary never wavered in his support of the Confederacy after having entered its service.[19]

It might also be related that two typed, unsigned, and undated articles apparently prepared by Colonel McCreary and found among his papers in his office after his death, in 1918, shed some light on this Kentuckian's Civil War experiences. One contains a graphic account of his suffering and fortitude while a prisoner of war in the penitentiary at Columbus, Ohio, in 1863, after the capture of General Morgan and his raiders. For steadfastly refusing to disclose the name of a guard who had given him a case knife which he used in helping General Morgan and some other officers escape from this prison, he was placed in an underground cell where he came near dying from exposure. The other article is a vivid description of an interview with his father in Fort Delaware, where some of Morgan's officers had been taken later to be exchanged. The father urged the son to accept a parole that he had obtained from Presi-

19. Knowledge of the McCreary incident is based largely on information given by the late Brutus J. Clay (minister to Switzerland, 1905-10), a son of Cassius M. Clay, who came to possess his father's papers in 1903, and who stated that the letter from McCreary applying for a position on General Clay's staff was among these papers. Furthermore, it might be noted that one of the General's daughters accidentally saw the letter of application on her father's desk and reported its existence to some young friends who subsequently related the incident.

Many years later this missive rose like Banquo's Ghost to plague its writer during his campaigns for office, once almost causing a riot at a political rally in Richmond, Kentucky. McCreary always denied having written the letter, and General Clay refused to commit himself one way or the other when asked about the matter, saying, in substance, that what had happened during the war should be forgotten since it had no bearing on one's fitness for office after the war. Moreover, it appears that McCreary, in due time, requested Clay by letter to return his application, but both letters remained in the General's possession. Perhaps McCreary regarded the recall as nullifying the application, and for that reason Clay may have preferred to remain noncommittal on the subject. The late Mrs. Brutus J. Clay told the author that McCreary requested the General to return his application for a place on his staff and that both letters were burned many years later.

dent Lincoln on condition that the boy (an only son) go abroad and remain until the war was over. The young man positively and eloquently refused his father's pleadings, which were supported by his invalid mother's request by letter, was later exchanged, and returned home at the close of the war a loyal Confederate.

The interesting subject matter and the rhetorical manner of statement in these articles are most remarkable. In fact, the informed reader is caused to suspect that McCreary expressed (or allowed to be expressed) his integrity in such glowing terms late in life in order to weaken any existing credence in the story of his applying for a position on the staff of a Union general before casting his lot with the Confederacy.[20]

The Military Oath and Persons Taking It

Naturally, Federal authorities met early overtures for clemency rather cautiously. Toward the close of 1861, however, there occurred instances where such requests were granted. A special order by the Assistant Adjutant General, on October 12, 1861, announced that a "number of prisoners of war taken from those Confederate States now confined in Washington and in New York Harbor will be released on taking the prescribed oath of allegiance to the United States." When the prisoner preferred not to swear allegiance to the Union, he was sometimes allowed his liberty on taking an oath not to bear arms against the United States. This oath of allegiance was similar to that taken by political prisoners. It was: "I do solemnly swear (or affirm) that I will not take up arms against the United States or serve in any military capacity whatsoever against them until regularly discharged according to the usages of war from the obligation."[21]

An officer's parole was worded somewhat differently, but it had the same binding effect. The significance of these obligations, however, was the clemency which the acts carried. When a prisoner was allowed to take the oath of allegiance, he was immune from punishment for rebellion against the government; for it should be remem-

20. The original articles are in the author's possession and are published in his *Old Cane Springs*, 217 ff.
21. *Offic. Rec.*, 2 Ser., III, 9, 10, 52.

bered that punishment for such conduct was provided by law all along. It has already been noted that the penalty of death, fixed by the law of 1790, applied at the time the policy of permitting prisoners to swear allegiance to the Union was adopted during the first months of the war. Even the treason (confiscation) act of July 17, 1862, did not deny prisoners—military or state—the privilege of declaring their loyalty to the Union when the administrative authorities were willing for them to do so. Furthermore, it should be noted that a mere obligation not to aid the rebellion (i.e., a parole) until regularly discharged from such obligation carried with it a considerable degree of clemency. At least the prisoner was released, and apparently there was no immediate likelihood of the existing laws against treason or rebellion affecting him. In other words, the Federal authorities virtually recognized the belligerent character of the Confederacy by applying measures of treating prisoners which were far more lenient than the treatment provided in the punitive laws described in the first chapter.

By the summer of 1862 requests for permission to take the oath of allegiance became more persistent. Such petitions came from every character of dis-Unionist. There was speculation, of course, as to the probable effect which the granting of these requests would have upon the Union cause. As early as April (1862), Andrew Johnson, Military Governor of Tennessee, expressed the opinion that the "reappearance of those released among their friends and relatives" would tend "to exert a great moral influence in favor of the perpetuity of the Union." A little later he stated that such clemency should have "a powerful influence throughout the state [Tennessee] in our favor, and to a great extent make the secessionists dependent upon Union influence. . . ." He added, however, that there were "many cases that ought to be well considered before releasing them. Many of them," he wrote, "should be dealt with severely, while others should be treated with great leniency." He asked permission, therefore, to exercise clemency when he deemed it advisable. Secretary Stanton replied that the President had "the question as to the time when executive clemency should be exercised under consideration." He also stated that it had always been the intention of the government to leave the exercise of that clemency to the President's judgment and discretion whenever the time came when it could be properly exercised.[22] In this manner, Johnson was restrained in his desire to grant requests for clemency until Lincoln thought the time had arrived to warrant such leniency.

In general, during the early period of the war there were three classes of persons in a region like Kentucky or Tennessee who desired to disclaim sympathy for the Confederacy by taking the oath of allegiance to the Union. Later the number might properly be increased. First, there were the ordinary prisoners of war, many of whom had always been Unionist at heart and who welcomed the first opportunity to manifest disapproval of the rebellion. Then there were recruits from the state itself who had cast their lot with the dis-Unionists during the recent Confederate occupation but remained behind when the Southern army withdrew. They now deemed it prudent to acquiesce in the Northern victory in order to avoid punishment and save their property from confiscation. Lastly, there were the ordinary civilians who had aided the rebellion during the Confederate occupation but who now desired to be restored to favor in the community. This third element really belonged to the class known as political prisoners, considered above. A more extensive classification of deserters is given in the discussion of the effects of Lincoln's proffer of amnesty in Chapter IV.

In 1862, apparently, the military authorities made the taking of the oath of allegiance practically compulsory, requiring everyone to carry a certificate to prove his loyalty. If a Confederate soldier returned to his home in Kentucky or Missouri, he was most likely asked to take the oath. If he refused, he was arrested; or, if he was not arrested, he was denied civil and political privileges.

As might be expected, the Confederate military authorities protested against the acts of the Federals compelling persons to swear allegiance to the Union. Especially did they do so in Virginia, where General Lee complained to General McClellan of the alleged practice. The Federal authorities, however, denied having "authorized any extortions of oaths of allegiance or military paroles." They stated, on the contrary, that they had "forbidden any measures" tending toward such acts; but they did make it clear that persons

22. *Ibid.*, III, 335, 457, 642, 659; IV, 392; V, 19, 32.

suspected of disloyalty were expected to be arrested.[23] If these suspects chose to take the oath of allegiance or give their parole, they were permitted to do so. Furthermore, the Union authorities declared that persons found violating such obligations would be punished, notwithstanding any announcement by the Confederate authorities that they would not recognize such oaths as binding.

It should be noted that no general policy of authorizing commanders in the field to grant requests to take the oath of allegiance was adopted until after a cartel for the exchange of prisoners had been agreed upon with the Confederate authorities. To a request for such authority the Assistant Secretary of War replied on June 27, 1862, that "when a system of general exchange shall be established none of the prisoners of war who will take the oath of allegiance and as to whose future loyalty there is no question will be forced within the rebel lines." Nearly a month later (July 22), articles of agreement for the exchange of prisoners were made by General John A. Dix for the Federals and General D. H. Hill for the Confederates.[24]

In anticipation of this cartel, the commander of the prison camp (Douglas) at Chicago wrote the Adjutant General at Washington for instructions "to make the proper answers" to numerous requests from prisoners of war to take the oath of allegiance to the United States. He stated that many of them declared that they had "entered the rebel service unwillingly; some through fear of being drafted, some to escape from actual imprisonment and some from the impossibility of finding other employment." And there were others who admitted that they were not forced to take up arms but confessed that they "were tired of the rebellion" and desired "to return to their loyalty and to their homes." It was clearly evident that the chief motive of many of the petitioners was to evade exchange and restoration to the Confederate service. About the same time (July 31), Adjutant General Lorenzo Thomas wrote Stanton that there were 301 prisoners in Fort Delaware who desired to take the oath of allegiance.[25] He stated further that many of them said

23. *Ibid.*, IV, 28, 29, 146, 151, 251, 381.
24. *Ibid.*, 90, 265-68.
25. *Ibid.*, 312, 314.

that "they would be shot if exchanged," and that a number also expressed a desire to enlist in the Union service.

Early in August, 1862, the authorities began complying with these requests. The Military Governor of Tennessee, Andrew Johnson, was instructed to examine the Tennessee prisoners at their several places of confinement to determine which of them should be exchanged or released and the terms upon which they might be liberated. A few days after receiving this instruction Johnson informed the Adjutant General at Washington that "all prisoners not officers who are willing to take the oath of allegiance and give bonds will be released upon parole to report to the Governor of Tennessee, and all who refuse to do so will be retained in prison and exchanged."[26]

By the end of August other military officials had received instructions similar to those given Johnson. This policy was continued until the following May. During the interval, orders and instructions were issued from time to time to regulate the system. On February 18, the commandants of all the important prison camps were "authorized to release all prisoners of war . . . not officers on their taking the oath of allegiance in good faith." A careful examination was to "be made in each case to ascertain the sincerity of the applicant," who was to be informed "that by taking the oath of allegiance" he became "liable for military service as any other loyal citizen." The application was to be rejected if there was doubt of the applicant's sincerity. Guerrillas and other irregular organizations were to be denied the privilege.[27]

It should also be noted that an applicant took the oath of allegiance voluntarily and usually gave bond for his subsequent loyalty. He understood, of course, that if he violated his oath he would be "punished according to the laws and usages of war," and death was the severest penalty. He was also informed that he would henceforth be "liable to be called on for military service as any other citizen." It appears, however, that very few of those taking the oath were permitted to enter the Federal service. In fact, the rule of

26. *Ibid.*, 335, 336, 362.
27. *Ibid.*, V, 281. See also General Orders, No. 193, *ibid.*, IV, 746, which applied to political prisoners; and *ibid.*, V, 19, 20, 125, 146, 172, 629, 707, 708.

April, 1863, was to deny all such requests.[28] Records were kept of all oaths, paroles, bonds, etc., and reports of the same made to authorities higher up. The War Department supervised the whole business and held subordinates responsible for their acts. Caution was evidently taken not to administer the oath too freely in areas from which the Union forces were likely to retire and which would most likely be reoccupied by the Confederates.

Clemency was exercised chiefly with the expectation of lessening the man power of the Confederacy. Caution, of course, was constantly observed in order to act at the proper time and place and in the most effective manner. The Federal authorities assumed that there were many misinformed men in the Confederate armies whose interests would, in all probability, never be promoted by a Southern victory. If these men were approached under the sobering influence of imprisonment, especially in a Northern prison camp, many would renounce their allegiance to the Confederacy and declare their loyalty to the Union. This was most likely to occur when intimidation had been used at the time of enlistment or when the prisoners came to believe that the movement for independence was hopeless, and that the sooner the conflict ceased the better it would be for all concerned. Personal liberty, home, loved ones, property interests, and other human factors had their proportionate influence on the prisoner.

Furthermore, one should remember that there were foreigners in the Confederate service who were more likely than native Americans to transfer their allegiance to the Union after becoming prisoners of war. Commanders made mention of German, Irish, and even Polish prisoners, all claiming to "have been pressed into the rebel army," who desired to enter the Federal service.[29] It was a comparatively easy matter for these aliens to plead that they had been conscripted into the Confederate army or misled in espousing the Southern cause. Even native Americans made similar excuses for supporting the Confederacy. Finally, it should be noted that many Southerners sympathized with the Union or at least were opposed to secession. If such persons became prisoners of war, especially in

28. *Ibid.*, IV, 393; V, 281, 297, 446, 593.
29. *Ibid.*, V, 240, 287.

a camp hundreds of miles away in the North, they were likely to welcome an opportunity to take the oath of allegiance and enjoy any privilege which might come with it.

While the Washington authorities were attempting to diminish the resources of the Confederacy by allowing deserters and prisoners of war to take the oath of allegiance to the United States, the Richmond authorities were declaring such oaths of no force, so far as the Confederate government was concerned. Such persons were regarded as owing the same allegiance to the South that they had owed while in the Southern service. Moreover, they were expected to avail themselves of the first opportunity to re-enlist, and were otherwise regarded in the same light as deserters from the Union armies were held by the authorities at Washington. If they returned to the Confederate army, in violation of their oaths to the Union, or if they were apprehended and forced into the Southern army again, their status was declared to be what it had been during the earlier enlistment. Furthermore, if they were captured again, the Northern authorities were expected to hold them for exchange and not punish them for violating their oaths of allegiance to the United States. And yet it appears that the Confederate authorities allowed Northern prisoners of war to swear allegiance to the Confederacy, and even to enlist in the Southern armies if they desired.[30]

Administering the Oath

As previously indicated, the commanding officers in the field were directed in May, 1863, "that, unless specially authorized, no Confederate prisoners of war will be released upon taking the oath of allegiance to the United States." This general restriction was not removed until the following August, and it appears that very few special permits were given during the interval to allow prisoners to take the oath. In the latter part of June, General Burnside was authorized to enlist any prisoners who proved that they had been forced into the Confederate service. On August 4, the commander of a prison camp in Delaware was also advised that, in granting requests to take the oath, "it must be shown . . . that the applicant was forced into the rebel service . . . and has taken advantage of the

30. *Ibid.,* IV, 827; V, 845.

first opportunity to free himself from it. . . ." These instructions provided that permission to take the oath might be granted as a favor to the applicant's friends or relatives, "they being all loyal people and vouching for his sincerity. . . ." The youth of the applicant might also be considered, if it could be "shown that he was led away by the influence of vicious companions, his Union friends guaranteeing his future conduct."[31]

On August 17 an order was issued by the Adjutant General at Washington prescribing specific rules to be applied in releasing prisoners on their oaths of allegiance. These regulations were intended to correct the alleged irregularities which commanders had allowed in exercising discretionary power in discharging prisoners. In general, the War Department was to direct all discharges through the Commissioner-General of Prisoners, who should endorse all applications and recommendations preparatory to their disposition by the department through the commissioner for the exchange of prisoners. The applicant had to prove that he "was impressed into the rebel service, or . . . plead in palliation extreme youth, followed by open and declared repentance. . . ." Furthermore, the oath had to "be taken without qualification," and in no case was the person so discharged to be exempt "from any of the duties of a citizen." It should be clearly understood, however, that there were many applications for permission to take the oath which were not granted. The circumstances did not warrant the privilege, and the facts were often too evident that the applicant, if released, would soon re-enter the Confederate service.[32]

In October, 1863, practically all applications to take the oath were denied. The authorities gave as a reason for such denials the fact that there were many Union prisoners for whose exchange provision should be made. These unfortunate soldiers were regarded as deserving first consideration. If every deserving Confederate prisoner's petition to take the oath were granted, the means of securing the release of Union prisoners through the system of exchange in vogue would have been reduced. Judge-Advocate-General Joseph Holt described the condition thus: "It is true that by this process of releasing prisoners on their oaths of allegiance

31. *Ibid.,* V, 659; VI, 31, 175, 177.
32. *Ibid.,* VI, 212, 228, 239, 242, 256, 351, 356-57.

soldiers are withdrawn from rebel ranks, but this is not regarded as such a gain to our cause as is the ransom of our own tried troops from Southern prisons." Pursuant to this situation, the Commissioner-General of Prisoners instructed the commanders of the twelve prison camps to inform all prisoners of war under their charge that no more discharges would be granted. Those who did not wish to be sent south for exchange might make application for this exception. Frequent reports of these requests and other information concerning the applicants were to be made in such manner that the merits of each case would be clearly understood.[33] The instructions, which were only "for the present," indicated that some prisoners of war might still take the oath and be paroled.

In some such fashion, therefore, the Federal authorities continued to encourage desertions from the Confederate service, even to the end of the war. But before the close of 1863 President Lincoln announced a policy of amnesty and a plan of reconstruction which were intended to weaken the general morale of the enemy and cause wholesale desertions from every field of service in the Confederacy. Consequently, clemency in dealing with the Confederates thereafter deserves separate consideration.

33. *Ibid.*, 394-95, 427. These prison camps were at Louisville, Ky.; Columbus, O.; Baltimore, Md.; Sandusky, O.; Point Lookout, Md.; New York Harbor, N. Y.; Boston, Mass.; Alton, Ill.; Saint Louis, Mo.; Fort Delaware, Del.; Indianapolis, Ind.; and Chicago, Ill. *Ibid.* See Ch. IX, first division, for other prison camps.

CHAPTER THREE

A PLAN OF AMNESTY

———◆———

ITS DEVELOPMENT

AN AMNESTY may be either general or universal. When it is general there are persons who are excepted from its benefits; when it is universal there are no exceptions and everyone is pardoned. These aspects of the words will be maintained throughout the remaining chapters, though such discrimination is unusual. Writers commonly use the term general amnesty in either a limited or a universal sense.

A general amnesty to those engaged in the rebellion was suggested as early as the summer of 1862. The probability that such clemency would be granted sometime during the war has already been referred to as provided in the Confiscation Act of July 17 of that year. The idea, however, that conditions warranted such leniency at this early date had been expressed more than a month earlier (June 10) by General B. F. Butler, who commanded at New Orleans. Butler wrote Stanton that many people in Louisiana were "tired and sick of the war . . . and would gladly return to their allegiance if, by some authoritative act, they could be assured that the past would be forgiven." He reported that many prominent men from all walks of life assured him of their willingness to submit to the Union, if their personal safety and the security of their property from confiscation could be guaranteed. It was his opinion, therefore, that, if "a declaration of amnesty under certain conditions could be made," Louisiana would desert the Confederacy within sixty days. Stanton referred this recommendation to the President and assured Butler that an answer would "be announced . . . with the least possible delay."[1]

It appears that Butler received no other word from Washington

1. *Offic. Rec.,* 1 Ser., XV, 466, 494, 516.

concerning his recommendation of amnesty. Nevertheless, on September 24, he announced at New Orleans that "every person who shall in good faith renew his or her allegiance to the United States previous to the first day of October next and shall remain truly loyal will be recommended to the President for pardon for his or her previous offenses." Evidently Butler was encouraged to make this announcement by the instructions which generals received early in August to permit prisoners of war to take the oath of allegiance.[2] The clement section in the Confiscation Act of July 17, 1862, may also have encouraged him. At any rate, in view of the fact that he had been dealing rather severely with dis-Unionists in his quarter, his desire to extend amnesty indicated that he was not opposed to a policy of milder treatment of the Confederates, especially if such clemency would hasten the end of hostilities. Butler acted at once on the policy recommended and soon (August 6) had some 11,723 citizens registered as having taken the oath of allegiance.[3] Apparently it was on the strength of these oaths that representatives to the United States Congress from the first and second Louisiana districts were elected in December, 1862, and the men chosen seated.

Why did the President not follow Butler's suggestion regarding an amnesty in 1862? Evidently he doubted its efficacy at that time. He expressed this opinion a few months later (December 12) to Mayor Fernando Wood of New York City, who had recommended to Lincoln at the beginning of hostilities that New York be made a "free city" and permitted to remain neutral during the war.[4] The Mayor had written to the President on December 4 that he had been recently "advised" by good authority "that the Southern States would send representatives to the next Congress, providing a full and general amnesty should permit them to do so. No guarantee or terms were asked for," he said, "other than the amnesty referred to." Lincoln replied that he understood this to mean that if "a full and general amnesty" were proclaimed, "the

2. *Ibid.*, 576; 2 Ser., IV, 365, 570,387, 393.
3. It appears that this number was increased to 61,382 by the end of Butler's administration in New Orleans. See William A. Russ, Jr., "Disfranchisement in Louisiana, 1862-70," *Louisiana Historical Quarterly*, XVIII, No. 3 (July, 1935), 557-80.
4. Noah Brooks, *Abraham Lincoln, a Biography for Young People*, 353.

people of the Southern States would cease resistance" and forthwith submit to the Federal authorities. He told Wood, however, that he suspected his information could not be substantiated, but assured him that the government would cease hostilities if the Confederates would thus submit, and that he was willing to grant an amnesty within a reasonable time if it would hasten the desired end. This he believed the secessionists already knew, and informed the Mayor confidentially that he thought the proper time had not yet arrived to announce any disposition on his part to proclaim an amnesty.[5]

It was undoubtedly Lincoln's intention all along to proclaim an amnesty when conditions made it appear certain that it would have the desired effect. Most assuredly the second year of the war was not the time for such action; nor was the first half of 1863 much more favorable. The victory at Antietam, September 17, 1862, may have warranted the Emancipation Proclamation five days later, but a more effective blow was required to give unmistakable evidence that the Confederacy was doomed to destruction. Such a victory would cause the Confederates to respond more readily to a proposition embodying amnesty. In this wise the President must have reasoned.

After the victories at Gettysburg and Vicksburg early in July, 1863, there appeared conclusive evidence that the spirit of resistance in the Confederacy was greatly shaken. The Washington press announced the disaffection in certain quarters as revealed in newspapers of the South.[6] The entries which Gideon Welles, Lincoln's Secretary of the Navy, made in his *Diary* for July and August, 1863, show that the Federal authorities understood the disintegrating influences at work in the Confederacy. On July 18 Welles wrote: "The whole political, social, and industrial fabric of the South is crumbling. They see and feel the evil but dare not attempt to resist it." On August 21 he also stated: "North Carolinians are just now beginning to discuss the subject of disconnecting their State from the Confederacy." The next day he expressed the degree of amnesty which he considered advisable to extend to the Con-

5. John G. Nicolay and John Hay (eds.), *Abraham Lincoln; Complete Works*, II, 280-81, hereafter cited as Nicolay and Hay, *Lincoln, Works*.
6. *National Intelligencer*, July 14, August 5, 1863.

federates in the following words: "We could now exact of Rebels the oath of allegiance before pardon, and could perhaps grant conditional or limited pardons, denying those who had been active in taking up arms the right to vote or hold office for a period. Such as came in on the terms granted would build up loyal communities."[7]

The authorities at Washington, therefore, kept informed of the disintegration going on in the Confederacy and were able to determine when and how to take advantage of it. That Lincoln was considering the probable effect of a proffer of amnesty is shown in his telegram on October 4 to General Rosecrans in East Tennessee. The General had suggested that such clemency be offered to all Confederate soldiers and officers. The President reminded Rosecrans of the unfavorable military condition existing at that time in his quarter, and assured him that he intended to grant an amnesty "whenever the case shall appear ripe enough to have it accepted in the true understanding rather than as a confession of weakness and fear."[8]

Lincoln was cautiously studying the military situation to make sure that an offer of pardon and amnesty would appear when it would materially weaken the enemy. At the time of proclaiming such clemency, he also expected to announce a plan for the restoration of the seceded states.[9] Amnesty, therefore, was to be a basis for reconstruction, i.e., the restoration of persons to their former rights and privileges must precede the restoration of a given state to its former position in the Union.

In this connection it should be noted that the Emancipation Proclamation had not been announced until the time seemed opportune. Having determined on such a course in the summer of 1862, the President withheld the measure until the North had gained a substantial victory (Antietam). He then proclaimed it in such

7. *Diary of Gideon Welles*, ed. John T. Morse, Jr., I, 376, 378, 402, 410, 411, 412, 413, 429, cited hereafter as Welles, *Diary*.

8. Nicolay and Hay, *Lincoln, Works*, II, 419. See also *Private and Official Correspondence of Gen. Benjamin F. Butler, during the Period of the Civil War*, ed. J. A. Marshall, III, 110 (Shaffer to Butler, September 2, 1863), cited hereafter as *Butler's Correspondence*.

9. John G. Nicolay, *A Short Life of Abraham Lincoln*, 423-24.

manner that its operation remained in abeyance until January 1, 1863.[10] The delay was largely due to Seward's advice. It was the Secretary's opinion that such a proclamation immediately after the Peninsula Campaign in Virginia would seem "as our last shriek on our retreat." In other words, Seward feared that such an act after this military failure might be interpreted as an appeal to the slaves for aid instead of a determination to emancipate them. In yielding to Seward's counsel, Lincoln stated: "It was an aspect of the case that, in all my thought upon the subject, I had entirely overlooked."[11] He surely expected, therefore, the ultimate effect of the Proclamation to be commensurate in no small degree with the consideration exercised in determining the time of its issue.

Evidently, Lincoln was just as cautious in proclaiming an amnesty and a plan of reconstruction as he had been in announcing his Emancipation Proclamation. Indeed, choosing the time to announce these measures required an even greater evaluation of conditions, since their efficacy would be determined by the certainty of victory and the final restoration of the Union. He evinced his grasp of the situation in his message to Congress on December 8, 1863, when he referred to the recent military gains in East Tennessee, to the separation of the Confederacy by the opening of the Mississippi, to the good fruit borne by the Emancipation Proclamation, to the improvement of foreign sentiment, to the successes in the fall elections, and to the favorable conditions in some of the seceded states, which called for a plan of restoration.[12] These calculations, he believed, justified the announcement of a proffer of amnesty and a plan of reconstruction. The time was now "ripe" for such action, and a "true understanding" would surely accompany its acceptance. Welles states that these clement provisions in the President's message were unanimously approved in a special meeting of the Cabinet, and that Lincoln's contribution to the document displayed "sagacity and wisdom."[13]

10. Nicolay and Hay, *Lincoln, Works,* II, 213, 285, 287; Rhodes, *History of the United States,* IV, 71-72, 157-62.
11. John G. Nicolay and John Hay, *Abraham Lincoln; a History,* VIII, 130, cited hereafter as Nicolay and Hay, *Lincoln.*
12. Richardson, *Messages . . . of the Presidents,* VI, 188-89.
13. Welles, *Diary,* I, 480.

AMNESTY AND RECONSTRUCTION

The proclamation which accompanied the President's message to Congress was of a dual character. In the first place, it offered pardon, with certain exceptions, to those engaged in the rebellion; and, in the second place, it outlined a plan by which the seceded states could be restored to the Union. The amnesty part referred first to the executive's constitutional power to pardon, to the punishment which Congress had provided for treason and rebellion, to the power authorized by Congress to extend clemency to participants in the rebellion, and to the desire of "some persons . . . to resume their allegiance to the United States and to inaugurate loyal State governments. . . ." In this manner the President justified his action.

The significance and scope of his next statement warrant its quotation. It was: "Therefore, I Abraham Lincoln . . . do proclaim, declare, and make known to all persons who have, directly or by implication, participated in the existing rebellion, except as hereinafter excepted, that a full pardon is hereby granted to them and each of them with restoration of all rights of property, except as to slaves and in property cases where rights of third parties shall have intervened, and upon the condition that every such person shall take and subscribe an oath and thence-forward keep and maintain said oath inviolate. . . ."

The oath prescribed then followed. It should be read carefully to appreciate the serious obligations recipients of pardon and amnesty were obliged to assume. Its phraseology was: "I _____ _____, do solemnly swear, in the presence of Almighty God, that I will henceforth faithfully support, protect, and defend the Constitution of the United States and Union of the States thereunder; and that I will in like manner abide by and faithfully support all acts of Congress passed during the existing rebellion with reference to slaves, so long and so far not repealed, modified, or held void by Congress or by decision of the Supreme Court; and that I will in like manner abide by and faithfully support all proclamations of the President made during the existing rebellion having reference to slaves, so long and so far as not modified or declared void by decision of the Supreme Court. So help me God!"[14]

Thus it was understood that an oath of allegiance to the United States had to be taken before a pardon would be granted. The oath, then, contained the terms necessary to obtain a pardon. As the President put it, "The man is only promised a pardon in case he voluntarily takes the oath." The oath also contained obligations of great significance when the items relative to slaves were considered. Lincoln based his right to fix such far-reaching terms upon his constitutional power "to grant or withhold a pardon at his own absolute discretion." He also explained that this obligation in the oath to support the government in all its proceedings relative to slavery was necessary to give the proclamations, laws, and other legal measures "their fullest effect." Moreover, he believed that he might claim the obligation "in return for pardon and restoration of forfeited rights." In this wise Lincoln's proclamation of amnesty was closely related to his Emancipation Proclamation.

Not everyone, however, was to be permitted to enjoy the benefits of amnesty. There were six classes of persons whom the proclamation excepted. They were: ". . . . all who are or shall have been civil or diplomatic officers or agents of the so-called Confederate Government; all who have left judicial stations under the United States to aid the rebellion; all who are or shall have been military or naval officers of said so-called Confederate Government above the rank of colonel in the army or of lieutenant in the navy; all who left seats in the United States Congress to aid the rebellion; all who resigned commissions in the army or navy . . . and afterwards aided the rebellion; and all who have engaged in any way in treating colored persons, or white persons in charge of such, otherwise than lawfully as prisoners of war. . . ."

It was to be expected that Lincoln would except the leaders of the Confederacy from the benefits of his amnesty. According to his way of thinking, they were responsible for the rebellion and surely deserved special consideration which might result in some degree of punishment. This was a logical conclusion and one which his successor came to make. Moreover, public sentiment in the North

14. Richardson, *Messages . . . of the Presidents,* VI, 213.

would have condemned an act of clemency universal in its scope. Nevertheless, as in the case of offenders of all kinds, a Southern leader might make special application for, and receive, an individual pardon, though the proclamation did not so specify. In a supplementary measure the following March the President did suggest the possibility of such clemency.[15] It might also be noted that Lincoln's willingness to grant special pardons to the excepted classes was shown in individual acts of clemency subsequent to the announcement of his amnesty and in his fourth annual message to Congress.

Lincoln manifested his willingness to pardon repentant Confederate leaders near the time of the announcement of his amnesty policy by pardoning Colonel E. W. Gantt of Arkansas. Becoming discouraged with the prospect of the independence of the Confederacy, Gantt declared his belief in the futility of the secession movement and expressed a desire to enter the Federal service.[16] On taking the oath of allegiance, he was granted a pardon and soon received a general's commission in the Federal army. The Springfield, Illinois, *State Journal* stated on December 11, 1863, that this special pardon would convince Southerners who were "sick of secession, of the merciful disposition of the President toward them." Naturally Gantt's transfer of allegiance affected the Southern press differently. The Savannah *Republican* denounced the man as a traitor, who, having deceived his countrymen into electing him a colonel and having failed to obtain a general's commission from the Confederacy, had deserted to the United States (December 29, 1863).[17] At any rate, the South lost a colonel and the North gained a general, while a presidential pardon operated in the transition.

As already stated, the President's proclamation also offered a plan of restoration to the seceded states. The plan provided that when, in any state, "a number of persons, not less than one-tenth in number of the votes cast in such state at the Presidential election" of 1860, had taken the amnesty oath and qualified as voters under the election laws existing prior to the state's act of secession, such persons

15. *Ibid.*, VI, 281.
16. Nicolay and Hay, *Lincoln*, VIII, 410.
17. D. Y. Thomas, *Arkansas in War and Reconstruction 1861-1874*, 394; General Clement A. Evans (ed.), *Confederate Military History*, X (*Arkansas*, by J. M. Harrell), 310.

and no otners might re-establish a loyal state government.[18]

Amnesty and reconstruction, therefore, were to be closely associated. The oath of allegiance became the test of loyalty to the Union and of fitness to participate in the reorganization program. At the same time, those who thus qualified were pardoned for any part which they had taken in the rebellion. Moreover, whenever the number of amnestied persons of a given state equaled one-tenth of the number of votes cast in that state in the last presidential election, such persons might form a loyal state government.

The President's proclamation was also expected to allay the fears of those engaged in the rebellion who believed they would be severely punished if they failed in their effort at independence. To them it had appeared that abject subjugation was certain if their cause was lost. This fear was indeed justifiable. The punitive measures of Congress and the threatening expressions of Northern Radicals naturally aroused such apprehensions. Furthermore, the Confederate leaders and press contrived to keep these fears before the Southern people in order to stimulate their utmost resistance and to counteract any development of sentiment for peace without independence. General Lee's proclamation, as the Army of the Potomac crossed the Rapidan in November, 1863, is an example of such efforts. In part, it ran as follows: ". . . a cruel enemy seeks to reduce our fathers and our mothers, our wives and our children, to abject slavery, to strip them from their homes. Upon you these helpless ones rely to avert these terrible calamities and to secure to them the blessings of liberty and safety."[19]

The President's proffer of pardon and his simple plan of reconstruction were expected to combat such sentiment. Surely, it was believed, the Confederate soldier or civilian, if the proclamation was brought to his notice, would be impelled to look with favor upon the proposition and be less inclined to expect disaster to follow Northern success. This expectation, however, was not realized to any considerable degree, at least immediately. It was not likely that the Southerner who had cast his lot with the movement for independence and who followed his leaders so willingly would allow himself to be diverted by such promises. Moreover, the ex-

18. Richardson, *Messages . . . of the Presidents*, VI, 214.
19. Cincinnati *Daily Commercial*, December 11, 1863.

clusion of his leaders from the benefits of the proclamation did not please him.

SOUTHERN OPPOSITION

The distribution of the proclamation was a rather difficult task, since the information was especially intended for those in arms against the government. The authorities determined to distribute copies of the measure "throughout the rebel country in such numbers that it could not be suppressed." The mails, where possible, were used, and scouting parties made special expeditions for that purpose. Raiding and reconnaissance parties were to contain men especially "detailed for the purpose of distributing the proclamation broadcast among the rebel soldiers and people. . . ." Copies were even distributed among the Indians of the West who had joined the Confederacy. Those in the field who were responsible for the distribution were warned that they would be called on from time to time for reports of their operations and success in distributing the proclamation.[20]

In a state like Tennessee, newspapers were easily utilized in advertising the proffer of amnesty. On December 24 the editor of the Nashville *Daily Press* announced his intention of printing the proclamation for some time, and the next day he earnestly urged the acceptance of the President's proposition. A little later he published a long letter by E. H. Ewing, who lived near Murfreesboro, advising acceptance of Lincoln's offer as the proper thing to do under the circumstances. The writer meant to avail himself of the opportunity, but he doubted the President's wisdom in excepting any persons from his amnesty, unless they were the leaders of the rebellion, who should be punished as a future warning. This letter was expected to be read widely and have a wholesome effect in influencing supporters of the Confederacy to renew their allegiance to the Union.[21]

20. *Offic. Rec.*, 1 Ser., XXXII, pt. 3, pp. 177-78; XXXV, pt. 2, p. 80; 3 Ser., IV, 90-91; also *Butler's Correspondence*, III, 463 (Colonel Alger to Butler, February 23, 1864).

21. Nashville *Daily Press*, December 24, 25, 1863, and January 9, 1864. Ewing's letter had been written on December 17, 1863. On July 10, 1864, the Nashville *Union* criticized Ewing severely for accepting amnesty as a commercial bargain instead of an act of patriotism and love for his country.

An interesting correspondence took place in January, 1864, between General James Longstreet (Confederate) and General John G. Foster (Federal) concerning the latter's method of distributing the proclamation among the former's soldiers. Longstreet suggested to Foster the propriety of circulating such information through him, "rather than by handbills circulated" among his soldiers. He also expressed the opinion that such procedure would "be more likely to lead to an honorable end" than the methods being followed. When Foster sent Longstreet a number of handbills to place where his soldiers could see them, the Confederate returned them with a complaint that the Federal had misunderstood him and had feigned levity in sending him copies of the proclamation to post within his lines. He also accused the Union authorities of violating the rules of civilized warfare. "And now," he continued, "the most ignoble of all, you propose to degrade the human race by inducing soldiers to dishonor and forswear themselves." Foster in his courteous reply yielded again to Longstreet's contention that Union generals should communicate through Confederate generals information intended for the soldiers of the Confederacy, and closed with a statement of the object of the proclamation.[22]

It might be said parenthetically that Longstreet was hardly fair to Foster in this correspondence. He admonished the Federal general "against trifling over the events of this great war," and so betraying "the dignity of his high station as to fall into a contest of jests and jibes." But the only part of Foster's brief and courteous letter which could have been so construed ran thus: "I accept, however, your suggestion that it would have been more courteous to have sent these documents to you for circulation, and I embrace, with pleasure, the opportunity thus afforded to enclose to you twenty copies of each of these documents, and rely upon your generosity and desire for peace to give publicity to the same among your soldiers."[23] Under the circumstances, of course, Longstreet could hardly appreciate Foster's zeal in distributing copies of the proclamation.

As might be expected, the Confederate civil authorities were

22. *Offic. Rec.*, 3 Ser., IV, 50-54; Frank Moore (ed.), *Rebellion Record*, VIII, 296-97.
23. *Offic. Rec.*, 3 Ser., IV, 51.

greatly incensed by Lincoln's amnesty measure. The Congress at Richmond considered a resolution which denounced it in scathing terms and referred to its author as an "imbecile and unprincipled usurper, who now sits enthroned upon the ruins of unconstitutional liberty. . . ." The resolution declared that it was the "undivided sentiment of the people of the Confederate States . . . that there never has been a day or an hour when the people of the Confederate States were more inflexibly resolved than they are at the present time never to relinquish the struggle of arms in which they are engaged until" they have achieved their independence. In debating this motion one member regretted that the resolution had been introduced and stated, "The true and only treatment which the miserable and contemptible despot, Lincoln, should receive at the hands of this house was silent and unmitigated contempt." He then moved to table the resolution. Another member favored this action as an indication of "the unqualified contempt of the House for Abraham Lincoln and his message and proclamation alluded to." The motion to table was in this manner unanimously adopted.[24]

The Virginia House of Burgesses also contemptuously spurned Lincoln's terms of clemency and declared that the Commonwealth would regard as traitors "all who seriously entertained them."[25] President Davis, of course, considered the proffer as entirely unacceptable. He denounced the proclamation and its author in the spirit expressed by the two legislative bodies referred to.[26]

The press of the Confederate capital also condemned the proclamation. The *Dispatch* for March 19 declared that it was designed "to protract the war" and to further the extermination of the Southerners. It regarded the terms as far more severe than "Christian Princes" were accustomed to accord rebellious subjects at the time of putting down a revolt. They were made more ridiculous as an offer, "not to a crushed rebellion, but to a powerful government." This paper closed its long and bitter denunciation of Lincoln's proffer of amnesty by declaring: "We desire no compromise upon any terms. . . . The miscreants, whose atrocities in

24. Moore, *Rebellion Record*, VIII, 21.
25. *Ibid.*, 24. See also the Chicago *Times*, January 5, 1864.
26. McPherson, *Rebellion*, 306-7; Varina Howell Davis, *Jefferson Davis . . . A Memoir by His Wife*, II, 458-60, cited hereafter as *Jefferson Davis, A Memoir.*

this war have caused the whole civilized world to shudder, must keep henceforth their distance. They shall not be our masters, and we would not have them for our slaves." The *Sentinel*, on December 14, after likening the proclamation to the British commissioners' offer of conciliation to the American revolutionists, asked this question: "Is even Lincoln base enough to imagine that brave people, such as the Confederates have proven themselves, would . . . prove traitors to the men whom they have called to lead them?"[27]

The unfavorable criticism of the Raleigh *Standard* is worthy of notice, since its editor, W. W. Holden, had deserted the Confederate cause and was advocating the restoration of the Union. In fact, President Johnson appointed him Provisional Governor of North Carolina in June, 1865, to promote his plan of amnesty and reconstruction in that state. After complaining of a "pardon based on an oath to support certain acts" of the Federal government to free the slaves as being "strange and absurd," Holden attacked Lincoln's 10 per cent plan of reconstruction. He believed that a government based on "one tenth of the people of a state" was "opposed to the fundamental principles of the right of the majority to govern, and would if carried into effect, lead to" civil war in North Carolina. Furthermore, he would "tell Mr. Lincoln that the people of" North Carolina would "take no oaths which their state in convention assembled" did "not require them to take." In fact, he declared that the people of his state "would not rally around a tenth to do anything."[28]

Nevertheless, to the Savannah *Republican* (December 16, 1863) the President's proffer of amnesty seemed to have an ominous meaning. After applying uncomplimentary terms to Lincoln and scorning his offer, the editor prophetically reminded his readers that, even though the assumption of the Washington government seemed ridiculous, it exhibited confidence of victory over the Southern people. "It may be a delusion with them," the paper continued, "but they believe in it and it may be death to us. . . . It shows that we are a doomed people unless we arouse a true sense of our condition and

27. New York *Tribune*, March 29, 1864; Cincinnati *Commercial*, December 21, 1863. The latter paper also quoted the Richmond *Enquirer* as attributing Lincoln's proclamation and message to a recent attack of the smallpox.
28. Raleigh *Daily Standard*, December 11 (?), 1863.

summon all our patriotism and energies for the battles yet to come. It proves that the Yankees consider us nearly whipped, and will use all their exertions in the next few months" to hasten the termination of the struggle.

At the close of the war Edward Albert Pollard expressed (1867) the ultra-Southern historian's opinion of the immediate effect of Lincoln's proclamation of amnesty. He attributed the measure "to those . . . factions which in North Carolina and in some parts of Georgia and Alabama [had] hinted" at peace and the restoration of the Union. To him the President's proposition was "the sound of a trumpet to every brave man in the South to meet and to contest a question of life and death." Pollard believed, therefore, that "the consequences of Southern submission could no longer be misconstrued; they were proscriptions, universal poverty, the subversion of our social system, a feudal allegiance to the Abolitionists and the depth of dishonor."[29] This was indeed the darkest interpretation that could be placed upon a measure which was intended to indicate the determination of the Federal President, at least, to deal leniently with the Confederates.

Thus it appears that Lincoln's proclamation of amnesty and plan of reconstruction received no favor whatever from the leaders of the rebellion. The ultimate effect of the measure, especially that part of it involving pardon, upon the rank and file of the Confederates will be discussed in the following chapter.

Northern Criticism

The Chicago *Times* reflected the most adverse criticism of the proclamation in the North. In speculating on the probability of its being accepted, this paper stated: "Perhaps the South will consent to these terms. If she does, the degradation they offer will not be half as severe as should be inflicted upon a people who could accept that degradation. If she does, she is not fit to be in the Union upon any terms of equality with other states. . . . If she does, her people should be compelled to change positions with the slaves, and be governed only by the overseer's lash. No true American could propose such degradation to his fellow citizens, and the fact

29. Edward Albert Pollard, *The Lost Cause; a New Southern History of the War of the Confederates* . . . , II, 192-95.

that they have been made is proof that their author is either insane with fanaticism, or a traitor who glories in his country's shame. If the Confederates are not dogs, they will free, arm, and marshall their slaves for conflict, by offering still greater bribes than are offered them by Abolitionists, before they will think of submission to the President's terms."[30] The editor was certainly exercising his constitutional right of freedom of the press, and, as might be expected, the *Times* advocated mild measures in dealing with the Confederates after the war.

Indeed, there was a diversity of opinion in the North as to the merits of the President's amnesty. The newspapers of New York City illustrate this divergence. The adverse attitude was taken by the *Daily News*, which called the measure "The Despot's Edict"; by the *Journal of Commerce*, which pronounced it "a ukase from the chambers of an autocrat" and "a device to perpetuate the effect of the abolition measures in the Southern States"; by the *World*, which declared it unconstitutional and intended for "political effect," and believed that it would aid the cause of the South; and by the *Staats Zeitung* and the *Courier des Etats Unis*, both of which declared that no person of influence would take advantage of the amnesty measure, and that the real purpose of the President was to insure his renomination for the presidency.[31]

Other papers of the nation's metropolis, however, spoke very favorably of Lincoln's proffer of amnesty. The *Tribune* believed that "henceforth, it can be neither truthfully nor plausibly said that those who have once been Rebels have no inducements to return to loyalty, and no hope but in the triumph of disunion." Surely, this paper continued, the administration's policy, with Northern support, will "go far to break the back of the Rebellion" and induce the "masses of Europe" to declare more emphatically for the Union because of the President's liberality. The *Times* stated that the executive's plan caused the desire to escape the penalties of treason to become an incentive to resume loyalty to the Union. The *Commercial* thought the proffer of amnesty was "marked by all that tenderness of feeling toward his misguided fellow citizens

30. Quoted by the Savannah *Republican*, January 19, 1864.
31. See the New York *Tribune*, December 11, 1863, for these unfavorable opinions.

that had characterized Mr. Lincoln's former utterances"; and the *Evening Post* believed that "nothing . . . could be more magnanimous or lenient toward the Rebels."[32]

Praise of the President's amnesty policy may also be found in the Washington *National Intelligencer*, which was glad that it contained no "pestilent political heresy" that proposed "to obliterate state lines in the South."[33] The Springfield, Illinois, *State Journal* approved the proclamation and expressed the opinon that the plan would insure a permanent and lasting peace. The editor of the Cincinnati *Daily Commercial* was certain that such leniency would tend to dispel the fears of the Southerners who believed a Northern victory would cause them irreparable injury; and the Philadelphia *Inquirer* expressed the idea that "the most potent agency in giving a happy issue" to the existing conflict would "be found to lie in the pardoning power of the President."[34]

The London papers, like those of New York, were not agreed as to the wisdom of the President's clemency. The *Times* pronounced his terms unacceptable and warlike; the *Morning Post* thought Mr. Lincoln "joking," and advised him to remember that a Confederate army was encamped within a hundred miles of Washington; but the *Morning Star* applauded the President's honesty and rejoiced at his liberality.[35]

It was quite natural that apprehension should be expressed as to the fate of the President's proclamation, if it should ever be reviewed by the Supreme Court. The author had hinted at this in the text. Since Roger B. Taney was still a member of that tribunal, those who disagreed with him in the Dred Scott decision (1857) might well fear an unfavorable opinion in any case involving matters pertaining to the rebellion. Wendell Phillips voiced this sentiment in Cooper Union Institute fifteen days after the appearance of the proclamation.[36] He stated that men of prominence had declared to him that as far as the legal character of the measure was concerned it was "not worth the paper on which it is written." He

32. *Ibid.*, December 9, 10, 11, 1863.
33. December 10, 1863; also the Nashville *Union* for January 2, 1864.
34. December 11 for the *State Journal*, and December 10 for the other two papers (1863).
35. *National Intelligencer*, December 31, 1863.
36. New York *Tribune*, December 23, 1863.

declared further that if the proclamation had "to be filtered through the secession heart of a man [Chief Justice Taney] whose body is in Baltimore and whose heart is in Richmond," then "God help the negro." However well founded this fear may have been, it should be noted that the Supreme Court in due time rendered opinions favorable to the executive's policy of amnesty both during and after the war. Taney, however, died in October, 1864, and did not sit on the bench when these decisions were made.

Phillips also expressed disapproval of that part of the amnesty which restored property to those who were pardoned. The landed aristocracy, he believed, should have been left destitute, if the free Negro was to prosper. He declared, therefore, that the Confiscation Act of July 17, 1862, was "a jewel of Congressional policy," which should be freely applied to those for whom it was intended.

One is not surprised to find disapproval of the President's clemency expressed in the Federal Congress. Especially was there opposition to that phase of the proclamation which permitted the restoration of a state by so few of its citizens. In reality, the Republicans had only a small majority in the thirty-eighth Congress (1863-1865). There was likelihood, so they believed, that senators and representatives from restored states would unite with the Democrats to repeal the punitive laws for rebellion, the laws affecting slavery, and any other measures growing out of the war. This possibility, the critics of the President's policy insisted, should be prevented, or the states in rebellion would ultimately determine the course of events after the war.

The immediate supposition, however, was that practically all members of Congress approved the President's message and the accompanying proclamation of amnesty and plan of reconstruction. John Hay, one of Lincoln's private secretaries, wrote later that "conservatives and radicals vied with each other in claiming that the message represented their views of the crisis," and that the President was well pleased. It has been revealed still later that he confided to his *Diary* at the time such expressions as: "Whatever may be the verdict of history the immediate effect of this paper is something wonderful. . . . Men acted as if the millennium had come. [Senator] Chandler was delighted. [Senator] Sumner was beaming, while at the other political pole [Senators] Dixon and

Reverdy Johnson said it was highly satisfactory. . . ." Perhaps Congress did, for a very brief period, appear to be unanimously in accord with the executive. And why should it not? As Hay also said, the President had kept within his constitutional bounds, and furthermore, he had complied with the amnesty clause of the Confiscation Act.[37]

Nevertheless, there were members of Congress who very soon came to regard that part of the proclamation having to do with restoration of the states as entirely unsatisfactory. They believed that 10 per cent was too small a basis for the organization of a loyal state government. One of the opposition, Henry Winter Davis, just one week after the President's plan was read, secured the passage of a motion by the House to refer that part of the message having to do with the reconstruction of the seceded states "to a select committee of nine to report the bills necessary and proper for carrying into execution the foregoing guarantee."[38]

This narrative need not contain any extensive consideration of the political phase of the problem of reconstruction. It is sufficient to explain that Representative Davis's initiative resulted in a bill which passed both houses early in July, 1864, and which the President received for his approval less than one hour before Congress adjourned *sine die*. The measure provided a very different plan of restoration from that offered by the executive. In general, reconstruction was to begin with the appointment of a provisional military governor in each state, who, as soon as hostilities had sufficiently ceased, was to allow a majority of the white males of a state to organize a loyal state government. Such persons were required to take the oath of allegiance; but office holders under the Confederacy were to be excluded from participation in the plan of reorganization and from the legislatures and the office of governor of the new state governments. Slavery, of course, was to be abolished in the reconstructed states.[39]

President Lincoln failed to sign this bill, and on July 8 gave his reasons for not doing so in a proclamation in which he stated that

37. Nicolay and Hay, *Lincoln*, IX, 109-10, 112. See also Tyler Dennett (ed.), *Lincoln and the Civil War in the Diaries and Letters of John Hay*, 131-32, cited hereafter as Dennett, *Lincoln and the Civil War*.
38. McPherson, *Rebellion*, 317-18; Nicolay and Hay, *Lincoln*, IX, 112 ff.
39. Nicolay and Hay, *Lincoln*, IX, 112 ff.

he did not want to commit himself to any definite plan of restoration. He gave as one reason for this pocket veto his unwillingness to discourage the loyal people in Arkansas and Louisiana, who had already installed governments in compliance with his plan. Furthermore, he also stated that he believed emancipation in an absolute and inclusive form should be provided by constitutional amendment.[40] Consequently, the Chief Executive remained free to carry out his policy of clemency and plan of restoration, as far as he could during the war, without congressional interference.

40. Richardson, *Messages . . . of the Presidents,* VI, 222-23.

CHAPTER FOUR

APPLICATION OF THE AMNESTY

---◆---

Administering the Oath

A S IN THE case of all new measures of an administrative or
legislative character, questions of interpretation and application arose as soon as persons began seeking advantage of the President's offer of clemency. Before whom must the oath be taken? Are
those who have remained steadfastly loyal to the Union obliged to
take the oath before voting? Does the proffer of amnesty apply to
persons already indicted or convicted? Does a person obtaining a
pardon regain possession of his property when it has already been
confiscated? These were the most important questions the authorities were called upon to answer.

The President, realizing the difficulties involved in administering
the oath, sent special agents to some localities with the necessary
blanks. These agents were to assist in enrolling those desiring to
take the oath. He even sent one of his private secretaries, John Hay,
on such a mission. Hay went first to Point Lookout, Virginia,
where General Butler explained "how he was administering the oath
at Norfolk; and how popular it was growing. . . ."[1] Later (February, 1864) he reported from Jacksonville, Florida, that he had
posted copies of the proclamation so that the general public could
see them, that he had also explained the purpose of the measure
to the Confederate prisoners there, and that he had announced his

---

1. Charles H. McCarthy, *Lincoln's Plan of Reconstruction*, 27, cited hereafter as McCarthy, *Lincoln's Plan*; W. R. Thayer, *The Life and Letters of
John Hay*, 142, cited hereafter as Thayer, *John Hay*.

readiness to register those who desired to take the oath. He stated further that sixty oaths were administered the first day, in some instances to "men of substance and influence."

It is interesting to note Hay's description of the broken spirits of these men as they accepted the offer of pardon. "They soon came," he said, "a dirty swarm of grey coats, and filed into the room escorted by a negro guard. Fate had done its worst for the poor devils. Even a nigger guard didn't seem to excite a feeling of resentment. They stood for a moment in awkward attitudes along the walls. . . . I soon found they had come up in good earnest to sign their names. . . . They all stood up in line and held up their hands while I read the oath. As I concluded, the negro sergeant came up, saluted and said: 'dere's one dat didn't hole up his hand.' They began to sign—some still stuck, hesitated and asked questions, some wrote good hands, but most bad. Nearly half made their mark." On the whole, however, Hay found no general disposition among the citizens of Florida to take the oath, so he soon returned to Washington, expressing the opinion that the "President's 10th" could not be obtained in that state.[2]

Andrew Johnson, Military Governor of Tennessee, soon desired to have the first two questions mentioned above answered. He was informed that the "oath might be administered by the Military Governor, the military commander of the Department, and by all other persons designated by them for that purpose."[3] The answer to the second question was of greater moment. Those who remained loyal to the Union protested vigorously against taking the oath and being classified with the secessionists. As John Lellyett put it, were the "host of noble East Tennesseans who have languished in prisons, and have been hunted in the mountains, and fought and bled in their country's armies," denied the privilege of participating in reconstruction until they had taken the amnesty oath? Must the fearless Parson William G. Brownlow swear allegiance to his country before being allowed to vote? Surely the tens of thousands of loyal men of Tennessee who had "voted for the Union in the dark days of 1861" would not be required "to take a certain oath or be excluded from the exercise of the right of suffrage . . . in the

2. Thayer, *John Hay*, 162-66, 170-80.
3. *Offic. Rec.*, 3 Ser., IV, 31, 46.

reconstruction of their State Government."[4] Such protests, however, were in vain, for Lincoln said: "Loyal as well as disloyal shall
take the oath because it does not hurt them, clears all questions as
to right to vote, and swells the aggregate number who take it, which
is an important object."[5]

It was quite natural that loyal Tennesseans should feel highly
indignant on being required to take the oath of allegiance with those
who had been notoriously disloyal. Their protests were so insistent
that a plan was proposed, but not adopted, to place "a sharp distinction between them and the disloyalists who had recovered the ballot
with amnesty . . . by dividing the oathtakers into two separate lists—
a loyal men's record and a disloyal men's record. . . ." The first
list would have constituted a "roll of honor" from which those who
had aided the Confederacy would have been excluded.[6]

There were also those in Tennessee who believed that one-tenth
was too small a number to be permitted to restore the state to its
former condition. The provision, they said, might operate so as to
permit some fourteen thousand former secessionists to govern a
million people, fifty thousand or more of whose voters had remained
loyal to the Union.This estimate, of course, was based on the assumption that the loyalists would refuse to take the oath on the
grounds that it was not fair to require it of them.[7] Many of these
objectors also believed that the President should have excepted
many others from his amnesty. Such exceptions would have lessened
the likelihood of amnestied Confederates' getting control of the
government in a state where there was a considerable loyal population, as there was in Tennessee.

Governor Johnson was of the opinion that the President's oath
was too liberal as a test for permission to participate in the reor-

4. Nashville *Dispatch*, January 8, 1864. See also *National Intelligencer*,
December 31, 1863, January 4, 1864; C. R. Hall, *Andrew Johnson, Military
Governor of Tennessee*, 113, cited hereafter as Hall, *Andrew Johnson*; James
Walter Fertig, *The Secession and Reconstruction of Tennessee*, 47.

5. Stanton Papers (Library of Congress), XX (Johnson to Horace Maynard, January 14, 1864); Lincoln Photostats (Library of Congress; Lincoln
to Johnson, January 25, 1864); *Offic. Rec.*, 3 Ser., IV, 46; Hall, *Andrew
Johnson*, 113.

6. Hall, *Andrew Johnson*, 113.

7. Nashville *Dispatch*, January 8, 1864. John Lellyett voiced this objection
in the *Dispatch*.

ganization of Tennessee. In preparation for the first elections, therefore, he announced a more stringent oath for the privilege of participation therein. One was required to swear that he would henceforth support and defend the Federal Constitution; that he would freely and faithfully observe all the obligations of citizenship in the United States; that he desired the success of the Northern armies and the speedy enforcement of the laws of the United States throughout the Union; and lastly that he would "aid and assist . . . in the accomplishment of these results."[8]

The question immediately arose as to whose amnesty oath should be administered. Some objected to the President's oath as a test not required by the laws of Tennessee. The Governor's test was still more objectionable, because it required a declaration of one's "desires." "I own it," John Lellyett complained, "as an unheard of inquisition, contrary to the genius of our institutions, to swear one concerning his desires. It brings the citizen to a confessional— a sworn confessional." And yet this objector advised all "honest citizens . . . to allow no paltry scruples . . . to deter them from resuming their position as the Sovereigns of this country. Take the oath," he said, "and vote."[9]

A week earlier (February 23) the Nashville *Dispatch*, in discussing the merits of the two oaths, had said: "The truly loyal who sincerely wish the restoration of the Union . . . will take Governor Johnson's oath, while those who have no such sympathies may possibly take the amnesty oath in order to save their property; but not without the forfeiture of self-respect. No discrimination is perfectly just. None but true men should be allowed to vote, while amnesty may be granted to all who will honestly pledge themselves to be faithful in the future to the laws and Constitution." Nevertheless, when the President was asked to set aside Johnson's proclamation, he refused, saying that there was "no conflict" between the two oaths and that the use of Johnson's plan would avoid "conflict and confusion."[10]

Apparently Johnson was not at all satisfied with the operation

8. Hall, *Andrew Johnson*, 113-19; McCarthy, *Lincoln's Plan*, 27; Moore, *Rebellion Record*, VIII, doc. 340; *Offic. Rec.*, 3 Ser., IV, 31.

9. Nashville *Dispatch*, February 5, March 2, 1864.

10. Lincoln Photostats (Library of Congress; Lincoln to Johnson, February 21, 1864); Nicolay and Hay, *Lincoln, Works*, II, 486-87.

of the President's amnesty measure in his state. He believed that it did not cause those for whom it was especially intended to manifest the proper respect for the power from which it came. He told Lincoln, therefore, "that Tennessee should be made an exception," and that those who deserved pardon should apply "directly to the President." This procedure, he believed, would cause them to "feel under a much greater obligation to the government."[11]

Lincoln, apparently, saw no reason for such an exception and allowed his plan to operate in Tennessee. Nevertheless, when the time came to choose presidential electors, Johnson, encouraged by a convention in which he had been the dominant personality, proclaimed another oath to be taken by those desiring to vote in this election. It differed from his first by requiring a greater expression of submission on the part of those who were not exactly in accord with the strong Unionists. One was required to swear that he would "henceforth support the Constitution of the United States"; that he was "an active friend" of the Union; that he rejoiced "in the triumph of its armies and navies"; that he would oppose all efforts for peace until the former status of the Union was achieved; that he would do his utmost toward "the attainment of these ends"; and that he took the oath "voluntarily and without mental reservation."[12]

There was considerable dissatisfaction with parts of this oath. The affirmations "to rejoice in the triumph" of the Union forces and to refrain from all efforts to establish peace until authority at Washington was re-established throughout the Union were especially objectionable. Such complete transformation could hardly be expected of many whose sympathies had once been with the Confederacy, or who had not been in sympathy with the policies of the administration at Washington. Furthermore, the Governor's proclamation was denounced as an unauthorized modification of the election laws of the state, and therefore entirely illegal. Many of the objects of the proclamation had taken the President's amnesty oath, had received a "full pardon," and consequently regarded themselves as "fully entitled to vote and exercise all other rights belonging to loyal citizens, without let or hindrance. . . ."[13]

11. Stanton Papers, XXI (Johnson to Lincoln, May 17, 1864).
12. Hall, *Andrew Johnson*, 143-45; McPherson, *Rebellion*, 436.
13. McPherson, *Rebellion*, 438-39.

The President, however, could not be induced to interfere with the Governor's procedure, justifying his refusal on constitutional grounds. He also suggested the impossibility of conducting an election in Tennessee "in strict accordance with the old Code of the State"; and for that reason he permitted Johnson to carry out his plan, reminding his petitioners that only Congress could determine whether the electors chosen in their state would be "entitled to be counted." Consequently, the President's refusal to interfere in Tennessee was interpreted as a declaration on his part to support Johnson, whose methods were regarded by many as revolutionary and intended to insure the re-election of Lincoln. Those who were opposed to Lincoln's re-election, therefore, announced the withdrawal of the "McClellan electoral ticket in Tennessee";[14] and Congress, exercising the power which Lincoln said it possessed, refused to count that state's electoral vote.

Determining the Scope of Pardon

As one might expect, persons under Federal indictment or conviction began at once to seek pardon under the President's proclamation. On December 15, the President informed a judge in San Francisco that the amnesty oath was "not for those who may be constrained to take it in order to escape actual imprisonment or punishment." A little later (December 31), when the case of a man under conviction to be hanged as a spy and for violating his oath of allegiance was brought to his attention, he decided that his offer of amnesty did "not extend to prisoners of war, or to persons suffering punishment under the sentence of military courts, or on trial or under charge for military offenses." The official who made known this decision stated that a "general jail clearing" could certainly not have been contemplated in the proclamation, and that such a result was in every way to be deplored.[15]

But it has never been within the province of the Chief Executive to pass upon the legality or constitutionality of his acts. The President's interpretation of the application of his proclamation, therefore, did not stand the test of the courts. Ridgely Greathouse,

14. *Ibid.*, 425, 441.
15. *Offic. Rec.*, 2 Ser., VI, 705, 802, 803.

serving a sentence in California for treasonable acts, desired to take advantage of the proclamation to secure his freedom. His action was opposed on the ground that the proffer of pardon did not apply to those already convicted and incarcerated. This stand conformed to the President's instructions noted above. The Federal circuit court for northern California, however, overruled this argument and allowed the proclamation to apply, there being nothing in the document to the contrary. The measure, the court declared, "embraces not only rebels in arms . . . but also such as are already arrested and incarcerated." The proclamation, therefore, was to be construed "like any other public act or law . . . irrespective of any opinion or . . . unexpressed intention of its author."[16]

The effect of a pardon on the application of the confiscation laws was also questioned. The proclamation promised "restoration of all rights of property except as to slaves, and in property cases where rights of third parties shall have intervened. . . ." The latter exception applied, of course, to property which had already been sold under the law and a bona fide title acquired by the purchaser. It was reported at Washington, however, that Confederate officers told "their men that the amnesty . . . if taken by individuals would still leave property liable to confiscation." To give greater assurance, therefore, that a pardon would restore a person's property, it was suggested, but not acted upon, "that Congress pass a resolution approving the President's amnesty proclamation."[17] Such sanction would have strengthened confidence in the executive's measure.

So many questions arose over the application of the proclamation that the Department of Justice addressed a circular letter, on February 19, 1864, to the United States district attorneys, which was to regulate the disposition of pardon cases.[18] In the first place, those who had taken the oath in good faith were "entitled . . . to all rights of property, except as to slaves and where rights of third parties" had intervened. Furthermore, a pardon removed an indictment or conviction and became sufficient reason for discontinuing criminal proceedings against the accused. This was con-

16. *Federal Cases*, No. 15254.
17. *Offic. Rec.*, 2 Ser., VI, 937.
18. McPherson, *Rebellion*, 148-49.

trary to the President's explanation of December 31, but it was in harmony with the decision in the Greathouse case.

These instructions also stated that, notwithstanding "any other sources of power in the President," the executive was authorized by section 13 of the Confiscation Act of July 17, 1862,[19] to grant, at his own discretion and by proclamation, pardon and amnesty at any time and on such conditions as he might think advisable. This provision, the letter continued, was without doubt intended to free "persons from the penalty of loss of their property by confiscation." Pardon was also explained as arresting and ending "all penal proceedings founded thereon, whether they touch the persons or the property of the offender."

The district attorneys were instructed, therefore, to dismiss cases of persons charged with acts of rebellion when they showed evidence of having complied with the President's proclamation, provided they were not of the excepted classes. The pardon itself was not necessary to stop proceedings; the mere taking of the oath in good faith and the placing of one's self "within the condition set forth in the proclamation" were all that was necessary. When it appeared that the oath was taken for the purpose of regaining the possession of "property seized under the confiscation acts, with intent to remove it from the subsequent reach of the officers of the law," the case was to be submitted to the Attorney-General's office before taking final action.

Lastly, the letter stated that the President, under his amnesty measure, might not remit forfeitures classified as prizes of war as specified by the law of July 13, 1861.[20] This power was "not within the scope of his proclamation of pardon," since the law provided otherwise. Nevertheless, attorneys were informed that, when owners of property affected by this act complied with the proclamation, the authorities would remit such forfeitures in the same generous spirit that inspired the President's liberality.

These instructions were extensive in their scope, giving magisterial power where there was any question concerning the President's amnesty. To be sure, the proclamation stated plainly what should constitute a bona fide application for pardon and what classes were

19. See Ch. I for this law.
20. *U. S. Stat. at Large*, XII, 255-58.

excepted from its benefits. It also defined the conditions under which property would be restored. Nevertheless, there were often complications requiring judicious discrimination. As one editor said, the district attorneys were "not only to decide in what cases the rights of third parties have intervened, but also whether the party seeking to be relieved has taken the oath in good faith or not."[21]

It does not require much effort to perceive the difficulties which might be involved in a pardon case. Contracts, leases, confiscations, sales, oaths, etc. suggest litigation of a complicated character, especially when property rights were at stake. One is not surprised, therefore, to find objectors to this delegation of authority. "Everybody abides by the judgment of a regularly constituted judicial tribunal," the critics said, "acquiescing in it, [even] if he does not approve it. But who will consent to be bound, or who *is* bound, by a decision proceeding from an office invested with magisterial functions unknown to the law?"[22] They believed, of course, that such questions should be determined in a regular law court.

The foregoing shows that the proclamation of pardon and amnesty was not satisfactory even to its author. It was regarded as being too liberal in its application to "insurgent enemies" who were being prosecuted, or who were already convicted and in confinement. It also failed to state who might administer the oath, and what provision was to be made for the certification and disposition of the oath after it had been administered. Furthermore, it should be noted that the court in the case of Greathouse annulled the President's interpretation of the application of his plan of amnesty.[23] Moreover, the pressure of prisoners of war for permission to take the oath was becoming insistent. These conditions made it plain that the proclamation needed supplementing. Accordingly, the President issued an explanatory proclamation on March 26, 1864, defining the application of his former measure.[24] In this manner his

21. New York *Tribune*, February 24, 1864.
22. *Ibid.*
23. See also the case of *United States* vs. *Hughes, Federal Cases*, No. 15416 (Bond 574).
24. Lincoln Papers (Library of Congress; Lincoln to Stanton, March 18, 1864); *Annual Cyclopedia*, 1864, p. 778; Richardson, *Messages . . . of the Presidents*, VI, 218.

act had the force of law, which his instructions of the previous December did not have.

The second proclamation stated that the first did "not apply to the cases of persons who, at the time when they seek to obtain the benefits thereof . . . are in military, naval, or civil confinement or custody," or otherwise under the restraint of the Federal authorities. It applied "only to those persons who being yet at large and free from arrest, confinement, or duress, shall voluntarily come forward and take the said oath with the purpose of restoring peace and establishing the national authority." Thus a seventh exception was added to the earlier proclamation. Those in the excluded classes, however, might "apply to the President for clemency, like all other offenders," and they would "receive due consideration."

The proclamation also provided that the oath might "be taken and subscribed before any commissioned officer . . . in the service of the United States," or any loyal state officer "qualified for administering oaths." Such officers were to issue certificates to those taking the oath, and "to transmit the original records of such oaths . . . to the Department of State." This proclamation, therefore, supplemented the previous one and, in reality, was defined by the courts as in effect a part of the first.

PRISONERS OF WAR

Notwithstanding President Lincoln's decision of December 31 that his proclamation of amnesty did not extend to prisoners of war, he chose to pardon such prisoners when he saw fit. Two days after this order he instructed General Butler, at Fortress Monroe, "to discharge of the prisoners at Point Lookout, Virginia," the following classes: "*First.* Those who will take the oath prescribed in the proclamation of December 8, and . . . will enlist in our service. *Second.* Those who will take the oath and be discharged and whose homes lie safely within our military lines." In fact, it appears that Butler was encouraged to assemble prisoners from other places at Point Lookout, not only for the purpose of exchange but also with the intention of encouraging them to desert the Confederate cause. The prisoners were to arrive "there in time enough to have the four questions directed by the President put to each one of them. . . . Every prisoner at Point Lookout," Butler reported, "had recorded his name under one of the four questions." At the same time, he also reported that he had nearly a regiment recruited of such persons.[25]

The test the President had provided for the disposition of these prisoners consisted of four questions which everyone was obliged to answer. They were: "First. Do you desire to be sent South as a prisoner of war for exchange? Second. Do you desire to take the oath of allegiance and parole, and enlist in the Army or Navy of the United States; and if so, in which? Third. Do you desire to take the oath and parole, and be sent North to work on public works, under the penalty of death if found in the South before the end of the war? Fourth. Do you desire to take the oath of allegiance and go to your home within the lines of the United States?"[26] In this manner the prisoners were to be classified and disposed of.

Butler was of the opinion that many would take the oath and break it immediately, "if by that means they could get out of prison." Nevertheless, he had the proclamation of amnesty fairly read and explained to squads of prisoners. "The object," he said, "is that no rebel prisoner shall go South who desires to take the oath. But the offer must not be made to them until they are paroled and ready to go South, in order that they may not seem to take it under duress."[27]

The nature of the operations at Point Lookout may be found in a communication from General Lew Wallace at Baltimore and the answer thereto. The General inquired of the authorities at Washington (April 15, 1864) to know what to do with "150 rebel soldiers here who have taken the oath of allegiance under the President's proclamation of December 8." These prisoners had been sent to Baltimore by General Butler and had evidently answered affirmatively the third question above. Wallace was instructed to send the men North and thereby comply with the general orders covering such conditions.[28]

It should be noted that the President's second proclamation

25. *Offic. Rec.*, 2 Ser., VI, 768, 808, 1033.
26. *Ibid.*, 823; *Butler's Correspondence*, III, 507.
27. *Butler's Correspondence*, III, 238 ff.
28. *Offic. Rec.*, 2 Ser., VII, 56.

stated that his plan did not admit to amnesty, except by special application, any "persons . . . in military, naval, or civil confinement. . . ." One is not surprised, therefore, to find that Butler's instructions "directing the discharge of prisoners of war on taking the oath of allegiance" were soon suspended (May 29, 1864). This policy was adhered to pretty closely during the remainder of the war. Military officers, of course, at times paroled prisoners who enjoyed their liberty until they were exchanged; but the privilege of passing upon applications for pardon they no longer enjoyed. Instead, they were informed that "rolls of prisoners desiring to take the oath" should be forwarded "to Washington for consideration"; and it might be added that apparently all bona fide petitions were acted upon favorably.[29]

As might be expected, prisoners who expressed a desire to transfer their support to the Union were not very popular among their fellows who remained loyal to the Confederacy. The following complaint illustrates the point. A private, imprisoned in Camp Douglas, Chicago, wrote his parents in Madison County, Kentucky, on December 3, 1863, as follows: ". . . I am sorry for our regiment. I do not know what we will do if all the commissioned officers take the oath. I believe it will play out entirely."[30] Evidently the writer was displeased with desertions among his fellow prisoners, even before the proclamation of amnesty was announced. Indeed, complaints of intimidation and violence toward those taking the oath became rather serious. A commander of a Northern prison camp, for example, wrote that "a persistent effort to intimidate men in the prison who show the least disposition to yield to the United States" was being made. "Their roommates drive them out of the quarters at night," he said, "and personal violence is . . . often inflicted on those who are suspected of wishing to take the oath of amnesty."[31]

The management of the prison posts often recommended that separate quarters be provided for such prisoners until their petitions were acted upon. The Commissioner General of Prisoners wrote

29. *Ibid.*, 177, 1158.
30. *Ibid.*, VI, 903, 954; II, 221, 766, 803. See the author's *Old Cane Springs*, 227, for a published letter by Nathan B. Deatherage, one of Morgan's men.
31. *Offic. Rec.*, 2 Ser., VI, 903; VII, 221, 776.

the commander of the post at Rock Island, Illinois, in June, 1864, as follows: "Your letter of the 26th ultimo with list of prisoners who have expressed a desire to enter the United States Navy is received. It is desirable that these men, and all others who have made applications to be permitted to take the oath of allegiance, should be treated with as much kindness as possible, while at the same time they must be held as prisoners. You will, therefore, place them in barracks by themselves as much isolated from the other prisoners as practicable. . . . When offenders can be detected, punish severely any prisoner who threatens or insults them in any way for expressing a desire to return to their allegiance." Sometimes, however, instructions were given to protect prisoners who desired to desert the Confederate cause without segregating them.[32]

It is difficult to determine the number of Confederates who were liberated from Northern prison camps on taking the oath of allegiance to the United States during the war. One instance early in 1865 indicates what surely occurred many times at these prisons. In January and February the law firm of Curtis F. Burnam (First Assistant Secretary of the Treasury for a time during Grant's administration) and James W. Caperton of Richmond, Kentucky, was engaged by a number of citizens of Madison County, Kentucky, to secure the release of their Confederate kinsmen from Camp Douglas and other prison camps. The loyalty of these lawyers to the Union and their known friendship with Lincoln apparently encouraged this action. At any rate, they agreed to obtain the release of thirty-four prisoners. It was strictly a business proposition in every instance, and the fee was one hundred dollars in nearly every case. Burnam went to Washington and secured the President's order for the releases, and Caperton took the approved list to Camp Douglas. In this manner, after they took the oath of allegiance to the Union, liberty was obtained for twenty prisoners. Others whose freedom the lawyers had undertaken to secure were released before Caperton arrived in Chicago, and consequently his firm received nothing for those cases.[33]

32. *Ibid.*, VII, 221, 954.
33. The "Fee Book," law firm of Curtis F. Burnam and James W. Caperton, 1863 to 1869, in the possession of Caperton's daughter, Mrs. Paul Burnam, Richmond, Kentucky. See also the author's *Old Cane Springs*, 210-11.

It might also be noted in this connection that Burnam and Caperton received (February 21, 1865) three hundred dollars for obtaining permission from the Federal authorities in Madison County to allow three escaped Confederate prisoners to take the oath of allegiance to the United States. These soldiers, who had been confined in Camp Douglas with the private whose letter was quoted above, were "hiding out" in the country near Richmond and were in danger of being arrested and returned to prison. Relatives of the men paid the lawyers for their service. Some of the prisoners in whose interest Burnam and Caperton were active had been in John Hunt Morgan's brigade, which was captured in the summer of 1863 and whose soldiers and minor commissioned officers were confined in Camp Douglas, from which many were not released until the spring of 1865.[34]

Whether or not the President's amnesty policy was a considerable contributing cause of desertion from the Confederate armies after 1863 is rather difficult to determine. The number of deserters increased, of course, as the end of the war approached, and the increase was undoubtedly due, in some degree, to the existing proffer of clemency. Dr. Ella Lonn has thoroughly discussed the circumstances which operated to decimate the Southern armies through desertion.[35] She first considers conditions that were largely personal in character. There were, of course, illiterate backwoodsmen and mountaineers who hardly knew what the war was about and who soon tired of fighting for a cause of little interest to them. There were aliens (Germans, Irish, Mexicans, especially) who could not care much about the final outcome of the struggle. There were also Southerners whose Northern ties tended to weaken their allegiance to the Confederacy. Another group comprised persons, in the border states at least, whose bankrupt condition influenced them to espouse the Confederate cause very early, hoping thereby to profit from a disruption of the Union. The impetuosity and inconstancy of youth was also a factor in causing desertion. Lastly, there were the conscripts and substitutes whose loyalty could not be

34. *Ibid.*, 123-28, 210-12, 218-30. Caperton and his father, W. H. Caperton, supported Lincoln and spoke in the interest of his election in 1860.
35. See Dr. Lonn's *Desertion during the Civil War*, Ch. 1, "Causes of Confederate Desertion," cited hereafter as Lonn, *Desertion*.

guaranteed because of the compulsion and indirection exercised in their enlistment. That was not all, for there were causes of desertion produced by conditions relating to the war itself. Dr. Lonn's second emphasis, therefore, is placed upon the hardships, anxieties, and disappointments occasioned by the prolonged civil conflict. The ever increasing lack of food and clothing, a condition which naturally contributed to the demoralizing discomforts of army life, caused much dissension, especially during inclement weather. Anxiety over the welfare of loved ones at home, whose misfortunes were often augmented by invading armies, was also a condition that caused many to desire to serve in local military units rather than in more remote detachments. Moreover, dissatisfaction with the decreasing value of the currency, which the soldiers were obliged to accept, weakened enthusiasm for the Confederacy. Then there were grievances against Confederate officials for apparent discriminations in applying tax measures, in administering the draft, and in executing other war measures. Finally, the growth of sentiment in the South for peace at any price, as the ultimate failure of the Confederacy to win independence became more apparent, contributed to the decimation of the armies.

When the foregoing is understood, one readily expects to find a considerable number of deserters from the Confederate armies. The figure has been conservatively placed at 104,428 for the entire war; but other estimates suggest a much larger number. A Confederate war clerk put the number at 136,000 in July, 1863, and early in 1865 another Southern official complained of the difficulty of returning 100,000 deserters from an area of 300,000 square miles.[36] Dr. Lonn states that "the full flood of desertion seems not to have set in until the fall of 1864, when sweeping down all barriers, it rushed on to high water mark during the concluding months of the war in 1865. From October 1, 1864, to February 4, 1865," she continues, ". . . it was stated in Richmond that nearly 70,000 had taken French leave from the Confederate armies east of the Mississippi."[37] A book called *Deserters Who Have Taken the Oath*

36. *House Exec. Doc.*, 29 Congress, 1st sess., Nos. I and IV, pt. 1, p. 141; Lonn, *Desertion*, 29, 231; *Offic. Rec.*, 4 Ser., III, 1119-22.
37. Lonn, *Desertion*, 27.

of Allegiance at Little Rock, Arkansas, now in the National Archives, gives the names of some 2,500 persons thus classified with detailed personal descriptions. There were scores of women and some boys recorded as taking the oath. Others were soldiers and officers.

The Confederate authorities vainly resorted to threats, executions, and amnesties to stem the tide of desertion and strengthen the morale of their armies. On February 11, 1865, Lee issued what he said would be his last amnesty to deserters who would return to the service in twenty days, and on the twenty-eighth of the same month he offered clemency again to those who had deserted to join other Confederate military units. Three days earlier he had written: "I cannot keep the army together unless examples of the death penalty are made in such cases."[38]

Lincoln's proclamation of amnesty received favorable consideration by many in the foregoing categories of disgruntled soldiers, especially as the end of the war approached. Naturally, the offer of clemency was attractive because of its guarantee against the application of the drastic punitive measures which Congress had provided for rebellion and which are described in the first chapter. Four days after the appearance of the proclamation, General Grant announced that deserters might remain at liberty, providing their homes were within the Federal lines; that they might be employed, when advisable, by the engineer and quartermaster's departments; that they might have passes and transportation to their homes; and that they would be exempt from military service. Such deserters, of course, were to take the usual oath of allegiance. This policy was virtually adopted in a general order by the War Department on February 18, 1864,[39] and the amnesty proclamation was applied whenever there was an occasion for it. Many times, however, deserters proved to be spies and informers, so that extreme caution was necessary to determine who should be trusted. Nevertheless, officers were often deceived and unworthy applicants accepted.

Apparently prisoners of war whose homes were within the Union

38. *Offic. Rec.*, 1 Ser., XLVI, pt. 3, pp. 1228-30, 1259; cf. Lonn, *Desertion*, 28.
39. *Offic. Rec.*, 1 Ser., XLI, pt. 4, pp. 818-19; 3 Ser., IV, 118.

lines gave the authorities in the field and at Washington the most concern. This problem became most acute early in 1864 and apparently distressed Lincoln, who recommended to Stanton on March 18 a general policy of action. "I am so pressed," said he, "in regard to prisoners of war in our custody, whose homes are within our lines and who wish to not be [*sic*] exchanged, but [who wish] to take the oath and be discharged, that I hope you will pardon me for reviving the subject. My impression is," he continued, "[first,] that we will not ever force the exchange of any of this class; [secondly,] that taking the oath and being discharged, none of them will again go to the rebellion, but the rebellion, again coming to them, a considerable percentage of them, probably not a majority, would rejoin it; thirdly, that by a cautious discrimination, the number so discharged would not be large enough to do any considerable mischief in any event, will relieve distress in some meritorious cases, [and] would even give me some relief from an intolerable pressure. I shall be glad, therefore, to have your cheerful assent to the discharge of those whose names I may send, which I will [choose] only with circumspection."[40] This communication to Stanton was surely reflected in Grant's announcement above, though it appears to have been only for the benefit of deserters from the Confederate service whose homes were within the Federal lines. Yet it must often have been difficult to discriminate between deserters and prisoners of war.

EFFORTS TO PREVENT FRAUD

So much evidence of fraud had come to Washington by August, 1864, that the War Office issued a general order defining cases where applicants were "entitled to the benefit of the amnesty proclamation. . . ." The instructions emphasized the explanatory proclamation of March 26, 1864, defining those who might not take advantage of the proffer of amnesty. It also reviewed the current charges that persons in Tennessee, Kentucky, and Missouri had "endeavored fraudulently and treacherously to obtain the benefits of the President's amnesty by taking the prescribed oath, without any purpose of restoring peace and establishing the national au-

40. Lincoln Papers, Robert Todd Lincoln Collection (Library of Congress), microfilm, reel 70, Nos. 31645-9 (Lincoln to Stanton, March 18, 1864).

thority, but with the purpose of preserving their property from the penalty of their crimes, or of securing themselves from punishment for the commission of arson, robbery, treason, and murder." Kentucky was represented as having "already suffered incomparably by the depredations of returned rebel soldiers, who shelter themselves under the President's amnesty proclamation." Consequently, officers were instructed to consider those who were guilty of violating their oaths as having committed "substantive offense against the government" in doing so. Such persons, as a consequence of their fraud, were to have "no protection . . . either in their persons or property," and they were also to be deprived "of all claim to immunity, protection, and clemency."[41] The order further authorized military commanders to prescribe such regulations as would prevent the fraudulent taking of oaths. Officers were also instructed to bring to justice any person administering oaths to those not entitled to amnesty under the proclamation of March, 1864.

In accordance with these instructions, departmental commanders issued the necessary rules for use in their respective districts. Those adopted by the Department of the Gulf, with headquarters at New Orleans, may be taken as a type.[42] They provided that persons would be permitted to take the amnesty oath only on certain conditions. The applicant had to describe the aid he had given the rebellion and the penalties from which he wished to be relieved. He also promised unreservedly to comply with the spirit of the oath. The commanding officer, on being satisfied with the examination of the applicant, sent him to the provost marshal, who administered the oath. After declaring his allegiance to the Union, the man received a certificate stating that he was "admitted to amnesty" for the specific acts set forth in his petition. Any fraudulent statement made in the petition invalidated the protection and privileges guaranteed in the amnesty and subjected "the party making such false statements to trial for his former treasonable acts."

The Nashville *Union* for April 3, 1865, contains an interesting account of a perfidious oathtaker in Arkansas, named William C. Woodruff. The man's correspondence had been intercepted and his unworthy or questionable motives in seeking amnesty revealed. On

41. *Offic. Rec.*, 2 Ser., VII, 145-55.
42. *Ibid.*, 1 Ser., XLI, pt. 4, pp. 818-19.

one day he wrote: "I shall probably take the oath tomorrow. If I do, it will be a matter of necessity, not of choice, and I shall be quite as strong a rebel after taking it as before." After taking the oath, he wrote his correspondent again in the same spirit: "Please put me right with my friends South. Tell them I am not less a sympathizer with them than heretofore, but feel mortified and chagrined. . . ." Woodruff was sent beyond the Union lines into territory occupied by Confederates when his perfidy was discovered.[43]

It was no wonder that deception was practiced in seeking advantages from the proffer of amnesty. Human nature has ever been the same, and the war had not improved morals in the United States one whit. Since absolute pardon meant the restoration of property threatened by, or in the process of, confiscation, the temptation to deceive was great. Moreover, when it removed all likelihood of punishment for participation in the war and at the same time allowed one to remain at home with his family, the temptation was still greater.

One is not surprised, therefore, to find a general order, even in South Carolina, late in the war relating to the taking of the oath and the subsequent restoration of property. This announcement, in reviewing conditions as they appeared to exist, stated that applications for the restoration of property, accompanied with certificates of amnesty, were so numerous "as to lead to a suspicion that the desire to receive a horse or mule may have induced some unprincipled persons to profess loyalty and take and subscribe to the oath, with no intention of being truly loyal citizens." The order provided that property would be restored to claimants under the amnesty only when they could "prove that they had remained loyal to the United States during the present rebellion or that they held, at the time of the seizure, a certificate that they had already complied with the terms of the proclamation [of amnesty]."[44]

In this connection some indication of Lincoln's increasing willingness to pardon those excepted from the benefits of his amnesty should be given. Such information may be found in a letter he di-

---

43. This man may have been a relative of W. E. Woodruff, who was Treasurer of Arkansas in the 1880's.

44. *Offic. Rec.*, 1 Ser., XLVII, pt. 2, p. 737. See also the example of fraud in the case of John Williams given in *Butler's Correspondence*, III, 16-21.

rected Stanton to write General Canby in March, 1865. The Federal commander had admitted General Smith P. Bankhead within his lines with the assurance that he would recommend him for pardon if the Southerner gave information valuable to the Union cause. Canby also wrote that, since other "similar overtures" for clemency had been made to him, he desired "some general instructions with regard to that class of persons excepted" from the proclamation. He stated further that there was "no difficulty in treating with persons" who were "entitled to the benefit of that amnesty," but he needed to be instructed as to how far he might "take preliminary steps in cases that required the action of the president."[45]

In due time Canby received the following reply from Stanton: "The President approves your action in regard to Brigadier-General Bankhead, and any engagements you have with him will be fulfilled. The President further directs me to say, in respect to the classes of persons excepted from amnesty by his proclamation, that any engagements you . . . may deem beneficial to the public interest to make with individuals belonging to such classes, you are authorized to make, and such engagements will be carried out by the Government."[46] This was probably as much authority to act in such cases as Lincoln ever delegated to generals in the field during the war. Bankhead had been serving under E. Kirby Smith west of the Mississippi, but, on becoming convinced that further efforts at independence would be futile, he determined to return to his former allegiance to the Union. Canby, being in charge of the Federal troops in that area, accepted the Confederate's oath and assured him of presidential clemency.

EVALUATING THE AMNESTY

One of the first persons of prominence to be pardoned under the amnesty proclamation was General E. W. Gantt of Arkansas. After the Union victories, beginning in July, 1863, he seemed to realize that the cause for which he had been fighting was certain to fail, and that hostilities should end at once. Consequently, he issued an address to the people of his state giving the reasons why he was abandoning the Confederacy. "Our armies," he said, "are melting,

45. *Offic. Rec.*, 2 Ser., VIII, 320 (Canby to Lincoln, March 1, 1865).
46. *Ibid.*, 1 Ser., XLVIII, pt. 1, p. 1216 (Stanton to Canby, March 20, 1865).

and ruin approaches us. The last man is in the field, half our territory [is] overrun, our cities gone to wreck—. . . while deserted towns, and smoking ruins, and plantations abandoned and laid waste meet us on all sides; and anarchy and ruin, disappointment and discontent lower over all the land." He advised therefore submission to the government at Washington as the certain and honorable course to take in hastening a return to prosperity. Of course, Gantt welcomed the amnesty, and was pardoned just one week (December 15) after it was proclaimed. His pardon was sent to him in Arkansas by General B. F. Rice.[47]

Gantt's pardon suggests the advisability of giving the contents of a Lincoln pardon warrant, especially when issued to a deserting Confederate. The war President did not use a definite printed form as did his successor, whose two forms are described in Chapter VIII. Instead, each pardon was written and made to fit the case to which it applied. Of course there was much similarity in the wording of the warrants, exact copies of which were carefully written in appropriate books with pardons of all persons receiving presidential clemency. The following pardon of a Tennessee brigadier general, late in 1864, illustrates the usual contents of warrants under the amnesties of December 8, 1863, and March 26, 1864:

"Abraham Lincoln,
"President of the United States of America.
"To all to whom these Presents shall come, Greeting:

"Whereas, one James W. McHenry, a citizen of Tennessee, by holding the office of Brigadier General of Militia in the service of the insurgent enemies of the United States, has committed a high crime, and made himself liable to heavy pains and penalties both civil and criminal;—

"And whereas, the said James W. McHenry has long since heartily repented of his error; taken the oath of allegiance to the United States, and given bond with proper security for the faithful observance of the same;—

47. Thomas Kettell, *History of the Great Rebellion . . .* , 607, for quotation; Thomas S. Staples, *Reconstruction in Arkansas, 1862-1874*, 12, 13; Dennett, *Lincoln and the Civil War*, 139.

"Now, therefore, be it known, that I, Abraham Lincoln, President of the United States of America, in consideration of the premises, divers other good and sufficient reasons me thereunto moving, do hereby grant to the said James W. McHenry, a full and free pardon for all treasons, felonies and misdemeanors by him committed against the Government of the United States and the remission of all penalties incurred by reason of his participation in the existing rebellion prior to the date of these presents.

"In testimony whereof, I have hereunto signed my name and caused the Seal of the United States to be affixed.

"Done at the City of Washington, this Sixteenth day of December,

"A.D. 1864, and of the Independence of the United States the Eighty-ninth.

ABRAHAM LINCOLN

"By the President:

WILLIAM H. SEWARD,
Secretary of State."[48]

It is rather difficult to determine whether the President's amnesty proclamation really hastened the end of the Confederacy. Though the measure did serve as a basis for Lincoln's plan of restoration, it is doubtful whether it alone caused desertions from the enemy in sufficient numbers seriously to weaken the opposition to the Union. Nevertheless, a fair estimate of the response to the President's offer may be given. Quite naturally, soldiers who were suffering from hunger and fatigue, and who were discouraged over the outlook for the success of the Confederacy, might be expected to look with favor upon the proffer of amnesty. A report for February, 1865, states that Confederates called across the line at night requesting that a member of the Masonic Order be sent to consult with one of their number belonging to that fraternity, to ascertain the terms deserters were offered by the Federals.[49]

The editor of the Nashville *Union* stated, January 31, 1864, that every mail captured was filled with letters relating to the amnesty,

48. Pardon Records, National Archives (Lincoln's Administration), VII, 621.
49. *Offic. Rec.*, 1 Ser., XLVI, pt. 2, p. 587.

and that nearly every writer longed for the hour when he or she could "escape the further calamities of the war by accepting a pardon." About six months later (July 12) this editor stated further that he had ascertained from the local provost marshal that more than 15,000 persons in Tennessee had taken the oath of allegiance to the Union since October, 1863. No one "who had subscribed to this oath," he advised, "need hesitate to accept the oath of amnesty offered by the President." On March 1, 1865, he gave "the most gratifying assurance that the people of the South" were anxious to accept the President's amnesty. He also said that a letter from Missouri stated that the offer of amnesty was playing mischief with the rebel armies west of the Mississippi, especially with Missourians.

As the end of the war approached, the Union authorities utilized every opportunity and means to encourage desertions. "Subsistence and free transportation to their homes" if they were within the Union lines, or, if not, "to any point in the Northern States," were offered to those who would desert. Employment continued to be promised to those who would take the oath of allegiance, and immunity from capture by the Confederates was also guaranteed. As a material inducement the Federals offered, on January 4, 1865, to pay market prices for "arms, horses, mules, or other property" which deserters would bring into their lines and turn over to the quartermaster. Similar inducements to desert were held out to "railroad employees, telegraph operators, mechanics, and other civilians employed" by the Confederacy.[50]

Was the President's proffer of amnesty accepted by any considerable number of persons in both the military and civil service of the Confederacy? Not as many, it might be said, as Lincoln expected. A report from Nashville, Tennessee, gave 2,207 deserters as having taken the oath from September 7, 1864, to January 20, 1865, and a Chattanooga dispatch gave 1,048 for January 20, 1864. It is interesting to note the comment of the Illinois *State Journal* on this second number: "If the advice of those papers which opposed the amnesty measure had been taken, these men would still be in the rebel army fighting against the Union and seeking the lives of loyal

50. *Ibid.*, 828-29 (Special Orders No. 3, January 4, 1865, and No. 44, March 4, 1865). Also *ibid.*, 2 Ser., VIII, 242.

men."[51] On March 10, 1864, a report from Little Rock, Arkansas, gave 4,000 voters as having qualified; 8,000 more were expected to qualify. On the same day Joseph Segar wrote Lincoln from Norfolk that the amnesty proclamation had done much good in Virginia, and recommended that certain eastern counties of the state be no longer considered as insurrectionary.[52] The *Annual Cyclopedia* for 1864 indicates that "a large number of persons originally from the South who were within the Union lines" received benefits from the amnesty proclamation. It also states that some of them "whose property had been seized for confiscation complied with the terms of the proclamation in order to save their property." Horace Greeley, however, states, in his *American Conflict*, that only a small number accepted the proffer of amnesty.[53]

The reports made to the Department of State at Washington give the best estimate of the number of all classes who accepted Lincoln's offer of clemency. A number of books in which the oaths were registered at the different places where they were taken may now be found in the National Archives at Washington. These records give a total of about 10,500. But the four volumes with the title "Oaths under Proclamation, Dec. 8, 1863," made from the reports sent to Washington, show some 22,659 names and addresses of persons who took the amnesty oath. Tennessee, North Carolina, and Arkansas lead with the largest numbers. This total, however, runs through May, 1865, when hostilities were over, but before Johnson proclaimed his amnesty (May 29). Nevertheless, a large majority were taken before April, 1865. A few Lincoln oaths were administered as late as July, 1865. It is interesting to note that no record of an oath from South Carolina appears before 1865.

The second figure above is large when compared with the entire number of Confederate deserters, which has been put at 104,428. The comparison becomes more significant, however, when 20,000

51. *Ibid.*, 1 Ser., XLV, pt. 1, p. 48; Springfield, Illinois, *State Journal*, February 10, 1864. For other reports see *Offic. Rec.*, 1 Ser., XXXII, pt. 1, pp. 12-13; XLIX, pt. 1, p. 349.
52. Lincoln Papers, R. T. L. Coll., microfilm, reel 70, U. of Ill. Lib.
53. *Annual Cyclopedia*, 1864, p. 778; Horace Greeley, *The American Conflict: A History of the Great Rebellion* . . . , II, 529, cited hereafter as Greeley, *American Conflict*.

to 30,000 of these deserters are reported as having returned later to the Confederate service. The appeal, of course, had been made to the great body of supporters (civil and military) of the Confederacy, and of this number those who accepted the proffer of amnesty were in reality a very small percentage.[54]

In the spring of 1864, the President sent General Daniel E. Sickles on a tour through the South to observe and report the success of the plan of amnesty. He was "to call at Memphis, Helena, Vicksburg, New Orleans, Pensacola, Key West, Charleston Harbor, and such intermediate points" as he might think proper. His instructions were to "ascertain at each place . . . how the proclamation works—if at all; what practical hitches, if any, there are about it; whether deserters come in from the enemy, what number had come in at each point since the amnesty, and whether the ratio of their arrival is any greater since than before the amnesty; what deserters report generally, and particularly whether, and to what extent, the amnesty is known within the rebel lines." Sickles made this trip, but no record of his report appears to exist. He undoubtedly brought the President considerable information concerning the operation of his amnesty measure.[55]

President Lincoln estimated the response to his proclamation of amnesty in his last annual message to Congress (December, 1864). He stated therein that "during the year many [had] availed themselves of the general provision, and many more would have done so, only that the signs of bad faith in some [had] led to such precautionary measures as rendered the practical process less easy and certain." He also said that he had granted "special pardons . . . to individuals of the excepted classes," and that "no voluntary application" had "been denied."

This statement was too general and perhaps too early to satisfy the desire for a more definite conclusion as to the results of the policy of clemency in operation during the war. Nevertheless, as Lincoln approached the close of his rather long message, he focused attention on the cardinal virtue of his policy in dealing with per-

54. See Lonn, *Desertion*, 232, for table of deserters, taken from *House Ex. Doc.*, 39 Cong., 1st sess., No. 1, Vol. IV, pt. 1, p. 139.
55. Nicolay and Hay, *Lincoln, Works*, II, 482-83; Ida M. Tarbell, *The Life of Abraham Lincoln*, IV, 14.

sons in rebellion against the government. "Thus practically," he said, "the [pardon] door has been for a full year open to all except such as were not in condition to make free choice; that is, such as were in custody or under constraint. It is still so open to all." Then he gave an ominous warning: "But the time may come, probably will come, when public duty shall demand that it be closed and that in lieu more rigorous measures than heretofore shall be adopted." Some speculation on the meaning of this last statement will be given near the close of the next chapter.[56]

Finally, it might be said that the President's proclamation of pardon and amnesty undoubtedly weakened the loyalty of many thousands of minor supporters of the Confederacy, both civil and military. Especially was it welcomed by those who saw in its acceptance a guarantee against molestation by the Federal authorities. Its merit as a test of fitness for participation in the restoration of a state justified its application; and, in this respect, it should be noted that Tennessee, Arkansas, and Louisiana, at least, were considerably affected.[57] This was manifested in their progress toward restoration according to the plan of amnesty. The proclamation's greatest merit, however, was the manifestation of a very liberal policy of clemency which the Chief Executive proposed to apply in dealing with those in rebellion against the government—a generous offer which remained unmodified when death overtook its author. Moreover, it was this constitutional application of executive clemency which was likely to function after the war in mitigating the severe punitive laws that many avenging Northerners desired to have enforced. The condition to be lamented was the unfortunate change of presidents that occurred when the problem of pardon and amnesty became more serious.

56. Richardson, *Messages . . . of the Presidents*, VI, 254.
57. Charles H. Wesley, *The Collapse of the Confederacy, passim,* gives an excellent account of factors contributing to the failure of the Confederate states to win independence.

CHAPTER FIVE

PRESIDENT LINCOLN'S CLEMENCY

———◆———

ONE of the most recent stories of Lincoln's clemency was written for the *Lincoln Herald* by Dr. Robert Stephens, a grandnephew of Alexander H. Stephens.[1] At the time of the Hampton Roads peace conference in February, 1865, Vice-President Stephens told President Lincoln that he had a nephew who, when last heard from, was a prisoner of war at Johnson's Island in Lake Erie. Stephens hoped that Lincoln would learn something about the young man and let him know that all was well at home. The upshot of the request was an order the next day to the officer in command of the prison camp to parole "Lieutenant John A. Stephens to report" to the President in Washington. "It is in pursuance of an agreement," Lincoln wrote (February 4), "I made yesterday with his uncle, Hon. A. H. Stephens."

The surprised and apprehensive officer soon reported at the White House, as instructed, and was ushered into the presence of Lincoln, who told him that he had seen his uncle recently and had promised to send his nephew to him. John Stephens was elated. He was free and could go home! After visiting friends in Washington a few days, he reported to the President again, receiving from him a remarkable letter to his uncle in Georgia. "According to our agreement," Lincoln wrote the uncle (February 10), "your nephew, Lieut. Stephens, goes to you bearing this note. Please, in return, to select and send to me that officer of the same rank imprisoned

1. See *Lincoln Herald*, XLV, No. 2 (June, 1943), for "An Incident of Friendship," by Dr. Robert Stephens.

at Richmond whose physical condition most urgently requires his release."

"Folding this letter without drying the ink," Dr. Stephens says, "the President handed it to Lieutenant Stephens. . . . Then turning again to his desk, he took from a pigeon hole a small profile of himself and taking his pen, wrote under the likeness, 'A. Lincoln.' Handing this to Stephens, he said, 'Suppose you take this along with you. I don't expect there are many of them down South.' "

John Stephens did not go home right away, but was exchanged and served on the staff of General John Echols, with the rank of major, until Lee's surrender in April. He then went to his home in Taliaferro County, Georgia. When he delivered the note to his uncle, Abraham Lincoln was dead, and Alexander H. Stephens was soon thereafter imprisoned in Fort Warren, Boston Harbor.

The nephew framed the letter relating to his release "and in the lower right hand corner of the frame, he placed the autographed photograph" given him by the merciful President. "For over seventy years it has hung on the wall of the Stephens' home," Dr. Stephens states, "a silent reminder of a most unusual event in history, showing the kind impulses of a man's heart. The incident woven around this letter has done much to soften the feelings of the South for Abraham Lincoln. It always alleviates the pain of the old sores and tends to bind two once warring sections closer to each other." Dr. Stephens closed his article with this singular and significant statement: "The incident further shows how alike were the leaders of the North and South, despite the divergent political views which culminated in war."[2]

DENIALS OF CLEMENCY

The foregoing story indicates only one aspect of Lincoln's sympathy for the unfortunate. Indeed, the President was importuned many times to extend clemency to offenders of every description and from everywhere, North and South. Not only did Lincoln have to consider individual pleas for mercy, but he was also obliged to determine in a large measure the treatment en masse of persons whose irregular conduct made them liable to punishment.

2. *Ibid.* John Stephens became a lawyer and a leader of the Georgia bar, serving as state senator and adjutant general of the state in later years.

In this larger sense whole states may be regarded as coming within the scope of the executive's pardoning power. Lincoln's clemency, therefore, may be considered in three different aspects. First, there was his pardon or stay of prosecution of persons indicted or convicted in the civil courts; second, his interference with court-martial proceedings, his commutation of court-martial sentences, his pardon of persons sentenced by court-martial, and his general leniency in dealing with deserters from the Union army; and third, his attitude toward persons and states in rebellion against the government. The nature of this general study requires the consideration of only the last phase of Lincoln's clemency.[3]

Perhaps no other Confederates caused the authorities at Washington more concern than those operating in Canada and in the Northern states. Captain John Y. Beall was such a person. Late in 1864 this youthful officer and other Confederates undertook the liberation of the prisoners of war on Johnson's Island near Sandusky, Ohio. Beall had already seen much service as a privateer in the vicinity of Cheaspeake Bay, and on being captured in November, 1863, had barely escaped trial for piracy.[4] His act was in pursuance of the desperate policy adopted by the Confederate authorities as Federal gains continued to sap their ever-weakening strength. When the Union authorities, in 1864, disregarded the cartel with the Confederates providing for the exchange of prisoners, in order to drain the Confederacy of its human resources, the government at Richmond resolved upon the questionable course of inciting insurrections in the North and liberating and arming the soldiers in the Union prison camps. Beall acted as one of the agents employed by the commission, including Jacob Thompson and Clement C. Clay, sent to Canada to direct such operations. In November he and twenty other men, dressed as ordinary citizens, overpowered the crew of the "Philo Parsons," on which they had taken passage at Detroit for Johnson's Island. A little later they captured the "Island

3. See J. T. Dorris, "President Lincoln's Clemency," *Journal of the Illinois State Historical Society*, XX (January, 1928), 547-68; and *Lincoln Herald*, LV, No. 1 (Spring, 1953), for a considerable extension of these aspects of Lincoln's clemency by the author.

4. *The Trial of John Y. Beall as a Spy and Guerrilla by Military Commission, passim*, cited hereafter as *The Trial of John Y. Beall*; William M. Robinson, Jr., *The Confederate Privateers*, Ch. XVIII.

Queen" and put ashore the passengers of the two boats, paroling thirty-two Union soldiers taken on the latter vessel. The Confederates then undertook the capture of the "Michigan," which defended the island; but most of the men deserted when they saw that this boat had been warned of their approach. Thereupon, Beall discharged the others, sank the boat which he occupied, and abandoned the attempt to liberate the prisoners. Subsequently, he took fifteen men, crossed Lake Erie, and tried to destroy the railroad between Dunkirk and Buffalo, New York. Again he failed; but this time he was captured, though his men escaped.

Under the circumstances, the civil and military authorities considered Beall's offenses as being very serious, although committed in the name of recognized warfare by a regular commissioned officer. Soldiers and sailors, however, were required to wear uniforms while in the service and to conform to certain accepted rules of espionage. Thus, although President Davis and others at Richmond attested to the prisoner's military status and assumed responsibility for the belligerent character of his movements in Lake Erie, nevertheless, Naval Solicitor John A. Bolles, in concluding his able address before the military commission, charged Beall with being a robber, brigand, and pirate. "There is nothing of Christian civilization," he said, "nothing of regular warfare, nothing of a high, noble, manly chivalrous character about it. . . ." James G. Brady, an able attorney of New York, was engaged as counsel for Beall, but despite his learned argument that his client was not a spy, and that his activities came within the scope of international law, the accused man was convicted and sentenced to be hanged.[5]

Much sympathy was manifested for the exemplary, young, educated Virginian, whose family was wealthy and prominent socially, and a tremendous effort was made to have his punishment commuted to life imprisonment. Men of great personal influence were enlisted to save him from the gallows, and President Lincoln was urged to prevent the execution. Senator Orville Hickman Browning advised clemency and presented a petition in behalf of the prisoner signed by ninety-one members of Congress. Postmaster-General Montgomery Blair, John Andrew, and even Thaddeus Stevens desired leniency. Six United States Senators formally petitioned Lincoln to

5. *The Trial of John Y. Beall*, 88.

commute the sentence, since it was admitted that Beall was "a Captain regularly commissioned in the rebel service and that Jefferson Davis . . . assumed all responsibility for his actions." A letter by Beall to Confederate Agent of Exchange Robert Ould, dated February 15, was not delivered until February 27, after the execution. Had Ould received it when he should have, he might have prevented the death sentence from being carried out. He said that the "cruelty of the enemy was so swift" that nothing could be done to stay the execution.[6]

General John A. Dix, commanding in New York State, and the Naval Solicitor, Major John A. Bolles, insisted on the execution, however, and Lincoln declined to interfere, though it was evident that his conscience was greatly disturbed. On the day before the execution (February 24, 1865), Senator Browning reveals in his *Diary*, in a last personal appeal to the President for clemency, he found Mr. Lincoln looking and feeling "badly—apparently more depressed than I have seen him since he became President." After the assassination of Lincoln, the Senator, in speculating on the probable assassins, wondered "whether it was the rebel leaders . . . or the friends and accomplices of Beall who was recently hung at New York. I am inclined," he wrote, "to the latter opinion."[7]

Beall's case certainly reveals Lincoln in a role that forcibly refutes the general impression of his over-leniency. If there ever was an instance when he could have justified mercy, it was on this occasion. With the President of the Confederacy assuming responsibility for Beall's acts, and with such an array of august petitioners for clemency, Lincoln's refusal was a reliable testimony to his strength of purpose when death appeared the proper penalty for conviction, notwithstanding extenuating circumstances that might have justified contrary action on his part.

There appears to be no connection whatever between Lincoln's assassination and Beall's execution. The "weird and lurid story" which was current for years that the assassination "was inspired by

6. Isaac Markens, *President Lincoln and the Case of John Y. Beall, passim;* *Offic. Rec.*, 2 Ser., VIII, 400 (Ould to President Johnson, March 11, 1865).
7. John B. Castleman, *Active Service*, 161-67; T. C. Pease and J. G. Randall (eds.), *The Diary of Orville Hickman Browning*, II, 7, 8, 19, cited hereafter as Browning, *Diary*; Carl Sandburg, *Abraham Lincoln; the War Years*, IV, 132-33; William E. Barton, *The Life of Abraham Lincoln*, II, 263.

the President's broken promise" to Booth to pardon Beall apparently had no authentic foundation. Booth himself, as shown in his diary, dissipated such belief. His plan to kill the President "antedated Beall's operations by quite a remote period." Seven days after his heinous deed he wrote: "I knew no private wrong. I struck for my country and that alone."[8]

Senator Browning relates two other instances of Lincoln's constancy in refusing petitions for concessions and clemency. The first had to do with one Mrs. Fitz, a rich widow in Mississippi, who claimed loyalty to the Union, but whose slaves and ten thousand bushels of corn the Federals had taken. The woman, who was then a refugee in St. Louis, wanted the government to give her a sufficient number of Negroes from those in its custody to enable her to raise a crop of cotton the ensuing season. She agreed to pay them the wages which the government paid those it employed. Browning himself counseled the President to grant the request, believing "it reasonable and just and worthy at least of being considered." Lincoln, however, positively refused, saying, "with great vehemence, he had rather take a rope and hang himself than do it." He declared that "there were a great many poor women who had never had any property at all who were suffering as much as Mrs. Fitz—that her condition was a necessary consequence of the rebellion, and that the government could not make good the losses occasioned by rebels." The fact that the widow was loyal to the Union and that the government was using her property made no apparent difference; and, according to Browning, the President declared "that she was entitled to no compensation," even though "a portion of her slaves, at least, had been taken in 1862, before his proclamation and put upon our gun boats. . . ."[9] Browning states that he left Lincoln "in no very good humor" after this interview.

The other case involved a young French surgeon named Shiff, who had been captured in the Wilderness Campaign and later paroled after taking the oath of allegiance to the United States. The man had subsequently gone to Paris with his widowed mother. The Shiffs had considerable property in the South which they feared the Confederates would confiscate if they learned that the son had

8. Quoting Markens, *President Lincoln and the Case of John Y. Beall*, 11.
9. Browning, *Diary*, I, 659 (entry for February 6, 1864).

taken the oath of allegiance to the Union. The boy's deceased father had "once lived in New Orleans and had invested in Southern stocks, and loaned money on mortgages." Consequently, there was "a large indebtedness from the rebels to the family," members of which were then in France. In petitioning the President to allow him to withdraw the oath, Dr. Shiff stated "that he was not fully aware of what he was doing" when he took it, and had "supposed that he did only what would entitle him to be paroled."

Browning states that "the President was very amiable, and seemed inclined to grant the request, but said he would consult Secretary Seward, and see what his views were." Seward, however, "became much excited, boisterous and profane" to a Mr. La Forge, who went with the Senator to intercede with the Secretary in the Frenchman's behalf. When La Forge "asked if Shiff, being a Surgeon and noncombatant, was not entitled to be paroled without taking the oath," Seward vehemently declared "that Shiff had no right to be paroled —that we had a right to have taken his head off, and that he ought to be thankful that he was allowed to go away [to Paris] with it on his shoulders, etc." Nothing, therefore, was gained in this interview, and the petition was renewed the next day. When Browning and La Forge called at the White House the following morning, the President told them that "Seward had been over to see him about it, and had urged his objections to the request"; consequently, "he believed he would do nothing about the matter."[10] Apparently no further consideration was ever given to Shiff's petition.

PARTIALITY TOWARD KENTUCKIANS

Lincoln was better known for his leniency in dealing with Confederates. He may also have been especially merciful when they were from his native state. An interesting case of his granting a request for clemency is that of the son of George D. Prentice, editor of the Louisville *Journal*.[11] The instance is also worthy of mention because Lincoln may have taken into consideration the influence the *Journal* probably had had many years earlier in causing him

10. *Ibid.*, 689-91 (entries for October 27, 28, 1864).
11. See Malcolm Bayley, "How the Louisville Journal's Editor Got His Son Paroled by Lincoln," Boston *Christian Science Monitor*, February 12, 1937, reprinted in the Louisville *Courier-Journal*, February 14, 1937.

to espouse the principles of the Whig Party. Moreover, the editor had done much for the Union cause in Kentucky, and that was something to be appreciated. At any rate, Prentice's twenty-year-old son, Clarence J., had entered the Confederate service, had quickly won a major's commission, and had been a serious menace to the Federals in eastern Kentucky. The youthful officer's fortune had suddenly changed, however, for one night in April, 1863, he slipped into Louisville to see his parents and baby, and in a few hours was captured. He was confined in Camp Chase, near Columbus, Ohio, and was soon ordered to be tried as a spy.[12]

The young Major's parents had already lost their other son while he was fighting with General John Hunt Morgan, and now became frantic over the prospect of losing their only living child. The father first implored the President by telegram to allow Major Prentice to be exchanged as a prisoner of war. Three days later he followed with a long letter describing his son's predicament. "I do not suppose, Mr. Lincoln," he concluded, "that you can parole my boy upon his taking the non-combatant's oath to remain in the United States, though I should be most happy if you could; but I fervently appeal to you to let him go, upon his taking that simple oath, anywhere outside of the United States and the rebel Confederacy. I know his plans. His mother will go with him and he will never bear arms against us again. I will be surety for this with my fortune and life. I have written to General Burnside to let my son remain at Camp Chase till I hear from you. Please let it be soon, for I am most unhappy."

The President, however, was advised by Judge-Advocate Joseph Holt not to grant the petition for a parole, but to allow the prisoner to be exchanged instead. On May 6 the father wrote Lincoln again, emphasizing his own past sacrifices for the Union cause and stating that he was "likely, even at the best, to suffer and sacrifice much hereafter." He also stated that he had requested General Burnside, at Cincinnati, not to permit his son to be exchanged unless the President refused a parole. He closed this petition with these words: "And now, Dear Sir, pray grant me what I ask in behalf of my only son. His mother is half delirious, and so am I. I am scarcely capable of performing my daily duties to the country, but if my request

12. *Offic. Rec.*, 1 Ser., pt. 2, p. 230 (Burnside to Halleck, April 11, 1863).

were granted, I feel I should be buoyant with new life. Please let me know your decision soon, for, if my son cannot be paroled upon either of the conditions I have mentioned, I want him sent forward as soon as possible to City Point to be exchanged, as he is extremely uncomfortable in his present condition. Is it too much to ask that you will telegraph me upon the receipt of this?"[13]

The letter had the desired effect. Notwithstanding Holt's recommendation that the petition not be granted, President Lincoln instructed Stanton to order General Burnside "to parole Major Clarence Prentice . . . to remain outside the limits of both the loyal and disloyal States . . . during the present rebellion, and to abstain from in anywise aiding or abetting said rebellion." On this condition the parole was granted. Nevertheless, as the Judge-Advocate had predicted, young Prentice soon appeared on the Kentucky-Virginia border, authorized by the Richmond authorities to raise a battalion or regiment for the Confederacy, and for more than a year longer he fought against the Union.[14] In December, 1864, Lincoln again went to the editor's aid to get his son out of trouble by granting him a pass through the Union lines to visit the boy in Richmond, Virginia, where he was charged with murder.[15]

Another Kentuckian in dire distress whom Lincoln proposed to befriend was Captain John Breckinridge Castleman of Fayette County, who had been an officer under General John Hunt Morgan. Like John Y. Beall, Castleman was caught while operating under the direction of the Confederate commission in Canada, whose purposes were to incite insurrection in the North and liberate and arm the prisoners in the prison camps there. Castleman tells the story in his *Active Service*, a book to which reference has been made in the account of the more unfortunate Beall. Posing under the assumed name of Clay Wilson, he moved about in the region from Chicago to St. Louis. A number of men operated under him,

13. The original letter is in possession of Hon. William H. Townsend, Lexington, Kentucky.
14. *Offic. Rec.*, 1 Ser., XXVII, pt. 3, p. 1007. For an account of Clarence J. Prentice's later service for the Confederacy, see *ibid.*, XXIX, XLII, XLIII, XLV.
15. *Ibid.*, XLV, pt. 2, p. 504. Sandburg, *Abraham Lincoln; the War Years*, has no mention of this case.

doing what mischief they dared without being apprehended. Their activities were frustrated, however, by the arrest of Castleman at Sullivan, Indiana, on October 1, 1864, and his incarceration in the military prison at Indianapolis. The young Captain's mother soon visited the prison and left with her son a Bible, in which a fellow officer, Captain Thomas H. Hines, another Morgan man, had caused a sympathetic bookbinder in Chicago to secrete three small saws and three thousand dollars in currency. The Holy Bible, the little saws, and the good United States money were intended to be both consoling and useful to the anxious prisoner, who was charged with the serious offenses of being a spy, of distributing money for malicious and incendiary purposes, and of conspiring to free and arm prisoners of war. As in the case of Beall, conviction would certainly have been followed with a death sentence.

On returning home, Mrs. Castleman engaged Judge Samuel Breckinridge of Lexington to secure her son's release. Breckinridge soon went to Indianapolis and, after interviewing Castleman, employed the able law firm of Porter and McDonald to defend the prisoner, who was his kinsman.[16] Late in November, 1864, the Judge went to Washington to enlist the President's beneficent interest in the case. Being a Kentuckian and a Union man, Breckinridge expected his mission to be favorably considered, and he was not disappointed. Lincoln was glad to receive the visitor from his wife's home town, and the two men talked until late about subjects of mutual interest. Finally the President said: "Sam, I have so much enjoyed having you with me that I have been glad for the time to forget grave questions that beset the country, but we have neglected the interest that brings you here, and have seemed to forget Castleman. In fifteen minutes we have a Cabinet meeting and I will give you now a note only to be used in case of emergency. Meanwhile from what I learn, it would be best to have that boy's attorneys endeavor to postpone the trial, for those young Confederates have caused the government annoyance and expense." Then he penned the following note: "Major General Hovey, or Whoever may have charge at the proper time: Whenever John B. Castle-

16. Albert Gallatin Porter of this law firm later became first Comptroller of the United States Treasury and then Governor of Indiana.

man shall be tried, if convicted and sentenced, suspend execution until further order from me, and send me the record."[17]

This order that Lincoln entrusted to Judge Breckinridge was written on November 29, 1864. Evidently the procedure the President advised was pursued, for Castleman was never brought to trial. Instead, an exchange was arranged between Grant and Lee, and the prisoner was taken to Washington for that purpose. Before this could be effected Lincoln was assassinated, and Castleman was soon taken from the Old Capitol Prison and returned to Indianapolis. There the determination to try him as a spy was revived.[18] Generals Halleck and Hovey and Judge-Advocates Joseph Holt and Guido Norman Lieber demanded that "the same justice which required the trial and execution of Beall" be applied to Castleman. Hovey wrote the authorities at Washington on May 25, 1865: "From the facts presented I cannot but regard Major Castleman as a dangerous and daring spy. There can be no doubt that he was connected with the contemplated burning of property in the North. I am constrained to recommend that he be tried or banished from the country."

The latter recommendation was followed, and Castleman was paroled, banished, and sent across the border at Detroit. He went to Europe, and, since he was excepted from President Johnson's amnesty of May 29, 1865, his friends, in due time, sought his pardon. Seventeen citizens of Lexington, Kentucky, petitioned President Johnson, reminding him that Lincoln's plan to have Castleman exchanged should have been carried out. Even Governor Thomas E. Bramlette of Kentucky endorsed the petition to pardon the exile, whose parole Johnson revoked on August 27, 1866, on condition that he return to the United States and take the oath of allegiance.[19] This he did, and thus the will of the martyred President was ultimately carried out, though not in the manner he had anticipated.

Lincoln's leniency in dealing with Captain Castleman incites some speculation as to the causes therefor. Lincoln allowed Captain Beall to be executed, even though pressure for clemency greater than that

17. Castleman, *Active Service*, 184 ff. The Boston *Christian Science Monitor*, February 16, 1935, reproduced this letter of November 29, 1864.

18. The order to take Castleman back to Indianapolis was dated April 25, 1865.

19. Castleman, *Active Service*, 188, 200.

exercised in Castleman's behalf was brought to bear upon him. Beall, of course, was tried and convicted, while Castleman, who was certainly a spy, was never even brought to trial, but was to be exchanged as a prisoner of war. Perhaps Beall's actual offenses were more serious; but certainly there should not have been such difference in the treatment of the two offenders. It could not be that the effect of Beall's execution on February 24, 1865, influenced Lincoln to be more clement toward Castleman for it should be noted that Lincoln entrusted his order concerning Castleman to Breckinridge nearly three months before the execution of Beall; thus no conscientious scruples on that account could have influenced him to write the note of the previous November. Nevertheless, the hanging might have had something to do with the later proposed exchange of prisoners in Castleman's case. Finally one might suppose that the request of a loyal Kentucky Breckinridge had much weight with Lincoln, also a native of Kentucky, although not all Breckinridges were supporting the Union. Moreover, was not Mrs. Lincoln also a Kentuckian—even a Fayette County Kentuckian, whose kin were neighbors of the Breckinridges and Castlemans?

Kentuckians undoubtedly enjoyed a choice place in Abraham Lincoln's affections and were likely to be recipients of his extraordinary beneficence. But who really knows why Lincoln allowed Beall, a Virginian, to be shamefully hanged as a spy, while he was willing that Castleman, a Kentuckian who was also a spy, should be exchanged as an honorable prisoner of war?[20] Indeed the acts of the great Civil War President were often enigmatical and hardly understandable according to the standards applicable to ordinary persons. Castleman's final parole and banishment, however, were surely due to the fact that the war was over and no more spies were to be tried as such. Nevertheless, Lincoln's plan to have the Kentuckian exchanged as a prisoner of war ultimately worked to his advantage when Johnson was petitioned to allow the exile to return and take the oath of allegiance.

20. Castleman became a prominent lawyer and served as Brigadier General during the Spanish-American War. Hines became Chief Justice of Kentucky's highest court. The men were lifelong friends. See Randall, *Lincoln and the South*, Ch. I, for Kentucky influences on Lincoln.

LENIENCY TOWARD CONFEDERATES

Perhaps Lincoln's greatest manifestation of clemency may be found in his general attitude toward those engaged in the rebellion, especially the leaders of the Confederacy. Consideration of this subject is closely associated with his policy of restoring the seceded states to their former position in the Union. Early in the war he had given his assent to the laws which Congress enacted to punish persons adjudged guilty of "treason." The severest of these measures provided that every person convicted of such crime "shall suffer death" or imprisonment "for not less than five years, and be fined not less than ten thousand dollars." In addition to this his slaves were to be freed; he was to be disqualified for holding office; and his property was to be confiscated. Nevertheless, in the passage of this law a message from Lincoln, indicating his displeasure with its severity, caused Congress to pass a joint resolution declaring that "no proceedings under said act shall be so construed as to work a forfeiture of the real estate of the offender beyond his natural life." It should be noted also that section 13 of the law authorized the President "by proclamation to extend to any persons who may have participated in the existing rebellion . . . pardon and amnesty, with such exceptions and at such time and on such conditions as he may deem expedient for the public welfare." In reality, President Lincoln had this power under the Constitution. The clement section, therefore, was intended to mitigate the severity of the law and suggest to those in revolt the possibility of returning to their former allegiance to the Union with impunity.

The sentiment expressed in the mitigating section of this punitive law is indicative of Lincoln's attitude toward persons who supported the Confederacy during the war. From the very beginning his administration applied a policy intended to encourage desertions from the enemy without fear of punishment by the Federal authorities. Especially was this done in Northern prison camps and occupied areas of the South. By 1862 it became the established policy to allow such disaffected persons to take an oath of allegiance to the United States and obtain their release on parole.[21] This procedure,

21. *Offic. Rec.*, 2 Ser., I-VIII, give much information bearing upon the treatment of political and military prisoners during the war.

however, was applied with varying degrees of intensity. In October, 1863, for example, when practically all applications for permission to swear allegiance to the Union were denied, the reason given for such denials was the great number of Federal prisoners for whose exchange provision should be made. Nevertheless, the records contain abundant evidence that many persons took advantage of the clemency in vogue during the first three years of the war.[22]

Apparently, however, Lincoln was ready at any time to grant a general amnesty with a remission of all penalties except the loss of property in slaves, if the measure would hasten the return of peace and the end of the Confederacy. By December, 1863, such a policy appeared feasible, and so he issued his well-known proclamation of general amnesty and his 10 per cent plan of reconstruction simultaneously with his annual message to Congress.[23] The only emphasis that needs to be given here to these clement measures is to pronounce them as embodying the magnanimous attitude which Lincoln had maintained all along toward his "dissatisfied countrymen" and as the index to the policy which he would have tried to administer during the period of reconstruction. It should be noted, however, that his proffer of pardon and amnesty did not apply to certain classes of persons, including the leaders of the Confederacy. But even they might make special application to him for pardon, which he would freely grant if it seemed prudent to do so—a promise that he fulfilled many times before his death.

President Lincoln, in proclaiming his program of restoration and amnesty, announced that he was committed to no one plan of reconstruction. His mind was open to new situations and possibilities that might contribute to the accomplishment of the main objective of the war, which was to save the Union. As far as dealing with the leaders of the Confederacy was concerned, his government had hanged no one for treason during the war, as Secretary Welles said, and it was not likely that anyone would be put to death for treason after the war. This diarist predicted early in June, 1864,

22. *Ibid.*, V, 19, 20, 125, 146, 173, 659, 707, 708; VI, 14, 31, 91, 175, 190, 212, 228, 242, 256, 294-95.
23. Nicolay and Hay, *Lincoln, Works*, II, 280-81, 419; *Butler's Correspondence*, III, 110; Richardson, *Messages . . . of the Presidents*, VI, 188-89.

that "very gentle measures in closing up the Rebellion" would be used. "The authors of the enormous evils," he said, "will go unpunished, or will be but slightly punished." A little earlier than this, it was stated that Lincoln had discussed the possibilities of "universal amnesty" in dealing with the South.[24]

So the questions in every Unionist's mind, as the end of the war approached, were: What plan of restoration would prove the most satisfactory? And what punishment, if any, should be inflicted on the leaders of the Confederacy? The President's 10 per cent plan appeared to be his answer to the first question, and his proffer of pardon and amnesty, his answer to the second. He had made it plain, however, that this policy was subject to modification.

But Lincoln's plan of reconstruction and his policy of clemency were announced long before the end of the conflict. Another question, therefore, naturally arises: Was he becoming more disposed, or less disposed, to leniency in dealing with the Confederates as time passed? One answer may be found in his annual message to Congress in December, 1864.[25] As far as the matter of reconstruction was concerned, he expressed his satisfaction with the plan then in effect one year. As to the treatment of persons engaged in the rebellion, in either civil or military capacity, he stated that his proffer of amnesty was still open to all. "But the time may come—probably will come—," he warned, "when public duty shall demand that it be closed; and that in lieu more rigorous measures than heretofore shall be adopted."

A little more than four months after this message, Abraham Lincoln was dead and the war practically over. Did his heart harden toward the Confederates during the interval? Did the time come when public duty demanded that "more rigorous measures . . . be adopted?" Apparently it did not. As far as Lincoln's subsequent acts were concerned, the door to his system of clemency remained open to the time of his death. The report of the Hampton Roads conference (February, 1865) shows that he still considered general

24. Nicolay and Hay, *Lincoln, Works*, II, 545; Welles, *Diary*, I, 43 (June 1, 1864); Isaac N. Arnold, *The History of Abraham Lincoln, and the Overthrow of Slavery*, 656-57.

25. Richardson, *Messages . . . of the Presidents*, VI, 188-89.

amnesty and restoration on practically the same plan as that in effect. As to the matter of enforcing the confiscation and other punitive acts of Congress, he said, their enforcement was left entirely to him; but he gave assurance that he would "exercise the power of the Executive with the utmost liberality."[26]

General Sherman states in his *Memoirs* that he asked Lincoln at City Point, on March 27, 28, 1865: "What was to be done with the rebel armies when defeated? And what was to be done with the political leaders? . . . Should we allow them to escape? . . ." Sherman says that "all he wanted of us was to defeat the opposing armies, and to get the men composing the Confederate armies back to their homes at work on their farms and in their shops. As to Jefferson Davis, he was hardly at liberty to speak his mind fully, but estimated that he ought to clear out, 'escape the country,' only it would not do for him to say so openly." Sherman also states that the President "distinctly authorized" him "to assure Governor Vance and the people of North Carolina, that, as soon as the rebel armies laid down their arms, and resumed their civil pursuits they would at once be guaranteed all their rights as citizens of a common country. . . ." In fact Sherman says that Lincoln outlined to him, in this conference, the magnanimous terms which he allowed General Joseph E. Johnston, on April 18, 1865, when he surrendered to him near Durham, North Carolina. This noted convention, which the authorities at Washington promptly disallowed, provided that "the war was to cease; and that a general amnesty, so far as the Executive of the United States can command, was to be granted, on condition of the disbandment of the Confederate armies, the distribution of arms, and the resumption of peaceful pursuits by the officers and men hitherto composing said armies."[27]

Lincoln, of course, was not alive to support Sherman's contention that the President had authorized this liberal agreement with

26. Nicolay and Hay, *Lincoln*, X, 118-31; Rhodes, *History of the United States*, V, 71; A. H. Stephens, *A Constitutional View of the Late War between the States . . .*, II, 617, cited hereafter as Stephens, *War between the States*.

27. William T. Sherman, *Memoirs of General William T. Sherman*, II, 326-31, 356, cited hereafter as Sherman, *Memoirs*; A. K. McClure, *Abraham Lincoln and Men of War-Times*, 236 ff,

Johnston. Admiral Porter, however, who was present at the City Point conference, stated, in 1866: "Mr. Lincoln did, in fact, arrange the so-considered liberal terms offered General Joseph E. Johnston, and, whatever may have been General Sherman's private views, I feel sure that he yielded to the wishes of the President in every respect. It was Mr. Lincoln's policy which was carried out, and had he lived long enough, he would have been but too glad to have acknowledged it." The Admiral also said of Lincoln at City Point: "His heart was tenderness throughout, and as long as the rebels laid down their arms he did not care how it was done. I do not know how far he was influenced by General Grant, but I presume, from their long conferences . . . that the terms given Lee after his surrender were authorized by Mr. Lincoln."[28]

Two days after the Hampton Roads conference the President prepared a message to Congress recommending that Congress pass a joint resolution providing that $400,000,000 be given the slave states on two conditions. Stephens says that Lincoln suggested this remuneration in the Hampton Roads conference, but John H. Reagan declares he did not make any such recommendation.[29] First, half the amount suggested was to be paid if "all resistance to the national authority shall be abandoned and cease on or before the first day of April next." Second, the remainder was "to be paid only upon the thirteenth amendment of the National Constitution recently proposed by Congress becoming valid law, on or before the first day of July next." If Congress acted favorably upon his suggestion by passing the "resolution" and the states complied with its terms, the President would proclaim that "war will cease and armies be reduced to a basis of peace"; that "all political offenses will be pardoned"; that "all property, except slaves, liable to confiscation or forfeiture, will be released there-from"; and that "liberality will be recommended to Congress upon all points not lying within executive control."

Lincoln submitted this measure to his Cabinet, whose disapproval

28. Sherman, *Memoirs*, II, 329-30.

29. Stephens, *War between the States*, II, 617; John H. Reagan, *Memoirs of John H. Reagan, with Special Reference to Secession and the Civil War*, Ch. VIII, cited hereafter as Reagan, *Memoirs*.

was unanimous, and consequently he never sent the message to Congress.[30] Its provisions, however, indicate the very great clemency which their author entertained, at the time, in trying to arrive at a solution of the problem confronting the nation at the close of the war. Welles said that "the earnest desire of the President to conciliate and effect peace was manifest in this proposed message, but there may be such a thing as so overdoing as to cause a distrust or adverse feeling." Furthermore, he did not think Congress "in its present temper" would approve the recommendation. "The rebels," he believed, "would misconstrue it if the offer were made." Moreover, if it were "attempted and defeated it would do harm."[31]

The amount which the President was willing to pay was not of very much consequence. The war was costing $3,000,000 a day in addition to untold suffering and destruction of property. Besides, he believed both the North and the South were responsible for slavery, and, according to his way of thinking, the North should be willing to tax itself to compensate the South for the loss of property in slaves. It was far better, he believed, to spend such a sum in conciliation and in rendering justice than in any further effusion of blood. But his will was not to be done. The day of compensated emancipation was gone forever, and Lincoln's effort to "dissolve sectional hatred and plant fraternal good will" was in vain.

If Lincoln desired to grant "universal amnesty" at the close of the war, he probably deemed it unwise to do so, since public sentiment in the North was in favor of punishing "Davis, Hunter and Company." He was aware "that he had already done more favors for the rebels than was exactly popular with the radical men of his own party."[32] He would most likely have granted a "general amnesty" at the close of hostilities. Grant was of that opinion. He says in his *Memoirs* that he believed "Mr. Lincoln wanted Mr. Davis to escape because he did not wish to deal with the manner of his punishment. He knew there would be people clamoring for the punishment of the ex-Confederate president for high treason.

30. Nicolay and Hay, *Lincoln, Works*, II, 635-36; Nicolay and Hay, *Lincoln*, X, 133-37; John T. Morse, Jr., *Abraham Lincoln*, II, 309-11.
31. Welles, *Diary*, II, 237 (entry for February 6, 1865).
32. *Harper's Weekly*, IX (April 8, 1865), 210; Springfield, Illinois, *State Journal*, July 5, 1865.

He thought enough blood had been spilled to atone for our wickedness as a nation."[33]

Grant says again: "I also know that if Mr. Lincoln had been spared there would have been no efforts made to prevent anyone from leaving the country, who desired to do so," and "he would have been equally willing to permit the return of the same expatriated citizens after they had time to repent of their choice." Charles Sumner was equally of the opinion that Lincoln could not bring himself to the point of punishing the leaders of the Confederacy. He said that he "was with him for four days, shortly before his death . . . and during all this period he was not for a moment tempted into any remark indicating any desire to punish even Jefferson Davis. In refutation to a statement that Davis should be hanged Lincoln said again and again, 'Judge not, that ye be not judged.' "[34]

Lincoln closed his last public address (April 11, 1865) with an argument in favor of the plan of restoration then in vogue. He indicated that he was just as lenient as ever, as far as his attitude toward the political problem of reconstruction was concerned. In the last two sentences of this same speech he intimated that he was contemplating "some new announcement to the People of the South. I am considering," he said, "and shall not fail to act when satisfied that action will be proper."[35] At his last Cabinet meeting a plan of reconstruction was discussed and left for subsequent consideration. Welles says that the President requested the members "to deliberate and carefully consider the proposition. He remarked that this was the great question now before us, and we must soon begin to act." The Secretary of the Navy stated at another time, in referring to this Cabinet session, that the President "was particularly desirous to avoid the shedding of blood, or any vindicativeness of punishment. He gave plain notice that morning that he would have none of it. No one need expect that he would take any part in hanging or killing these men, even the worst of them.

33. Ulysses S. Grant, *Personal Memoirs of U. S. Grant*, II, 522, cited hereafter as Grant, *Memoirs*.
34. *Ibid.*, II, 533; Edward L. Pierce, *Memoir and Letters of Charles Sumner*, IV, 239.
35. Nicolay and Hay, *Lincoln, Works*, II, 675. Also Greeley, *American Conflict*, II, 747.

'Frighten them out of the country, open the gates, let down the bars, scare them off,' said he, throwing up his hands as if scaring sheep. 'Enough lives have been sacrificed; we must extinguish our resentments if we expect harmony and Union.' "[36] These are the last recorded utterances of Abraham Lincoln on the subject of punishing the leaders of the Confederacy. Had he lived he would have dealt with Davis, Lee, Toombs, *et al.* in the most merciful manner consistent with the exigencies of the time. A general amnesty with fewer exceptions than in his proclamation of December, 1863, would probably have been granted; confiscations would have stopped; and the leaders of the Confederacy would most likely have gone into voluntary exile for a time, after which they would have returned, taken the oath of allegiance, and resumed their former privileges as citizens of the United States. The manner of restoring the states to their former political position in the Union would have been little different from that announced in his proclamation of December, 1863. It might have been even more generous.

The murmurings against Lincoln's policy of leniency were silenced in the general rejoicings over Lee's surrender to Grant. At that time sentiment was very strong in favor of dealing very liberally with the South. The President's policy had certainly given the Confederates no cause to fear. His assurances at the Hampton Roads conference indicated that his attitude of clemency and liberality toward them had not changed. They were expecting his program of mercy, always so evident, to continue to function. As General John B. Gordon so aptly states in his *Reminiscences*, the government would have dealt generously with the South, "because Abraham Lincoln was at its head."[37]

The door of mercy at the White House was open while Lincoln lived. Was the time to come—did the time "come, when public duty" demanded "that it be closed. . . ?" The most unfortunate event which occurred during the rebellion was the assassination of

36. Welles, *Diary*, II, 298 (April 14, 1865); Nicolay and Hay, *Lincoln*, X, 283-85. See Randall, *Lincoln and the South*, Ch. IV, especially the last paragraph, for an excellent, extensive appraisal of Lincoln's probable clemency in dealing with the South after the war.

37. John B. Jones, *A Rebel War Clerk's Diary at the Confederate States Capital*, 475; Stephens, *War between the States*, II, 614-17; General John B. Gordon, *Reminiscences of the Civil War*, 450-52.

the President. Was it in case of such an event as this that Lincoln had warned, in his fourth annual message to Congress, that "more rigorous measures than heretofore" might be adopted?

The magnitude of the opposition to Lincoln's policy in dealing with the Confederates now became evident. The death of the President was regarded by many as a godsend to the country. Declarations were made all over the North that too much mercy had been shown the Southerners. The New York *Herald* for April 16, while deploring Lincoln's cruel death, predicted that the policy of the new President in dealing with the South would "be more tinctured with the inflexible justice of Andrew Jackson than with the prevailing tenderness of Abraham Lincoln."

President Johnson received letters from many sources saying, in substance, that Lincoln's death was an act of providence; that his work of saving the Union was finished; and that a man of stronger parts was needed to punish those responsible for the rebellion. A man in Ohio wrote: "We believe that Abraham Lincoln's work was done; he was not the man to administer justice, he was always too merciful and kind." Another in Massachusetts said: "When news came of the assassination of President Lincoln, and my family were in tears around me, I rallied them, as myself, by the thought, Providence has given the work of justice into the hands of Vice-President Andrew Johnson to be better done than it would have been done by good President Lincoln."[38]

Thus in life and in death Abraham Lincoln was regarded by many as inherently too disposed to leniency to deal justly with those who sought to destroy the Union. Now that he was gone and his place taken by one who had shown every indication of being far less lenient, the punishment of the Southerners seemed assured.

38. These letters are among the Amnesty Papers for Jefferson Davis, now in the National Archives at Washington. See Ch. VIII for a description of the Papers. Myrta Lockett Avary, *Dixie after the War*, 90-100, and *Harper's Weekly*, IX (May 6, 1865), 274, indicate such confidence in Johnson.

CHAPTER SIX

AMNESTY AFTER THE WAR

An Avenging President

THE DAY after Lincoln's death a delegation of Radicals in Congress called at the White House to pay their respects to the new President. Evidently they were well pleased with the change of presidents, for their spokesman, Senator Wade, said: "Johnson, we have faith in you. By the gods, there will be no trouble now in running the government!"[1] This was strong language, indeed, but, under the circumstances, it was to be expected of Benjamin Wade in addressing Andrew Johnson at that time. Wade had bitterly opposed Lincoln's amnesty policy and plan of reconstruction. He had fostered the Wade-Davis bill and had joined Henry Winter Davis in the famous "Wade-Davis Manifesto" of August 5, 1864, a severe denouncement of Lincoln for refusing to sign the Wade-Davis bill and for persisting in applying the lenient policy of reconstruction announced in his proclamation of December 8, 1863.[2] Wade had also voted to refuse to count the electoral votes from the newly reconstructed states in the presidential election of 1864, and had opposed the admission to Congress of senators and representatives from these same states. Consequently, he now exulted in the apparent assurance that a punitive or retributive policy would soon be administered in dealing with persons who had supported the Confederacy.

Indeed, from the earliest days of secession, Johnson had evinced a desire to have at least the leaders of the rebellion punished. Notwithstanding Tennessee's act of secession, he had answered the

1. Norman Hapgood, *Abraham Lincoln, Man of the People*, 408.
2. See McPherson, *Rebellion*, 332. The "Manifesto" was published in the New York *Tribune*, August 5, 1864.

Southern senators' farewell speeches by declaring: "Were I the President . . . I would do as Thomas Jefferson did in 1806 with Aaron Burr, who was charged with treason. I would have them arrested and tried for treason; and if convicted, by the Eternal God, I would see that they suffered the penalty of the law at the hands of the executioner."[3] Johnson's stirring words had also helped to inspire and unite the North to support the Union when many Northerners of influence were passive or counseled Lincoln to let the "erring sisters" go in peace. Tennessee had disowned and persecuted Johnson during the early days of the war, but in 1862 this state had felt his rigorous administration as Military Governor. Moreover, when he came to administer Lincoln's plan of reconstruction in Tennessee he had insisted on applying a more stringent oath of allegiance than the President had provided—an oath that permitted only those who had stood unswervingly by the Union to participate in any program of reconstruction.

Johnson's strong desire to make treason odious caused Senator Wade and others of like intent to acclaim the new President as the proper person to deal with those so lately in rebellion against the government. Such sentiment was expressed to Johnson by Samuel McFarland, a prominent Democrat and politician of Pennsylvania, who had been considered as a candidate for the vice-presidency in 1856.[4] McFarland had written a letter to Lincoln, but had not mailed it when the assassination was announced. This letter he enclosed with one to Johnson about a month later. In his letter to Lincoln he advised "unlimited confiscation and disfranchisement" in dealing with the South. "According to the rules of civilized warfare," he stated, "the conquering party has a right to demand of the conquered, 'indemnity for the past and security for the future.'" As to the leaders of the Confederacy, he wished to tell Lincoln, they had no rights "under the Constitution except to be hung or banished."

McFarland told Johnson in his second letter that he was free to admit he was not so concerned about the subject of recon-

3. *Congress. Globe*, 36 Cong., 2 Sess., 1354-56; George F. Milton, *The Age of Hate: Andrew Johnson and the Radicals*, 104, cited hereafter as Milton, *Age of Hate*. Cf. *Harper's Weekly*, for May 13, 1864 (IX, 289).

4. John C. Breckinridge received the nomination and was elected.

struction as he had been in Lincoln's lifetime. He was sure that the former understood the Southerners and the spirit of the rebellion much better than the latter. "Your advantages for obtaining knowledge in this particular," he told Johnson, "far exceeded his, because you were where you could not only read and hear but you could see and feel the rebellion. And your late speeches have not shaken my faith in your ability to close up the infernal rebellion . . . in the right way." McFarland then went on excoriating the leaders of the rebellion in the strongest possible polite language. He would have them "roam as vagabonds upon the earth . . . as did Cain, who imagined everyone who saw him would slay him. Let them feel," he said, "that they have no rights which white men or black men are bound to respect. . . ."[5]

McFarland's letter indicates the tenor of many other communications on the subject of reconstruction which Johnson received before he formally announced his policy of dealing with the Confederates. One other example, but from a lesser source, will suffice. T. Scott French, writing from Hopkinton, New Hampshire, believed that Lincoln "was removed from this world to show the wickedness of the rebels and to place" Johnson at the head of the government to punish them. He told the new President that he was "just such a person as the times" demanded, who would "mete out to these rebels the punishment that they deserve and which the true interest of the country demands for millions yet unborn." French believed that Lincoln could have saved the lives of thousands by being less lenient toward the Confederates.[6]

Such counsel as the above harmonized with the policy Johnson had advocated during the war. Now, as President, he appeared—for a time at least—to be determined to apply that policy in dealing with the leaders of the rebellion. In his brief inaugural address he uttered these ominous words: "The only assurance that I can now give of the future is reference to the past. The course which I have taken in the past in connection with this rebellion must be regarded as a guaranty of the future."[7] To Wade's committee, the day after taking the oath of office, Johnson declared: "I hold that

5. Amnesty Papers, Jefferson Davis.
6. *Ibid.* (French to Johnson, May [?], 1865).
7. Richardson, *Messages . . . of the Presidents* (1913 ed.), V, 3503.

robbery is a crime; rape is a crime; treason is a crime; and crime must be punished. Treason must be made infamous, and traitors must be impoverished." Two or three days later he assured a delegation from Illinois of his determination to teach Americans "that treason is a crime and must be punished."[8] In other speeches during the early weeks of his administration, he made similar utterances.

On assuming the duties of President, Johnson manifested a retributory policy in matters pertaining to the close of the war. His reaction to the Sherman-Johnston convention is a case in point. The liberality accorded the Confederates in this measure was too much for his temper. In fact, the terms were generally unacceptable to the North. This agreement which Generals W. T. Sherman and Joseph E. Johnston made near Durham, North Carolina, on April 17, 1865, was in substance a treaty intended to be accepted by the two governments concerned. It provided that all the Confederate armies were to be disbanded and their arms held at the several Southern state capitals to await the disposition of the Federal authorities; that the existing state governments were to be recognized, subject to determination by the Supreme Court; that the Federal courts were to be re-established in the South; that civil, political, personal, and property rights were to be guaranteed to the inhabitants of the states lately in rebellion; and that the Southern people were not to be disturbed "by reason of the late war," on condition that they remain peaceful and lawful.[9]

This agreement, which the disintegrating Confederate government readily approved, was, in reality, intended to be a universal amnesty. The last article announced that the war was to cease, and that "a general amnesty" was to be proclaimed by the President "on [the] condition of the disbandment of the Confederate Armies, the distribution of arms, and the resumption of peaceable pursuits by [the] officers and men hitherto composing such armies." The measure would have placed the late Confederate states in their former status in the Union. There would have been no punishment for treason or rebellion, and the Confederate leaders would soon have been admitted to the counsels of the nation, barring, of course, any

8. New York *Herald*, April 19, 1865.
9. The original document is in the Stanton Papers (Library of Congress), **XXVI.**

adverse decisions of the Supreme Court. But to President Johnson,
General Grant, and the Cabinet, the Sherman-Johnston convention
was anathema.[10] General Grant was therefore sent to instruct
Sherman to treat with Johnston on such terms as Grant had allowed
Lee at Appomattox.

Sherman was much chagrined at this annulment of the convention, but complied, of course, with instructions. Supported by
Admiral Porter and others, he insisted, however, that his agreement
with Johnston conformed to Lincoln's intentions expressed to him
at City Point, where on March 27, 1865, the President had confided to Sherman his sentiments on reconstruction. The terms were
indeed somewhat in advance of Lincoln's earlier views on reconstruction, but they were in line with the general tendency of his
policy. Nevertheless, Sherman deserves commendation for his
liberality, especially in view of his recent destructive campaigns
in Georgia and the Carolinas. His letter to Grant enclosing a copy
of the convention shows the magnanimous spirit of the man who
characterized war as Hell. He stated that the measure, "if approved
by the President," would "produce Peace from the Potomac to the
Rio Grande . . . and if you will get the President to simply endorse
this copy, and commission me to carry out the terms, I will follow
them to the conclusion. You will observe that it is an absolute submission of the enemy to the lawful authority of the United States,
and disperses his armies absolutely. . . . I know," he concluded,
"that all the men of substance in the South sincerely want peace and
I do not believe they will resort to war again during this century.
I have no doubt that they will in the future be perfectly subordinate
to the laws of the United States. . . ."[11] Further allusion to the
Sherman-Johnston convention is not germane to the general theme
of this study; moreover, others have well discussed its various
aspects.[12]

The rejection of the Sherman-Johnston convention suggests by

10. Stephens, *War between the States*, II, 806-7; McPherson, *Rebellion*,
121; Welles, *Diary*, II, 294-97.
11. Stanton Papers (Library of Congress), XXVI (Sherman to Grant,
April 18, 1865); Lloyd Lewis, *Sherman, Fighting Prophet*, 540-48.
12. See Jefferson Davis, *The Rise and Fall of the Confederate Government*, II, 678-94; Sherman, *Memoirs*, II, 336; Grant, *Memoirs*, II, 514-17;
Stephens, *War between the States*, II, 589-618; Milton, *Age of Hate*, 151-75.

contrast the government's treatment of the Indians who had supported the Confederacy. After the war, the Choctaw and Chickasaw nations, as well as other Indians of the Southwest, found themselves in a condition somewhat similar to that of the states which had rebelled against the Union. In joining the Confederate States they had forfeited privileges guaranteed them in treaties with the United States. At least, this anomalous condition was recognized as existing. A new treaty with the Choctaw and Chickasaw, therefore, appeared advisable, and the Federal government, while refusing to treat with the Confederate States in any manner resembling a treaty, extended this privilege to the Indians so lately in rebellion. The policy thus adopted was "to act with clemency toward them in the hope that they might thereby be deterred from future aggressions."

Accordingly, the President sent commissioners to Fort Smith, Arkansas, in September, 1865, to confer with delegates from all the nations of the Southwest. In that month a treaty was made, in which the Indians acknowledged "themselves to be under the protection of the United States" and promised that thereafter they would "recognize the Government of the United States as exercising executive jurisdiction over them." They also agreed never again to "enter into any allegiance . . . with any state, nation, power, or sovereignty whatsoever." For the United States, the commissioners guaranteed to "reestablish peace and friendship with all nations and tribes of Indians within the so-called Indian Territory," and to "afford them ample protection for the security of person and property." The government also declared "its willingness to settle all questions . . . growing out of former treaties of such nations with the so-called Confederate States."[13]

As suggested in this agreement, another treaty soon followed to which the first was only preliminary. On April 28, 1866, commissioners for the government signed an agreement with the Choctaw and Chickasaw nations whereby "permanent peace and friendship" were declared established between the United States and these Indians. Article V of this treaty is remarkable, since it

13. *Annual Cyclopedia* (1865), 783. See Annie Heloise Abel, *The American Indian as Slaveholder and Secessionist*, I, *passim*, for an account of the secession of the Indians and their alliance with the Confederate States.

differs so greatly from the qualified amnesty by proclamation granted the whites after the war. It declared a universal amnesty for all past offenses against the United States committed before the signing of the treaty by any Choctaw or Chickasaw. A request was also expressed in the agreement that Missouri, Kansas, Arkansas, and Texas grant like amnesty to the Choctaw and Chickasaw for all offenses committed in those states during the war. The Indians, on their part, declared "an amnesty for all past offenses against their respective governments" and agreed to abolish slavery in their domain.[14]

Another example of President Johnson's early punitive policy was the Milligan-Bowles treason case. Four men, Lamdin P. Milligan, William A. Bowles, Stephen Horsey, and Andrew Humphreys, had been convicted of treason by a military tribunal in December, 1864. Their offenses as "Sons of Liberty" were committed in Indiana, where they were also tried. Milligan, Bowles, and Horsey had received death sentences, and Humphreys was to be imprisoned for life. Lincoln had been petitioned to pardon the men, but he had done nothing about the matter except to give assurance that he would pardon them after the war. Johnson, on becoming President, approved the death sentences and ordered the three men to be executed on May 19, 1865. He was influenced later (May 2) to suspend the execution of Milligan and Bowles to June 2 and to commute Horsey's punishment to life imprisonment. Yielding again to entreaties for clemency, he commuted (May 31) the sentence of the first two men to life imprisonment, and ordered the three prisoners to be taken to the penitentiary at Columbus, Ohio, on June 2.

Governor Oliver P. Morton of Indiana and others came to believe that the men should have been tried by the civil authorities and

14. *U. S. Stat. at Large*, XIV (Treaties, United States, Foreign Nations and Indians), 85. Similar treaties were made with other Indian nations: with the Creek, June 14, 1866; with the Cherokee, July 19, 1866. *Ibid.*, 102, 115.

The petition for pardon by General Douglas H. Cooper (Amnesty Papers for Arkansas), Confederate agent for the Indians, contains much information about the activities of the Indians during the war, especially at the beginning, when they felt themselves abandoned by the United States and left only the choice of joining the Confederate States. The Indians desired Cooper's pardon, and, on the recommendation of persons of much influence, his petition was granted late in April, 1866.

that the military court which convicted them had no legal status in Indiana. For this reason they urged Johnson to set aside the sentence on constitutional grounds as well as for good policy, the war being over and peace having returned. Morton, though having been much perturbed over the activities of the men, concluded that he did not want Johnson to begin making "treason odious" by inflicting the death penalty in his state, especially since the constitutionality of the convictions was in doubt. The case, thereupon, was taken to the Supreme Court, which declared (April 3, 1866) against the military commission that had convicted the men. Before the decision was announced (December 17, 1866), however, Johnson yielded again (April 10, 1866) to an application for clemency and ordered the sentences remitted and the men discharged from prison.[15] By the late summer and autumn of 1865, however, he had in general become rather lenient in dealing with supporters of the Confederacy, as will be shown later.

QUESTIONS OF TREASON AND AMNESTY

Before stating the amnesty policy adopted by the new President, it might be well to observe that such a serious and weighty matter as dealing with the supporters of the Confederacy should have been largely determined at the outset by judicial precedent, or opinion, and international law. There were Southerners, of course, who thought so, and the President of the Confederate States was one of them. To quote Dr. John J. Craven: "Mr Davis said it was contrary to the law of nations to treat as a rebellion, or lawless riot, a movement which had been the deliberate action of an entire people through their duly organized state governments. To talk of treason in the case of the South was to oppose an arbitrary epithet against the authority of all writers on international law." Craven also stated that Davis believed, from "the clamor about 'treason' in the Northern newspapers," that the editors of those papers were poorly informed. None of them "seemed to remember that treason to a

15. *Offic. Rec.*, 2 Ser., VIII, 7-10, 523, 543-48, 583, 586, 637-38, 896-97; 3 Wall. 776; 4 Wall. 2; *Ex parte Milligan*, 71 U. S. 2. Cf. Kenneth M. Stampp, "The Milligan Case and the Election of 1864 in Indiana," *Mississippi Valley Historical Review*, XXXI, No. 1 (June, 1944), 41-58. See also William D. Foulke, *Life of Oliver P. Morton*, I, 419-32.

State" was just as possible as to the United States. Consequently, "between the horns of the dilemma there could be little choice."[16] According to both municipal and international law the Confederates had a legal status that the authorities at Washington might well have considered. The belligerent character of the Confederacy had been established, as far as the highest American tribunal could determine the legal status of any organization, early in the war. The Supreme Court, in December, 1862, interpreted certain acts of both the executive and legislative departments of the government as recognizing the belligerency of the Confederacy. In what are known as the Prize Cases, the Court held that the President's proclamations of April 19 and 27, 1861, ordering the blockade of the Southern ports, and certain laws of Congress passed July 13 and August 6, 1861, to increase the pay of the United States soldiers were evidences of the recognition of the belligerency of the Confederacy, even though these acts were not intended as such. Furthermore, the decision contained the opinion that the attitude of foreign powers had given the conflict a status of legalized warfare between two belligerents. This meant, of course, that declarations of neutrality by European powers were, in effect, recognitions of a belligerency between the United States and the *de facto* government of the Confederate States which the administrative authorities at Washington should respect.

In this case the Court further defined the struggle as a civil war, and the Southern participants as "enemies" and not "traitors." Moreover, the law of nations was declared to contain "no such anomalous doctrine . . . that insurgents who have risen in rebellion against their sovereign, expelled his courts, established a revolutionary government, organized armies and commenced hostilities [all of which the Confederacy had clearly done], are not *enemies* because they are traitors; and a war levied on the Government by traitors, in order to dismember it and destroy it, is not a war because it is an 'insurrection.' " In other words, as Dr. Randall states, the Supreme Court's opinion as to the relationship of the Confederate States to the government might "be called the double-status theory—i.e. that the United States 'sustained [toward the enemy]

16. Colonel John J. Craven, M.D., *Prison Life of Jefferson Davis*, 122-23, 291-2, cited hereafter as Craven, *Davis*.

the double character of a belligerent and a sovereign, and had the rights of both.'" This meant that the authorities at Washington were invested both with sovereign powers against parts of the country and with belligerent powers as in a recognized war with a sovereign power.[17]

Thus the highest tribunal in the nation took the position very early that the organization of the Confederate States and the long war that ensued were not actually treason against the United States. There was nothing new in this opinion; for more than a century earlier the great international legalist, Emmerich de Vattel, had not only described civil war in such terms as to remove the American "war between the States" from the category of treason, but he had also prescribed certain rules which the sovereign power should apply in dealing with rebellious subjects. "If they have rebelled without cause," he stated, ". . . the sovereign must even then . . . grant an amnesty to the greater number of them on the return of peace." He admonished the sovereign, however, to observe carefully "whatever promises he has made even to . . . those of his subjects who have revolted without reason or without necessity." Nevertheless, he made it clear that the sovereign "may except from the amnesty the authors of the disturbance, the leaders of the party, and may judge them according to the laws, and punish them if they are found guilty." But even here Vattel made a qualified exception which is worthy of notice. The sovereign, he said, "may follow this course especially when dealing with those disturbances which are occasioned less by popular grievances than by the designs of certain nobles, and which deserve rather the name of *rebellion* than *civil war*."

This principle, if applied to supporters of the Confederacy, would mean a nearer approach to universal amnesty than if the struggle had been of lesser significance and magnitude. In other words, if the President regarded the leaders of the Confederacy as acting without sufficient cause and as merely desiring to further their unworthy and selfish motives, he would be justified in punishing them; but if he placed the conflict on the higher plane of a

17. *Prize Cases*, 67 U. S., 635; James G. Randall, *The Civil War and Reconstruction*, 384 (quoting *Miller* vs. *U. S.*, 78 U. S., 306-7). The decision in the Prize Cases was five to four.

civil war, he would be justified in pursuing a more lenient policy in dealing with them. Vattel made it very plain that in an effort to "split" a "Republic," the obligation upon the two parties to observe toward each other the customary laws of war is "absolute and indispensable, and the same which the natural law imposes upon all nations in contests between state and state."[18]

If Vattel in his day (1758) clearly placed organized and material internal resistance to a sovereign power on the plane of legitimate warfare and stated that both parties should observe the recognized rules of warfare commonly applying to struggles between belligerents, it appears that such consideration might have been exercised a century later under similar circumstances. That consideration would surely have placed the supporters of the Confederacy, in the seceded states at least (including Kentucky and Missouri), beyond the pale of treason.

In this connection it is instructive to note the opinion expressed somewhat later (1905-6) by the great English authority in international law, Lassa F. L. Oppenheim. While admitting that in "Federal States war between member-states, as well as between any member-state and the Federal States, is illegal," Oppenheim says that such "armed contentions . . . ought to be considered as war in International Law."[19] This would place the acts of the Confederates outside the category of treason. Furthermore, he states: ". . . One of the effects of every peace treaty is the so-called amnesty. . . . But here again the amnesty grants immunity only for wrongful acts done by the subjects of one belligerent against the other." And then he makes this significant statement: "Wrongful acts committed by the subjects of a belligerent against their own government are not covered by it [amnesty]. Therefore, a belligerent may after the conclusion of peace punish treason, desertion, and the like committed during the war by his own subjects, unless the contrary has been stipulated in the treaty of peace." The application of this principle to the Civil War would have meant amnesty to the supporters of the Confederacy who were citizens of the

18. E. de Vattel, *The Law of Nations; or the Principles of Natural Law* (1758), trans. Charles G. Fenwick (1916), III, 337-40.
19. Oppenheim, Lassa F. L., *International Law, a Treatise* (3rd ed.), II, 368-70.

states that actually comprised the Confederacy. This would have caused the punitive laws to be applied only to disloyal persons in the border states and in the rest of the Union. Yet this line would have been hard to draw, since the Confederate government recognized Kentucky and Missouri as having seceded from the Union and admitted senators and representatives from these states to its congress.

Therefore, in the light of international law as expressed later by Oppenheim, the Confederates were in reality belligerents and came within the scope of the rules of warfare applying to such contests. Amnesty, universal or general, should have been the recognized procedure by both belligerents at the close of the war. This would have meant that no one would have been indicted for treason. Oppenheim suggested further that a treaty of peace containing an amnesty is not out of place at the close of a civil war, as in the case of the Indian nations in 1866. It is interesting to note also that a treaty similar to the Sherman-Johnston agreement containing a universal amnesty provision was made in 1902 between the British and the Boers of South Africa, who had fought for independence from Great Britain.[20] Consequently, since the Confederate States of America were certainly a belligerent power with a *de facto* government, it is easy to deduce from the foregoing that those who had supported the Confederacy might reasonably have believed that the Federal government would deal very leniently with them.

Perhaps the able lawyer and distinguished Confederate soldier, Bradley T. Johnson, expressed the best contemporary Southern viewpoint on the question of treason as it touched the supporters of the Confederacy. He set forth his opinion in a long "Statement of the Case" of Jefferson Davis in his *Reports of Cases Decided by Chief Justice Chase, 1865-69,* published in 1876.[21] Much of Johnson's reasoning suggests the opinion of the Supreme Court and the arguments of Vattel and Oppenheim. "When traitors and rebels oppose their government by open violence," said the legalist, "and are summarily put down, those not slain in the combat may fairly

20. *Annual Register,* 1902, 402-3; *New Learned History for Ready Reference* (1924), X, 7859.
21. Dunbar Rowland, *Davis,* VII, 138-227.

be tried for treason in the civil courts and dealt with as ordinary criminals. . . . But far different results ensue when rebellion maintains itself so long and so effectively as to compel between itself, its people and their territory, on the one hand, and the lawful government on the other, an . . . acceptance of the rules and usages which obtain in regular wars between independent nations." The only difference was to be found in the result of the revolt. "If successful, the rebels acquire the power of establishing an independent state . . .; if they fail, the victor may be as indulgent as far as he will or as far as he dare. . . ." Public opinion should determine the severity of the treatment of the vanquished.

Attorney Johnson also believed that "trials for treason in the civil courts were not remedies adapted to the close of a great civil war" like the American War between the States. He advanced the logical opinion that such tribunals have no "functions suitable" in cases pertaining to the leaders of the late conflict as though they were classed as common criminals. On the contrary, honor forbids trials for treason "after combatants in open war have recognized each other as soldiers and gentlemen engaged in legitimate conflict." Moreover, since treason could only exist "in levying war against the United States or in adhering to their enemies," the leaders of the Confederacy could not be traitors, because they had *waged* war and not *levied* it as defined in the Constitution. Such conclusion was due to the actual treatment of the Confederates as belligerents waging war, and not as rebellious citizens levying war against their own government.

The cogency of Johnson's reasoning is rather compelling, but space forbids the long, minute details of his argument. Briefly, he insisted that Themis, the goddess of harmony, and not Mars, presided "over all intercourse between the parties" during the war. He admitted, however, that the United States, having the power, could "inflict upon the vanquished any punishment their faults may merit." Nevertheless, as a "responsible member of civilized society," the government was perforce constrained to do otherwise. Any attempt, therefore, to punish Jefferson Davis and other leaders of the Confederacy would be considered disgraceful to the American people.

PRESIDENT JOHNSON'S FIRST AMNESTY

International law is not likely to be applied by a sovereign power in dealing with its subjects who have revolted, even when the rebellion has assumed major proportions and the opposition has been recognized as a belligerent power. Municipal law is likely to have greater weight. Such was the case immediately after the close of the American Civil War. The organic law of the United States defines certain acts, when committed by citizens of the nation, as treason, and gives Congress the power to determine the punishment therefor. According to this definition, the acts of the supporters of the Confederacy could be regarded as treasonable. The punitive laws which Congress had passed in 1861 and 1862, as already shown, were intended for persons convicted of "levying war" at that time against the United States. No provision was made for any other kind of warfare. The maximum penalty had been fixed at death. Minor sentences of confiscation of property, of disfranchisement, of imprisonment, and of heavy fines might be imposed. Furthermore, the Federal executive authorities had not accepted the principle that the Confederate States was a belligerent power with a *de facto* government (as had been expressed by the Supreme Court in the Prize Cases), had made no treaty with it, and had insisted rather on regarding its adherents as insurgents and liable to punishment as such, except, of course, in the case of the treaty with the Choctaw and Chickasaw Indian Nations in April, 1866, which provided for a universal amnesty.

In this connection, the significance of "General Orders of the War Department, No. 100," issued on April 24, 1863, might be noted. These "Instructions for the . . . armies of the United States in the field" contained the following ominous clause: "Treating in the field the rebellious enemy according to the law and usages of war has never prevented the legitimate Government from trying the leaders of the rebellion or chief rebels for high treason unless they are included in general amnesty."[22]

When hostilities ceased in the South, therefore, Johnson's government had perforce to solve the problem of dealing with the

22. *Offic. Rec.*, 2 Ser., V, 681.

adherents of the Confederacy. Most naturally there were persons who insisted on the enforcement of the municipal laws intended for this occasion. Just as naturally there were others—and Northerners, too—who, as already stated, advocated the application of more liberal measures, such as came within the range of international custom.[23] Authority (Vattel most often) was quoted to prove that the Southerners were not traitors, but were belligerents, and should be accorded the utmost liberal treatment as such. But the excitement and animosity engendered by the assassination of Lincoln made it less likely that clemency would prevail in the first acts of the administration in dealing with the Southerners.

On April 21 President Johnson formally asked his Attorney-General, James Speed, to advise him concerning the power of the President to grant pardon. He also desired to know the "construction and effect" of Lincoln's proclamations of December, 1863, and March, 1864, and whether or not another amnesty proclamation should be offered and how inclusive it should be. On May 1, Speed gave a long opinion concerning the information requested.[24] He first advised Johnson that he had the constitutional right to issue such a proclamation, and emphasized the propriety and benevolence of clemency. He then defined the meaning and effect of such an act of mercy. Furthermore, he declared that Lincoln's proclamation was only a war measure intended "to suppress the insurrection and to restore the authority of the United States, and was applied with reference to those objects alone." This meant, of course, that Lincoln's pardons were valid, but that his proffer of amnesty ceased to function with the end of the war.

The Attorney-General also stressed the former President's tendency toward leniency. He quoted from his fourth annual message to Congress the entire paragraph on "general pardon and amnesty." He wanted especially to emphasize the words: "But the time may come, probably will come, when public duty shall demand that it [the 'door' of mercy] be closed and that in lieu more rigorous

23. See *Harper's Weekly*, IX, 289, 386-87; *New Englander*, XXIV, 781-83; New York *Tribune*, May 6, 1865.

24. Welles, *Diary*, II, 294; *House Exec. Doc.*, No. 99, 39 Cong., 1 Sess.; *Opinions of the Attorneys-General*, XI, 227-35.

measures than heretofore shall be adopted." Speed declared his great respect for his former President's profound wisdom, but he was impelled to say that "all who had the good fortune to know him well must feel and know that from his very nature he was not only tempted but forced to strain his power of mercy. His love for mankind was so boundless; his charity so all embracing, and his benevolence so sensitive that he sometimes was as ready to pardon the unrepentant as the sincerely penitent offender. Clearly and positively," he continued, "does the above paragraph from his annual message show to the world that such was his nature."

Thus the Attorney-General paved the way for his forthcoming recommendation that Johnson grant an amnesty with a much wider range of exceptions than Lincoln's proclamations contained. He was certain that the former President "had no power to make an offer of pardon which could be relied upon as protection for offenses committed after notice of the offer." His conclusion, therefore, was that another proclamation of pardon and amnesty "covering a new past" was advisable. "Such [persons] as have been affected by their treasonable associations," he said, "should be absolutely forgiven." But the leaders of the effort to sever the Union should be denied clemency. Lincoln's proclamation had served to suppress the "rebellion." "Now one was desired to restore order and reorganize society" in the South. "Mercy must be largely extended. Some of the great leaders and offenders only must be made to feel the extreme rigor of the law, . . . not in revenge, but to put the seal of infamy upon their conduct." Punishment, therefore, would become a preventative means and not a retributory act.

Welles indicates that the Cabinet shared with the President the task of shaping the proclamation of pardon and amnesty. Speed and Stanton appear to have been the chief factors in determining the contents of the document. Senator Preston King of New York, who was largely responsible for Johnson's nomination in 1864, also counseled the President as to the procedure of dealing with the South. The group evolved a plan of reconstruction for North Carolina which became a model for the other states of the late Confederacy. Having recovered from the attempt made on his life when Lincoln was assassinated, Secretary Seward returned to the councils of the President on May 23, and added his benevolent influence in shaping the policies under consideration. He vainly advised against excepting those worth more than twenty thousand dollars from amnesty.[25]

Eventually the amnesty measure and its reconstruction supplement were completed, and on May 29, 1865, Johnson issued his first proclamation of pardon and amnesty.[26] He gave as the reasons for his act the failure of many to take advantage of Lincoln's proffer of amnesty, and the fact that many others who had been "justly deprived of all claim to amnesty and pardon" under the earlier proclamations by reason of their participation in the rebellion after the date of the previous amnesty "desired to apply for and obtain amnesty and pardon." The proclamation further stated: "To the end, therefore, that the authority of the Government of the United States may be restored and that peace, order, and freedom may be established," the President grants, "to all persons who have directly or indirectly participated in the rebellion, except as hereinafter excepted, amnesty and pardon, with the restoration of all rights of property except as to slaves and except in cases where legal proceedings under the law of the United States providing for the confiscation of property of persons engaged in the rebellion have been instituted."

The oath which Johnson required of those seeking benefit from his amnesty was briefer and less inclusive than that in Lincoln's proclamation. Its meaning, however, implied as much. It was: "I, _____, do solemnly swear (or affirm) in the presence of Almighty God, that I will henceforth faithfully support, protect, and defend the Constitution of the United States and the Union of the States thereunder, and that I will in like manner abide by and faithfully support all laws and proclamations which have been made during the existing rebellion with reference to the emancipation of slaves. So help me God."

Johnson excepted fourteen classes from the benefits of his amnesty, eight more than Lincoln excluded in his first proclamation (see p. 35). Johnson's twelfth exception (those under restraint

25. Welles, *Diary*, II, 294, 299, 300, 301, 305, 307 (May, 1865).
26. Richardson, *Messages . . . of the Presidents*, VI, 310-12.

of the Federal authorities) is in his predecessor's explanatory proclamation of March, 1864, given in Chapter IV. The seven additional classes which Johnson excluded were: "All persons who have been or are absentees from the United States for the purpose of aiding the rebellion"; all Confederate military and naval officers who were educated at West Point or Annapolis; "all persons who held the pretended offices of governors of states in insurrection against the United States"; "all persons who left their homes within the jurisdiction of the United States" to aid the Confederacy; "all persons who have been engaged in the destruction of the commerce of the United States, and . . . who have made raids into the United States from Canada"; all voluntary participants in the "rebellion and the estimated value of whose taxable property is over $20,000"; and all who had taken and subsequently violated the previous amnesty oath or the oath of allegiance to the United States.

Probably the most significant provision of the proclamation, as far as the present study is concerned, provided: "That special application may be made to the President for pardon by any person belonging to the excepted classes, and such clemency will be liberally extended as may be consistent with the facts of the case and the peace and dignity of the United States." This meant that the President could determine at will which of the influential Southerners he would pardon and which he would refuse to favor, providing, of course, that those excepted from his general amnesty chose to make individual application to him for clemency.

Simultaneously with his proclamation of pardon and amnesty, the President announced a plan of restoration for North Carolina.[27] This plan appears to have been foreshadowed by Lincoln and his Cabinet at their last meeting.[28] There was a noticeable difference, however, between it and Lincoln's measure of December, 1863. Instead of a ratio of at least one-tenth of the number of voters in 1860 being required to take the amnesty oath before proceeding further with the work of reconstruction, no percentage at all was

27. *Ibid.,* 326.
28. Hugh McCulloch, *Men and Measures of Half a Century,* 378; Hilary A. Herbert, et al., *Why the Solid South?,* 5-6. Cf. Howard K. Beale, *The Critical Year; a Study of Andrew Johnson and Reconstruction,* 35, cited hereafter as Beale, *The Critical Year.*

needed. Johnson merely required the taking of his oath without any specification as to numbers necessary to participate in the program of reconstruction. It was clearly evident, however, that a satisfactory number would thus qualify.

It can readily be seen that a close relationship existed between the process of pardon and amnesty adopted and the plan of reconstruction put into operation. Pardon not only restored a citizen to his former civil rights and stopped further confiscation of his property, but it also gave him political standing in his state. This political power was so desirable that the most obstinate supporter of the Confederacy could not afford to allow any sentimental scruples to restrain him from seeking a pardon even at the hands of Andrew Johnson.

In proclaiming a plan of reconstruction for North Carolina, the President appointed William W. Holden of that state Provisional Governor. Holden was to prescribe such rules and regulations as might be necessary and proper for a convention to alter and amend the constitution of the state.[29] In the main he was granted rather liberal authority to carry out the provisions embodied in the plan of restoration. Since the amnesty oath was a prerequisite for participation in the program of reconstruction and in the politics of the state after restoration, and since the Provisional Governor was authorized to pass upon, or approve, the petitions for pardon of those in the excepted classes, Holden held a position of considerable power in his state. He could grant or withhold such recommendations for pardon at will, and thereby determine, unless the President disregarded his action, who of his fellow-citizens might participate in the state government. Holden's partiality in recommending pardons is discussed in the chapter on "Pardoning North Carolinians." A failure for any reason to receive a pardon left the applicant, of course, liable to punishment for his part in the late effort at Southern independence.

The North Carolina plan was soon applied to six of the other

29. Richardson, *Messages . . . of the Presidents*, VI, 313. For details of the plan of reconstruction, see Rhodes, *History of the United States*, V; E. P. Oberholtzer, *A History of the United States since the Civil War*, I; Randall, *The Civil War and Reconstruction*, Ch. XXX.

states of the Confederacy;[30] and, therefore, practically the same conditions obtained as to the working of amnesty in those states. The other four Confederate States, as did all the rest of the United States, came, of course, within the scope of Johnson's scheme of clemency. Louisiana, Arkansas, and Tennessee had been reorganized under Lincoln's plan. Moreover, the Alexandria government of Virginia, which had made a new constitution for the state in 1864, was allowed to continue to function after Johnson's accession, until Congress took over the work of reconstruction in 1867.

Johnson's proclamation of amnesty provided that the Secretary of State should "establish rules and regulations for administering and recording the said amnesty oath, so as to insure its benefits to the people and guard the Government against fraud." In compliance with this provision Seward issued a circular on May 29, stating "that the oath prescribed in the proclamation may be taken and subscribed before any commissioned officer, civil, military, or naval, in the service of the United States, or any civil or military officer of a loyal state or territory, who by the laws thereof may be qualified for administering oaths." Certified copies were to be given to those taking the oath, the originals being sent at once to the State Department at Washington, where certificates of their registry might be obtained.[31]

On June 7, Attorney-General Speed announced the following rules which should apply in passing upon the validity of applications for pardon from persons in the excepted classes: the certificates of amnesty were void and of no effect until the recipient had taken the oath prescribed in the proclamation; applications should be made in writing and be accompanied by the original oath; the certificate became invalid if the recipient "shall hereafter at any time acquire any property whatever in slaves, or make use of slave labor." Furthermore, the person pardoned must first pay all costs accrued because of proceedings against him or his property "be-

30. The proclamations for these states are in Richardson, *Messages . . . of the Presidents*, VI, Mississippi, 314; Georgia, 318; Texas, 321; Alabama, 323; South Carolina, 326; Florida, 329.
31. Edward McPherson (ed.), *The Political History of the United States of America during the Period of Reconstruction*, 10-11, cited hereafter as McPherson, *Reconstruction; House Exec. Doc.*, No. 99, 39 Cong., 1 Sess., 9; *Offic. Rec.*, 2 Ser., VIII, 538.

fore date of acceptance of" the pardon. Moreover, the recipient forfeited all claims to property sold under the confiscation acts.[32]

THE PLIGHT OF THE SOUTHERNERS

While the preliminaries of reconstruction were under way the people of the Southland were in a state of great anxiety over their immediate future. Chaos and ruin were all about them. They were in the midst of an economic, social, and political revolution, not of their choice but in spite of their vigorous resistance. The abolition of slavery itself meant the end of an economic and social system that had developed over a period of nearly two and a half centuries. On the agricultural economy, of which Thomas Jefferson had been the most distinguished advocate, a caste social system had developed similar to the manorial life of medieval England, notwithstanding the democracy of the sage of Monticello.[33] Actually the slave was on a lower economic and social plane than the serf. Now all this crumbled rapidly without time for adjustment.

Indeed, so great was the cost of the war through the destruction of property, the emancipation of the slaves, and other harmful concomitants of the conflict and the downfall of the Confederacy, that the eleven seceded states sank far below their economic level of 1860—a level not recovered until 1900.[34] At the same time the Northern states continued to increase in wealth and economic strength. Moreover, the dominant political influence that Southerners had come to exercise in national affairs prior to 1860 had apparently ended. Never again (in the nineteenth century at least) would Southern statesmen enjoy such prestige as in the days of Polk, Tyler, Pierce, and especially Buchanan. Even if the Whigs had been victorious in 1844 and 1852, the presidents would have come from slave states. Furthermore, were not even Frémont and Lincoln Southerners by birth?

All this must have occurred to the Southerners. Their present condition was miserable, and the immediate future boded little improvement. Truly, their plight was calamitous. They were aware

32. *House Exec. Doc.*, No. 99, 39 Cong., 1 Sess., 8-10.
33. See Thomas Jefferson's *Notes on the State of Virginia* (1801), 165-66 (Query XIX).
34. James L. Sellers, "The Economic Incidence of the Civil War in the South," *Mississippi Historical Review*, XIV, No. 2 (September, 1927), 179-91.

of the laws providing punishment for rebellion. They knew that Northerners regarded them as traitors, for which the extreme penalty was death. Confiscations of property had already occurred, and arrests on charges of treason had been and were being made. Especially were the arrest and imprisonment of leaders of the Confederacy ordered as the Confederate States disintegrated. Soon Davis, Stephens, Campbell, Reagan, Hunter, Mallory, Trenholm, Vance, Clay, and a number of others were behind prison bars. But not every civil leader was caught. Benjamin, Breckinridge, Toombs, and others fled to Europe and elsewhere to escape the punishment they thought awaited them. Of course, the Confederates could not go West and acquire land under the Homestead Act, which had been passed during the war (May 10, 1862).[35] To augment the seriousness of the situation, Jefferson Davis, Clement C. Clay, and other prominent Confederates were charged with complicity in the assassination of President Lincoln! Apparently the worst of all dangers was the accession to the presidency of Andrew Johnson. Everyone knew of his long-standing desire to punish the leaders of the Confederacy. Now he was in position to do that very thing, as far as the power of the President would permit.

Naturally many Southerners considered emigrating to other lands. In Alabama the Huntsville *Advocate* announced, on December 14, 1865, that a boat that could carry five hundred emigrants would soon sail for Para on the Amazon River. Rev. Ballard S. Dunn's *Brazil, the Home for Southerners* was published in New York and New Orleans in 1866, giving much information about conditions in Brazil favorable to colonization. Perhaps ten thousand finally did go, Brazil and Central America receiving the largest numbers. These Southern exiles soon tired of their new homes, and, after many hardships, most of them returned to the United States.[36]

35. See A. J. Hanna, *Flight into Oblivion, passim.*; *U. S. Stat. at Large,* XII, 392.

36. Lawrence F. Hill, *The Confederate Exodus to Latin America, passim;* and "Confederate Exiles to Brazil," *Hispanic American Historic Review,* VII, No. 2 (May, 1927), 192-210. See also Charles Sweet's pamphlet on *A Trip to British Honduras and to San Pedro in the Republic of Honduras* (1868); also Blanche Henry Clark Weaver, "Confederate Immigrants and Evangelical Churches in Brazil," *Journal of Southern History,* XVIII, No. 4 (November, 1952), 446-68.

To many Southerners the President's proclamation of amnesty was an encouraging proposition. Johnson's plan of reconstruction was equally heartening, especially since it continued Lincoln's policy, under which Louisiana, Arkansas, and Tennessee (and Virginia, too) were recognized as restored. The fourteen exceptions in the amnesty, of course, left many thousands disfranchised and disqualified from performing legal contracts until they obtained the President's special pardon. Moreover, the punitive laws for rebellion affected some persons in loyal as well as in the late Confederate States. Applications for clemency, therefore, came from states which had not been members of the Confederacy. Naturally, when the amnesty was clearly understood, thousands of persons began seeking the President's pardon.

Many in the excepted classes, apparently, engaged in business as if they had been pardoned, while others hesitated to act thus until they were relieved. Applications for special pardon reveal the desire of some for clemency so that they might sell property or engage in a lucrative profession or business. An unpardoned man like General Howell Cobb, for example, returned to his profession hoping that no one would disturb him. In December, 1865, Cobb, a lawyer, wrote his wife (see page 169) that he was doing well. In August, 1865, General Robert E. Lee accepted the presidency of Washington College, though desiring a pardon so that he could transact business in court to settle the Custis estate on the Potomac.

The following chapters will reveal other uncertainties and confusion attending the resumption of business due to the unpardoned status of persons whom, under the laws providing punishment for rebellion, the President excepted from amnesty. Confiscation proceedings against property owned by such persons were often expected until the owners were pardoned. Other penalties might also be inflicted. Of course, the thousands in the thirteenth exception (owners of property worth more than twenty thousand dollars) had perforce to promote the success of their plantations or other businesses. Doubtless a diligent and extensive search among county records, local newspapers, correspondence, and diaries would contribute much information relating to the efforts of Southerners to adjust themselves to the exigencies of the time. Certainly a pardon was necessary to qualify one for participation in the program of restoring the states to their former connection with the government at Washington, and even to participate in local government. Indeed pardons were much desired by those disabled under Johnson's amnesty and reconstruction program. Many, of course, rather ignored the President's policy and did the best they could under the circumstances.

CHAPTER SEVEN

GENERAL ROBERT E. LEE AND AMNESTY

———◆———

An Application for Pardon

THE CONDUCT of General Lee after the end of hostilities and Johnson's offer of amnesty was highly commendable.[1] In May, 1865, some prominent Federals favored allowing the great Southern military leader the privilege of taking Lincoln's amnesty oath and receiving the benefits therefrom. General Henry W. Halleck, in Richmond, wrote Grant on the fifth of the month that all classes were offering to take the oath and that those excluded from its benefits were taking it and applying for pardon. A few days earlier Grant had instructed General W. S. Hancock to arrest several civil leaders in Virginia. Halleck doubted the wisdom of making so many arrests for fear of checking this general desire for amnesty. "Many of Lee's officers," he wrote, "have come forward to take the oath, and it is reported that even Lee himself is considering the propriety of doing so and petitioning President Johnson for pardon. Should he do this the whole population with few exceptions will follow his example."[2]

Apparently pleased with Halleck's statement, Grant replied the next day: "Although it would meet with opposition in the North to allow Lee the benefit of amnesty, I think it would have the best possible effect toward restoring good feeling and peace in the South to have him come in." He predicted that practically all

---

1. For a similar, but briefer, treatment of Lee, see J. T. Dorris, "Pardoning the Leaders of the Confederacy," *Mississippi Valley Historical Review,* XV, No. 1 (June, 1928), 3-21.

2. *Offic. Rec.,* 2 Ser., VIII, 534 (Halleck to Grant, May 5, 1865).

Southerners would accept whatever Lee did as right and would "be guided to a great extent by his example."[3]

Nevertheless, sentiment increased for the arrest of Lee and his indictment for treason, notwithstanding his military parole. This condition so alarmed him that he appealed to Grant to counteract the movement. In fact, he had gone to Richmond soon after reading Johnson's proclamation of amnesty to learn what he should do. In a letter to Grant, on June 13, he complained of the apparent unwillingness of some Federal authorities to respect the paroles given him and his officers at Appomattox. He stated that he did "not wish to avoid trial, but if I am correct as to the protection granted by my parole, and am not to be prosecuted," he continued, "I desire to comply with the provisions of the President's proclamation, and therefore inclose the required application [for pardon], which I request in that event may be acted on."[4]

Three days later (June 16) Grant forwarded Lee's petition to the President through Stanton's office, "with the earnest recommendation that this application . . . be granted him." He excused the General's failure to enclose the amnesty oath with his petition by saying that General Edward O. C. Ord had informed him that the order requiring the oath had not reached Richmond when the application was forwarded. Grant also admonished the authorities at Washington to respect the terms of the convention at Appomattox in every detail, which meant, he said, that neither Lee nor his generals could "be tried for treason so long as they observe the terms of their parole." He believed such action would have produced "a feeling of insecurity in the minds of all the paroled officers and men," which might have caused them to regard "such an infraction of terms by the Government as an entire release from all obligations on their part."

Believing Federal Judge John C. Underwood's arrests and indictments at Norfolk were injurious to the interest of peace and tranquillity, Grant asked that all indictments found against paroled prisoners of war be quashed and that Underwood be ordered "to desist from the further prosecution of them." When President Johnson insisted on allowing the indictment proceedings to con-

3. *Ibid.*, 535-36 (Grant to Halleck, May 6, 1865).
4. *Ibid.*, 1 Ser., XLVI, pt. 3, p. 1275 (Lee to Grant, June 13, 1865).

tinue, Grant threatened to resign. The President thereupon yielded, and the prosecutions ceased.[5]

Lee's application for pardon was a simple statement of fewer than one hundred words. Others (in the Confederate civil service especially) wrote hundreds and even thousands of words asking for pardon. Often these men defended their actions in supporting secession, and sometimes, as in the case of former Associate Justice of the United States Supreme Court John A. Campbell, they used an honest lawyer's technique in presenting their cases.[6] Many times the civil applicants ably argued the position of the Southern states in claiming the right of secession, hoping thereby to influence the hand of the President in shaping the policy of clemency and restoration in dealing with the late Confederates and their Confederate States. General Lee's motives were not less worthy; brevity is characteristic of the genuine soldier. Few applications for pardon were briefer. Lee wrote:

"Richmond, Virginia, June 13, 1865.
"His Excellency Andrew Johnson,
   "President of the United States.
"Sir: Being excluded from the provisions of the amnesty and pardon contained in the proclamation of the 29th ult., I hereby apply for the benefits and full restoration of all rights and privileges extended to those included in its terms. I graduated at the Military Academy at West Point in June, 1829; resigned from the United States Army, April, 1861; was a general in the Confederate Army, and included in the surrender of the Army of Northern Virginia, April 9, 1865. I have the honor to be, very respectfully,
      "Your obedient servant, R. E. LEE."[7]

Other reasons besides his own personal welfare prompted Lee to apply for pardon. One of his sons, Custis Lee, copied the father's petition evidently before it was forwarded to General Grant. Later

5. *Ibid.*, 1276, 1286-87; Adam Badeau, *Military History of Ulysses S. Grant . . .*, III, 654.
6. See Ch. XII for Campbell's petition.
7. Captain Robert E. Lee, *Recollections and Letters of General Robert E. Lee*, 164-65, cited hereafter as Lee, *Recollections and Letters*. The original has not yet been found. See also Douglas Southall Freeman, *R. E. Lee: A Biography*, IV, 204, cited hereafter as Freeman, *R. E. Lee*.

Custis wrote his brother, Captain Robert E. Lee, that when their father had requested the copy he had said that "it was but right for him to set an example of making formal submission to the civil authorities, and that he thought, by doing so, he might possibly be in a better position to be of use to the Confederates who were not protected by military paroles, especially Mr. Davis."[8]

Apparently at every opportunity Lee urged those coming under Johnson's proclamation "to take the oath of allegiance and accept in good faith the amnesty offered." In this statement he had in mind the tens of thousands not excepted from the benefits of amnesty. To the multitude in the fourteen excepted classes he also recommended that they apply to the President for clemency, as especially provided in the proclamation. "I believe it to be the duty of every man," he wrote in September, 1865, "to unite in the restoration of the country and the reestablishment of peace and harmony. Those considerations governed me in the counsels I gave others, and induced me on the 13th of June to make application to be included in the terms of the amnesty proclamation. . . ."[9]

At the time of the writing above (September, 1865), Jefferson Davis was in Fortress Monroe, accused by many of treason, prison atrocities, and even complicity in the assassination of Lincoln.[10] Lee's concern for the welfare of Davis and for the appeasement of the whole nation caused him to say: "It appears to me that the alloyment of passion, the dissipation of prejudice, and the restoration of reason will alone enable the people of the country to acquire a true knowledge and form a correct judgment of the events of the past four years." Then to be more specific, he continued: "It will, I think, be admitted that Mr. Davis has done nothing more than all the citizens of the Southern States, and should not be held accountable for acts performed by them in the exercise of what had been considered by them [an] unquestionable right." Believ-

8. Lee, *Recollections and Letters*, 165.
9. Walter L. Fleming, *Documentary History of Reconstruction . . .*, I, 63-64 (letter to Captain Josiah Tattnall of the "Merrimac," September 7, 1865), cited hereafter as Fleming, *Documentary History*; Lee, *Recollections and Letters*, 163; James C. Young, *Marse Robert, Knight of the Confederacy*, 327-33, cited hereafter as J. C. Young, *Marse Robert*.
10. See Ch. XIII, "Pardoning Jefferson Davis."

ing that common sense and justice would ultimately triumph, he concluded with these optimistic words: "I have too exalted an opinion of the American people to believe that they will consent to injustice, and it is only necessary, in my opinion, that truth should be known, for the rights of everyone to be secured. I know of no surer way of eliciting the truth than by burying contention with the war."

Lee revealed another reason for desiring a pardon in a letter to Reverdy Johnson on January 27, 1866. After referring to the distinguished jurist's plea before the Supreme Court in the case of *Ex parte Garland* concerning the constitutionality of the test oath,[11] he wrote: "I have been awaiting the action of President Johnson upon my application to be embraced in his proclamation of May 29, and for my restoration to civil rights, before attempting to close the estate of Mr. G. W. Custis, of which I am sole administrator. . . ." The estate in question was the "Arlington," Virginia, which the United States claimed by tax title and had begun to use as a national cemetery on the Potomac opposite Washington. The Supreme Court gave title to the Custis-Lee family in 1882, and Congress allowed George Washington Custis $150,000 for the estate a year later.

Anxiety over the disposition of "Arlington" to the advantage of the Custises and Lees caused Lee to complain to Johnson again, on July 7, 1866, of his predicament. "If it was not for the interest of others which is involved," he wrote, "I should have no anxiety in the matter, but I should not like them to suffer on my account." Then, after despairing of any early abatement of passions and restoration of reason in the nation, he said: "Knowing how the President's time is occupied in public matters, and how his acts are turned by his opponents to operate against him, I have been unwilling to intrude upon him my private affairs, preferring to wait for some general action of his in which they might be embraced." He closed by soliciting Johnson's aid, saying: "If you can suggest anything proper for me to do, I will be very much obliged to you. . . ." By "some general action" Lee meant a more general, or a

11. See division, "The Ironclad Test Oath," in Ch. XVII.

universal, amnesty which would remove the disability disqualifying him from functioning as administrator in settling the Custis estate.[12]

The Oath Omitted

Lee's failure to submit the amnesty oath with his petition for pardon was mentioned above with Grant's apology for the omission. In reality, the omission appears hardly excusable. The oath was a part of the proclamation and a requirement for a favorable consideration of an application. Lee stated that he had read the proclamation before he prepared his petition. Surely there was someone in Richmond who could have administered the oath. Subsequently he could have taken the oath and forwarded it to Washington, but there appears to be no record of his having done so. Yet he advised all others similarly disabled to take the oath. Why did he not do as he advised others? As early as September 7, 1865, he had told Captain Josiah Tattnall, a former United States naval officer who had commanded the Confederate "Merrimac," that he had not received an answer to his petition and could not inform his correspondent of the President's decision.[13]

Could Lee have had some poignant uneasiness about taking the amnesty oath? Tens of thousands of others, much less responsible for the tremendous effort to sever the Union than he, took the oath. In fact, a multitude took two oaths—an oath of allegiance on being released from military prisons and later the amnesty oath, either Lincoln's or Johnson's. And yet a third oath was required by, and administered under, the Congressional Reconstruction Act of March 23, 1867. Oathtaking was indeed the order and measure of one's loyalty to the United States and fitness for suffrage in the 1860's.

General Lee had no good reason to expect favorable action on his application for pardon without his having taken the amnesty oath. He surely did not think the requirement should have been waived in his case. Certainly, if it should have been required of anyone, it should have been required of him. Perhaps taking a

12. The Reverdy Johnson Papers (Library of Congress; Lee to Johnson, January 27, July 7, 1866). For a good brief account of the case involving the Custis estate see Freeman, *R. E. Lee*, IV, 385 ff.

13. Fleming, *Documentary History*, I, 63-64; J. C. Young, *Marse Robert*, 333.

second oath to support and defend the United States government was distasteful to Lee because he had taken a similar oath as an officer in the United States army and then, after resigning, had sworn to support the Confederacy as an officer. In all probability, however, his petition would not have been granted even if he had again sworn fidelity to the government which he had earlier disowned. He may have realized that, but the thought does not excuse him, since he advised all others to swear fealty to the United States.

Perhaps a reason for Lee's never taking the oath of allegiance or the amnesty oath may be found in his statement on the subject to General George Gordon Meade on May 5, 1865. The Federal General was passing through Richmond with the Army of the Potomac on the way to Washington for the grand, triumphant army review at the close of the war. In a spirit of conciliation and to renew old friendships, Meade visited Lee, whom he urged to take "the oath of allegiance, not only on his own account, but for the great influence his example would have upon others." Lee replied that he "had no personal objections" to taking the oath and "that he . . . intended to submit to the Constitution and laws of the United States, but that . . . he was unwilling to change his present status [as a paroled prisoner of war] until he could form some idea of what the policy of the Government was going to be toward the people of the South." Meade stated that the government could not decide how to treat the Southerners "until it was satisfied [that] they had returned to their allegiance, and that the only practicable way of showing this was by taking the oath." Lee admitted the logic of his visitor's argument but evidently took the position then that he would defer swearing allegiance again to the United States until he was certain of the government's policy of restoration.[14]

Evidently General Lee was pleased with the course reconstruction took in the summer of 1865, for he applied for pardon on June 13 and later advised all others to comply with the proclamation of amnesty. But why did he not take the amnesty oath? The answer may be found in his statement above to General Meade.

14. George Meade, *The Life and Letters of George Gordon Meade, Major-General United States Army*, II, 278-79. Cf. Freeman, *R. E. Lee*, IV, 195.

Since he never again swore allegiance to the United States, he probably regarded himself as a paroled prisoner of war until the President formally declared hostilities at an end, on April 2, 1866, in all the late Confederate States except Texas.[15]

By that time Congress was launching a program of reconstruction which most Southerners could not approve. Indeed, the refusal of the Radicals of that body to seat representatives from the late seceded states in December, 1865, was displeasing to Southerners like Lee. Nor did conditions improve as time passed, for by March and April, 1867, ten state constitutions and governments had been brushed aside and a military regime imposed on the states thus affected to supervise the holding of elections, the making of constitutions, and the inauguration of governments more satisfactory to the Radicals in Congress and the North. (This was something, it should be noted, that Presidents Lincoln and Johnson had done earlier in setting aside the state governments of the Confederate States, even to the requirement of the ratification of an amendment to the Constitution for restoration. The Thirteenth, however, was not as objectionable to Southerners as the Fourteenth Amendment.) Whites were disfranchised and Negroes enfranchised by Federal law. Moreover, another oath, more comprehensive than the others, was required of the participants in this reconstruction program,[16] and the ratification of the Fourteenth Amendment, first submitted in June, 1866, was required for restoration.

By April, 1866, therefore, and certainly by March, 1867, the government's treatment of the South was far from what Lee had desired in 1865. According to his statements to Meade on the subject of an oath, he surely concluded that, as far as he was concerned, the revolutionary policy of the government, thus forced upon the South, did not justify his ever taking another oath of allegiance of any kind to the United States. Had he taken an oath in 1865 or after the end of his parole, on April 2, 1866, and obtained a pardon, the action of Congress in March, 1867, would

15. Richardson, *Messages . . . of the Presidents* (1913 ed.), V, 3627-30. Not until August 20, 1866, was the war declared ended in Texas. *Ibid.*, 3632-36.
16. *U. S. Stat. at Large*, XIV, XV.

have revoked the political benefits of the amnesty—for a time, at least.

The oath, it should be noted, was required in Johnson's more generous amnesty proclamation of September 7, 1867. Lee, remaining excepted, must have noted the retention. The oath, however, was omitted from the President's third general amnesty, proclaimed July 4, 1868. The General still remained unpardoned until Johnson's universal amnesty on Christmas Day, 1868, when every person remaining disabled under the laws providing punishment for supporting the rebellion was relieved, except for the disability provided in the third section of the Fourteenth Amendment, which became a part of the Constitution on July 26, 1868.[17]

Actually Lee did not need a pardon very badly. His parole exempted him from molestation for nearly a year, and he was allowed to do pretty much as he pleased. He was soon (August, 1865) chosen President of Washington College at Lexington, Virginia, and on October 2 took the oath required by the trustees of the college to discharge the duties of his office "without favor, affection or partiality," and called upon the Almighty to help him keep the faith.[18] Apparently he functioned in that capacity as though he had been pardoned. What more liberty did he need, since he had no desire to participate in politics? Indeed he did want to administer the Custis estate, which he had the authority to do after being amnestied on December 25, 1868. But the Fourteenth Amendment, on becoming a part of the Constitution, in July, 1868, denied such men as he the privilege of holding any kind of military or civil office in the United States until the disability was removed by Congress. Lee's position, fortunately, was president of a private college and needed no sanction by a two-thirds majority of both houses of Congress. Had Washington College been otherwise, the presidency could easily have been classified as a public office, and Lee could not then have been its president until he had been pardoned by Johnson and relieved by Congress of the disability provided in the third section of the Fourteenth Amendment.

17. See third division of Ch. XIV and second division of Ch. XV.
18. The oath is in the archives of Washington and Lee University, Lexington. For Northern opposition to Lee's presidency of Washington College, see Freeman, *R. E. Lee*, IV, 350 ff.

Of course there was opposition, in the North especially, to the freedom allowed Lee. One man, writing on October 1, 1865, shamed the President for permitting him to become president of a college. In fact, he regarded the General's military parole as equivalent to a pardon. He was so unreasonable in his criticism that he hoped some calamity would overtake Johnson in this or the next world for neglecting to have the leaders of the rebellion punished, as he had declared earlier he would do if he were President.[19] His radical declaration will suffice here for the statements of all other opponents to favors allowed General Lee and other leaders of the Confederacy.

Some Southerners believed Lee felt much humiliated in petitioning for pardon. "Had the General considered his own feelings alone," ran the Savannah *Republican* for August 31, 1865, "he would have died sooner than humble himself and a just cause by a seeming admission that it was wrong. His application was one more proof of his love for his country. . . ." The writer then gave Lee's action as an example of what the Virginian desired all others to do. It is very doubtful, however, that General Lee was as remorseful as some believed him to be when he applied for pardon. He was too sensitive to the exigencies of the time, and his obligation to Virginia in promoting her restoration and the part she should take in the development of a greater United States surely lessened any compunctions of conscience that he otherwise might have felt in petitioning "plebeian" Andrew Johnson for pardon. Would taking the amnesty oath to "support, protect, and defend the Constitution of the United States and the Union of the States thereunder" have been more painful than the application for pardon? It should not have been to a man of Lee's character and capability.

Lee in no wise approved of the emigration of any Confederates, and advised all, especially the leaders, to remain to share the fate of their respective states and to contribute to the restoration of the Southland to tranquillity and prosperity. When a British nobleman "desired him to accept a mansion and an estate [in England] commensurate with his individual merits and the greatness of an historic family," he declined the offer. "I am deeply grateful," he

19. Cf. Fleming, *Documentary History*, I, 36.

replied; "I cannot desert my native State in the hour of her adversity. I must abide her fortunes, and share her fate."[20]

How different were John Cabell Breckinridge, Judah P. Benjamin, Robert Toombs, and many other leaders of the Confederacy! They scurried out of the country as best they could, "fleeing from the wrath to come" as the Confederate States rapidly disintegrated. It should be noted, however, that Lee was protected by his military parole, a privilege not enjoyed by the civil leaders of the Confederacy.[21]

Before we leave the consideration of Lee's favorable attitude toward "bind[ing] up the nation's wounds" and achieving "a just and lasting peace," the contents of a letter by Charles A. Dana to Stanton, on April 12, 1865, and another letter by Stanton to Grant, on March 3, 1865, might well be considered. The first is indeed remarkable, if Dana related correctly what General Lee had said to Grant at Appomattox. Wrote Dana: "General Grant had a long private interview with Lee, who said that he should devote his whole efforts to pacifying the country and bringing the people back to the Union." This statement is in accord with the General's sentiment expressed above. The next sentence especially arrests the attention: "He had always been for the Union in his heart and could find no justification for the politicians who had brought on the war, whose origin he believed to have been in the folly of extremists on both sides." This is in accord with Freeman's account of Lee's love for the Union and abhorrence of secession, and of his greater love for Virginia, which, after a struggle, caused him to serve the Confederate States.[22]

Perhaps Grant did not accurately relate just what Lee said, or perhaps Dana failed to state correctly what Grant told him. Dana's next statement, however, surely pertains to Stanton's message to Grant on March 3. "If General Grant had agreed to the interview he [Lee] had asked for some time ago," the Assistant Secretary of

20. Quoted by Lee, *Recollections and Letters*, 170. Also see Freeman, *R. E. Lee*, IV, 208.
21. See Freeman, *R. E. Lee*, IV, opposite p. 150, for a photoengraving of General Lee's parole, signed by himself and also by six of his staff officers. For a good account of the emigration of certain leaders of the Confederacy, see A. J. Hanna, *Flight into Oblivion, passim*.
22. Freeman, *R. E. Lee*, I, Ch. XXV.

War wrote, "they would certainly have agreed on terms of peace then, as he [Lee] was prepared to treat for the surrender of all the Confederate armies. . . ." Dana went on to relate that the war had left Lee a poor man, whose "wife would have to provide for herself until he could find some employment."[23]

Dana's official relationship to Stanton and Grant gives his letter some importance, and his earlier and later prominence and success as a journalist enhance interest in the message. But when did Lee ask for the interview referred to? According to Stanton's letter to Grant, the time was surely March 2 or 3. Apparently Grant asked Stanton at once for instructions relative to peace negotiations with Lee, and received the following reply: "The President directs me to say to you that he wishes you to have no conference with General Lee unless it is for the capitulation of General Lee's army, or on some minor, and purely military matter. He instructs me to say that you are not to decide, discuss, or confer upon any political question. Such questions, the President holds in his own hands; and will submit them to no military conferences or conventions. Meanwhile you are to press to the utmost your military advantages."[24]

No other reference to a proposed interview between Lee and Grant early in March, 1865, appears extant. Grant might have asked for instructions without having been approached by Lee. Nevertheless, these two letters indicate the contemplation of such a conference by the two generals and its denial by Lincoln. If the correspondence has a valid basis, it sheds some interesting light on Lee's thinking at that critical time—early March, 1865. Moreover, Stanton's message to Grant expresses exactly the attitude Lincoln's successor took toward General Sherman's negotiations with General Joseph E. Johnston for the surrender of the latter's army nearly two months later.[25]

23. *Offic. Rec.*, 1 Ser., XLVI, pt. 3, pp. 716-17 (Dana to Grant, April 12, 1865).

24. Stanton Papers (Library of Congress), XXV (Stanton to Grant, March 3, 1865). Evidently these letters had no connection with the Hampton Roads conference of February 3, 1865.

25. See the first division of Ch. VI; also Randall, *Lincoln and the South*, 135-39, for Grant's recommendation to Lee, on April 10, 1865, that Lee and Lincoln confer on terms of reconstruction.

AN EVALUATION

One other observation will suffice. Lee's most eminent biographer, Freeman, in eulogizing the great General, exclaims: "Had his sense of duty held him to the Union, as it held Winfield Scott and George H. Thomas, how much easier his course would have been! Never, then, after the first mobilization, would he have lacked for troops or been compelled to count the cost of any move. He would not have agonized over men who shivered in their nakedness or dyed the road with shoeless, bleeding feet. . . . The superior military would have been his, not his adversary's. On his order new locomotives and stout cars would have rolled to the front, swiftly to carry his army where the feeble engines and groaning trains of the Confederacy could not deliver men. . . . His simplicity, his tact, his ability, and his self-abnegation would have won the confidence of Lincoln that McClellan lost and neither Pope, Burnside, nor Hooker ever possessed. He would, in all human probability, have won the war, and now he would be preparing to ride up Pennsylvania Avenue, as was Grant, at the head of a victorious army, on his way to the White House."[26]

This eulogy stimulates thought. Did the old veteran, Winfield Scott, or the younger veteran, George H. Thomas, feel any less a sense of duty in 1861, when they chose to defend the Union, than did Robert E. Lee, when he declined the opportunity to command a United States army to maintain the Union and instead resigned his commission and accepted later a commission in the Confederate service? Indeed, was not the decision of those two worthy sons of the Old Dominion more commendable than that of General Lee? Scott and Thomas had been nurtured in the same soil that had nourished Lee. Thomas had been schooled in the same atmosphere (West Point) that had made Lee a superior military officer, and the "Rock of Chickamauga," too, won many laurels.

It should be noted parenthetically that Virginia voted eighty-eight to forty-five, on April 4, against a motion to formulate an ordinance of secession, and that it was not until the firing on Fort Sumter and especially Lincoln's call for troops that sentiment crys-

26. Freeman, *R. E. Lee*, IV, 165-66.

tallized sufficiently to cause a Virginia convention, on April 17, to secede by a vote of eighty-eight to fifty-five. Lee would certainly have voted against secession if he had been in the convention on April 17, as Scott and Thomas would also have done if they had been members. The three were strong Unionists; but Lee was a Virginian first and then a nationalist, and, though he did not approve of the separation of his state from the United States, he chose to follow the Old Dominion, regardless of the course she took. Scott and Thomas were nationalists first and last, and wisely acted accordingly.[27]

The three Virginians were doubtless familiar with the growth of American nationality. They were surely familiar with the ideals of the statesmen of that day and the previous generation, diverse though they were. They had all fought in the Mexican War, and now they were faced with a military choice that demanded the wisdom of a seer and prophet. If Lee had been victorious, the result would have been a nation founded on the waning principle of states' rights and a weak central government, and on the outmoded institution of human slavery with its concomitant, an agrarian economy and civilization. Such a conclusion of the conflict as Lee envisioned would have been disastrous to the South, to the United States, and to the world at large, as has been clearly shown by subsequent history. Never would the Confederate States have prospered and received world-wide approbation in the rapidly developing scientific, technical, and humanitarian age, with a weak central government, with a preponderance of slave labor, and with only an agrarian economy. Actually the Confederacy would most probably have strengthened its central government after it had gained independence, and have abolished slavery in order to guarantee human rights and make possible modern industries to supplement its agricultural system. All this surely would have happened; but is not one great Union far more desirable today than two comparatively small nations would have been in defending

27. Randall's Ch. IX, "The Plight of the Upper South," in *The Civil War and Reconstruction*, gives a good account of Virginia's early resistance to the forces of separation in the South. General Scott retired from service October 31, 1861, on account of age and ill health.

the ideals of Western civilization? Moreover, in the light of what has just been stated, would a successful effort at independence in the 1860's have justified the enormous human and material cost? Let the competent economists, political scientists, statesmen, historians, and humanitarians answer the questions—if their answers are necessary to convince dubious questioners.

But to be more specific: admitting that Lee deserves all the honor that is his today, the historian is justified in believing he could have deserved even greater honor if, like Scott and Thomas, he had stood by the Union and not tried to go out with Virginia. The value of a man's life should be measured by evaluating the service he has rendered to society for all time. As the scholarly Freeman suggests, suppose Lee had been a nationalist instead of a states' rights devotee—a progressive instead of a conservative or reactionary.[28] He would have decided differently in April, 1861, and most likely have been given command of the Army of the Potomac. Consequently, Richmond would probably have fallen to the Federals two years earlier, maybe sooner. Or was Lee far more successful fighting on the defensive than on the offensive? It has not been proven so. Following Freeman's suggestion, the student must conclude that Lee could have caused the war to end much earlier. What a great service that would have been! What a saving in lives and property! Lincoln would most likely have lived, and the nation would have escaped the crime of congressional reconstruction. Lee could have marched up Pennsylvania Avenue at the head of a victorious army two years or more before General Meade (for Grant)

28. Despite his nationalism and disapproval of Virginia's act of secession, Lee must be classified as conservative and reactionary because he supported the Confederacy. A man's classification should be determined by the cause for which he voluntarily fights. Freeman (*R. E. Lee*, IV, 367) quotes Lee as saying, in May, 1868: "I did only what my duty demanded. I could have taken no other course without dishonor. And if all were to be done over again, I would act in precisely the same manner." Perhaps his ultimate opinion would have been different if he could have lived a generation longer; but by that time there would probably have been no reason for Virginia's act of secession. Had Lee lived, he would most likely have subscribed to Jefferson Davis's concluding statement, in 1881, to *The Rise and Fall of the Confederate Government*. See the division "Refusal to Ask for Pardon" in Ch. XIII ("Pardoning Jefferson Davis").

enjoyed that distinction; and he, instead of the incompetent President Grant, would probably have been trusted and honored with the presidency!

Finally, would not Robert E. Lee have rendered greater service to his native Virginia and the United States if he had made the decision in April, 1861, that Winfield Scott and George H. Thomas made? Could not Scott and Thomas have offered as good reasons for supporting the Confederacy as Lee offered? Did they not exercise better judgment than their fellow Virginian by choosing to remain loyal to their country? Is it not fortunate that they did not turn away from the government at Washington to support "pretending" state and "usurping" separatist governments?

Washington was an American first and then a Virginian. His ideals and services were those which Scott and Thomas promoted, defended, and made enduring. Would not Lee occupy a position today in the minds of Americans equaled or excelled only by Washington if he had served his country as faithfully and valiantly as he did the Old Dominion? Lee, however, followed a different course of action, and for his superb character as a man and superior ability as a soldier deserves the honor of being the one outstanding hero of the War between the States. *So mote it be.* But, in the light of the foregoing words, should not Scott and Thomas be advanced to a place nearer the top of the pinnacle of adoration, universally accorded Lee, than has generally been awarded them? The eloquence of the discerning and penetrating Dr. Freeman certainly suggests what the future, carefully evaluating historians will surely do.[29]

29. This departure from the subject of the chapter and the main theme of the book was suggested and encouraged by Freeman's chapter, "The Sword of Robert E. Lee," in *R. E. Lee: A Biography*, Vol. IV. The digression surely has some value. The author has no desire, of course, to cast any aspersion on Robert E. Lee. The "Evaluation" above should prove the contrary. He agrees with Freeman, who wrote, after reading this chapter: "He [Lee] can stand the scrutiny of all critics, I take it, without losing any of the nobility of his character." (Letter to the author, December 15, 1950.) Moreover, the author hopes with Dr. Frank L. Owsley, who has read this and other chapters of the manuscript, that readers and reviewers of the book will not "take up too much space arguing" the point of "Lee's decision to go with the Confederacy and Virginia." (Owsley to the author, December 18, 1950.)

CHAPTER EIGHT

PARDON SEEKERS AND BROKERS

———◆———

THE AMNESTY PAPERS

IN THE National Archives at Washington are manuscripts very properly called the Amnesty Papers. At least that is what they were labeled in the War Department, which received them from the Department of Justice in 1894 and kept them in eighty boxes, or files, until transferring them to the National Archives a few years ago. These papers are the "special" applications for pardon by many thousands of persons excepted from the benefits of President Johnson's first proclamation of amnesty. Their use has been neglected by historians of the period, though they contain much interesting information of both private and public import.

There are some fifteen thousand of these individual petitions in the collection. This number is a rough estimate. There may be many more, but only about 13,500 petitions were granted. Some applications never reached Washington, since they had to pass through the offices of the governors of the states in which the petitioners lived, and others that did reach the capital were never placed with the great mass of petitions. Moreover, there are numerous letters relating to the pardoning business that may be found among the papers of many prominent persons of the period. With each request for clemency is (or should be) filed the writer's oath of allegiance to the United States. Often there is also filed with the application at least one memorial (often that of the governor of the petitioner's state) to the President by interested persons imploring clemency for the petitioner. Sometimes these memorials are very strong appeals and have many signatures.

Naturally the disfranchised and otherwise proscribed Southerner was anxious to be pardoned and have his rights and privileges restored. Until this was done, he could neither acquire nor transfer titles to properties; nor could he obtain copyrights and patents. The New York *Herald* for November 16, 1865, states that the first West Point man to be pardoned was a certain Major Echols, who desired a patent on something which the government wished to use. The authorities were anxious for Echols's services as an inventor and advised clemency. The Southerner often found it difficult to secure employment and to engage in any business whatsoever. He even hesitated to marry. Moreover, his property was in danger of confiscation; and, worst of all, he was threatened with indictment and conviction for treason. The desire to participate in the program of reconstruction, however, was the impelling motive in the applications of many.

The petitioners represented every activity in the South during the rebellion. From the lowest to the highest officials—save one— in the Confederacy came requests for clemency. Jefferson Davis never asked for pardon, but Vice-President Stephens and other civil leaders did; and Robert E. Lee very early set the example for those who had led the armies in the futile struggle for independence. The late Professor Walter L. Fleming gave forty-nine occupations in Alabama that excepted the people engaged in them from the benefits of amnesty.[1] His list indicates the wide range of those thus disabled in all the states. There were tax assessors and receivers, postmasters and mail contractors, cotton agents and commissioners of appraisement, enrolling officers and generals in the armies, district attorneys and state and Confederate judges, graduates of West Point and Annapolis, state printers and custom officers, wealthy planters and businessmen, Confederate governors and congressmen, and many others whose activities placed them under the displeasure of the government.

Women as well as men were affected, and special provisions were sometimes made as to when they might take the amnesty oath. In Savannah, for example, men were instructed to apply at the provost

1. Walter L. Fleming, *Civil War and Reconstruction in Alabama*, 357, n. 2.

marshal's "office on Bryan Street between 9 and 12 A.M. and Ladies
. . . at . . . the Custom House between 1 and 4 P.M. each day."[2]
In fact, all were obliged to obtain pardons if they were to escape
punishment and again enjoy civil and political rights and privileges
in their respective states and in the nation, for it must be remembered
that the punitive laws passed during the rebellion and described in
the first chapter were still in force and applying to those in the
excepted classes until they obtained pardons. The sensible thing for
these people to do, therefore, was to recognize the exigencies of the
time and ask for clemency. Of course, there were many who did
not apply, but waited instead for further developments, which
might include another amnesty with no exception at all.[3] It was
more than two years, however, before Johnson proclaimed a
second amnesty, and it was not universal, as will be explained in
Chapter XV.

Often the petitions to the President were brief requests for pardon,
accompanied only by the applicants' oaths of allegiance. Many
times, however, they were long and well-prepared defenses of the
Southern cause with suggestions of the proper course to pursue in
dealing with the South now that the war was over, the Union pre-
served, and the end of slavery assured. And in this connection it
might be noted that the Amnesty Papers indicate, first, that Negro
slavery was generally regarded as having been the paramount cause
of the Civil War, and, second, that the failure of the Confederacy
to gain independence was also regarded as ending forever the
existence of that institution in the United States. Nevertheless, there
were persons who endeavored to excuse themselves for supporting
the Confederacy. Some also declared that they had remained steadfastly loyal to the Union and should therefore receive immediate,
favorable consideration. Others stated that they had been forced to
aid the South and consequently deserved clemency. Only a few
apparently misrepresented their part in the rebellion in order to
receive favor more readily.[4]

2. Savannah *Republican*, September 1, 1865.
3. Fleming, *Civil War and Reconstruction in Alabama*, 356.
4. See J. T. Dorris, "Pardon Seekers and Brokers: A Sequel of Appomattox," *Journal of Southern History*, I, No. 3 (August, 1935), 276-92, for
the character of many petitions by the rank and file of the Confederates.

THE MAGNITUDE OF THE TASK

Many petitioners went to their respective state capitals to influence their governor to approve and forward their applications to the President. Others remained at home and depended on friends or agents to look after their interests. In fact, the provisional governors were soon very busy receiving petitioners and their friends, and examining applications. William W. Holden of North Carolina left a good account of his "very heavy task" in performing this duty, which is given in the chapter on "Pardoning North Carolinians." The Provisional Governor of South Carolina, Benjamin F. Perry, also left an interesting account of his experience in administering the President's amnesty. "One mail," he states, "brought me no less than one hundred and fifty letters! They were mostly for offices and pardons. . . . This utter destitution of the country seemed to make everyone ravenous for office. . . .⁵ But the applications for pardon were more numerous than even those for office. . . . All were anxious to be made 'new men' again. These applications were very troublesome," he continues. "I had to read them and see that they were in proper form, approve or reject them, and mail them to the President. I had also to give the petitioner a certificate that his application had been received and forwarded. . . ." Perry states further that he approved every petition and that during the first six months of his administration as Provisional Governor he "received, examined and forwarded to Washington between two and three thousand applications for pardon. . . ."⁶

It is easily perceived, therefore, that a considerable task confronted the governors and especially President Johnson and certain of his aids, if due consideration was to be given every petition and a pardon granted or delayed or refused, as each case merited. The plan of amnesty was expected to operate simply and honestly, but it did not. So many factors affected its administration, so many benefits were derived from a pardon, and so many persons petitioned for clemency that the pardoning business became a colossal national spectacle, affording opportunities for chicanery and money-making.

5. The sequence of this and the following sentence has been reversed for the sake of coherence.
6. See Benjamin Franklin Perry, *Reminiscences of Public Men*, 263-88.

If state and national administrative officials wearied during the ordeal, and if the President suffered much from vituperation by his opponents as his amnesty policy unfolded, these tribulations should be charged to just such an unfortunate aftermath as might be expected to follow the national travail of a long and injurious civil war.

It appears that only a small number of petitions had been granted by the middle of August, 1865. When the subject of amnesty was discussed in a Cabinet meeting on the eleventh of that month, "the President . . . said that few pardons had been granted notwithstanding the clamor that was raised. No one who had been educated at public expense . . . no officer of the Army or Navy, no member of Congress who had left his seat, no member of the Rebel government who had deserted and gone into the service had been pardoned, nor did he propose to pardon anyone of that class. It was understood that neither Davis, Stephens, nor any member of the Rebel Cabinet should be pardoned."[7]

The above statement shows that Johnson had not yet departed very far from his earlier position in respect to punishing some of the Confederates. Nevertheless, the approaching conventions authorized under Johnson's plan of reconstruction caused many in the excepted classes to try to hasten action on their petitions so that they might qualify to sit in these conventions. Furthermore, there would soon be many state and national offices to be filled, and they were something to be desired. So, as August passed and September days came, there was much activity in Washington, which indicated that pardons ere long would be granted in large numbers. Another desk was placed in the Attorney-General's office, and M. F. Pleasants was appointed pardon clerk. It was this official's duty to examine the petitions and arrange them for his superior's consideration.

General L. C. Baker, Chief of the National Detective Police in the District of Columbia, was a close observer of all that was going on in Washington at the time. In 1869 he included in a *History of the United States Secret Service* an account of what he observed in connection with the granting of pardons. Concerning the ap-

7. Welles, *Diary*, II, 358.

pointment of the pardon clerk, Pleasants, he states: "To obviate this difficulty [delay in granting pardons] the President appointed as an agent for this purpose, a man reported to have been a rebel colonel. It was advertised throughout the South that such an agent had been appointed, and consequently those desiring pardons were requested to forward their applications to said agent. In pursuance to this notice, applications came forward in great numbers."[8] Baker's disapproval of the pardoning business and his trouble with Johnson over the activities of pardon agents may sometimes have caused him to exaggerate somewhat. Yet there is no doubt of his accuracy in describing the general rush for pardons and the activity of pardon agents in the capital during the months of July, August, September, and October, 1865. There is plenty of contemporaneous evidence of that exciting and deplorable spectacle—deplorable because such were the wholesale applications for pardon and the numerous visitations of both petitioners and their friends or agents to the source of clemency that considering and granting pardons became, so it appeared, the chief business of the executive and his departments of State and Justice.

By September pardons began to be granted rather freely, causing much displeasure to those who believed that retribution should be required in the cases of Johnson's fourteen excepted classes. The newspapers kept the public informed of the President's increasing leniency, announcing that pardons were being granted daily by scores and hundreds. There appeared in the New York *Tribune* for July, August, and September statements like the following: "One hundred and ninety pardons, mostly Virginians and North Carolinians, were granted today, on recommendations of the Governors of their respective states." "About ninety pardons were granted today and two hundred applications received at the Attorney-General's office." "There were several hundred pardon seekers thronging the President's mansion today. The city is filled with those of the twenty thousand dollar stamp and daily arrivals are greatly in excess of the departures." "The notorious Albert Pike of Arkansas, now residing in Canada, has applied for pardon. Two hundred of the Masonic Fraternity endorse him." "Between 300

8. General L. C. Baker, *History of the United States Secret Service*, 691, cited hereafter as Baker, *Secret Service*.

and 400 applications for pardon were received today." "Hotels are unusually crowded today with Southern patriots yearning for forgiveness. Among the more demonstrative is McMullen, a late Congressman."

On July 31 the New York *Herald* stated: "The scene at the President's reception today was most remarkable. The ante-room was crowded with Senators and Representatives of the late rebel Congress, seeking interviews with the President and beseeching that their pardons might be hurried up." This was in July, however, and before Johnson began pardoning the leaders of the Confederacy. Just one month later the *Herald* stated that some of the pardon seekers acted "as if they had an indisputable right to the pardon . . . and are correspondingly importunate. This retards rather than facilitates their object; for the President continues to act in such a manner as to assure them that pardon is a deed of clemency and not of right."

The newspapers, apparently, were not always correct in their numbers, sometimes exceeding the facts in the case. The *Tribune* appears more extravagant in its statements than the *Herald*. The former estimated, on September 5, 1865, that 50,000 petitions were on file; and on March 10, 1866, it was of the opinion that from 25,000 to 30,000 had already been granted. These numbers are entirely too large, as only some 13,500 pardons were actually granted, and the number of applications on file appears to be not more than 15,000 to 20,000. It should be noted, in this connection, that the scores of thousands of amnesty oaths received and recorded in Washington from persons not in the excepted classes and consequently pardoned outright may have confused reporters and caused them to overestimate the number of petitions for special pardon actually received and also the number of pardons really granted. These oaths were not referred to the Attorney-General and his pardon clerk for their consideration as the oaths and petitions of those applying for pardon were. They remained instead in the Department of State without any special consideration.

The oaths of those not in the excepted classes may now be found in the National Archives at Washington. An estimate of their number while they were in the custody of the Department of State indicated that there were some two hundred thousand. Two books now in the National Archives, however, contain 181,034 names of these oath takers. Many of the amnesty oaths may not have been recorded. Moreover, there were also tens of thousands of oaths of allegiance administered to men released from prison camps, as explained in the first division of Chapter IX. Requisition Books A and B of the Attorney-General's office, now in the National Archives, give the names of those receiving special pardons day by day during the months of 1865-66, the requisitions becoming very few as 1866 passed. July, August, September, and October were the most fruitful months in 1865.

Naturally, much time was required of the President and his aids in considering petitions and granting pardons. If they had had little else to do, it would have been different. But for the Chief Executive and a Cabinet officer or two to give so much attention to such matters was certain to arouse adverse criticism, even by those who favored the President's increasing leniency. The New York *Herald* repeatedly stated that Johnson was unwell, owing to the press of business, and that the ever-increasing number of pardon seekers made his condition worse. It was to be expected, therefore, that a solution of the difficulty would be offered. A pardon board was soon advocated as the proper agency to handle this business.[9] Senator Henry Wilson was expected to head this bureau, but such an organization was never created.

On August 23 the New York *Tribune* manifested its disapproval of a pardon board by advocating "a simple proclamation setting forth that certain Rebels for the good of the country are expatriated, and all the rest admitted to the rights of citizens." A little later (September 21) the *Herald* presented two current opinions concerning the President's pardoning activity. "One class of men feel vindicative," it said, "and believe no pardons should be granted until the people of the rebellious states have at least passed through a severe probationary period. The others are in favor of pardons, but believe the present laborious method of examining cases wholly impracticable. The President's lifetime would not suffice for a moiety of the work. Why, then," the editor continued, "does he not submit to the irremediable necessities of the case, designate by

9. New York *Herald*, June 27, 28, 29, 30, August 25, 1865; New York *Tribune*, August 18, 1865.

name or by class the few whom he does not intend to pardon, and declare a sweeping amnesty for all the others? To this complexion it must come at last." Even the Savannah *Daily Republican* (September 21, 1865) comments on this serious situation. But murmurings did not turn Johnson from his course. Neither did he establish anything like a pardon bureau, nor did he issue another amnesty proclamation for two years. By that time only a comparatively small number of those in his excepted classes remained unpardoned, unless the original number in the thirteenth exception (those whose property exceeded twenty thousand dollars) was sixty to eighty thousand, as had been estimated.[10]

By September, 1865, the form of pardon warrants was changed somewhat. The second form was an improvement in style and contained an additional condition. On December 8, for example, the terms under which William P. Miller of Dallas County, Texas, was pardoned were as follows:

"1st. This pardon to be of no effect until the said William P. Miller shall take the oath prescribed in the Proclamation of the President, dated May 20th, 1865.

"2d. To be void and of no effect if the said William P. Miller shall hereafter, at any time, acquire any property whatever in slaves, or make use of slave labor .

"3d. That the said William P. Miller first pay all costs which may have accrued in any proceedings instituted or pending against his person or property before the date of the acceptance of this warrant.

"4th. That the said William P. Miller shall not, by virtue of this warrant, claim any property or the proceeds of any property that has been sold by the order, judgment, or decree of a court under the confiscation laws of the United States.

"5th. That the said William P. Miller shall notify the Secretary of State, in writing, that he has received and accepted the foregoing pardon."

The pardon requisitions began to designate the use of the second form in September, 1865. The twenty-five volumes of duplicates of pardon warrants, or certificates, contain only these two forms.

10. See the first division of Ch. XI for this estimate and the second division of Ch. XV for Johnson's second proclamation.

Lincoln's pardons for supporting the rebellion had no definite style, nor did they contain uniform terms or conditions.[11]

The fourth condition of Johnson's second pardon certificate, given above, did not appear in the first form, nor were the conditions numbered in the earlier warrants. The phrase "before the date of the acceptance of this warrant" was omitted from the third condition in the first warrants. It was added in writing a few times, however, to the earlier printed warrants, as in the pardon of Isaac Newell of Milledgeville, Georgia, on August 25, 1865. Notwithstanding the restriction provided in the fourth term, such beneficiaries of pardon might bring suit in the United States Court of Claims to recover the proceeds of the sale of their property, if claims were filed within two years after the close of the war. This subject is considered in the last chapter, "Pardon and Amnesty in the Courts."

PARDON ATTORNEYS

Special consideration should be given to a class of participants in the pardoning business who were denominated pardon brokers and attorneys. It was presumed, of course, that such a matter as obtaining a pardon from the President should in no wise be tinctured with anything that savored of irregularity or undue influence. One should remember, however, that the need of a pardon was often so urgent and the congestion of petitions so great that an applicant was certain to become anxious and impatient over the fate of his case. It was only natural that such a person would welcome the assistance of any agency that could secure his pardon quickly.

Many persons accepted aid in their respective states in getting their petitions through the local authorities to Washington. In fact, an examination of the amnesty papers shows that many applicants received assistance in preparing their petitions. But at the capital there was greater need, it seemed, for assistance. The reasons, then, are quite obvious for the appearance of pardon attorneys; the exigencies of the day produced them, and their assistance was welcomed by everyone whose pardon they were instrumental in securing. The New York *Tribune* gives the following account of

11. See the last division of Ch. IV for the wording of a Lincoln pardon.

the activities of these agencies during the busiest pardoning season:[12] "If we look over the Southern papers we find advertisements about these agencies for procuring special pardons. One especially sets forth that Wright and Gibson, in Georgia, 'have secured the services of able and influential gentlemen at Milledgeville and Washington.' At Milledgeville Gov. Johnson's friends are to be fixed and at Washington President Johnson is to be approached by 'able and influential gentlemen.' Who these gentlemen are we are not told, but Wright and Gibson have confidence in them for they say, 'our facilities for securing a speedy decision in all cases presented by us are such as to offer inducements to parties interested to make their applications through us.' " The editor then mentions an attorney at Augusta who announced that he was giving his personal attention to the business. The Milledgeville, Georgia, *Southern Recorder* announced, on July 25, that attorneys Briscoe and Graffenreid would "give special attention to the preparation of applications for pardon," and that arrangements were "being made with professional parties at Washington City to attend . . . to all such cases."

The pardon brokerage business existed and functioned to a considerable degree wherever there were many pardon seekers. It appears that one hundred and fifty dollars was the usual fee charged by these agents. The New York *Herald* gives an instance in which five hundred dollars was paid for such service.[13] It relates that a certain citizen of Richmond, Virginia, knowing that his warrant had been forwarded to the Chief Executive, became overanxious when he learned that his paper remained in the President's office with hundreds of others waiting for his signature. Finally he offered a pardon attorney five hundred dollars to procure the President's signature. This agent, who was a man of prominence, asked Johnson at one of his receptions to sign his friend's pardon. The President did so promptly, not knowing, of course, about the money consideration in the matter or that it was an agent who had solicited the pardon. It can be readily understood how subordinates in the Department of Justice and the White House could easily bring an applicant's case to the attention of the Attorney-General or the

12. New York *Tribune*, September 8, 1865.
13. New York *Herald*, July 21, 1865; also New York *Tribune*, August 19, 1865.

President at the solicitation of some outside agency. Except for such action many petitions and warrants for pardon would have remained much longer without attention.

Of course, neither Johnson nor his immediate aids received money for granting pardons. But the agents of the impatient petitioners often received compensation for managing in some way to get the pardons granted sooner than the authorities might otherwise have acted. Not every applicant for clemency, however, would engage a broker to present his petition. One Alexander Dudley, for example, denied having told anyone, while he was applying for pardon, that he "could obtain a pardon by paying five hundred dollars or any sum for it." He also said that "no one in or about" the President's office had "at any time stated" that he "could obtain a pardon by paying for it." He wrote further that he had "said repeatedly that a proposition had been made" to him by others "applying for pardon to unite with them in employing a pardon broker," which he had refused to do.[14]

President Johnson and his immediate assistants took note of the activities of pardon agents in Washington and elsewhere, and endeavored to discourage the business. The pardon clerk, Pleasants, wrote to Governor Francis H. Pierpont of Virginia, on August 27, 1865, stating that the Attorney-General had authorized him to say "that the only influence possible to be exerted in the matter of pardons by the agents, or attorneys, whoever they may be, is to delay the petition. All cases coming under the thirteenth exception and all petty civil officers having your recommendation need nothing further. They are approved by the Attorney-General as a matter of course. The President declares that any intimation that money can assist a petition is a gross insult of his whole office from himself to his humblest messenger."[15] Nevertheless, the business continued.

Pardon Brokeresses

The activities of certain women operating as pardon brokers in Washington caused much unfavorable comment. The press at times was pointed in its criticism of these "Lady Lobbyists at the White

14. Johnson Papers, LXXV, No. 6413. Dudley's letter was dated at Washington, D. C., August 30, 1865.
15. New York *Herald*, September 2, 1865.

House." In contrasting Lincoln's and Johnson's susceptibilities to the influence of female petitioners, one organ stated that Lincoln's "courtesy and chivalry did not prevent the plain expression of his disgust for the character and pertinacity of such women as have earned in this day so enviable a notoriety as 'pardon brokers.'" This magazine, after commenting on the few "noble and devoted women . . . who always had free access to Mr. Lincoln" on deeds of charity and mercy, stated: "It may be that the many anecdotes in circulation of the manner in which lady applicants were thus received stimulated the professional sisterhood to their apparently extensive and successful assault upon the susceptibilities of Mr. Lincoln's successor."[16]

The most notorious pardon brokerage case grew out of the activities of Mrs. L. L. Cobb, who apparently boasted of her ease in gaining access to President Johnson and her skill in obtaining pardons. She and a few other women engaged in this business were considered by some as having questionable characters. Among those who felt that this practice should be discouraged and that the President should be given conclusive evidence of its baneful influence was the Chief of the National Protective Police (United States Secret Service), General LaFayette C. Baker. This man had become noted during the war for his activity, especially in the District of Columbia and its vicinity, in apprehending and causing the punishment of persons opposing the administration at Washington. He also claimed to have had a conspicuous part in the capture of Lincoln's assassin and in the disposition of his body. The chief suspected Mrs. Cobb of irregularities in obtaining pardons and resorted to strategy to catch her. He intended to use the evidence thus obtained to influence the President to refuse the woman any further admission to the White House.

Baker's plan worked well.[17] His assistant in the ruse approached Mrs. Cobb and obtained her written promise to deliver his own pardon the next day. He also took her receipt for two marked fifty-dollar bills which he gave her as a retainer's fee. Mrs. Cobb failed

16. See cartoon and information in *Harper's Weekly*, X (October 27, 1866), 673.
17. Baker gives more than one hundred pages to this Cobb pardon episode in his *Secret Service*.

to have the pardon the next day and gave as her excuse the President's illness, Seward's absence from the city, and the absence of a friend in the Treasury Department. The second day, however, she delivered the pardon, duly signed by the President, and gave a receipt for four more marked fifty-dollar bills, the remainder of the contract price for the pardon. Immediately after this transaction Baker appeared and demanded of the woman the four bills, which he obtained after she and her husband had accompanied him to his office, where they were detained until Baker persuaded them to give up the money. Mrs. Cobb, before leaving General Baker, denounced his action and stated that she would have him indicted for false imprisonment and cause the President to have him discharged.[18]

Soon after his experience with Mrs. Cobb, Baker had three interviews with the President in which he tried to persuade Johnson that pardons were being obtained irregularly. On the third visit the President told Baker that it was impossible for him to "know the character of the females visiting his house." He stated that Mrs. Cobb and a certain Mrs. Washington had been to see him frequently, but he declared that "if he could be convinced that the character of these women was bad, he certainly would not tolerate their presence at the Executive mansion a moment."[19]

According to Baker, Mrs. Washington was the indiscreet widow of a deceased enemy of the government. The chief stated that she occasionally entertained in her home certain officials of the government, thereby affording herself better opportunity to obtain pardons for her clients. On a certain evening when she entertained a member of the Cabinet, the President's private secretary, and other distinguished guests, one of Baker's detectives "was unceremoniously enjoined to leave" when Mrs. Washington learned of his presence. A short time before the party the widow had promised to get a pardon for one of the chief's agents and had accepted one hundred dollars as a retainer's fee. Knowledge of the Cobb episode

18. *Ibid.*, 589-96.
19. *Ibid.*, 596-99. Mr. Cobb defended his wife's integrity in a letter published in the New York *Times*, on April 10, 1866. He stated in part: "This famed pardon brokeress, a Yankee girl, gave months of her best strength as a nurse . . . in the Union hospitals, and also the sacrifice of . . . an only brother, who fell as color bearer . . . at Gettysburg."

appeared to be responsible for her displeasure on finding the detective among her guests.[20]

Baker's complaints caused the President to ask him to submit a report of his investigation on which Johnson could base an order directing his subordinates to exclude bad characters from the White House. On the following day Baker submitted the desired report,[21] which apparently did not cause the President to discourage Mrs. Cobb's visits. When Baker learned that the woman was continuing her calls at the White House, he placed a detective at the main entrance to prevent her admittance. But she was not to be frustrated in her work and entered the house through the kitchen.

Nevertheless, the Washington correspondent for the New York *Herald* for August 28, 1865, reported that the Attorney-General had limited "the hours of receiving personal applications on business connected with pardons" from nine to eleven in the forenoon, and that visitors would be received from eleven to one. After these hours all persons were to be denied admission. Of these regulations the *Herald* said: "A new leaf has been turned over at the White House. A certain feminine *habitué* of the East room and lobbies, who is generally understood to have been engaged in the pardon brokerage business, was to-day refused permission to ascend the stairway or further importune the President. Visitors to the President's mansion have not missed the familiar features of the fair *literatura* a single day for many weeks. The rule that gives everyone access to the White House will, in her case, be more honored in the breach than the observance." Mrs. Cobb was not to be outdone, however, and reported her treatment to the President, who summoned Baker and lectured him roundly for his interference with matters not pertaining to his business. The General thereupon resigned his commission and prepared his defense for his impending trial for false imprisonment.

It should be noted that the President's private secretary, Colonel A. K. Long, on being examined by the Judiciary Committee of the House during an investigation of charges against Johnson in 1867, reported somewhat differently concerning this episode. He stated that Mrs. Cobb obtained only three pardons from the Presi-

20. Baker, *Secret Service*, 598-606.
21. Johnson's Papers, LXXXI, LXXXIV, contain the original report.

dent, who did not even see or know the woman. The petitions had been prepared in regular form, and the pardons were secured through the assistance of third parties. Long also testified that Johnson did not act violently in speaking to Baker, as that man had stated, but that he respectfully ordered him to remove his detectives from the White House and to tell Stanton, who, according to Baker, had caused them to be placed there, that he would send for the chief when he needed him.[22]

Much has been found to discredit Baker's statements of his relations with the President. Doubtless some visitors at the White House dealt with Johnson's son, Robert, who has been called a "notorious debauchee."[23] If there were women of questionable character seeking pardons, they naturally courted favor with Robert. This reacted unfavorably on the father, who, according to Welles, sought to send the young man on an ocean mission as one means of getting him out of Washington and perhaps curing him of his inebrious habit.[24] Of course, the President's enemies—and General Baker was surely one—took advantage of this condition to slander the father. Maybe the chief of detectives was somewhat vindictive and even distorted the facts in his report of the Cobb episode. Quoting from an *Impeachment Investigation*, published in 1867, George Fort Milton gives an unfavorable estimate of Baker's integrity. His statement concerns Baker's testimony in the preliminary impeachment proceedings against the President, and certainly reflects on the chief's veracity.[25]

Actually Baker had done his work during the war so thoroughly that he was very unpopular in the District of Columbia. The very character of his responsibilities and activities had naturally aroused antagonism toward him. Policemen and detectives are often not appreciated even in normal times; and the vigilance of such officials in Washington during the war had reacted very unfavorably on their leader. Consequently, attempts had been made to discredit Baker's bureau and cause his downfall, but Lincoln and

22. Charleston *Mercury*, May 31, 1867 (clipped from the Baltimore *Sun*).
23. See Beale, *The Critical Year*, 16-18, especially note 27.
24. Welles, *Diary*, II, 468, 472, 479, 491, 604, 605 (March 31, April 2, 10, 24, September 26, 1866).
25. Milton, *Age of Hate*, 406-9.

Stanton had stood by their chief of detectives, and he had retained his position. Such confidence is surely some evidence of his integrity, notwithstanding anything that might be stated to the contrary. Public sentiment, however, was against him during the trial, and in his account of the case he states that there was constant communication between the White House and the prosecution, indicating that President Johnson desired his conviction. The jury did convict him of false imprisonment, which cost him, for fine and costs, thirty-six dollars. So ended this noted trial which came out of the activities of a pardon brokeress.[26]

CHARGES FOR PARDON

The governors of at least some of the states appointed agents to look after their applicants' interests in Washington. A. J. Taylor of Dawsonville was Georgia's representative at the capital for a time, while George Jenkins was appointed "to represent in the premises" at Milledgeville. The Atlanta *Daily Intelligencer* (April 15, 1865) reported that Georgia's agent was to charge those able to pay for the service a reasonable fee, but those unable to pay, nothing. Dr. Robert J. Powell, on being relieved of his duties as agent for North Carolina, remained at the capital to engage in obtaining pardons on his own account. His experience, of course, was a considerable asset, and many petitioners preferred his services to the assistance of his successor, who was also inclined to seek his aid.[27] Since the paramount object of the petitioners was to obtain pardons

26. Baker, *Secret Service*, 607-50. As further evidence of the defendant's integrity, it might be stated that, during the 1850's, Baker had been a member of a vigilance committee in restoring order in the city of San Francisco. He happened to be in New York when the war began and, instead of returning to California, went immediately to Washington to offer his services to the authorities there. It appears that General Winfield Scott sent him to Richmond, where he had interviews with President Davis and, in spite of his arrest on suspicion of being a spy, returned to Washington with much valuable information. He soon demonstrated his ability as a superior detective and was placed at the War Department in February, 1862. (*Appleton's Cyclopaedia of American Biography*, I, 145.)

27. Jonathan Worth Executive Papers, Raleigh, N. C. (B. S. Hendrich to Jonathan Worth, May 2, 1866). See Ch. X for more information concerning Dr. Powell.

as quickly as possible, it made no particular difference who performed the service.

As has been stated, the policy of the government was to grant pardons gratuitously, but the Attorney-General's office apparently allowed others to make money out of the business. Chief of Detectives Baker says that agents received pardons from the Department of Justice and sent them to the persons pardoned through the Adams Express Company, "with instructions to collect on delivery, one hundred dollars." The books of that company, he also states, "show that over thirteen thousand pardons were procured by this agent and forwarded through the express." If one hundred dollars was collected on each, as Baker implies, the Adams people handled more than $1,300,000 of pardon money.[28] This apparently went to the "brokers," or agents, who obtained the pardons, while the company, of course, received fees for delivery.

But Baker's estimate of the magnitude of business which the express company did in delivering pardons is surely too large, for many were evidently delivered by other means, although there is an abundance of additional evidence that many pardons were delivered by express. Furthermore, it is extremely doubtful that the fees were always collected on delivery, since a great number were distributed from the governors' offices.[29] In any case, there were objectionable features involved in obtaining these special pardons, whose delivery restored both civil rights and political privileges to the recipients, stopped or prevented confiscation proceedings against their property, and, until Congress interfered, obliterated any offense against the government caused by their support of the Confederacy.

28. Baker, *Secret Service*, 692. The General gives a list of twenty-nine persons, with their addresses, the dates the pardons were sent, and the fees charged (one hundred dollars in each case), taken from a page of the express company's books. The company's records appear not to be extant, and the author was unable to verify Baker's statements. The page used was doubtless one of many like it in the company's books.

29. A number of pardons remain uncalled for among the executive papers at Jackson, Mississippi; or perhaps they were collected in more recent years by the Department of Archives of that state.

CHAPTER NINE

OATHS, RELEASES, PAROLES, AND PARDONS

———◆———

THE RANK AND FILE

PERSONS in the armed service, with some exceptions, were in a more favorable condition at the end of hostilities than those in the civil service of the Confederate States. According to Johnson's first proclamation of amnesty (May 29), a large number whose sole offense had been service in the Southern army or navy and whose rank had not been above colonel in the army or lieutenant in the navy were pardoned by merely taking the amnesty oath, providing they were not included in any of the fourteen exceptions. On the other hand, all civil and diplomatic officers of the Confederacy were obliged to make special application to the President for pardon if they desired to regain their former rights and privileges in the United States. A seaman or ensign in the navy and a private, captain, or colonel in the army, for example, might be pardoned by taking the amnesty oath, while a petty postmaster, tax-collector, or recruiting officer had to make special application for clemency, and the application, under the rules soon prescribed, had to be approved by the governor of the state in which the applicant lived. Moreover, the excepted ranking Confederate army and naval officers enjoyed freedom guaranteed in their paroles when they surrendered, while many high civil officers were imprisoned for a time upon the disintegration of the Confederate States. Generals like Robert E. Lee and E. Kirby Smith remained at liberty (though not pardoned), while civil leaders like President

Jefferson Davis and Governor Zebulon B. Vance of North Carolina were arrested and imprisoned for a while.

There were three conditions, by the middle of June, 1865, under which men who had served in the Confederate army or navy had been, or were being, released to return to their homes. Many had been liberated from prison camps on taking Lincoln's amnesty oath; a much larger number had been paroled without taking any oath, as armies surrendered in April and May; and the remainder were being liberated from prison camps on taking the oath of allegiance without any benefit of amnesty. Of this last class, at the time of Johnson's first proclamation of amnesty, there were nearly sixty thousand Confederate prisoners of war, notwithstanding the resumption of exchanges in January, 1865.[1]

To facilitate the release of prisoners of war, Commissioner-General of Prisoners William Hoffman recommended to Lieutenant General Grant (May 31) that "the commanding officers of the military prisons be directed to release, on their taking the oath of allegiance, fifty or more" men per day. Soldiers charged with offenses and the five thousand officers in confinement were to be excepted. In this manner Hoffman estimated that the prison camps could be evacuated in nearly sixty days. There were also citizens in confinement who deserved similar consideration. Hoffman suggested that those confined without charges and others charged with offenses and awaiting trial be released, especially, he significantly but erroneously stated, since "all who have been tried and sentenced during the war have been pardoned. . . ." He believed a few of those awaiting trial might be retained for further consideration. Two days later Hoffman informed General John E. Mulford that all prisoners of war who had made application to take the oath of allegiance before the fall of Richmond had "already been ordered to be discharged." "For those below the rank of colonel in the army or lieutenant in the navy," he said, "special applications are

1. By 1863 the whole system of exchange practically broke down. Only a few exchanges were made thereafter, until December, 1864, when General Butler resumed the policy existing before the cartel, and General Grant, realizing the approaching end of hostilities, ordered (January, 1865) the policy of "even exchange" observed again. William Best Hesseltine's *Civil War Prisons; a Study in War Psychology* is the best account of this subject. See also Randall, *The Civil War and Reconstruction*, 436-43.

received through this office . . . and unless there is some special objection the release is generally granted." He expected a "general order" for releases in a few days.[2]

Hoffman's recommendation was not strictly followed. On June 6 the Adjutant General's office in Washington issued "General Orders, No. 109 for the discharge of certain prisoners of war." All enlisted men of the army and petty officers and seamen of the navy were to "be discharged on taking the oath of allegiance." Officers of the army "not above the grade of captain," and of the navy "not above the grade of lieutenant," were to be released on taking the oath, unless they were graduates of the military or naval academy. When these discharges had been completed, regulations for the release of higher officers would be issued. As many prisoners were to be liberated each day as could be conveniently released, and certified rolls of the same were to be forwarded to Washington. Commanders were to give preferment for liberation to those "longest in prison and from the most remote points of the country. . . ." Only the oath of allegiance was to be administered, but notice was given that all who desired might take the amnesty oath "after their release, in accordance with the regulations of the Department of State respecting the amnesty." The first oath, a mere declaration to defend the government, would permit their parole, or release; the second, a promise to defend the government and to support all laws and proclamations made during the rebellion to emancipate the slaves, would restore their rights and privileges. Furthermore, the quartermaster's department was instructed to furnish transportation to all released prisoners of war to such states as Kentucky and Missouri. These men had left loyal states to aid the Confederacy. Attorney-General Speed had ruled that men of this class could not return to their former homes in the loyal states. This ruling was in keeping with the tenth exception of the amnesty of May 29, which denied the benefit of the proclamation to "all persons who left their homes within the jurisdiction and protection of the United States and passed beyond the Federal military lines into the pretended Confederate States" to aid the rebellion.[3] Evidently Speed's opinion was not allowed to operate.

2. *Offic. Rec.*, 2 Ser., VIII, 585, 636.
3. Richardson, *Messages . . . of the Presidents*, VI, 310.

When destitute, paroled Confederate troops arrived in Memphis, Tennessee, on the way to their homes north of the recognized boundary of the Confederacy, the Federal authorities at first denied them aid on their journey. The refusal was in accord with Speed's ruling, but contrary to the instructions (Order 109) of June 6, which had made no exceptions whatever to the benefits of transportation. The distressed men claimed therefore the aid given soldiers returning to homes in the seceded states. General John E. Smith at Memphis, though admitting the justice of Speed's opinion, thought it wiser to furnish the men transportation to their homes than to allow them "to encumber and deprecate upon the community, which their destitute condition" would compel them to do, unless they were assisted in going home. "It is true," he stated, "that they might be billeted on the people here—rebel sympathizers, if you please—but this would not be just, as nearly all [citizens of Memphis] have complied with the conditions imposed by [the] Government." He asked therefore that all soldiers who were not excepted in the amnesty proclamation be permitted to take the oath of allegiance and receive transportation to their homes in the loyal states. His communication was returned with the indorsement that, under the agreement made by General Edward R. S. Canby with General E. Kirby Smith when the latter surrendered the Trans-Mississippi Department on May 26, 1865, all paroled prisoners of war were "entitled to transportation [and subsistence] to the nearest practicable points to their homes. . . ." Of course, such aid was to be at public cost.[4]

Paroled and released Confederate soldiers and prisoners of war were aided, therefore, in returning to their homes, even though they had left loyal states or passed through Union lines to aid the rebellion. There were instances, of course, where the men did not need, or wait for, such assistance. When exchanges and paroles were made earlier, i.e., before General Orders No. 109 went into effect, released Confederates often went home by foot. For example, Private Nathan B. Deatherage of Madison County,

4. *Offic. Rec.*, 2 Ser., VIII, 651. This indorsement is dated June 26 in the *Official Records*, but the time was surely June 16, four days after General Smith's recommendation. For the Canby-Smith agreement see *ibid.*, 1 Ser., XLVII, pt. 2, pp. 600-1.

Kentucky, captured with Morgan's Brigade in July, 1863, and soon taken to Camp Douglas, Chicago, was sent with others to Richmond, Virginia, early in March, 1865, to be exchanged. He was one day late in arriving for the exchange, and before another could be arranged, General Lee had surrendered (April 9). Consequently Deatherage was paroled and with many others allowed to walk to Mt. Sterling, Kentucky, whence he and his comrades rode horses to Lexington, Kentucky, arriving there on May 1; "and," as he said, "that ended the last day of our service for the Confederacy."[5]

The plight of three or four thousand Union prisoners near Jacksonville, Florida, should also be noted to show the misfortune that at least once attended the return of Union prisoners of war to their homes. A Confederate escort had left the men to shift for themselves while conducting them to Lake City, where they might be received by Federal authorities. General Israel Vogdes, commanding at Jacksonville, had declined to receive the prisoners until properly authorized to do so. In urging Vogdes to accept the soldiers, General Sam Jones stated "that he was unable to care for the prisoners . . . and that he was somewhat fearful that they would not longer submit to control. . . ." While Vogdes waited for instruction, the escort deserted the men near Baldwin, and some of the prisoners soon appeared in Jacksonville. They "were in a miserable condition," and a number died after arriving there. Vogdes informed General Hitchcock at Washington that he had sent the able survivors north and placed "the last sick and disabled . . . on board the hospital ship Cosmopolitan on the 20th of May."[6]

As the number of privates and officers diminished in the Northern camps, Hoffman seemed disposed to assemble at fewer places all officers not released. On June 14, he instructed the commander at Camp Chase, near Columbus, Ohio, to send officers who were not to be liberated under the existing Order 109 to Johnson Island

5. Dorris, *Old Cane Springs*, 165-67, 227. According to Deatherage's account in the *Confederate Veteran*, XXXVI (August, 1928), 305, there were "about 750 old soldiers in the gang" returning at this time to Kentucky.

6. *Offic. Rec.*, 2 Ser., VIII, 642 (Vogdes to Hitchcock, June 6, 1865). An exchange of prisoners of war occurred as late as May 26 between Colonel William M. Dye at New Orleans and Major Ignatius Szymanski at the mouth of the Red River. *Ibid.*, 643.

in Lake Erie. Two days later he reported to Grant that there would probably not be more than "250 officers to be held" at Rock Island, Illinois, after the execution of this order. On the same day, he recommended that "citizen prisoners in confinement at various military prisons without charges," and those against whom there were no serious charges, "be at once released on their taking the oath of allegiance." The next day, on Grant's approval, Hoffman ordered the release of such citizen prisoners on their taking the oath; doubtful cases were to be referred to his office. The day following, the order was restricted to prisoners not arrested "in connection with the assassination of the late President."[7]

By June 27 all soldiers and officers coming under existing orders had been released from Fort Delaware, and Grant was willing to have all other officers remaining at that place discharged on taking the oath. Furthermore, he recommended "that general direction for the discharge of all remaining prisoners be given" and executed by commanders of prisons in accordance with the plan in operation. "This will enable us," he stated, "to discharge a great many soldiers and diminish expenses materially." By July 5 Hoffman was able to report the release of all prisoners of war, except the sick, from the nine prisons which had held the most men.[8]

It was not until July 20, however, that the President directed the discharge of "all the prisoners of war of the rebel Army and Navy except those captured with Jefferson Davis and any others where special reasons . . . exist for holding them." The old conditions of release were required—the oath of allegiance and parole on good behavior. Transportation by railroad or steamer was to be furnished, and the names and places of confinement of persons excepted were to be given. The scope of this order included Old Capitol Prison in the District of Columbia, which had been the subject of much bitter criticism during the war and which was ordered to be abandoned and destroyed four months later.[9]

7. *Offic. Rec.*, 2 Ser., VIII, 653-58.
8. *Ibid.*, 673, 700-1. These prison camps were Point Lookout, Md.; Newport News, Va.; Hart's Island, N. Y.; Elmira, N. Y.; Camp Chase, Ohio; Camp Morton, Ind.; Camp Douglas, Chicago; Rock Island, Ill.; and Alton, Ill.
9. *Ibid.*, 709-10; also Marshall, *American Bastile: A History of the Illegal Arrests and Imprisonments of American Citizens during the Late Civil War*, *passim*.

Two weeks earlier (July 5), on the recommendation of General Grant, Stanton had issued an order especially beneficial to paroled Southern prisoners of war in the South. Such men were expected to remain at home during the operation of their paroles. There were those, of course, who desired to seek employment or business in other communities or states. Stanton's order allowed them to take the oath of allegiance and "to leave their homes to obtain civil employment elsewhere; but taking the oath," he stated, "will not restore them to citizenship." Only the benefits of the amnesty oath would do that. A second clause of this order removed all restraints upon prisoners of war in the North, whether paroled or not, and upon all others "under orders to remain in the North during the existence of the rebellion." As in the first instance, these persons were to swear allegiance to the United States and could then go where they pleased.[10]

As might be expected, there were prisoners who were too ill to be released. On the approval of Grant and Stanton, Hoffman ordered (June 30) such prisoners remaining in hospitals at Newport News transferred to the hospital at Hampton, Virginia, and those at Elmira, Chase, Morton, Douglas, and Rock Island to the "post hospitals at those several places. . . ." Prisoners attending the sick were allowed to go with them or be discharged on taking the oath of allegiance as appeared "most desirable."

It is interesting to note the rapid decrease in the numbers of ill prisoners in the Northern camps during the period from May to October, 1865. The report for the first month gave 4,188 ailing prisoners of war and 1,299 ailing citizen prisoners in twenty-three prisons. Fort Lafayette apparently had none to be reported. By the end of June there were only 374 military prisoners and 832 citizen prisoners remaining, and by the end of July only 7 of the first and 218 of the second class remained. The total number of prisoners of war in the camps in May was 70,974, in June, 49,385, and in July, 2,498. The figures indicate, therefore, that ailing men were released much faster than those not so classified. Moreover, the authorities were much slower in discharging citizens than in releasing men in the military class.

10. *Offic. Rec.*, 2 Ser., VIII, 682, 683.

Some other interesting details in connection with the release of all classes of prisoners should be related. On June 30 seventy-two citizen prisoners, who had been convicted of violating "the laws and customs of war" and "military orders," were discharged from the prison at Alton, Illinois. Confederate Surgeon William S. Wright was the seventy-second on this list of men who had been confined "for the duration of the war." Three days later the prison was reported vacant, when 231 Federal prisoners, 34 citizens, and 4 prisoners of war were sent to the prisons in St. Louis and Jefferson City, Missouri. The last four declined to take the oath, but they were surely later released, for by September no prisoners were reported at St. Louis. Moreover, they probably soon realized the prudence of declaring their loyalty to the United States and being discharged.[11]

The inspector of prisons, Lieutenant Colonel O. E. Babcock, found "one citizen and seven prisoners of war" at Camp Morton on July 10. He recommended that the citizen, Lieutenant William E. Munford, arrested as a spy with Major John B. Castleman on the same charge, "be released on taking the oath of allegiance or required to leave the country." Lincoln had disposed of Castleman by allowing him to be exiled. Munford was probably released on taking the oath. The seven other prisoners were deserters from the Union army who had enlisted in the Confederate service. Babcock recommended "their discharge on taking the oath . . . as their trial would be attended with many difficulties and great expense, and . . . they can do no harm if released." Evidently this was done, for no prisoners were reported at Camp Morton in August. Babcock also reported finding "some forty [United States] Veteran Reserve Corps prisoners in the guardhouse" at this camp, charged with mutiny. The commanding general said they were clearly guilty, but recommended their dishonorable discharge without pay as both judicious and economical.[12] Apparently his advice was followed.

Thus by the close of 1865 the military prisons and camps had

11. *Ibid.*, 691-4, 1003. The prison fund remaining at the Alton post was $35,000; on July 6, at Rock Island, Ill., $174,068.15; and on June 10, $100,000 at Camp Morton, Ind. *Ibid.*, 694, 704-5.

12. *Ibid.*, 704-5, 1003.

been practically cleared of all prisoners, and every Confederate soldier and sailor in the field after April 8 had been paroled to his home—never, fortunately, to be called to arms again in the cause of the Confederate States of America. On June 15, 1866, Stanton reported to the President that since April 15, 1865, 5,501 officers, 53,679 enlisted men, and 1,220 citizens had been discharged from imprisonment of some sort; and that 1,953 persons, sentenced by military commission or court-martial, had been pardoned.[13] The remarkable result, or sequence, to note, however, is the fact that many tens of thousands of citizens who had fought desperately against their country—not to overthrow the government of the United States, but, on the other hand, to establish a new, independent government and nation in at least eleven contiguous states of the Union—were scarcely punished at all, as will be seen in this and the following chapters. Temporary embarrassments and disabilities under the presidential and congressional plans of reconstruction are not considered in this estimate of punishment.

GENERAL AND MRS. RICHARD S. EWELL

General Lee naturally sought to have the parole privileges given his officers and men at Appomattox extended to those of his army who had surrendered a few days earlier. He asked Grant on April 25, therefore, to allow this to be done, saying he could see no benefit that might result by retaining them in prison. On the contrary, he thought "good might be accomplished by returning them to their homes." At least invalid officers and men should be paroled at once. He mentioned particularly General Richard S. Ewell, who had surrendered with eight to ten thousand troops at Sailor's Creek, on April 6.[14] General Custis Lee was among the officers thus embarrassed. Ewell had been taken to Fort Warren, Boston Harbor, and was not in the best of health; he had lost a leg in August, 1862, and apparently needed an artificial limb.

As indicated above, high-commissioned Confederate officers were not discharged from prison camps very soon after the end of hostilities. Consequently, some applied for pardon after learn-

13. *Ibid.*, 929. A checking of numbers in *ibid.* indicates variation in estimates.
14. *Ibid.*, 1 Ser., XLVI, pt. 3, pp. 596, 625, 1003.

ing of the President's amnesty proclamation of May 29. Ewell petitioned Johnson the day following. In fewer words than Lee's application, he merely asked to be permitted to take the amnesty oath and be released, saying he was excluded from the general amnesty for having been educated at West Point, for having attained the rank of lieutenant general in the Confederate service, and for being a prisoner of war.[15] He might also have mentioned a fourth exception, namely, his resigning a commission in the Federal army to serve the Confederacy; and, since he had recently married a woman worth well over twenty thousand dollars, he also came under the President's thirteenth exception.

Near the close of the war, General Ewell had married Mrs. Lizinka Campbell Brown, a childhood playmate and cousin, whose son, Campbell Brown, was also a prisoner of war in Fort Warren. Mrs. Ewell was a woman of much wealth; consequently the Federals took possession of her estates in Maury County, Tennessee, and elsewhere after her marriage to General Ewell. Evidently in order to regain her property, Mrs. Ewell sought and obtained permission to take Lincoln's amnesty oath late in March, 1865. There was delay, however, in allowing her to take possession of her estate and home in Nashville, and on April 10 she wrote Mrs. Andrew Johnson a peculiar and incoherent letter. Apparently the Johnsons and Mrs. Ewell had been good friends earlier. At any rate, Mrs. Ewell addressed the President's wife as "Dear Mother," informed her of having arrived in Nashville from St. Louis "a week ago," and asked to be allowed "the use of one or two rooms in my [her] house," since she was expecting her daughter and needed a place for the two of them to lodge. She also referred to the President familiarly as "Gov. J.," apparently using a term applied to Johnson in Nashville while he was Military Governor of Tennessee.[16]

Of course, Mrs. Johnson, who was really an invalid and who even left the management of the White House to her daughter, Mrs. David Trotter Patterson, could not be expected to have anything whatever to do with the disposition of property anywhere; and Mrs. Ewell doubtless knew that. Weeks before Johnson's proc-

15. *Ibid.*, 2 Ser., VIII, 582 (Ewell to Johnson, May 30, 1865).
16. The Richard S. Ewell Papers (Archives, University of North Carolina; Mrs. Ewell to General Ewell, Baltimore, June 28, 1865).

lamation of amnesty, therefore, the indiscreet Mrs. Ewell found
herself arrested and detained in St. Louis, with her Tennessee property in jeopardy and her husband and son prisoners in Fort Warren. On May 30 she read the President's amnesty proclamation and,
noting its exceptions, immediately petitioned Johnson to pardon
her dear ones. Her wealth, of course, placed her beyond the reach
of the general benefits of the amnesty and made it necessary for her
to apply for a special pardon also.

In writing Johnson, Mrs. Ewell said that two months earlier she
would have appealed confidently to him with "memories of former
friendship," but her subsequent arrest indicated that such appeal
would be "presumptuous." She added that she was "suffering very
much, and fearfully anxious for the future." She had carefully observed the spirit of Lincoln's amnesty oath and had tried diligently
to conform to what she supposed to be Johnson's wishes. She
closed by imploring freedom for her Richard and Campbell and
for herself, so that they might find happiness and show gratitude by
being useful to their benefactor.[17]

Generals of the army, as already noted, were the last to be discharged from prison camps. Campbell Brown indicated such delay
when he wrote to his mother on June 10 that about thirty majors
were released that day, "leaving only two or three [others] besides the Generals." Six days later it appears that General Ewell's
oath and application for pardon went to the President, and on
June 21 General John Pope sent a copy of a dispatch from Stanton
to Mrs. Ewell, stating that the President was "willing for her to
visit Washington or go farther north or wherever she pleases, except into the State of Tennessee." Three days later Mrs. Ewell
went to Baltimore and thence to Washington to see the President.
Johnson was ill, and Mrs. Patterson arranged for the visitor to see
her father on June 28.

Mrs. Ewell described her interview with Mrs. Patterson as painful, especially when she was informed that a family occupying
her home in Nashville had taken Governor William Ganneway
Brownlow "to board." Evidently the rather aristocratic and
wealthy Mrs. Ewell was not an admirer of the eccentric, able, and
famous "Parson Brownlow." She reported Mrs. Patterson as being

17. *Ibid.* (Mrs. Ewell to Johnson, St. Louis, May 20, 1865).

very kind to her, but as stating that "she had been hurt" by the note which Mrs. Ewell had written her mother asking for lodging accommodations in Nashville. After being assured that the President "would be just, and disposed to be lenient," she returned to Baltimore to await the day when she might see Mrs. Patterson's father.

Mrs. Ewell wrote her husband a long letter after her three-hour interview with the President on June 28. She had dined with the Johnsons (or with some of them) on bread and butter, cold chicken, crackers and cheese, with green tea for drink. The food was pretty hard to swallow, she related, for she had been told that her Richard could not yet be released. Johnson did promise to pardon her and Campbell if she would return in three days with petitions. This puzzled her somewhat and caused her to observe to her husband: "If a special amnesty from Mr. Lincoln is not binding or effective, why should one from Mr. J[ohnson] be more so?" Nevertheless, she thought it "folly to complain of the form if the end is obtained; but the truth is," she continued, "I am so disappointed at being refused your release that the proffer to give binding force to an act of Mr. Lincoln's, so kindly done by him two months ago, seems like mocking."[18]

As the President suggested, Mrs. Ewell petitioned at once for pardon. She first quoted Lincoln's telegram of March 23, 1865, allowing her the benefit of his amnesty. She then reminded Johnson of his assurance that there was no charge of disloyalty against her since the date of Lincoln's pardon, and appealed to him to "carry into execution the amnesty of the late lamented President Lincoln. . . ."[19]

True to his promise, Johnson allowed Mrs. Ewell a pardon, but instead of granting it under his own proclamation, he recognized Lincoln's pardon under date of March 23, 1865. He directed therefore that the lady be "permitted to return to Nashville, Tennessee, free from arrest, or other detention by Military Authorities, and to take possession of her property, as decreed by the U. S. District Court for the Dist. of Middle Tennessee. . . ." This order was dated July 15, but not until September 14 did General Otis O.

18. *Ibid.*, for letters of June 10, 16, 21, 24, 25, 28, 1865.
19. *Ibid.* (Mrs. Ewell to Johnson, Baltimore, July 1, 1865).

Howard of the Freedman's Bureau instruct a subordinate to allow her to possess her farms (one of forty-five hundred acres and another of two hundred) in Maury County and her home in Nashville. The property, however, was to be restored on two conditions: first, lessees were to "remain in possession until the expiration of their leases"; and, second, the order of restoration was "not to be construed as giving any claim upon the Government for damages, or rents."[20] Thus, after nearly six months, the benefits of a late Lincoln pardon were finally realized, but not without much discomfort to the beneficiary, due largely to a change of presidents.

General Ewell and Major Campbell Brown, however, remained in prison, while Mrs. Ewell continued efforts to cause their release. At least, she tried to encourage them with cheerful letters, eatables, and money. She believed, however, that some unfortunate circumstances had injured her husband's case. One unfavorable condition was a letter the General had written, on June 13, 1865, to a man in St. Paul, Minnesota, who had served as a noncommissioned officer in a company under Ewell's captaincy years earlier in the United States army. The New York *World* had published the message as Ewell's "Reasons for Deserting the Old Flag."

The effect of the letter on the writer's status is not certain. Mrs. Ewell feared that it was injurious, but the person to whom it was written evidently thought that he would mitigate his old captain's embarrassment by allowing it to be printed. Many others were recommending Ewell's release and pardon, and on July 7 President Johnson telegraphed Mrs. Ewell, who he supposed was in Baltimore, to come to Washington to arrange for the release of her husband and son. The lady was in Wakefield, Rhode Island, however, where a written message of similar import was sent on July 12.

Before Mrs. Ewell received the second message, she wrote the President a very impatient letter, full of anxiety and pathos. She had visited Fort Warren, where she saw her "husband and son haggard from three months' confinement in stone cells. . . ." "A single line from you," she told Johnson, "can give them back to liberty and me to happiness—Will you write it? Or are your pro-

20. *Ibid.*, Special Orders, No. 4, Asst. Commissioner's Office, Nashville, September 8, 1865; General Howard's order, Bureau of Refugees, etc., Washington, September 14, 1865.

fessions of kind feelings towards me merely air—intended to deceive one too miserable and insignificant to be worthy of such artifice from such a man? I am afraid to write to you," she railed, "afraid of rendering their condition harder by making some mistake as in my note to Mrs. Johnson." Then she made an impassioned appeal to the President "as a weak woman to a strong man" to liberate her husband and child. "I am afraid to write more —I could not write less," she concluded, "but if Richard dies in Fort Warren, how I will hate you—wicked as it is to hate anyone." She signed herself, "Your miserable friend, Lizinka C. Ewell."

Mrs. Ewell's efforts to secure the release of her husband from prison suggest Mrs. Clement C. Clay's experience in persuading Johnson to liberate her husband, related in a later chapter on "Pardoning Civil Leaders" of the Confederacy. Both the women were highly spirited and determined, but Mrs. Clay was apparently more tactful and resourceful. Each accomplished her purpose, for General Ewell and Major Brown were paroled from Fort Warren late in July, 1865.

At first General Ewell's liberty was limited only to Virginia. Other generals who were released from Fort Warren a few days earlier than he were given a much larger range of activity. On September 23 he politely protested to the President against such discrimination. Some of these more favored officers had entered the Confederate service with higher rank than Ewell, and had been, according to him, "instrumental in bringing about secession." The list included other West Pointers, but he was the only one who had attained the rank of lieutenant general. Under the circumstances, he could see no good reason why he should not "be placed on the same footing with them." In a little while his liberties were extended, and he was permitted to go to Tennessee to obtain an artificial limb.[21] His parole surely expired with Johnson's announcement, in April, 1866, that the war was over. Of course, he needed a pardon, which he received through the operation of the President's amnesty of July 4, 1868, for it appears that he was never given a special pardon.

21. The Ewell Papers contain the letters indicated above.

GENERAL HOWELL COBB

Having been an influential secessionist, Major General Howell Cobb became an interesting applicant for pardon. He had been congressman, Governor of Georgia, and Secretary of the Treasury under Buchanan, resigning the last position in December, 1860, to promote secession. He was president of the Confederate provisional congress at Montgomery and probably would have been a member of Davis's cabinet if he and the President of the Confederate States could have agreed. As it happened, he never became an outstanding military leader like Lee, Longstreet, Johnston, and others.

Late in April, 1865, Cobb surrendered his troops at Macon, Georgia, under the terms Sherman had granted Johnston a little earlier. He became therefore a paroled officer, and soon began to co-operate with Governor Joseph E. Brown and others to establish proper relations between his state and the government at Washington. About the middle of May he wrote to General J. H. Wilson, commanding the Georgia area, a very comprehensive, useful statement describing conditions that should be understood in restoring the state. Wilson forwarded this letter to the War Department with a long diagnosis of its contents, in which he particularly stressed Cobb's constructive attitude toward the existing problem.

Wilson stated, however, that the "people of Georgia" did not want "Brown, Toombs, and Cobb to escape." Then he said that Cobb had "conducted himself . . . strictly in the spirit of his communication" enclosed therewith, and evidently thought the seceder deserved favorable consideration. Since he was an original secessionist and had led his state in the effort at independence, Cobb believed he could not justly ask for more favor than was granted to others of his class of secessionists. He asserted, however, that, having caused his people to be in their present deplorable condition, he desired "sincerely to see them lifted once more upon their feet and established in prosperity." Nevertheless, Cobb was ordered to be arrested, on May 29, and sent to Fort Lafayette; and preparations were made to execute the order. He claimed immunity under the privileges of his parole, but General Wilson, in compliance with fresh orders, started him and other prominent prisoners north-ward. An examination of a copy of his parole at Washington, how-ever, caused Stanton to instruct General George H. Thomas, at Nashville, to "release him from custody and send him to his home," where he was to remain subject to the terms of his parole.[22]

Cobb waited nearly four months after Johnson's first amnesty before applying for pardon. As many other petitioners stated, he said that the election of Lincoln, in 1860, had caused him to feel "that the future welfare and prosperity of the South demanded a separation of the Southern States from the Federal Union." Since Johnston's surrender, however, he had "counselled an uncondi-tional submission to the results of the war" and the adoption of such measures as would restore "Georgia to her former status in the Union." He regarded the institution of slavery as abolished and had urged his people to abandon all ideas of its restoration.[23]

On October 11, Cobb asked Seward to present his application to the President, stating that he had not sent recommendations be-cause he was so well known to both Johnson and the members of his Cabinet. Having learned "with equal surprise and regret" that he was believed by some to have mistreated prisoners of war, he emphatically denied the charge, and thought an exception might be made of him because of his "uniform and unusual kindness to prisoners. . . ." Six days later Cobb wrote the President again, re-minding him of his petition, endorsed by Provisional Governor James Johnson of Georgia and General James B. Steedman, com-manding in Georgia. Fearing that he would never be favored with an interview with the President, he stated further that he had dele-gated a kinsman, General Henry R. Jackson of his state, to convey this letter to him and to press his application for pardon.[24]

General Jackson had more than one interview with the Presi-dent pertaining to Cobb's petition. According to George Hillyer, an appreciative beneficiary of Cobb's kindness, who was present at

22. *Offic. Rec.*, 1 Ser., XLIX, 429, 783-86, 802, 839, 859, 861, 883, 901, 922, 923.

23. Amnesty Papers, Georgia (Cobb to Johnson, Athens, Ga., September 25, 1865).

24. Miscellaneous Letters, State Department (perhaps now in the National Archives; Cobb to Seward, Atlanta, October 11, 1865); *Annual Report, Am. Hist. Assoc.*, 1911, II, 668.

one and who kept in touch with Jackson, Johnson appeared disposed to favor Cobb if he came to Washington quietly for a personal conference. Hillyer told his correspondent, however, that there was a "general disposition" in Washington to hold him "responsible as the only accessible man, and in truth the chief man, of Buchanan's administration against whom the accursed venom of the saints can vent itself. . . ." He had concluded, therefore, that, if Cobb should come to the capital, his presence should hardly be known, for fear that an unkind press and the general excitement his moving about might cause would discourage favorable action on his petition.

On November 18, 1865, Cobb wrote to his wife that General Jackson had advised against his going to Washington to interview the President. Conditions there appeared to have become worse since the fall elections in the North. Moreover, Johnson had not yet reached the class of cases to which Cobb belonged. It was Jackson's belief, therefore, that his "time would come when Mr. Davis was pardoned; and my opinion is," said Cobb, "that it will not come sooner." He disliked to discourage Mrs. Cobb with such information, but consoled her with the resolution: "I shall now turn my attention to my business, and if permitted shall give it my earnest and undivided attention. I hardly expect to be interfered with but it is hard to say what these people will or may do. . . ." Evidently Cobb was not molested as he began the practice of law in Macon, Georgia, for early in December he reported pretty good business. "Two fees, one of five hundred dollars and another of two hundred, with some smaller ones, have been ensured, and I doubt not others will follow," he wrote to Mrs. Cobb. That was indeed encouraging to an unpardoned Confederate, and illustrates what many disabled Southerners did before their disabilities were removed.

During all these passing months, Jefferson Davis was imprisoned in Fortress Monroe, Virginia (see Chapter XIII). Cobb was not unmindful of the desire of a multitude of Southerners to secure his release—and his pardon. Whatever he may have thought of Davis personally, he sympathized with the natural desire of the distinguished prisoner to be liberated and with the longing of the tens of thousands of adoring petitioners who were entreating the President to set him free. Cobb looked about, apparently, to find some influential person who might intercede with Johnson to discharge Davis from prison. At any rate, on September 12, 1866, he made a strong appeal to General Daniel E. Sickles to cause the desired liberation. In the light of his statement above, he may have thought that amelioration of Davis's more serious condition would hasten the granting of his own petition for pardon. He gave, however, a more worthy reason for writing to General Sickles, and for that he should be commended. His affirmed objective was to hasten the closing of the schism between the two sections of the nation by liberating Jefferson Davis.

No more eloquent, earnest, and reasonable plea was made during Davis's two years' imprisonment to cause the prisoner's liberation and to encourage a wise course of reconstruction. But Cobb's effort, in thus writing Sickles, was in vain, for Davis remained in prison more than eight months longer; and reconstruction went from bad to worse, until it assumed the ugly, wounding character of a crime upon the South. Thus the whole nation suffered, for a country can be no healthier, happier, or more prosperous, at a given time, than its most ailing section.

A visit which Cobb made to Washington early in 1867 apparently availed nothing. Davis was paroled from prison in May, but reconstruction approached its worst stages as the year wore on. On September 7 the President proclaimed his second general amnesty, but its benefits did not reach Howell Cobb. It excepted army officers above the rank of brigadier general and naval officers above the rank of captain. Jeremiah S. Black of Pennsylvania, who had also been a member of Buchanan's Cabinet, soon expressed to Cobb his disappointment with the proclamation. The former Attorney-General and Secretary of State declared that it was not what the South needed. "Justice is the supreme necessity," he declared. "This hollow show of *mercy* postpones the restitution of their rights. I told the President that I disliked it for the reason above stated and because it was useless to my friend Cobb." Johnson told Black that it would be "easier now to relieve Cobb by a special pardon than it was before," and intimated that he would "not have to wait much longer" for a pardon. The former counsel for the Department of Justice believed that Johnson "had no in-

tention of allowing" Cobb to suffer, but that he delayed pardoning him because of his fear of Congress. "He feels that he must
husband the power that is left him for self defense," Black opined.
"If he does not they will depose him, perhaps hang him."[25] But
the effort, in 1868, to "depose" Johnson failed by one vote. Had
he been removed from the presidency, he most likely would not
have been tried for any criminal act.

Black did not allow his discouragement over national affairs to
stay his efforts to obtain his friend's pardon. But, like a few others,
Howell Cobb was not to receive a special pardon. He was included in the President's third general amnesty (July 4, 1868),
which did not except from its benefits officers of the army and
navy unless they were under presentment or indictment. He died
October 9, 1868.

OTHER GENERALS

Space does not allow much consideration of any other Confederate generals. Only a few of the many who sought special pardon
will be considered. Their cases illustrate the embarrassment in
which the high officers of the army found themselves and the
manner in which they approached the President in seeking
clemency.

As has already been noted, not every general applying for pardon had his petition granted. Lee, James Longstreet, and E. Kirby
Smith were among those who had to wait until a proclamation of
amnesty gave them relief. They had been too prominent in the
movement to divide the United States to receive special favor very
soon. Johnson expressed his attitude in that respect by what he
told Longstreet when that General, on the advice of General
Grant, made a personal appeal for pardon early in November,
1865. Grant and Longstreet had attended West Point together
and had served in the same regiment after graduation. The Federal, who had married Julia B. Dent, Longstreet's first cousin, had
a very high opinion of the Confederate, and praised Longstreet
highly to the President, in a personal interview and in a letter, for his
conduct during the war. "I will further state," he added, "that my

25. *Annual Report, Am. Hist. Assoc.,* 1911, II, 668-88, for the letters.

opinion of him is such that I shall feel it as a personal favor to myself if the pardon is granted."

Before going to the White House, Longstreet called on Stanton, who referred him to Johnson. According to Longstreet, after a "long pleasant talk," the President said: "There are three persons of the South who can never receive my amnesty: Mr. Davis, General Lee, and yourself. You have given the Union cause too much trouble." When Longstreet replied, "You know, Mr. President, that those who are forgiven, love the most," Johnson retorted, "You have very high authority for that, but you can't have amnesty." Having been a major general, Longstreet had to wait until relieved by the President's general amnesty of July 4, 1868.

According to Longstreet, Grant had his name placed on a list of Georgians whom General John Pope recommended to Congress for relief from the disability of the third section of the Fourteenth Amendment. The list was approved, and Longstreet could then regard himself as entirely relieved of all disabilities that he had incurred in supporting the Confederacy.[26]

Another Georgian, Brigadier General A. H. Colquitt, told the President in his petition that he had encouraged secession and earnestly desired the success of the rebellion. Since the effort to secede had failed, he yielded "in good faith to the fortunes of war" and recognized "that the institution of slavery was extinct." Furthermore, he had proclaimed freedom to his former slaves and was employing those who desired to work for him. A majority of the petitioners who recommended Colquitt to the President and General Grant for clemency were citizens of Illinois, who spoke in the highest terms of his treatment of Union prisoners. Most of the sixty-four who signed one petition were from Springfield, twenty-five being members of the state's legislature. The list of prominent peti-

26. See James Longstreet, *From Manassas to Appomattox: Memoirs of the Civil War in America*, 632-38. Longstreet's statement implies that Grant was President when he had the Southerner's name placed on Pope's list. Longstreet's name appears, however, among the 1,350 persons whose disability under the Amendment was removed June 25, 1868 (see the division, "Early Removals," in Ch. XVI). Longstreet also states that this removal by Congress took place soon after relief "was given to General R. E. Lee." Evidence does not seem to exist that the disability was ever removed from Lee.

tioners also included Generals J. A. McClernand and John M. Palmer, and Colonel Robert G. Ingersoll. Colquitt, who was also in the twenty-thousand-dollar exception, applied for pardon on August 30, 1865, but Johnson apparently was not influenced to grant his request until the strong recommendations from Illinois came to him in January, 1867. At any rate, on the eighth of the following month he ordered the pardon issued.[27]

Alabama had many brigadier generals. One of them, Alpheus Baker, applied rather early (August 3) for pardon. Though Provisional Governor Lewis E. Parsons and others recommended prompt action, the President, who was not in a hurry to pardon generals, deferred granting his petition. General Baker stated that he had favored secession "as a peaceful termination to the 'conflict.' " He "did not think separation would produce war," and he "was satisfied the South would never consent to yield slavery." Furthermore, he believed that "the two sections which lived together only in strife, would live apart in amity and prosperity." He had fought hard for independence, but the end of slavery, which he had hoped would be averted by secession, had been "accomplished by the war which it [had] produced." "It is gone forever," he stated, "and with it the motive which prompted me to desire separation." So he submitted willingly "to the inevitable result," and desired "to conform, in good faith, to the altered condition of affairs" and become a peaceful and loyal citizen of the United States. The war had reduced him to poverty, and, having a wife and two children depending on him for support, he wished to have all his former rights and privileges restored. Months passed, and Baker remained unpardoned. On June 15, 1866, Governor R. M. Patton, who had been elected to succeed Provisional Governor Parsons, wrote the President that as far as he knew General Baker was one of only two "prominent officers in the rebellion from this state whose embarrassment has not been removed." The other was General Henry D. Clayton. Nearly a month later (July 10) Baker was pardoned.[28]

Another ranking officer who had voluntarily and conscientiously embraced the Southern cause was Major General J. Patton Anderson of Florida. He told the President, in his petition for pardon,

27. Amnesty Papers, Georgia.
28. *Ibid.*, Alabama.

that he had not believed, "until blood was shed, that war would result from secession." Accepting defeat gracefully, he gave assurance that he was determined to aid in restoring "the country to a condition of peace and prosperity." His application, endorsed by Provisional Governor William Marvin, was filed December 4, 1865, but favorable action on it was not taken until nearly a year later (December 1, 1866). About that time Attorney-General Stanbery and his chief clerk, M. F. Pleasant, recommended clemency. The latter was a relative of Anderson, whose pardon he urged so that the beneficiary could "sell a little property," worth three or four thousand dollars, to support his family.[29] Had a relative and the Attorney-General not intervened, and ill health and the dire need of disposing of property not been given as good reasons for pardon, Anderson would probably have remained disabled months longer.

Brigadier General W. G. M. Davis of Florida waited until early in 1866 to petition for pardon. He had entered the service in 1861 but was obliged to resign in 1863 on account of ill health. In his brief, straightforward letter he said that, in seeking pardon, he was "actuated by a sincere desire to be and remain a loyal citizen of the United States," and to give thereto his "unqualified obedience." Furthermore, he was determined to instruct his "children to perform their duties" as good citizens. His application was filed on January 9 with the President's prompt endorsement, "Issue a pardon in this case"; and on that day the petition was granted. No oath or recommendation was filed with this petition in the Amnesty Papers. Even the Governor's endorsement was not in evidence. The omissions were very unusual.[30]

Not every Confederate general applied for pardon. General Robert Toombs of Georgia was one who did not. He had served in both houses of the Federal Congress, resigning from the Senate in January, 1861, to promote secession, and had been a member of the first Confederate congress. In fact, he was considered for the presidency of the Confederacy when Davis was chosen. After about five weeks as Secretary of State, he resigned to enter the military service, being commissioned brigadier general. President John-

29. *Ibid.*, Florida.
30. *Ibid.*

son ordered his arrest on May 19, 1865, but he eluded his would-be captors and fled to Cuba. Apparently, he was expected to be arrested with Alexander H. Stephens and taken to Fort Warren. Probably knowledge of Stephens's apprehension increased his determination to avoid arrest and imprisonment by escaping.[31]

From his safe retreat in Havana, Toombs railed at Congress and the President. He saw no material difference between their positions in the controversy over reconstruction, as far as the welfare of the South was concerned, and was not in sympathy with either. He felt secure and satisfied in exile at that time (December, 1865), for he believed that if he returned home only the President could keep him out of Fort Warren. Not even the Supreme Court could prevent his incarceration, if it wanted to, unless Johnson intervened. And Toombs was confident that Johnson believed the "life of the nation" would demand his imprisonment. And "if anything more was deemed necessary for the 'life of the nation,' " he said, "a military court could hang me much more rightfully than it" executed Mrs. Mary Surratt; "for I did try to take the life of the nation; and sorely regret the failure to do it."[32] Such spirit and temper were in marked contrast to the expressions of the petitioners for pardon above, and illustrate the difference between Toombs's character and that of nearly all other secessionists.

Mrs. Toombs joined her husband in Cuba, where they remained until the spring of 1866. She returned home in May, and he went to Europe, where Mrs. Toombs followed in July of that year. In December, 1866, Mrs. Toombs returned home again, on account of a daughter's illness. General Toombs shortly became homesick and soon notified his wife that he was returning too. " 'The worst that can happen to me is a prison,' said he, 'and I don't see much difference to choose between my present position and any decent fort.' " He returned home early in 1867 and had a satisfactory interview with President Johnson, who allowed him to return home, where he remained unmolested. He never took the amnesty

31. *Offic. Rec.*, 1 Ser., XLIX, pt. 2, pp. 750, 786, 839, 859, 902.
32. *Annual Report, Am. Hist. Assoc.*, 1911, II, 674 (Toombs to Stephens, December 15, 1865). Gamaliel Bradford's *Confederate Portraits*, Ch. VIII, "Robert Toombs," describes the violent and volatile character of this able, but "fire-eating," secessionist.

oath or any other oath of allegiance nor did he ever apply for pardon. He died in December, 1885, without having had the disability under the Fourteenth Amendment removed. In many respects his obstinacy suggests that of Jefferson Davis.[33]

Major General T. J. Churchill of Arkansas wanted a pardon soon so that the Freedman's Bureau could not take over his estate. He desired also to engage in business in Louisville, Kentucky. Another Arkansan, Brigadier General Thomas P. Dockery, was recommended strongly for clemency because he had been especially considerate of captured Union soldiers. After obtaining pardon, General Gideon J. Pillow of Tennessee wanted his captured mules restored so that he could begin the cultivation of a plantation near Helena, Arkansas. The President, sustained by General Sherman, denied his request, on the ground that the restoration of such captured property was not a benefit derived from amnesty. George R. Riddle of Pittsburgh, Pennsylvania, had opposed Pillow's pardon, fearing it would annul any right to damages against the General for the destruction of his steamboat and other property on the Mississippi River, valued at $100,000.[34]

The New York *Herald* exulted, on August 27, 1865, in announcing General Wade Hampton's petition for pardon in these words: He "has reconciled his sanguinary determination to die in the last ditch of the Southern Confederacy and now bellows lustily for pardon. . . . Who next?" Senator Orville H. Browning requested a pardon for General George E. Pickett on June 6, but the President told the Senator that "he thought he would hold some of the principal leaders [of the rebellion] in suspense for some time." General Grant spoke highly of Pickett and believed he should apply, but thought his hanging of some Union soldiers on the pretext of their being deserters from the Confederate army might be an obstacle in his obtaining pardon. On November 3, 1865, Brown-

33: U. B. Phillips, *The Life of Robert Toombs*, 256-57. While in Cuba, Toombs seriously thought of emigrating to Mexico. He was successful as a lawyer and as a business man, amassing a considerable fortune after the war.

34. Amnesty Papers, Arkansas; Stanton Papers, XXIX (Sherman to Stanton, November 7, Stanton to Sherman, November 8, Sherman to Stanton, November 14, 1865); MS Record Book B., 68, Dept. of Justice (in the National Archives).

ing and Grant expressed again the inexpediency of Pickett's petitioning the President, even though the General did need relief to engage in business to support his family. Grant expressed the opinion, however, that Pickett might go where he pleased, since he (Grant) had directed the issue of an order, after Appomattox, allowing the paroles of Lee's men to be suspended to "enable them to go when and where they pleased, and to embark in any business that was open to them. . . ."[35] Grant was certainly more disposed to leniency in 1865 than Johnson or Stanton.

While scores of other generals were enjoying paroles and petitioning for pardon, Lieutenant General Joseph Wheeler experienced an unprovoked attack upon his life. After learning of Johnston's surrender, he appears to have moved about in an uncertain manner seeking a Federal officer who would parole him. On May 11, he was reported captured near Atlanta under the assumed name of Lieutenant Sharp and with a forged parole on his person. While being taken to Fort Delaware for detention, he wrote General Halleck a letter detailing his activities after April 26 and claiming the privilege of parole under the terms granted Johnston. After some weeks' imprisonment, he was paroled and went to Nashville, where two Federal officers assaulted him with a club and pistol in his hotel room on August 21, 1865. Wheeler reported the attack to General George H. Thomas, who ordered an investigation, and the men, Lieutenant Colonel Joseph H. Blackburn and Captain Morton E. Quinn of the Fourth Tennessee cavalry, were informed that they would be arrested and court-martialed if their regiment had not already been mustered out of the service. They were also told that their "conduct at the time of the assault, as well as subsequently," was an "insult and a disgrace to the uniform they wore. . . ." Wheeler denied ever having given the men any cause whatever for the attack, though he had captured some of their men and had passed through the community where Blackburn's family lived.[36]

35. Browning, *Diary*, II, 32, 48.
36. *Offic. Rec.*, 1 Ser., XLIX, pt. 2, pp. 725, 726, 837, 845, 846, 857; 2 Ser., VIII, 726-29; MS, Duke University (letter, Wheeler to Halleck, Steamer Clyde, near Fortress Monroe, May 20, 1865).

Sometimes there were complaints that the President was more ready to pardon the civil than the military leaders of the Confederacy—politicians than generals. In reality, there were more of the former than the latter. Furthermore, the civil leaders were needed in the plan of reconstruction in vogue in 1865 and 1866. The able generals, too, had prolonged the war, and that probably made a difference. Moreover, 7,197 property owners, each worth more than $20,000 (the thirteenth exception), were reported, on May 4, 1866, as having been pardoned by special acts of the President. These pardons added to the evidence, therefore, that disabled civilians were favored more than the military.

There were scores of other generals, of course, who asked for clemency, and most of them received special pardons. In fact, sixty-four brigadier and eight major generals were thus amnestied between April 15, 1865, and January 8, 1867.[37] There were others whose cases were being considered when this report was made, some of whom, as indicated above, were not pardoned until Johnson's second and third general amnesties.

ADMIRAL RAPHAEL SEMMES

Raphael Semmes had an unfortunate experience after his surrender and parole as a prisoner of war late in April, 1865. A brief account of his activities subsequent to his escape from the sinking "Alabama" on June 19, 1864, is necessary to understand the excuse for his arrest and detention in Washington and the threat to try him before a military commission. He was threatened with civil trial also.

When Captain Semmes realized that the "Alabama" could no longer withstand the fire of the "Kearsarge," he determined to beach the vessel on the French coast, near Cherbourg. The sinking condition of the ship, however, soon caused him to strike his colors and dispatch "a boat to inform the enemy" of the necessity of surrendering. But the "Alabama" filled so rapidly that Semmes and his surviving seamen were obliged to go overboard to save

37. *House Exec. Doc.*, No. 31, 39 Cong., 2 Sess.

their lives, some in boats and others, including the captain, by jumping into the sea. The neutral English steam-yacht "Deerhound" rescued Semmes and others, and took them to Southampton, England.[38]

After enjoying a very pleasant experience in England and France, Semmes sailed in October, 1864, to Havana and thence to the coast of Mexico, from which he traveled by land to the Confederate capital. Davis promoted him at once to the rank of rear admiral and placed him in command of the fleet on the James River, where he fought again for the Confederacy. On the night Lee evacuated Richmond, Admiral Semmes burned his ships, organized his seamen into a naval brigade, received a brigadier general's commission, and moved rapidly southward to join General Joseph E. Johnston's army in North Carolina. On April 26 he surrendered to General Sherman under the terms granted Johnston's army at Greensboro.

Semmes was careful to prepare his parole so that it guaranteed protection to him as "Rear Admiral and Brigadier General," thus becoming a paroled prisoner of war from both branches of the Confederate armed service. With this double guarantee against molestation, he went quietly to his home in Mobile, Alabama. Nearly eight months later (December 15), Secretary of the Navy Gideon Welles had him arrested and taken to Washington where he was detained, first in the Navy Yard and then in the Marine Barracks, for nearly four months under threat of trial before a military commission.

Welles had Semmes arrested on the advice of all the members of Johnson's Cabinet. The charges were: "1. Fraudulently obtaining a cessation of firing on the part of the Kearsarge by showing a white flag, and then reopening his fire; 2. Perfidiously running away after overtures of surrender; 3. Reentering the rebel service without being exchanged." Personally, Welles would have been pleased if the prisoner had left the country in the interval between his surrender and the time of his arrest, and observed that the prisoner's

38. Admiral Raphael Semmes, *Memoirs of Service Afloat, during the War between the States*, 752 ff., 809 ff., cited hereafter as Semmes, *Memoirs of Service Afloat.*

case was "one of the most aggravated and least excusable of the whole Rebel host."[39]

Indeed there were probably more angles to the trouble that Semmes had given the authorities at Washington during the war than might have been charged against any other Confederate. The main grievance against him appeared to be his escape from Captain John A. Winslow when the "Kearsarge" sank the "Alabama." The Federal authorities, by the time of his arrest, had come to regard him as an escaped prisoner of war who had violated his status as such by returning to the Confederate States and fighting again without having been exchanged. Of course, the fact that Semmes had left the Union and become a terror to the shipping of the United States aggravated his case. As Welles put it: ". . . He was educated and supported by that government which he deserted in disregard of his obligations and oath; he made it his business to rob and destroy the ships and property of his unarmed countrymen engaged in peaceful commerce; when he finally fought and was conquered he practiced a fraud, and in violation of his surrender broke faith, and without ever being exchanged fought against the Union at Richmond; escaping from that city, he claims to have been included in Johnston's surrender, and therefore not amenable for previous offenses."[40]

Of course, Semmes protested vigorously against the violation of his parole. Grant, Sherman, and Johnston apparently approved of Semmes's contention that paroles given at Greensboro had the same force as those issued at Appomattox, and should be respected. Grant had insisted that Lee's parole be honored months earlier, as has been explained in Chapter VII. Nevertheless, according to Sherman, the arrest of Semmes had been made by order of the Navy Department, and of necessity the President, "being the common superior to both the Army and Navy," would have to dispose of the case.[41]

Just one month (January 15, 1866) after his arrest, Semmes

39. Welles, *Diary*, II, 404 (December 27, 1865); Naval Solicitor John A. Bolles, "Why Semmes of the Alabama Was Never Tried," *Atlantic Monthly*, XXX (August, 1872), 150.
40. *Ibid.* President John Quincy Adams appointed Semmes midshipman.
41. *Offic. Rec.*, 2 Ser., VIII, 842 (Sherman to Johnson, January 2, 1866).

wrote President Johnson a polite and scholarly letter of some three thousand words denying the charges against him. After emphasizing the binding force of the terms of Johnston's surrender and his own parole, he denied the charge that he had violated the laws of war in escaping from Captain Winslow. He claimed that the manner of his escape was unavoidable, and that, "according to the laws and usages of war," he could not be regarded as a prisoner of war, since his enemy did not take possession of him. He reminded the President that he could verify this statement "in almost every page of naval history," even though the Secretary of the Navy claimed the contrary.[42]

Semmes contended that, in reality, the important question in his case was whether the act for which he had been arrested was an act of war. If that was the cause of his detention and threat of trial before either a civil court or a military commission, then, he declared "there is an end to the question, and I must be discharged," for, if the convention at Greensboro meant anything, it was "an oblivion of all acts of war of whatever nature." Moreover, if his act came within the definition of treason, and treason consisted "only in levying war against" the United States, or "adhering to their enemies," then he could "neither be tried by a military tribunal during the war, nor a civil tribunal after the war, for any act of war, or for treason which consists only of acts of war." Attorney-General Speed had advised Johnson, on January 4, that treason cases belonged to the civil courts; but, since treason was an act of war which the convention had placed, in Semmes's case, in oblivion, the government should discharge the prisoner.

Speed had advised the President, however, that the convention under which Semmes claimed protection was not a continuing guarantee. Consequently, the prisoner might be turned over to a civil court for trial after the war ended. This might be correct if Semmes had surrendered unconditionally, but such was not the case. The agreement made by Sherman and Johnston "was not a mere release of prisoners on parole; nor, indeed, had it anything to do with prisoners, for none of the officers and men of General

42. Semmes, *Memoirs of Service Afloat*, 825-31 (Semmes to Johnson, January 15, 1866). See Bolles, "Why Semmes . . . Was Never Tried," 148 ff., for a strong denial of Semmes's contention.

Johnston's army *ever were prisoners*," as an examination of the convention would show. "On the contrary, it was expressly stated that the guarantees contained in it were to continue and be in force, so long as the parties to whom the guarantees were given should perform their part of the treaty stipulations." A contrary opinion, Semmes told the President, would "shock the common sense and love of fair play of the American people." Moreover, since the authorities at Washington knew of Semmes's "alleged illegal escape off Cherbourg," they should have excepted him from the benefits of the Sherman-Johnston convention.[43]

It should be noted that Semmes never offered a defense of the Southern cause in his message to the President, as many other Confederates did in petitioning for pardon or a release from imprisonment. His case was somewhat different. He confined himself, instead, to clarifying the legal elements that entered into his escape from Captain Winslow and his subsequent fighting against the Union, but he did not specifically cite laws or current usages of war to sustain his position. He did say that "nearly every page of naval history" sanctioned his actions. His letter was merely an able affirmation that the Greensboro convention guaranteed protection under his parole.[44]

Semmes's long letter to the President apparently had no immediate effect. Yet Welles's *Diary* indicates that much attention was given the case. For some time the authorities were uncertain whether the Confederate Rear Admiral and Brigadier General

43. Semmes, *Memoirs of Service Afloat*, 830-31.

44. Semmes was not lacking, however, in information to justify secession. The first seven chapters of his *Memoirs of Service Afloat*, copyrighted in 1868, contain as good a defense of the South as can be found anywhere else. He related therein Northern and Southern differences from the settlements of the Puritans in New England and the Cavaliers in the Southern colonies, during the seventeenth century, to the tariff issue and the controversy over slavery in the nineteenth century. Colonial Massachusetts and Virginia had received from the mother country the seed of separatism that had germinated in America and grown to the colossal effort of dividing the United States into two diverse and independent republics. In November, 1949, Dr. Roy F. Nichols of the University of Pennsylvania read a paper entitled "1461-1861: The American Civil War in Its True Perspective," before the Southern Historical Association, at Williamsburg, Virginia, showing that the War between the States began during the War of the Roses in England. See *Journal of Southern History*, XVI (May, 1950), 143-60.

should be tried before a military commission or a civil court. The choice depended upon the selection of charges to prefer against him. On February 1 the President refused to sign an order, prepared by Bolles and others, to proceed before a commission. He desired the case to remain in the hands of the Navy Department, saying, according to Welles, that he did not want Judge-Advocate Joseph Holt to have another opportunity for a cruel prosecution, since everything coming "from that quarter partook of the traits of Nero and Draco."[45]

Evidently if Semmes had been tried in either court much evidence would have been offered by the defendant that would have reflected unfavorably on practices and abuses by United States naval officers. At any rate, Bolles, in explaining some years later (1872) why Semmes was not tried, stated that he was "entitled to all the customary cheats, falsehoods, snares, decoys, false pretenses, and swindles of civilized and Christian warfare," and that "the records of the United States Navy Department effectually silence all right to complain of Semmes for having imitated our example in obedience to orders from the Secretary of the Confederate Navy."[46]

Seward accused John Lancaster, owner of the "Deerhound," of conspiring to liberate Semmes and his men when he rescued them and took them to England. He asked that the Confederates be turned over to the United States as prisoners of war. Lancaster clearly proved his neutrality, and Lord John Russell refused Seward's request. Apparently the English authorities had no difficulty in justifying Semmes's escape from Captain Winslow, even though the captain of the "Alabama" had signaled his desire to surrender.[47]

Nevertheless, Gamaliel Bradford, after discussing the various phases of the escape, says: "The only aspersion upon him here is that he did not give himself up as a prisoner after being rescued by the Deerhound. It is possible that Lee or Albert Sidney Johnston would have done this; but I do not believe there were many of-

45. Welles, *Diary*, II, 410, 414, 420, 423-24 (January 3, 13, 30, February 1, 1866).
46. Bolles, "Why Semmes . . . Was Never Tried," 150; also quoted by Bradford, *Confederate Portraits*, 221.
47. Semmes, *Memoirs of Service Afloat*, Chs. LIV, LV.

ficers in either the Union or Confederate service who would have strained honor to a point so quixotically fine."[48] Perhaps this is a fair statement of the merits of the case.

One apparent reason Johnson allowed Semmes's case to drag along was the increasing hostility of Congress toward him. According to Welles, the President seemed to fear a subversion of the government by that body, believing that the Radicals were plotting "to take the government into their own hands, and to get rid of him by declaring Tennessee out of the Union." This deferment of the trial was to Semmes's advantage. Bolles stated in 1872 that if the prisoner had been tried soon after his arrest he would have been convicted and executed. The information subsequently obtained revealed that the captain of the "Alabama" was not entirely "free from all violation of the law of war," but that he was "by no means the guilty monster" of the opinion that prevailed against him in 1865.

On March 30, Speed had recommended trial before a mixed commission of five naval and four army officers. Thus both phases of the case would be reviewed. But the President still wavered, and when Welles submitted Semmes's application for parole, endorsed by Bolles, whose advice he appreciated more than Speed's counsel, he still deferred action.[49]

By April 3, 1866, two important developments in Semmes's case had occurred. On April 2, the President proclaimed the Civil War at an end in all the late Confederate States except Texas, while the next day the Supreme Court declared, in *Ex parte Milligan*, that a trial by a military commission where the civil courts were open was illegal. Bolles recommended therefore that the prisoner be paroled, "unless the case was [to be] wholly abandoned." Welles thought abandonment preferable to a parole. He reasoned that, unless Semmes was tried for violating the laws of war, there was no case against him. He thought, however, that a trial before a military commission might please those who were complaining of the President's failure to discharge his duty in punishing "the worst Rebels." People would realize "that the courts were not as prompt as the

48. Bradford, *Confederate Portraits*, 240.
49. Welles, *Diary*, II, 432, 436, 457, 467 (February 13, 21, March 20, 31, 1866); Bolles, "Why Semmes . . . Was Never Tried," 154-55.

Executive" in discharging their respective duties, if Johnson insisted on trying Semmes.

Two days after his proclamation ending the war, the President appeared disposed to parole Semmes if trials before a military commission were illegal as the court had decided. He still had some doubts about the matter, but he wanted to be rid of the aggravating case somehow. Mrs. Semmes had been tearfully entreating him to release her husband, and that was annoying. After a Cabinet meeting on April 6, therefore, Johnson told Welles that, since Grant believed his own paroles covered almost everything and since the courts were against military commissions, Semmes might "as well be released on his parole." The Secretary thought the man had already been twice paroled, and that was enough, "one [time] on the surrender of the *Alabama* and another at the time of Johnston's surrender," and that if he could not be tried promptly, he should be released unconditionally. Johnson accepted his advice and instructed him to prepare a paper providing for the prisoner's release and to present it for his approval.

Welles's first thought was to justify the discharge on the grounds of both the President's proclamation of April 2 declaring the war at an end and the recent decision of the Supreme Court denying military commissions where the civil courts were functioning. On second consideration, however, he omitted the proclamation from the paper, because its inclusion would probably have caused those who had been imprisoned to criticize Johnson for delaying action to end the war, since that power was seemingly the President's prerogative.[50]

On being released, Admiral Semmes returned to his home in Alabama. Like many others, he was included in the benefits of the President's amnesty of July 4, 1868. Soon thereafter he concluded his monumental *Memoirs of Service Afloat* with the following caustic lines: "By the last of these proclamations, the writer of these pages, who was true to his State, was 'graciously pardoned' by Andrew Johnson, who had not only been a traitor to his State, but had betrayed, besides, two political parties. A glorious opportunity presented itself for him to show himself a statesman. He has proved a charlatan instead. He cowered in his struggle with

50. Welles, *Diary*, II, 471 ff. (April 2, 3, 4, 6, 1866).

Congress, and that body has shorn him of his prerogatives and reduced him to the mere position of a clerk. . . ."[51]

How different had been the feelings of the repentant engineer of the "Alabama," M. J. Freeman of New Jersey, when he applied for a special pardon more than two and a half years earlier! He stated that he hoped in the future to be able to erase "the Black Stains now recorded against" him. He assured the President that, if the country should ever need his services again, he could be depended on to serve her. He closed his petition by stating that he had been the "misguided tool and dupe of others" who were then at liberty. Captain John A. Winslow, who had captured the ship, recommended the engineer highly, saying that he was "the only officer of the *Alabama*" whom he "would feel warranted" in recommending for pardon. The engineer's petition was filed on August 16, and his pardon granted on November 7, 1865.[52]

51. *Memoirs of Service Afloat*, 833. See Naval Solicitor Bolles's bitter criticism of Semmes in "Why Semmes . . . Was Never Tried." Bolles stated that Winslow never found fault with Semmes until Semmes began criticizing Winslow.

52. Amnesty Papers, New Jersey.

CHAPTER TEN

PARDONING NORTH CAROLINIANS

———◆———

THE FAVORED STATE[1]

THE SPECIAL consideration that President Johnson gave North Carolina in his program of reconstruction deserves notice. He was doubtless influenced by the manifestations there of loyalty to the Union during the war, and by the fact that he had many acquaintances and old associates in his native state. Having been instrumental in restoring Tennessee, he was in a position to help North Carolina regain her former status in the Union. The proximity of his native to his adopted state, therefore, may have influenced the President to begin his plan of restoration in the former.[2] Other conditions, however, were ripe for such an undertaking.

Having introduced his program in North Carolina, the President was especially generous in a material way to that state. At the close of hostilities, he allowed Governor Holden to retain war property worth $150,000. He also paid all legislative and court expenses incurred during the Provisional Governor's term. Johnson did this for no other state. He also allowed Holden seven thousand dollars from the Treasury to cover the expenses of his office. Indeed, Johnson seemed "very desirous that his native state should

1. This chapter, in much longer form, appeared first in the *North Carolina Historical Review*, XXIII, No. 3 (July, 1946), 360-401. It is hoped that it will encourage similar studies of the subject in other states of the Confederacy.
2. Johnson was Military Governor of Tennessee from March 4, 1862, until late in 1864.

be the model . . . and outstrip all her contemporaries in the race for reconstruction and reunion."[3]

Apparently the Chief Executive consulted a number of North Carolinians before announcing his amnesty and plan of reconstruction. He summoned Holden to Washington as early as May 9, and by the latter part of that month the editor and a number of other prominent Carolinians had gone to the capital for conferences. Responding to their plea for "forbearance and kindness toward the Southern States," the President promised that he would be as generous as possible, especially when entreated by those excepted in his proclamation of amnesty. Though he would pardon them when he could, Holden quotes him as declaring, "treason must be made odious, and coming generations ought to know it and profit by it."[4]

Johnson allowed some of his visitors to press Holden upon him as Provisional Governor, despite the unfavorable reaction of former Governor David L. Swain and others. The editor himself states that Swain tried to persuade him not to accept, preferring instead that Vance remain in the office in compliance with the Sherman-Johnston convention. Between the President and Holden, however, "there was the bond of like social origin and like political opinions in the past, and this fact, coupled with their old friendship and communications during the war," probably made Holden the President's choice.[5] Consequently he accepted the appointment, though he could not meet the "ironclad" requirement, since he had, "more or less, aided the rebellion." In fact, he had been a strong secessionist before the war and had voted for separation in the North Carolina convention. As Provisional Governor he swore allegiance in August, as provided in the amnesty proclamation. This is worth noting, since other provisional governors were required to take the test oath also.[6]

3. *Memoirs of W. W. Holden,* 55-56, cited hereafter as Holden, *Memoirs;* J. G. de Roulhac Hamilton (ed.), *The Papers of Thomas Ruffin,* IV, 28-29 (David L. Swain to Judge Thomas Ruffin, September 15, 1865), cited hereafter as Hamilton, *Papers of Ruffin.*

4. Holden, *Memoirs,* 45-56.

5. Hamilton, *Papers of Ruffin,* IV, 28-29 (Swain to Ruffin, September 20, 1865); Hamilton, *Reconstruction in North Carolina,* 108.

6. Holden, *Memoirs,* 49; Hamilton, *Reconstruction in North Carolina,* 108 ff.

RULES AND REGULATIONS

Soon retiring from the *Standard*, Holden entered upon the duties of his office.[7] The President's proclamations of amnesty and reconstruction and Seward's rules pertaining thereto would now be complied with. In a presidentially approved proclamation of June 12 and August 2 explaining the plan of reconstruction, Holden invited the people to resume their accustomed pursuits with cheerfulness and confidence in the future. He also urged those who had left the state during the war or immediately thereafter to return, assuring all that they would "be protected in their persons and property, and encouraged in their exertion to improve their condition. . . ."[8] On August 8, Holden announced that delegates were to be elected to a convention to be held on October 2 for the purpose of making certain prescribed changes in the state's constitution and providing for the election of a legislature, governor, and other state officials under that constitution.

Among Holden's first acts was the appointment of justices of the peace to administer the amnesty oath, and other officers necessary to register voters and otherwise set in motion the plan of reconstruction. After taking the amnesty oath and also the customary oath required by North Carolina,[9] these officials received pledges of loyalty from those who were pardoned outright on taking the amnesty oath, and from those who were required to make special application for individual pardon. The great majority regained their civil rights and political privileges under the general plan. The selection of reliable justices and registering officials was no easy task. Many whom the Governor selected were not permitted to administer the oath. Holden explained to the President that inasmuch as "there are weak men among them . . . persons

7. Thereafter the paper carried, for a time at least, the names of Joseph S. Carman as editor and Joseph W. Holden as assistant editor. The latter was the Provisional Governor's son. Holden's paper had several names, but only one is used in this study.

8. Raleigh *Daily Standard*, August 2, 1865.

9. It appears that justices were also required to take a third oath. At least, the Governor's Papers for July 1-15, 1865 (in archives of State Department of Archives and History, Raleigh), indicate that the justices of Carteret County took a third oath.

would be qualified to vote who ought not to be," if all justices were authorized to administer the oath.[10]

On June 23, Johnson instructed Holden, through the Attorney-General's office, to use precaution in administering the amnesty proclamation. The communication pointed out that an "indiscriminate exercise of Executive clemency" was inadvisable, because both the state and the general government needed to be protected from certain persons in the excepted classes. Johnson became very generous in granting pardons before the end of the summer, but at first he appeared determined to move slowly in exercising clemency. The applicant was required to show that he would be a peaceful and useful citizen in the future, what confiscation proceedings had been instituted against his property, and whether the government held any realty belonging to him as "abandoned property." The President assured Holden that, when cases were referred to the Governor for careful consideration, all information pertaining thereto would be sent to him for "prompt and careful attention." The instructions closed with a detailed explanation of the reasons why the President wanted doubtful cases submitted to the Governor. First, it seemed desirable to avoid, if possible, any risk of granting pardons to disloyal persons, or to such as, judging from previous conduct and character, could not be trusted with the control of the freedmen. Second, Johnson desired to strengthen Holden's hands in the reorganization of the state by all constitutional means. A United States district attorney would soon be appointed to assist the Governor, who was reminded that the President looked to him to uphold law and order in the state.[11]

In considering the two classes of oath takers, the justices and registering officials gave special attention to those who had to make application to the President. Persons in the other class, of course, were pardoned when they renewed their allegiance and received certificates to that effect, while excepted persons had to enclose copies of their oaths with their applications for clemency. This meant delay in registering, because petitioners could not be

10. Johnson Papers, LXXI, No. 5666 (Holden to Johnson, July 24, 1865).
11. Governor's Papers, 1865, Raleigh Archives (I. Hubley Ashton to Holden, June 23, 1865).

registered as voters until they presented their pardon certificates. Inasmuch as carelessness in preparing petitions delayed consideration, specific instructions were published for the preparation of applications.[12] The applicant was directed to address himself to the President, giving his name, age, and residence, describing any conduct during the war rendering "his property liable to confiscation," stating the clause in the Amnesty Proclamation under which he came, and asserting that he had "taken the oath of Amnesty" and intended to observe the same. He was instructed regarding the selection and folding of paper, and was reminded to sign the petition and attach thereto a copy of his amnesty oath properly attested. By observing these directions, applicants would gain prompt consideration. Though these instructions were not always followed in detail, the pardons were often granted just the same.

Governor Holden appointed Dr. Robert J. Powell state agent in Washington to facilitate the granting of pardons.[13] The advantage resulting therefrom may be appreciated when it is understood that petitions the Governor approved went to the Attorney-General of the United States and then to the President. Powell's functions during Holden's incumbency were very important, because he was the medium of communication between Raleigh and Washington and often even between the offices of the President and the Attorney-General. Consequently, he was in a position to promote Holden's political ambitions, which appear to have depended largely on granting some applications and denying or delaying action on others.

<h3 style="text-align:center">PARDON SEEKERS AND PARDONS</h3>

As one might expect, Holden was kept busy during his term as Provisional Governor receiving petitioners and their friends and examining applications. To his office came supporters of the late Confederacy in every capacity—governors, legislators (state and Confederate), generals, judges, county and city officials, professional and business men, and planters—to secure endorsement of

12. Raleigh *Daily Standard*, August 3, 1865.
13. Powell was a native of North Carolina, holding a position in the patent office at the time of his appointment.

their petitions. "For the first five months," he stated, "I had not less than seventy-five visitors every day, which engaged my attention for hours. . . . I also received every day a large number of applications for pardon which I read carefully. I was the medium through which these applications went to the President, and my duty was to mark them Granted, Postponed, or Rejected. . . . During my time of seven months as governor about twelve hundred pardons (1,200), as well as I recollect, were thus obtained. . . ."

Furthermore, as already indicated, Holden "had to provide books with the amnesty oaths for all the counties, to appoint persons in various counties to administer those oaths," and to perform various other duties necessary in the reconstruction program then in operation. So closely did he apply himself to his duties that his health was impaired, and at one time during his incumbency he went to a resort called Kittrell Springs to recuperate. On June 21 the New York *Herald* described activities in the North Carolina capital in these words: "Since the promulgation of the Amnesty proclamation . . . there has been a great rush of the secessionists to Raleigh to solicit pardon. . . . They come from the east and from the west, from the north and from the south . . . and all at once they have discovered that Governor Holden is a remarkably proper man—the right man in the right place. . . ."[14]

Some applicants for pardon stated that they had accepted civil offices to avoid service in the Confederate army. One man became tithing agent; another, postmaster; a third, assessor and depot agent. Tod R. Caldwell, who later became Lieutenant Governor and Governor of the state, said that he avoided military service by accepting the office of solicitor for Rutherford County. He also stated in his petition that he was so active in opposing the "Davis Usurpation" that the rebel leaders threatened to destroy his property and do him personal violence.

Caldwell gave only one offense against the United States. He applied for pardon on July 25; Holden recommended pardon at once; and Johnson pardoned him on August 12, 1865. Sundry other petty offices had also been filled by persons to avoid military service, but most petitioners of this class seem to have been postmasters. These men usually stated their opposition to secession and

14. Holden, *Memoirs*, 57-65; New York *Herald*, June 21, 1865.

their satisfaction with the outcome of the war. Consequently their petitions were often granted with little delay.[15]

The Quakers found themselves in an awkward position when expected to take the amnesty oath. The inquiry of Joseph Newlin of New Market illustrates their predicament. He told Holden that he thought "it would be requiring too much of them" to swear "allegiance to the United States," since they had "never broken their allegiance thereto voluntarily," and could not, therefore, "consistently make the affirmation."[16] Newlin's contention, however, was better expressed in a formal petition to Holden by the Quakers at one of their annual "Sufferings." After giving their religious scruples against rebellion and stating that not one of them had favored the rupture of the government, they related the hardships inflicted upon them for opposing the war. They had been imprisoned, whipped, suspended by the thumb, and had suffered other penal indignities and abuses. Consequently they believed that they should not be required to swear allegiance to the United States. The Quakers also feared that taking the oath might be construed to mean defending the Constitution by the use of arms, a practice in direct violation of a primary principle which had always characterized their society. If they might not be released entirely from the amnesty oath, they desired "it to be so modified as not to violate" their conscientious scruples.[17]

Holden asked Johnson to excuse the Quakers from swearing at all. If this might not be done, he requested that they be allowed to take the North Carolina oath, which did not have some parts that the complainants found objectionable in the amnesty proclamation. If neither of these requests could be granted, Holden asked that it might "be stated by authority in the newspapers that when Quakers take the oath of amnesty it is not expected that they bind themselves to defend the Government with arms."[18] But the President did not grant the Governor's request, for the Quakers were obliged to take the amnesty oath. Perhaps he took the position that Lincoln had maintained when loyal Tennesseans objected

15. Amnesty Papers, North Carolina.
16. Governor's Papers, 1865 (Newlin to Holden, June 13, 1865).
17. *Ibid.*
18. Johnson Papers, LXVIII; Governor's Papers, 1865 (Holden to Johnson, June 27, 1865). Holden sent Johnson a copy of the Quakers' petition.

194   *Pardon and Amnesty under Lincoln and Johnson*

to taking the oath provided in the amnesty proclamation of December 8, 1863. Such persons had protested vigorously but vainly against taking it and being thus classified with rebels. Having insisted in 1864 on applying a more rigid test of loyalty in Tennessee than Lincoln had required, he was at this time not likely to except anyone merely on account of religious scruples.[19]

HOLDEN'S PARTIALITY

The records show that Holden carefully scrutinized the lists forwarded to Washington and indicated thereon those whose pardons he desired deferred and those whom he desired released at once.[20] Evidently he withheld his recommendation when he regarded the applicant as likely to oppose his administration as Provisional Governor and later his candidacy for Governor. Such persons, of course, could neither sit in the convention soon to assemble nor vote in the forthcoming election, unless they had previously obtained pardons. Furthermore, he appeared to favor petitioners who had been ardent secessionists in 1860 and 1861, and to oppose (for a time at least) those, like Zebulon B. Vance, John A. Gilmer, Josiah Turner, Jr., William A. Graham, and John M. Morehead, who had been for the Union until influenced by the first seceders to cast their lot with the Confederacy. Original secessionists, therefore, like A. H. Arrington, Burton Craige, John L. Bridgers, William Lander, and Abram Venable were recommended for pardon.

Those discriminated against accused Holden of seeking to promote his own political fortune by such partiality. Jonathan Worth wrote two years later that all Holden's "actions were shaped to bring about his election by the people as Governor. He never failed to recommend for pardon anyone . . . who gave him satisfactory assurance of support. He recommended for suspension or rejection everyone, regardless of his political antecedents, who would not assure him of support." Even Lewis Hanes, who was for a time Holden's private secretary, stated that "in everything that he did,

19. See first division of Ch. IV.
20. Amnesty Papers, North Carolina.

he kept constantly in view no object but his own political advancement."[21]

It should be noted, however, that Holden did favor pardoning some prominent persons who had opposed secession and had later supported the Confederacy, and Jonathan Worth was one of these. In fact, Worth said of himself: "As to getting into the war or getting out of it, I have a better record than any [other] man in the State."[22] He had been pardoned early (August 11) so that Holden might appoint him provisional treasurer of the state. Former Governor David L. Swain, Dr. James G. Ramsey, and Judge Thomas Ruffin were three other men in this class whose pardons Holden favored. Swain, whose petition contained an account of his Union sentiment during the war, was needed as President of the University of North Carolina. He had declined a seat in the Confederate States senate, had never been a real secessionist, and believed Buchanan could have prevented the war. Holden recommended his pardon on September 24, and Johnson granted it two weeks later. Ramsey supported his long petition so well with newspaper comments on his opposition to secession that Holden recommended his pardon on June 30, and Johnson pardoned him a few days later.[23]

Holden stated in his *Memoirs* that he refused to recommend for pardon only four persons, but the records show that he marked many applications to be suspended or deferred. For example, on August 18, 1865, his agent at Washington, Dr. Powell, submitted a list of some 290 persons who had applied for pardon. Six were marked for immediate action, 232 for pardon without any time indicated, and 40 others were to be suspended. Seven more were to take effect on January 1, 1866. John A. Gilmer was among those to be pardoned, but James R. McLean's petition was marked "rejected," and that of Landon C. Haynes of Iredell County (formerly

21. J. G. de Roulhac Hamilton (ed.), *The Correspondence of Jonathan Worth*, II, 977 (Worth to Colonel W. G. Moore, June 9, 1867), cited hereafter as Hamilton, *Jonathan Worth*; Hamilton, *Reconstruction in North Carolina*, 133.
22. Hamilton, *Jonathan Worth*, I, 204 (letter to Jesse Walker, September 14, 1865).
23. Amnesty Papers, North Carolina.

of Tennessee) was sent to the President without any recommendation at all.[24]

Furthermore, as will be related more fully later, Holden left some three hundred petitions not attended to on file in his office at the close of his term as Provisional Governor. He said nothing about these papers or the six hundred pardons which he advertised as granted on the eve of the election in November, 1865, which will be discussed later. Certainly he should have explained why these petitions were not forwarded to Washington and why the larger number advertised as having been granted were not delivered as expected. The avalanche of criticism heaped upon him because of these omissions and commissions should have caused him to make some explanation in his own account of pardoning North Carolinians. Perhaps the thought of the subject was so unpleasant that he concluded it would be better not to mention it. His own story thus puts him in a more favorable light than the actual facts justify.

GILMER, TURNER, AND GRAHAM

Holden was eventually prevailed on to recommend the pardon of John A. Gilmer, who, after serving in the United States Congress, had been tendered the place of Secretary of the Treasury in Lincoln's Cabinet. Gilmer was a strong Union man, who had exerted himself to keep North Carolina from seceding. In seeking pardon, he wrote former Governor Thomas Corwin of Ohio, whose influence with the President he sought, claiming that he had helped defeat an effort to call a convention to consider secession in his state in February, 1861, by printing and distributing over 100,000 copies of "speeches and documents, fully one-third of which were by Andrew Johnson." Gilmer also told Corwin that he had worked faithfully for the Union until Lincoln called for troops after the attack on Fort Sumter; then he could "do nothing more with the people." It was only when "the whole South declared for independence" that he was obliged to support the Confederacy by serving in its congress. In his depressed condition and the confusion of the times, he also said that if he sustained any other losses besides that of his slaves he would "feel that an innocent man had suffered." But if he could be released from his existing distress and difficulty,

24. *Ibid.*

he would endeavor to sell what he had left and take his wife and children to some free state, where even at his advanced age of sixty he would begin life again.[25]

Governor Holden's administrative staff, including his private secretary, Lewis Hanes, also requested Gilmer's pardon. Even a dozen or more army officers, among whom were Generals Jacob Dolson Cox of Ohio and Thomas Jefferson Henderson of Illinois, petitioned the President in behalf of the popular North Carolinian. Finally sentiment in both the North and South became so strong for Gilmer that Holden recommended clemency, telling the President that the man appeared "sincerely repentant and much depressed," and that he was "so 'good a fellow' personally" that many "old line Whigs" were inclined to believe that he (Holden) refused to recommend his "pardon on account of past political differences." Consequently Holden advised leniency, but he desired that the pardon not be issued until January 1, 1866. This would be too late for the recipient to participate in the October convention and the election that followed. In the meantime, however, Holden hoped that Gilmer's estate would not be libelled.[26] Nevertheless, it appears that Gilmer was pardoned much earlier. On October 14 he told Vance that Dr. Powell had informed him that the President had pardoned him. He also assured Vance that he could now work much more efficiently for Vance's pardon, which he was certain would also be granted.[27]

Another person, as stated above, whose pardon Holden wanted deferred was Josiah Turner, Jr. The Governor recommended that the man's father, who was very old and included in the thirteenth exception, be pardoned at once; but the son's petition, seemingly "a bill of indictment against" the Democratic Party, he thought should be suspended.[28] Indeed, the former Confederate Congressman charged both Southern and Northern Democrats with erroneous interpretations of the Constitution in advocating the principles of states' rights and nullification. His four-thousand-word application for pardon, therefore, deserves some consideration, since it

25. Amnesty Papers, North Carolina (Gilmer to Corwin, June 4, 1865).
26. *Ibid.*
27. Vance Papers, VIII (Gilmer to Vance, October 14, 1865). Cf. Hamilton, *Reconstruction in North Carolina*, 115.
28. Amnesty Papers, North Carolina.

contains an unusual presentation of the Confederate cause by a pardon seeker.

Turner pointed out the "error of the Jeffersonian school" in continuing to interpret the Constitution in the light of the Virginia and Kentucky resolutions of 1798-99, which South Carolina later developed into the right of peaceful secession. Yet he stated that Hamilton had agreed that armed coercion could not "be executed upon the states collectively." Then he asserted that Buchanan had merely followed the precepts of Washington, Hamilton, Madison, and other framers of the Constitution when he refused to coerce South Carolina. Turner also declared that these Fathers had erred by their actions in the Convention, and that Buchanan had probably acted unwisely in following the debates in the Convention instead of the Constitution itself and his oath of office. Furthermore, he asserted that the Democrats had endorsed the Kentucky and Virginia resolutions in their platform of 1848 and in later campaigns; and thus, he reasoned, "The Northern as well as the Southern democracy was committed to secession."

But Turner did not stop here. He went on to analyze Buchanan's policies to show his mistakes, which, however, he declared to be in conformity with the faulty teachings of the Democratic Party from 1798 to 1860. He quoted Jefferson freely and then affirmed that both North and South had "laid down platforms and inculcated principles calculated to weaken the Government and bring it into contempt." The people, he said, had been taught "that the Federal Government was only an agency or a co-partnership to be dissolved by secession when the states wished." They had been "taught the impotency of the Federal Government. It could not create a bank, improve a river, make a railroad, or a turnpike. It was reserved for sovereign states to do these things." Then he pointed out the fact that Calhoun had remained in favor with Northern Democrats long after he drafted the nullifying ordinance of 1832.

Turner wrote all this and much more of similar import in presenting his plea for clemency. As a Captain in the Confederate army and later as a member of the Confederate Congress he had only acquiesced in a long-standing but fallacious party leadership that had finally precipitated a national catastrophe. Nevertheless, he expected to provoke to anger a host of its followers rather than cause them to be "thankful for the occasion of correcting them." As an opponent of secession and castigator of the party responsible for his mistake, he expected his petition to be freely granted. But his facile pen and ready tongue seemed to hinder favorable action, for Holden stated that "under all these circumstances it was not to be reasonably expected that I would . . . write the President to forward" his pardon.[29]

Former Governor William A. Graham's failure to qualify for office in 1865 was a great disappointment to his friends. He had been United States Senator, Governor of North Carolina, Secretary of the Navy, candidate for Vice-President, and Confederate States Senator. Naturally, his services were desired in the program of reconstruction, and in due time he applied for pardon. In his well-prepared petition of some three thousand words, he told of his early strong attachment to the Union and opposition to secession, until North Carolina found herself "completely insulated among the seceded states with no loyal members of the Union nearer to her than Pennsylvania and Ohio. . . ."

As a member of the state legislature during the first years of the war, Graham had "uniformly opposed all propositions to abridge the freedom of speech . . . or otherwise impair the common rights of the citizen." He was "mainly instrumental," he told the President, "in defeating an ordinance proposing to disfranchise and banish every citizen of the State who should not submit to a test oath to uphold and defend the Confederate Government with arms, and abjure his allegiance to the United States." Likewise he succeeded in defeating a measure intended to penalize severely persons advocating the restoration of the Union. Though he came sincerely to desire the success of Confederate arms, he sternly refused "to make public addresses in which he was expected to give assurance" of the final success of the movement for independence. For all this, as might be expected, he was censured by the press throughout the contest.

Later, as a member of the Confederate Congress, Graham advocated the mild policy which had characterized his efforts in the state legislature. Believing his counsels were in some degree re-

29. Holden, *Memoirs*, 60. See also Raleigh *Daily Standard* for October 20, 26, 1865. Turner had severely criticized Holden's policies.

sponsible for the Hampton Roads peace conference, he had urged another effort at conciliation after the failure of that meeting. Yet he had advised North Carolina "to forbear premature attempts at peace through the instrumentality of a separate convention of the State . . . until the refusal of the Confederate authorities to treat according to the necessities of the situation should be definitely ascertained." But when he became satisfied that the Confederate government would not treat for peace, except on the basis of independence, he counseled the authorities of his state "to interpose promptly for the termination of the war."

Graham also stated in his petition that he had a large dependent family. Nevertheless, he trusted that his five sons, who had fought for the Confederacy, had "performed their parts" creditably. Having cheerfully resumed his obligations to the government, he prayed that, in consideration of the premises, pardon and amnesty might be extended to him for having opposed "the authority of the United States."[30] Graham could not represent Orange County in the state convention because the Governor had recommended the deferment of his pardon; but, as in Gilmer's case, proceedings against his property were discouraged. Hesitating to believe that Holden had blocked Graham's plea, the *Sentinel* was confident that, if Johnson "could know the truth" about Graham, "he would at once sign his pardon."[31]

In November the state legislature petitioned for Graham's pardon, and a little later elected him United States Senator. He had already been elected to the state senate. Holden, however, still withheld his recommendation; and apparently he encouraged Powell to return to Raleigh to work against Graham's election. In reporting the result of the campaign to Vance, Swain stated significantly that Dr. Powell was still in Raleigh, and that he had "left no stone unturned to thwart Graham," whose victory had left his opponents deeply mortified.[32] Nevertheless, the day Graham was elected the President signed his pardon, but it was not delivered

30. Amnesty Papers, North Carolina. Graham's petition is dated July 25, 1865.

31. Raleigh *Daily Sentinel*, September 1, 1865.

32. Vance Papers, VIII (F. E. Shiber to Vance, November 30, 1865, Swain to Vance, December 4, 1865). Vol. XXV of the Pardon Duplicates gives December 4, 1865, as the date of Graham's pardon.

until 1867. Nor was Graham or any other ex-Confederate admitted to a seat in the United States Senate during the sessions of the Thirty-Ninth Congress (1865-67). In fact, both houses denied representation to all the states lately in rebellion (except Tennessee) until they had conformed to the congressional plan of reconstruction.

FORMER GOVERNOR VANCE'S PETITION

Perhaps the most important pardon case in North Carolina concerned Zebulon Baird Vance, who had been Governor of the state from 1862 until the close of hostilities. He declined an invitation to participate in the Sherman-Johnston surrender negotiations near Durham. He might also have tried to escape with Jefferson Davis, but he chose to remain with his people to do what he could to prevent the destruction of state property and archives and otherwise help adjust the affairs of the state to the new order. When it appeared that he could do nothing more, he offered to surrender to General Schofield, who declined to receive him as a prisoner and advised him to go to his home at Statesville. This he did, but not until he had made a futile effort to send a commission to Washington and had urged the people in a public address to abstain from excesses, assuring them that he would do all he could to restore normal conditions in the state.[33]

On May 13, Vance was arrested by order of the President, taken to Washington, and placed in a cell at the Old Capitol Prison with Governor John Letcher of Virginia. Clement Dowd gave the best reason for the arrest and imprisonment of Vance, as well as the other civil leaders of the Confederacy. After discrediting any desire on the part of Johnson "to settle some old grudge he may have had against Vance," he expressed the belief that the assassination of Lincoln not only "excited and exasperated" the authorities at Washington, but also left them in doubt as to the "temper and purposes" of the Confederate leaders. Dowd concluded, therefore, "that it was thought the public peace and safety would be better secured by imprisoning the Governors of the several states for a time, and thus effectually preventing the further prosecution of the war by

33. Clement Dowd, *Life of Zebulon B. Vance*, 95-101; Hamilton, *Reconstruction in North Carolina*, 95-101.

guerrilla parties or otherwise." Indeed, Davis himself admitted that his attempt to escape from Richmond was in order to join the forces of E. Kirby Smith and others in the South and West and continue the struggle.[34]

But such was not Vance's desire. Seeming to recognize the utter futility of further resistance, he set about at once to restore his state to its former place in the Union. Kemp P. Battle stated, in a commencement address on "The Duties of Defeat" at the University of North Carolina during these days, that "his Counsels, like those of General Lee on the same subject, were eminently wise and timely, a sincere acceptance of the decisions of the war, loyalty to our governments, national and state, [and] faithful labor for the reconstruction of society. . . ."[35]

Vance was a man, therefore, whose pardon was widely sought. Influenced also by Mrs. Vance's illness in Statesville, Holden yielded to pressure and recommended his parole from prison. So, on July 6, Vance was allowed to proceed to his home, where "he was to remain subject to the order of the President." This privilege was later extended so that he might do as he pleased, subject to the conditions of his parole.

Paroles and their extension, however, did not remove the most serious disability from Vance. He needed to be pardoned so that he might engage in some lucrative business. Moreover, his many friends wanted him to become eligible to serve the state in some useful, official capacity. Petitions for the restoration of his rights and privileges, therefore, began to be made shortly after his imprisonment and continued until far into 1867. The President probably received more requests to pardon Vance than for any other ex-Confederate, except Jefferson Davis. As early as January, 1866, Johnson told William A. Graham and David L. Swain that he supposed fifty persons had spoken to him of Vance's case.[36]

Vance prepared his petition for pardon on June 3, 1865, while confined in the Old Capitol Prison. Its 1200 words contain a sim-

34. Dowd, *Life of Zebulon B. Vance*, 97; Davis, *The Rise and Fall of the Confederate Government*, II, 696-97.

35. Kemp P. Battle, *History of the University of North Carolina*, 753.

36. Vance Papers, IX (Graham to Vance and Swain to Vance, January 20, 1866).

ple statement of his devotion to the Federal Union and the individuality of the states until the beginning of the war. He reminded Johnson that, as a member of Congress, he had had the honor, during the session of 1860-61, of cooperating with him in trying to save the Union. On returning home after March 4, 1861, he had become "a candidate for reelection on the Union ticket, amid such persecutions and threats of personal violence as it was customary to heap upon Union men in that day." It was during this canvas, he stated, that actual hostilities began and Lincoln called on North Carolina for troops to put down the "rebellion."

The President's action produced an instantaneous and overwhelming revolution of public sentiment in that state, and caused the people to clamor for disunion, "declaring if they must fight, it should be for and not against their Southern neighbors and kindred." Consequently, in less than three weeks a convention assembled and unanimously passed an ordinance of secession. Under these circumstances, Vance told Johnson, there were only two choices open to him, namely, to leave North Carolina and "levy domestic war at the head of such persons as would follow him, or to abide by the action of his State. He chose the latter alternative," serving the Confederacy in military and civil capacities until the end of the conflict.

The prisoner reviewed his futile efforts to cooperate with Generals Sherman and Schofield in an effort to place the state in its former position in the Union. Then he told the President that he did not desire to secure a pardon "by any false or mean pretenses, or to mitigate the offence of abandoning one government by showing that he was likewise false to another." Vance also thought that he should truthfully state that, though he yielded reluctantly "to circumstances in the beginning, his feelings became in time thoroughly and earnestly enlisted in behalf of the cause his State had espoused." Naturally the threatened abolition of slavery and the horrors of war affected him, and caused him to labor "zealously in every honorable way to repel an invasion of his state . . . and to avoid results, which seemed to him equivalent to the absolute subjugation of his people." Now he fully appreciated "the actual condition of affairs," and contemplated "no further resistance whatever to the authority of the United States." Furthermore, he accepted the restoration of

the Union and the abolition of slavery, and was willing "to take
and faithfully observe the oath prescribed" in the President's proclamation of amnesty. He desired, of course, to be permitted to
return home, so that he might "assist an almost ruined people in the
restoration of law, and assume all the duties of a quiet and law
abiding American citizen." Humbly concluding his petition, Vance
asserted that he had very little property, and that his wife and four
small children were "totally dependent upon his personal exertions," and that they were then "living upon the charity of personal
friends."[37]

Of course, there was considerable effort on the part of many
to get the President to pardon Vance. The petitions from individuals
and groups were numerous. As has already been stated, the first
efforts resulted in his parole from prison, but full suffrage was
desired. Naturally his leadership was needed. Former Governor
Letcher of Virginia wrote Vance that he would out-distance all
competitors in political influence were he free to act. Holden, however, remained adamant in refusing to endorse his application. In
recommending deferred action on Gilmer's and Graham's petitions,
he expressed the opinion that they could make no disturbance even
if disposed to do so as long as Vance remained unpardoned.[38]

HOLDEN *versus* VANCE

To understand why Holden refused to recommend Vance's
pardon, a brief review of the political activities and relations of the
men prior to the summer of 1865 appears desirable. During the
1850's the editor of the *Standard* had been one of the strongest
advocates of secession in the state, and through the columns of his
paper, which he had edited since 1843, he was one of the most
ardent supporters of the doctrine of states' rights in the South.[39]

37. Amnesty Papers, North Carolina (Vance's petition for pardon).
38. Vance Papers, VIII (Letcher to Vance, October 16, 1865, Holden to
Johnson, August 9, 1865).
39. Holden's life as a journalist, from 1843 to 1865, has been well told
by Edgar E. Folk in a doctoral dissertation (two bound volumes) at George
Peabody College. See also Dr. Folk, "W. W. Holden and the North Carolina
Standard, 1843-1848: A Study in Political Journalism," *North Carolina Historical Review*, XIX, No. 1 (January, 1942), 22-47, and "W. W. Holden and
the Election of 1858," *Ibid.*, XXI, No. 4 (October, 1944), 294-318. Dr. Horace

Politically ambitious, he vainly attempted to secure Democratic support for Governor in 1858, but John W. Ellis was nominated and elected. In 1860, however, Holden appeared rather uncertain for a time in his attitude toward secession, addressing the Democratic national convention at Charleston on its dangers, and announcing a little later "that he was 'for the Constitution and the Union, and against all who would trample on the one or dissolve the other.'"[40]

Nevertheless, on June 2, Holden declared again for secession. In anticipation of the autumn election, he asserted that the people of the South would never be troubled by the decisions of Black Republican judges, if they were true to themselves. But in these trying times constancy was not one of Holden's virtues, for he was loath to support secession after Lincoln's election, until the call to arms. Then, as a member of the secession convention of his state, he "is reported to have held up the pen with which he signed [the ordinance] and said that he would hand it down to his children as their proudest heritage."[41]

Holden did not support the war policies of Governor Ellis, who died in July, 1861, nor those of Henry T. Clark, who, as speaker of the state senate, succeeded Ellis as Governor. In fact, he became the main leader of the opposition to President Davis's administration which developed early in North Carolina. Moreover, as the gubernatorial election of 1862 approached, he sought a candidate who, if elected, would be anti-Davis and pro-Union; for, by the second year of the war, Holden was denouncing the policies of the Confederate government and again advocating the Union cause. His candidate was Zebulon B. Vance, formerly an ardent Union man and now the most popular man in the state.

Vance said little or nothing about peace during the campaign, and was elected by a large majority; but he soon disappointed Holden. In his inaugural address, the new Governor declared that he would support the Confederacy. "Speaking of secession, he said,

---

Raper, State College History Staff, Richmond, Kentucky, completed a biography of W. W. Holden in 1951, as a doctoral dissertation.
40. Hamilton, *Reconstruction in North Carolina*, 10-12.
41. *Ibid.*, 12, note 2; 32. On October 19, 1865, the Raleigh *Daily Standard* declared vehemently that Holden had never been a secessionist.

'It was not a whim or sudden freak, but the deliberate judgment of our people. Any other course would have involved the deepest degradation, the vilest dishonor, and the direst calamity. . . .' " Then, in an exhortation for unanimity of action, he continued: " 'To prosecute this war with success is quite as much for our people as for our soldiers to do. One of the vital elements of our success is harmony. On this great issue of existence itself let there, I pray you, be no dissentive voice in our borders.' "[42]

The Governor's new position was a great departure from his policy of two years earlier. Then, according to Burton Jesse Hendrick, "he engaged in a kind of campaign resembling a religious revival. . . . He appeared in churches, even at street corners, shouting always: 'Keep North Carolina in the Union! Let it not follow the example of other Southern States!' " But a great change of heart and purpose came over him after Lincoln's call for troops to put down the rebellion, and his energy and prowess in the Confederate army soon made him a hero. After his election, he gave assurance of his continued loyalty to the Confederacy, but his former declarations for the Union were not forgotten in the North or in Richmond. Consequently, his policies as Governor were not always understood or appreciated in the Confederate capital.[43]

Vance's vigorous and able support of the state war party, therefore, was a keen disappointment to Holden. By the summer of 1863, the editor of the *Standard* was urging peace and the Union, fearing, as he said, "that a prolongation of the war" would "obliterate the last vestige" of slavery.[44] This fear was doubtless due to Lincoln's Emancipation Proclamation and to the probability of further action to liberate the slaves.

Holden's strong advocacy of peace and the return of North Carolina to the Union greatly exasperated Vance. This annoyance became a serious aggravation as the year 1863 passed and the peace movement increased. At first Vance tried to get along with Holden, but finally concluded to oppose him cautiously. He prepared, there-

42. Hamilton, *Reconstruction in North Carolina*, 43, quoting from Vance's inaugural address.
43. Burton J. Hendrick, *Statesmen of the Lost Cause; Jefferson Davis and His Cabinet*, 342-49.
44. Hamilton, *Reconstruction in North Carolina*, 50.

fore, a long article for publication attacking the editor's policies, but he was considerate enough to allow Holden to see the paper before publishing it. Since Graham advised against publication, he never allowed it to go to press. This was in August, but by September Vance firmly determined to counteract the peace movement and published a proclamation to discourage dissension and division among the people. His position, however, was not satisfactory to the war party, since he did not clearly define the line between himself and Holden, whose printing house was molested by infuriated Georgia soldiers on the night of September 9. The sequel to this mob attack on the *Standard*, whose editor sought protection in the Governor's home during the night, was the destruction, the next morning, of the equipment of the war-sympathizing Raleigh *State Journal* by some of Holden's friends.[45]

As yet there had been no open break between Holden and Vance. The rupture came, however, when the *Standard* began advocating a state convention to consider peace, stating on January 19, 1864, that, unless Vance favored such action, he could not be re-elected. Peace meetings followed in several counties, and the situation became so serious that President Davis suspended the writ of habeas corpus in the state. Highly displeased, Vance began an angry and profitless correspondence with Davis. Nevertheless, the Carolinian remained firm in his support of the Confederacy, declaring on January 1 to his close friend, Graham, that he would see the peace party blown into atoms "and Holden and his under-strappers in hell" before he would consent to a course that "would bring dishonor and ruin upon both state and Confederacy." Consequently, on Washington's Birthday, he delivered a carefully prepared and widely-published speech announcing his stand against peace and also his candidacy for re-election.[46]

Vance's address was a pungent challenge to Holden, who, on March 3, announced his candidacy for Governor through the columns of the *Standard*. An acrimonious campaign was soon in full swing, but Holden was no match for his resourceful and able opponent, who stumped the state in a rather dramatic and winning

45. Richard E. Yates, "Governor Vance and the Peace Movement," Part I, *North Carolina Historical Review*, XVII, No. 1 (January, 1940), 1-25.
46. *Ibid.*, No. 2 (April, 1940), 89-113.

manner, often ridiculing the editor unmercifully. The wily Governor won a great victory, but his defeated opponent became his implacable enemy. The two men, therefore, were utterly irreconcilable when the Confederacy fell and Holden became Provisional Governor. During Holden's incumbency Vance could hardly expect to be pardoned unless Johnson ignored the Governor's desire, which he was not likely to do. Yet Vance was treated no worse in this respect than Graham, Turner, and other North Carolinians, as well as prominent citizens of other states. Johnson himself had reasons for deferring pardons and acted accordingly. Vance naturally resented the Governor's refusal to recommend him to the President. At one time, in complaining to his friend, David L. Swain, he accused Holden of being ungrateful for protection "from . . . infuriated soldiers, and still oftener from incarceration in Castle Thunder. . . ."[47]

THE CONVENTION AND ELECTION

Inasmuch as the convention which met to comply with the President's plan of reconstruction did not convene until October 2, 1865, there was plenty of time for many persons to obtain pardons and to participate in the election of delegates. Early in August Governor Holden issued specific instructions for the election. Every voter had to exhibit a copy of his amnesty oath, "signed by himself and witnessed and certified by at least two Justices of the Peace." He called the attention of justices appointed to administer the amnesty oath to the President's fourteen exceptions, which were given in full, the first, seventh, and thirteenth being explained. "No certificate," he stated, "will be granted . . . to any person who is included within the fourteen excluded classes, unless on exhibition by the party of his pardon. . . ." All election officials were enjoined to perform their duties faithfully, and persons taking the oath were expected to keep it. Lastly, the newspapers of the state were to publish the proclamation twice a week until the day of the election.[48]

Nevertheless, eleven candidates who had not been pardoned were

47. Vance Papers, IX (Vance to Swain, January 8, 1866). See also Hamilton, *Reconstruction in North Carolina*, 54-55. This reference was to threats on Holden's life during the excitement in the autumn of 1863.
48. Raleigh *Daily Standard*, August 10, 1865.

elected as delegates. Since a pardon was necessary before one could sit in the convention, Holden immediately asked the President to forward certificates for these men.[49] Having promised clemency to candidates who were elected, Johnson complied with Holden's request. Former Governor Graham, declining the virtual assurance of a seat from Orange County because of his ineligibility, had to wait nearly two years for the full restoration of his rights.

The convention met as arranged and passed ordinances rescinding the act of secession, abolishing slavery, repudiating the state's war debt, and otherwise paving the way for final restoration to the Union. The act of repudiation was urged by both the President and the Provisional Governor, but it aroused bitter opposition in the convention. Nevertheless, the delegates passed a resolution thanking the two executives for their efforts in behalf of the state and adjourned to meet again the following May. Political rivals were active during the session, and Holden and Jonathan Worth were virtually placed in nomination for Governor at the forthcoming election.

Now that the convention had done its work the next important step in reconstruction was the election of state officials on November 9, 1865. Apparently Holden desired to succeed himself, and, on being petitioned by some 53 of the 120 members of the convention, he became a candidate. Jonathan Worth, the popular state treasurer, was persuaded to oppose him, and actually announced his candidacy first. In Raleigh the *Standard* supported Holden and the *Sentinel*, Worth. The President was regarded as desiring the election of his Provisional Governor and the candidates he favored. Holden's supporters, therefore, declared that the election of Worth and his opposition ticket would certainly delay the restoration of the state to the Union. Even the unpardoned Josiah Turner had the temerity to run for Congress and support Worth. So the issue, according to the *Standard*, was: "W. W. Holden . . . and live again under Washington's government, or Jonathan Worth and perish."[50] Such declarations gave Worth so much uneasiness that "he appealed to

49. Hamilton, *Reconstruction in North Carolina*, 119-120.
50. Hamilton, *Jonathan Worth*, I, 436-40; Raleigh *Daily Standard*, October 25, November 7, 1865; Hamilton, *Reconstruction in North Carolina*, 136.

friends in Washington to try to find means to efface the impression which was being created by the friends of Holden that the President preferred the latter's election." A telegram from Johnson to Holden after the election, however, indicated the President's satisfaction with Holden's administration and his keen disappointment with the outcome of the election.[51]

Evidently Holden expected those whom he had befriended to support his administration and doubtless his candidacy. Early in October the *Standard* told some thousand applicants for pardon, seven or eight hundred of whose petitions had already been endorsed and forwarded to Washington, that they should "congratulate themselves on their success"; but warned them that the governor had the "power, if he chooses to exercise it, to assess their estates . . . for the support of the State government . . . and that the exercise of this power" would depend upon the manner in which they and their friends conducted themselves until the provisional government ended. Moreover, there were hundreds of persons whose petitions had not yet been forwarded to the President, and many others who had not yet applied for pardon. This was a condition that might be utilized to Holden's advantage. In fact, his paper suggested late in October, 1865, that a universal amnesty might be declared in North Carolina if certain candidates were elected in November.[52]

Two days later the *Standard* announced that voters would be required to present only their oath certificates, meaning, of course, that some persons would be allowed to vote whose pardons had not yet been granted. This privilege complied with an act of the convention providing that those "whose pardons should be announced by the Governor, although the pardon should not have been received, should be entitled to vote in the" forthcoming election.[53] A little while before the election, therefore, the press published a list of names of some six hundred persons who might vote. Thus the citizens of North Carolina were to be convinced that

51. Hamilton, *Reconstruction in North Carolina*, 136, 141.
52. Raleigh *Daily Standard*, October 7, 25, 1865.
53. Hamilton, *Jonathan Worth*, II, 505, 631 (Worth to Hedrick, March 3, and Worth to Seward, June 18, 1866).

Holden had been a friend of "his native state and his people," who would surely "not desert him and Andrew Johnson."[54]

Worth won the gubernatorial election of 1865 by a good majority. Most of the voters also expressed their preference for the anti-Holden candidates for Congress, all of whom had been pardoned except Josiah Turner, whose election, in the minds of many, made it still less likely that any of the seven men elected would be admitted to their seats. In fact, only one of all the aspirants could take the "ironclad" test oath. Disappointed over the results of the election, Johnson feared that the prospects of the state's restoration were greatly injured. "Should the action and spirit of the legislature be in the same direction," he said, "it will greatly increase the mischief already done and might be fatal."[55]

The *Standard* saw in its candidate's defeat the "unmistakable work of unpardoned traitors." The President refused Holden's request to set aside the election, but directed the Provisional Governor to remain in office until relieved. Worth assumed the office of Governor on December 27 and assured Johnson of his cooperation. Holden's defeat caused some who had supported Worth to expect the President to be inclined to vindictiveness. Though Vance had not opposed Holden openly, he had "earnestly desired his defeat."[56] His name, moreover, had "been used more or less in the campaign," and he feared reincarceration in the Old Capitol Prison, unless he could see the President personally, a privilege that had already been denied him several times. Others, like Graham and Turner, also had reason to expect deferment of clemency, for the new Governor was not likely to influence Johnson in their behalf. Yet the President soon instructed Worth to approve or disapprove all petitions forwarded by him, saying, "Your knowledge of the parties is of great worth to us here in issuing pardons." Nevertheless, the Governor complained just five months after his election that "not a single pardon" had been granted on his recommenda-

54. Raleigh *Daily Standard*, October 30, 31, 1865. On the first day the *Standard* published a list of 244 pardons and the next day, another list of 400 or 500.

55. Hamilton, *Reconstruction in North Carolina*, 137-42; Raleigh *Daily Standard*, November 29, 1865.

56. Vance Papers, IX (Vance to Swain, January 8, 1866).

tion. Yet the North Carolina Amnesty Papers show that Worth made recommendations for pardon early in January, 1866, and that the pardons were granted early in February, 1866.[57]

THE ADVERTISED PARDONS; OTHER PETITIONS

But what of the six hundred or more pardons that had been advertised to influence the November election? The persons concerned were greatly disappointed when the certificates did not come, subjecting Worth to much effort in explaining why they had not been delivered. The pardons had actually never been granted. Apparently the certificates had gone through the Attorney-General's office, but for some reason were sent to the "garret of the State Department instead of going to the Executive Mansion" for the President's signature; and in the garret they remained. Even though Worth sent Johnson a copy of the *Standard* containing the names, there was no immediate action. The exasperated Governor repeatedly tried to get the papers signed and delivered. A little while later he declared the "publication of the 500 to 600 pardons just before the election" to be "an incredible instance of official villainy. . . ."[58]

Why did President Johnson hold the papers of those whom Holden had caused to be advertised as having been pardoned? Perhaps it was not his policy to grant clemency in such wholesale fashion, especially to citizens of one state. Furthermore, in all probability, the advertisement had been made only on Holden's authority. Under the circumstances, therefore, Johnson could not deliver them without prejudice to himself, even though Worth urged him to act.

Dr. Powell's successor, Benjamin S. Hedrick, probably threw some light on the business late in January, 1866. In relating to Worth his futile attempt to see the Attorney-General, he expressed the opinion that the President was reluctant to act just then because of the demands on his time. Congress was in session, and it was well to wait until that body had given "some expression of opinion

57. *Ibid.*, VIII (Vance to Swain, November 14, 1865); Governor's Papers (Johnson to Worth, December 29, 1865); Hamilton, *Jonathan Worth*, I, 537 (Worth to Hedrick, April 9, 1866).
58. Hamilton, *Jonathan Worth*, I, 550, 624, 628.

in regard to what had been done." Hedrick advised supplicants to be patient. "There is no disposition to put them on trial or hang them," he said, "and the President has so clearly indicated his policy in regard to the South, that . . . no one can doubt his desire to restore peace and harmony with as little harshness as possible." Dr. Powell also told Worth that Johnson thought "it was a bad time to be issuing pardons,"[59] so these North Carolinians had to wait a while longer.

But this was not all, for there were some three hundred applications for pardon in the Governor's office when Worth entered. Of course, the change of executives caused the petitioners, many of whom had been petty officials, to renew their efforts. Some had interviews with Governor Worth, while others wrote him earnest entreaties. One man who came under the thirteenth exception sought clemency in order to transact some business in the North. Another complained impatiently that it had been almost six months since his first petitions, that other similar offenders had been pardoned, and that he feared the confiscation of his property.[60]

On January 15, 1866, at the President's request, Worth forwarded the petitions with the recommendation that they be acted on at once. Thus there were at least eight hundred persons in North Carolina early in 1866 impatiently seeking clemency. Those whose pardons had been falsely advertised naturally deserved first consideration. Worth was more successful, however, with the three hundred petitions that he himself had sent to Washington in January. Though some attention was given them in the Attorney-General's office soon after they were received, final action was delayed. Worth wanted the pardons in time to distribute them through the members of the assembly, which was then in session; but he was disappointed.[61]

A month later Hedrick wrote that Johnson had some five hundred North Carolina papers ready for the official signature. The

59. *Ibid.*, 479, 550; Governor's Papers (Powell to Worth, January 15, 1866).
60. Governor's Papers (Worth to W. S. Mason, January 8, 1866, Donald MacRae to Worth, February 22, 1866, Du Brutz Cutlar to Worth, February 17, 1866).
61. Hamilton, *Jonathan Worth*, I, 483, 497, 585-93; Governor's Papers (Hedrick to Worth, January 3, 1866).

President was willing, however, to favor at one time only petty officials, those in the thirteenth exception, and such other cases as appeared urgent. The agent then made the ominous statement that, from proceedings in Congress, it appeared that the President was likely to be impeached on account of his many pardons.[62] In fact, threats to impeach him because of his leniency had been made many months earlier, and conditions in that respect had not improved.

Thus it is seen that the President did not at that time dare to grant so large a number of pardons at once. Inquiries and complaints, of course, continued to come to the Governor's office. It was about this time that Worth sent the President, through Hedrick, a list of five hundred names published in the *Standard* just before the previous November election, saying that he supposed Holden did not submit the other three hundred petitions to Washington because he was not willing to trust the petitioners to vote for him. Eight days later (April 26) Worth sent Johnson the names of those in the first and thirteenth exceptions from the list of three hundred he had forwarded in January, with instructions to have Hedrick forward their pardons to him. But the authorities continued to procrastinate, and the pardon seekers waited.[63]

Finally, Hedrick informed Worth that about three hundred certificates were being prepared for early delivery. Soon the agent received them in three batches, expressing them all in separate shipments to Raleigh for delivery. Thus by the middle of May, 1866, pardons were issued to the three hundred persons whose petitions were found in the Governor's office when Worth succeeded Holden.

Efforts continued to be made, of course, to cause the delivery of the large number of advertised pardons. Worth seems to have been less interested in these and other applications which Holden had forwarded than in those he himself had submitted. When the case of Judge Asa Biggs was presented, the Governor stated that he did not feel like appealing to the President for anyone whose

---

62. Governor's Papers (Hedrick to Worth, March 3, 1866, Mason to Worth, March 8, 1866); Hamilton, *Jonathan Worth*, I, 562, 564 (Worth to Johnson, April 26, 1866, and Worth to T. X. Kenan, May 5, 1866).

63. Hamilton, *Jonathan Worth*, 543, 562 (Worth to Hedrick, April 18, 1866).

petition had been forwarded by Holden, "especially while the pardons of such men" as Graham and Turner were withheld. Biggs had been more prominent in the secession movement than the other two; Worth felt justified, therefore, in assisting those whom he regarded as having been "always anti-secessionists." In all probability, however, the Governor did not know that Holden had recommended that favorable action on Biggs's petition be deferred, for the paper had been on file in Washington since early in October, 1865.[64] At any rate, he thought more deserving men should receive first consideration.

Worth, Hedrick, and others continued to press the matter of delivering the pardons which Holden had advertised; and at last their efforts were rewarded. Near the middle of June, Hedrick, realizing that it was "impossible to get the whole [lot] issued at once," selected about fifty certificates at random and presented them for final attention. Worth urged Seward to act immediately, complaining again of being grievously annoyed with inquiries relating to these pardons. Consequently, the Secretary of State sent the Governor 121 pardons on June 29 and 335 others about a month later.[65] With the ones already forwarded these deliveries about equalled the estimated number of names published. The pardons, therefore, that had been falsely advertised to influence voters in the election of a Governor late in 1865 were finally delivered in June and July, 1866. It had taken about nine months of persistent effort to dislodge the certificates from the "garret" of the State Department, to secure the President's signature, and to cause their delivery.

The Last Pardons

The story of clemency in North Carolina, however, does not end here, for there were many still under the ban. Former Governors Graham, Clark, and Vance, together with Josiah Turner, William Dortch, and A. W. Venable were perhaps the most prominent. Venable was soon pardoned on the recommendation of Holden

64. Amnesty Papers, North Carolina; Hamilton, *Jonathan Worth*, I, 593 (Worth to Biggs, May 21, 1866). Also Hamilton, *Reconstruction in North Carolina*, 26.
65. Hamilton, *Jonathan Worth*, II, 602, 624 (Hedrick to Worth, June 7, 14, 1866), 631 (Worth to Seward, June 18, 1866); Governor's Papers (Seward to Worth, June 29, July 24, 1866).

and the new Attorney-General, Henry Stanbery. Worth was eager to have three of the other five eligible to participate in political affairs more freely. Indeed, he repeatedly complained of the status of Graham, Turner, and Dortch, regarding their continued disability as a serious "political blunder" on the part of the President. In his opinion, Johnson should pardon these three men "without a moment's hesitation after pardoning Bridgers, Arrington, Lander and Venable," whom he called "original Secessionists." Such action, during the existing crisis, he believed, would make the President "more popular in the State" than anybody else had "been since the days of General Washington."[66]

It is interesting to note that Worth failed to mention Vance at this time or on other occasions in 1866 when urging action in the cases of the favored trio. Evidently the Governor was less enthusiastic over Vance's political future than over Graham's. Probably thinking Johnson would delay passing on the popular war Governor to the last, he believed it useless to ask for his pardon. Besides Holden had never appeared to want Vance pardoned, and that was something to be considered in approaching Johnson.

Indeed, Worth thought Holden influenced the President to defer granting the pardons he most desired, accusing his immediate predecessor with prejudicing Johnson against "Graham, Turner and all other true Union men of the State." Furthermore, according to Hedrick, Seward "always stood up for Holden," who made a futile attempt to defeat Worth for re-election late in 1866, General Alfred Dockery being the defeated candidate.[67] Holden himself was elected Governor in 1868 under the congressional plan of reconstruction; but, largely because of his extreme efforts to suppress activities of the Ku Klux Klan, he was impeached late in 1870 and removed from office early in 1871. He later edited the *National Republican* in Washington, D. C., and afterward was postmaster at Raleigh. He died in 1892; Worth, in 1869. Worth remained Governor, therefore, until some time after Congress took over the task of reconstruction.

66. Amnesty Papers, North Carolina; Hamilton, *Jonathan Worth*, II, 667, 752, 841, 926, 977, 981.
67. Hamilton, *Jonathan Worth*, II, 666, 675 (Worth to Hedrick, July 4, Hedrick to Worth, July 8, 1866).

Apparently the heated political contest between Johnson and the Radicals in Congress during the late summer and autumn of 1866 did not materially affect clemency to North Carolinians. But there seems to have been a lull in the pardoning business after the national election in November, 1866, owing perhaps to Johnson's repudiation at the poll and the censorious activities of Congress. Nevertheless, clemency was extended to persons of importance in North Carolina during the spring of 1867, despite the unfavorable report in Congress on presidential clemency, the repeal of the amnesty section of the Confiscation Act, and the beginning of extreme congressional reconstruction. Worth continued to urge the President to lift the ban from Graham and Turner, and repeatedly asked for the pardons of Colonel Owen R. Kenan and Burton S. Gaither, both former Confederate congressmen.[68] Early in 1867, he also recommended Vance, whose relief many prominent persons had been earnestly seeking ever since his imprisonment and later parole.

For a long time after being paroled from prison, Vance remained quietly "at home as retired and silent as it was possible for a man to be." He also told Johnson's son-in-law, David T. Patterson, that his numerous requests for an interview with the President, whose policies he earnestly supported, had not received any attention, notwithstanding the fact that this "favor [had been] granted to both Governors Letcher and Brown," war governors of Virginia and Georgia, respectively. He naturally sought a reason for Johnson's discrimination, and believed Holden to be at the root of the matter, charging the editor with influencing the President to refuse to see him in Washington. Vance also blamed Secretary Stanton for the unfavorable situation, declaring him to be "the worst of the whole batch." At this writing he seemingly despaired of ever receiving a pardon, saying Johnson had begun his policy of clemency so late that his opponents had discouraged his proclaiming another general amnesty or even granting special pardons. He expected no more pardons for men of prominence, except for those who might resort to methods to influence the President which he would feel ashamed to use. Yet it appears that Johnson had already extended Vance's

68. See Ch. XIV, "Efforts to Curtail Presidential Amnesty"; Hamilton, *Jonathan Worth*, II, 752, 841, 926.

parole to permit him to go anywhere and to engage in any business to support his family.[69]

The movement to obtain Vance's pardon was accelerated late in 1866 and early in 1867 by the irrepressible missionary, Paul Bagley, who also tried hard to obtain a pardon for Jefferson Davis. Bagley, a returned missionary from China and Japan, told the President that Vance had caused the railroads to allow him to ride all over the state without charge while he preached the gospel, an act which he believed should have some weight with the President in considering Vance's petition for pardon. At Frankfort, Kentucky, he obtained Governor Bramlette's recommendation, which was later endorsed by John T. Hoffman, Mayor of New York City (later Governor of New York), Horace Greeley, Hugh M. McCullough, and forty other prominent citizens. About the same time, Bagley wrote Johnson that Senators John Sherman, Lewis W. Ross, and Waitman T. Willey also recommended clemency. Governor James L. Orr of South Carolina and Attorney-General Stanbery also advised the President to pardon Vance.[70]

In this manner Johnson was soon influenced to act, and on March 11 he granted the long-desired pardon.[71] The document was carefully prepared and signed (not stamped) by the Secretary of State and the President. Vance was further honored by having the names of many prominent persons who had recommended his pardon carefully written on the upper margin of the certificate, a unique consideration that was probably not given anyone else. He later became Governor of North Carolina and United States Senator, and is generally regarded today as having been one of the state's most prominent citizens.

Perhaps former Governor H. T. Clark was the most prominent person whose petition Holden had failed to send on to Washington. He had applied for pardon on July 17, 1865, stating in substance what many others had said in justification of their support of the Confederacy. In a letter to Worth in September, 1866, he stated

69. Vance Papers, IX (Vance to Swain, January 8, 1866, Swain to Vance, January 20, 1866).

70. Amnesty Papers, North Carolina.

71. Vance Papers, Vol. IX. It appears that, when Worth saw that Vance's pardon was coming, he endeavored to receive some credit for obtaining it. See Hamilton, *Jonathan Worth*, II, 927, 935.

that Holden had promised to give his petition immediate attention. Since the Provisional Governor had left the application with the many others which Worth found on becoming Governor, Clark's case had been in an unfavorable light before the President, for it appeared that the former Governor had not applied for pardon. Consequently, when Swain and others presented his case to Johnson, their efforts were in vain, for they were told that Clark "had asked for nothing."[72]

Clark needed clemency for business advantage. The Confederacy had sequestered a trust fund of $14,000 which he held for citizens of Rhode Island. After the war he paid the obligation in full from his own means. Fearing that his unpardoned condition might cause him to lose what property he still possessed, especially if power should somehow fall into Radical hands, he desired his case to be attended to without further delay. Worth wrote to Johnson on September 31, 1866, recommending that the petition be granted, but it was not until June 10, 1867, that the pardon was issued. Naturally, Clark was greatly provoked at the delay, since so many others of his class had been relieved. Therefore, when Worth invited him to join in welcoming the President to Raleigh in June, 1867, he ironically declined the invitation. The pardon clerk had sent Clark's certificate to Johnson on January 23, 1867, so it appeared that sheer indifference on the President's part was responsible for the delay. Of course, Holden was also blamed. Johnson penciled his instructions for the pardon on the envelope enclosing Clark's caustic letter, which Worth had forwarded to Washington.

Josiah Turner still remained disabled, but he was soon relieved. Worth desired to reappoint him director of the North Carolina Railroad, but feared that if he did so Holden and his followers would cause General Sickles to object, on the pretext that he had appointed an unpardoned rebel. Sickles had become Military Governor of the Carolina district, and this condition made Worth cautious in his appointments. Consequently, he asked Hedrick, on June 14, 1867, for Turner's "pardon as a personal favor," believing that it would be entirely "gratifying to every friend of the President in North Carolina." One week later the necessary warrant was

72. Amnesty Papers, North Carolina; Governor's Papers.

forwarded to Turner, who was told that its immediate issuance was "due to the efforts of Col. W. G. Moore, the President's Private Secretary, who had made prompt efforts in the matter at the request of Gov. Worth." He had been free to engage in business for some time, and Worth had first appointed him railroad director a year earlier.[73]

With Turner's relief the account of pardoning North Carolinians might well be concluded. The number remaining disabled by the midsummer of 1867 is uncertain. Of those who had applied for clemency there were not many whose petitions had not been granted and the certificates delivered. Late in June, 1867, Worth asked Hedrick to "get a duplicate" of a pardon for J. S. Means of Mecklenburg County and forward it to him for delivery. Means, disabled under the thirteenth exception, had refused to pay a pretending Philadelphia friend, named Wallace, who had obtained the pardon and asked first $350 and later $100 for his services.

Johnson's general amnesties of September 7, 1867, and July 4, 1868, left only a few North Carolinians disabled. Yet Worth, who was no longer Governor, wrote the President's secretary, Colonel Moore, on July 16, 1868, that he earnestly desired the petitions of certain persons attended to. If there were any citizens of the state still unrelieved late that year, they were pardoned by the President's universal amnesty of Christmas Day, 1868. This last act of presidential clemency, however, did not remove the disability from North Carolinians who were affected by the third section of the Fourteenth Amendment, which had become a part of the Constitution in July, 1868, and which Congress had made operative in 1867. This phase of the subject will be treated in the chapter on "Congressional Amnesty."

73. Hamilton, *Jonathan Worth*, II, 981, 984, 985.

CHAPTER ELEVEN

PARDONING THE PROPERTIED CLASS

---◆---

THE THIRTEENTH EXCEPTION

APPARENTLY the exception in Johnson's proclamation of amnesty which was most objected to was the thirteenth, which left unpardoned those whose property was worth more than $20,000. Indeed, this thirteenth provision directly affected more people than any other exception made from the benefits of the amnesty. Avery says the tax books of Georgia gave the names of 12,470 in that state who were worth $20,000 or more. The Nashville *Dispatch* estimated the total number in all the states at 60,000, while the Washington *National Intelligencer* placed the figure at 80,000.[1] The first general estimate was probably too high, when property depreciations were considered. Nevertheless, the number was considerable; and the embarrassment thus occasioned surely gave plebeian Andrew Johnson much satisfaction, since the rich Southern aristocrats would have to make special application to him for pardon.

The President was urged not to except persons from his general amnesty merely on the basis of wealth. General Grant testified before the House Judiciary Committee in July, 1867, that he objected not only to that exception but also to the one excluding West Point and Annapolis graduates. James G. Blaine stated still later that Seward opposed the thirteenth exception on the ground

1. I. W. Avery, *The History of the State of Georgia from 1850 to 1881*, 340. The Nashville *Dispatch*, June 7, 20, 1865, estimated the total number in all classes excepted from amnesty at 150,000 to 200,000.

that thrift and wealth were not especially responsible for the war. But Johnson firmly believed, so Blaine said, "that the rebellion was the work of the slaveholders; and . . . [that] he was sure . . . to catch in his twenty-thousand-dollar drag-net some great offenders" not in other classes. Therefore, the President "was merely striking at the class whom he personally hated when he . . . excluded them from all benefit of amnesty." Seward did not think the number thus affected was very large, since the war and the abolition of slavery had reduced the value of Southern estates considerably. Consequently, he believed special pardons "would cure the evil and repair the injustice which the singular and vindictive action of Mr. Johnson might entail." Blaine also believed that the object of the thirteenth exception "was to draw the line between the men who could exert influence in their respective communities, and those who were necessarily led by others. . . ." Those who had been loyal, therefore, as well as the disloyal were opposed to its application.[2]

Nevertheless, the twenty-thousand-dollar exception was a serious disability. Estimates or assessments were likely to be made on the basis of values in 1861, "at which time," according to Fleming, in describing conditions in Alabama, "slaves were included and a slaveholder of very moderate estate would be assessed at $20,000. In 1865, however, there were very few [people in that state] worth $20,000."[3] Similar changes had taken place in other Southern states. Unfortunately, this exception seriously restricted business and was even injurious to persons of very limited means and others whose loyalty had been satisfactory. On June 20, the New York *Herald* emphasized this business embarrassment by complaining that "many large manufacturers, like Jo Anderson, of the Tredegar Iron Works, and Haxall and Crenshaw, of the Richmond Flouring Mills, who are personally . . . amenable to punishment, are but part owners of their immense establishments, and have loyal and deserving men for partners. Some rule separating such interests is imperatively demanded," the editor continued, "so that the manufacturing and

2. James G. Blaine, *Twenty Years of Congress: From Lincoln to Garfield*, II, 73-5.
3. Fleming, *Civil War and Reconstruction in Alabama*, 349-50. Fleming says fewer than fifty thousand persons of all classes, including those not in any of the fourteen exceptions, took the amnesty oath in Alabama.

production interests of the South may be put in motion, and thousands of employees and artisans now idle be enabled to earn their sustenance." The next day the *Herald* reported an effort "to induce the President to suspend the processes issued under the confiscation law against property in Richmond" until owners could obtain action on their applications for pardon.

Commerce was also hampered. Four days after the *Herald*'s complaint, *Harper's Weekly* offered the opinion that one reason cotton was not being sold on the market in the South was that most of the owners were "expressly excluded from the benefit of President Johnson's Proclamation of amnesty." The natural motive for sale, of course, was jeopardized by the exclusion of the owners from pardon and the consequent probability of their punishment under the existing punitive laws for rebellion. "As well let the cotton rot where it lies," the editor said, "as send it to market for the benefit of the conquerors." *Harper's* gave two other reasons why cotton was not being sold, namely, the 25 per cent government tax on sales after the close of hostilities and the want of money to get the cotton to market.[4]

The Amnesty Papers, particularly described in Chapter VIII, indicate the plight of thousands of petitioners for pardon who came under the thirteenth exception. Many of them, of course, desired pardon not only for business advantage but also for political privilege. The chief need for clemency, however, was to regain all civil rights, especially the right to engage in normal business.

Conditions were so serious that a committee of Virginians went to Washington early in July "to present a memorial of the citizens of Richmond asking the President to annul, or at least to modify the [thirteenth] clause of his amnesty proclamation. . . ." Johnson was ill, so Senator Oliver H. Browning took the gentlemen to the Attorney-General's office. There Speed told them that this objectionable "exception had been intentionally inserted because that class comprised most of the slaveholders," and that it was "intended to put them under bonds to abide by the President's [Lincoln's] proclamation of emancipation." He informed the committee that the authorities were determined to prevent the courts from testing

4. *Harper's Weekly*, June 24, 1865.

the validity of that proclamation. Speed also stated that those in the thirteenth exception would have no difficulty in obtaining clemency, but "that when the pardon was delivered a receipt would be taken acknowledging that" it was accepted with the understanding the recipient "would never again employ slave labor."[5]

Doubtless the Attorney-General told the committee pretty nearly what the President himself would have said. This delegation or another from Virginia apparently did interview Johnson. The newspapers, in presuming to quote him in their accounts of the visit, put their own interpretation on the nature of the reply. Much they said was absurd. The following by the New York *Herald* is typical: "The President reminded them that the amnesty proclamation did not cause" existing hardships; "it was the commission of treason and the violation of law that did it." The President was also represented as telling the committee that in making the thirteenth "exception he had acted on the natural supposition that men had aided the rebellion according to the extent of their pecuniary means." Moreover, he did not believe his visitors were so much interested in relieving the poor by causing a revival of business as they were in making money for themselves. If they were so interested in relieving the destitute, why did they not give them of their substance and thereby reduce their wealth below twenty thousand dollars? In this manner they would eliminate the need for a special pardon. Finally, the editor quoted Johnson as saying: "I am free to say to you that I think all of you ought to be taxed on all over twenty thousand dollars, to help the poor. When I was governor of Tennessee, I assessed such taxes on those . . . leaders of the rebellion, and it had good effect."[6]

The character of the statements the editors quoted Johnson as uttering was such as they would naturally expect him to say under the circumstances. At least, the utterances were what many who did not sympathize with the purpose of the committee would have said. A report came from Richmond that the delegation returned disappointed, and that much dissatisfaction was expressed in certain

5. Browning, *Diary*, II, 36 (July 3, 1865).
6. New York *Herald*, July 10, 1865. Probably these newspaper comments pertained to the committee Browning mentioned on July 3.

quarters with the President's apparent "Jacksonian" stand in applying the thirteenth exception.[7] Consequently, persons thus disabled
were obliged to seek relief by applying for special pardon.

There was a feeling in some quarters that the twenty-thousand-
dollar clause had a salutary effect. Edmund Langley of southwest
Virginia thought so when he wrote that it worked well by holding
"the hand of the national power firmly upon a large class of influential men" who were impelled to respect the government. "It is
true," he said, "that the trammeling of capital and business which
the treason of these men has superinduced, is a serious, public evil,
but there are more serious, public evils than the temporary inertness of capital. . . ." Langley also believed that special clemency
would forever hold the recipients under such "tangible obligations
to the Executive and the nation" that they would be strictly loyal
thereafter. Having in mind loyalists and repentant rebels who had
taken the oath prior to May 29, 1865, but who were in areas not
then under control of the Federal authorities and thus not accessible
to executive clemency, he suggested that those who had complied
with Lincoln's proclamations, as far as they could under the circumstances, be granted the benefits expected therefrom.[8]

In a similar recommendation a few days earlier, Governor
Francis H. Pierpont favored "the extension of the amnesty to the
people of Virginia without reservation." He believed that some
ten thousand persons in that state had taken Lincoln's oath prior
to May 29, 1865, and consequently should be regarded as pardoned
and not affected by Johnson's exceptions. An effort was also reported to have been made to obtain pardons for a group of twenty-
five prominent citizens of Richmond known as the "Ambulance
Committee," on the ground that their benevolence during the war
merited clemency.[9] Not all of this number, of course, belonged to
the propertied class. Such magnanimity, however, could not then
be expected, though there was a desire for a reasonably early restora-

7. New York *Herald*, July 12, 1865. See also Washington *Evening Star*,
July 10; Springfield, Illinois, *State Journal*, July 12; Huntsville *Advocate*,
July 19; Milledgeville *Southern Recorder*, July 25, 1865.
8. Johnson Papers, LXX, No. 5345 (letter dated July 12, 1865).
9. New York *Herald*, June 23, July 9, 1865. Cf. Hamilton J. Eckenrode,
The Political History of Virginia during the Reconstruction, 32-37.

tion in Virginia, but not by any such extension of amnesty as Pierpont and Langley suggested. This policy of delay and selection was also manifested in dealing with the same problem in other states.

About this time, Senator Browning asked for the pardon of certain manufacturers of Richmond who could not obtain funds to resume operations until they were relieved. Johnson refused the request, saying it was not yet time to pardon men in the twenty-thousand-dollar class. He "would leave them, for the present, where the law and the rebellion [had] placed them," and allow "new men" to do the manufacturing in Richmond. The President stated further that he believed these Virginia petitioners "were still rebels at heart, and only anxious to make money [so] that they might give more trouble."[10]

As many believed, therefore, Johnson had the peculiar satisfaction of having the wealthy aristocrats of the South apply to him for pardon. The records indicate, however, that most of those who were worth twenty thousand dollars or more made no such approach to the President for clemency. If there were as many as sixty or eighty thousand in this class as was estimated, only a small per cent (certainly less than twenty) applied for pardon. Johnson was rather generous, however, and in most instances granted such petitions without much delay.

On September 21, he pardoned General Joseph R. Anderson of the Richmond Tredegar Iron Works. Anderson was a graduate of West Point and worth more than twenty thousand dollars, thus coming under three exceptions of the President's amnesty. The press in other states noted the injury to business in Virginia because of the thirteenth rule. The Columbia *Daily Phoenix* complained of the disability early in July, and the Savannah *Republican*, in appreciation of the evidence of relief, reported later that "Governor Pierpont's urgent recommendation" caused Johnson to pardon Anderson. Stanton was not pleased, however, and when asked to suspend the sale of some railroad iron until the claim to it by the Tredegar Company could be investigated, stated "that he had rather suspend their pardons, and send them to the penitentiary—and that

10. Browning, *Diary*, II, 38 (entry for July 20, 1865). On this visit to the White House, Browning did obtain "a pardon for Andrew Johnson, Esqr., of Richmond."

he would recognize no title resting on a contract made in Virginia in 1862."[11]

The President's leniency in granting relief from the disability under the thirteenth exception so alarmed his critics that the House of Representatives, on March 5, 1866, asked for "the names of persons worth more than twenty thousand dollars to whom special pardons" had been granted. The House also indicated its antipathy to Johnson's clemency by requesting "a statement of the amount of property . . . seized as belonging to enemies of the government or as abandoned property and returned to those who claimed to be the original owners."

By May 4 Seward reported that, according to the Attorney-General, 7,197 pardons had already been granted to persons in the thirteenth exception. He stated further that 707 other petitions of persons in this class remained in Speed's department as "not yet having been disposed of," and had therefore "been stricken from the accompanying list" of names.[12] The inference was, of course, that other pardons would be granted and delivered later.

Even though several thousand wealthy Southerners had been pardoned in the first ten months after Johnson had proclaimed his amnesty, the fact that the thirteenth exception remained in effect for more than two years surely retarded the economic recovery of the South. Johnson's satisfaction in exacting some retribution from the class of which he had always appeared jealous, and which he believed was largely responsible for the rebellion, was rather costly. Yet he seemed to befriend the pardoned claimants to the land taken over by the Freedmen's Bureau rather than the freedmen whom the Bureau endeavored to aid, thus favoring the whites rather than the blacks.

THE FREEDMEN'S BUREAU

On March 3, 1865, Congress enacted a law creating a Bureau of

11. Columbia *Daily Phoenix*, July 3, 1865; Savannah *Republican*, September 19, 1865; Browning, *Diary*, II, 53 (December 11, 1865). Stanton was wrong about the legality of contracts in Virginia during the war. See Browning, *Diary*, II, 53, n. 1, for citation of court decisions to the contrary.
12. *Cong. Globe*, 29 Cong., 1 Sess., pt. 2, p. 1190; also *House Exec. Doc.*, No. 99, 39 Cong., 1 Sess., 14-15. See Ch. XIV, "Efforts to Curtail Presidential Amnesty," for more information concerning reports on pardons.

Refugees, Freedmen and Abandoned Lands, which was to provide for the support and protection of all emancipated Negroes. This organization was authorized to take charge of abandoned and confiscated realty in the rebelling states, and assign "to every male . . . refugee or freedman . . . not more than forty acres of such land." The occupants were to "be protected in the use and enjoyment of the land for the term of three years" at a fair annual rent. At the end of the period the occupants might buy the property and receive a title to it from the United States.[13]

The President appointed General Oliver O. Howard Commissioner of the Bureau, and, on June 2, ordered "all abandoned lands and property contemplated" by Congress to be turned over to the Bureau. General Howard and a corps of assistants immediately undertook to carry out the provisions of the law. Not a great amount of land, however, was available under the confiscation and abandoned property acts. Howard states in his *Autobiography* that "Only about one five hundredth . . . of the entire amount of land in the States seceding" could thus be allotted.[14] It was generally supposed by those interested in the successful operation of the Bureau, of course, that the property thus entrusted would remain in such control "until the purposes for which it was granted were accomplished."[15] Unfortunately this was not to be. One of the benefits of pardon was the restoration of the recipient's property. Persons pardoned, therefore, insisted that this right be respected at once, even though their land had been allotted to freedmen for a term of three years.

Late in July, 1865, Commissioner Howard issued a circular "quoting the law and limiting and regulating the return of lands to former owners." Such land in the possession of the Bureau as

13. *U. S. Stat. at Large*, XIII, 507-9. The Bureau was later continued by act of Congress for two years after July 16, 1866. *Ibid.*, XIV, 173-77.

14. Richardson, *Messages . . . of the Presidents*, VI, 340; *Autobiography of Oliver Otis Howard, Major General, United States Army*, II, 229, cited hereafter as Howard, *Autobiography*. Howard gives the amount of land in the possession of the Bureau "till near the close of the first year" as follows: "cultivated, 161,331 acres; uncultivated, 143, 219 acres; unclassified, 464,040 acres; aggregate, 768,590 acres; number of pieces of town property, 1,596. Number of acres returned to owners, 88,170; number of pieces of town property returned, 1,177." *Ibid.*, 231-35.

15. *House Exec. Doc.*, No. 99, 39 Cong., 1 Sess., 12.

had not actually been abandoned was to be restored. Other lands that had been confiscated and abandoned were to be used immediately "for the life and comfort of refugees and freedmen." "Surely the pardon of the President," he said, "would not be interpreted to extend to the surrender of abandoned or confiscated property which in strict accordance with the law had been 'set apart for refugees and freedmen' or was then in use" in such manner. Thus he acted on the assumption that the law as he himself understood it would be carried out, and that legal occupants of such lands would be protected against the owners, at least until the three years were up. Apparently, he expected the government "to indemnify ... those Confederates who were pardoned," and certainly not aid them by dispossessing the freedmen who were lawfully holding the land.

At first, therefore, the Bureau refused to restore property to owners who claimed it merely by right of pardon. Something more than evidence of a special pardon, or a certified copy of the amnesty oath which persons not in the excepted classes were also expected to have, was required. Proof of absolute loyalty to the Union during the war was necessary before the Bureau would restore property. Of course, there was much dissatisfaction among pardoned claimants, and it was not long until Johnson was appealed to. On the day (July 27) Howard issued his circular of instructions to the assistant commissioners of the Bureau, B. B. Leake of Tennessee "was specially pardoned," but he was denied possession of his property. The denial was plainly contrary to one important benefit derived from a pardon. Consequently, about the middle of August, the President directed Howard to have his assistant at Nashville restore Leake's property immediately. Furthermore, the Commissioner was instructed to take "the same action ... in all similar cases."[16]

Early in August, 1865, General James B. Steedman, writing from his headquarters in Georgia, advised the President to pardon persons in the thirteenth exception as quickly as possible, especially businessmen. Such clemency, he believed, would cause many of this

16. McPherson, *Reconstruction*, 13 (Johnson to Howard, August 16, 1865); *House Exec. Doc.*, No. 99, 39 Cong., 1 Sess., 12, 13. Cf. James W. Garner, *Reconstruction in Mississippi*, 257-58.

class to "join earnestly and sincerely in the work of restoration and in sustaining" Johnson's policies in general. Steedman also recommended the release of "Stephens at once as a means to hasten conciliation in Georgia." Such counsel from a Federal major general who was in a position to appreciate the wisdom of pardoning men of wealth surely had the desired effect on the President.[17]

At any rate, Howard's policy toward pardoned claimants to land in possession of the Bureau was not satisfactory to the President. The Commissioner said that Johnson compelled him "to draw up another circular worded better to suit this policy and submit it to him before its issue." This paper was not satisfactory to the President, who had "a totally different object in view." Johnson, therefore, had the document redrawn and instructed Howard, on September 12, 1865, "to send it out as approved by him." Howard did this reluctantly, for the order "in great part rescinded former land circulars." His chief objection to it was that it not only allowed "assistant commissioners to return all land not abandoned, but [it] also instructed them to return all abandoned land to owners who were pardoned by the President, and provided no indemnity whatever for the occupants, refugees or freedmen, except a right to the growing crops."[18]

To be more specific, the President's circular defined both abandoned lands and confiscated lands. The former were described according to an "act of Congress approved July 2, 1864, as lands 'the lawful owner whereof shall be voluntarily absent therefrom, and engaged either in arms or otherwise in aiding the rebellion.'" Land in the latter class was not to "be regarded as confiscated until it had been condemned and sold by decree of the United States court for the district in which the property may be found, and the title thereto thus vested in the United States." Monthly reports of lands under control of the assistant commissioners were also to be made to the Commissioner, and only such lands as were actually under control of the Bureau were to be set apart from the use of the freedmen. Furthermore, every pardoned claimant was required to show "evidence of a special pardon . . . or a copy of the oath of

17. Johnson Papers, LXXXIII, No. 6037 (Steedman to Johnson, August 6, 1865).
18. Howard, *Autobiography*, II, 234-35.

amnesty," when he was not among the fourteen classes excepted from the proclamation of amnesty. The last provision of the circular assured the "loyal refugees or freedmen" that lands would not be restored to the rightful owners until the crops growing thereon could "be secured for the benefit of the cultivators" of the land. If restoration was made earlier, the tenants were to be paid a "full and just compensation . . . for their labor and its products, and for their expenditures."[19]

According to Howard, these instructions appeared "fair and right enough," but they defeated the intention of Congress to allow the freedmen the privilege of acquiring title to the land they were tilling. Nevertheless, some consideration appears to have been shown the freedmen in at least one state. "In Virginia, a considerable amount [of land] had been libeled and was about to be sold, when Mr. Stanton considerately suspended sales, [in order] that these lands might be turned over more directly to the Bureau for the benefit of the freedmen." When Howard contended that the lands "were already the property of the Government," the President, supported by the Attorney-General, insisted on inserting the word "sold" in the definition of confiscated property in preparing the circular of September 12, 1865. Howard stated later that "this was what caused the return to former owners of *all property* where sales had been suspended and never consummated."[20]

In determining the final policy for the Bureau, Johnson appeared disposed to favor the pardoned owners of land, while Howard sought the advantage of the emancipated tenants of that land. The former, of course, was merely insisting that the recipients of pardon should receive the full benefit of such clemency. The President "was amused," therefore, "and gave no heed" to Howard's urgent recommendation "that all men of property to whom he was offering pardon should be conditioned to provide a small homestead or something equivalent" for each head of a family among their former slaves. "My heart ached for our beneficiaries," said the sympathetic Commissioner, "but I became comparatively helpless to offer them any permanent possession [of their property]."

Howard's recommendation had much support from certain quar-

19. McPherson, *Reconstruction*, 12-13.
20. Howard, *Autobiography*, II, 236.

ters. Senator Samuel Clark Pomeroy of Kansas, writing in September, 1865, would have withheld all pardons of those in the twenty-thousand-dollar class until the recipients agreed to deed ten acres of land to every head of a family or able-bodied single person held as a slave at the time Lincoln first announced his Proclamation of Emancipation. Of course, those who advised confiscating the property of the leaders of the Confederacy approved such a policy. Believing the Negroes deserved something from the estates which their labor had produced, Senator Sumner secured the passage of a resolution in the Senate, on July 3, 1867, expressing the opinion that "reconstruction would be hastened . . . if the President . . . in the exercise of the pardoning power would require every landed proprietor . . . before receiving his pardon" to give his former slaves homesteads, "so that the disloyal master may not continue to appropriate to himself the fruits of their toil."[21] The President never heeded such counsel. In fact, he omitted the thirteenth exception entirely from his next general amnesty, which he proclaimed on September 7, 1867. Henceforth the possession of property was no barrier whatever to a pardon.

According to Howard, Johnson's September circular put the Bureau somewhat at a disadvantage. The burden of proof thereafter was upon the assistant commissioners to determine whether "property had ever been voluntarily abandoned by a disloyal owner." This condition operated to the advantage of the pardoned claimants, for no great amount of land had been actually confiscated and sold by court action. Consequently, "wholesale pardons in a brief time completed the restoration of the remainder" of the lands under the control of the Bureau. Howard's statement implies, of course, that, since many persons were pardoned outright by Johnson's first amnesty and since many others in the excepted classes were pardoned before the close of 1865, the process of returning lands to the owners was practically over in a few months after the President determined the final policy of restoration.

In this connection, it should be noted particularly that there were pardoned claimants of property who did not come under the twenty-thousand-dollar exception of the amnesty measure. Never-

21. Johnson Papers, LXXVII (Pomeroy to Harlowe, September 16, 1865); *Cong. Globe*, 40 Cong., 1 Sess., 467.

theless, Howard lamented that "all was done for the advantage of
the late Confederates and for the disadvantage and displacement of
the freedmen. Very many [of these poor people]," he continued,
"had in good faith occupied and cultivated the farms guaranteed
to them by" act of Congress. His solicitude for the freedmen was
in vain, however, and by April, 1866, 430,104 acres of land had
been surrendered to pardoned owners. Only 30,104 acres of this
amount had been restored before Johnson issued the circular of
restoration in September, 1865.[22]

Sometimes it was difficult to get the emancipated tenants and
the pardoned owners of the land in question to cooperate in a satisfactory plan of restoration. In October, 1865, the President sent
Howard to adjust a serious condition existing on "certain tracts of
land, situated on the coast of South Carolina, Georgia, and Florida."
General Sherman had encouraged freedmen following his army to
occupy some of these lands, especially those of the islands south of
Charleston and inland for thirty miles.[23] The returning pardoned
owners, however, desired to regain their properties, "promising to
absorb the labor and care for the freedmen." On arriving in Charleston, Howard soon concluded that the prudent thing to do was to
appease the freedmen by explaining the will of the government to
them in a general meeting.

The situation seemed to be most acute on, and in the vicinity of,
Edisto Island. Howard arranged, therefore, to meet the freedmen
"in a large meeting house" on the island. Several officers and a
representative of the planters accompanied him. Rumor of the purpose of his coming preceded him, and there was "strong evidence
of dissatisfaction and sorrow" manifested in every part of the large
assembly. Naturally the freedmen did not like "the President's
orders to restore the lands to the old planters. . . ." Both sexes were

22. Howard, *Autobiography*, II, 237-47. See McPherson, *Reconstruction*,
13, for figures of land disposals. Cf. Eckenrode, *The Political History of
Virginia during the Reconstruction*, 54 ff.
23. F. B. Simkins and R. H. Woody, *South Carolina during Reconstruction*, 31-32, 227-31, give a good brief account of this Edisto Island episode.
See C. Mildred Thompson, *Reconstruction in Georgia . . .*, Ch. II, and
Fleming, *Civil War and Reconstruction in Alabama*, Ch. XI, for good accounts of the Freedmen's Bureau in two other states. Also *Sen. Exec. Doc.*,
No. 27, 39 Cong., 1 Sess., 138-40.

present, and the situation was tense. The noise and confusion was such that no progress was made until "a sweet-voiced negro woman" began singing, "Nobody knows the trouble I feel; nobody knows but Jesus." Many others joined the good woman, and the singing "had a quieting effect on the audience."

The apprehensions of the freedmen on Edisto Island were confirmed, for Howard was obliged to tell them that they must allow the owners to take possession of the plantations. Nevertheless, the freedmen were given some consideration. A board of supervisors was created "to secure and adjust contracts" between them and the planters, and to settle disputes and controversies arising therefrom. Before land was restored the owner signed an agreement "in which he promised substantially: To leave to the freedmen the existing crop; to let them stay at their present homes so long as the responsible freedmen among them would contract or lease; to . . . make new contracts or leases, with the provision that freedmen who refused would surrender any right to remain on the estate after two months; the owners also [were] engaged to interpose no objections to the schools; all the obligations [were] to hold for only one year unless renewed."

In this manner the Freedmen's Bureau endeavored to establish a satisfactory relation between the pardoned planters and their former slaves. In fact, the system was encouraged wherever there was need for it. Was it a wise policy? Later Commissioner Howard himself answered this question. He concluded his account of the subject by saying: "After years of thinking and observation I am inclined to believe that the restoration of their lands to the planters proved for all their future better for the negroes."[24] This meant the approval of a system for the freedmen in which they had to begin at the lowest free economic level, where they had to learn lessons in independent action, in frugality, and in the principles of good business, before they could expect to acquire and retain possession of property. They have not yet gained social and political rights and privileges at the same level.

EXAMPLES OF RESTORATION

Sometimes the pardoning of an individual was delayed because of

24. Howard, *Autobiography*, II, 238-44.

property considerations. One of the most interesting cases of this sort was that of Richard L. Cox, a native and citizen of the District of Columbia. Cox had served the Confederacy first as a paymaster and later as quartermaster with the rank of major, and at the close of the war he had promptly taken (June 12) both Lincoln's and Johnson's amnesty oaths and applied for pardon. Favorable action on his application, however, was delayed on the advice of Judge Underwood of the United States District Court of Virginia, because his property in Georgetown was being used as a "Colored Orphans' Home." The Attorney-General offered assistance in securing the pardon if Cox "would make a donation to the institution in a sum to be fixed by two parties designated by him." This, Cox declined to do; so the pardon was withheld. Subsequently the trustees of the Colored Orphans' Home offered to vacate the property on condition that the owner would pay the institution ten thousand dollars. Major Cox refused this proposition also and insisted that, since he had not abandoned the property, his family having been driven away from it, he was entitled to its return with a pardon, according to the terms of the President's proclamation. An account of these negotiations, including the original propositions made by the Department of Justice and the trustees, was sent to the President on October 11, 1865. The communication, however, was referred to the Attorney-General for his consideration, apparently without the President's ever having seen it. Several weeks later the authorities again deferred action on Cox's petition until persons could return to Washington "whose testimony," to quote a representative of the Colored Orphans' Home, "will sustain the several matters heretofore stated as reasons why Richard L. Cox should not be pardoned."

Far along in 1866 the matter was taken up again. On May 30, the Attorney-General inquired of General Howard whether there was any "prospect of making some adjustments with" Major Cox "in regard to his property in Georgetown." The General replied the following day that the property was "only nominally in the possession of this Bureau being really in the hands of 'the National Association for the Relief of Destitute Colored Women and Children.'" He said, however, that he believed that, since "several thousand dollars" had been spent in improving the property, "the buildings and at least five acres of land should be reserved to said Association. . . ."

It appears that the occupants of the estate were regarded as having leased the property from the Bureau of Refugees and Abandoned Lands. In compliance with the amnesty proclamation, therefore, especially with the provisions of the special pardon to be granted the petitioner, their rights had to be respected in the restoration. At this time, however, Cox's brother appealed to the President, who, after a conference with the Attorney-General, ordered the pardon warrant issued. The Major, therefore, received his pardon on June 12, 1866, just one year from the day he had filed his petition. Apparently, the pardon would not have been granted at this time, if ever, had Johnson not been appealed to directly.

Nevertheless, some months passed before the property was vacated. Another home for its inmates had to be secured, and there was a natural disposition on the part of those in possession to procrastinate their withdrawal. A former employee of the Treasury Department was farming the land, and two clerks of the government occupied the gardener's house on the estate. It was not until late in 1866 that the owner took possession, and then, on December 27, he had to permit Federal agents to remove the frame addition which the Association had built to his home; but this was the only consideration, or "donation," he was obliged to allow the Colored Orphans' Home.[25]

There is an interesting case of the revocation of a wealthy man's pardon. The recipient, John Overton, of Nashville, had fled from Tennessee when the Union army occupied the state's capital, and thus had abandoned his property. Later he apparently lost confidence in the success of the Confederate cause and took Lincoln's amnesty oath in February, 1865, before the clerk of the Federal district court in Kentucky. When he returned to Nashville, General George H. Thomas, whose headquarters were in that city, refused to recognize the validity of the oath, because Overton had

25. Amnesty Papers, Dist. of Columbia; also Serial 22, Endorsements and Memoranda, II (1866), entry 145; Asst. Com. Bureau of Refugees and Abandoned Lands, Serial 1, Vol. I (1865-1866), 275; and *ibid.*, Serial 2 (1866). Sometimes Cox's name appears as Richard S., instead of Richard L.

taken it in a state of which he was not a citizen. Thomas also claimed that Overton had taken the oath only "to save his property," and that his taking it in Kentucky "showed that he feared that he would be unsuccessful if he applied to" him to administer it. General Halleck, on being appealed to, sustained Thomas, who later (April 26, 1865) sought and obtained the approval of the Secretary of War.

All this occurred before Johnson's first proclamation of amnesty, of which Overton soon took advantage. His petition was granted, and he was pardoned in August, 1865. In the meantime, however, the Freedmen's Bureau disposed of his estate in the usual way. Overton claimed his property under the terms of the pardon, but refused to respect the leases of it. His controversy with the Bureau caused his pardon to be revoked in November, 1865, but he regained it two months later, with the understanding that he would refrain from making claims against the Bureau and respect the unexpired leases on his property.[26]

Another interesting case concerns Joseph E. Davis of Mississippi, a much older brother of Jefferson Davis. The elder Davis easily came under the thirteenth exception of Johnson's amnesty. In due time his property, consisting of "Hurricane" and "Brierfield" plantations, was appropriated for use by the Freedmen's Bureau. Apparently, the desire to regain possession of the estates caused him to apply to President Johnson late in September, 1865, for a pardon. Joseph Davis's lack of prestige at the Capital prompted him to say in his petition: "I have no friends in Washington, nor the means of making such. I must rely, therefore, upon the justice of my claim. In the year 1818 I purchased of the United States some lands on the Mississippi River, below the Walnut Hills, now Vicksburg; upon the land I fixed my residence and occupied it forty years." It was not until March 28, 1866, however, that Joseph Davis was pardoned, and from that date he "claimed and received rents" from the use of his plantations.

26. *Offic. Rec.*, 2 Ser., VIII, 319, 336, 501, 513; Johnson Papers, LXXXI, LXXXV; *Nation*, II, 335. John Overton built the hotel in Nashville still known as the "Maxwell House," which Dr. A. L. Crabb of Nashville used in his novel, *Supper at the Maxwell House*, and which has also given its name to a popular brand of coffee.

Naturally Joseph Davis desired actual possession of his estates. There was also a circumstance probably not existing in the case of any other pardoned claimant for the restoration of property. In 1835, Joseph had given "Brierfield" to his brother, Jefferson, who occupied and controlled the plantation "as his own, although he never secured title to it." Since Jefferson was imprisoned in May, 1865, and soon indicted for treason, any property he had was in danger of confiscation and sale. Apparently realizing that his unfortunate brother was likely to be punished, Joseph willed "Brierfield" to Jefferson's children in 1865. This act would tend "to conceal from the Federals any right that Jefferson Davis had to the land." Nevertheless, early in September, 1866, Joseph applied again for the restoration of "Hurricane" and "Brierfield" plantations. This time he employed an agent, J. H. D. Bowmar, "to go to Washington to see the President about the restoration of the property." The authorities approved, and the plantations were turned over to the rightful owner.

Soon after receiving "Brierfield" from the Freedmen's Bureau, Joseph Davis sold the plantation to Bowmar. The elder brother died in September, 1870, and some years later Jefferson Davis brought suit against the purchaser, in the name of his children, to obtain the property on the ground that his brother had given it to him. The court held (April, 1878), however, that title to the estate had remained in Joseph E. Davis, and decided against the plaintiff.[27]

OTHER DETAILS

The cases just cited are typical of the difficulties which sometimes became involved in the granting of pardon and the restoration of property to the average person of means. Other examples with different causes of delay might be given. It would be strange, indeed, if instances had not occurred where state authorities, for personal or partisan reasons, retarded the progress of certain applications for pardon. Such cases were not uncommon. The chapter

27. This information was obtained from 55 Mississippi Reports, 671-814, in the case of *Jefferson Davis* vs. *J. H. D. Bowmar, Executor et al.* Dr. William D. McCain, Director of the Department of Archives and History, State of Mississippi, kindly furnished excerpts from the case.

on "Pardoning North Carolinians" contains evidence of many such examples in one state. Delay occasionally was due to negligence or clerical error. The applicant's apparent obstinacy in accepting defeat or his failure to make adequate expression of loyalty to the Union, apart from the oath, was regarded as sufficient cause for delaying favorable action on his petition. There were those, too, who hesitated to take the oath and thereby qualify for pardon because they believed this act would preclude their ever receiving any compensation for the loss of property in slaves. A tendency also existed on the part of a few Texans "to keep the Negro in some sort of bondage and to talk of 'gradual emancipation' even after having subscribed to emancipation in their oaths of amnesty."[28]

In Texas the poor mail service delayed the announcement of the amnesty proclamation in many communities and thereby deferred the taking of the oath provided therein. For some months in Alabama the military authorities administered the oath and controlled the granting of pardons. During this time many persons were denied the privilege of the amnesty. When the civil authorities took over the pardoning business, a more liberal policy was adopted in that state.[29]

Once in a while the President received a warm expression of gratitude from a person whom he had pardoned. Joseph Holt's help in obtaining pardons was also appreciated. Nevertheless, there were often manifestations of insincerity on the part of those pardoned. Such persons accepted the program of clemency because they were obliged to do so in order to enjoy the benefits accruing therefrom. Some remained rebellious in spirit and often gave expression to their seditious feelings.[30] Occasionally a pardon was recalled for some reason or other. The recipient may have been too

28. C. W. Ramsdell, *Reconstruction in Texas*, 57, 62, 66. Evidence of delays in delivering pardons due to clerical negligence and error may be found in the Archives at Atlanta, Georgia, Executive Letter Book, June 28, 1866, to November 13, 1867.

29. *Ibid.*, 62; Fleming, *Reconstruction in Alabama*, 409-10.

30. New York *Tribune*, August 24, 1865; *Nation*, I, 334-67; New York *Herald*, July 15, October 6, 1865; W. L. Fleming (ed.), *Documentary History of Reconstruction* . . . , I, 36-37, 39; Johnson Papers, LXVII, LXXXIII; Holt Papers, L (Harrison to Holt, October 12, 1865, Payne to Harrison, November 16, 1865).

boastful of his prowess in securing executive clemency, or new evidence of his conduct during the war may have come to light. His enemies might also have influenced the authorities to recall his pardon, or he might have disagreed with the Freedmen's Bureau in adjusting the restoration of his property, as has been related above.

The records show some interesting data relative to the offenses for which special pardons were issued. There were more offenders in the twenty-thousand-dollar class than in any other of the fourteen exceptions.[31] As has already been stated, a report prepared in the spring of 1866 gave the names of 7,197 persons in the thirteenth exception whose petitions had already been granted, and 707 others whose applications were under consideration. Of course, in many instances, these persons also came under other exceptions of the amnesty. In some states the number of those worth more than twenty thousand dollars exceeded that of those under all other exceptions. Such appears to have been the condition in Texas, Louisiana, Mississippi, Alabama, Georgia, North and South Carolina, and Virginia.

A report for March, 1867, shows that most of the special pardons granted to Marylanders went to persons who had left a loyal state to aid the Confederacy. The same condition appears also to have existed in Kentucky and Missouri. The latter state and Tennessee each received 40 per cent or more of its pardons for indictments for treason. The largest percentage in Arkansas was for violations of the oath of allegiance. Alabama and South Carolina led the states in showing the most brigadier generals, having in this report eleven and ten respectively.[32]

By June 5, 1866, there had been 12,652 special pardons granted. The following December, on the request of the House, other reports began to be made, the last being given on December 4, 1867,

---

31. *House Exec. Doc.*, No. 99, 39 Cong., 1 Sess. This report gives the number of special pardons to persons of this class by state as follows: Virginia, 2,070; Alabama, 1,361; Georgia, 1,228; Mississippi, 765; South Carolina, 638; North Carolina, 482; Texas, 269; Louisiana, 142; Tennessee, 93; Arkansas, 41; West Virginia, 39; Florida, 22; Kentucky, 11; Missouri, 10.

32. *House Exec. Doc.*, No. 116, 39 Cong., 2 Sess., Nos. 31, 116.

and covering 147 pages.[33] In all there were some 13,500 persons who received special clemency. The reports also contained information pertaining to the pardons, one (July, 1867) giving the names of those recommending clemency and the date it was granted.

It must be kept in mind that indictments for offenses against the United States and for other charges growing out of the war continued to be made throughout 1865 and 1866. The amnesty measure had contemplated that situation. Indictments existing before Johnson's proclamation appeared excluded from its general application some persons who would otherwise have enjoyed that privilege. Such individuals, therefore, were obliged to stand trial or to secure a special pardon.

At the same time the local authorities, especially in the border area, including Tennessee and Arkansas as well as Kentucky and Missouri, were active in securing indictments. This was done, it appears, without much regard for the amnesty measure. The New York *Tribune* (September 27, 1865), in discussing conditions in Tennessee, stated: " 'Old Rebels and young ones,' says Brownlow's paper, 'who took a leading part in running down the loyalists, imprisoning and starving them, have been spotted, and in defiance of "Amnesty" are being held fearfully responsible for their crimes.' " In March, 1866, for example, the United States District Attorney for Kentucky, Joshua Lewis, sent Speed a list of 232 indictments for treason in his district.[34] He desired instructions as to the course to pursue, especially "against persons paroled by the military authorities." "Many," he said, "will plead [guilty] and rely on their pardons."

In this connection it should be explained that many Confederate soldiers had been paroled in April and May, 1865, before Johnson's proclamation had appeared, and had taken the oath of allegiance to the United States. In fact, General Grant had written to Gen-

33. Johnson Papers, XCV, report of Attorney-General Speed to Johnson, June 6, 1866; *House Exec. Doc.*, No. 16, 40 Cong., 2 Sess. Other reports were given on December 31, 1866, March 2, 1867, and July 8, 1867.

34. Attorneys-General's Papers, Library of Congress. One hundred and forty-seven of these indictments were made at Frankfort, and eighty-five at Louisville.

eral Thomas, on May 6, 1865, that "paroled prisoners surrendered by
Lee and Johnston and others entering into the same arrangements"
were to be permitted "to return to their homes if within any of the
seceded states," but if they belonged "to other states they must take
the oath of allegiance first, under the decision of the Attorney General." Two days later these instructions were issued from Washington as "Special Orders, No. 215."[35] This order applied to General Johnston's and General Smith's armies, and other soldiers surrendered in like manner. President Johnson's proclamation amnestied, therefore, all who did not come under any of his fourteen exceptions; and a copy of the amnesty oath, properly executed, became a certificate of pardon.

On April 30, 1866, United States District Attorney C. W. Hall
sent to Washington a list of fifty-four indictments for treason recently made at Knoxville, Tennessee. The list contained some of
the most prominent men of the Confederacy, including Jefferson
Davis and Generals E. Kirby Smith and Simon Bolivar Buckner.
Such activity on the part of Federal attorneys and grand juries was
in response to information received from Attorney-General Speed
three weeks earlier (March 19) that "the President deemed it important that a 'few' persons indicted for high treason should be
punished," especially those who had been "prominent, conspicuous,
and influential in the rebellion."

Notwithstanding such indictments and prosecutions, as well as
confiscation proceedings, the operation of the system of granting
special pardons continued, diminishing, of course, the number of
possible prosecutions. The records give instance after instance of
indictments and prosecutions thus set aside and property restored
to the recipients of pardon.[36]

After the issue of the amnesty proclamation there seems to have
been a disposition at times to stop or delay proceedings of confiscation until the owners of the property concerned could obtain action on their applications for pardon. For the most part, such
suits were encouraged; but as the number of special pardons in-

35. *Offic. Rec.*, 2 Ser., VIII, 536, 539. See also New York *Tribune*, May 11,
1865. The oath was the one in Lincoln's proclamation.
36. Amnesty Papers, *passim; House Exec. Docs.*, No. 99, 39 Cong., 1 Sess.;
Nos. 31, 116, 39 Cong., 2 Sess.

---

creased, these prosecutions became fewer. There were instances, however, when such proceedings were continued against property after the owner had been pardoned.[37] In the case of Bryce Wilson, for example, proceedings were continued on the ground that Wilson had taken the oath before a notary public, and that the oath bore date after the acceptance of pardon. A notary had not been designated as one who might administer the oath. The Secretary of State, however, waived the defect, thereby allowing the man a full pardon. The local authorities, in such cases, were informed that a pardon relieved one from any punishment whatever on account of his support of the Confederacy.

Where property was actually condemned and sold, the proceeds of the sale were deposited in the United States Treasury, and there could be no restoration of what was sold, since ownership had become vested in a third party. The Abandoned Property Act (March 3, 1863), however, provided that a claimant might bring suit within two years after the close of the war in the Court of Claims to recover the proceeds of such sales. Cases of this sort are properly treated in the last chapter of this study.

37. New York *Herald*, July 21, 1865; Attorneys-General Office Letter Book E, 96 (Attorney-General to Samuel Robb, July 10, 1865); Johnson Papers, LXXXI, LXXXIV; Attorneys-General Office Letter Book F, 591 (Assistant Attorney-General to U. S. Attorney Francis Bugbee, December 6, 1867).

CHAPTER TWELVE

PARDONING CIVIL LEADERS

THE DESIRE FOR PARDON

SOON after the close of hostilities the President of the Confederacy and many of his chief civil officers, including governors of the Confederate States, were in prison awaiting the disposition of the Federal government. Others who were not in confinement were in voluntary exile. Among the latter were Robert Toombs, John C. Breckinridge, and Judah P. Benjamin. Benjamin fled to England, where he remained and became a prominent citizen and jurist. The military leaders (army and navy), with a few exceptions, were more fortunate than the civil ones, since they enjoyed parole and consequently were not subject to arrest and imprisonment. They have been considered earlier, and the next chapter will be devoted to Jefferson Davis.

It should be remembered that treason was the current definition in the North for complicity in the effort of disunion, and death was the extreme penalty. Moreover, the assassination of President Lincoln had intensified the feeling that "traitors" should be severely punished, and for a time, at least, it really appeared that the severest punishment might be inflicted on the most prominent secessionists. The only hope was in the President. Johnson apparently had the power to pardon or allow to be punished, as he might think advisable, any persons charged with, or convicted of, violating laws providing punishment for rebellion. His proclamation of amnesty indicated that. An examination of this measure, therefore, revealed the possibility of his pardoning even Jefferson Davis and Alexander H. Stephens if they would ask him for clemency. In their present predicament, however, the Confederate leaders could do nothing more than follow Lincoln's advice—encourage others "to bind up the nation's wounds" and "achieve and cherish a just and lasting peace" in the United States. From positions of disadvantage, therefore, they naturally felt very keenly their forced incompetency. It was galling to them to see places of leadership which they had so recently occupied held by other men, often of lesser prominence and ability. Consequently, even before President Johnson announced his plan of amnesty and reconstruction, some civil leaders of the Confederacy applied for pardon, and others eventually did likewise.

As has already been shown, the necessity of asking for clemency also afforded these men an opportunity to plead the general cause of the South in the hope of influencing the authorities at Washington to adopt a liberal policy of reconstruction. It may be stated, however, that the petitions sometimes reveal efforts of the petitioners to put their respective cases in as favorable light as possible. If they had opposed secession or accepted the final action of the states unwillingly; if they had mitigated the horrors of war in any way or worked for peace during the conflict; if they had disapproved of the policy of Davis's administration or felt that the object of secession had not been realized because of maladministration at Richmond, they were prone to stress their actions and feelings with the apparent purpose of winning the President's favor. Men like Alexander H. Stephens, John H. Reagan, and John A. Campbell, however, did not exaggerate or misrepresent. They were justified in writing as they did, and their motives were most commendable. Perhaps some of them would not have written such long petitions if they had not been in prison and had so much time to write. Their applications and other matter pertaining thereto contain much interesting information, and, as with the North Carolinians discussed in an earlier chapter, some of them deserve consideration in this narrative.

REAGAN AND STEPHENS

One of the first of the Southern leaders to apply for pardon was John H. Reagan of Texas. He had been Postmaster-General of the Confederate States and was very early confined in Fort Warren, Boston Harbor. From his prison cell, on May 28, he sent President Johnson a long and able letter stating the position of the Southern states in their effort at independence, and counseling moderation in the program of reconstruction. Five days later, on learning of the new amnesty measure, he applied for special pardon under its provisions.[1] These two communications, having a total of some nine thousand words, were not written merely to obtain a pardon for their author, but rather to encourage the amelioration of the dismal state of affairs in the South and to secure a lasting peace between the two sections.

Reagan explained in his first letter that secession resulted from the logical development of principles of government originating in the very foundation of the nation. He said that Jefferson and Madison were the authors of the doctrine of states' rights and that their Virginia and Kentucky resolutions had "always been the standard by which this doctrine has been tested." "Can it be a crime," he asked, "for men to believe doctrines so old, so promulgated, and accepted and believed, by men of such ability and character? God forbid. Shall men be imprisoned, or exiled, or hanged, or have their property confiscated, or be disfranchised for believing political doctrines and acting on them, which have been the basis of the creed of the Democratic party during its whole existence, and the profession of which was the test of its political orthodoxy?" The writer closed by suggesting that, inasmuch as the states lately in rebellion appeared ready to renew their allegiance to the Union, it would be "better to extend amnesty to all," rather than to increase "the sorrow and suffering of the country by the employment of a harsh and vindictive policy." It was his opinion, therefore, that such procedure would "sooner and more perfectly secure the pacification of the country and the fraternization of the people" than any other policy.

The distinguished Texan had four small motherless children, ages four to eleven, who needed his care. In his second letter, therefore, he pleaded for immediate action on his petition so that he might go home to them. Nothing was done, however, so he wrote to the President again on July 18, urging favorable action on his petition. At the same time he also wrote to Attorney-General Speed, hoping that he would expedite action on his case. Even earlier he had entreated others, including Governor A. J. Hamilton of Texas, to influence the President to act. He told Johnson in his third letter that

1. Originals of these letters are among the Amnesty Papers for Texas. The letter of May 28 may be found in Reagan, *Memoirs*, Appendix B.

he recognized and believed "that if the case of the South had met the approval of the Almighty its people would have succeeded in the establishment of their independence," and consequently he accepted "the result of the war as the will of God." Furthermore, he acquiesced "in the abolition of slavery, and in the principle that the federal government had the right to preserve itself against disintegration by secession or separation of the states from it."[2] These earnest efforts to secure clemency, however, had no immediate effect.

On August 11, Reagan wrote a long letter urging the people of Texas to acquiesce in the existing reconstruction program.[3] His earnest and comprehensive statement had a wholesome effect, for the press gave the message publicity. Indeed, his course so pleased Governor Hamilton and former Governor E. M. Pease that they advised the President to parole the writer so that his good influence might be exercised to greater advantage in the state. Consequently, Johnson included Reagan among the few leaders whom he released from prison on October 11, 1865.[4]

Vice-President Alexander H. Stephens, who was also imprisoned in Fort Warren, began preparing a petition for pardon soon after learning of Johnson's amnesty. He finished and mailed a second copy of it to the President on June 10. In some five thousand words Stephens ably stated his own position and the cause of the South. He told Johnson that he had not sympathized with the secessionists in 1861 or later. "No living man," he wrote, ". . . exerted his powers to a greater extent . . . to prevent these troubles and the late deplorable war than I did; and no man in the United States is less responsible by any intentional act for the consequences than I feel myself to be." He declared further that he professed no sense of guilt for anything he had done, nor was he trying to shun responsibility for his "acts under the Constitution and laws of the country—even though the end should be the scaffold or the gallows."

Stephens stated that he "was brought up in the strictest sect of the Crawford, Troup, and Jefferson State Rights School of Politics,"

2. Amnesty Papers, Texas.
3. See Reagan, *Memoirs*, 286-95, for this letter; also Ramsdell, *Reconstruction in Texas*, 87-88 and n. 2, and the New York *Tribune*, October 20, 1865.
4. *Offic. Rec.*, 2 Ser., VIII, 763.

and that the Virginia and Kentucky resolutions were the first lessons of his "political creed." He became therefore a firm believer in the doctrines set forth therein. Consequently, when Georgia seceded, he believed that, "being a citizen of Georgia," he was no longer a "citizen of the United States." He related how he became hostile to the Davis administration when it subverted the rights of the states. Secession, he said, had been resorted to in order to guarantee those rights. "The war was inaugurated against my judgment," he continued. "It was conducted on our side against my judgment. I do not feel myself morally responsible or accountable in any way [,therefore,] for any of the appalling evils attending it." He further stated that he accepted the issues and results of the war and declared his entire willingness to abide by them. He desired to be paroled from prison, however, if it appeared unwise to pardon him.[5]

The prisoner seemed to doubt the propriety of this letter and wished that his brother, Linton, were present to advise him as to its contents. He thought "of many things that would have improved it," and wondered how he would feel if it were "rejected or unnoticed."[6] This uncertainty increased until he was prompted to write the President on June 29, saying: "I therefore now address you for the purpose of withdrawing that special application for amnesty in my behalf. . . . I did not and do not wish to be considered or looked upon in any manner or form as a base supplicant for mercy. I have not the slightest sense of being a criminal before God or man for anything I have done in the late armed conflict and most lamentable war between the States." Stephens concluded this letter by reminding Johnson that his constitutional rights were being denied, since he had been "imprisoned . . . without any judicial process, warrant or legal authority whatever."[7]

The only immediate effect that these communications appear to have had was to cause the release of Stephens from the close confinement to which he had been subjected. Late in July and again in

5. Johnson Papers, LXXIII, No. 6061. See also Alexander H. Stephens, *The Recollections of Alexander H. Stephens . . .*, 187-204.
6. *Ibid.*, 201-5.
7. Johnson Papers, LXXIII, No. 6061.

August, he expressed his deep gratitude for this relaxation and begged the President to allow him to come to Washington for an interview. The purpose of the proposed visit was to obtain a parole from prison so that he might go to "Liberty Hall," his home in Crawfordville, Georgia, which was the dearest place on earth to him. Stephens assured the President that under no possible contingency would he attempt to escape, and that he would promptly return to prison if the privilege were refused.[8]

Of course, many persons recommended that Stephens be paroled and pardoned. On August 29, former Governor Brown of Georgia and Linton Stephens interviewed Johnson in his behalf.[9] He himself wrote Seward at length about the subject on September 19, saying that he would like to interview the President upon the subject of his release and other matters. Ten days later he told Seward that unless he was paroled or admitted to bail by the middle of October, such clemency, if allowed later, would avail very little. The ostensible reason for desiring Stephens's parole or pardon was the wholesome influence he might have in Georgia.

No doubt Stephens's Union speech in the city hall park of Augusta, Georgia, on September 1, 1860, and his celebrated speech delivered in opposition to secession before the Georgia legislature on November 14, 1860, had some influence in causing his liberation from prison. It might be stated also that his intelligent address on Washington's Birthday in 1866 before the Georgia legislature on reconstruction undoubtedly had a salutary effect on conditions in Georgia.[10] Stephens's testimony before the Reconstruction Committee of Congress, April 16, 1866, doubtless increased his favor with authorities at Washington. Of course, his responsibilities and activities before and during the war must have had much influence in determining his treatment after the war. At any rate, the leniency toward Stephens was in marked contrast to the harsh treatment of Davis after the end of hostilities. One had opposed secession, applied for pardon, and offered to do what he could toward restora-

8. *Ibid.*, Nos. 6059, 6063.
9. *Ibid.*, LXXIV, Nos. 6264, 6268, 6270; LXXVII, No. 6889; Amnesty Papers for Georgia; New York *Herald*, August 29, 1865.
10. Henry Cleveland, *Alexander H. Stephens, in Public and Private*, 674, 694, 804.

tion, while the other had encouraged secession, remained adamant in his refusal to ask for clemency, and did little or nothing toward solving the problems of reconstruction.

On October 10, 1865, the New York *Tribune* suggested "that the influence of such men as Stephens and Reagan was too valuable to be longer compressed within four stone walls. They ought to be at liberty," the paper asserted, "because the country has urgent need of their aid in correcting and enlightening Southern opinion." The next day the two men were paroled to their respective states.

JOHN ARCHIBALD CAMPBELL

The Confederate Assistant Secretary of War, Judge John A. Campbell, also deserves special consideration. In fact, if space permitted, a considerable chapter might well be given to efforts to secure his pardon. He had resigned from the United States Supreme Court in May, 1861, after having been a member of that tribunal since March, 1853, and had immediately begun the practice of law in New Orleans. A year later he went to Virginia to rejoin his family, members of which had remained in the East for educational advantages. In the autumn of 1862, however, he accepted the position of Assistant Secretary of War under James A. Seddon in Davis's Cabinet, and served in that capacity until the end of the Confederacy.

Early in May, 1865, Campbell applied for special pardon under Lincoln's proclamation. While his application was under consideration he remained at home under the surveillance of General Halleck. This precaution was due to a "strong impression" in the North that his "conduct after the capture of Richmond was not fair or candid; and that he labored as far as he dared to keep the rebellion alive." Moreover, according to Stanton, evidence was soon found in the Confederate records which made it advisable that he "be placed in strict confinement." It appears that the former United States Supreme Court judge was first placed in Libby Prison, but, on General Halleck's recommendation, he was removed in a few days to Fort Pulaski as a more suitable place for his imprisonment.[11]

In reality, Campbell deserved more favorable consideration than imprisonment, but, of course, the Federal authorities could not ap-

11. *Offic. Rec.*, 2 Ser., VIII, 550, 551, 562, 567, 570, 576, 583.

preciate that until much later. He had not only served the Confederacy with increasing unwillingness as time passed, but he had also sought to hasten the termination of hostilities, especially after the Hampton Roads conference early in February, 1865, where he and others met Lincoln and Seward in the interest of peace. He had remained in Richmond after Lee's evacuation to cooperate with the Federal authorities in restoring Virginia to her proper place in the Union. He had conversations on that subject with Lincoln in the city early in April, receiving from the President a memorandum, which he interpreted too liberally as containing plans and procedure for the state's restoration. In fact, he believed that Lincoln had implied in the conversations that a "universal amnesty would be granted if peace were now concluded."[12]

Not long after his confinement in Fort Pulaski, Campbell renewed his application for pardon. This time he had his son-in-law, Colonel George W. Lay, prepare a memorial to the President from "a blurred and unsigned original in his own handwriting."[13] Campbell's two long petitions for clemency are especially interesting because of the high Federal judicial position the prisoner had held, because of his early vigorous opposition to secession and his later serious efforts at conciliation, and because of his apparent desire to show that he had served the Confederacy only half-heartedly. He stated that he did not resign from the Supreme Court to aid the rebellion, and that he had administered his Confederate office, which was of a judicial character, in such manner as to exempt many persons from military service and to lessen the "severities of the war" to others. In fact, he wanted to make it clear that his office and services had had nothing to do with the activities of the armies, but

12. *Ibid.*, 1 Ser., XLVI, pt. 3, pp. 655-57. For details concerning Campbell's misinterpretation of Lincoln's intentions, see *ibid.*, 595, 612, 724, 725; Henry G. Connor, *John Archibald Campbell . . .* , 188-92; *Dictionary of American Biography*, III, 458-9. Cf. Eckenrode, *Political History of Virginia during the Reconstruction*, 28; and Randall, *Lincoln and the South*, 128-32, for a justification of Campbell. See also Lewis, *Sherman, Fighting Prophet*, 540-48.

13. The "blurred and unsigned original" was evidently Campbell's rough copy of his application in May, for the two petitions in the Amnesty Papers for Alabama contain many similar statements. See J. W. DuBose, *The Life and Times of William Lowndes Yancy*, 689 ff., for a good account of Campbell's opposition to secession in 1861 and the criticism of him in the South resulting therefrom.

that his duties were of a peaceful nature as nearly as possible. He also said that his work was "irksome" and "uncongenial," and that he had offered to resign three times; but Davis had urged him to remain, since his services could not be dispensed with.

In this connection it might be noted that Campbell wrote Benjamin R. Curtis on July 20, 1865, that Davis had erred seriously in not encouraging his recommendations for peace after the Hampton Roads conference. "The idiosyncrasy of one man," he complained, "defeated the design to treat for a settlement of the war. . . . The result is that each citizen of the Confederacy is making his separate treaty on the basis of President Johnson's merciful amnesty policy." Campbell stated further that he did not believe that Davis had had any part in the plot to slay Lincoln, but he did say that the Confederate President was "unfitted to manage a revolution or to conduct an administration."[14]

Campbell made it very plain in his petition for pardon that he was never an adviser of the Confederate President, and stated that he "had only six conversations with him" after October 2, 1862. Three of these concerned the peace conference early in 1865, one pertained to his proffered resignation, and the two others were occasioned by the absence of Secretary Seddon. He quoted from a long letter that he wrote to Associate Justice Samuel Nelson, in December, 1864, commending Nelson's plan of conciliation in 1861 and suggesting communications between himself, Judge Nelson, and others, and finally a conference, which would have been likely to promote "an exchange of views and opinions that might" have been productive of good. Apparently, he regretted Nelson's failure to answer this letter and to comply with its suggestions. He believed, however, that the Federal confiscatory legislation of 1862 and the Emancipation Proclamation a little later had multiplied the obstacles to a settlement of the differences between the sections and had prolonged the war.[15]

The petitioner denied any suspicion of an alleged plot to slay President Lincoln or any other officials of the United States. His

14. See *Century Magazine*, XXXVIII (1889), 905-54. Cf. Clifford Dowdey, *Experiment in Rebellion*, passim.

15. See *Offic. Rec.*, 2 Ser., VIII, 838-49, for this letter and the significance which Judge-Advocate-General Joseph Holt gave it.

denial was occasioned by a current newspaper account of a letter said to have been found in the Confederate archives, written by one Lieutenant W. Alston, proposing an interview with President Davis to plan to abduct President Lincoln. The letter appeared to have received Campbell's endorsement before it was referred to the Adjutant General's office for further consideration. Campbell asked in his first message to the President that the records be examined to determine the facts in the case. In due time General Samuel Cooper, Confederate Adjutant General, reported that he had never seen the original or heard of it until asked to investigate the subject. Furthermore, he stated that such endorsements of papers received from the War Department as Campbell was said to have made on Alston's letter were "never understood as implying sanction or demanding report of their contents."[16] This matter, therefore, was evidently disposed of satisfactorily.

Naturally there were many persons who supported Campbell's plea for clemency. Early in June, former Governor William A. Graham of North Carolina told the President that during the war he had conversed repeatedly with the former Federal judge "on the subject of . . . reunion with the United States"; and ex-Confederate Senator Allen T. Caperton of West Virginia attested to Campbell's early belief that the Confederacy would prove to be abortive. Caperton also stated that the former Federal jurist had administered his office under Seddon in such manner as to mitigate the severities of the war. Others gave similar testimony to Campbell's conduct.

Honorable Thomas Ewing, father-in-law of General William T. Sherman, wrote that Campbell was largely responsible for saving the public offices in Washington from control by the enemies of the government during the winter of 1860-61. Campbell, it appears, told Ewing of the danger from "a combined movement of the clerks within and the Knights of the Golden Circle without"; and General Winfield Scott, on being informed of the situation, forthwith applied to Secretary of War John Floyd for a sufficient force to pre-

16. Amnesty Papers, Alabama (General Samuel Cooper to Colonel George A. Lay, June, 1865). Colonel Lay reported the findings of General Cooper in his memorial to the President. The Alston letter had been reported found in accumulating evidence against Lincoln's assassins.

vent the movement from materializing. Floyd refused the request, and consequently Scott called personally on the President for "the means of defense or a discharge from his duty." Troops were promptly supplied by bringing in a thousand men from Fort Washington. Ewing said further: "That the city was not captured at that time I think we owe to Campbell as fully and absolutely as we owe to Stanton that it was not surrendered to the Rebels by the President and Cabinet a few days later."[17]

Many other noted persons recommended Campbell's release from prison. Perhaps the most able pleas for clemency were made by the distinguished lawyers and brothers, George Ticknor and Benjamin Robbins Curtis. The latter had served on the Supreme Court with Campbell until his resignation soon after dissenting in the Dred Scott decision. One hundred and twenty-eight members of the bar of Louisiana, and even the Society of Dunkards of North Carolina, recommended clemency. People of Alabama were also active in his behalf, and a citizen of Philadelphia emphasized Campbell's failing health and advised liberation.[18]

Mrs. Campbell wrote that she feared imprisonment would impair her husband's health, and stressed the necessity of his "freedom for the protection and support of his family, upon whom the pressure of the times" was very heavy. She and her daughter, Mrs. Henrietta Lay, had previously visited the President in seeking clemency for the husband and father. Late in July, the daughter wrote the distinguished journalist, Thurlow Weed, a long letter in her father's behalf, stating that it had been intimated by high authority that Seward was her father's enemy because of "some statements of Judge Campbell's on political matters in 1861," and stood, therefore, in the way of his freedom. She said, however, that she gave no credence to the report, since Seward was "incapable of mean revenge."[19]

Perhaps Mrs. Lay was somewhat mistaken in her estimate of Seward's attitude toward her father. Secretary Welles stated that the

17. Amnesty Papers, Georgia (letter written by Ewing on June 29, 1865, in the interest of clemency for Campbell and Alexander H. Stephens).
18. *Ibid.*, Alabama.
19. Johnson Papers, LXXV (Mrs. Campbell to Johnson, September 2, 1865); Amnesty Papers, Alabama (Henrietta Campbell Lay to Thurlow Weed, July 29, 1865).

prisoner's condition was discussed in a full Cabinet meeting on July 11, while Campbell's petition to be released from imprisonment was being considered. Seward, he said, advised against Campbell's immediate release and declared the former Supreme Court Justice to be "a fool," who "lacked common sense and had behaved singularly." Welles stated further that he himself said that Campbell, as a judge of the highest court in the land, "had failed in his duty at a critical moment, that he was the only judge on that bench that had been recreant and a traitor, and [that] he would be one of the last" to recommend him for pardon. The other members of the Cabinet agreed with Welles, "and some were even stronger" in their statements.[20] Thus Campbell was not liberated until Reagan and Stephens were released, and his pardon remained in abeyance much longer.

The Confederate Secretary of the Treasury, Christopher G. Memminger of South Carolina, waited until December 4, 1865, before applying for pardon. Two months earlier he had written the President a long letter discussing the status of the freedmen and offering a solution for the problem occasioned by freeing the slaves. He said nothing at this time about a pardon.[21]

Memminger had served the Confederacy till June, 1864, resigning when his financial program failed to receive the support of the Confederate Congress. Having no official connection with the Confederacy thereafter, he was not arrested and imprisoned as others were after the fall of the Confederacy. Nevertheless, his wealth and his earlier official connection with the Confederate government caused him to be excepted from the President's general amnesty. Moreover, his fine mansion in Charleston had been appropriated by the Freedmen's Bureau for use as a home for colored orphan children. The desire to cause the return of this property and to regain his former rights and privileges of citizenship finally influenced him to apply for clemency. It is interesting to note also that he had just received

20. Welles, *Diary*, II, 330. The two other judges on the Supreme Court from the seceded states were John Catron of Tennessee, who served from 1837-1865, and John M. Wayne of Georgia, who served from 1835-1867.
21. For this letter (November 27) see Henry D. Capers, *The Life and Times of C. G. Memminger*, 373-78, cited hereafter as Capers, *C. G. Memminger*.

a letter from General Robert E. Lee expressing hope that his house at Charleston would soon be restored, and "that a new field of usefulness" would be opened to him. This message probably encouraged him to apply for pardon without further delay. Moreover, there was evidence as time passed that Johnson was becoming more lenient in dealing with the Confederates, and Memminger now had good reason to hope for favorable consideration.

The former Confederate Treasurer's petition is interesting because of the consistency with which the author adhered to the doctrine of states' rights even in applying for pardon. He reminded the President that his earnest convictions had caused him to support South Carolina in her effort to separate from the Union. His state, he said, had asserted, in 1834, "the doctrine that paramount allegiance was due her," and by a constitutional amendment had "required a corresponding oath from her citizens." This oath he had repeatedly taken as a state official. Moreover, in 1851, another convention had asserted the state's "right to secede from the Union, and in 1860 that assertion" had been "practically put in operation by an ordinance of secession." Then again, in 1865, after the failure of the effort at independence, the state, by still another convention, had "repealed this ordinance and resumed her place in the Union." And that was not all, for by a change in her constitution South Carolina had "receded from the position taken in 1834 and 1851," thereby relieving "her citizens from the conflicting duties of obedience to the Federal and State authorities." The consistent thing for Memminger to do, therefore, was, as he said, to proffer "his submission to the authorities of the United States" in the "same sincerity and conviction of duty which had hitherto governed him."[22]

Memminger's memorial was recommended by many prominent persons, including Governor Benjamin F. Perry of South Carolina and former Governors Peter D. Vroom and Charles S. Olden and Governor Joel Parker of New Jersey. Pending consideration of the petition, friends made efforts to secure the restoration of the petitioner's home in Charleston. The Freedmen's Bureau, however, remained in control, and there was no prospect of return until the owner was pardoned.

22. Amnesty Papers, South Carolina; also Capers, *C. G. Memminger*, Ch. VIII.

Johnson began pardoning men in Memminger's class late in 1866. George A. Trenholm, who succeeded Memminger as Secretary of the Confederate Treasury, was pardoned on October 25, 1866. On June 14, 1865, he had been arrested near Columbia, South Carolina, and confined in the Charleston jail. Stanton soon frustrated an attempt to parole the ailing prisoner to the healthful environments of the city, and ordered him sent to Fort Pulaski, near Savannah. Like other distinguished Confederates in that prison he made satisfactory submission to the authority of the United States and soon applied for clemency. Believing that conditions in the Southern states justified the prisoner's relief from close custody, the President paroled Trenholm to South Carolina on October 11. It was a little more than a year later, however, before he was fully pardoned.[23]

Early in November, 1866, Memminger wrote Seward that he understood that others of like prominence had already been pardoned and urged favorable action on his own case, emphasizing the dire need of recovering his property in Charleston and resuming the legal profession as a means of livelihood. Seward, Stanbery, and others soon recommended pardon, which was granted on December 19, 1866. Early the next month Memminger's property was ordered restored, but on condition that the former Confederate treasurer relinquish "all claims against the United States for damages" done while it was used by the Freedmen's Bureau.[24]

MALLORY, YULEE, AND ALLISON

On the evacuation of Richmond, the Secretary of the Confederate Navy, Stephen R. Mallory, fled southward with President Davis. At Washington, Georgia, however, he left Davis's party and went to his family at Lagrange, Georgia, where he was arrested late in May and soon imprisoned in Fort Lafayette, New York Harbor. On June 21, he applied for pardon, declaring his opposition to secession in any form during his ten years in the United States Senate, and calling on both Johnson and Seward, who had been his colleagues in the Senate, to testify to his loyalty. He stated further that his

23. *Offic. Rec.*, 1 Ser., XLVII, pt. 2, pp. 647-48, 52; 2 Ser., VIII, 664, 763. Cf. A. J. Hanna, *Flight into Oblivion*, 191, 239, 249.
24. Amnesty Papers, South Carolina; Capers, *C. G. Memminger*, Ch. VIII.

retirement from Congress late in January, 1861, "on the command of the [secession] convention" of Florida, "was the most painful" experience of his life, and that he could in no wise "be regarded as a leader of secession."[25]

In his petition for clemency, Mallory also claimed to have exerted himself before his resignation from the Senate to facilitate a reconciliation between the North and the South. Dreading the horrors of civil war, he had remonstrated against an attack on Fort Pickens in Pensacola Bay by "armed bands of Alabamians and Floridians" and had thus averted "a dire calamity." For this interference and his opposition to disunion he had "endured the bitter hostility of leading men" in his state. He further stated that he accepted the office of Secretary of the Confederate Navy only after "repeated and urgent requests" by President Davis. A year later he had offered to resign, but Davis had refused to accept his resignation. Evidently to strengthen his plea for clemency, Mallory also expressed the opinion that at its beginning the Confederacy "contained the fruitful elements of its own destruction," which, "as the will of Almighty God," he had come to accept "as decisive of the question of slavery and secession." He closed his petition by denying any responsibility of the Confederate Cabinet for alleged inhuman treatment of Federal prisoners. On the contrary, he claimed for himself "acts of kindness and consideration" to such men whenever possible.[26]

The case of former United States Senator David Levy Yulee was connected somewhat with that of Mallory and may properly be considered here. Like Mallory, Yulee had heeded the instruction of his state and had resigned his seat in the Senate (January 21, 1861), but, unlike Mallory, he had retired to his home in Florida, where he remained in private life during the war. Nevertheless, he was arrested in June, 1865, and confined in Fort Pulaski, from which he soon (June 24) sent the President an application for pardon. He feigned surprise at his arrest and detention, since he had not "been connected with the civil or military action of the Confederate Gov-

25. For Mallory's arrest and imprisonment see *Offic. Rec.*, 1 Ser., XLIX, pt. 1, pp. 369, 379, 571, pt. 2, pp. 883, 902, 923, 927; 2 Ser., VIII, 577, 640, 652, 720. Mallory had been a member of the Committee on Naval Affairs in the United States Senate, where he had served from 1851 to 1861.

26. *Ibid.*, 2 Ser., VIII, 662-64.

ernment" and had left Congress only on the demand of his state and "not 'to aid the rebellion.' " Yulee also denied having done anything to encourage secession, though he had sympathized with the "feelings" of the "wronged section" of the country and approved the action of his "state as a social and political necessity and duty." Moreover, he claimed particularly not to have done anything while a United States Senator to encourage secession.[27]

General Israel Vogdes, of Jacksonville, Florida, forwarded Yulee's petition to the President on July 11, saying that from conversations with Yulee and others he inferred that the petitioner "belonged to the peaceful secession party, and was bitterly opposed to any resort to arms, desiring [instead] to have the question of secession settled by the courts or by a general convention to amend the Constitution. . . ." He stated further that Yulee had lived quietly at home during the war, refusing all offers of office under the Confederates. The General believed that the President would not regret having extended clemency to Yulee, whom he would find to be "a peaceable and law-abiding citizen." This recommendation had no effect, for Stanton and Johnson refused, at the time, even to release the man from prison.[28]

Throughout the summer and autumn of 1865 efforts were made to obtain pardons for Mallory and Yulee and especially their parole from prison. In due time Provisional Governor William Marvin of Florida recommended their pardon, and finally, on November 7, Secretary Stanton asked Judge-Advocate Joseph Holt to report on the desirability of approving Marvin's recommendation. Holt, a loyal Kentuckian, had become very active in accumulating evidence against Jefferson Davis, Clement C. Clay, and many other leading Confederates, and in a little more than two weeks he was ready with evidence from the archives of Washington and Florida to show why Mallory and Yulee should be denied clemency. In fact, his experience as Secretary of War from January 1 to March 4, 1861, and as Judge-Advocate-General of the army after September 3, 1862, had given him an opportunity to observe pretty closely

27. *Ibid.*, 668-71. Yulee had also been a member of the Senate Committee on Naval Affairs. Senator Yulee had wide railroad interests, which, according to some, appear to have lessened his earlier belief in secession and doubtless caused him to retire to private life in 1861.

28. *Ibid.*, 702, 703.

what transpired in Washington during his incumbency in these positions. He had also been Postmaster-General under Buchanan.

Holt positively denied the claims of Mallory and Yulee that they had not encouraged secession while United States Senators. He told Stanton that on January 9, 1861, he had declined to furnish them information which they had requested seven days earlier concerning the strength of the garrisons in Florida. Such detailed information had been prepared by the Captain of Ordinance and sent to Holt to be given to Mallory and Yulee. Moreover, Holt offered two letters written by Yulee on January 5 and 7 advising General Joseph Finegan of Florida to hasten the organization of the state to oppose forces of the United States, while he remained in Washington to help defeat legislation which might be passed to "put Mr. Lincoln in immediate condition for hostilities." Yulee also proposed to keep Buchanan's hands tied until the fourth of March. This action was in conformance with resolutions Mallory, Yulee, and ten other Senators, including Jefferson Davis, Robert Toombs, and Clement C. Clay, had signed on January 4, recommending secession and the organization of the Confederacy by February 15, 1861.[29]

During these first days of the new year Mallory and Yulee telegraphed Governor Madison S. Perry of Florida that Federal troops were to be sent to unoccupied Pensacola forts and urged action to prevent such occupancy. On January 7, Florida and Alabama troops seized Fort Marion and the arsenal at St. Augustine, and five days later Forts Barrancas and McRee and the navy yard at Pensacola suffered the same fate. The attitude of the Senators toward the occupancy of Fort Pickens on St. Rose Island in Pensacola Bay soon changed. On January 18, Mallory joined several others, including Davis and Clay, in advising Governor Perry that nothing of the sort should be done; and two days later Yulee joined Mallory in telling Perry that "no assault should be made" on Fort Pickens, since its possession would not be worth the cost and since the human

29. *Ibid.*, 1 Ser., I, 349, 351, 442-44; 2 Ser., VIII, 862-66; McPherson, *Reconstruction*, 391-92. In sending a copy of the resolutions to General Finegan, who was a member of the Florida secession convention, Yulee wrote: "I shall give the enemy a shot next week before retiring. I say *enemy!* Yes, I am theirs, and they are mine. I am willing to be their masters, but not their brothers." *Offic. Rec.*, 1 Ser., I, 442-43.

sacrifice necessary might be fatal to their cause.[30] The next day (January 21) the Florida Senators retired from Congress. Apparently Mallory and Yulee determined to use peaceful tactics in dealing with Buchanan's administration until more progress could be made in promoting secession. On January 29, the President yielded to Southern pressure and receded somewhat from his earlier decision to strengthen Fort Pickens. In fact, there developed what has been called the "Fort Pickens Truce." Though the defense was finally strengthened by Lincoln and though a considerable Confederate army was assembled at Pensacola, fighting in that vicinity did not occur again until late in 1861. By that time Pickens was strong enough and otherwise protected by Union ships to prevent Pensacola Bay from ever being controlled by the Confederates.[31]

Thus Mallory and Yulee felt that some consideration, or credit, should be given them for causing the Confederates to refrain from attacking Fort Pickens early in 1861 when they might have taken it. Vindictive Joseph Holt felt otherwise. With the spirit of a prosecuting attorney, determined to secure the conviction of an accused criminal before the bar, he likened the two men to the Roman senator, "Catiline, whose name is a synonym for infamy," and earnestly recommended that they be tried for treason as soon as possible.[32] Yet, when the evidence against them is considered, he can hardly be blamed. They had denied, in their petitions for pardon, that they had plotted secession while in the United States Senate. Holt had found conclusive evidence to the contrary. They also claimed undeserved credit for the failure of Southern troops to attack Fort Pickens.

Governor Marvin also included Abraham Allison in his recommendation for the pardon of Mallory and Yulee. Allison's case, as Holt observed, differed considerably "from those of Yulee and Mal-

30. *Ibid.*, 1 Ser., I , 444, 445.
31. See William Watson Davis, *The Civil War and Reconstruction in Florida*, Chs. IV, V, for a good account of the "conspiracy" of Southern Senators at Washington, in December and January, 1860-61, and the occupation of Federal forts, etc., in Florida.
32. *Offic. Rec.*, 2 Ser., VIII, 862-66. Cf. Dowdey, *Experiment in Rebellion*, 71-2.

lory, in that he was not a member of Congress or so conspicuous in his treason as they were." On April 1, 1865, the war-time Governor of Florida, John Milton, committed suicide. Allison, being president of the state senate, became *ex officio* Governor of the state, and, in compliance with the state's constitution, proclaimed an election to choose a successor to Milton. He also called a meeting of the legislature and contemplated sending commissioners to Washington to assist in restoring order in the state. The local Federal military authorities, however, objected to his plans, which he abandoned forthwith. Nevertheless, he was arrested and confined in Fort Pulaski early in May, and soon applied for clemency.[33]

In applying for liberation and pardon, Allison stated his belief that his condition did not come within the President's ninth exception relating to the governors of the seceded states. He considered instead that his political status had been simply that of president of the Florida state senate, which should put him in the class benefited by the amnesty. He pledged his loyalty to the government and his disposition to acquiesce in the new order of things, and reaffirmed his resolution not "to exercise the function of Acting Governor of Florida."[34]

On August 5, Governor Marvin requested that Allison be released from prison while his application for pardon was under consideration, so that he might assist in restoring order in Florida. A month later the prisoner's son, Charles E. S. Allison, offered to become "a hostage for the good conduct of his father," if his act would "relieve the government of any embarrassment in granting the pardon." On October 6, Allison reminded the President again of his application and enclosed a second letter in his behalf from Governor Marvin. Though anxious to return home to his family, he stated that he was neither ill nor an invalid, and that he was being "kindly and humanely treated."[35] Marvin recommended his pardon again on October 22 with a plea for Mallory and Yulee; but, as has

33. *Offic. Rec.*, 2 Ser., VIII, 769, 862; Amnesty Papers, Florida; W. W. Davis, *The Civil War and Reconstruction in Florida*, 333-36.

34. The Amnesty Papers for Florida show that Allison first applied for pardon at Jacksonville on June 18, 1865, and that four days later he petitioned again.

35. *Ibid.*

been stated above, Holt included Allison in his unfavorable report on the other two men a month later. Nevertheless, Allison was finally paroled to Florida on January 20, 1866, and was apparently pardoned nine months later (October 19).[36]

The condemning evidence against Mallory and Yulee that they had encouraged secession while in the United States Senate apparently caused them to be detained in prison a while longer than Allison. They were paroled late the following March (1866), after General Grant had interceded for the release of Yulee.[37] Many persons continued to petition for the pardon of the two men. In May, 1867, eighty-one prominent citizens of Connecticut, including several members of the state's legislature, requested Mallory's pardon.[38] Mallory himself wrote other letters to the President and to persons who might influence Johnson in his behalf; and Governor Marvin, who had been Mallory's law partner for a time, continued his efforts to influence Johnson. Finally, on September 14, 1867, Seward addressed a letter to Attorney-General Stanbery recommending clemency, and the next day the President granted the request. Apparently Yulee had already been pardoned.

CLEMENT C. CLAY

The cases of Clement C. Clay and Jefferson Davis might well be considered together. A long chapter, however, will be devoted later to Davis, while a much briefer account here will suffice for Clay.

The Alabamian was a typical secessionist, who had been expelled from the United States Senate in March, 1861, and soon thereafter elected to the Confederate States Senate. As a member of the secret commission sent to Canada in 1864 to aid the Confederacy from that quarter, he was charged with serious offenses contrary to the laws of war. The Bureau of Military Justice also charged him with

36. *Offic. Rec.*, 2 Ser., VIII, 870.
37. See *ibid.*, 893, 895, for Yulee, and *Appleton's Cyclopedia of American Biography*, IV, 184, for Mallory. Cf. *Dictionary of American Biography*, XII, 224-25; XX, 638.
38. Amnesty Papers, Florida.

encouraging the assassination, and the President had offered $25,000 for his arrest.[39]

Unlike Davis, Clay voluntarily surrendered to the Federal authorities as soon as he learned that he was wanted for alleged complicity in the assassination of Lincoln. He and Mrs. Clay were in the party of captives, including the Davises, who were taken in the "Clyde" to Norfolk, Virginia, where Clay and Davis were placed in Fortress Monroe on May 22, 1865. The men were securely confined in separate cells and at once subjected to the closest surveillance, which in itself was punishment. One of the many regulations provided that a light be kept burning in each room at night, so that the guards would always have the prisoners in view. The officer on guard was also to observe the presence of the prisoners every fifteen minutes. Moreover, General Nelson A. Miles, in charge of the Fortress, was authorized to "place manacles and fetters upon the hands and feet of" the prisoners whenever he thought it advisable. The next day this humiliating and needless precaution was partially applied to Davis by fettering his ankles, an indignity which the prisoner "violently resisted," so Miles reported. Five days later Stanton ordered the shackles removed and requested the cause for such action.[40]

Clay was never treated so harshly, but the close confinement, the constant burning of a light in his room, and the eternal presence and vigilance of the guards were very irritating. He soon complained, and, in consideration of his poor health and his voluntary surrender, General Miles recommended, on June 17, that the guards be posted outside the grated doors of the prisoner's cell. About ten days later this change was made, and Clay was also allowed to exercise in the open air after giving his parole of honor not to try to escape. At the same time, Miles said of Davis: "The case of the other prisoner is different, as I think him to be as strong now as he was the day he entered the fort." In October, however, both Davis and Clay and also John Mitchell, editor of the Richmond *Examiner*, were given more comfortable quarters in the fortress,

39. *Offic. Rec.*, 1 Ser., XLIX, pt. 2, p. 566; and 2 Ser., VIII, 696-98, 847-61, 867-69, 890-92, 931-45.
40. *Ibid.*, 2 Ser., VIII, 563-66, 570-71, 577. See also *Jefferson Davis, A Memoir*, II, 655-64.

where they awaited further consideration. Mitchell had been placed in Fortress Monroe in June, but on October 31, 1865, he was liberated on promising to leave the country, never to return except by permission of the Secretary of State.[41]

During the five months prior to Clay's transfer to "Carroll Hall," Mrs. Clay worked incessantly to obtain some amelioration of her husband's condition. In her *Belle of the Fifties* she left a full account of her unceasing efforts to get Clay out of prison.[42] During the first three months of his imprisonment she received information about him only from General Miles. Not until August 20 did Clay receive his first letter from his wife. He replied immediately, giving a favorable description of his quarters and treatment. Evidently he desired to relieve his wife's anxiety over his welfare and also to satisfy or deceive the censors of his letter, for he had already begun a long serial paper to be delivered to Mrs. Clay in the event of his death in prison. He concluded it on October 16 and sent it to her by trustworthy guards. The communication could hardly have been delivered before his transfer to "Carroll Hall," and the ill effects of its melancholy contents were surely softened by the knowledge of his recent assignment to more desirable quarters.

Not only did Clay tell his wife of the horrors of Fortress Monroe, but he also advised her what to do if he died in prison. Seeing no likelihood of future profit from their property in Alabama, he advised her to go where there were not so many Negroes. The inclusion of his views on public affairs suggests that he desired others to know what he still believed. He declared that he had not changed his "opinion as to the sovereignty of the States" and the right of secession, and that the sudden liberation of four million slaves was "one of the most terrible calamities that ever befell any people." He then expressed the ominous opinion that the Negroes of the South would be as oppressed and afflicted as the Jews of other

41. *Offic. Rec.*, 2 Ser., VIII, 657, 673, 715-17, 725, 746, 755, 756-59, 761, 767, 775, 782.

42. This effort was rewritten and published in 1905 by Miss Ada Sterling as *A Belle of the Fifties; Memoirs of Mrs. Clay, of Alabama, Covering Social and Political Life in Washington and the South, 1853-66*, cited hereafter as *A Belle of the Fifties*. See also "The Clays of Alabama: Two Generations in Politics," cited hereafter as Ketring, "Clays of Alabama," a doctor's thesis prepared in 1934 for Duke University by Ruth Anna Ketring (Nuermberger).

lands had been. Had he foreseen all this, he would have been willing to endure lesser wrongs from the North until a more favorable time for separation, since the effort was certain to be made. He believed delay would have given time for such preparation as would have ensured independence.[43]

Mrs. Clay proved to be her husband's greatest advocate in urging his petition for liberation. Clay had hardly entered Fortress Monroe before she placed his case before Judge Holt. Her emotional appeal to him on the grounds of earlier cordial friendship availed nothing. She was more successful in appealing to Benjamin Wood, editor of the New York *Daily News*. He helped her secure the services of George Shea, Charles O'Connor, and Jeremiah Sullivan Black, who were also counsels for Jefferson Davis. As in the case of the President of the Confederacy, Johnson and Stanton at first refused to allow the lawyers to see Clay, informing Black, late in July, that further communication on the subject should be with the Attorney-General.[44]

By this time (July 5) the misguided Bureau of Military Justice, with the aid of vindictive and gullible Judge Holt, had concluded that Clay, Davis, Jacob Thompson, and others had conspired to assassinate Lincoln. In June, 1866, the House of Representatives revealed the fraudulent evidence on which this unfortunate charge was made, but during most of the interval Clay was in prison fearing further punishment. This fear was largely due to, and augmented by, the testimony given during the trial of others charged with the assassination and the convictions and executions resulting therefrom.[45]

Events during the summer of 1865 increased Mrs. Clay's early determination to see the President in behalf of her husband. Many influential persons tried to arrange an interview, but it was not until late in November that she gained the privilege. She stated many years later that Mrs. Stephen A. Douglas accompanied her to the White House and, on her knees, pleaded tearfully with Johnson to permit Mrs. Clay to visit her husband. Mrs. Clay refused Mrs.

43. *A Belle of the Fifties*, 295-99; Ketring, "Clays of Alabama," Ch. X.
44. *Offic. Rec.*, 2 Ser., VIII, 712 (Townsend to Black, July 26, 1865).
45. *Ibid.*, 696-700, 921-23. In the specification, Clay, Davis, Jacob Thompson, and others were charged with encouraging those convicted of the crime. *Ibid.*

Douglas's request that she should entreat the President in like manner, saying later: "I had no reason to respect the Tennessean before me. That he should have my husband's life in his power was [to me] a monstrous wrong, and a thousand reasons why it was wrong flashed through my mind like lightning as I measured him, searing it as they passed. My heart was full of indignant protest that such an appeal as Mrs. Douglas's should have been necessary; but that having been made, Mr. Johnson could refuse it, angered me still more. I would not have knelt to him even to save a precious life." This dramatic scene paralleled Mrs. Davis's interview with the President some months later.[46] Mrs. Davis, however, never visited Johnson again, while Mrs. Clay stated that she went on more than fifty other missions to the White House during the next few months. Often she sought clemency for friends, and in February, 1866, she obtained a pardon for her husband's father, Clement C. Clay, senior.[47]

About the time Mrs. Clay arrived in Washington, Clay wrote to the President setting forth again the merits of his case and asking for immediate trial. The contents of his long, well-written letter suggest the spirit in which many others had petitioned for clemency. He complained of not having received answers to three previous letters, disclaimed any responsibility whatever for the assassination, and denied having been in Canada for nearly six months before Lincoln's murder. He sought freedom until his trial could be arranged, but, if "public interest" required his confinement, he begged to be sent to a prison farther South, where he would suffer less bodily pain on account of cold weather.[48] The letter was of no avail, and Clay remained in Fortress Monroe during the winter of 1865-66.

In December, 1865, Charles O'Conor, Horace Greeley, and others advised Mrs. Clay to secure a trial or a parole for her husband as soon as possible. Obtaining Johnson's permission to visit Clay, she asked Holt for a copy of the report of the Bureau of Military Justice

46. *A Belle of the Fifties*, 302-6, 310-11. See division, "Varina Howell Davis," in Ch. XIII.
47. *A Belle of the Fifties*, 354. This pardon certificate is now in the library of Duke University.
48. See *Offic. Rec.*, 2 Ser., VIII, 812-14, for the entire letter, dated November 23, 1865. Clay's other letters were of June 20, August 19, and October 1, 1865.

on Clay and Davis to take along. She thought her husband should know the nature of the evidence offered the Secretary of War concerning his alleged complicity in the crime. When her request was refused, she borrowed the report from the President and copied it before setting out for the Fortress.[49]

The contents of the document astonished and terrified Mrs. Clay. In it Holt gave the names of several witnesses who had testified to the Bureau, of which he was the head, that Clay and Davis had plotted and encouraged Lincoln's assassination and sanctioned certain other crimes not allowed in civilized warfare. Holt apparently accepted the statements of the witnesses and declared that either the denials of the accused were "utterly false or the body of testimony of all the witnesses who have been enumerated and of others not herein alluded to must be wholly discredited." Then, after emphasizing at length his confidence in the reliability of the evidence, he advised that it was the opinion of his "Bureau that as soon as preparations shall be completed this party [Clay] be brought before a military commission upon charges, not only of complicity in the plot of assassination, but also of violation of the laws of war. . . ."[50]

Mrs. Clay was frightened by what she interpreted as a spirit of malice in Holt's report. On returning it to the President, she entreated him tearfully to give her his solemn oath that he would never yield Clay and Davis "into the hands of that blood-seeking Military Commission" before which the Bureau of Military Justice recommended that they be tried. She stated further that Johnson raised his hand and swore that he would not.[51]

Fortunately, Holt was not President, and Mrs. Clay could take a copy of his report to Stanton on her first visit to Fortress Monroe. Her husband now, some seven months after his imprisonment, learned of the serious charges against him and the fraudulent evidence on which they were based. Of course, the information increased his uneasiness, and he soon sent Mrs. Clay secretly the names of persons who could help her get him out of prison. "Judge

49. *A Belle of the Fifties*, 314-15, 320-21; Ketring, "Clays of Alabama," Ch. X.
50. *Offic. Rec.*, 2 Ser., VIII, 855-61 (Holt to Stanton, December 6, 1865).
51. *A Belle of the Fifties*, 328-29.

Holt," he told his wife, "is determined to sacrifice me *for reasons I have [given you]*. He may do it if I am not allowed liberty to seek witnesses and prepare my defense. . . ."[52]

Neither Clay nor Davis, as it happened, was to be tried before any court; but Clay was more fortunate than Davis, for he was released from prison more than a year before the former Confederate President. Mrs. Clay deserved much credit for the earlier parole of her husband. Had Mrs. Davis beseiged the White House as assiduously as did Mrs. Clay, her husband might have been released sooner. Mrs. Clay had gained an audience with the President, visited her husband, and secured his release nearly five months before Mrs. Davis had obtained even the first two of these privileges. Of course Davis's leadership of the Confederacy, his flight from Richmond, and his obstinacy in refusing to apply for clemency surely contributed to the delay in paroling him from prison. Clay, on the other hand, had occupied a minor position in the Confederacy and had hastened to surrender on learning that his arrest had been ordered, riding 170 miles from Lagrange to Macon, Georgia, to surrender, while others were fleeing from the United States.

Mrs. Clay obtained another interview with the President soon after her first conference with her husband. Her anxiety was so great that she almost overwhelmed Johnson with pleading. The only consolation she received, however, was instruction to prepare a letter for the Cabinet, setting forth her case in detail. This appeal elicited the President's praise, but neither it nor the letter following produced the desired result, even though she postscripted the second message with the plea that her memorial be granted as a "precious gift of *Parole*" on her birthday. Stanton obtained the first of these letters and kept it for weeks, ignoring several requests for its return.[53]

As time passed, Mrs. Clay enlisted influential Northerners in her cause. Late in November, 1865, she had taken a letter to the President from General Grant recommending clemency. Even Thaddeus Stevens denied belief in Clay's complicity in the assassination, and early in March, 1866, Senator Henry Wilson recom-

52. *Ibid.*, 337-38.
53. *Ibid.*, 340-44; Ketring, "Clays of Alabama," Ch. X.

mended the prisoner's release. Mrs. Clay also obtained the support of the statesman-financier, Robert J. Walker, in her campaign. Furthermore, the Northern press, as indicated by the New York *Herald*, began to sympathize with her. Consequently, during a two weeks' visit at the Fortress in March, 1866, she was able to obtain the freedom of the prison without guards for her husband.[54]

Finally Mrs. Clay's faithfulness was rewarded. Her last visit to the White House was on April 17, 1866, when, summoning every worthy art at her command, she cajoled and argued so persistently that Johnson, late at night, ordered Clay's parole from prison. Mrs. Clay immediately telegraphed her husband, and the order was transmitted at once through the War Department to Fortress Monroe. The next day Clay was paroled after taking the oath of allegiance and promising to report for trial if any charges were thereafter preferred against him. He was not required to give bail, however, while more than a year later a bond of $100,000 was posted to guarantee Davis's appearance in court.[55]

The day before Clay's parole the House Judiciary Committee inquired of Stanton to ascertain whether there was "probable cause to believe that any persons named in" the President's proclamation calling for the arrest of Davis, Clay, Thompson, and others were guilty of complicity in the assassination. The committee also desired to know whether any legislation was "necessary . . . to bring such persons to a speedy and impartial trial in the district where such crime may have been committed." No immediate reply from Stanton appears to exist. Apparently, however, the information desired was contained in the reports of Holt to Stanton dated December 6, 1865, and January 18 and March 20, 1866, referred to above.[56] The contents of these papers were further set forth in another communication to Stanton on July 3, 1866, withdrawing certain testimony found to be false by the House Judiciary Committee.

Holt had appeared before that committee and had aided in the review of the testimony offered before the military commission which convicted Lincoln's assassins. Notwithstanding the eliminated

54. *A Belle of the Fifties*, 317; Ketring, "Clays of Alabama," Ch. X; also *Offic. Rec.*, 2 Ser., VIII, 890 (Townsend to Miles, March 19, 1866).

55. *A Belle of the Fifties*, 370 ff.; *Offic. Rec.*, 2 Ser., VIII, 899; Ketring, "Clays of Alabama," Ch. X.

56. *Offic. Rec.*, 2 Ser., VIII, 898-99 and note, also 931-45.

testimony, he asserted that sufficient reliable evidence remained "to show how strongly and impressively the findings of the military commission against Davis, Clay and others" were supported. Evidently, Holt still felt that Davis and Clay should be tried on charges of encouraging the assassination. The House committee, however, reported differently,[57] and no "blood-seeking Military Commission," as Mrs. Clay called it, was ever created to try them. Clay and Davis, being excluded from Johnson's general amnesties and never receiving individual pardons, awaited the President's universal amnesty (December 25, 1868) to absolve them for supporting the Confederacy.

SEDDON AND BRECKINRIDGE

Davis's fourth Secretary of War, James A. Seddon (November, 1862, to January, 1865), had served in the United States House of Representatives and the Confederate provisional congress before accepting a place in the Confederate Cabinet. He was living in retirement at the time of his appointment, and had resigned and retired again to his country estate on the James River when he was arrested, late in May, and placed in Libby Prison. He was soon transferred to Fort Pulaski, where, by June 27, Hunter, Campbell, Magrath, Allison, Yulee, Trenholm, and Clark of Mississippi were also confined. On August 21, Seddon and the other prisoners were allowed the freedom of the island (with a few restrictions), after the eight of them signed a "parole of honor not to attempt, under any circumstances, to leave the post without permission from" the authorities. Three months later (November 23) he and Magrath took the amnesty oath and were paroled to Virginia and South Carolina, respectively.[58]

Seddon was one of those whose pardon came rather late. Perhaps his position for more than two years as Confederate Secretary of War caused delay in favorable action on his application. Stanbery presented his petition to the Cabinet early in October, 1867, stating, according to Welles, that the applicant "had opposed extreme

57. *Ibid.*, 944; *House Report*, No. 104, 39 Cong., 1 Sess.
58. *Offic. Rec.*, 2 Ser., VIII, 566 ff., 723, 724, 815. Campbell, Clark, and Trenholm had been released on October 11. Hunter was released by January 4, Allison on January 20, and Yulee on March 25, 1866. *Ibid.*, 763, 844, 870, 893, 895.

measures" and had done "what he could to mitigate the calamities of war" while in Davis's Cabinet, making "himself unpopular thereby."

Apparently, the discussion was brief. Seward thought a consideration of the petition should be deferred until after the coming November elections. Then, he believed, the pardon might be granted, "for Seddon was a harmless old man and undoubtedly true to the Union." Welles believed that it was "unwise and unjust to continue this proscription," and that the pardon should be granted. "General Grant said very curtly and emphatically that he was opposed to granting any more pardons, for the present, at least." A year or two earlier he had felt different toward the Confederates, Welles confided to his *Diary*, but he had become "pretty strongly committed to the Radicals," and was "courting and being courted." Grant's strong stand, therefore, chilled the others present, and the subject was dropped. Evidently Seward's counsel prevailed, for, soon after the elections, the pardon was granted. Seddon's acknowledgment on November 9 was the 11,378th special pardon accepted by a beneficiary.[59]

John Cabell Breckinridge's experiences before and after the war were most singular. Though himself a candidate for the presidency in 1860, as Vice-President he presided over the joint session of the House and Senate when Congress counted the electoral vote, and announced the election of Lincoln. Having been the candidate of the Southern Democrats, he probably would have been a seceder much earlier if he had lived in the deep South. As it was, he remained a Unionist until rather late in 1861, working for compromise between the two sections and supporting a neutral position of mediation when Kentucky adopted that policy.

Being available, Breckinridge was chosen, early in 1861, to succeed the retiring veteran statesman, John J. Crittenden, in the United States Senate. His term began March 4, so he attended the special session of Congress during the summer of 1861. He strongly

59. Welles, *Diary*, III, 230-31 (October 8, 1867). See also Browning, *Diary*, II, 162. Two volumes marked "Acceptance of Pardons, Amnesty, Department of Justice," now in the National Archives, contain acceptances of pardons under Johnson's proclamation of May 29, 1865.

opposed Lincoln's war measures in the Senate, thereby indicating, perhaps unconsciously, what was to be his ultimate decision to support the Confederacy. One example will suffice. On August 1, he declared Kentucky would have to be represented in the Senate "by some other man" if she abandoned her position as mediator and approved and sustained "the policy of the Federal Administration" in what he believed "to be a war of subjugation and annihilation." Nevertheless, he wanted it known that he was a son of Kentucky and would "share her destiny."[60]

As late as August, 1861, therefore, Breckinridge seemed resolved to stand by the Union if his state cast her lot on that side. John Forney, editor of the Washington *Daily Chronicle*, thought differently, and told the Senator, on the evening of the last day (August 6) of the special session, that he would never sit in the United States Senate again. Breckinridge appeared surprised, and asked Forney what he meant. When told that he would follow his doctrine into the Confederate army, the Kentuckian replied: "If I go over the line it will be to bring back . . . my son Cabell, who has gone into the other army wholly against my will; but we shall meet, if we live, in the winter."[61] The implication was, of course, that he expected to return to the Senate in December.

Forney was right, for Breckinridge found sentiment in Kentucky turning fast (in the newly elected legislature) toward the Union and against him when he went home in August. On September 18, the state abandoned the position of neutrality, and her most distinguished citizen since Henry Clay, fearing arrest, went "over the line" to the Confederate army, but not "to bring back" his son Cabell. At Bowling Green, Kentucky, on October 8, he complied with his state legislature's instructions to resign his seat in the Senate. In doing so, he exclaimed: ". . . I exchange, with proud satisfaction, a term of six years in the Senate of the United States for the musket of a soldier." Early in November the Federal district court at Frankfort indicted him for treason, and, about the

60. Lucille Stillwell, *John Cabell Breckinridge*, 99-100 (quoting much of the speech).
61. Samuel M. Wilson, *History of Kentucky*, II, 356 (using an editorial in the *Daily Chronicle*, headed "The Two Breckinridges," meaning Robert J. and John C.).

same time, Davis commissioned him Brigadier General. Early in December the United States Senate "resolved that the traitor Breckinridge be expelled."[62]

Breckinridge was soon promoted to Major General, and in February, 1865, he succeeded Seddon as Secretary of War. Upon the evacuation of Richmond he fled south, and, when the Federal government refused to treat with the Confederate civil authorities, he escaped to Cuba and thence to England. He soon went to Canada, where his wife joined him. Realizing that England was a safer and more satisfactory place to be in exile, he crossed the Atlantic again. Had he entered the United States he would certainly have been arrested, but his fate would probably have been no worse than that of any other Confederate.[63]

After much travel in the Old World, Breckinridge went to Canada again (June, 1868), where he waited for an opportune time to return home. All along there were expressions of desire that he be pardoned and encouraged to return. On February 10, 1866, seventy members of the Kentucky legislature petitioned the President to pardon him. Horace Greeley expressed the opinion, in April, 1867, that his "presence and counsel" were needed in Kentucky. The city council of Louisville, in January, 1868, urged the Kentucky contingent in Congress to insist that the authorities at Washington permit him to return free to resume his former rights and privileges.[64]

Perhaps Breckinridge would have been better off and Kentucky have profited thereby if he had remained in the United States and endured the consequences. His condition would not have been any worse than that of many other leaders. Even Davis did pretty much as he pleased after his liberation in May, 1867. The Kentuckian

62. Moore, *Rebellion Record*, III, 254-59, for the entire address, which was published for the benefit of the people of Kentucky; also Stillwell, *John Cabell Breckinridge*, 101-9. A short-lived Confederate state government was organized at Bowling Green late in 1861. Cf. E. M. Coulter, *The Civil War and Readjustment in Kentucky*, 118 ff.

63. Hanna, *Flight into Oblivion*, 230 ff., gives a good account of Breckinridge's exciting and hazardous escape to Cuba. Stanton ordered the General's arrest on September 14, 1865, if he returned to the United States. *Offic. Rec.*, 2 Ser., VIII, 747.

64. Stillwell, *John Cabell Breckinridge*, 152-53.

might have returned home as soon as Toombs did (early in 1867) and have made a satisfactory arrangement with President Johnson (see Chapter VIII). But Breckinridge's case was different from that of any other Southern leader. Not only was he from a state that did not actually secede, but he had lingered in the United States Senate until the adjournment of Congress in August, 1861, and had been expelled as a "traitor" by that body in December. Breckinridge may have had some compunctions of conscience as time passed during his exile, and he might be excused for remaining away so long, since he was under indictment for treason. After Davis's release from prison and the increasing evidence of the President's leniency, however, there appears to be no good reason why he should have continued his absence when he was really needed at home. He surely knew that no one had been or was being tried for treason, and indications were that no one ever would be so tried.[65]

Early in December, 1868, General Breckinridge wrote to his friend James B. Beck of Kentucky (later United States Senator) concerning the prospects of obtaining his pardon. Beck, accompanied by Judge L. D. Trimble of Kentucky, interviewed the President on December 11 in the interest of the exile. Johnson was interested and inquired "somewhat eagerly" whether the fugitive had petitioned for pardon. Beck expressed the opinion that the President would have granted the request "then and there" if Breckinridge had already applied for clemency. Beck's long account of this interview contains the salient elements in Breckinridge's case. President Johnson spoke kindly of the Kentuckian and thought he ought to return to the United States at once and apply for pardon. When told that Breckinridge feared arrest if he returned, Johnson stated that he thought there was no danger of that.[66]

65. The late Judge J. W. Cammack of a Kentucky circuit court district told the author, many years ago, that older men who knew General Breckinridge personally had expressed to him the opinion that Breckinridge regretted, during his last years, that he had ever espoused the cause of the Confederacy.

66. James B. Beck to Breckinridge, Washington, D. C., December 11, 1868, Breckinridge Papers, Library of Congress, Vol. 263, No. 17644. Copied by James P. Gregory, Tulane University.

Beck stated that he told the President that Breckinridge had hoped that his pardon would be covered in a universal amnesty, and for that reason he had not petitioned for clemency. Johnson then made it clear that petitioners must be within the jurisdiction of the United States to have their applications considered, and that "deserters and others had frequently applied from Canada and had always been refused, though they had been afterward pardoned as soon as they returned." At this point in the conversation the President expressed concern about Jefferson Davis and informed his visitors "that before the holidays" were over something would "be done in a general way" that would "have a decided influence" on Breckinridge's case. Beck interpreted this to mean a universal amnesty was in the offing and advised his correspondent "to wait until after the holidays to see what" Johnson intended to do.

After leaving the White House, Beck and Trimble called on Francis Blair (in the now famous "Blair House"), to whom they related their interview with Johnson. Beck told Breckinridge that Blair thought he "ought to return to New York at once," so that he might be "in the country when an amnesty" was granted. If Breckinridge did not come that quickly, then he proposed to accompany Beck and Trimble to urge the President to grant the pardon when the exile did return.[67]

Beck's encouraging letter did not cause Breckinridge to return home. Even after the President's universal amnesty on Christmas Day (1868), he still remained away. Evidently he feared that the amnesty did not apply to him since he had not been in the United States when it was granted. Moreover, he apparently did not want any special grace shown him through an interview with Johnson, as Blair had suggested to Beck. Breckinridge waited therefore until he had been assured at Washington that he would not be molested when he entered the United States. He arrived in Lexington, Kentucky, on March 9, 1869, having been given an ovation all the way from the Ohio River, at Covington, to his home in Fayette County.[68] Breckinridge was included in Johnson's universal amnesty.

67. *Ibid.*
68. Stillwell, *John C. Breckinridge.* President Grant favored removing

By January 8, 1867, eighty-six members of the lower house of the Confederate congress, a smaller number of the upper house, and perhaps a dozen Confederate governors had been pardoned.[69] Besides these, there were many others of lower rank among the civil leaders who had sought and obtained special clemency. There were also many whose petitions were under consideration; the general contents of such applications are to be found in this and other chapters. The experiences of the Confederate governors and lieutenant governors after the war and their pardon cases alone would require a chapter. John Milton of Florida (as stated above) committed suicide, April 1, 1865; Pendleton H. Murrah of Texas and Henry Watkins Allen of Louisiana fled to Mexico and died in exile. John J. Pettus of Arkansas fled to the swamps of his state and then, under an assumed name, to his home, where he soon died. But the examination of additional cases, except that of Jefferson Davis, would add very little to the information already obtained from petitions for pardon.

---

the disability under the Amendment from Breckinridge (who died in 1875), but the radical Republicans refused to do it. *Ibid.*, 154.
69. *House Exec. Doc.*, No. 31, 39 Cong., 2 Sess., (January 9, 1867).

CHAPTER THIRTEEN

PARDONING JEFFERSON DAVIS

———◆———

JOHNSON *versus* DAVIS

PERHAPS Jefferson Davis endured more hardships immediately after the Civil War than any other leader of the Confederacy. Indeed, a full account of his arrest and imprisonment, of his indictments for treason and the attempts to try him therefor, of his liberation from prison on bail, and of his final pardon late in 1868 would fill a large volume. A considerable book on the first six months of his life in prison was published in 1866.[1] Only a chapter, however, concerning the efforts to obtain his pardon and release from prison and the opposition thereto, is needed here. Accounts of attempts of the government to bring him to trial have already been well told,[2] the recent description by Dr. Robert McElroy being the most satisfactory.

As has previously been stated, the assassination of Lincoln and the alleged conspiracy of Davis and others in the plot added fuel to the existing indignation in the North against the Southern people, especially their leaders. The authorities at Washington shared this bitterness and sought to bring the President of the late Confederacy and his alleged accomplices to justice. On May 2, 1865, President Johnson, in a proclamation based on what appeared to be

1. Craven, *Davis.*
2. See Judge Charles M. Blackford, *The Trials and Trial of Jefferson Davis*, a pamphlet of some 15,000 words published in 1901; Dr. Roy Franklin Nichols, "United States *vs* Jefferson Davis, 1865-1869," *American Historical Review*, XXXI, 266-84; and Robert M. McElroy, *Jefferson Davis; the Unreal and the Real*, II, Chs. XXVII-XXIX, cited hereafter as McElroy, *Jefferson Davis.*

"evidence in the Bureau of Military Justice," charged Davis with complicity in the assassination and offered a reward of $100,000 for his capture.[3] A little later (May 23) the fleeing President of the Confederacy was arrested and imprisoned in Fortress Monroe, Virginia, where he remained until admitted to bail on May 13, 1867. The reward for his capture was paid, but no indictment for murder was ever returned against him. In fact, the evidence upon which the atrocious charge was made proved to be absolutely fraudulent. Unfortunately, the ill-advised proclamation was never rescinded, but remained a source of irritation to Davis and many others.[4]

It appears that Johnson allowed himself to be unduly influenced by Secretary Stanton and Judge Joseph Holt in issuing this proclamation.[5] Yet it may be said to his discredit that he never did anything to remove the defamation of Davis's character which resulted from his unfortunate act. Subsequently, he could, with good grace and at an opportune time, have expressed his confidence in Davis's integrity and thus disavowed the shameful charge his proclamation carried. Perhaps, under the circumstances, such magnanimity was too much to expect of Andrew Johnson. Indeed, Johnson and Davis were extraordinary persons, whose experiences and fortunes had placed their appreciations and sympathies in entirely different categories. Diverse conditions in life and heated controversies of long duration had driven them far apart. A terrible civil war had left a bloody chasm between them. Such rugged individualities, therefore, could hardly approach any appreciable degree of conciliation during the "Age of Hate" in which they lived.

This estimate of the public relationship between Johnson and Davis is supported by a conclusion of Dr. McElroy, who relates a verbal encounter between the two men in 1846. The occasion was an unfortunate reference to tailors which Davis made in the House of Representatives while supporting a resolution of thanks to General Zachary Taylor for his recent victories in Mexico. In giving credit to West Point for the General's success, Davis "rhetorically

3. Richardson, *Messages . . . of the Presidents,* VI, 307-8.
4. *Offic. Rec.,* 2 Ser., VIII, 921-23, 964-65, 978-80. See *Jefferson Davis, A Memoir,* II, 769-71. Also Dunbar Rowland, *Davis,* VII, 126-29.
5. Milton, *Age of Hate,* 196.

challenged any critic to say whether 'a blacksmith or a tailor could have secured the same results. . . .' " Johnson, who had been a tailor in early life, thought the allusion was intended to ridicule him, and immediately "poured scorn and contempt upon the 'illegitimate, swaggering, bastard scrub aristocracy' of which he declared Davis a member." Davis professed surprise that Johnson had taken his comparison as a personal taunt, and "at once disavowed any intention of personal reference in his remark. . . ." Two days later, in the House, he sincerely apologized again, meticulously explaining "that his sole aim had been to point out 'the results of skill and military science,' and to call attention to the fact that these could not be expected from men without military education."

Apparently Johnson was not appeased. "To the average man," Dr. McElroy states, "this apology would have removed all sense of injury . . .; but in capacity for cherishing hatreds Andrew Johnson was far from average, and he hated Jefferson Davis from that time forth and for evermore, elevating him to the position of the very incarnation of the superiority complex which he always saw in the leaders of the slaveocracy."[6] This is indeed very severe criticism, but if the opinion needed support it might be noted that as late as 1879 Colonel L. B. Northrop wrote Davis that Johnson never forgave him for this reference to a tailor. In reminding Davis of his "haughty and sarcastic style of younger days," Northrop said in part: "You were terrible sometimes. Andrew Johnson never forgave your alluding to his having been a tailor and took his revenge on you at Fortress Monroe."[7] All this and more, therefore, should be kept in mind in considering Johnson's attitude toward Davis and other leaders of the Confederacy.

There is evidence also that Jefferson Davis entertained no liking for Andrew Johnson. Mrs. Davis indicates as much in her account of her husband's first reaction to the startling news that the President had offered a reward for his "capture as accessory to Mr. Lincoln's assassination. I was much shocked," she states, "but Mr. Davis was quite unconcerned, and said, 'the miserable scoundrel who issued that proclamation knew better than these men [his

6. McElroy, *Jefferson Davis*, I, 69-71.
7. Dunbar Rowland, *Davis*, VIII, 378-80 (L. B. Northrop to Davis, April 17, 1879). *Ibid.*, 383, for Davis's answer.

captors] that it was false. Of course, such an accusation must fail at once. . . .' " About the same time, in a conversation with General James H. Wilson, at Macon, Georgia, Davis stated again that "there was one man in the United States who knew that proclamation to be false . . . and that person was the one who signed it, for he at least knew that I preferred Lincoln to himself."[8]

In 1876 Davis again expressed his earlier aversion to Johnson. The occasion was a letter to Crafts J. Wright concerning the story of Davis's alleged complicity in the assassination of Lincoln. The particular item that elicited the criticism of Johnson was a reference to what Davis said when he received a telegram from General Breckinridge announcing Lincoln's death. "The news was to me very sad," Davis wrote, "for I felt Mr. Johnson was a malignant man and without power, or generosity which I believed Mr. Lincoln possessed."[9]

Thus it has been shown that there had long been considerable enmity between Andrew Johnson and Jefferson Davis. Undoubtedly this feeling had some baneful influence on the fortune of the latter until his liberation from prison in May, 1867, and his pardon more than a year later. In the meantime, however, Johnson's earlier bitterness toward Davis appears to have waned somewhat; or the exigencies of later days, at least, made it advisable to adopt a more lenient policy in the treatment of the man who had been President of the Confederacy.

DEMANDS FOR PUNISHMENT

As might have been expected, the ultra-Radicals in the North were influenced by Johnson's serious charges against Davis and the offer of a reward for his capture, and when the Confederate leader was apprehended and placed in prison they exhibited a venomous desire for his punishment. Sometimes their relish for revenge was expressed most diabolically. Perhaps more evidence of such sentiment remains in the Amnesty Papers than elsewhere, for during 1865-66 the President received a hundred or more mes-

8. *Jefferson Davis, A Memoir*, II, 641-44.
9. Dunbar Rowland, *Davis*, VII, 513. See Craven, *Davis*, 96, 97, for a summary of Craven's interpretation of Davis's characterization of Johnson.

sages recommending punishment which ranged from the ridiculous to the inhuman and barbarous. Accusations of murder and treason were hurled at the prisoner, who was often charged with the abuses at Andersonville and Libby prisons. Most of the writers were bent on revenge that called for humiliation and the shedding of blood.

An account of these virulent petitions to the President is not as pleasant to relate as that of the memorials for mercy which follow, but such hatred for Davis existed in the North as surely as there was intense devotion for him in the South. A consideration of the efforts to obtain his pardon, therefore, must include the malevolent demands for his death as well as the most eloquent and earnest prayers for his pardon. Perhaps no person now lives who harbors any ill will toward Jefferson Davis; but history must be related as it was made.

As indicated above, the most violent outbursts of passion and hatred for the fallen leader were manifested in letters to the President during the three or four months following the assassination. Four days after Johnson offered a reward for the capture of Davis, a rope maker of Quincy, Illinois, asked for the privilege of making a rope to hang "the scoundrel," as he called him, "or any of his co-assassins." Even women were thus affected, for the daughter of the man who had built the first ropewalk in Boston sent to Washington a rope which she had made from South Carolina hemp, with "the ardent desire to have it used as soon . . . as proper." Thirty-seven other "daughters of the Bay State" urged the President to have the prisoner hanged, and another petitioner in Pierce County, Wisconsin, advised perpetual imprisonment at hard labor and branding on the forehead with his own name as a "Christian" punishment.[10]

Three men from Massachusetts would have had Davis hanged with the rope used in hanging John Brown; while six others from Paradise, Pennsylvania, recommended "that, as Haman . . . has heretofore, been the standard for hanging, Jefferson Davis be suspended . . . so high that henceforth, Haman may be allowed to rest in peace and the text be 'Hung as high as Jeff. Davis, the great American Traitor.'" And in this hanging business a citizen from

10. Amnesty Papers, Davis.

Danbury, Connecticut, who had suffered much in Andersonville, desired the pleasure of building the scaffold.

Perhaps the most inhuman and ridiculous punishment recommended for Davis was exhibition throughout the country in female attire so that admission might be charged and money raised toward paying the national debt.[11] Other strong protests against pardoning Davis contain similar inhuman recommendations. A citizen of Lafayette, Ohio, offered to purchase the prisoner "from the government for a specific sum with the agreement to pay two millions of the war debt." He proposed to put the recent President of the Confederacy in a cage with a Negro "and show him through the United States at one dollar a sight." A like proposal was made by a little girl of Lawrence, Massachusetts, who also recommended that the leaders of the Confederacy be hanged on the Fourth of July as a national celebration. This unique disposition of Davis on the birthday of the nation was also advised by a citizen of Mt. Zion, Illinois. Another protester would have freed Lincoln's assassins rather than pardon the leaders of the Confederacy, while a grief-stricken mother at Centralia, Illinois, enclosed a photograph of her son, who had suffered at Andersonville and had died soon after his release from prison. She desired that Davis be punished to atone for her boy's death.

Other memorials to the President against Davis were somewhat milder in tone, but insisted that the Confederate leader be punished in order that treason might be made forever odious in the United States. Thirty-five soldiers of Liberty City, Iowa, desired Johnson to use his "influence and official position" to have Davis tried and punished "if found guilty"; while thirty-three citizens of Summit Hill, Pennsylvania, stated that they were "witnesses of his most cruel barbarity" and admonished Johnson not to be influenced by those seeking clemency. Sixty-nine petitioners of Leland, Illinois, believed that a pardon would have a bad effect on the country and

11. *Ibid.* Colonel B. D. Pritchard's report of the capture, which may be found in the archives of the War Department, contains no reference to the prisoner's attire. The fact that Davis was wearing his wife's long rain cape, or shawl, when captured caused some Northerners to ridicule him as though he had purposely tried to escape dressed as a woman. See *Offic. Rec.*, 2 Ser., VIII, 555-69; McElroy, *Jefferson Davis*, II, 510-17; and Dunbar Rowland, *Davis*, VII, 405, 441 n., 443 ff., VIII, 35, 53, 74, 176.

desired Davis tried and punished, if convicted. This sentiment was also expressed in memorials signed by 147 men of Johnson County, Indiana; by 1,000 soldiers of Meadville, Pennsylvania; and by 80 veterans of Council Bluffs, Iowa.

Apparently the most concerted effort to influence the authorities at Washington to punish Davis was made in Indiana. One of Governor Morton's aids at Indianapolis, Major John Hogarth Lozier, wrote a poem entitled "A Protest against the Pardon of Jefferson Davis and other leading traitors and murderers." Copies were used as a petition and signed by some fifteen or twenty thousand "soldiers and citizens of the state. . . ."[12] Its eight stanzas implored the President to inquire of every group of persons, including the dead, who had suffered or who were suffering because of the war, to learn whether the Confederate leader should be punished. The supposition was, of course, that after reviewing the tragedies of the conflict as thus described, he would refuse to pardon Davis. It ended with a personal appeal to the President:

> "Heed no 'petition' framed by hands
> That yesterday had gladly slain thee!
> But rather heed those loyal hands
> Whose lives were periled to sustain thee.
> Heed those poor stricken ones who weep,
> Who but for *him* had not been weeping.
> Heed those who sleep the dreamless sleep,
> Who but for *him* had not been sleeping."[13]

PLEAS FOR CLEMENCY

Meanwhile there was much concern in the South over the prisoner's physical condition and the apparent determination of the Federal authorities to prosecute him for treason. When it was reported that he was in chains and that his health was becoming impaired through lack of proper care and from the foul prison air, anxiety over his condition became intense.[14] This concern was evidenced in numerous memorials to the President imploring clemency,

12. Amnesty Papers, Davis. This number was given by Lozier, but an examination of the petition by the author indicated that ten or twelve thousand was a more nearly correct number.

13. *Ibid.*

14. Craven, *Davis, passim;* also *Jefferson Davis, A Memoir,* II, Chs. LXV-LXXIII.

especially after the announcement of the amnesty proclamation of May 29, 1865, and during the following autumn. Southerners were undoubtedly encouraged by the apparently increasing leniency of the President. Furthermore, it should be remembered that they did not regard themselves as traitors. Nevertheless, their chief civil leader was languishing in prison, from which Johnson at the stroke of his pen could liberate him.

The womanhood of the Confederacy responded nobly to the situation, memorializing the President from hamlets, towns, and cities all over the South. More than seven thousand women of Richmond, Virginia, petitioned for the prisoner's release, and twelve hundred of Scott County, Kentucky, asked Johnson to let "the bloody past bury its dead, and as a seal to its sepulcher, open the prison doors and lead the illustrious Captive forth." Like sentiment was expressed by some two thousand women of New Orleans, who rightly declared that Davis was "no more responsible for initiating the war than hundreds of other public men in the South." They assured the President that a pardon from him "would fill with lasting gratitude the heart of a nation. . . ." Two hundred and thirty "Ladies of the town of Aiken," South Carolina, "humbly but hopefully" approached his "Excellency in behalf of the great, the good and the beloved Jefferson Davis." They said: "Fallen though he be by the fortunes of war, yet our hearts yearn for his deliverance. . . ."[15]

Scores of other petitions of similar content, signed in the aggregate by tens of thousands of persons, were sent to the President. Sometimes the pleas for clemency contained passages from literature and the Bible emphasizing the desirability of showing mercy. Nearly three hundred admirers of Davis in Virginia reminded the President that:

> "The quality of mercy is not strained:
> . It droppeth as the gentle rain from heaven
> Upon the place beneath; it is twice blessed;
> It blesses him that gives and him that takes. . . ."

While Virginians quoted Shakespeare in their plea for executive

15. Amnesty Papers, Davis. Davis wrote Mrs. Davis that the Richmond petition "was not ineffectual, for it refreshed my burdened heart as the shower revives a parched field." Dunbar Rowland, *Davis,* VII, 67.

clemency, more than fourteen thousand Marylanders approached the "throne of grace in the name of Him who hath said 'Blessed are the merciful for they shall obtain mercy' to ask pardon for the illustrious prisoner. . . ."[16]

Perhaps no more pathetic plea was made than the memorial of Virginia and Bessie Davison and more than six hundred and fifty other "Ladies of the Valley of the Shenandoah." These grief-stricken and apparently destitute women of the Old Dominion implored the President to "look over the history of this valley. Remember the trails of fire of Hunter and Sheridan have passed over us. . . . The old and young, the noblest and fairest are hewers of wood and drawers of water. Want and sorrow clasp hands with us everywhere. . . . We are cut off from the sympathies of Christendom, and seemingly forsaken by God himself. In this hour of misery give us, we beseech you, the comfort of seeing Mr. Davis restored to his family. . . ."[17]

Mention of other petitions from the women of the Confederacy is not necessary. Their contents indicate the faithfulness of the supplicants in their support of the Lost Cause and their earnestness in trying to hasten the adoption of a policy which they believed would restore prosperity and happiness to their war-ridden homeland.

The men of the Confederacy also sought to obtain Davis's liberty. One of the most eloquent petitions in behalf of the prisoner was presented by seventy-five pioneers of Texas. Early in October, 1865, these men directed David G. Burnett, the first President of the Texan Republic, to go to Washington to present their petition to the Chief Executive. Their instructions contained a statement of the clemency which they claimed Burnett had exercised in dealing with the Mexican President, Santa Anna, after his capture at San Jacinto in April, 1836. They recounted the cruelties of the Mexicans during the struggle of the Texans for independence and then reminded their spokesman that he had not treated Santa Anna with the "just vengeance" that the latter's atrocious methods of warfare justified.

16. See James S. Jones, *Life of Andrew Johnson*, 331, for comment on this petition.
17. Amnesty Papers, Davis.

Instead of detaining their distinguished prisoner, Burnett and General Houston had discharged him "to return to Mexico without any act derogating [detracting] from his honorable distinction. . . ."[18] The Texans thus emphasized by implication the contrast between their alleged magnanimous treatment of Santa Anna and the present imprisonment of Jefferson Davis, who had for five days been needlessly and cruelly placed in irons.

If Burnett failed in his mission, he was instructed to remain in Washington to aid in the defense of Davis and otherwise endeavor to ameliorate his condition. On October 16, he wrote to President Johnson defending the veneration of "the Pioneers of Texas" for Davis, telling Johnson that Davis's exalted position as President of the Confederacy had been imposed upon him by those who were just as guilty as he. He then asked this pertinent question: "But wherefore impute *guilt* to a political offense by a similitude to which, in all its essential properties, our immediate [Revolutionary] ancestors constituted you and all of us members of a free and independent government? The whole moral difference in the two series of events," Burnett reasoned, "is involved in the one simple fact of failure! . . ."[19]

This favorable comparison of the efforts of the Confederates to the work of the revolutionists of 1776 was ingenious, and equally significant was Burnett's contention that the struggle of the Texans for independence in the 1830's differed from the attempt of the Confederate States at independence only as victory differs from defeat.

An argument similar to that offered by the Texans, that they had as much right to declare their independence in 1861 as they had in 1836, may be found in a speech by Abraham Lincoln before the lower house of Congress on January 12, 1848. Edward Foster of Surrey, England, writing to Andrew Johnson on June 3, 1865, re-

18. *Ibid.* Actually, the Texans had held Santa Anna captive for some eight months, part of that time in irons, after which they sent him to the United States, where he was released in February, 1837, and allowed to return to Mexico. Letter, President Burnett to Captain W. H. Patton, October 8, 1836, museum, San Jacinto Battlefield Monument, Houston, Texas.

19. Amnesty Papers, Davis. The Savannah *Republican* for September 30, 1865, printed the letter.

minded the President of the wholesome effect of the clemency shown the English Chartists in 1848.[20] This prominent Britisher, who had been active in anti-slavery movements in England, then quoted Lincoln as having said:

"Any people anywhere being inclined and having the power, have the *right* to rise up and shake off the existing government, and form a new one that suits them better. This is a most valuable and sacred right—a right which, we hope and believe, is to liberate the world. Nor is this right confined to cases in which the whole people of an existing government may choose to exercise it. Any portion of such people that *can may* revolutionize and make their own of so much of the territory as they inhabit. More than this, a *majority* of any portion of such people may revolutionize, putting down a *minority*, intermingling with, or near about them, who may oppose their movements. Such minority was precisely the case of the Tories of our own Revolution. It is a quality of revolutions not to go by *old* lines, or old laws; but to break up both, and make new ones. . . ."[21]

Jefferson Davis could not have spoken more to the point in supporting the right of the Southern States to secede from the Union. But it should be noted that Lincoln also emphasized the equal right of the majority to coerce the minority, which, in the case of the Civil War, justified the action of the Federal government in putting down the rebellion and maintaining the integrity of the Union. Foster lamented what he regarded as Lincoln's later departure from the position thus taken in discussing the Texan revolution. He expressed the opinion that the war-time President failed to live up to his earlier position in discussing the revolt of Texas from Mexico. The burden of the Englishman's argument, therefore, was that the Confederates should not be treated as traitors.

The able plea of the pioneers of Texas availed nothing toward securing the immediate release of Davis. The petition was merely

20. Six days later, Henry Thompson, an English clergyman, wrote the President that beheading Charles I "was Cromwell's [one] great error, which finally brought ruin upon his party," and warned Johnson that he and his party would ultimately be ruined if he allowed Davis to be executed. He recommended exiling the Confederate President as punishment. Amnesty Papers, Davis.

21. *Ibid.; Congressional Globe*, Appendix, 30 Cong., 1 Sess., 94; Pollard, *The Lost Cause*, 85-86.

filed in Washington with a resolution, passed by their state legislature early in November and addressed to Johnson, invoking clemency for the Confederate leader.

Other states also petitioned for Davis's pardon. Sidney Andrews, a correspondent for the Boston *Advertiser* and the Chicago *Tribune*, left an interesting description of the exciting proceedings of the Georgia reconstruction convention (1865) in passing such a memorial. His detailed account of the long debate suggests what surely took place in other similar groups. Finally, the convention created a committee, which soon reported a petition invoking clemency for Davis "and all others similarly circumstanced." Andrews stated that the petition "was adopted without debate or objection," and that it indicated that the people of Georgia were not likely to fail in their efforts "through any excess of modesty."[22]

The legislature of Georgia met soon after the convention adjourned and transmitted the memorial to Washington. The President was commended for allowing Stephens to return "to the grateful people of his state," and was asked to pardon Davis. The petitioners said further that, though the Confederate President had originally been opposed to the sectional policy to which public opinion had finally driven him, he had become the exponent of their principles and the leader of their cause. In brief, the Georgians claimed the responsibility for Davis's action and claimed for him the "liberal clemency" which the government had already extended to them.

The legislature of Mississippi unanimously adopted a similar petition, which had been signed (but not approved) by nearly all the members of the state's recent convention, asking clemency for Davis. Likewise, the general assembly of Virginia, in December of the same year (1865), recommended "the release of all political prisoners and the restoration of the Habeas Corpus . . . as a solid guarantee of restored peace." The South Carolina reconstruction convention had already, in September, memorialized the President to release Davis, Stephens, Magrath, and Trenholm from prison.[23]

22. Sidney Andrews, *The South since the War; as Shown by Fourteen Weeks of Travel and Observation in Georgia and the Carolinas* (1866), 247-52.

23. Amnesty Papers, Davis; Garner, *Reconstruction in Mississippi*, 151-52; John Porter Hollis, *The Early Period of Reconstruction in South Carolina*, 41.

ARGUMENTS FOR AND AGAINST CLEMENCY

One of the strongest arguments that leniency should be shown Davis and other leading secessionists was that they had merely applied the compact theory of the Federal government advocated by certain distinguished founders of the Republic and subsequently accepted and developed by later prominent statesmen of the nation. Had not Thomas Jefferson and James Madison thus interpreted the Constitution? And had not John C. Calhoun and others further expanded this theory? Davis, therefore, should not be made to suffer for following such learned leadership.

James Chestney of South Carolina was one of many who expressed this opinion. On June 14, 1865, he reminded President Johnson that for a long time the doctrine that treason could not be committed under the sanction of a sovereign state, like any one of the United States, had been taught with much success, especially in the South. He stated that forty years earlier he and others had vainly raised their warning voices against the authority of Jefferson, Madison, Calhoun, and other advocates of states' rights. Consequently, he believed that no secessionist could be justly "tried for treason unless Mr. Jefferson and Mr. Madison be first convicted for leading millions of people into error...."[24]

Perhaps Chestney's thesis was even better stated in Albert Taylor Bledsoe's book, *Is Davis a Traitor; or, Was Secession a Constitutional Right Previous to the War of 1861?* The author explained in the preface that his sole purpose was to discuss the right of secession in such manner as to vindicate the South and dispel the charges of treason against Davis and other leaders of the Confederacy. After admitting that the right of secession no longer existed and that these Southerners may have been misled "by the passions of the hour," he declared that they were loyal to the spirit of the Constitution of 1787.

Bledsoe not only stated that Hamilton and Madison had eloquently recommended the Constitution as a compact among the states, but he also said that such constitutional authorities as Alexis de Tocqueville, Thomas Spence, and Henry Brougham had later adopted the Southern interpretation of the Constitution and pro-

24. Amnesty Papers, Davis.

nounced the American Union a confederation of states. He then wanted to know if it was treason to believe that the Constitution was a compact among the states as those who had made it believed it to be. Or was it loyalty, he asked, to denounce the makers of the Constitution "as inventors of modern rebels and blood thirsty traitors?" He did not believe anyone would "venture to answer this question in the affirmative." [25]

The writer then went on to show that secession had been approved and condemned by both North and South. Consequently, each section was to be denounced and commended, if secession was wrong. New England had threatened the Union in earlier times and had been condemned by the South; and the South had more recently threatened the Union and had been condemned by the North. "For if the South in 1815 condemned secession," Bledsoe asserted, "it was the secession which New England had approved; and if the North in 1861 denounced secession, it was precisely the right which the South had asserted. Hence, it is just as true," he concluded, "that all parties were committed *for,* as that all parties were committed *against,* the right of secession." [26] The government of the Union, therefore, should be influenced by the experiences of the past in dealing with the leaders of the Confederacy, and such consideration ought to result in a policy of leniency.

Perhaps the *Nation* voiced the most logical argument against the early defenses of Davis that can be found in the press of the time. The London correspondent of this periodical had written in July, 1865, that even the English who never sympathized with the Confederacy were opposed to inflicting capital punishment on the President of the Confederate States. They believed that there was "a real moral difference between crimes committed by a man in his public capacity, as the head of a government or army, and those committed by him as a private individual." They also pronounced capital punishment barbarous, and asked the Americans "to place Davis in the same category as Napoleon," whom the English and their allies imprisoned, but did not put to death.

The *Nation* did not agree with this English opinion. It pointed

25. A. T. Bledsoe, *Is Davis a Traitor. . . ?* (2nd ed., 1879), 153-56, 186-87. The first edition was published in 1866.
26. *Ibid.,* 201.

out what it believed to be a marked difference between Napoleon's claim to immunity from punishment and that of Davis. Not only had Napoleon been the "head of a belligerent power," but he had also owed his high position to a revolution that was "morally justifiable." Moreover, since the Bourbon dynasty was regarded as rightfully overthrown and not restored until many years later (1814-15), and then only by the aid of foreign bayonets, the returned monarch of France, Louis XVIII, had "no valid claim to the allegiance of Napoleon or any other Frenchman." The Corsican deserved, therefore, a degree of clemency that Davis had not earned.

Furthermore, the case of the American was not similar to that of any leader of the French Revolution. Davis had led a revolt against a government, the *Nation* asserted, that had been "established after full and fair discussion by the free will and consent of the governed." Moreover, the American Civil War "was the only revolt on record which had not been caused by solid palpable grievances, capable of being, or actually enumerated, on paper." The editor probably had in mind the American Declaration of Independence and the French Declaration of the Rights of Man, which the Southerners appeared not to have imitated in justifying their effort at independence.[27] Furthermore, the late war "was the only revolt ever set on foot avowedly to avoid a remote and only probable risk of interference with the institution of slavery." Hence, there could be no excuse whatever for rebellion against the free government of the United States, and if one could "deserve hanging" for such action, the *Nation* believed Jefferson Davis deserved it.[28]

During the early months of reconstruction other Northern periodicals also thought Davis should be punished. *Harper's Weekly* (June 30) tried to stir its readers to demand the punishment of Davis by contrasting the prisoner's condition in Fortress Monroe with that of the unfortunate Union soldiers in Southern prisons during the war. "Let us not forget," it pleaded, "that this man, for whose comfort sentries must tread softly, for whose stomach the bill of fare must be daily changed . . . is the same man who could see from his

27. Dr. Frank L. Owsley states, in a communication to the author, that Southerners made frequent references to the Declaration of Independence during the war.
28. *Nation*, I, 330.

home in Richmond the island upon which Union soldiers were slowly starved and frozen, and who knew that thousands of his fellow men . . . were being pitilessly tortured into idiocy and death." Then, in stinging sarcasm, it continued: "Not the least pang of their terrible bodily suffering would we have retorted upon Jefferson Davis; not one touch of retaliation should the American people allow to be visited upon him. . . ."[29]

There were, also, at least some of the religious publications of the North which vehemently demanded that the leaders of the rebellion be punished. One example from the *Central Christian Advocate* will suffice. On May 3, it likened the acts of those who had attacked the government to the deeds of those who had killed the President and wounded the Secretary of State. "Shall, then, these assassins of the State escape?" the editor asked. "We demand that the assassins of liberty be hunted out of their hiding places and driven ignominiously from the face of the earth. The nation cannot forget," he continued, "the bones of her sons bleaching on Southern soil, and that it required her richest blood, even that of her noble President, to wash away the stains of slavery and treason. . . ."[30]

But not every printing press was turning out demands for Davis's punishment. A few days after the capture of the Confederate President, Aaron Bang expressed in the Richmond *Republic* the sentiment that ultimately prevailed in disposing of the case against the distinguished prisoner. R. W. Latham, another advocate of clemency, clipped this article and sent it to the President, assuring him that no stone would be left unturned by the writer or himself to place Johnson on the highest possible pinnacle of fame, with "not even Washington or Lincoln" by his side.[31]

Since Bang was a Northern sympathizer, his opinion was very pertinent to the question. He rejoiced, of course, over the capture of Davis, but he dismissed consideration of the charge of treason

29. *Harper's Weekly*, IX, 289, 386; X, 433. See Randall, *Civil War and Reconstruction*, 436 ff., and Hesseltine, *Civil War Prisons*, for true accounts of Southern prisons.

30. See also *Central Christian Advocate*, May 10, 17, June 21, November 24, 1865; *Western Christian Advocate*, July 19, 1865; *New Englander*, XXIV, 783-84.

31. Clipping in the Amnesty Papers, Davis (Latham to Johnson, May 17, 1865).

against him "as the wildest phantom of imagination." He predicted, therefore, that Davis would never be executed, since the preponderance of feeling in the North was against any further "effusion of blood." Bang did say, however, that Davis's property and that of others would probably be confiscated and "their persons banished forever from this continent." But he wrote when sentiment was most bitter against the leaders of the Confederacy. As time passed, this spirit of retribution gave way to a more benevolent attitude. Even in June, 1865, such Northern papers as the New York *Tribune* and the Chicago *Times* counseled leniency in dealing with the leaders of the Confederacy. It should be remembered, however, that Greeley, the humanitarian editor of the *Tribune*, advised the authorities at Washington in November, 1860, to let "the Cotton States . . . go in peace," and that the *Times* had been critical of Lincoln's administration throughout the war.

INDICTMENTS FOR TREASON

While these early demands for punishment and pleas for clemency were being made, Davis remained carefully guarded in Fortress Monroe. In due time the judicial committee of the House of Representatives found the ill-founded charge against him of complicity in Lincoln's assassination to be untenable. In fact, those who had plotted to implicate Davis in the heinous crime were reported to have conspired to deceive the authorities and thus obtain money from the government. Fortunately the nefarious plot was frustrated; but it was not until the House reported unfavorably on the case, in April, 1866, that the fraudulent evidence against him was brought to light.

The chief conspirator to implicate Davis, and even Johnson, in the plot to assassinate Lincoln was Sanford Conover (or Dunham), who was convicted of perjury in August, 1867, and sentenced to the penitentiary. Conover began paving the way for a pardon during his trial and petitioned the President for clemency on being found guilty. His plea was approved by Judge Joseph Holt and others because of his services in securing the conviction of Lincoln's assassins before the military commission created to try them. Johnson denied the petition, and a little later received a communication from

Conover in prison exposing a plot by Representative James W. Ashley, Judge Holt, and others, who had promised to secure a pardon for Conover if he would help implicate Johnson in Lincoln's assassination. In fact, the pardon was to be used as evidence against the President. Conover remained in prison, however, until Johnson pardoned him in February, 1869, on the ground of ill-health.[32]

As time passed, the case against Davis weakened. In January, 1866, an examination of Confederate records showed clearly that he had steadfastly refused to allow Union prisoners to be treated harshly.[33] Moreover, the idea of trying him before a military commission was also abandoned. This disappointed the too credulous Joseph Holt, who had been easily influenced to believe that the President of the Confederacy had encouraged Lincoln's assassination. Perhaps Secretary Stanton was also displeased with the more favorable turn the prisoner's case had taken.

Actually, Davis had been indicted for treason at the May, 1865, term of the United States Circuit Court at Norfolk, Virginia. Somehow this indictment soon disappeared and was never found. A later indictment against him in the District of Columbia was not processed, since the authorities in Washington became convinced that he should be tried in Virginia, where his alleged offense had been committed.[34] Consequently, in May, 1866, Davis was again indicted for treason by a Federal grand jury at Norfolk. His case might have been tried at Richmond in June, for both he and his able attorneys, Charles O'Conner, George Shea, James T. Brady, and others, desired a speedy trial. But the existing military custody of the prisoner (whose health was reported to be unequal to the ordeal of a trial), and the inability of Chief Justice Chase to attend, caused a deferment until a special term of the court in October. This influenced Davis's counsel to ask for the prisoner's liberty on bail, offering a million dollars, with Horace Greeley as one surety, to guarantee his

32. *Offic. Rec.*, 2 Ser., VIII, 899, 921-23, 964-65, 978-80; Dunbar Rowland, *Davis*, VII, 159-60. See also D. M. DeWitt, *The Impeachment and Trial of Andrew Johnson* . . . , 138-42.

33. McElroy, *Jefferson Davis*, II, 553-55.

34. Blackford, "The Trials and Trial of Jefferson Davis," 19. See also *Offic. Rec.*, 2 Ser., VIII, 844-45, for Attorney-General Speed's opinion of January 4, 1866, that Davis should be tried in the civil courts and in "some one state or district" where he had committed the crimes with which he was charged.

appearance in court; but the petition was denied on the ground that Davis was a military prisoner.[35]

The United States had not had another criminal case of such importance since the indictment of Aaron Burr for treason in 1807. Burr, however, secured a speedy trial and acquittal, while Jefferson Davis had been imprisoned more than a year without trial, on the serious charges of treason and assassination. Such delay appeared inexcusable. Yet his case did not come to trial in October (for the special term of the court did not convene), or during the short regular session in November—or ever, for that matter.

VARINA HOWELL DAVIS

During the two years of Davis's imprisonment Mrs. Davis was active, sometimes rather plaintively, at other times rather bitterly, in endeavoring to obtain amelioration of her husband's condition or his release from prison. Her activities in this role were comparable to the efforts of Mrs. R. S. Ewell and Mrs. Clement C. Clay, whose valor in interceding for the liberation of their husbands has been related in chapters IX and XII, respectively. It might be noted, however, that Mrs. Davis's behavior under such trying circumstances was at all times becoming to the woman who had been the First Lady of the Confederacy. Any bitterness—and naturally there was some—that she may have expressed was owing to the unjust treatment which she rightly felt was being accorded to herself and to her husband.[36]

There is some evidence that the President thought Mrs. Davis rather defiant in her first letters seeking clemency. When Judge Davis L. Wardlaw of South Carolina asked Johnson to permit her to leave Georgia to visit friends in South Carolina, the President stated that he had received letters from Mrs. Davis which, with one exception, were not very commendable. When the Judge reminded the President that she was a woman of strong feeling, he replied: "Yes, I suppose she is . . . but there . . . is as much magnanimity and

35. Dunbar Rowland, *Davis*, VII, 150-67. Davis was also indicted by a Federal grand jury at Knoxville, Tennessee, early in 1866.

36. McElroy, *Jefferson Davis*, II, 542 ff.; *Jefferson Davis, A Memoir*, II, Ch. LXXII.

independence, and nobleness of spirit in submitting, as in trying to
set the Government at defiance. . . ."[37]
An estimate of Mrs. Davis's influence in securing her husband's
liberty, however, is hard to make, since she was only one of many
working toward that end. She and the children had accompanied
him by water from Savannah to a point near Fortress Monroe after
their capture at Irwinsville, Georgia. Mrs. Davis left a graphic description of the parting in her *Memoir*.

When Davis was reported to be in chains and still later in declining health, his wife naturally became exceedingly anxious for his
welfare. But for a time she was denied the privilege of even com-
municating with him or with those who offered to become his
counsel.[38] At this remote period such denials are not easily appreciated. Maybe the authorities were overcautious in guaranteeing the
prisoner's security from escape or intrigue; but it should be noted
in their defense that under no circumstances could Davis have been
allowed to encourage a continuance or renewal of the rebellion. It
might be said, however, that there were harsh prison regulations
early in his incarceration which were unbecoming to one of his
late high position and the cause he had represented.[39] Yet it should
always be remembered that Davis, at the time of his capture and for
a long time thereafter, was believed by many to be a traitor and an
assassin, and to have allowed, and even encouraged, cruelties to
Union soldiers in prison camps near Richmond. Certainly this was
enough to cause him to be made "the scapegoat" of the Confederacy, as McElroy has so aptly termed him in discussing the unfair
treatment of Jefferson Davis for having been the President of the
Confederate States of America.

Mrs. Davis relates that the authorities finally gave her permission
to attend to certain business in Louisiana. Later she was allowed to
go to New York City, where she hoped to receive permission from

37. John Savage, *The Life and Public Service of Andrew Johnson*, Appendix, 98.
38. *Jefferson Davis, A Memoir*, II, Chs. LXX-LXXXIII; McElroy, *Jefferson Davis*, II, Ch. XXVII. On December 28, 1865, General Grant recommended "that Mrs. Davis and her family be put precisely on the same
footing as the families of other state prisoners." Johnson Papers, LXXXIII.
39. See Craven, *Davis, passim;* McElroy, *Jefferson Davis*, II, Ch. XXVII;
Dunbar Rowland, *Davis*, VII, *passim; Jefferson Davis, A Memoir*, II, *passim;*
Offic. Rec., 2 Ser., VIII, *passim*.

the President to visit her husband. Not being allowed this privilege at that time, she went to Canada in January, 1866, to join her children, who had been sent thither some months earlier. Soon thereafter rumor reached her that Davis could not live much longer. She thereupon telegraphed the President: "Is it possible that you will keep me from my dying husband?" Johnson replied by granting her permission to visit Fortress Monroe, "subject to conditions to be stated at the fort." At the same time he assured her "that her husband was in his usual health."[40]

Late in the afternoon of May 3, 1866, Mrs. Davis arrived at Fortress Monroe with her youngest child and, after signing a "parole of honor" not to take "any deadly weapons" to the prisoner or aid him in attempting to escape, gained admission. It had been almost a year since she had last seen her husband, and naturally she was quite overcome by the emaciated condition in which she now found him. She was unable to get General Miles to improve his accommodations. Instead, she described the General as "using his power to insult and annoy to the utmost, and in ways previously unknown and not to be anticipated by gentlefolk."

Alarmed at the condition of her husband's health, Mrs. Davis went to Washington to try to persuade the President to have the prison accommodations improved. She had a cordial interview with Johnson. When she complained of his proclamation for the arrest of Davis as accessory to the assassination of Lincoln, he admitted that he did not credit the charge, but stated that at the time he "was in the hands of wildly excited people and must take such measures as would show he was willing to sift the facts." Since the attempt to implicate Davis in the assassination had been thwarted, Mrs. Davis naturally thought that the President "owed Mr. Davis a retraction as public as his mistake" in issuing a proclamation had been. But to her astonishment, Johnson "said that he was laboring under the enmity of both houses of Congress," which would impeach him "if they could find anything upon which to hinge an impeachment." Then with apparent feeling he declared that he would retract the proclamation if he could.

40. Johnson Papers, Nos. 6035, 6037; *Jefferson Davis, A Memoir*, II, 757. Numerous reports of Davis's health while in Fortress Monroe may be found in the *Offic. Rec.*, 2 Ser., VIII, *passim*.

Mrs. Davis had found Johnson somewhat puzzling. "I felt sorry for a man whose code of morals I could not understand," she related, "and so we parted, with kind words and courteous manner on his part, and much sympathy for his miserable state [of mind on my part]." Thus ended the rather trying interview between the suppliant wife of former President Jefferson Davis and President Andrew Johnson—the entreating patrician and the ruling plebeian. How changed were conditions from the time twenty years earlier when, in the House of Representatives, Davis had angered Johnson by referring to the incompetence of tailors as compared with men trained at West Point! Seldom does history reveal such ironies.

Varina Howell Davis was never again a personal supplicant to President Johnson.[41] Several months before her visit to Fortress Monroe, Dr. John J. Craven had been removed as prison physician, apparently because of his solicitude for Davis's welfare. His successor, Dr. George Cooper, was just as concerned for the comfort and health of the distinguished prisoner, and soon gained the liberty of the fort for Davis. Further complaint caused the removal of General Miles and the assignment of General Henry S. Burton as commander of the fortress. General Burton's sympathy for the prisoner ultimately resulted in the provision of an apartment of four rooms for the Davises. Many visitors came, Mrs. Davis related, and "generally remained for dinner, and . . . wine and delicacies of all kinds were pressed upon us by friends."[42] This was a great improvement over the treatment of the early months of Davis's imprisonment, and indicated something of the general change in the attitude of the public toward the former President of the Confederacy.

LATER VIEWS ON PUNISHMENT

The controversy over the question of allowing Davis clemency continued throughout the period of his imprisonment and impending trial. When the President released Stephens, Reagan, Semmes, Trenholm, Campbell, and others from prison in October, 1865, many feared that he would ultimately give Davis the same liberal

---

41. *Jefferson Davis, A Memoir*, II, 767-71.

42. Craven, *Davis*, 359-68; *Jefferson Davis, A Memoir*, II, 771-75. Apparently, by July, 1866, Mrs. Davis was permitted to assist the surgeon in attending to her husband.

consideration. But by 1866 a more merciful attitude began to be manifested in the North. A lawyer of Ohio begged Johnson to pardon Davis, reminding the President that Davis had fought valiantly for the United States in the Mexican War, and urging that for this and other services to the Union he should be shown clemency. And in similar spirit Bishop Little, writing a few weeks earlier from Mechanicsburg, Ohio, advised clemency. The clergyman claimed to have counseled "Mr. Lincoln on important topics of the time," and, in his letter of nearly six thousand words, stated his views on reconstruction. In his opinion, Johnson should liberate Davis for fear lest "he die in prison by the slow and murderous torture of nervous irritability and neuralgic distress."[43]

One of the most impressive manuscripts in the Amnesty Papers for Davis is Horace Greeley's "Memorial" to the President, of August 11, 1866. By this time the noted journalist, like many others, had become exceedingly impatient over the delay in bringing Davis to trial. Greeley stressed the fact that it was now some fifteen months since the President of the Confederacy had been placed in Fortress Monroe, and, even though he had been charged with complicity in the assassination of Lincoln and accounted guilty of other high crimes and misdemeanors, he had not yet been brought to trial. Moreover, he observed that the prisoner had not been indicted for anything but treason, nor was he ever likely to be indicted on any other charge. The memorialist also pointed out the fact that, even though Davis's learned counsel had endeavored to have their client brought to trial, there appeared to be no certainty that he would ever be tried. Lastly, Greeley emphasized the danger of a prolonged confinement to Davis's health and demanded that, "in the interests alike of Humanity, Public Justice, and the rights of persons secured to every citizen by law," the prisoner be either speedily tried or admitted to bail.[44]

Harper's Weekly appears to have remained rather hostile toward Davis until early in 1866. In April of that year it offered the opinion that there was as much cause to release Davis from prison as there

43. Amnesty Papers, Davis (Little to Johnson, June 10, 1866, James E. Cox to Johnson, August 4, 1866).
44. In the New York *Tribune*, November 21, 1866, Greeley complained again about the delay in disposing of the case against Davis.

had been for liberating Vice-President Stephens. One was as guilty as the other, and if they were both guilty, treason could not be made odious by imprisoning one and releasing the other. Then, after speculating on the more recent release of Admiral Raphael Semmes from prison and the continued imprisonment of Clement C. Clay, the editor presumed that a universal amnesty was in the offing. Yet pages of this magazine contain much, especially in its illustrations, to indicate a sort of fiendish glee in referring to Davis as guilty of, or suffering from the consequences of, alleged wrongful acts committed during the war. In a June issue there are two pictures, one showing the horrors of Andersonville Prison and the other, in contrast, showing Davis in Fortress Monroe receiving every consideration necessary for his welfare. Then, as if this were not enough to arouse the punitive instincts of the reader, the words, "Treason must be made odious," are printed under the picture.[45]

Nevertheless, as the year 1866 passed, animosity against the leaders of the Confederacy continued to wane. The *Nation* indicated the growing spirit of clemency when it stated in May that the "holy horror of treason and traitors" of the early days of Johnson's administration had "died out long ago" and that its place had been "taken by a mild desire to have . . . treason tested before a court, and to get rid of Davis somehow." The editor stated further that, of those who had charged the President of the Confederacy with treason, the number who thought that he should be punished had "probably diminished one half."[46]

The foregoing should indicate sufficiently the demands for the severe punishment of the President of the Confederacy and the contrary urgent pleas for his complete pardon. Since Johnson held, for a time at least, the destiny of the accused in his hands, he was surely greatly concerned over the ultimate disposition of the distinguished prisoner. His responsibility for the enforcement of the punitive laws against rebellion required that much consideration for Davis's plight. Moreover, the volume of appeals, for and against Davis, far exceeded that concerned with any other ex-Confederate. It may be taken for granted, therefore, that the case of the former Secretary of War, United States Senator, and recent President of the Confed-

45. *Harper's Weekly*, X (April 21, June 30, July 7, 1866), 243, 409, 428.
46. *Nation*, II (May 17, 1866), 625.

erate States of America was uppermost in Johnson's mind until near the close of his administration.

REFUSAL TO ASK FOR PARDON

Mention has been made above of Johnson's asking Mrs. Davis in May, 1866, whether her husband had thought of asking for pardon. There may be some indication, therefore, that Davis would have been pardoned earlier if he had petitioned for clemency. It should be remembered, however, that the President did not pardon General Lee any sooner than he did Davis, though the General promptly applied for pardon (June 13, 1865) and was held in greater esteem than Davis. Paul Bagley's success (as he estimated his own efforts) in obtaining Vance's pardon in March, 1867, encouraged him, the next month, to urge Davis to apply for similar consideration. A little later the missionary wrote Davis again asking him to sign an enclosed petition to Johnson and expressing confidence of favorable action on it. Bagley's philosophy as a Christian minister prompted him to assume that pardon would result from properly approaching the authority which claimed to have been offended and which had the power to forgive. About this time, eleven other Southerners earnestly entreated Davis to accept the situation by applying for clemency. In reality, their communication was in itself a petition to the President praying for leniency.

But Davis signed no such petition. Indeed, he must have read one of Bagley's letters with some misgivings as to its probable effect in obtaining a pardon. The would-be advocate told his self-chosen client that most of the Senators who had signed for Vance refused in his case, and that others who wished to sign were afraid to do so. One Senator, he said, had declared that his people would hang him if he signed the petition, and that they would hang Davis if they caught him in their state. Yet, notwithstanding these and other discouraging statements, Bagley told Davis that he believed Johnson would pardon him if he were to petition for clemency.[47]

Perhaps Bagley was overconfident of Johnson's susceptibility to acts of clemency when appealed to by persons on missions of mercy. At any rate, he wrote Davis four days later that he had asked the

47. Dunbar Rowland, *Davis*, VII, 93, 96 (Bagley to Davis, May 1, 1867).

President for an assurance that he would pardon him if he would ask for clemency. Johnson stated that he could not pardon Davis unless he asked for clemency and that he had offered terms from which he could not deviate; but, in reality, he thought Davis ought to be tried for treason. Thereupon, Bagley said that his client had already been tried "at the Bar of War and condemned by the God of Battles," whose decision no court might reverse. The President encouraged Bagley in his reply by declaring: "If the case comes before us I claim the right to decide it as I think right irrespective of the opinion of any man. . . ."[48]

Nevertheless, Davis steadfastly refused to indicate his acceptance of the verdict of the God of Battles by petitioning for clemency. Evidently he wanted his cause tried before a more earthly tribunal to determine whether he had committed treason and deserved punishment therefor. Many years later (1876) he referred to the stand he had taken by saying: "When closely confined at Fortress Monroe, I was solicited to add my name to those of many esteemed gentlemen who had signed a petition for my pardon, and an assurance was given that on my doing so, the President would order my liberation. Confident of the justice of our cause, and the rectitude of my own conduct, I declined to sign the petition, and remained subject to the inexcusable privation and tortures which Dr. Craven has but faintly described."[49]

In one important respect, therefore, Davis's case was rather singular. Unlike others for whom pardon was sought, the former President of the Confederacy refused to petition for clemency, believing that he had done nothing for which he should seek pardon. In this attitude he remained till death. Mrs. Davis was apparently of the same spirit. Though she had already begun to exert herself to the utmost to have her husband liberated from prison, she asserted vehemently in a letter of July 14, 1865, to George Shea, that the Davises would never ask for pardon or amnesty for themselves. Her

48. *Ibid.*, 98. In a speech at St. Louis on September 8, 1866, Johnson stated, in referring to Davis: "Before the case comes to me, and all other cases, it would have to come on application as a case for pardon." McPherson, *Reconstruction*, 140.

49. Dunbar Rowland, *Davis*, VII, 483 (Davis to James Lyons, January 27, 1876). Cf. *Jefferson Davis, A Memoir*, II, 777.

pronouncement on the subject is indeed characteristic of both of them.[50]

It might be observed here that Mrs. Davis lived forty-one years after writing this letter. Following her husband's death in 1889, she traveled extensively, losing much of her early animosity and spending considerable time in the North, where she was widely appreciated, even by Mrs. U. S. Grant. When she died on October 16, 1906, in New York City, she was honored as though she had been the distinguished wife of a great President of the United States, and was buried beside her beloved husband near St. Paul's Church in Richmond.

On March 10, 1884, Davis asserted in a speech before the Mississippi Legislature: " 'Tis been said that I should apply to the United States for a pardon, but repentance must precede the right of pardon, and I have not repented. Remembering as I must all which has been lost, disappointed hopes and crushed aspirations, yet I deliberately say, if it were to do over again I would again do just as I did in 1861."[51] Although Davis uttered this statement after being urged to petition Congress to remove the disability imposed by the Fourteenth Amendment so that he might become a candidate for office, the declaration indicates that there had been no change in his attitude since the years he was in prison and under indictment for treason. Nevertheless, three years earlier (1881) he had concluded his two-volume *The Rise and Fall of the Confederate Government* with this significant paragraph: "In asserting the right of secession it has not been my wish to incite its exercise: I recognize the fact that the war showed it to be impracticable, but this did not prove it to be wrong; and, now that it may not be again attempted, and that the Union may promote the general welfare, it is needful that the truth, the whole truth, should be known, so that crimination and recrimination may forever cease, and, then, on the basis of fraternity and faithful regard for the rights of the States, there may be written on the arch of the Union, *Esto Perpetua.*"

Thus the former President of the Confederate States acknowledged the perpetuity of the Union and expressed the fervent prayer

---

50. See Mrs. Eron Rowland's *Varina Howell, Wife of Jefferson Davis,* II, 456-62. Cf. Dunbar Rowland, *Davis,* VII, 75-80.
51. Dunbar Rowland, *Davis,* IX, 280.

that there would never be another effort to destroy it. This was indeed a fitting conclusion to his monumental treatment of the subject of states' rights and the constitutionality of secession, but it was no expression of penitence or apology for the past.

Late in August, 1867, Paul Bagley told Johnson that it appeared to be impossible in the nature of the case for Davis to apply for pardon so long as the proclamation for his arrest on the charge of complicity in the assassination of Lincoln remained against him. Furthermore, those who had conspired to implicate Davis in the crime had admitted their fraud. An application for clemency, therefore, would appear to admit an accusation to be true which those who had made it had subsequently shown to be false.[52] But the prayer of the missionary was not answered, and the unfortunate proclamation was never revoked. Nor was it likely that the withdrawal would have caused Davis to apply for pardon at any time later.

RELEASE FROM PRISON AND PARDON

The President's headstrong and vindictive subordinates were often more culpable than the real head of the government. It should be remembered, however, that the circumstances under which Johnson became President were bound to affect his early reactions to certain serious situations. He was inclined to defer, for a short time at least, to the opinions of strong-willed and vengeful men like Secretary Stanton and Judge Holt, who had been very influential under Lincoln. Then, as he told Mrs. Davis, there was also the general clamor for vengeance immediately after the assassination, sentiment which, it may be said, Johnson shared. After two years as President, however, he was able to see things in a clearer light.

Indeed both Andrew Johnson and the general situation changed somewhat between 1865 and 1867. Much had happened in the interval to cause the President to be more considerate. The rising tide in the North against him and the threats of impeachment, which began with his acts of clemency in 1865, undoubtedly affected his attitude. Nevertheless, there was an increasing demand that the consideration which had been shown to other leaders of the Confed-

52. *Ibid.*, 127, 129.

eracy be also given to Davis. At least he should be released from prison while his trial was pending. No other civil leader of the Confederacy remained imprisoned, and surely something should be done with Davis. Finally, through the efforts of Mrs. Davis, Horace Greeley, Reverdy Johnson, Charles O'Connor, George Shea, Burton N. Harrison, and others, President Johnson and Secretary Stanton were prevailed upon in May, 1867, to have the distinguished prisoner given over to the civil authorities for trial.[53]

Through a writ of habeas corpus, therefore, Davis was taken to Richmond, Virginia, and placed in the custody of the United States Circuit Court for that district, with Judge John C. Underwood on the bench. Harrison was assigned to go to the fort to accompany his former chief to Richmond. Attorney-General Evarts, however, announced to the court that it was not the government's "intention to prosecute . . . the prisoner at the present time," and the trial was deferred to the following November.[54] Nevertheless, the movement for trial brought much relief to Davis, for he was not returned to prison. The case was bailable under the Confiscation Act of July 17, 1862, providing penalties less than death for treason, and so the court was willing, on O'Connor's motion, to release the prisoner on bail. The bond was fixed at $100,000, and Horace Greeley, Cornelius Vanderbilt, James Lyons, and more than a dozen other prominent and public-spirited men were accepted as guarantors for Davis's subsequent appearance in court.[55]

Not everyone, however, approved this action of the court. Perhaps a resolution of the East Baptist Association of New Jersey, one month later (June 14), well expressed the most unfavorable opinion. It declared "that the indiscriminate pardon of prominent traitors . . . with the practical release of the chief traitor without trial is sure to encourage treason in the future. . . ."[56] The view of the *Nation* was

53. McElroy, *Jefferson Davis*, II, 568-83. The Reverdy Johnson Papers contain two letters from Mrs. Davis, of July 19 and October 16, 1866, pleading with Johnson to induce the President to release her husband.

54. Dunbar Rowland, *Davis*, VII, 165-70; *Southern Historical Society Papers*, XXXVII, 243-52. See also *The Harrisons of Skimino*, 199-206, for Burton N. Harrison's mission to Fortress Monroe and his account of Davis's reception by the police in Norfolk and Richmond.

55. Dunbar Rowland, *Davis*, VII, 171-76. A facsimile of this bail bond may be found in McElroy, *Jefferson Davis*, II, 585.

56. Amnesty Papers, Davis.

somewhat saner. "We are glad," it said, "that this step has been taken, both as an act of justice in itself and as an indication that his trial is approaching." Then, after endeavoring to justify his treatment, the editor stated that Davis should be tried for treason so that future generations in the United States might know whether such acts as his during a rebellion constituted treason. Others, however, were more hopeful than the *Nation's* editor. Roy Franklin Nichols says that O'Connor was so elated over the release of Davis that he wrote to his wife: "The business is finished. Mr. Davis will never be brought to trial."[57]

Though Davis was now out of prison, he remained under indictment with prospects of being tried for treason. He and his counsel, however, apparently desired a trial, in order that a jury might determine whether he, or any other person who had supported the Confederacy, was guilty of treason. On the other hand, the authorities of the United States appeared less desirous of continuing the prosecution, since no jury in Virginia was likely to vote for conviction. An acquittal or a hung jury would probably have been embarrassing to the government. Furthermore, the spectacle of such a trial was not encouraging, especially when the argument expected from the defense was contemplated. It appears, for example, that James Lyons stood ready to tell Chief Justice Chase, as he had stated to him when he obtained his own pardon from the President in 1865, that "the evidence upon which I shall rely for defense of Mr. Davis ... will be your message to the Legislature of Ohio ... declaring that, if the Government of the United States attempted to coerce Ohio, you would bring into the field to meet her the whole military force of the State." It is not likely that Chase ever forgot this statement by the man who would confront him if the case were ever actually tried.[58]

57. *Nation*, IV (May 16, 1867), 297; Nichols, "United States *vs* Jefferson Davis," *American Historical Review*, XXXI, 274.
58. Dunbar Rowland, *Davis*, VIII, 362. An authority on Chase, Dr. William Baringer, University of Florida, in discussing Lyons's statement, stated: "I do not find that Chase as governor actually threatened to call out the militia for such a purpose. He implied that he would use all Ohio's power, and his as governor, to uphold *state* powers against federal encroachment. That is quite a different thing from defiance of federal authority in the federal field of power. Chase's position was that federal power *should not* be used to assist slavery. But the distinction was lost on Chase's enemies,

Meanwhile, President Johnson, after much consideration, proclaimed a second amnesty on September 7, 1867, two months before
the time set for Davis's trial. The proclamation was not universal,
however, and among its exceptions were those "legally held to bail
either before or after conviction."[59] Davis was not tried in November since Chase could not attend court, nor the following March,
the time conditionally set again for a hearing. Instead, a more satisfactory indictment was found against him on the twenty-sixth of
that month, and the case was arranged for May 2. The impeachment
of the President, however, required the presence of the Chief Justice, and the trial was deferred until June 3, 1868.

There was so much apprehension over what Davis's fate would
be if Johnson were found guilty and removed from office that
O'Connor advised his client to flee the country, since his life would
probably be in danger if Benjamin Wade, President Pro Tem of the
Senate, succeeded to the presidency. Fortunately, Johnson was acquitted, and Davis's trial remained in abeyance. Chase might have
been ready to hear the case in June, but apparently other Federal
officials were in no hurry; so, on May 28, the defendant was given
until late in October to appear before the court. On June 23, parties
to the case agreed for his appearance on November 4, 1868.[60]

Even while the impeachment trial was in progress, Johnson considered proclaiming another amnesty that would have embraced
every remaining disabled ex-Confederate. In fact, there is evidence
that he had contemplated a universal amnesty as early as the preceding August.[61] Such action would have ended the efforts to try Davis
for treason. It might also, in the opinion of some advocates of absolute clemency, have enhanced Johnson's chance to succeed himself
as President. Owing to the close impeachment vote, Johnson probably thought that a universal amnesty might provoke another attempt to remove him. Consequently, the proclamation excepted

who thought he was, wrongly, an abolitionist like Garrison who cared
nothing for law." Letter to the author, May 10, 1951.

59. See Ch. XV for an account of this amnesty; also Browning, *Diary*, II,
165 (November 12, 1861).

60. Dunbar Rowland, *Davis*, VII, 195-6. Davis visited Europe during this
interval.

61. *Ibid.*, VIII, 127-8 (Paul Bagley's letters).

such "persons as may be under presentment or indictment . . . upon a charge of treason. . . ." The Fourth of July amnesty, therefore, left Davis to the further consideration of the Federal judiciary.

Soon after Johnson proclaimed his third conditional amnesty, a new factor entered the movement to try Davis for treason. The Fourteenth Amendment to the Constitution went into effect on July 28, 1868, and the disability imposed by its third section (forbidding office-holding by those who had sworn to defend the United States and had later rebelled against the Union) came to be regarded as a punishment for rebellion superseding any previous penalty provided by law. Hence, as the time approached for the trial in November, Davis's counsel planned to show that he had taken an oath to support the Constitution of the United States previous to engaging in the recent rebellion. An affidavit to this effect, therefore, was made to the court on November 30, and an order obtained for its execution. This motion to dismiss the case was heard on December 3, but the court was divided, Chase being for, and Underwood against, dismissal. Thereupon, at the request of the counsel for Davis, the fact of the disagreement was certified to the Supreme Court at Washington for further consideration.[62]

While efforts were being made to have the indictment against Davis quashed, Johnson was considering a universal amnesty. When the subject was discussed at a Cabinet meeting on November 6, Attorney-General Evarts said that for two years he had believed that nothing could be gained by trying Davis, that if tried he would not be convicted, and if convicted he would not be punished. Evarts stated also that Charles A. Dana, who was to assist in the prosecution, was of the same opinion, and that he and Dana were not willing for Judge Underwood to preside at the trial because of his prejudice against the defendant.[63] Furthermore, the Attorney-General thought the time had come for the President to issue a proclamation of universal amnesty. If this was done, he would have the indictment against Davis set aside. Thus Evarts expressed his belief in the folly

62. Dunbar Rowland, *Davis*, VII, 196-97, 226-27.
63. Paul Bagley wrote to Davis in August, 1867, that he had informed Johnson that Judge Underwood had told him "that he could get negroes enough on a jury with a few white men to convict him. . . ." Dunbar Rowland, *Davis*, VII, 128.

of any further pretense to bringing the case to trial. The logical method of disposing of it, he reasoned, was to pardon the accused and others similarly disabled.

Senator Browning, who was attending the Cabinet meetings, stated that Seward and Welles did not agree with Evarts's recommendation. The President was favorable, however, and, after due consideration, instructed his Attorney-General to prepare a proclamation of universal amnesty to be presented at the next meeting. Two weeks later the Senator mentioned the matter again.[64] As the time for Davis's trial approached, Evarts continued to believe that the ordeal should be either obviated through a pardon or at least postponed. Johnson, however, was still undecided about the matter, and Evarts allowed the case to come up for consideration as planned.

Apparently, Davis's counsel was not so eager for the trial as formerly. Since the Fourteenth Amendment offered a satisfactory alternative, the attorneys resolved to ask the court to dismiss the case on the ground that the punitive section of the Amendment had annulled the law under which their client had been indicted. The forthcoming trial, therefore, was an opportunity to present this phase of the case; but the court actually disagreed, and the case remained undetermined when the long desired amnesty was proclaimed.

Evidently, Johnson was finally convinced that every person remaining disabled under the laws providing punishment for supporting the rebellion should be pardoned, as far as that power existed in the Chief Executive. John Cabell Breckinridge and others were still in exile, apparently unwilling to return under existing conditions. Moreover, a few other leaders of the Confederacy also remained unpardoned, and their exact status uncertain. The argument of Davis's counsel for the dismissal of the indictment against their client most likely influenced the President to act without further delay. It was also pretty certain that the other Justices of the Supreme Court would support Chase if the question of dismissal ever came before that tribunal. Moreover, Johnson was approaching the end of his unhappy administration and probably desired to have the last word in disposing of the case against the former President of the Confederacy. At any rate, on Christmas Day he proclaimed universal

64. Browning, *Diary*, II, 225, 227 (November 6, 20, 1868).

amnesty to all who remained unpardoned for aiding the rebellion.

And yet President Johnson wrote Benjamin C. Truman as late as August 3, 1868: "I shall go to my grave with the firm belief that Davis, Cobb, Toombs, and a few others of the arch conspirators and traitors should have been tried, convicted, and hanged for treason. . . . If it was the last act of my life, I'd hang Jeff Davis as an example. I'd show coming generations that, while the rebellion was too popular a revolt to punish many who participated in it, treason should be made odious and arch traitors should be punished."[65] This did not mean, of course, that he ever favored an unfair trial of the accused.

Nevertheless, the President's Christmas amnesty finally disposed of the case against Jefferson Davis. No motion for a hearing was ever made after it. Instead, at a subsequent term of the court, the indictment was dismissed. With this ends Bradley T. Johnson's account of the famous case, which, for three and a half years after the end of the Civil War, had received the serious consideration of the three departments of the Federal government. Not only was Davis affected, but the amnesty and subsequent quashing of the indictment on February 15, 1869, also similarly benefited "Generals Lee, Rooney, Custis, and Fitzhugh Lee, fourteen other general officers of the Confederacy and nineteen other persons, or thirty-seven in all."[66]

The universal amnesty affected Jefferson Davis as though the President had pardoned him individually in response to an application for such special favor. In other words, Davis was the beneficiary of clemency as was Confederate Governor Vance of North Carolina, who received a special pardon in March, 1867 (see page 218). The Supreme Court had declared the words pardon and amnesty as being synonymous and as affecting beneficiaries in exactly the same way. The courts, therefore, were obliged to drop the charge against Davis, regardless of any effect the Fourteenth Amendment may have had on his condition.

At last Jefferson Davis was pardoned and all his privileges were restored, except that of holding any office in the United States, state or national, civil or military. He might vote and enjoy civil privi-

65. *Century Magazine*, LXXXV (1913).
66. Dunbar Rowland, *Davis*, VII, 227; Freeman, *R. E. Lee*, IV, 381.

leges in his home state or in any other state without legal hindrance, but until Congress removed the disability imposed by the Fourteenth Amendment, he could never hold any public office. This disability will be further considered in the chapter on "Congressional Amnesty."

Perhaps the New York *Herald*, on the day of the proclamation, expressed the true significance of the amnesty by stating that it ended "the farce of the Jefferson Davis trial," and released Horace Greeley, Gerrit Smith, John Minor Botts, and others of their bail bond for the due appearance of Davis in court when called for. Carl Schurz later gave greater significance to this action of the President. "There is not," he asserted, "another single example of such magnanimity in the history of the world, and it may be truly said that in acting as it did, this Republic was a century ahead of its time."[67]

Moreover, when the summary executions of political offenders in Europe during the present century are considered, the clemency of the government of the United States, during and after the Civil War, may be regarded as the essence of traditional American justice, liberalism, and democracy, notwithstanding the hangings of Mrs. Mary Surratt and Henry Wirz,[68] the long imprisonment of Jefferson Davis without trial, and the regrettable errors of Congressional Reconstruction.

67. *The Reminiscences of Carl Schurz*, III, 149, cited hereafter as Schurz, *Reminiscences*.

68. For the doubtful guilt and unjustifiable executions of Mrs. Surratt and Wirz, see Milton, *Age of Hate*, Ch. X, and Randall, *Civil War and Reconstruction*, 803.

CHAPTER FOURTEEN

EFFORTS TO CURTAIL PRESIDENTIAL AMNESTY

———◆———

Johnson's Increasing Clemency

PRESIDENT Johnson's early attitude toward the leaders of the Confederacy has already been given. It might be stated further, however, that he had declared his determination to punish them, and many persons who approved his policy had hailed his accession to the presidency as an act of Providence. It appeared, therefore, as if his administration would quickly bring to justice a considerable number of secessionists. The rapidity with which some Southerners sought exile at the close of hostilities is evidence that they, too, feared punishment. And well they might, for numerous arrests and imprisonments seemed to indicate the President's intention to carry out his threats to make "treason odious." General Grant later characterized the feeling in the South at the time of Johnson's becoming President by saying: "He uttered his denunciations with great vehemence, and, as they were accompanied with no assurance of safety, many Southerners were driven to a point almost beyond endurance."[1]

How far Johnson intended to go in avenging the attack on the Union was defined in his proclamation of May 29, 1865. His fourteen exceptions surely included all who the Radicals believed should make retribution for supporting the Confederacy. The twenty-thousand-dollar provision especially appealed to those who felt that

1. Grant, *Memoirs*, II, 510, 523. Oberholtzer, *History of the United States since the Civil War*, I, 23, 49-50, gives a brief description of the state of mind among the Southerners at the close of hostilities.

men of wealth in the South should be punished through the application of the confiscation acts.

The more liberal element in the North also found the President's policy rather satisfactory. Those who favored punishing only a few of the more responsible leaders expected that large numbers in the excepted classes would ultimately find little difficulty in obtaining executive pardon by complying with the amnesty proclamation.[2] The liberals, therefore, expected a policy of leniency finally to prevail. There were others, of course, who saw in Johnson's policy a disposition to treat the South with undue severity through a program of subjugation and confiscation. This sentiment emanated naturally from Southern sympathizers who took the President at his word when he declared himself in favor of punishment. They also interpreted his words as indicative of the general feeling in the North, and expected him to administer his amnesty policy rigorously. Circumstances in June and July, 1865, hardly justified any other conclusion. Furthermore, Johnson's refusal, early in July, to stay the execution of Mrs. Mary Surratt, whose lodging house had sheltered President Lincoln's assassins, must have augmented the fear of many of those whom he had excepted in his amnesty.

Yet, as has already been shown, the President's proclamation had a safety valve which soon began to operate in such a manner that all its severity eventually disappeared. Its author was no longer the avenger he had earlier appeared to be. By September he was saying: "I know I love the Southern people . . . and [will] do all in my power to restore them to that state of happiness and prosperity which they formerly enjoyed."[3]

A combination of circumstances operated to turn Johnson to a course of leniency in dealing with the South. Perhaps the first and most significant influence was Lincoln's clemency, which, in a sense, became the new President's heritage. President Johnson could hardly avoid adopting, in the main, his predecessor's program of reconstruction. He doubled Lincoln's number of excepted classes in his amnesty measure, and to that extent his policy was more severe than his predecessor's; but, on the whole, as in Lincoln's plan, the

2. New York *Herald*, May 30, 1865; New York *Observer*, June 1, 1865.
3. *Annual Cyclopedia*, 1865, pp. 805-6, quoting from an address to a delegation of Virginians, September 11, 1865.

states of the Confederacy were to return as quickly as possible to their former condition in the Union. Furthermore, Lincoln's apparent willingness to pardon anyone who properly applied for clemency was plainly incorporated in Johnson's proclamation. This mitigating proviso soon caused the measure to lose its severity, and Johnson eventually became as lenient as Lincoln had been.

Probably the new President's most significant inheritance from his predecessor was the Secretary of State, William H. Seward, whose pacific disposition was undoubtedly a determining factor in Johnson's administration.[4] Seward had learned much in his association with Lincoln, and was now able to temper the avenging zeal of his new chief with something of that spirit of clemency so characteristic of the late President. Fortunately, the harmony and mutual confidence which had developed between Lincoln and Seward were soon manifested between Johnson and Seward, and the persuasive and conciliatory Secretary very early influenced the President to adopt a milder course in dealing with the Confederates. Apparently, Seward desired his inclination toward leniency to be appreciated, for he is quoted as saying in referring to those excepted in Johnson's proclamation of amnesty: "They come to me . . . as if I were more inclined to tenderness than others, because I have been calm and cool under political excitement."[5] Lincoln's policy of mercy surely had a wholesome influence on Seward, who hardly seemed like the fiery abolitionist of former days. Even the attempt on his life appeared to lessen his vindictiveness.

A third factor in diverting Johnson from his original intention of dealing harshly with the Confederates was the compliant spirit of most of their leaders. Their arguments in defense of the Southern cause and their apparent willingness to abide by the consequences of their defeat could hardly help affecting anyone of intelligence. The logic of men like Reagan, Campbell, and Stephens from the South, supported by such men as the Curtises from the North, certainly influenced Johnson as he faced the problems of reconstruction.

4. G. E. Baker, *The Works of William H. Seward*, V, 517-18, 523-24; Pierce, *Memoirs and Letters of Charles Sumner*, IV, 299; J. W. Burgess, *Reconstruction and the Constitution, 1866-1876*, 32; Foulke, *Life of Oliver P. Morton*, I, 464.

5. Quoted by Bancroft, *Life of William H. Seward*, II, 446 ff. Cf. Blaine, *Twenty Years of Congress*, II, 63-76; and Bancroft, II, 447, n. 1.

Then there were political motives behind Johnson's measures. It would have been strange indeed if he had not considered his own interests in acting on matters pertaining to the dominant issue of his administration—the restoration of the late Confederate States and the treatment of their leaders. Johnson had been a politician a long time and owed his present position largely to the fortune of politics. There were also state and national elections which he might influence, and, of course, the possibility of his nomination and election to the presidency in 1868 occurred to him.[6] Nevertheless, in justice to him, it should be said that he did earnestly desire to do what would contribute to the most satisfactory settlement of the controversial problem of dealing with the leaders of the Confederacy.

Effects of Pardon and Amnesty

As Lincoln had sent General Sickles on a tour of inspection to report the efficacy of his amnesty measure, so Johnson sent General Carl Schurz, in July, 1865, to observe and report conditions in the South, with the apparent desire of obtaining information to support his policy. Schurz was gone nearly three months and made a thorough investigation, but he reported unfavorably.[7] On the matter of oathtaking and amnesty he stated that many persons who accepted the President's proffer did so as a political convenience. "Persons falling under any of the exceptions of the amnesty proclamations," he said, "made haste to avert the impending danger; and politicians used every means of persuasion to induce people to swell the number of votes by clearing themselves of all disabilities." Newspapers sometimes recommended this taking of oaths "with sneering remarks," and in many instances the amnesty "was treated with contempt and ridicule." Schurz understood that Johnson's policy "was merely experimental" and that it would be changed "if the experiment did not lead to satisfactory results." He concluded, therefore, by stating: "A historical examination of the subject of political oaths

6. Blaine, *Twenty Years of Congress*, II, 75-76, 396; Burgess, *Reconstruction and the Constitution, 1866-1876*, 98-99.
7. See division, "Evaluating the Amnesty," in Ch. IV; Frederic Bancroft (ed.), *Speeches, Correspondence and Political Papers of Carl Schurz*, I, 279 ff., cited hereafter as Schurz, *Speeches, etc.*; *Sen. Exec. Doc.*, No. 2, 39 Cong., 1 Sess.

will lead to the conclusion that they can be very serviceable in certain emergencies and for certain objects, but that they have never insured the stability of government and never improved the morals of a people." It was his opinion that the experiment was not working very satisfactorily, a condition which meant, of course, that a modification of the plan in vogue ought to be made.

Apparently, about the time of Schurz's return and report, there was a lull in the granting of pardons. This was "understood to be occasioned by the flagrant breach of faith committed by" many amnestied persons.[8] Whether this was true or not, Johnson was certainly disappointed in Schurz and treated him rather coldly on his return. Apparently there was belief in some quarters that Schurz had spent part of his time in the South in the interest of the Republican Party and, as a result, had alienated the President.[9] The President expected a report which would support his amnesty policy, and such a report he meant to have before Congress met in December. What he did, therefore, was to send General Grant into the Southern states "to learn as far as possible the feelings and intentions of the citizens of those states toward the general government." Grant returned in about two weeks and gave a brief report of his observations. He said nothing about pardon and amnesty, but stated that there was "much universal acquiescence in the authority of the general government throughout the portions of the country" which he visited.[10] Thus, while Schurz found "an entire absence of that national spirit which forms the basis of true loyalty and patriotism," Grant reported that "the mass of thinking men of the South accept the present situation of affairs in good faith."[11]

Soon after Grant's return, the President, in response to a call from the Senate, sent to that body the two reports on the success of his reconstruction policy. In his message accompanying these papers, he expressed an opinion on conditions in the South which coincided with Grant's report. That he regarded Grant as his most reliable authority may be seen in the following statement from his message: "From all the information in my possession, and from

8. Cincinnati *Commercial*, November 9, 1865; also New York *Herald*, October 31, 1865.

9. Schurz, *Speeches, etc.*, I, 272-76; Schurz, *Reminiscences*, III, 185.

10. *Sen. Exec. Doc.*, No. 2, 39 Cong., 1 Sess., 106.

11. Quoted by Pierce, *Memoir and Letters of Charles Sumner*, IV, 271-73.

that which I have recently derived from the most reliable authority, I am induced to cherish the belief that sectional animosity is surely and rapidly merging itself into a spirit of nationality...."[12]

In his annual message to Congress a little earlier, the President had endeavored to justify his use of pardon and amnesty as the proper course to take in the plan of reconstruction. "In exercising that power," he stated, "I have taken every precaution to connect it with the clearest recognition of the binding force of the laws of the United States and an unqualified acknowledgement of the great social change of Conditions in regard to slavery which has grown out of the war." Furthermore, he believed an invitation to the states lately in rebellion to participate in amending the Constitution should be accompanied by a liberal exercise of amnesty. He thought his policy of clemency, therefore, to be entirely consistent with the pressing needs of the South.[13]

But Congress proposed to do its own investigating and then determine the proper course to take in dealing with the Southerners. One of the first things it did, upon assembling in December, was to appoint a joint committee to inquire into the condition of the late Confederate States "and report whether they or any of them are entitled to be represented in either house of Congress." This body sat for several months and examined persons on the status of affairs in the South.[14]

Forty-four witnesses were asked to express an opinion on the effect of the President's amnesty proclamation and the pardons which had been granted. The questions asked were something like this: Do you think that President Johnson's liberal policy in granting pardons and amnesties has made the masses of the people more or less respectful toward the government of the United States than they were before? Of the total number questioned, forty-two answered in the negative. The substance of their evidence was that the measure was unwise and that the Southerners had far less respect for the Federal government after being pardoned. One man be-

12. *Sen. Exec. Doc.*, No. 2, 39 Cong., 1 Sess. Johnson also submitted to the Senate a number of letters from Schurz bearing upon conditions in the South. *Ibid.*

13. Richardson, *Messages ... of the Presidents*, VI, 357-58.

14. *Report of the Joint Committee on Reconstruction*, 39 Cong., 1 Sess. (a separate volume), *passim*.

lieved that they mistook "leniency as an evidence of weakness and not an evidence of generosity." Another made the significant statement that pardons had not drawn the people closer to the government, but that he believed that they drew them closer to President Johnson. In general, the witnesses testified that the Southerners appeared crushed and penitent until they obtained their pardons; then most of them became arrogant, aggressive, and abusive of the national government.

The two witnesses who believed that the measure was beneficial qualified their statements. One (from Alabama) stated that most of those pardoned in his section of the state were in the twenty-thousand-dollar class. "Some of them," he said, "acted very differently before they were pardoned" from the way they behaved later. The change, perhaps, could be accounted for by their natural feeling of independence after receiving their pardons, rather than from any feeling of antagonism toward the government.[15] Thus it is seen that the preponderance of this testimony was against Johnson's policy of clemency.

While the joint committee was carrying on its investigation, the House asked the President for "the names of persons worth more than twenty thousand dollars to whom special pardons" had been given and a statement of the amount of property which had been "seized as belonging to the enemies of the Government or as abandoned property and returned to those who claimed to be the original owners." The information was submitted on May 4, 1866, and showed that 7,197 persons in this class had been pardoned and that considerable property had been restored to its former owners. Three days later Johnson submitted to the Senate a report by Benjamin C. Truman, who, as the President's special commissioner, had spent seven months investigating conditions in the South. Truman's conclusions supported the executive's policy, but the report had no more influence in Congress than Grant's.[16]

THE FOURTEENTH AMENDMENT

Long before these reports were submitted, the President and the

15. *Ibid.*, pt. 3, pp. 66-67.
16. *Sen. Exec. Doc.*, No. 43, 39 Cong., 1 Sess., 4; Oberholtzer, *History of the United States since the Civil War*, I, 158-59.

Radicals in Congress had been denouncing each other. On February 22, 1866, for instance, Johnson had said publicly that he regarded Charles Sumner, Thaddeus Stevens, and Wendell Phillips "as being opposed to the fundamental principles of this government, and as now laboring to destroy them." At the same time, however, he stated that he was in favor of punishing a few of the Southern leaders whom he designated as "conscious, intelligent traitors"; but to those who had "been forced into the rebellion" he believed "clemency and kindness" should be shown. Nevertheless, just when, where, and whom the President was going to punish was becoming more uncertain. He had admitted earlier "that his disposition had been to go faster than he had done restoring them to their rights, but [that he] had slackened his hand in deference to others."[17]

As time passed, therefore, the number Johnson professed to be reserving for punishment became smaller and smaller. This caused the Radicals much apprehension, especially since the amnestied Southerners seemed to be running their state governments in such manner as to deny the Negroes the fruits of their newly gained freedom. Furthermore, the opposition feared that the pardoned secessionists, if admitted to representation in Congress, would unite with the Democrats of the North and obtain control of the government.[18] This the President's enemies determined never to permit, as they had already clearly indicated in December, 1865, by refusing to seat representatives chosen by the states lately in rebellion. Even before the Joint Committee on Reconstruction reported, they evolved the Fourteenth Amendment to the Constitution. Briefly stated, this proposed measure guaranteed citizenship to "all persons born or naturalized in the United States . . . ," reduced representation in Congress from any state denying the franchise to any of its citizens, assured the payment of the Federal public debt, and outlawed any obligation assumed in support of the rebellion. The third section of the amendment was particularly intended to deny the right to hold any public office, civil or military, to those who, "having previously taken an oath . . . to support the Constitution . . .

17. McPherson, *Reconstruction*, 60-61; Browning, *Diary*, II, 57 (January 2, 1866).
18. Blaine, *Twenty Years of Congress*, II, 233-34; Pierce, *Memoir and Letters of Charles Sumner*, IV, 269 ff.

shall have engaged . . . in rebellion against the same, or given aid or comfort to the enemies thereof." Thus the political effect of the President's pardons would be nullified, since the proposed amendment further provided that the imposed disability could only be removed "by a two-thirds vote of each House" of Congress.

While Thaddeus Stevens was introducing the amendment to the House, the question of its conflict with the President's power to amnesty, as conferred in Section 13 of the Confiscation Act, arose. James G. Blaine wanted to know if the proposed action did not place the members in the attitude of rescinding by constitutional amendment what had previously "been given by Act of Congress and by Presidential proclamation issued in pursuance of the law." He also suggested that such a course could "be justly subject to the charge of bad faith on the part of the Federal Government." In short, he desired to know what would be the condition of those who had been amnestied before the ratification of the amendment. Would they return to their former criminal status under the punitive laws? Stevens finally extricated himself from the confusion by stating that "those who had been fully pardoned" would not be affected by the amendment. But Blaine reminded him that many thousands had no documentary proof of their pardons; and James A. Garfield further vexed him by stating that, since most of the Confederates had already been amnestied, the third section would apply to so few that it would be practically useless.[19]

Thus there developed early in 1866 a serious problem involving the effect of the disability clause in the proposed amendment on the President's pardons already granted under the mitigating clause of the Confiscation Act. Furthermore, the situation was further complicated by the recognized constitutional right of the President to grant reprieves and pardons. Since Johnson was charged with using his pardoning power to re-establish the rebels in control of the South, the controversy had a real political significance, to which the Radicals were obliged to give immediate attention. They deemed it mandatory, therefore, to distinguish between presidential and congressional pardons. Did the President have the constitutional power to proclaim amnesties, or was he limited to reprieves and

19. *Cong. Globe*, 39 Cong., 1 Sess., 2460 ff. (May 8, 1866). Also Blaine, *Twenty Years of Congress*, II, 205 ff.

pardons except when authorized by Congress to grant amnesties? Just what was meant by pardons in the Constitution anyway? The document did not include the word amnesty; hence, did the power to pardon also include the power to amnesty? In short, were the terms "pardon" and "amnesty" synonymous, or did they have different meanings and applications? Moreover, did Congress have the power to bestow pardon and amnesty? The Radicals were impelled to define the words so that the power to pardon would work to their advantage and not to the interest of the President.

The great debate on the delegated power to grant pardon and amnesty and the scope of such clemency came in the Senate during the following session when the bill to repeal Section 13 of the Confiscation Act was passed. The essentials of the argument, however, were asserted in the House during this session and might well be given briefly here. Bent on reducing Johnson's political influence, Representative John W. Longyear of Michigan declared that something must be done to curtail presidential pardoning power so that no "traitor" would ever sit in Congress. Thaddeus Stevens readily took the position that a pardon only nullified a crime and did not restore political privilege. He called for precedents and proofs that it did more than free one from such punishment as imprisonment, fine, or confiscation of property. Some Senators endeavored to answer him during the next session. General Nathaniel P. Banks of Massachusetts supported Stevens in the House by arguing that the President could not restore political privileges; and General Robert C. Schenck of Ohio declared that, since the Southerners had lost their political rights by rebelling, the President could only remove their criminal status and relieve them from any likelihood of punishment for violating laws providing punishment for supporting the Confederacy. This position was also taken by Thomas D. Eliot of Massachusetts, who asserted that Congress alone could grant the late rebels the privilege of participating in national elections.[20]

It should be noted that the Senate omitted a significant clause in the House resolution containing the Fourteenth Amendment. The third section of this measure, as formulated by the Representatives, provided that all persons who had voluntarily supported the Confederacy should be denied the privilege of voting for members of

20. *Cong. Globe*, 39 Cong. 1 Sess., 2470, 2511-12, 2532-37.

Congress or presidential electors. The Senate, however, without a dissenting vote, modified the section and cast the amendment in the form in which it was later submitted for ratification. The disability thus imposed, therefore, was not as inclusive in its application as the House majority first desired to have it. Congress did legislate against voting by ex-Confederates in the first supplemental reconstruction act (March 23, 1867), as will be shown later.

Notwithstanding the apparent enthusiasm for the Fourteenth Amendment, an effort was made in the Senate to save the President's pardoning prerogative. Senator Saulsbury of Delaware would have authorized either Congress by a two-thirds vote, or the President by the exercise of the pardoning power, to remove the disability proposed in the third section; but his proposition failed by a large vote. Finally, Senator Doolittle of Wisconsin offered a proviso to the effect that the disability should not apply to those whom the President had already pardoned. His effort was also futile, for it received the support of only ten Senators. As Blaine stated many years later: "The effect of this vote unmistakably settled," in the judgment of Congress, "that the operation of the Fourteenth Amendment would not in the least degree be affected by the President's pardons." [21]

The argument over the power to grant pardon and amnesty, however, and about the effect of the third section of the Fourteenth Amendment on presidential pardons and amnesties was not yet closed. This will be shown presently when the repeal of the clement section in the Confiscation Act is discussed. In June, 1866, the amendment was sent to the states for ratification. With the exception of Tennessee, all members of the Confederacy (and Delaware and Kentucky) rejected the amendment until they were forced, in 1867, to ratify in order to regain representation in Congress. In the meantime, other matters germane to the quarrel between the executive and Congress were attended to. Nevertheless, Johnson pursued his original policy of clemency in spite of laws and the amendment, though his clemency lost most of its original potency.

The Joint Committee on Reconstruction rendered a full report on June 18, 1866, though its findings, of course, had been made

21. *Ibid.*, 2914-21 (May 31, 1866); Blaine, *Twenty Years of Congress*, II, 211.

known to members of Congress as the investigation progressed. On the matter of the President's clemency the Committee reported "that after the collapse of the Confederacy the feeling of the people of the rebellious states was that of abject submission," but that "the general issue of pardons to persons who had been prominent in the rebellion, and the feeling of kindness and conciliation manifested by the Executive" and the Northern press had caused whole communities to forget their crimes and to become defiant toward the Federal government. "The bitterness and defiance exhibited . . . ," the report ran, "is without parallel in the history of the world. In return for our leniency we receive only an insulting denial of our authority. . . . The crime we have punished is paraded as a virtue, and the principles of republican government which we have vindicated at so terrible a cost are announced as unjust and oppressive."[22]

This report and the Fourteenth Amendment, then, were formal protests of Congress against the President's policy of leniency. With these measures might also be included the Civil Rights and the Freedmen's Bureau bills, which were passed over the executive's veto on April 9 and July 16, respectively. But Johnson did not allow these measures to restrain him, and former Confederate leaders continued to receive his pardon along with men of lesser prominence.

The President's opposition to the ratification of the amendment and his vigorous activity in the congressional election of 1866 augmented the breach between him and Congress. Johnson hoped, of course, that candidates who opposed his policy would be defeated. In his "swing around the circle," as his speechmaking tour during the campaign was called, he allowed himself to be provoked into saying many things which angered his adversaries and put him in an unfavorable light before the voters.[23] Moreover, the failure in 1866 of the states of the late Confederacy, except Tennessee, to ratify the Fourteenth Amendment, and the Memphis and New Orleans riots in July, still further discredited Johnson with many people. The election, therefore, resulted in a victory for the Radi-

22. *Report of the Joint Committee on Reconstruction*, 39 Cong., 1 Sess., 18.
23. Blaine, *Twenty Years in Congress*, II, 239-48; Pierce, *Memoir and Letters of Charles Sumner*, IV, 299-301; Oberholtzer, *History of the United States since the Civil War*, I, 396-413; DeWitt, *Impeachment and Trial of Andrew Johnson*, 124-26.

cals, who became more determined than ever to curtail the President's pardoning power—if they could.

REPEAL OF THE AMNESTY CLAUSE IN THE CONFISCATION ACT

As soon as Congress met in December, 1866, the House hurriedly passed and sent to the Senate a bill to repeal Section 13 of the Confiscation Act. This measure was intended to rescind the authority which Congress had given the President (July 17, 1862) to extend pardon and amnesty by proclamation, and its advocates believed its passage would restrain Johnson in his career of leniency. The repeal, at least, would register the preponderating sentiment in Congress against the President's policy of clemency. Furthermore, it would leave Johnson to rely solely on his disputed constitutional power to grant amnesty by proclamation; and if he endeavored to grant such clemency again, his act would subject him to grave charges of high crimes and misdemeanors. In this manner the Radicals in Congress reasoned as they planned the undoing of the President.

The debate on the bill in the Senate is worthy of consideration from both historical and constitutional standpoints. The friends of the measure desired its immediate passage "to prevent an unwise restoration of property" to persons whom the President might yet pardon. To Senator Howard of Michigan the power to restore forfeited property seemed "to be a distinct and separate function conferred on the President by the confiscation act" of 1862. Now, he believed, the country desired that power withdrawn at once. His colleague, Chandler, insisted that the bill to repeal should be passed to stop the restoration of property to persons whose pardons were being obtained by women of "doubtful reputation." Senator Trumbull of Illinois was at first in favor of immediate action, but late in the debate of the first day he expressed the thought that the bill should be referred to a committee for consideration.

The opposition to the measure, led by Reverdy Johnson of Maryland, pointed out the fact that, if the President could grant only general amnesty under the power conferred by Congress, a repeal of Section 13 of the Confiscation Act would still leave him the authority under the Constitution to issue individual pardons to any persons who might want them. Fessenden of Maine could see no advantage in immediate action. Such haste, he thought, might cause the consummation of that which the repeal was intended to prevent. The President "has ten days in which to consider every bill," the Senator said, and in this interval "he might do whatever he chose to do" before approving the bill. In other words, Johnson might proclaim a universal amnesty—a power existing under the very law whose repeal was under consideration.[24]

In the debate the next day on a motion to refer the bill to the Committee on the Judiciary, Chandler renewed his charge that pardons were for sale in Washington by disreputable women, and declared that such disgraces and abuses of the pardoning power should be curtailed by the immediate passage of the bill. The President, he insisted, should be allowed only the power to pardon conferred by the Constitution. Senator Grimes of Iowa, however, did not see how such precipitate action could head the President off if he were about to issue another general proclamation of amnesty. Furthermore, he feared the immediate passage might be regarded by the people generally as causing the President "to do something of the kind."

Senator Henderson of Missouri rightly doubted that the "Act of 1862 . . . conferred any additional power upon the President." Repeal, in that event, was unnecessary. He also stated that the Supreme Court had recently decided that a pardon granted at any time restored to an individual all his former rights, and that "all the rights which had not been taken entirely from the individual, by a decree of a court," were restored to him as a necessary consequence of the pardon. It was his opinion that the bill should go to the judicial committee. Senator Dixon of Connecticut denied emphatically that pardons were on sale and stated that the bill should not be passed in "hot haste . . . with such a charge preferred against the President of the United States."[25]

At the conclusion of the debate, the motion to refer the bill to the judicial committee was passed without the yeas and nays. On the following day, this committee reported in favor of enacting the

24. *Cong. Globe*, 39 Cong., 2 Sess., pt. 1, pp. 8, 9.
25. *Ibid.*, 14, 15.

measure; but, owing to other pressing business, further consideration was not given it until December 17.

In the next debate, Trumbull spoke at great length in favor of
the bill. Admitting the President's power to pardon and recognizing
all the benefits therefrom, he said questions relative to such had
been "settled by decisions of the Attorney-General and of the
Supreme Court . . . years ago." But why repeal this measure? He
answered by stating "that this thirteenth section is broader than
the Constitution; it authorized the President by proclamation to
grant pardon and amnesty." By this he meant that the President had
the constitutional right only to grant individual, or special, pardons,
and that Congress alone could empower him to extend amnesty by
proclamation. The Senator also sought to explain the difference between the terms pardon and amnesty. The second word did not
appear in the Constitution; hence his ground for giving it a broader
application than pardon. He stated: "A pardon is an act of mercy
extended to an individual; it must be by deed; it must be delivered—
an amnesty on the contrary is a general pardon proclaimed by
proclamation." Then he continued to argue that, since the President "had already issued general proclamations of amnesty and
pardon," and since "no occasion for the exercise of that power"
then existed, there was good reason for repealing Section 13 of the
Confiscation Act. He did not want Congress to assume any responsibility for further clemency to persons who had already shown
themselves "so undeserving of the mercy which has been extended
to them."[26]

Senator Johnson refuted Trumbull's argument by declaring that
the "power conferred upon the President by the Constitution is as
comprehensive as words can make it." Since this power is conferred
upon him absolutely in general terms, "it is for him to decide as to
the manner in which he will execute it." He may "execute it by
granting" individual pardons or by extending amnesty to groups
of individuals at his own discretion. The Senator then went on to
substantiate his argument. He gave Washington's amnesty to the
participants in the Whiskey Rebellion as an example of executive

26. *Ibid.*, 143-45. See Ch. XVII for opinions of the courts on the meanings
of the words pardon and amnesty.

328 *Pardon and Amnesty under Lincoln and Johnson*

clemency to persons en masse without congressional sanction.[27] He also supported his proposition by quoting Hamilton as believing that when a crime is leveled at the state it appears proper to refer "the expediency of an act of mercy to the judgment of the Legislature," since the supposition of the connivance of the chief magistrate with the perpetrators of the crime ought not to be entirely excluded. "But there are also strong objections to such a plan," Hamilton concluded, "for one man of prudence and good sense is better fitted, in delicate conjunctures, to balance the punishment, than any numerous body whatever." Hamilton believed, therefore, that the Chief Executive, and not Congress, should grant amnesties.[28] In this manner the Senator argued that President Johnson ought to be left unhampered in the exercise of the power to pardon persons lately in rebellion against the government.

Other business in the Senate stopped the debate at this time, and the bill was not taken up again until January 4, 1867, when Senator Johnson continued his argument by giving English precedent. "The English monarch," he said "from time to time has granted pardon and granted amnesty by proclamation." This power, he insisted, belonged also to the President of the United States by heritage as well as by constitutional right.[29]

At this point an interesting turn was injected into the debate by Senator Saulsbury, who offered an amendment to repeal the whole of the Confiscation Act of 1862. In brief, he believed that, since the Confederates had established a *de facto* government, which had excluded the *de jure* government and compelled the obedience of those under its jurisdiction, those against whom the law of July, 1862, was directed were not guilty of treason and should not be subject to the penalties under that law. Its name, "an act to punish treason," he said, was a misnomer. "Will you tell me, sir," he continued, "that you can frame a bill of indictment like this against eight million people?" He answered by pointing out that Great

27. See Richardson, *Messages . . . of the Presidents*, I, 173, for Washington's amnesty. Other early precedents are John Adams's amnesty to the offenders in Fries's Rebellion of 1799 and Madison's to persons who, during the War of 1812, opposed the Federal authorities in certain warlike acts on the Island of Barataria at the mouth of the Mississippi River. *Ibid.*, I, 303-4, 558-60.
28. See *The Federalist*, edited by Henry B. Dawson, 517-19.
29. *Cong. Globe*, 39 Cong., 2 Sess., pt. 1, pp. 267-69.

Britain had done no such thing when the Thirteen Colonies rebelled against her. On the contrary, the *de facto* government set up by the revolting Colonies had regarded as enemies those citizens of the Colonies who claimed allegiance to Great Britain. Then, after quoting Blackstone, he declared: "A usurper [meaning the Confederate Government] who has got possession of the throne is a king within the meaning of the statute."

Saulsbury's argument, therefore, was that the act of separation of South Carolina from the United States in 1860 was similar to the separation of South Carolina from Great Britain in 1776. In other words, if the people owed allegiance to the state in 1776, they were obliged to support the action of that same government in its act of secession in 1860. He gave Madison as his authority, and insisted that the great mass of people in the South could not be guilty of treason and deserving of punishment. Notwithstanding Saulsbury's able argument, his motion to amend was lost.[30]

Senator Hendricks of Indiana offered a sensible objection to the repeal. It was his opinion that such action would be interpreted by the country at large "as an expression by Congress against a conciliatory course toward the Southern States. It will be understood," he said, "as an expression by Congress of its opinion that there ought not to be pardon extended to the people of the South, and that the policy which was understood to have been adopted by Mr. Lincoln before his death, and the policy which was subsequently pursued by Mr. Johnson . . . in extending pardons was an improper one." He believed also that the repeal of Section 13 would not affect the President's power to pardon one whit, and wondered whether conditions should not remain as they were.

The Senate (with eighteen members "absent") passed the bill on January 4 by a vote of twenty-seven to seven. President Johnson refused to sign it, but Congress quickly overrode his veto, and the measure became a law on January 7.

In this connection it should be noted that the Radicals had been determined for a long time to impeach Johnston. One ostensible reason for the repeal, therefore, was to deprive "the President of a plausible answer to one of the grounds of impeachment—his abuse of the pardoning power." Furthermore, his general amnesties, if

30. *Ibid.*, 273-74.

there were to be others, would also be put in an unconstitutional light before the country.[31]

DENIAL OF THE POLITICAL BENEFITS OF PARDON

Nevertheless, there were a great many persons already enjoying the political benefits of presidential clemency. The repeal alone, therefore, would not affect their status. Realizing this, the Radicals determined to resort to other means to gain their purpose.

It was true that Congress had refused to seat representatives elected by persons amnestied by Presidents Lincoln and Johnson; and in this manner the opposing members had disregarded political rights claimed under the mitigating section of the Confiscation Act. But something more had to be done to annul every phase of presidential reconstruction. Not only must there be no more amnesties proclaimed from the White House, but there must also be a partial annulment of the pardons and amnesties already granted. In short, there were to be no political benefits whatever resulting from any clement acts of the executive. Moreover, all the late Confederate States, except Tennessee, were to undergo another reconstruction before they would be fully recognized. The Radicals, therefore, soon evolved measures which revoked the political effects of previous clemency without constitutional amendment. Thus the principles of the second and third sections of the Fourteenth Amendment were applied even before ratification. Negroes were allowed to vote and hold office, and many whites were disfranchised, notwithstanding any previous or subsequent presidential pardons and amnesties. Henceforth, amnesty was to be a congressional prerogative to be exercised with the utmost caution.

In perpetrating this "monstrous thing," as John W. Burgess characterized that portion of the new reconstruction which "put the white race of the South under the domination of the negro race," Congress enacted four laws.[32] The first was passed on March 2, 1867, and the last on March 11, 1868, and all went into effect without the President's signature. The law of March 2 divided the ten unrecognized states into five military districts, each under control of a major general of the United States army (a brigadier general

31. DeWitt, *Impeachment and Trial of Andrew Johnson*, 136.
32. Burgess, *Reconstruction and the Constitution, 1866-1876*, 133.

might have been appointed), who was to maintain military rule until the states in his district had organized a satisfactory government, had ratified the Fourteenth Amendment, and were otherwise ready for proper recognition by Congress. Negroes might participate in this program, but persons "excluded from the privilege of holding office under the proposed amendment" might not.[33] Thus political benefits of presidential pardons and amnesties were annulled along with the destruction of all but one of the eleven state governments which Presidents Lincoln and Johnson had recognized.

The first law provided no machinery for putting its program in operation. The new Congress, therefore, reassembled on March 4 in special session without the call of the President, and on March 23 passed over Johnson's veto a supplemental law. This measure not only made provisions for the administration of the first act, but it also required of every voter, when registering, an oath that he had "never been a member of any State legislature, nor held any executive or judicial office in any State, and afterwards engaged in . . . rebellion against the United States," and that he had "never taken an oath as a member of any State legislature, or as an executive or judicial officer of any State, to support the Constitution . . . and afterwards engaged in . . . rebellion against the United States. . . ."[34] This drastic measure not only excluded a multitude of Southerners from holding office, but it also denied them the privilege of voting. The law of disfranchisement, therefore, was more extensive than the third section of the Fourteenth Amendment.

Here again amnestied Southerners were legislated against. Nevertheless, many still believed that the President's pardon had restored both their civil and political rights, notwithstanding any laws of Congress to the contrary. The Supreme Court encouraged them in this belief, for in December, 1866, it had declared in *Ex parte Garland* that the "power of the President is not subject to legislative control, [and that] Congress can neither limit the effect of his

33. *U. S. Stat. at Large*, XIV, 428-29. For fuller accounts of congressional reconstruction, see Rhodes, *History of the United States*, VI, Chs. XXXI-XXXIII; Oberholtzer, *History of the United States since the Civil War*, I, *passim*; Randall, *The Civil War and Reconstruction*, Chs. XXXII, XXXIII.

34. *U. S. Stat. at Large*, XV, 2-4. Election officers were required to take the iron-clad oath.

pardon, nor exclude from its exercise any class of offenders." Then, after further elucidation, the Court concluded that Congress could not "inflict punishment beyond the reach of executive clemency."[35] Since the opinion was in favor of a pardoned Confederate's claiming immunity from taking the iron-clad test oath, it meant that presidential amnesty could not be affected by the acts of congressional reconstruction.

Just a week before this decision the House had referred to its Committee on the Judiciary impeachment charges against the President, accusing him, among other things, of having "corruptly used the pardoning power."[36] Naturally, the Radicals attacked the Supreme Court for declaring executive clemency beyond congressional restriction. Representative George S. Boutwell, in urging legislation to make that tribunal more submissive to the will of Congress, had appeared to see some hidden influence of the President on the judiciary. From his seat in the House he had declared, on January 21, 1867, that it was "an offense to the dignity and respectability of the nation that the Supreme Court" did "not protect itself from the contamination of rebels and traitors. . . ." Then, after stating that Congress would have to do what the Court had failed in its duty to perform, he asserted that, although the President might open jails and penitentiaries and release criminals, while he occupied a place in the House a pardon by the President should never "be a certificate on which a felon enters into the sacred tribunals of the land, and assists in the administration of the law."[37]

Nevertheless, no legislation affecting the Supreme Court was enacted. It is not beside the general subject, however, to note a further attempt on the part of one member of Congress to restrict the President's power to pardon. On March 19, 1867, Thaddeus Stevens introduced a bill in the House to confiscate estates of persons worth more than five thousand dollars who could not take the oath of

35. See Ch. XVII, "Pardon and Amnesty in the Courts."

36. DeWitt, *Impeachment and Trial of Andrew Johnson*, 136; McPherson, *Reconstruction*, 188. The House, however, did not impeach the President until 1868.

37. *Cong. Globe*, 39th Cong., 2 Sess., pt. 1, p. 649; also the Richmond *Enquirer*, January 25, 1867. Other decisions which had also aroused the ire of the Radicals were *Ex parte Milligan* (Ch. VI) and *Cummings* vs. *Missouri* (4 Wall. 277). Cf. Oberholtzer, *History of the United States since the Civil War*, I, 463-67.

July 17, 1862. Such a law would certainly have rescinded existing property benefits derived from pardons and caused general consternation in the South on that score. In supporting his bill, Stevens said: "I must take the liberty to deny that any pardon, or any other power vested in the President, can withdraw the forfeited properties from the confiscation decreed by Congress. Nothing less than an act of Congress can divest them from the United States and bestow them on the pardoned belligerent." Stevens sarcastically credited the bill to Andrew Johnson, whose disciple he claimed to be in his determination to punish those who had tried to destroy the Union. He declared that the President had "favored confiscation while he was 'clothed and in his right mind,' but Seward [had] entered into him, 'and ever since they have been running down deep places into the sea.' "[38] Thus the beneficent Secretary of State was made to share the blame for Johnson's ever increasing leniency.

PARDON AND AMNESTY

The Reconstruction Act and its supplement of March 23 were not easily administered. The five generals nominated by Grant and appointed by the President were soon disagreeing with the existing state authorities in their respective districts. The civil officials naturally resented the assumed supremacy of the military. Serious dissatisfaction, for example, was manifested over the denial of registration to large numbers of whites. Negroes, of course, were encouraged to register; but the primary object of the Radicals was the disfranchisement of as many supporters of the Confederacy as could be classified under the disability provisions of the reconstruction measures.

Early in April a number of specially pardoned citizens of Atlanta vainly inquired of the editor of that city's *Daily Intelligencer* whether they were qualified to vote.[39] Pardoned individuals were denied registration; and others who insisted that their willingness to take the oath should admit them to register without stating their activities during the war were likewise refused. Moreover, persons

38. *Cong. Globe*, 40th Cong., 1 Sess., pp. 206-7; also Charleston *Mercury* and Richmond *Enquirer*, March 23, 1867, and Samuel W. McCall, *Thaddeus Stevens*, 325.

39. Atlanta *Daily Intelligencer*, April 10, 1867.

who declared that they had served the Confederacy under coercion and consequently deserved the franchise were also turned away. Boards of registration insisted on carefully reviewing the activities of all applicants during the war and were strict in applying the regulations.

But what caused the military authorities much concern was the scarcity of whites who qualified for service in the new program of reconstruction. One good example will suffice. General Sickles, in charge of the second district (the Carolinas), found it necessary to allow many who were disqualified to remain in office so that the new plan of state organization could be set up properly. On July 1, 1867, he further emphasized the seriousness of the situation in a letter to Senator Trumbull recommending universal suffrage and universal amnesty as "essential to the success of the congressional plan of Reconstruction. It will enlarge the range of choice," he continued, "for the important Judicial, Executive and Legislative departments of the State Governments, now inconveniently confined to classes very few of whom are fit to hold office."[40]

Such counsel, though coming from a Radical, was anathema to friends of congressional reconstruction. Perhaps General Miles best expressed the extreme view of the opposition when he wrote to Senator Sumner, on July 13, that "to declare a general amnesty for those who are openly and avowedly enemies [of the new plan of reconstruction] would be placing the knife again in the hands of the Government's assassins."[41] Nevertheless, Sickles's opinion was the practical conclusion of one who had found his task made exceedingly difficult by the disfranchising provisions of a law which he was obliged to execute and whose execution, unless modified, was likely to be disastrous to the best interests of the South.

So much confusion existed, therefore, that, in due time, the President was asked to determine the respective limits of the civil and military authorities in the districts and the extent of the disfranchise-

40. William A. Russ, Jr., "Radical Disfranchisement in South Carolina (1867-68)," *Susquehanna University Studies*, I (January, 1939), 148-60 (quoting letter from Sickles to Trumbull in Johnson Papers, Vol. CXVI, No. 16013).

41. Russ, "Radical Disfranchisement in North Carolina, 1867-1868," *North Carolina Historical Review*, XI (October, 1934) 277; also Sumner Papers, LXXXII, 79.

ment to be enforced by the registration officers. Johnson rightly referred the matter to his Attorney-General, whose opinions (May 24 and June 12, 1867) were approved by the Cabinet (Stanton excepted) on June 18 and properly announced two days later.[42] Stanbery's interpretation of the laws was favorable to the Southerners. He stated that when a person took the prescribed oath "his name must go upon the register. The board of registration," he continued, "cannot enter upon the inquiry whether he has sworn truly or falsely." If the registrant swore falsely, he could be tried later and punished for perjury. Furthermore, "a person forced into the rebel service by conscription," or otherwise coerced into supporting the Confederacy, was not to be disfranchised. He also stated that, until the new governments intended by Congress were organized, the existing governments should constitute the ordinary rule, to which the military authorities should be auxiliary.[43]

Other instructions which the President sent the five generals in charge of reconstruction need not be given. Stanbery did not directly mention the effects of pardons and amnesties, but the apparent inference was that the scope of his interpretation included the political benefits of such presidential clemency. At least, some law officials in the districts acted as if they thought so. The United States Attorney at Savannah, for example, stated that "a pardon by the President blots out all disfranchisement and restores the pardoned individual to all franchises of a citizen, including the elective. If a person thus pardoned," he continued, "is refused registration, let him enter a protest for the consideration of the commanding general." Influenced by this opinion, thirteen citizens of Savannah presented their pardons and demanded registration. On being refused, they published an account of the board's refusal in the press of the city.[44]

The reaction to these denials was so unfavorable that the president of the board informed the Savannah *Republican* that persons who had pardons might register on taking the prescribed oath. This apparent victory, however, was short-lived, for the authorities higher

42. Oberholtzer, *History of the United States since the Civil War*, I, 458.
43. Burgess, *Reconstruction and the Constitution*, 136-38.
44. New York *Times*, June 29, 1867; Fredericksburg *News*, July 2, 1867; Atlanta *Daily Intelligencer* and Charleston *Courier*, July 3, 1867.

up refused to allow the privilege, and the inspector for registration under General Pope, who commanded the third district, ordered the recall of the notice.[45] Thus again, in spite of the opinion by the Supreme Court and the implied opinion of the Attorney-General to the contrary, pardons were not allowed to re-enfranchise the recipients.

Nevertheless, the fear of Negro majorities in the approaching elections caused many to claim registration on the basis of presidential clemency. Such insistence, of course, was encouraged by the recent executive instructions through Stanbery's office. Meanwhile the Radicals, becoming alarmed at the turn of affairs occasioned by the Attorney-General's opinion, assembled Congress on July 3, 1867. To allow the President and his legal advisor to determine the extent of white enfranchisement in the military districts would defeat one of the most desired objectives of congressional reconstruction. Johnson's enemies were determined that "loyalty must govern," that the Negroes must vote, and that a "bad man" must be restrained. Such resolution had kept them in readiness for action ever since the adjournment of Congress on March 30.[46] Another supplemental reconstruction act, therefore, was deemed necessary to free the military from any interference whatever by the civil authorities.

The law that was soon formulated and hurriedly passed (July 19) over the President's veto expressly provided that the civil officers should "be subject in all respects to the military commanders of the respective districts and to the paramount authority of Congress." The generals were authorized "to remove from office all persons" who used "their official influence in any manner to hinder, delay, prevent or obstruct the due and proper administration" of the reconstruction measures. Rulings of registration boards were to be final in every respect, and contrary opinions of civil officers were to be disregarded. Moreover, to make it clear that presidential pardons carried no political benefits, this second supplemental law provided

45. Atlanta *Daily Intelligencer*, July 6; Charleston *Courier*, July 8; Savannah *Republican*, July 15, 1867.

46. Robert S. Henry, *The Story of Reconstruction*, Ch. XXVIII; Milton, *Age of Hate*, 216, 219, 226, 381, 432, 433.

that "no person shall, at any time, be entitled to be registered or to vote by reason of any executive pardon or amnesty for any act or thing which, without such pardon or amnesty, would disqualify him for registration or voting."[47]

Thus the influence of the President in the program of reconstruction became completely ineffectual, except through his obligation as Chief Executive to enforce the laws of Congress. Though he had not approved such legislation, Johnson instructed his Attorney-General to support the constitutionality of the reconstruction acts when they were reviewed and confirmed by the Supreme Court in April and May, 1867.[48] In reality, he could not do otherwise. Henceforth, therefore, presidential pardon of ex-Confederates in no wise restored political privileges to the recipients. At least, that was the expectancy of the Radicals; and, in fact, the letter of the law was strictly carried out, notwithstanding subsequent pardons and amnesties which some persons believed should have restored the franchise. It should be borne in mind, however, that when conditions provided in the reconstruction acts were complied with, and when the political disability contained in the third section of the Fourteenth Amendment was removed by Congress, all privileges of franchise were restored.

Nevertheless, Congress deemed it necessary to pass one other supplemental reconstruction act. The measure had nothing to do (at least, directly) with pardon and amnesty, but mention of it properly concludes this chapter. Under the existing law, the adoption of a new constitution in a reconstructed state required the approval of a majority of all the registered voters. When opponents of the proposed constitution in Alabama recognized that their failing to vote in such an election would probably prevent ratification, they appealed to those opposed to ratification to refrain from voting. The appeal had the desired result, for the vote cast (February 4, 1868) for the new constitution was less than a majority of the number of registered voters. Congress was in session at the time, so the Radicals passed (March 11) another law providing that "any elec-

47. *U. S. Stat. at Large*, XV, 14-16.
48. *Mississippi* vs. *Johnson* (4 Wall. 475) and *Georgia* vs. *Stanton* (6 Wall. 50). See also Milton, *Age of Hate*, 437-38.

tion authorized by the reconstruction acts . . . shall be decided by a majority of the votes cast. . . ."[49]

Nothing now could prevent the "Crime of Reconstruction" from being perpetrated.[50] Consequently, all but one of the eleven states that had formed the Confederacy suffered from calamitous governments administered by misguided and illiterate Negroes, by unscrupulous Northern adventurers, and by erring white Southerners. The absolute annulment of the political benefits of executive clemency left the Southland practically helpless, until those of her citizens who were most competent to govern were re-enfranchised and until a new and more reliable electorate had issued from the ashes of the Civil War and Reconstruction.

49. Randall, *Civil War and Reconstruction*, 759; McPherson, *Reconstruction*, 336.

50. David Saville Muzzey used this term for the heading of a chapter in his well-known high school text in American history.

CHAPTER FIFTEEN

OTHER PRESIDENTIAL AMNESTIES

———◆———

ANOTHER AMNESTY DESIRED

T HE NATION was to learn whether Congress had really curtailed the Chief Executive's power to proclaim amnesties. The repeal of the clement section of the Confiscation Act was certainly a challenge to the President. Would Johnson respect the will of the Radicals, so emphatically manifested in legislation, by confining himself to granting individual pardons? His opponents had left him, so they believed, only this constitutional prerogative; yet his numerous special acts of clemency were to them still very objectionable, since the reported lists contained so many persons of property and influence.

Executive clemency had become very alarming. It was largely the political activities of these specially pardoned Southerners that had caused Congress to set presidential reconstruction aside and to disfranchise those who could not prove that they had never taken an oath to support the Constitution and subsequently broken it. The actions of such persons might have become more threatening if they were allowed to reach Washington. The Radicals knew, of course, that there were thousands of persons in Johnson's fourteen exceptions who were still unpardoned, but who could meet the test for suffrage if they were pardoned. Most of them had not applied for clemency, as provided in the proclamation, and might delay doing so (if they applied at all) until it was too late for favorable action on their petitions before the coming elections. The repeal of Section 13 of the Confiscation Act, therefore, was expected by its proponents to remove the power of the President to proclaim another amnesty and thus keep these proscribed Southerners from participating in politics.

By the time congressional reconstruction was taking definite form, in the summer of 1867, some 13,500 special pardons had been granted. Since the estimated number of persons excepted from the benefits of Johnson's proclamation of May 29, 1865, was more than 150,000, there remained much that the President might do if he should conclude to proclaim another amnesty, especially a universal one. In Georgia alone there were supposed to be, at the outset, more persons in the twenty-thousand-dollar exception than the entire number of this class in all the South to whom special pardon had already been given. Judging from the alarming rate at which such people of means had already been pardoned (7,197 by March 15, 1866), another proclamation was not likely to except those worth more than twenty thousand dollars again. All this—and more—the Radicals had in mind all along.

Johnson had been urged from time to time to proclaim a universal amnesty.[1] Even while the measure to repeal Section 13 was on his desk for his approval—which he never gave—he seriously considered issuing another proclamation. In fact, the day (January 8) following the passage of the rescinding bill, he discussed with his Cabinet the advisability of another amnesty. Stanton, who had just received a copy of an act by the North Carolina legislature extending clemency to all classes of war offenders against that state, "thought it would be well if there should be a reciprocal presidential amnesty."[2] The other members favored the suggestion, but no action was taken. The President, therefore, allowed the spring and summer of 1867 to pass without another proclamation. As the autumn elections approached, however, he became more determined to extend clemency again in this manner. Since the registration officials followed closely the instruction of Congress, Negro rule seemed certain unless something was done before it was too late to act.

Thus, as time passed and congressional reconstruction progressed,

1. New York *Herald*, October 1, 1865, and December 26, 1866; *Confederate Records* (Georgia), IV, 348; Attorneys-General's Papers (Library of Congress), R. W. Perkham to Stanbery, November 26, 1866.
2. Welles, *Diary*, III, 9 (January 8, 1867).

the Southerners and their sympathizers saw that existing pardons and amnesties had as yet accomplished nothing politically for them. In desperation they concluded that their only hope was in another presidential amnesty, which, they believed, would re-enfranchise enough whites to counteract the Negro vote. Certain Northern newspapers came to sustain this idea. The New York *Herald* (August 27), in urging another such proclamation, stated: "With universal amnesty the reconstruction problems will be finished at a stroke; intelligence will replace ignorance . . . and the negro may take position second to the common sense of the country." A day earlier it had referred to Lincoln's emancipation of the Negroes and advised the President to proclaim, "by universal amnesty, an emancipation for the white portion of the population." Three days later this paper also declared that Congress could not limit the power of the Chief Executive to proclaim amnesties, since the Constitution gave him that prerogative. The Chicago *Times* would have had "all classes from Jefferson Davis down" pardoned, and believed: "A declaration of universal amnesty would be, for the most unpopular administration of Mr. Johnson, a master stroke of policy. It is, indeed," the paper continued, "the last move on the political chessboard that is left him if he expects to be President of the United States to the expiration of his official term."[3]

So, as September approached, Johnson became convinced of the necessity of another proclamation of amnesty. One way of extending clemency, of course, was by granting special pardons, but that method entailed too much individual consideration. Moreover, there were many thousands in the excepted classes who had not applied for pardon, and, according to the terms of the first proclamation, special pardons were to be given only to those who petitioned for clemency. There were civil benefits derived from pardon and amnesty besides the political privileges which congressional reconstruction measures now denied. Yet, apparently, another amnesty was desired because of the political benefits it was expected to confer. A second proclamation, therefore, seemed certain to be issued in the near future. On August 5, Reverdy Johnson encouraged the President to act, assuring him that the Constitution clearly gave him the necessary power; and on August 24 Secretary

3. August 30, September 5, 1867.

Welles and the President considered the "expediency of a general amnesty . . . before voting began in the proscribed States."[4]

DRAFTING THE PROCLAMATION

On September 2, Welles and Johnson compared their respective drafts of a proclamation. The President's document, apparently the work of Seward, was better prepared, and the Cabinet accepted it.[5] Evidently Welles wanted the proclamation to include more than Seward thought advisable. Even before the proclamation was approved, he had advised extending the franchise in the South by reducing the exceptions from amnesty as provided in the proclamation of May 29, 1865. It is apparent, therefore, that the Secretary of the Navy not only was interested in material benefits derived from amnesty but also wished the new measure to allow the restoration of the privileges of voting and holding office.

Furthermore, Welles desired to have the proclamation allude to General Grant's favorable report, in December, 1865, on the workings of presidential reconstruction. He would also have included a statement to the effect that congressional amnesty was allowed by Section 13 of the Confiscation Act at the end of hostilities, and that such clemency had been promised by the government and received by the Southerners "in good faith" after May 29, 1865, though Congress had later "in bad faith" denied it (January 7, 1867).

Notwithstanding his failure to get these ideas incorporated into the document, Welles found consolation in the fact that he had recommended a more inclusive and sympathetic proclamation than Seward would allow the President to issue. Of his colleague, he said: ". . . He prefers what he believes to be expedient to what he knows to be right."

The President and his two Secretaries did agree to point out in the proclamation certain aggravating conditions in the South that should be considered in extending executive clemency. After expressing the danger of maintaining standing armies and of suspending the writ of habeas corpus and the right of trial by jury in

4. Johnson Papers, XCIX, No. 12211; Welles, *Diary*, III, 183.
5. Welles, *Diary*, III, 193, 197 (September 2, 6, 1867).

time of peace, they emphasized the existing policy of vindictiveness attended by "unnecessary disqualifications, pains, penalties, confiscations, and disfranchisements." In their opinion, such disabilities delayed "reconciliation among the people" and seriously embarassed, obstructed, and repressed national prosperity. They resolved, therefore, to cause a "more perfect restoration of constitutional law and order" by modifying Johnson's first amnesty, so "that the full and beneficent pardon conceded thereby should be approved and further extended to a large number of persons" who had been excepted from its benefits.[6]

In due time, therefore, the President formulated a proclamation, to which both Welles and Seward had contributed, and issued it on September 7. This amnesty was not universal; but it is worth noting that wealth was no longer a hindrance to clemency, so that many in the twenty-thousand-dollar class who had not applied for pardon were now relieved. Furthermore, persons in other classes excepted in Johnson's first proclamation and not yet pardoned received the benefits of presidential clemency. In fact, the measure had only three general exceptions: (1) the President, Vice-President, heads of departments, foreign agents, those above the army rank of brigadier general and naval rank of captain, and the governors of the several Confederate States; (2) "all persons who in any way treated otherwise than as prisoners of war persons who in any capacity were employed in the military or naval service of the United States"; and (3) all who were "actually in civil, military, or naval confinement, or legally held to bail either before or after conviction. . . ." This last exception also included those who were implicated in any way in the assassination of President Lincoln. Those availing themselves of the benefits of the amnesty were required to take the oath to support the Constitution and to respect all matters pertaining to slavery contained in Johnson's first proclamation.

There were now, probably, only some three hundred persons remaining unpardoned. One newspaper, however, estimated that two hundred and seventy-seven were affected by the proclamation's first exception alone, namely, two admirals, forty-five generals,

6. Richardson, *Messages . . . of the Presidents*, VI, 549.

twenty governors, eight cabinet heads, two hundred foreign agents, and the President and Vice-President of the Confederacy.[7] A few of the leaders remaining proscribed, besides Davis and Stephens, were Breckinridge, Benjamin, Mason, Slidell, Maury, C. C. Clay, Thompson, Toombs, Cobb, Lamar, Lee, Johnston, Bragg, Longstreet, E. Kirby Smith, Buckner, Hood, Pemberton, Hampton, Pickett, Beauregard, Hardee, Forrest, and Magruder. Several leaders, including Reagan, Memminger, Mallory, Trenholm, and Campbell had already received special pardons, and, of course, were not affected by the second proclamation.

CRITICISM OF THE PROCLAMATION

As one might expect, Johnson's September amnesty angered the Radicals. Congress had repealed the law (Section 13 of the Confiscation Act) that authorized the executive to proclaim amnesties. It had also expressed disapproval of presidential reconstruction by superseding it with a plan of its own and by annulling the political benefits, in many instances, of earlier pardons and amnesties. The President's purpose in proclaiming another amnesty became a serious question. Did Johnson intend resuming registration so that newly amnestied voters might defeat congressional reconstruction at the polls? The Radicals believed that he did; and the Philadelphia *Press* declared the day after the appearance of the amnesty: "The animus of the proclamation, it is very plain to see, is an effort to impede reconstruction and to throw the control of the Southern States more fully into the hands of the rebels."

In New York City there was even greater dissatisfaction with the President's second amnesty and apprehension concerning his further probable course of action. The *Times*, in stronger language than that of the *Press*, declared the proclamation to be "a deliberate defiance of Congress and its authority, a repudiation of its enacted laws, and an assertion of the President's determination to take the work of reconstruction into his own hands. . . . What more flagrant form could Executive usurpation take short of dictatorship?" Three weeks later this paper said that Johnson would be

7. *National Intelligencer* as reported in the Atlanta *Daily Intelligencer*, September 18, 1867.

like the Tzar of Russia if he undertook to undo congressional reconstruction. It further declared that the "South would then pass under rebel rule and every state would be as much the paradise of traitors as Kentucky is, and the few who are still unpardoned would soon be restored to their forfeited rights."[8] The South Bend *Register*, previously edited by Speaker Schuyler Colfax, pronounced the proclamation "an outrage and insult to our loyal dead and their surviving relatives and friends" and hoped Congress would impeach the "drunkard" who had issued it.[9] The Chicago *Journal* (September 9) anticipated the impeachment of the President if he insisted on registering the persons just pardoned, and it characterized the amnesty proclamation as "the greatest rebel victory since Bull Run. . . ."

According to some other editors, Johnson had scored a great victory. The New Orleans *Times* was elated and said: "All honor to the statesman who has proved himself President, not of a party or a section, but of a whole people and an undivided Union." On the same day, the Charleston *Courier* declared: "We cannot but conclude, therefore, that all who had accepted and received the pardon . . . are entitled to register, and are competent for both suffrage and office. . . ." The Cincinnati *Enquirer* stated: "The President's power in this respect is more plenary than that of Congress, and his amnesty proclamation will compel the Registrars to register tens of thousands of Southern citizens whom the Reconstruction Laws of Congress say shall not be voters. . . ."[10] In the same spirit, the Chicago *Times* urged Southerners, the next day, to insist on their right to register and advised Johnson to provide for a new registration, while the Milledgeville *Recorder* speculated on the possibility of the President's deferring elections to permit recently amnestied Southerners to register.[11] The Vicksburg *Herald* said that the proclamation was not worth the paper it was written on unless the President came "practically to the aid of the oppressed South" by insisting on another registration. A week later it would have

8. September 9, 30, 1867.
9. Cited by the Chicago *Tribune*, September 13, 1867. The word "drunkard" referred to Johnson's inebriate condition at the inauguration on March 4, 1865.
10. September 10, 1867, for each of the three papers.
11. Reported in the Atlanta *Daily Intelligencer*, September 26, 1867.

allowed amnestied persons to vote without this requirement.[12]

Some editors went so far as to interpret the amnesty proclamation as the forerunner of another rebellion. They speculated on whether the President would use the army to resist impeachment and to compel officials to register newly amnestied citizens. Numerous papers called on Johnson to use force, and a *coup d'état* followed by a military dictatorship was even suggested.[13] The New York *Times*, deploring such extreme editorials, said of these wild rumors: "The setting aside of divers laws on the alleged ground of unconstitutionality, and the scattering of Congress at the point of the bayonet, are features of the entertainment which Mr. Johnson is said to have in contemplation for the inauguration of his Winter campaign. Of course, no man in the possession of his senses believes that the President, with all his rashness, seriously entertains the purposes which his newspaper friends persist in imputing to him. . . ." Ten days later this paper further described the situation by saying: "The President is suspected of intending to disperse Congress by force, as CROMWELL did Parliament, and as NAPOLEON I did the French Legislature."[14]

Not every editor sympathizing with Johnson expected him to resort to such rash measures. The New Orleans *Republican*, for example, affirmed (September 22): "He will not take the last fatal step. He will not resort to violence. He has lived too long and learned the temper of the people too thoroughly to risk the irretrievable." This statement implied that the President knew he would certainly lose if he resorted to such tactics in trying to thwart the will of Congress. Nevertheless, fear of military action caused Johnson's enemies to estimate their strength in case they should be obliged to combat force with force in maintaining their position. An officer of the newly organized order of veterans in the District of Columbia wrote to General Benjamin F. Butler: "We have a Soldiers' organization in this city [Washington] known as the

12. September 22, 29, 1867.
13. William A. Russ, Jr., substantiates these conclusions in his article, "Was There Danger of a Second Civil War during Reconstruction?" in the *Mississippi Valley Historical Review*, XXV, No. 1 (June, 1938), 39-58, by giving many newspaper references.
14. September 13, 27, 1867.

Grand Army of the Republic, which can be made of great use to Congress . . . if this thing should have to be settled by arms. We now number about 500, but are organizing colored posts, and think that within a Short time, with some encouragement, we will number Several thousand. . . . All our workings are entirely Secret."[15]

One Radical believed that in the event of armed conflict 500,000 men from Ohio, Pennsylvania, and New York alone could be depended on to rescue Washington "from the hands of rebels and traitors," meaning, of course, Johnson and his sympathizers.[16] There was also a feeling of security among the President's opponents in the belief that they had many of the generals, including Grant, Thomas, and perhaps Sherman, on their side. Maryland was expected to be the center of the *coup*, and Governor Swann of that state was regarded as the probable leader of the movement to coerce Congress and make the President a dictator.[17]

Notwithstanding the dire apprehensions the Radicals appeared to entertain, the President, in all probability, never thought of using force to hinder or obstruct the congressional program after its enactment. On the contrary, he manifested a disposition to enforce all laws, including, of course, those that had been passed over his veto. His oath of office included that solemn obligation; and it has already been shown that he respected the congressional reconstruction measures even before their confirmation by the Supreme Court. Andrew Johnson was an honest and courageous legalist who, as President, could be depended upon to use the military only when it was necessary to enforce the laws and maintain the government. Just four days (September 3) before issuing the amnesty under consideration, he proclaimed a comprehensive order "enjoining Obedience to the Constitution and Laws" of the nation, especially in the reconstruction area. After reviewing conditions necessary thereto, he called "upon the officers of the army and navy to assist and sustain the courts and other civil authorities

15. Butler MSS, Library of Congress (F. M. Thomas to Butler, September 18, 1867).

16. Chicago *Tribune*, September 27, 1867. See also Russ's "Was There Danger of a Second Civil War during Reconstruction?"

17. Cincinnati *Commercial*, September 21, 1867; Nashville *Press and Times*, October, 3, 5, 1867.

of the United States in the faithful administration of the laws thereof. . . ."[18]

This pronouncement should have been taken in good faith. It was a guarantee of the President's proper use of the armed forces at his command. It was also further assurance that Johnson would not use extreme measures to preserve the presidential prerogatives threatened by Congress. Many Radicals interpreted the closing paragraphs of his veto message of July 19, 1867, to indicate his intention to do so. Johnson most likely used the language thus grossly misconstrued in order to influence Congress to render to the Constitution the same respect that he as Chief Executive endeavored to exercise.[19]

EFFECTS OF THE SECOND AMNESTY

Several newspapers, while favoring re-enfranchisement by presidential amnesty, had misgivings about the proclamation's restoring the privilege of voting and holding office in the face of congressional legislation and opposition. The Vicksburg *Herald* and the Charleston *Courier* raised the question of whether it had actually done so.[20] The Columbus (Georgia) *Enquirer* expressed the opinion that "the work of reconstruction" had "been taken from the President" and that "Congress, in selecting persons for disfranchisement, had paid no regard to the exceptions made by the President. . . ." Even the New York *Herald*, wondering whether Johnson would push the issue, doubted that he would win if he did. Other papers were more certain of the proclamation's failure to improve political conditions in the South. According to the Nashville *Press and Times* and the New Orleans *Republican*, it would augment political victories in the North and increase lawlessness in the South.[21] The foreign press contained similar speculations. On October 3, the Louisville *Journal* quoted the London *Times* as saying that amnesty had failed, as had most of Johnson's policies, and that "the Southern

18. McPherson, *Reconstruction*, 82; Richardson, *Messages . . . of the Presidents* (1913 ed.), V, 3743-44.

19. Burgess, *Reconstruction and the Constitution, 1866-1876*, 141-42; Richardson, *Messages . . . of the Presidents* (1913 ed.), V, 3734-43.

20. September 11, 1867, for both papers.

21. September 12, for the *Enquirer* and *Herald;* September 10, the *Press and Times;* and September 10, 11, 21, 1867, for the *Republican*.

citizen is disfranchised by the federal legislature, and it can afford him little comfort to be told that the President pardons him."

Some Southerners who had expected much from Johnson's second amnesty soon became fearful that it would not bring them any political benefits. Yet there were those who hoped to the very last that the President could and would do something to increase the size of the white electorates in the coming elections. One Matthew Tyler, who had been elected to a state office in Mississippi before presidential reconstruction was overthrown, complained to Johnson as late as September 30 that, notwithstanding his election by "Citizens of the State who had availed themselves of the first amnesty, his qualifications were not recognized."[22] Four days earlier, Judge Rice of Montgomery, Alabama, was reported as having been denied registration; and when General Imboden of Virginia was not allowed to register, reports were circulated that he would take his case to the Supreme Court.[23] In this manner the constitutionality of congressional reconstruction could be tested and perhaps an opinion obtained that pardon and amnesty re-enfranchised the recipients. To the Chicago *Times*, early in September, this plan had appeared feasible, but it was never carried out.

Perhaps it was the administration's organ, the Washington *National Intelligencer*, which best expressed the true worth of the President's September amnesty. It stated very early the possibility that the proclamation would cause the constitutionality of the reconstruction laws to be tested by the courts, but it also pointed out the civil benefits derived from the amnesty.[24] After all, removing the threat of the penalties which the punitive laws described in the first chapter provided for those who engaged in rebellion against the United States was sufficient reason for the proclamation, regardless of any political privileges that the recipients might or might not be allowed. It was well, therefore, that this paper emphasized the civil benefits of amnesty and the restoration of business confidence which the act of clemency was doubtless expected to cause.

22. Johnson Papers, CXXI, No. 17238.
23. Augusta *Constitutionalist*, September 26, 1867; Chicago *Times*, October 20, 1867.
24. September 11, 12, 1867.

One cannot state exactly what influence Johnson's September amnesty had on the elections required by the new order of reconstruction. By October the registrations were over, and soon thereafter balloting on the propositions to call constitutional conventions and the selection of delegates thereto began. There were many, of course, who, notwithstanding the removal of their disabilities by presidential clemency, could not take the oath and consequently were denied suffrage. One estimate for South Carolina placed the number thus disabled at 8,244.[25] There were many whites, moreover, who registered but refrained from voting because they were opposed to congressional reconstruction. Furthermore, in five states (Alabama, Florida, Louisiana, Mississippi, and South Carolina) there were more Negroes and mulattoes registered than whites; while in the remaining states undergoing reconstruction the white majorities were not large. The questionable manner in which elections were held needs no further consideration here; sufficient information on that travesty of democratic government can be found in Burgess and Russ.[26]

THREATS OF IMPEACHMENT

It should be related, however, that Johnson's disregard of the repeal of the clement section of the Confiscation Act whetted the desire of the Radicals for impeachment. On the day the proclamation appeared in the press Welles wrote: "There is a little obscurity, perhaps, on the subject of amnesty and pardon in the measure, of which the Radicals will try to take advantage. . . . They believe the President has the power by the Constitution to grant pardons, but not amnesty." Welles then went on to state that the Radicals claimed British law and custom as established precedents in the United States. Consequently, they reasoned that, since in England "the King grants pardons to individuals, and the Parliament grants amnesty, or general pardon, to the masses," the power in the United States to proclaim amnesty was reserved to Congress. According to Welles, the Radicals were wrong, for in this country no such

25. McPherson, *Reconstruction*, 374; also Russ, "Radical Disfranchisement in South Carolina (1867-68)."

26. Burgess, *Reconstruction and the Constitution, 1866-1876*, 144-56; Russ, "Radical Disfranchisement in Georgia, 1867-71," *Georgia Historical Quarterly*, XIX (September, 1935), 176-209.

distinction exists, since the entire pardoning power, in all forms, is vested in the executive. The Radicals, therefore, were mistaken in assuming for Congress the powers of Parliament. Johnson's enemies in Congress, however, were "so imbued with British law and British precedent" that the diarist wrote two days later: "The Radicals are full of sensation and malignity over the 'Amnesty' Proclamation. They see in it incipient monstrosities, and the leaders declare that the President shall now certainly be impeached. . . ."[27]

Nevertheless, no specific charge of exceeding his power to grant pardons or amnesty was included in the indictment against the President. In the preliminary impeachment proceedings, complaints of such abuses had been made; and "General Benjamin F. Butler had exulted in the discovery of what he believed to be a damning offense in the pardoning of about two hundred deserters in order to render them available as voters for the President's policy"—a charge he was unable to prove. Johnson's bank account had even been examined to see if he had received money for pardons,[28] and the committee of the House which in 1867 investigated Johnson's reconstruction activities had listened to General L. C. Baker's account of the President's connections with the pardon brokeress, Mrs. L. L. Cobb. But all this had availed the Radicals as little satisfaction as did the investigation of the charges that Johnson had been implicated in the assassination of Lincoln.[29]

Indeed, there was little likelihood of the President's being impeached until his disregard, in February, 1868, of the Tenure of Office Act. Johnson had suspended Stanton from the office of Secretary of War the previous August, but now he dismissed him from that position. This had nothing to do with pardon and amnesty, though the failure in September, 1867, to respect the action of Congress in repealing Section 13 of the Confiscation Act undoubtedly augmented the rising indignation against the President. The Radicals now believed they had other sufficient causes to prefer impeachment charges against the Chief Executive, and if they had in mind his alleged abuse of the power to grant pardons and

---

27. Welles, *Diary*, III, 198, 199.
28. DeWitt, *Impeachment and Trial of Andrew Johnson*, 153, 221-23, 298-313. See also *Cong. Globe*, 39 Cong., 2 Sess., 319-21.
29. Milton, *Age of Hate*, 410-16.

amnesty in formulating their articles of impeachment, such allegation was hidden in the preamble, or title, to the articles in the general term "high crimes and misdemeanors in office."[30] Therefore, since the subject of pardon and amnesty does not enter into the actual impeachment of the President, no further account of the trial needs to be given in this narrative.

THE THIRD PROCLAMATION OF AMNESTY

While Congress was engaged in the impeachment, the President was considering another proclamation of amnesty. He was cautious enough, however, to wait until the trial had ended before acting. Apparently hoping to increase the prospect of acquittal, he also hesitated to grant individual pardons as the time approached for the senators to vote.[31] Fortunately Johnson was not convicted, but was cleared by actions of the Senate on May 16 and 26, 1868. It might also be observed that during all this bitter controversy a vituperative press kept public interest at high pitch by predicting undesirable developments, even to a kidnaping of the President and an armed rebellion.[32]

On June 26, President Johnson found all members of his Cabinet in favor of another amnesty. Seward, however, advised excepting those against whom legal proceedings were pending, and McCulloch and Schofield, the New Secretary of War, thought that those who had gone abroad and had not returned should be excepted. McCulloch also insisted on excepting John C. Breckinridge, whom he called "a double traitor," meaning that he had been disloyal both to his native state of Kentucky and to the nation. This session of the Cabinet ended with the understanding that a "proclamation would be prepared and submitted for consideration at an early day."[33]

A few days later the Cabinet considered a proclamation prepared by Seward, which excepted only Jefferson Davis and John H. Surratt. The mother of the latter had been convicted and hanged for complicity in the assassination of President Lincoln. Her son had

30. McPherson, *Reconstruction*, 266.
31. Browning, *Diary*, II, 196 (May 11, 1868).
32. See Russ, "Was There Danger of a Second Civil War during Reconstruction?"
33. Browning, *Diary*, II, 293-94.

been tried late in 1867 for the same offense, but the jury had disagreed, and a new trial was now impending. The President, according to Welles, objected to the exceptions, saying there was "really but one man, Davis," excepted, since "Surratt was arraigned for a criminal, personal matter, rather than treason." After everyone had left the conference but Welles and Browning, Welles advised the President to revise Seward's document in such manner as to emphasize the fact that there had been no armed rebellion in the United States since the amnesty proclamation of May 29, 1865. This Johnson promised to do, adding that he "particularly desired" that the Cabinet should "consider the subject of an unqualified amnesty to all, without any exception." Senator Browning, however, advised against this, stating that such universal clemency might "expose the President to violent partizan abuse and put some political capital into the hands of unscrupulous partizans."[34]

Probably Browning had more influence than Welles in persuading the President not to make the amnesty universal. He agreed with Johnson that Davis was no more culpable than other leaders of the rebellion; but, since the question of pardon was one of policy and expediency, and since Davis had been indicted and was in the hands of the law, he believed the Radicals would make the Confederate's pardon a pretext for another impeachment. Excitement, he said, might be aroused over Davis's pardon, which might cause Congress, with the aid of recently admitted carpetbaggers, to impeach Johnson again and cause his removal from office. Browning believed this to be "too great a risk for the President to take in the present condition of the country." He stated further that Welles supported this argument and that Johnson promised that "he would duly consider" it and confer with him the next day.[35]

On July 3 there was a full Cabinet meeting, and the contents of the proclamation were definitely determined. The exception that Browning had urged was incorporated in the document, and each member, "in turn, expressed his full and unconditional approval of it, except General Schofield . . . who said his only objection to it was that it made any exceptions whatever." He would not dignify

34. Welles, *Diary*, III, 394-95 (July 1, 1868); Browning, *Diary*, II, 204 (June 30, 1868).
35. Browning, *Diary*, II, 205 (July 2, 1868).

Jefferson Davis by making him an exception; for "if he should chance to be tried he would be acquitted, and this last blunder would be worse than the first."[36]

These frequent considerations of a third proclamation of amnesty were in keeping with the interest Johnson's friends had in his candidacy for the Democratic nomination for the presidency in 1868. The convention was to convene in New York City on July 4, and they believed another amnesty might attract greater support from the Southern delegates. Johnson did not appear very enthusiastic about his candidacy and may not have expected the nomination. Nevertheless, while he outwardly expressed little desire for it on the eve of the convention, apparently he inwardly coveted the honor. One reason, perhaps, for his desire to make the contemplated amnesty universal was to gain more support for his nomination and, if nominated, to increase the prospect of his election.[37]

At any rate, the President did proclaim an amnesty on the day the convention convened, but it was not universal. If Johnson had any qualms of conscience over his one exception, perhaps he found consolation in the knowledge that some members of his official family had advised the omission and that because of it the Radicals would not find the proclamation so objectionable. At the last moment, therefore, he excepted "such person or persons as may be under presentment or indictment in any court of the United States having competent jurisdiction upon a charge of treason or other felony. . . ." To all others he granted "unconditionally and without reservation . . . a full pardon and amnesty . . . with restoration of all civil rights of property, except as to slaves, and except also as to any property of which any person may have been legally divested under the laws of the United States." The President stated that he believed this amnesty would "tend to secure a complete and universal establishment and prevalence of municipal law and order . . . in the United States, and to remove all appearances presumptuous of a retaliatory or vindictive policy on the part of the Government attended by unnecessary disqualifications, pains, penalties, con-

36. *Ibid.*, 206 (July 3, 1868); also Welles, *Diary*, III, 395.
37. DeWitt, *Impeachment and Trial of Andrew Johnson*, 600-1; Milton, *Age of Hate*, 637-39. Johnson Papers, CXLI (Fred P. Powell [colored] to Johnson, July 3, 1868).

fiscations, and disfranchisements, and, on the contrary to promote and procure complete fraternal reconciliation among the whole people, with due submission to the Constitution and laws."[38] A noticeable difference between this proclamation and the preceding ones was the omission of an oath of allegiance to the United States. This was probably because such an oath was already required in the congressional reconstruction measures.

Johnson's friends desired that the proclamation should be read before the convention in order to influence delegates to vote for his nomination. It was not read, but knowledge of it apparently "highly pleased" a large number of delegates.[39] However, one of them, W. W. Warden, wrote to the President on July 5 that some of the Southerners in the convention were disappointed with his amnesty, since it did not include "Jefferson Davis and all others." The day following, Johnson received a telegram from New York urging him to write a letter stating, among other things, that he favored a universal amnesty. Consequently, a letter of this kind, apparently from the President, appeared in the New York press on the morning of July 7; but, according to one of his friends, it was too late. "Had that letter appeared 60 days ago . . . ," the friend wrote, "there would have been no doubt about your nomination."[40]

Notwithstanding Johnson's amnesty and his manifested desire for the nomination after the convention assembled, he never received more than 65 votes out of a total of 317, and they were on the first ballot. Welles's entry for July 7 says: "The President was evidently gratified with the vote he received, and the cheers when it was announced"; but Browning's entry for the same day is: "I could form no opinion, from his manner or speech, whether he desired a nomination or not." The following day Johnson received this telegram from New York: "Resolution passed today indorsing the amnesty. I suggest to you to make it universal. As it is you have made some capital."[41] Nevertheless, Horatio Seymour was finally unanimously nominated during the fifth day of the convention.

The amnesty measure apparently gained very little for its author.

38. Richardson, *Messages . . . of the Presidents*, VI, 655-56.
39. Johnson Papers, CXLI (Wm. Thorpe to Johnson, July 4, 1868).
40. *Ibid.* (R. W. Lathram to Johnson, July 7, 1868).
41. Browning, *Diary*, II, 206; Welles, *Diary*, II, 397; Johnson Papers, CXLI. See also Milton, *Age of Hate*, 634-39.

Even if it had been universal, the result would most likely not have been different, as far as Johnson's nomination for the presidency was concerned. All that can be said for the proclamation is that it received the endorsement of the Democratic convention, which also recommended in its platform "amnesty for all political offenses. . . ."[42] In this manner the party went on record as being in favor of pardoning everyone who had supported the Confederacy.

The Radicals, of course, received Johnson's July proclamation of amnesty with execrations. Had not Congress denied the President's power to proclaim amnesties eighteen months earlier by repealing the clement section of the Confiscation Act? That certainly was the purpose of the repeal. A citizen of Detroit, Michigan, wrote to Seward as soon as he read the proclamation, denouncing the Secretary and the President for "trifling with justice." He wanted to know why twenty-five or fifty "bad men" who were responsible for half a million "cases of deaths and desolation in the homes of this country" had not been "punished capitally," and then he continued to rail: "You have sided with the rebels. You have done all in your power to encourage another war. Your threats of punishment the rebels now know were basely disregarded. . . ."[43] Thus it was to be expected that the Radicals in the lower house of Congress would be thoroughly provoked when, on July 21, Representative Thomas L. Jones of Kentucky asked unanimous consent to offer a resolution requesting the President to proclaim a universal amnesty "to all persons engaged in the late rebellion. . . ."[44] Of course there was objection, and the resolution was not considered; but Jones had suggested the scope of the next proclamation of amnesty. The Republicans had already condemned Johnson in May, in their party platform, for abusing the pardoning power, and there were numerous individual condemnations.[45]

THE LAST PRESIDENTIAL AMNESTY

Since the development of sentiment for Johnson's fourth and

42. T. H. McKee, *The National Conventions and Platforms of All Political Parties, 1789-1900*, 132, cited hereafter as McKee, *National Conventions and Platforms*.

43. Johnson Papers, CXLI (Elisha Taylor to Seward, July 4, 1868).

44. *Cong. Globe*, 40 Cong., 2 Sess., pt. 5, p. 4501 (July 25, 1868).

45. McKee, *National Conventions and Platforms*, 138.

last proclamation of amnesty has been adequately treated in the chapter on "Pardoning Jefferson Davis," only the remaining aspects of the measure need be given here. The third proclamation left Jefferson Davis, John C. Breckinridge, Robert E. Lee, Simon Bolivar Buckner, and a few others unpardoned. Davis, as has already been shown, was under indictment for treason. His trial had been deferred in June to November, then to December, and then to no particular date at all. The indications for some time had been that he would be pardoned before he was actually brought to trial. This eventually happened, for on Christmas Day, 1868, the President proclaimed "unconditionally and without reservation, to all and to every person, who directly or indirectly, participated in the late insurrection or rebellion a full pardon and amnesty for the offense of treason against the United States. . . ."

Johnson plainly stated his reasons for this universal amnesty. Since "the authority of the Federal Government" had been re-established throughout the United States, he believed there was no further need for "such presidential reservations and exceptions" as he had provided in the other proclamations. He also thought "that universal amnesty and pardon for participation in the rebellion" would tend "to secure permanent peace, order, and prosperity throughout the land, and to renew and fully restore confidence and fraternal feeling among the whole people, and their respect for and attachment to the National Government. . . ."[46] Thus the few remaining unpardoned leaders of the Confederacy were finally restored to all their former civil and political privileges in the nation, except for the disability placed on them by the Fourteenth Amendment, which had gone into effect on July 26, 1868, and will be discussed in the next chapter.

It is interesting to note that in each of his last two proclamations Johnson proclaimed amnesty "for the offense of treason." He had used the word "rebellion" in his other two, as had Lincoln in his proclamations of December 8, 1863, and March 26, 1864. "Treason" was an exceedingly odious term to the Confederates. Indeed, it was so offensive that they appeared to be particularly anxious to have Davis tried on the indictment for treason in the Federal courts in order to test the validity of the term as it was

46. Richardson, *Messages . . . of the Presidents*, VI, 708.

applied to those who had supported the Confederacy.[47] It was the opinion of the Confederate leaders, and even of men like Chief Justice Chase, that participants in a movement of such magnitude as the effort of the Confederate States of America to establish their independence had not committed treason.[48] Nevertheless, treason was the offense for which Davis had been indicted again, for a new indictment had been found against him on March 26, 1868. It may have been this recent emphasis on the odious term that caused Johnson to use the word in his last two amnesties. Nevertheless, the apparent desire to have Davis acquitted of treason was followed, after the promulgation of the Fourteenth Amendment, by a movement to have the indictment against him quashed, an aim which was accomplished shortly after Johnson proclaimed his universal amnesty.[49]

Of course the opposition took exception to the President's universal amnesty. The day following its appearance the New York *Herald* reported: "Radicals like General Butler think the issuing of the proclamation an unwarranted act of authority on the part of the President. They threaten to treat it as of no effect, and some of them even go so far as to talk of a new impeachment of the President." The editor stated, however, that Senator Trumbull believed that Congress could "do nothing to set the proclamation aside, even if they were so disposed." Yet, on January 5, the Senate by resolution asked Johnson to submit for its consideration "a copy of any proclamation of amnesty made by him since the last adjournment of Congress and also to communicate to the Senate by what authority of law the same was made." The ostensible purpose of the request was to obtain information so that the Committee on the Judiciary could pass upon the propriety of the President's power to grant his Christmas amnesty. In about two weeks Johnson replied, declaring that he issued the proclamation "by virtue of the power and authority in me vested by the constitution, and in the name of the sovereign people of the United States." He stated also that his amnesty was in accordance with precedents "established by Wash-

47. See Ch. XIV.
48. Robert B. Warden, *Account of the Private Life and Public Services of Salmon Portland Chase,* 696.
49. See closing paragraphs of Ch. XIII.

ington in 1795, and followed by President Adams in 1800, Madison in 1815, and Lincoln in 1863, and by the present Executive in 1865, 1867, and 1868."[50]

Only brief mention need be made of the debate in the Senate on the President's power to grant his last amnesty. The argument was largely a restatement of that given in the debate on the measure to repeal Section 13 of the Confiscation Act of 1862.[51] The controversy hinged again on the general power of the executive to grant pardon as defined in the Constitution; on the difference in meaning between the words pardon and amnesty; on the power of the President to stop judicial proceedings by an act of amnesty; and on the effect of the repeal of Section 13 of the Confiscation Act.[52]

On January 19, the Senate referred the question to the Judiciary Committee, which submitted its report about a month later.[53] The committee denied the President's right under the Constitution to grant his recent proclamation; insisted that the words pardon and amnesty were "not synonymous or equivalent"; and gave English law and custom to support their contention that the executive could grant pardons only to individuals and not to persons en masse. The report stated further that Washington, Adams, and Madison did not purport to grant amnesty or any restoration of lost rights, as Johnson's Christmas proclamation had done. The amnesties of these early Presidents, the committee believed, did "purport to grant general pardon and remission of penalties, and so far they certainly would have great weight in justifying the motives of the President in this act; but as authority for an executive act, which would be illegal without them, they have little or no force, for the reasons stated above."

This rather weak argument in the report was followed by the citation of a decision by the great jurist John Marshall, who, near the close of his career as Chief Justice, had stated: "A pardon is an act of grace, proceeding from the power intrusted with the

50. *Cong. Globe*, 40 Cong., 3 Sess., pt. 1, p. 168; Richardson, *Messages . . . of the Presidents*, VI, 767; *Senate Reports*, No. 239, 40 Cong., 3 Sess. (February 17, 1869).
51. See division "Repeal of the Amnesty Clause . . ." in Ch. XIV.
52. *Cong. Globe*, 40 Cong., 3 Sess., pt. 1, pp. 168-70, 438-39.
53. *Ibid.*, 170; *Senate Reports*, No. 239, 40 Cong., 3 Sess.

execution of the laws, which exempts the individual, on whom it is bestowed, from the punishment the law inflicts for a crime he has committed. It is the private, though official, act of the executive magistrate, delivered to the individual."[54] These words were construed to mean that the President could not grant a proclamation of amnesty. In other words, the committee asserted that Marshall's opinion had been that the executive's power to pardon, under the Constitution, was limited to individual cases and did not apply to persons en masse. But the report did not end here. After referring to the repeal of the section of the Confiscation Act which authorized the President to proclaim an amnesty, the committee concluded by offering a resolution "that in the opinion of the Senate the proclamation of the 25th of December, 1868 ... was not authorized by the Constitution or laws." The opinion, however, was not unanimous, and one member, Senator Hendricks, notified the Senate that he would submit a minority report when the resolution of the majority came up for consideration.[55] The work of the committee, however, never received any further consideration in the Senate.

A writer in the *American Law Register* for September, 1869, who signed himself "L. C. K.," very learnedly discussed this judiciary report and the English precedents for the President's proclamation of amnesty. In the October issue of the publication he continued the discussion by showing that the makers of the Constitution intended that the executive should exercise the power of granting general pardons, or amnesties, and that three of them—Washington, Adams, and Madison—actually supported the President's side of the controversy.[56]

Presidential clemency during the period of Reconstruction had run its troubled course by the close of 1868. Johnson had courageously granted pardons to individuals and amnesties to groups when he had considered such clemency advisable. At least, he had been magnanimous in the face of menacing opposition. Perhaps, on the whole, he had acted wisely; and he had certainly kept within

54. 7 Peters 150 (*United States vs. Wilson*).
55. *Cong. Globe*, 40 Cong., 3 Sess., 1281.
56. *American Law Register*, VIII, 513-32, 577-89. See Richardson, *Messages ... of the Presidents* (1913 ed.), IX, 6718-20, for President Theodore Roosevelt's general amnesty proclamation of July 4, 1902.

his constitutional rights, for the Supreme Court has never rendered a contrary opinion thereon. Henceforth, however, amnesty was solely a congressional responsibility, since the Fourteenth Amendment had imposed a disability on certain participants in the rebellion that could only be removed by a two-thirds vote of both houses of Congress. Due consideration, therefore, will be given to "Congressional Amnesty" in the following chapter.

CHAPTER SIXTEEN

CONGRESSIONAL AMNESTY

◆

CLEMENCY AND POLITICS

BEFORE the passage of the reconstruction acts in March and July, 1867, persons began appealing to members of Congress for relief from disfranchisement. There were those, of course, whom the President had not yet pardoned, and doubtless some people believed that Congress, rather than the President, should remove disabilities incurred by supporting the rebellion. Perhaps many were influenced by the repeal, early in January, 1867, of the clement section of the Confiscation Act. The proposed Fourteenth Amendment, whose ratification had failed late in 1866, was also evidence of the determination of the Radicals to cause the ex-Confederates to petition Congress for the privilege of holding office. In fact, the drastic plan of congressional reconstruction, soon created and administered, provided no alternative. Even the privilege of voting was seriously curtailed by the act of March 2, which made the ratification of the amendment a condition of restoration, and by a second law enacted to implement the first.

Some appeals came from Southerners who professed to have supported the Confederacy unwillingly, or who at least were not among the leaders of secession. Simeon Corley of South Carolina told Senator Sumner (January 21, 1867) that a distinction should "be made between the people of the South and their disloyal leaders," leaving, if possible, "a majority of the white population in possession of the franchise and their real estate." Judge J. M. Wiley of Pike County, Alabama, wrote Senator Fessenden that he had labored for the Union until his state seceded, after which he supported the Confederacy, though expecting its failure. Having taken the oath of allegiance and desiring the prosperity of the whole coun-

362

try, he urged the immediate relief of a few prominent men to encourage others to believe that they too would "someday be relieved."[1]

Many petitioners expressed sympathy for the growth of the Republican party in the South. Judge Wiley was thus disposed, and Robert P. Dick, a pre-war Democrat of Greensboro, North Carolina, told Senator John Sherman that he "was never a rebel" and that he still loved the United States government "better than any other on earth. . . . I would be content to remain disfranchised for a time," he continued, "but I know that I can render very efficient service to the Republican party in the coming canvass. . . ." Dick actually became one of the organizers of that party in his state late in 1867.[2] Indeed, one competent student of this period states that letters from thoroughgoing Democrats can hardly be found among the papers of Radicals who received appeals for mercy.[3] First consideration, apparently, was likely to be given to those whose relief would augment the strength of the Republic Party in the South.

When it became known that Senator Sherman had promised to introduce a resolution to relieve former Governors Brown of Georgia and R. M. Patton of Alabama, who had accepted congressional reconstruction, others asked to have their names placed in the measure. Such persons usually minimized their support of the rebellion. Thomas W. Alexander of Rome, Georgia, in asking to be included with Brown, stated that his transgressions just barely placed him in the disfranchised class, thereby leaving him "in bad company from which" he desired to escape. G. Mason Graham of Louisiana, in requesting relief for himself and for W. H. Hough, said that his offense had consisted only in succoring starving Confederate soldiers, until a Federal brigade had exasperated him by camping on his property and consuming his entire stock of provisions for both man and beast.[4]

1. Sumner Papers, CLIV; Fessenden Papers (Wiley to Fessenden, March 21, 1867).
2. Sherman Papers, CXXI, No. 27971. President Johnson had appointed Dick a Federal judge in 1865, but, since he was unable to take the oath, he became a provisional judge instead. Hamilton, *Reconstruction in North Carolina*, 116, 241, 244, 249.
3. Russ, "Congressional Disfranchisement, 1866-1898" (doctoral dissertation, University of Chicago, 1936), 145.
4. Sherman Papers, CXVIII, Nos. 27269, 27286.

Like the petitions to President Johnson for clemency, similar requests to members of Congress were often supported by recommendations. Governor J. D. Cox of Ohio, in recommending Robert P. Dick, told Sherman that the North Carolinian had incurred disfranchisement merely by accepting a small office to evade service in the Confederate army.[5] Dr. R. J. Powell, who had previously been a state pardon agent in Washington, requested relief for nine men whose qualifications for office would strengthen the Radical party in the Tarheel State. One was W. W. Holden, for whose relief John N. Bunting and others memorialized the Senate on July 10, 1867. In March, the next year, the North Carolina constitutional convention asked to have the disabilities removed from a list of about 525 persons, who had indicated their "hearty accord with the reconstruction measures of Congress."[6]

The Radical leaders were admonished to proceed cautiously in removing disabilities in order to promote the interests of the Republican party. In December, 1867, a member of the convention to form a new constitution for Florida wrote Sumner that Southerners who had enriched themselves during the war by purchasing property belonging to Unionists should not be given office. Only those who were Union men at heart should be chosen. About the same time, A. W. Tourgee, a power in North Carolina politics, advised against relieving large numbers, many of whom might turn against the Republicans. In another letter, he urged the relief of Holden, on the plea that it would give the Republicans "almost invaluable advantage."[7] But O. W. Dennis of Charleston, South Carolina, opposed qualifying former Governor A. G. Magrath because of his haste in espousing secession and the likelihood of his failing to cooperate with the Union party.[8] From Georgia, Texas, Virginia, and other Southern states came similar pleas for such removals of disabilities as would insure Republican domination.

By the summer of 1868, when most of the Southern states were

5. *Ibid.*, CXXI, No. 27969.
6. *House Misc. Doc.*, No. 108, 40 Cong., 2 Sess.
7. Sumner Papers, CLIV (C. R. Mobly to Sumner, December 10, 1867), CLV, CLVI (Tourgee to Sumner, December 23, 1867, March 28, 1868). See Hamilton, *Reconstruction in North Carolina, passim,* for Tourgee's extensive activities.
8. Sumner Papers, CLIV, No. 91.

ready for admission, appeals naturally became more numerous. Interest in the election of Grant undoubtedly accelerated the movement, but, as has been stated in the preceding chapter, the need for white men to fill offices increased the desire for removals. Still other conditions encouraged petitions, such as former friendships, family influence, and fraternal ties.

At the time Congress met in regular session in December, 1867, much progress had been made in the movement to obtain relief from the disabilities imposed in the legislation of the previous March and July. A test case was soon made in the Senate in a measure to relieve former Governor Patton of Alabama, for whom clemency had been recommended by Generals John Pope and Wager Swayne and by thirty-seven members of the Alabama constitutional convention.[9] Patton, who had been Johnson's Provisional Governor of Alabama, was regarded as representing many Southerners who had involuntarily supported the rebellion in some manner. Moreover, he had favored the ratification of the Fourteenth Amendment, which could hardly be said of any other Johnson governor.

The bill to relieve Patton aroused opposition from both Radicals and Moderates. Since the amendment had not yet been ratified, some believed that only the President could exercise the clemency desired. Others contended that the measure had nothing to do with executive prerogative, "for it merely concerned the removal of disabilities imposed by Congress itself." Especially was this so after the repeal of Section 13 of the Confiscation Act, even though the Fourteenth Amendment had not yet been ratified. Some believed that ratification could not take place until men like Patton had been re-enfranchised, while others thought Patton was still a traitor, deserving treatment as such. Nevertheless, the bill passed the Senate on January 27, 1868, by a vote of twenty-six to five (twenty-two senators not voting); but in the House Thaddeus Stevens prevented a hearing by having it referred (February 4, 1868) to the Committee on Reconstruction.[10]

9. General Pope was Military Governor of the district under congressional reconstruction embracing Alabama, Georgia, and Florida. General Swayne became a commissioner of the Freedmen's Bureau in Alabama.

10. *Cong. Globe*, 40 Cong., 2 Sess., 650 ff., 766, 776, 978-79.

If a mild offender like Patton could not be relieved, there was little prospect of clemency for real rebels. Yet, on February 19, Senator Oliver P. Morton of Indiana presented a bill in behalf of Holden. The measure was referred to the Judiciary Committee. On March 15, John A. Bingham of Ohio offered the House a bill to relieve Holden, General Longstreet, James L. Orr, former Governor Joseph E. Brown, and John A. Gilmer. Others were added to the list later. Again the question of the status of the Fourteenth Amendment arose when it was known that three-fourths of the states, not counting those undergoing reconstruction, had ratified it, but that the President had not yet proclaimed it a part of the Constitution. Did ratification depend on the approval of three-fourths of all the states that had ever comprised the Union? Evidently Johnson thought so, for he waited until that number had ratified before announcing, on July 28, 1868, that ratification had been accomplished. According to James F. Wilson of Iowa, before the President's proclamation only a majority vote of each House was necessary to remove disabilities. Men like Representative James B. Beck of Kentucky, however, waived all considerations pertaining to the amendment and to acts of Congress. They insisted that the Chief Executive had the power to restore the franchise and offered the decision in *Ex parte Garland* to prove the point.[11]

The inclusion of Gilmer in the bill caused some wrangling. Representative John Covode of Pennsylvania had added the worthy North Carolinian, who petitioned on the grounds that he had always been loyal to the Union and had attended sessions of the Confederate congress only in the interests of the Union. Yet Horace Maynard of Tennessee called him a traitor and desired his name removed from the bill, a request which Covode allowed in the interest of harmony. This did not hasten action, however, for there were objectors to Longstreet, Orr, Brown, and Holden, and so the debate dragged on. Representative John F. Farnsworth of Illinois emphasized the plight of Southerners generally by stating that fifty newly elected men in Alabama were waiting for the removal of disabilities, so that they could serve in the state's

11. *Ibid.*, 1906 ff. See Ch. XVII for this decision.

legislature.[12] No general amnesty law was passed for several years, however; Congress enacted special relief measures instead.

EARLY REMOVALS

The first person to be relieved by Congress was R. R. Butler of Tennessee. In March, 1868, the House quickly passed a bill to remove his disability so that he might represent his district in that body. When the Senate came to consider the measure, certain technicalities arose which delayed action. Although Butler was a Tennessean who had served creditably in the Union army from September, 1863, to May, 1864, he had been disfranchised because he had, earlier in the war, been a member of the Confederate state legislature. For this he was disabled under the third section of the Fourteenth Amendment, even though there was no doubt of his subsequent loyalty. Party jealousies caused the bill to be recommitted, but on June 19 it became a law. Perhaps it was not necessary for the President to sign the measure, although it had received a two-thirds vote of both houses. The amendment had not yet been proclaimed a part of the Constitution, and he might have exercised the right to veto the bill. He signed it, however, after receiving the approval of his Cabinet with the exception of Welles, since the majority believed it would not be best for him "to interpose and assert" his power under the Constitution by vetoing or ignoring the measure.[13] But why should not the President approve the measure? Had he not already restored the franchise to nearly all whom Congress had later disfranchised?

In relieving Butler, Congress set a precedent for more removals, and six days later it passed a bill thus affecting about 1,350 others. The hazardous course of this measure through Congress illustrated the questionable nature of this method of exercising re-enfranchisement by legislation. Much time was consumed in reading lists of names and discussing the merits of individual requests for relief. A conference committee finally omitted G. S. Houston of Alabama

12. *Cong. Globe*, 40 Cong., 2 Sess., 1906 ff.
13. *Ibid.*, pt. 3, pp. 1708-11, 2192, 2218-20, 2559, 3058-69; Welles, *Diary*, 386 (June 19, 1868); Blaine, *Twenty Years of Congress*, II, 512. The act removing the disability required Butler to take an oath more applicable to the period after the war than the oath prescribed by Congress (see Ch. I), July 2, 1862. *U. S. Stat. at Large*, XV, 360.

and George W. Jones of Tennessee because they were Democrats. The men deserved to be qualified to hold office, but they could not be trusted to support Republican policies. The passage of the bill on June 25, 1868, however, enabled hundreds of men to fill offices to which they had been elected, and thereby accelerated the progress of reconstruction.[14]

The beneficiaries of this act could not take the ironclad oath of June 2, 1862, which required them to swear that they had never voluntarily supported a rebellion against the United States. At first a modified form of this oath was administered, but on July 11, 1868, Congress supplied an easier affirmation for removals under the amendment. The new oath provided that persons thus relieved should swear "to support and defend the Constitution of the United States against all enemies, foreign and domestic," and to discharge faithfully the duties of the offices on which they were entering. The act did not affect persons who were not disabled by the third section of the amendment (i.e. those who had not "previously taken an oath . . . to support the Constitution of the United States" and later supported the Confederacy) and who still had to take the ironclad oath, because they had aided the rebellion. Nearly three years later (February 1, 1871), but not without opposition, Congress applied this oath (of July 11, 1868) to them.[15]

For nearly ten years after the promulgation of the Fourteenth Amendment, Congress gave much time to the removal of disabilities thus imposed. Sometimes these private acts, as in the case of R. R. Butler, applied to only one person; at other times, as in the law of July 25, 1868, they applied to many. In every such measure the names of the beneficiaries were given, even when the lists were long; and as in the case of petitions to the President for pardon in 1865 and 1866, the requests to Congress for removals were numerous. Each appeal was expected to receive special consideration to determine its merits. This required much time that might well have been devoted to other needed legislation, but Congress continued

14. *Cong. Globe*, 40 Cong., 2 Sess., April, May, June, 1868; *U. S. Stat. at Large*, XV, 360; Blaine, *Twenty Years of Congress*, II, 512.

15. *Cong. Globe*, 40 Cong., 2 Sess., 3733, and Appendix, 514; *U. S. Stat. at Large*, XVI, 5-11.

to make removals in special acts until, by March 4, 1871, 4,616 persons had been relieved.[16]

For a time (June to December, 1868), the relief acts of Congress were in juxtaposition with the President's removals of disabilities. As has been shown, while Johnson was in the midst of his pardoning program, Congress tried to curtail the executive's power to restore the franchise by reserving to itself that prerogative through the repeal, early in January, 1867, of the clement section of the Confiscation Act. This policy matured with the ratification of the Fourteenth Amendment, in July, 1868, though the Reconstruction Act of March 23, 1867, disfranchised Southerners who could not take the ironclad test oath. The President could, and did, continue to restore civil rights by special pardons and by amnesty, but after ratification there was no question as to the power of removing the disability imposed in the third section of the amendment. Congress—not the executive—was to dispense clemency in this particular.

It might also be stated again that the President's amnesties and special pardons, until Congress interfered, removed all disabilities imposed by Congress in the punitive laws of 1861 and 1862. The special acts and general amnesty of Congress (to be described later), therefore, restored only the privilege of holding any civil or military office, either state or national. Jefferson Davis, for example, was restored, on December 25, 1868, to all his former privileges as a citizen except that of holding office. He might even vote (after the removal of the disability under the congressional Reconstruction Act), but, unless Congress removed the disability provided in the Fourteenth Amendment, he could not be elected or appointed to any office whatever in the United States. It was nine years after his death, in 1889, before Congress passed an amnesty act that would have affected him. Yet that body might have re-enfranchised him before Johnson pardoned him in his universal Christmas amnesty.

16. Oberholtzer, *History of the United States since the Civil War*, I, 269; *Private Acts of Congress* (1868-1872) in *U. S. Stat. at Large*, XV-XVII, *passim*. The Fortieth Congress (1867-69) relieved 1,431, and the Forty-first Congress (1869-71), 3,185.

GENERAL AND UNIVERSAL AMNESTY BILLS

Opposition existed at the outset to the disabling clause in the Fourteenth Amendment, and a desire for a universal amnesty act was expressed as long as anyone remained disqualified. Sometimes this sentiment was formally stated by political organizations. Even the Republicans were favorable, in their platform of May, 1868, to an appreciable degree of leniency, which would be manifested "in the same measure as the spirit of disloyalty" in the South died out, and as might "be consistent with the safety of the loyal people." This was not as encouraging as it might have been, but it was at least indicative of a disposition toward liberality. Blaine stated later, somewhat approvingly, that the rule to relieve everyone who asked for clemency, either through himself or his friends, was freely applied.[17] For several years, however, relief came only in special acts of Congress.

It should also be noted that removals of disability could be made only with a considerable Republican support of Democratic measures, a support given with party advantage in view until a cleavage occurred in the Republican party. Then removals were sometimes approved by conservatives to counteract the liberal movement among the Republicans. Especially was this true after the Liberal Republican victory in Missouri in 1870. Indeed, at least three Republican state conventions, two of which were Southern, declared in July, 1869, for universal amnesty. They were the California Republican, the Mississippi Republican, and the Mississippi Conservative Republican state conventions.[18] By 1870 Maryland, Kentucky, Tennessee, and West Virginia had repealed their disfranchising acts. The example of Missouri, however, was most potent, for that state not only re-enfranchised all its ex-rebels in 1870, but it also elected B. Gratz Brown as Governor on a platform of universal amnesty. From then on, Senator Carl Schurz of Missouri was one of the most effective champions of liberalism in Congress.

Dissatisfaction with partisan re-enfranchisement of some and continued disfranchisement of others increased when Democrats

17. McKee, *National Conventions and Platforms*, 139; Blaine, *Twenty Years of Congress*, II, 512.

18. McPherson, *Reconstruction*, 478, 481, 482.

charged the disorders of the Ku Klux Klan and other similar organizations in the South to Republican illiberality. In fact, the preponderance of evidence was that the Klan movement was accelerated by the operation of the third section of the Fourteenth Amendment and the encouragement of Negro suffrage. Even though leading Southerners were reluctant to admit that persons disfranchised supported the Klan, they believed that re-enfranchisement would lessen the disorders. At any rate, qualifying the better element of the South would tend to improve local and state government generally, and thereby remove the most prevalent excuse for bad conditions.[19]

As might be expected, therefore, efforts were made from time to time to enact an amnesty law, either general or universal in scope. The Senate refused a gesture in that direction as early as December 9, 1868, by rejecting a motion to "add the words, 'and all other citizens of . . . South Carolina' " to a bill to relieve Franklin J. Moses, who had been elected chief justice of his state, but who had been a state senator for a long time before the war. About eighteen months later (June 13, 1870) the House also refused "to suspend the rules and put upon its passage a bill" to grant universal amnesty. The time was not yet ripe for even a general amnesty law, much less one with no exceptions.[20]

Yet, in December, 1870, the House struggled with a bill for which eccentric and vindictive Ben Butler was the chief sponsor. It took more than three columns of the *Congressional Globe* to contain this curious measure, whose contents aroused such fierce opposition that only rancorous debate resulted. Consequently the Forty-first Congress came to an end on March 4, 1871, without any solution of the distressing problem, except through the passage of special relief acts.[21]

19. Russ, "Congressional Disfranchisement, 1866-1898," 186-88, 200-12. See also Oberholtzer, *History of the United States since the Civil War*, II, 268-72. Schurz had been largely responsible for the amnesty clause in the Republican platform in 1868.

20. McPherson, *Reconstruction*, 393, 583; Russ, "Congressional Disfranchisement, 1866-1898," 173, 180.

21. See *Cong. Globe*, 41 Cong., *passim*, for the various phases of the "Butler Bill." Russ devoted one division of his dissertation on "Congressional Disfranchisement" to this proposed monstrous piece of legislation.

A few days later James B. Beck of Kentucky was defending a universal amnesty bill in the House. This asked for too much, so he accepted a compromise measure that excepted men who had left seats in Congress in 1860-61, who had resigned commissions in the army or navy to aid the Confederacy, and who were members of secession conventions. The bill failed, and Eugene Hale of Maine offered another bill (April 10) in the House with the same provisions, but also providing that beneficiaries should take an oath of allegiance. The measure passed without debate, but the Senate deferred action until the next session, so it never became a law.[22]

By this time the pressure for relief had become so great and the process of passing special acts covering individual cases so unsatisfactory that President Grant recommended a general amnesty in his annual message of December, 1871. He stated that he did "not see the advantage or propriety of excluding men from office merely because they were before the rebellion of standing and character sufficient to be elected to positions requiring them to take oaths to support the Constitution. . . ." Nevertheless, he recommended that if there were "any great criminals, distinguished above all others for the part they took in opposition to the Government, they might in the judgment of Congress, be excluded from such amnesty."[23]

The President's words indicated truly that complete relief from the disqualifying clause of the Fourteenth Amendment was still far off. Nevertheless, sentiment for the immediate restoration of the full privilege of citizenship to thousands of persons was sufficient to demand the early enactment of a general amnesty law. Blaine later described the situation thus: "The impossibility of examining into the merits of individuals by tens of thousands, and establishing the quality and degree of their offenses, was so obvious that representatives on both sides of the House demanded an act of General Amnesty, excepting therefrom only the few classes whose names would lead to discussion and possibly to the defeat of the beneficent measure."[24]

22. *Cong. Globe*, 42 Cong., 1 Sess., 107, 561-65, 832; Blaine, *Twenty Years of Congress*, II, 512-13.
23. Richardson, *Messages . . . of the Presidents*, VII, 153.
24. Blaine, *Twenty Years of Congress*, II, 513.

Blaine's phrase "tens of thousands" suggests an estimate of the number disabled by the third section of the Fourteenth Amendment. There is reason to believe that the number thus affected has been over-estimated when given as high as 150,000 or more. Blaine stated that, "when the [Fourteenth] Amendment was under discussion in Congress, the total number affected was estimated at fourteen thousand," but he also said that "subsequently it was ascertained to be much greater." He stated further that the House passed a bill early in the Forty-first Congress containing some seventeen thousand names, to which the Senate added approximately three thousand more. The implication was that there were others disabled besides these twenty thousand persons. Yet a special report, made to the Fifty-fifth Congress, of the total number disabled by the amendment placed the figure at only eighteen thousand.[25] In 1898, while speaking on the universal amnesty measure, John J. Jenkins of Wisconsin, quoting Blaine's statement, said: "It has been variously estimated that this section, at the time of the original insertion in the Constitution, included somewhere from 14,000 to 30,000 persons. As nearly as I can gather the facts of the case, it included about 18,000 men in the South."[26]

It appears, therefore, that when a careful estimate of those disabled under the third section of the Fourteenth Amendment was made, the number found was less than 20,000. The actual number, of course, was not easily obtained, but it was surely much less than 150,000 and was probably not more than 20,000, as the report just mentioned and Blaine's estimate suggest. Yet information concerning the number expected to be relieved by the act of 1872, as will be given presently, implies a larger number.

In response to Grant's recommendation, a bill was introduced in the House, on December 11, 1871, providing for the removal of disabilities from everyone remaining disqualified. The Judiciary Committee, however, did not favor unconditional amnesty and

25. *Ibid.*, 511, 513. Rhodes, *History of the United States*, VI, 440, using the New York *Tribune* for May 23, 1872, as his authority, estimated the number disabled by the amendment as 150,000 to 160,000 before the passage of the general amnesty of May 22, 1872. He also referred to the *Life and Times of Samuel Bowles*, by George S. Merriam, II, 234, in making his estimate. See also *Annual Cyclopedia*, 1869, pp. 183-84.

26. *Cong. Record*, 55 Cong., 2 Sess., 5405.

reported a bill on January 15 excepting only members of Congress and army and naval officers who had resigned to aid the Confederacy. This was the measure of the previous April without the clause excepting members of state conventions who had voted for secession. The bill provided that those who would be relieved should take the oath of allegiance to the United States. The House suspended the rules and passed the measure by a vote of 171 to 31.[27]

When the bill came before the Senate, it was amended (February 9) by the casting vote of Vice-President Colfax to include a guarantee of civil rights to the Negroes, with the galleries applauding lustily.[28] The Radicals, led by Sumner, insisted in this manner that the welfare of the freedmen was a paramount issue and that there should be no general removal of disabilities from the Southerners until the Negroes were given equal privileges with the whites in such public places as hotels, theatres, schools, public conveyances, and in jury service.

The debate on this amended amnesty measure in the Senate reveals the peculiar situation, especially in the South, occasioned by the disability clause of the Fourteenth Amendment. Senator Pratt of Indiana voiced the sentiment of certain Northerners who approved passage of the bill. He would vote for removal, not because he believed the Southerners had repented; on the contrary, they were proud of their effort and regarded Jefferson Davis as a hero. On the other hand, he would support the bill "because the exclusion of these men from office" was "a fruitful source of discontent" in the South and an excuse "for bad government there." The Southerners argued, he said, "that if they were invested with the power of magistery again, some respect would be felt for the laws," and violence and bloodshed would cease. "It is claimed," the Senator continued, "and I think . . . that . . . some of the very best men of the South are still kept back, by reason of this amendment, from sharing in the responsibilities of office, their pride forbidding them to appeal to Congress. . . . As it is they do not consider themselves responsible for the disorders there, nor, I fear, make much effort to stop them. They are regarded as martyrs, and the magna-

27. *Cong. Globe*, 42 Cong., 2 Sess., pt. 1, pp. 56, 388, 389.
28. *Ibid.*, pt. 2, p. 919.

nimity of the Government is impeached for keeping on foot such distinctions."[29]

Senator Carl Schurz supported the bill by giving recent examples of amnesty in Europe. He stated that there were then sitting in the Austrian parliament men who had been pardoned for their part in the revolution of 1848-52. In his opinion, the United States ought to be even more generous than foreign nations in granting amnesty to political offenders. He then went on to say that failure to remove the political disabilities gave the leaders of the rebellion a distinction which they otherwise would not have. He stated that he "would not leave them the pitiable distinction of not being pardoned. Your very generosity," he continued, "will be to them the source of bitterest disappointment." He surmised, however, that some Democratic senators whom the disabled Southerners regarded as their friends would be filled with dismay at the thought of seeing Jefferson Davis once more a senator in their midst. Schurz closed his long and able argument with the observation that it was "the experience of civilized nations . . . [that], when an amnesty is to be granted at all, the completest amnesty is always the best. . . ."[30]

The friends of this bill could not muster the necessary vote to secure its passage. Southern senators would not support it with the amendment providing civil rights for the Negroes. Senator Francis P. Blair of Missouri, who opposed the measure in its amended form, believed it could have been easily passed if the civil rights feature had not been attached. He was of the opinion that the consideration for the Negroes was intended to delay action on, and ultimately to defeat, the bill. Furthermore, he believed that the solution of the Negro problem was not in political and social equality but in segregation, as in the case of the Indians. The Senate rejected the measure on May 10, 1872, by a vote of thirty-two to twenty-two.[31]

THE GENERAL AMNESTY LAW OF 1872

On May 13, 1872, Butler introduced another general amnesty

29. *Ibid.*, pt. 3, pp. 3252-53.
30. Schurz, *Reminiscences*, II, 338-45. Carl Schurz, Prussian by birth, came to the United States in 1852, after the failure of the 1848 revolution in the German Confederation.
31. *Cong. Globe*, 42 Cong., 2 Sess., pt. 4, p. 3249.

bill, which the House passed without debate and sent to the Senate. It excepted "Senators and Representatives of the Thirty-sixth and Thirty-seventh Congresses, officers in the judiciary, military, and naval service of the United States, heads of Departments, and foreign ministers of the United States," who had supported the Confederacy.[32] The simplicity of the bill indicated better judgment than its proponent had shown in proposing his earlier measure to the House of the Forty-first Congress. Butler could well afford to hasten the enactment of a straightforward, general re-enfranchisement law by the next Congress if he desired to obviate a condition that threatened the defeat of his party at the polls the following November.

The measure was certain of enactment, since the time was ripe for action reflecting public sentiment for such legislation.[33] The Liberal Republican victory in Missouri, in 1870, had indicated the direction of political thinking, and the Republicans were mindful of the forthcoming presidential election. Perhaps Grant had his own party interests in mind when he recommended a qualified amnesty in December, 1871. Now, in May, 1872, the time for party conventions and nominations was drawing near, and the passage of some sort of law allowing mass re-enfranchisement was imperative.

It might be noted that immediately after approving the amnesty bill the House passed another measure, intended to remove the disability from a large number of persons. In supporting the resolution, the ex-slave, Joseph H. Rainey of South Carolina, "made an impressive appeal for magnanimity" toward those who had been the "former oppressors and taskmasters" of his race. "We foster no enmity now," said he, "and we desire to foster none, for their acts in the past to us or to the Government we love so well. But while we are willing to accord them their enfranchisement and here today give our votes that they may be amnestied . . . we would say to those gentlemen on the other side that there is another class of citizens in the country, who have certain rights and immunities which they would like you, sirs, to remember and respect. . . . We invoke you, gentlemen, to show the same kindly feeling toward us . . . and in demonstration of this humane and just feeling,

32. *Ibid.*, 3383; also *Ibid.*, pt. 5, p. 3744.
33. See *Harper's Weekly* for January 20, 1872, for such opinion.

I implore you, give support to the Civil-rights Bill, which we have been asking at your hands, lo! these many days."[34]

Rainey had prepared his speech for the debate which he anticipated on the other amnesty measure, but its later delivery was just as appropriate. It indicated the willingness of the Negro representatives in Congress to re-enfranchise their former masters if the friends of these Southerners in the two houses were willing to accord the Negroes equal civil rights. Civil rights and amnesty, however, were now to be put into separate measures, since only a bare majority was necessary to pass a bill favoring the colored people, while two-thirds of each house was required to re-enfranchise the whites.

On May 21 the Senate began considering civil rights for the Negroes in advance of amnesty for the late slave-owners. Sumner was ill and absent; consequently, not only were civil rights considered separately, but equality in public schools and jury service were more easily stricken from the bill. In this form the Senate passed the measure and immediately gave attention to amnesty. But before action was taken on the latter measure the obdurate Senator from Massachusetts was routed out of bed and taken to the Senate, where he criticised his colleagues for the change made in the civil rights bill and bitterly protested against its passage during his absence. He desired to amend the amnesty bill to guarantee equal rights in public schools and in jury service to the colored race. "Sir, the time has not come for amnesty," he declared in desperation. "You must be just to the colored race before you are generous to former rebels. . . ."[35]

In vain did Sumner plead his cause, for the Senate passed the amnesty bill, on the early morning of May 22, by a vote of thirty-eight to two. Thirty-four members were recorded absent. James Warren Nye of Nevada voted with Sumner, who was assured that the deleted civil rights measure, which had been passed separately, was as much as could be expected at that time. During this all-night session, the Senate did vote thirty-three to seventeen to re-

34. *Cong. Globe*, 42 Cong., 2 Sess., pt. 4, p. 2824; Blaine, *Twenty Years of Congress*, II, 513-14; Rhodes, *History of the United States*, VI, 439.
35. *Cong. Globe*, 42 Cong., 2 Sess., pt. 4, pp. 3737-38; Blaine, *Twenty Years of Congress*, II, 514-15.

consider the bill, but left it on the table. The House steadfastly refused to pass such a measure, so the Negroes got no relief.

The question arose in the House as to whether the amnesty bill should go to the President for his signature. The Fourteenth Amendment provided that the disability in the third section would be removed when two-thirds of both houses approved such action. What if Grant delayed signing? Sion H. Rogers, a newly elected representative from North Carolina, was waiting to be qualified before taking his seat. Should he wait until the President disposed of the measure? He was obliged to wait, but not long, for Grant signed the bill on May 23.

The general amnesty law of 1872 re-enfranchised many thousands. According to Rhodes and Oberholtzer, the disability had already been removed from nearly five thousand by previous special acts of Congress, and these two eminent authorities believed that from three to six hundred still remained disqualified to hold office. Others have placed the number as high as 750.[36] Nevertheless, after May 23, 1872, every seat in the House and Senate was occupied for the first time since 1861; and that was something to be appreciated.

At the time of the enactment of this amnesty law, there were *quo warranto* proceedings in several Federal circuit and district courts to remove from office certain persons who were alleged to be holding positions in violation of the third section of the Fourteenth Amendment. On May 31, 1870, Congress had authorized such removals. Believing that the clement act of May, 1872, relieved these persons, President Grant, on June 1, directed "all district attorneys having charge of such proceedings and prosecutions to dismiss and discontinue the same. . . ."[37] Evidently Grant believed that only Congress could grant amnesty and acted accordingly.

As a campaign measure the amnesty act surely had some bearing on the elections of 1872. It did not prevent the Liberal Republicans, however, from nominating separate state and national tickets.

36. Rhodes, *History of the United States*, VI, 440; Oberholtzer, *History of the United States since the Civil War*, II, 272. Blaine, *Twenty Years of 44 Cong.*, 1 Sess., 324; Rhodes, VII, 243, n. 2.

37. Richardson, *Messages . . . of the Presidents* (1913 ed.), V, 4130-31. *Congress*, II, 555, placed the number at 750 in 1876. Cf. *Cong. Record,*

They chose Horace Greeley and B. Gratz Brown as their candidates for President and Vice-President, respectively, and demanded "the immediate and absolute removal of all disabilities imposed on account of the rebellion . . . believing that universal amnesty" would pacify "all sections of the country." They also recognized "the equality of all men before the law," and believed it to be the duty of the government "to mete out equal and exact justice to all" regardless "of race, color, or persuasion, religious or political." These candidates and their platform were satisfactory to the Democrats, who resolved to accept the same.[38]

The regular Republicans renominated Grant, with Senator Henry Wilson for Vice-President. They pronounced their "glorious record of the past" eleven years to be "the party's best pledge for the future." They also declared that "neither the law nor its administration should admit any discrimination in respect of citizens by reason of race, creed, color or previous condition of servitude," thereby indicating their sympathy with equal civil rights throughout the nation for all races. And, of course, they heartily approved "the action of Congress in extending amnesty to those lately in rebellion . . .," a statement that meant that the party was not likely to aid in the passage of a universal amnesty law very soon. Grant and Wilson were chosen by a large majority.[39] The party also gained undisputed control of both houses of Congress, which the Liberal Republicans and the Democrats had seriously weakened in 1870. The Forty-third Congress, therefore, resumed the policy, adopted in 1868, of re-enfranchising individuals by special acts.

THE AMNESTY BILL OF 1876

The Forty-second Congress qualified twenty-seven persons to hold office, and the Forty-third and Forty-fourth qualified forty-seven and forty-three more, respectively. The beneficiaries were often men of considerable prominence, like former members of

38. McKee, *National Conventions and Platforms*, 143-47. There was also a "Straightout" Democratic labor platform and ticket, with Charles O'Conor, a member of Jefferson Davis's counsel, for President, which was in favor of granting universal amnesty.
39. Blaine, *Twenty Years of Congress*, II, Ch. XXII.

Congress Alfred Iverson of Georgia, Lucius Q. C. Lamar of Mississippi, and J. H. Reagan of Texas. Generals P. G. T. Beauregard and Joseph E. Johnston and former United States Senator and Confederate Secretary of the Navy Mallory were also relieved.[40] These men, like others, were re-enfranchised in order that they might qualify for certain high offices in the government which they had once served well and had later rebelled against.

Of course earnest efforts were made to enact another general amnesty law, and many wanted one that would have been universal in scope. Realizing that the number of persons remaining disqualified was "very small, but enough to keep up a constant irritation," Grant recommended a "general amnesty" in his message to Congress on December 1, 1873. "No possible danger," he said, "can accrue to the Government by restoring them to eligibility to hold office."[41] By "general" he doubtless meant an amnesty with no exceptions whatever. A week later Maynard introduced in the House a bill intended to qualify everyone remaining disabled under the Fourteenth Amendment, and to substitute the oath of July 11, 1868, for that of July 2, 1862. This measure would have qualified Jefferson Davis for office. And why not? The Vice-President of the Confederacy had already been relieved by the general amnesty of May 22, 1872, and was soon to be elected to Congress. The magnanimous House passed the bill, but obstinant Charles Sumner caused its defeat in the Senate by again insisting on civil rights for the Negroes as an exchange for the proposed re-enfranchisement of their former masters.[42]

The congressional election of 1874 gave control of the House in the Forty-fourth Congress (1875-1877) to the Democrats. Consequently, Maynard's amnesty bill became the dominant issue in that body during the first session of the new Congress, with Blaine, who had lost the speakership as a result of the election, its most formidable opponent. When this measure was finally brought to a vote by Samuel J. Randall of Philadelphia, on January 10, 1876, Blaine

40. Rhodes, *History of the United States*, VI, 440-41.
41. Richardson, *Messages . . . of the Presidents* (1913 ed.), V, 4209.
42. *Cong. Record*, 43 Cong., 1 Sess., 18. The *Congressional Globe*, a private publication, was discontinued at the end of the Forty-second Congress, and since then the *Congressional Record* has been published by the government.

made his notorious "bloody shirt" speech, in which he heaped all the vicious vituperation at his ready command upon the ex-President of the Confederacy. He desired to except Davis by name in the amnesty, though not because he was "the head and front of the rebellion. . . . But," said he, "I except him on this ground: that he was the author, knowingly, deliberately, guiltily and willfully, of the gigantic murders and crimes at Andersonville. . . . And I here before God, measuring my words, knowing their full extent and import, declare that neither the deeds of the Duke of Alva in the Low Countries nor the massacre of St. Bartholomew, nor the thumb-screws and engines of torture of the Spanish Inquisition begin to compare in atrocity with the hideous crime of Andersonville."

Blaine then entered upon a long, revolting, and vitriolic description of the horrors of Andersonville. He concluded by declaring "the prison house the ideal of Dante's Inferno and Milton's Hell," and vehemently protested "against calling back and crowning with full American citizenship the man" whom he charged with the deaths in that prison.[43]

Evidently Blaine was not enthusiastic about relieving others besides Davis. Recalling that Robert Toombs had said in Europe that he would never ask for clemency, he asserted: "Very well; we can stand it about as well as Mr. Robert Toombs can. And if Mr. Robert Toombs is not prepared to . . . swear that he means to be a good citizen, let him stay out. I do not think the two houses of Congress should . . . gushingly request him to favor us by coming back to accept of all the honors of citizenship."

Others were drawn into the debate, and perhaps Benjamin H. Hill of Georgia best expressed the Southern position when he rebuked Blaine and his followers by saying that they seemed "determined that the wounds which were healing shall be re-inflamed. . . . We feel it our imperative duty," he continued, "to vindicate the truth of history as regards the section we represent, feeling that it is a portion of this common country. We do not intend to say

43. *Ibid.*, 44 Cong., 1 Sess., 323 ff.; C. E. Russell, *Blaine of Maine; His Life and Times*, 266-69; Rhodes, *History of the United States*, VII, 243-45; Blaine, *Twenty Years of Congress*, II, 554-55. Cf. Hugh Craig, *The Biography and Public Services of Hon. James G. Blaine, passim.*

anything calculated to aid the gentlemen in their work of crimination and recrimination and of keeping up the war by politicians after brave men have said the war shall end."[44]

This clash of giants did the cause of amnesty no good. As Hill truly stated, they were hopelessly fighting the battles of the rebellion again in the halls of Congress long after the cannonading had ceased on the fields of valor. The resounding echoes of this debate were heard five months later in the national Republican convention in Cincinnati, when Robert G. Ingersoll eloquently placed Blaine's name in nomination for the presidency. It was for this hour, many believed, that Blaine had struck when he viciously, but eloquently, flayed Jefferson Davis in opposing the amnesty bill. At any rate, one of his biographers has stated that "when that day [of polemics in the House of Representatives] was done discerning men everywhere said that James G. Blaine had made inevitable his nomination by the next Republican convention. Nothing but death, they said, could prevent that elevation."[45]

The debate on the universal amnesty bill of 1876 ceased on January 10, when it became known that the Senate had just passed resolutions of sorrow for the death, on July 31, 1875, of Senator and former President Andrew Johnson. He had been elected to the United States Senate in January, 1875, where some Senators who had voted to remove him from the presidency were still sitting and where, a little later, he brilliantly defended his reconstruction policy and bitterly denounced President Grant. The polemic on the amnesty measure was resumed the next day and continued several days longer, despite the fact that probably a thousand other bills were on the calendar. The measure finally lost by a vote of 184 to 97. Another futile attempt was made on January 17 to secure a general amnesty excepting only Jefferson Davis.[46]

As has already been shown, Davis stolidly declined to do anything for himself in 1876. He regretted, however, that any of his

44. *Cong. Record*, 44 Cong., 1 Sess., 345 ff.

45. Russell, *Blaine of Maine*, 271. See David S. Muzzey, *James G. Blaine, a Political Idol of Other Days*, 100-11, for mention of a sunstroke which Blaine suffered June 11, 1876.

46. *Cong. Record*, 44 Cong., 1 Sess., 351 ff. See Blaine, *Twenty Years of Congress* II, 554-55, for charges that the Democrats defeated the amnesty bill of 1876.

"compatriots should suffer by being identified" with him in any refusal of amnesty. He expressed this regret to Dr. Luke P. Blackburn (later Governor of Kentucky), who had suggested to him in January, 1876, that he write an open letter to Congress, "declining to be a recipient of any favor from so infamous a source. . . ." In replying, Davis requested Blackburn not to allow any objection against clemency to the President of the Confederacy "to prevent others from enjoying whatever benefits" they might receive on the condition of his exclusion from amnesty. He also disclaimed any right to pardon, since he had not "in any wise repented, or changed" the convictions which had determined his political course, "as well before, as during, and since the war between the States."[47]

JURY, OFFICIAL, AND MILITARY DISABILITIES

In June, 1862, Congress enacted a law requiring Federal petit and grand jurors to swear that they had never given aid to any insurrection or rebellion against the United States. In April, 1871, this requirement was made applicable only to cases involving "any suit, proceeding or prosecution based upon or arising under the provisions" of the Fourteenth Amendment.[48] This rule greatly reduced the number of persons in the Southern states who could qualify for jury service. The requirement was also annoying to many Northerners who saw no good reason why a loyal man should take such an oath. Former Confederates who qualified for office by being relieved of the disability imposed under the third section of the Fourteenth Amendment could not serve as jurors because they could not take the oath. As has been explained above, after July 11, 1868, they were required to swear only "to support and defend the Constitution" and to discharge the duties of their offices faithfully.

Futile attempts were made in the Forty-fifth Congress (1877-79) to remove the disability from Federal jurors. Late in 1877 the Democratic House approved the proposed removal, but the Republican Senate refused to concur in their legislation. About the same time, efforts by Representatives John Goode, an ex-Confederate

47. Dunbar Rowland, *Davis*, VII, 485-86.
48. *U. S. Stat. at Large*, XVIII, 152. Section 822 of the revised code applied to the amendment.

of Virginia, and Charles C. Ellsworth of Michigan to secure the enactment of special relief laws removing disabilities under the amendment also failed, the latter's amnesty bill receiving no attention at all.

The Republicans were evidently not in very good humor after the Hayes-Tilden contest over the presidency and their losses in the South in the election of 1876. Their reluctance to pass individual relief measures caused Senator James Beck of Kentucky to observe that the sentiment for amnesty had been strong in 1873, but that politics had since killed the movement. Beck was assisted by Senators F. Bayard of Delaware and Augustus H. Garland of Arkansas and Representative Samuel S. Cox of New York in efforts to remove the jurors' oath and the disability of the third section of the amendment. Bayard's bill (April, 1879) to remove the test oath for jurors passed the Senate (June, 1879); but the Republican minority in the House defeated it a few days later by repeated roll calls.[49]

The Democrats now resorted to riders to secure the removal of the test oath for jurors. In supporting such an amendment to a bill for judicial expenses for the fiscal year beginning July, 1870, Senator John T. Morgan of Alabama stressed the fact that he could be a United States Senator, but not a juryman. A little earlier, Cox had said: "General Joseph E. Johnston and others who participated with him in the rebellion are only required to take the oath to the Constitution, while the gallant band of Union soldiers led by . . . General Garfield . . . must file down in platoons . . . and take the oath . . . swearing so help them God that they never, *never*, never did bear arms" against the United States. This poignant argument and the knowledge (which Senator Morgan had also emphasized) that the whites of the South were obliged to resort to Negro jurors had the desired effect. Both houses passed the bill, but President Hayes vetoed it because of this and other amendments. Failing to over-ride the veto, the House and the Senate quickly passed another similar bill, which the President was obliged to sign (June

49. *Cong. Record*, 45 and 46 Congs., *passim*. See Samuel S. Cox, *Three Decades of Federal Legislation, 1855 to 1885*, 601, and *Opinions of the Attorneys-General*, XVIII, 149-53, for the struggle over this measure in the Senate.

30, 1879) so that funds necessary for judicial expenses would be available.[50]

The task, however, had to be done over, for, in the revision of the laws, the disability sections slipped into the code again. The Forty-seventh Congress was unable to repeal either the juror's oath or the test oath required of United States officials.[51] The next Congress did better. Senator Beck offered a bill to allow former rebels to serve in the army and navy, to repeal the test oath for jurors, and to grant universal amnesty. Cox, in the House, and Garland, in the Senate, also tried to obtain the repeal of the part of the Revised Statutes which excluded former rebels from the army and the navy.

The House passed Beck's bill, but the Senate felt that it went too far. Thereupon, under the leadership of John A. Logan of Illinois, the Senators put through a threefold measure. It excluded from appointments in the army and navy those persons who had resigned commissions in 1861 to enter the Confederate service; it repealed the test oath for jurors; and it required all United States officials, except the President, to take the oath of July 11, 1868, to support the Constitution and perform their duties faithfully. The will of the Senate was acceptable to the House, and the bill became a law with President Arthur's approval on May 24, 1884.[52]

At last Federal jurors and civil officials were no longer obliged to swear that they had never aided a rebellion against the United States. But there still remained work to be done if disabilities were to be removed from every living person who had supported the late rebellion. Section 1218 of the revised code needed to be repealed so that former Confederates might be appointed to commissions in the army and navy. There were also those who had not yet been relieved of the disability imposed by the third section of the Fourteenth Amendment. Futile attempts were made during the

50. *Cong. Record*, 45 and 46 Congs., *passim; U. S. Stat. at Large*, XXI, 44; Richardson, *Messages . . . of the Presidents* (1913 ed.), V, 4493-96. The President did not mention the juror rider in his veto message, but gave his objection to other riders in refusing to sign.

51. *Cong. Record*, 47 Cong., 4772.

52. *Ibid.*, 48 Cong., 11, 17, 391, 551-54, 1420, 3936-37, 4174; *U. S. Stat. at Large*, XXIII, 22. See Cox, *Three Decades of Federal Legislation*, Ch. XXIV, for a scholarly account of "Test Oaths and Penalties."

next ten years (1885-95) to remove the restriction on military and naval service. Finally, on December 18, 1895, Democratic Senator David B. Hill of New York demanded the immediate repeal of section 1218 of the Revised Statutes. The fear of war with Great Britain over the Venezuelan boundary was one alleged reason for such action. Republican Senator Orville H. Platt of Connecticut thought Hill's measure was unwise and prompted solely by this fear. But Democratic Senator Daniel W. Voorhees of Indiana believed it was "an expression of nationality, of brotherhood, of total reconciliation and of the process of healing all that had passed" since the outbreak of the Civil War. The Senate's action may have been influenced by altruistic motives or by fear of a war with Great Britain. At any rate, the Senate passed the bill, without division, on December 24, 1895.[53] Late the following March the House unanimously approved the measure, and, with the President's approval, it became a law.

Apparently a war scare hastened the removal, in 1896, of the last disability on former Confederates in the military and naval service, and thereafter persons who had resigned commissions in the army or navy in 1861 to cast their lot with the Confederacy might fight for the Union. Representative John A. T. Hull of Iowa stated facetiously, in supporting the bill: "So far as I am concerned I have no objection whatever, in case of another war, to allowing the men who fought in the Confederate army to enter the Union service, if they desire to do so, and get shot in place of myself."[54] Of course, the law was practically useless, for nearly all who had worn the Gray in the early 1860's were too old to fight in another war. Moreover, President Cleveland and his Secretary of State, Richard Olney, happily accepted a peaceful settlement through arbitration of differences with Great Britain.

THE LAST REMOVALS AND UNIVERSAL AMNESTY

By 1896 there was still need for a final amnesty that would place in oblivion the disability that remained on anyone under the Fourteenth Amendment. Congress had gone along, too cautiously perhaps, relieving persons now and then during the twenty years

53. *Cong. Record*, 53 Cong., 2 Sess., 672.
54. *Ibid.*, 54 Cong., 1 Sess., 3149-59.

after the failure of the amnesty bill of 1876. Political rancor thereafter precluded any prospect of a law with universal application. One by one the disfranchised ex-Confederates had passed away, thereby diminishing the number remaining disabled. Their leader, Jefferson Davis, died late in 1889, still disqualified from holding any office in the land of his birth and of which he was a citizen. At the time of his death he was among the very few remaining disabled.

Of the estimated 750 excepted by the general amnesty of 1872, 212 had been re-enfranchised by special acts of Congress.[55] General Joseph Wheeler of Alabama, who had been relieved in June, 1874, was elected to Congress a few years later. He left his seat in 1898 to command a division in the war with Spain, returning, after gallant service in Cuba, to defend the Republican administration when it was charged with grossly neglecting the soldiers in the field. Generals E. Kirby Smith and John C. Pemberton were re-enfranchised in June, 1878, and June, 1879, respectively, but neither ever held an office thereafter.

Only one voice was heard in doubting the wisdom of removing the disability from Clement C. Clay. The former United States Senator had simply petitioned Congress as follows: "I respectfully ask that the disabilities imposed upon me under section 3 of the Fourteenth Amendment of the Constitution of the United States in consequence of my participation in war waged by Alabama and other states against the United States, or my having given aid or comfort to the enemies of the United States, may be removed." The petition was dated at Huntsville, Alabama, May 24, 1880, and the bill for the removal was introduced by Senator John T. Morgan of Alabama four days later.

In the House, Harry White of Indiana thought that Clay's petition was not "in the form contemplated by the" Fourteenth Amendment. When J. Warren Keifer of Ohio said that it was "better than usual," several other members urged White not to object. When White declared that "Clement C. Clay was a dangerous man," William M. Lowe of Huntsville, Alabama, said: "I hope the gentleman will withdraw his objection. Mr. Clay is not dangerous now." White yielded, and the bill was taken from the speaker's

55. See Rhodes, *History of the United States,* VI, 441, n. 1, for the numbers relieved by the Congresses following the general amnesty of 1872.

desk, read three times, and passed. The Senate had already acted without debate, and the President signed the bill on June 16, 1880.[56] Thus, nearly twenty years after his expulsion from the United States Senate in 1861, Clement C. Clay could again enjoy all the privileges of citizenship in the United States. He died about eighteen months later without ever holding office again.

The last two men to be relieved by special acts of Congress were John Taylor Wood of Louisiana, an officer of the "Merrimac," and Colonel William E. Simms of Kentucky. Wood was a grandson of Zachary Taylor, whose daughter had been Jefferson Davis's first wife, and the bill to relieve him was hurriedly passed by both houses and signed by President Cleveland on February 12, 1897.[57] A little more attention was given to Simms. In introducing the measure for his relief, Representative William C. Owens of Georgetown, Kentucky, said that the beneficiary was an old man who had but a few more years to live, and that he was anxious before his death to have "the ban of his country's disfavor" removed from his record. Two other Kentuckians, James B. McCreary of Richmond and Walter Evans of Louisville, recommended the petition, and the measure passed without reference to a committee.

When the bill reached the Senate, George F. Hoar of Massachusetts told his colleagues that Simms had been "a gallant officer of the Mexican War," that he was a member of a distinguished family, and that he was quite old and in feeble health. Hoar stated further that he had received no formal application for clemency from Simms, but that he did have a very touching letter by the Kentuckian to Justice John Marshall Harlan, in which Simms "expressed his love for his country and his desire to become fully a citizen of the United States again." By unanimous consent the bill was ordered to a third reading and passed, the President approving on February 25, 1897.[58]

No effort to relieve any individual appears to have been made after the relief of Simms. Evidently a few still remained disabled under the Fourteenth Amendment, but this study has not disclosed

56. *Cong. Record*, 46 Cong., 2 Sess., pt. 4, pp. 3896, 4314; *U. S. Stat. at Large*, XXI, 571.
57. *Cong. Record*, 54 Cong., 2 Sess., pt. 2, pp. 1486, 1762.
58. *Ibid.*, 1947; pt. 3, pp. 2048, 2070, 2267.

their names. The relief of these few was accomplished by a universal amnesty some sixteen months after the last two individual removals. As a war scare had hastened the qualification of all living ex-Confederates for military service in 1896, so, in 1898, actual war caused the passage of a universal amnesty law.

While sons of the Blue and the Gray were organizing under the Stars and Stripes to drive the last vestige of Spanish misgovernment from the Western Hemisphere, a universal amnesty bill was introduced in the Senate. In presenting the measure, William Morris Stewart of Nevada said that the "few persons . . . still unrelieved" were old and that "it would be a gratification . . . to the whole country, to have Congress do this act of kindness."[59] The Senate passed the bill without debate, but the House changed the measure a little when it came before that body with a report from the Committee on the Judiciary. This report was a remarkable document, especially when considered in the light of the thirty-three years of disfranchisement that had been imposed on supporters of the Lost Cause. "It is to be regretted," the committee said, "that it was ever in the mind of any persons that such extreme measures were necessary." The next sentence indicated that such Radicals as Charles Sumner, Thaddeus Stevens, and James G. Blaine had passed on and could no longer raise their voices to restrain the hand of clemency in Congress. "Years have rolled by since that great struggle closed, and the American people look at public matters growing out of the war of 1861 in calmer moments when their judgment can be trusted, and [they] are [now] willing . . . that this bill pass and the disability [be] wholly removed from the statute book."

But the most significant statement in this memorable report was the following: "The seeds of this war were sown when the Convention framed the Constitution . . . and it was only a question of time when the growth would be ready for the sickle, and the war was simply reaping the harvest. To the American people the war was worth the sacrifice. It accomplished at a terrible cost of life and money what could not be realized by any other means. . . ."[60]

The committee did not, of course, mean to say that the Fathers

59. *Ibid.*, 55 Cong., 2 Sess., pt. 5, p. 4833 (May 12, 1898).
60. *Ibid.*, 5404-5.

intentionally sowed the seeds of the Civil War. Perhaps it was the existence of states' rights in 1787 that caused the Convention to frame a government that made a civil war inevitable. A stronger argument, however, could not have been found against the charge of treason which had been made against the Confederates in earlier years. Such judgment from the most representative branch of Congress came too late, however, to give any satisfaction to the large number of Southerners who had contended that they had merely applied the principles laid down by the founders of the government when they organized the Confederate States of America. Jefferson Davis, Clement C. Clay, Zebulon B. Vance, Joseph Turner, Robert Toombs, Raphael Semmes, Howell Cobb, and many others who had earnestly contended that their support of the Confederacy was historically justifiable were no longer living. Nevertheless, the committee of the House had placed the Civil War in a more favorable light than had generally been accepted, and no doubt there were those then living who did find some consolation in the report and in the universal amnesty thus recommended.

A civil war is often the most deplorable, for it arrays neighbor against neighbor and brother against brother, and its aftermath is most certain to be hatred and vengeance. The American Civil War was certainly no exception, and the Crime of Reconstruction was its natural sequel. While the third section of the Fourteenth Amendment was in effect, public opinion gradually became more enlightened, and the war with Spain accelerated the manifestation of mutual appreciation of Americans of both sections. Since Generals Joseph Wheeler and Fitzhugh Lee (nephew of General Robert E. Lee) were leading Southern soldiers against the enemy of the United States, there was likely to be an overflow of enthusiasm when the House undertook to debate the universal amnesty bill. "Never in my life had I seen a more pleasing sight," said John Fletcher Lacey of Iowa, referring to Virginians who had gone forth to battle for the Union in 1898. "Their march proclaimed the new day of patriotic reconciliation and national unity."

Speaking for the South and pretending to hear both "Dixie" and the "Star Spangled Banner" being played in the army, Evan E. Settle of Kentucky eloquently exclaimed: "I thank God that I have lived to see this day. We sometimes thought that the war between the States was an unmitigated evil, but in the providence of God, it, accompanied by other agencies, has proved to be a great blessing." Then, in appreciation of the fraternal spirit occasioned by the war with Spain, he said: "We shall free Cuba, but we shall do more than that. We shall free ourselves."[61]

What a pity the leaders of both the Blue and the Gray did not live to see that day! Perhaps their passing was necessary to hasten the era of better feeling between the North and the South that dates from May and June, 1898. At least one of them had left a prophecy of a better time to come as he sat weakly penning the last of his *Memoirs* during the summer of 1885. "I feel," wrote General Grant, "that we are on the eve of a new era, when there is to be a great harmony between the Federal and the Confederate. I cannot stay to be a living witness to this prophecy, but I feel that it is to be so." Jenkins, in submitting the report and bill recommending universal amnesty, quoted these parting words of the victorious Union general, whose only equal wore the Gray at Appomattox, and then concluded: "We certainly can make no mistake when we follow the dying words of our great leader, Grant. Your committee believe that they but voice the sentiment of the people of the nation when they unanimously say: Let the disability be removed."[62]

Before action was taken on the bill, there was some bickering over filling quotas in the army. When Democratic states were charged with delay and neglect in this respect, their representatives proved that they were doing their part in filling quotas. It also appeared necessary to satisfy a few that General Wheeler was not retaining his seat in Congress while serving in the army.

The House passed the amnesty bill unanimously, and President McKinley signed it on June 8. The law provided: "That the disability imposed by section three of the Fourteenth Amendment to the Constitution of the United States heretofore incurred is hereby repealed."[63] No oath, no exception, and no reservation whatever were required of the beneficiaries—if there really were any persons remaining disabled. Perhaps the only benefit derived

61. *Ibid.*, 5404-17.
62. *Ibid.*; Grant, *Memoirs*, II, 553, for the quotation from Grant.
63. *U. S. Stat. at Large*, XXX, 432.

from the universal amnesty act was the spirit of amity and fraternity that it encouraged. It is exceedingly doubtful, of course, that the disability thus removed should ever have been given constitutional status in the first place. Certainly an earlier universal amnesty would have been better policy.

CHAPTER SEVENTEEN

PARDON AND AMNESTY IN THE COURTS

---◆---

EARLY DECISIONS

SINCE ACTS of executive clemency during the period under consideration were often tested in the courts to determine their efficacy, an account of the litigation attending the functioning of pardon and amnesty properly concludes this narrative. The courts were inclined at the outset to favor claimants of benefits derived from pardons.[1] As has already been shown in the case of Ridgely Greathouse, a California Federal court declared (February, 1864) that Lincoln's December proclamation extended "not only to rebels in arms ... but also to such as are already arrested and incarcerated." This decision allowed a broader application of the amnesty measure than the President had intended. Consequently, he issued a supplementary proclamation on the twenty-sixth of the following March, excluding from the benefits of his clemency persons under restraint by the Federal authorities at the time they applied for pardon.[2]

The explanatory measure was intended to obviate the decision in the case of *In re Greathouse;* and indeed it did, so far as subsequent applicants under Federal restraint were concerned. But at the time it appeared there were applicants for pardon whom this supplementary proclamation was intended to exclude from the benefits of amnesty. Edward L. Hughes, a citizen of Ohio, who had participated in Morgan's raid north of the Ohio River in the summer of

---

1. See Dunbar Rowland, *Davis,* X, 100, for a statement to that effect by John D. McPherson, an able attorney who practiced in the United States Court of Claims.
2. See the second division of Ch. IV.

1863, was such an applicant. Indicted for treason, he tried to avail himself, on March 1, 1864, of the President's proffer of amnesty. When his petition was denied, he brought suit in the United States district court of southern Ohio for his freedom under the proclamation of the previous December. The Federal counsel insisted that the benefits of the proffered amnesty did not extend to "citizens of a loyal state charged with treason," and that, if the defendant were "included in such proclamation, the amended explanatory proclamation excluded" him "from all its benefits." The court, however, decided that Hughes came within the scope of the first proclamation. Moreover, he had taken the oath of allegiance on March 1, and, therefore, was not affected by the measure of March 26, as such exclusion would "give the second proclamation a retroactive operation and thus doom the defendant to a punishment from which he had already been exonerated."[3] Consequently, the plaintiff was allowed a pardon (October, 1864), and others in similar condition were similarly affected by the court's opinion.

The question of the restoration of property condemned in a prize court to recipients of pardons arose very early. Attorney-General Edward Bates expressed the opinion on February 9, 1863, that international law applied in such cases and not municipal or national law. "The condemnation of a vessel and cargo in a prize court," he said, "is not a criminal sentence. No person is charged with an offence; and so, no person is in condition to be released and reinstated by a pardon. In fact," he continued, "there is nothing upon which a pardon, granted by the President in terms of the Constitution, can operate. . . ."[4]

Bates's successor, James Speed, expressed a similar opinion (April 2, 1866) in the case of the schooner "Adelso." This vessel and its cargo had been condemned on November 13, 1861, in the United States district court for Rhode Island. The sentence was confirmed in a Federal circuit court, but the case was dismissed by the Supreme Court, to which the claimants appealed but before which they failed to appear. Subsequently the claimants availed themselves of the President's amnesty and petitioned for the restoration of their property (or the proceeds of its sale) under the terms thereof. In

3. *United States* vs. *Hughes, Federal Cases,* XXVI, 15418.

4. *Opinions of the Attorneys-General,* X, 453-54.

his denial, Speed discriminated between the functions of prize and municipal courts. "The prize courts," he stated, "adjudicate the character and relations of things . . . brought within their jurisdiction. The municipal courts . . . judge of the acts of persons, and determine whether offences have been committed which superinduce the confiscation of property. . . . No one of the claimants was guilty of any offence against the United States in owning or shipping this cargo. There is, therefore, nothing in the case on which the President's pardon . . . could operate."[5]

The status of property condemned in a prize court is further illustrated in the case of the "Gray Jacket." One Timothy Meagher, in December, 1863, suffered the seizure and condemnation of his vessel and cargo for attempting to take cotton from Mobile to Havana. The following March, Meagher availed himself of the President's amnesty and sought the restoration of his property, claiming only his oath of allegiance as proof that his property should be restored. Under a law enacted on July 13, 1861, providing for the "Collection of Duties on Imports, and for other Purposes,"[6] the claim appeared plausible. This act allowed penalties for infraction to be mitigated or remitted, as conditions warranted. Consequently, Secretary Hugh McCulloch ordered the restoration of the property (March 21, 1866), since its owner claimed not to be running the blockade of the Southern ports.

The Supreme Court, however, decided against Meagher (December, 1866), declaring the seizure of the "Gray Jacket" to be "incurred by the public law of war and not by the statute of July 13, 1861." Furthermore, the court asserted that the case came only within the province of maritime warfare. Consequently, the proclamation of amnesty could not "extinguish the liability of a vessel and cargo running the blockade, and seized *flagrante delicto*. It would be a strange result in such a case," the court concluded, "if the subsequent oath of the claimant were allowed to establish his innocence and compel the restitution of his property."[7]

In December, 1864, the Supreme Court declared that enemy property taken on island waters was not good prize. The decision

5. *Ibid.*, XI, 446-51.
6. *U. S. Stat. at Large*, XII, 255-58.
7. 5 Wall. 367.

also concerned the operation of Lincoln's amnesty. The main facts of this unique case are as follows: In March, 1864, a certain Mrs. Alexander, living near the Red River in Louisiana, suffered the seizure of seventy-two bales of cotton by a naval force from a gunboat belonging to Admiral Porter's expedition. Soon thereafter she took the oath and claimed the restoration of her property. Her plea was granted by the United States district court for southern Illinois at Cairo, to which the cotton had been taken. The Federal authorities were not satisfied with the lower court's decision and forthwith appealed the case to the Supreme Court, on the ground that the cotton was good maritime prize and should be condemned as such. This tribunal, however, asserted that the property did not come under that classification. On the contrary, it affirmed "that the cotton in controversy was not maritime prize, but should have been turned over to the agents of the Treasury Department in order that the claimant, when the rebellion is suppressed, or she has been able to leave the rebel region, may have the opportunity to bring suit in the Court of Claims, and, on making the proof required by the act for the Collection of Abandoned Property, have the proper decree."[8] This meant, according to the law enacted on March 12, 1863, that Mrs. Alexander might, "at any time within two years after the suppression of the rebellion, prefer" her claim in the Court of Claims and, on proof of her loyalty, which her oath and subsequent actions should substantiate, obtain the proceeds of the sale of her cotton.[9]

THE IRONCLAD TEST OATH

The effect of presidential clemency on the various national and state laws commonly called test oaths is worthy of notice. The act of Congress requiring the "ironclad" oath of all Federal officers, except the President, that they had never supported the Confederacy was extended on January 24, 1865, to include attorneys and counselors admitted to practice in the United States courts.[10] The scope of this sweeping prohibitory law was challenged in the famous case

8. Mrs. Alexander's Cotton, 2 Wall. 404.
9. *U. S. Stat. at Large*, XII, 820-21.
10. *Ibid.*, 424.

of *Ex parte Garland,* the result of which came near precipitating the passage of drastic judicial measures by Congress.

In July, 1865, Augustus H. Garland, a former Confederate Congressman from Arkansas, received a special pardon, which he soon produced with a petition to practice law in the Federal courts without taking the prescribed oath. He had enjoyed that privilege before the war and now desired to be reinstated. The case was eventually settled in the Supreme Court. Garland "rested his petition principally upon two grounds: 1st. That the act of January 24, 1865, so far as it affected his station in the court, was unconstitutional and void; and, 2nd. That, if the act were constitutional, he was released from compliance with its provisions by the pardon of the President." A bare majority decided both points in his favor (December, 1866). The four dissenting judges and the government's counsel, Speed and Stanbery, insisted that Congress had a right to determine the qualifications of Federal court officials. They contended, also, that the required oath was not within the constitutional prohibition concerning bills of attainder and *ex post facto* laws, as Garland's counsel insisted and the majority ruled. Nevertheless, the court stated that the President's power to pardon extended "to every offence known to the law, and may be exercised at any time after its commission. . . . This power . . . is not subject to legislative control. Congress can neither limit the effect of his pardon, nor exclude from its exercise any class of offenders. . . . A pardon . . . releases the punishment and blots out the existence of the guilt, so that in the eye of the law the offender is as innocent as if he had never committed the offence. . . ." Garland, therefore, was declared restored "to all his civil rights," one of which was the privilege of practicing in the Federal courts.[11]

Naturally this decision infuriated the Radicals. And well it might, for young Garland (then only thirty-six and later Governor of Arkansas and Attorney-General under Cleveland) had argued his own case and had won a great victory, not only for himself but also for other ex-Confederate lawyers. So disturbed were the op-

---

11. *Ex parte Garland,* 71 U. S. 333 (1866); *American Law Register* (new series), VI, 284-96. See also *Cummins* vs. *Missouri,* 71 U. S. 277 (1866). S. S. Cox, in his *Three Decades of Federal Legislation,* 250-57, discusses the objectionable features of the Federal and state test oaths.

position that they undertook to curtail the power of the Supreme Court. A bill was soon introduced in the House requiring a unanimous decision to invalidate an act of Congress on constitutional grounds, and a measure requiring a two-thirds vote for such ruling was actually passed by that body. Threats were also made to deny the Court appellate jurisdiction, and even to abolish the tribunal by constitutional amendment.[12] Fortunately nothing of that nature was actually done.

A case similar to Garland's soon came before the Supreme Court of the District of Columbia, which had established a rule requiring counsel practicing before it to take an oath very much like that involved in the decision above. Allan B. Magruder had applied for permission to practice in the District's court without taking the prescribed oath, on the ground that the decision in the case of *Ex parte Garland* applied in like manner to the District. Inasmuch as the petitioner had never practiced before that tribunal, the judges were of the opinion that the fact of his pardon did not enter into the case, "as it is not the part of the office of a pardon to create in a criminal new rights which he did not before possess." The court also ruled that Magruder's case was not analogous to Garland's. Congress had determined the oath for the Federal courts, while the District court had exercised its "inherent right" in determining its own regulations for procedure. Magruder's petition, therefore, was denied, notwithstanding the President's pardon.

THE RESTORATION OF PROPERTY

Apparently the largest number of cases involving claims to benefits derived from pardon and amnesty concerned the restoration of property seized under the confiscation and abandoned property acts.[13] Provisions enacted for the return of such property have already been given in this chapter and elsewhere. Before some of the

12. *Cong. Globe*, 39 Cong., 2 Sess., pt. 1, pp. 646-49. See also Henry, *The Story of Reconstruction*, 215-16; and DeWitt, *Impeachment and Trial of Andrew Johnson*, 478-79.

13. This subject has been treated by J. G. Randall, *Constitutional Problems under Lincoln*, Ch. XIV. It should be noted that much information might be given concerning state amnesty laws and amnesty cases in state courts if space permitted. Such information may be found in state statutes and court reports, especially for North Carolina, Kentucky, and even Nevada.

litigation over the interpretation of these regulations is considered, several opinions of the Attorneys-General relating thereto might well be given.

In the "Adelso" case (July, 1865), Speed stated that he did not "see how any Southern man who is within the 6th section of the Confiscation Act of July 17, 1862, and who remains unpardoned, can make a valid sale or consignment, as against the United States, of any property belonging to him."[14] The restraining clause referred to declared null and void any conveyance of property by anyone who sixty days after the passage of the Confiscation Act continued to support the Confederacy. The law further provided that any person claiming classification under this section of the act would be barred from suing to recover "possession or the use of such property." A year later the new Attorney-General, Henry Stanbery, issued a statement intended to be a rule in determining the operation and effects of a pardon. This opinion embodied the features of amnesty as they were understood at that time. He asserted that a pardon was "applicable to the remission of fines, penalties, and forfeitures, which are imposed by law as punishment for offense." He made it clear, however, that a pardon did not restore to the recipients "by its own operation, any property, or the proceeds of any property sold under a judgment or decree of Confiscation."[15] As has already been stated, such persons might bring suit in the United States Court of Claims within two years after the close of the war to recover their property or the proceeds of the sale thereof. In order to gain their suits, however, they were required to prove their constant loyalty to the Union throughout the conflict.[16]

The following question then arose: What effect did a pardon have upon the requirement of proof of one's constant loyalty in a suit to recover property? At first the Court of Claims was unwilling to accept a pardon in lieu of proof of constant loyalty in such cases. This position was taken in denying the petition of John F. Pargoud of Louisiana for the recovery of the proceeds of the sale of eighty-

14. *Opinions of the Attorneys-General*, XI, 291.

15. Attorneys-General's Office, Letter Book E, 290; *Opinions of the Attorneys-General*, XII, 81.

16. On June 25, 1868, Congress re-emphasized this requirement of loyalty. *U. S. Stat. at Large*, XV, 75.

five bales of cotton. The claimant did not offer evidence of his constant loyalty, but insisted instead that, by virtue of his special pardon on January 11, 1866, his claim should be allowed. The court, however, in a two-to-one decision, refused his petition, on the ground that Congress under the act of March 12, 1863, had limited its jurisdiction in these cases to persons who had given no aid or support to the rebellion.[17]

The dissenting judge vigorously insisted that the pardon did affect Pargoud's condition, and that the majority opinion was a "confiscation pure and simple, and nothing else. Moreover," he continued, "it is confiscation by way of punishment for a crime which has been fully pardoned." He further averred that "to take a convicted criminal from his cell, with a full pardon in his hands, and hang him . . . would not be a whit more illegal and unconstitutional than to confiscate" Pargoud's "property as a punishment for a crime for which he" had been fully pardoned. Pargoud moved to appeal his case to the Supreme Court, but the Court of Claims overruled his motion. The majority, in their denial, declared that claimants, under the law allowing such suits, had no right of appeal from their judgment.[18]

Nevertheless, Pargoud was ultimately to receive consideration by the Supreme Court. On the twenty-fifth of December, the month his petition was denied, President Johnson announced his universal amnesty, without condition, to all supporters of the Confederacy. Soon thereafter, judgments in several cases were affected by this proclamation, among them that of Mrs. Hibernia Armstrong of Arkansas, who had fled southward with thirty or forty of her slaves on the approach of a Union army. The Federals had sequestered her cotton and placed it in the fortifications of Little Rock, from which it was later removed, shipped to Cincinnati, and sold, and the proceeds were deposited in the Treasury at Washington.

The Court of Claims denied Mrs. Armstrong's suit for the recovery of her property, on the ground that her flight with her slaves had constituted aid to the rebellion. The Supreme Court, upon appeal, held that the President's proclamation of December 25,

17. *Pargoud* vs. *U. S.*, 4 Ct. of Cl. 337 (December, 1868).
18. *Ibid.*

1868, made it unnecessary for it to express an opinion on the nature of the claimant's act in fleeing on the approach of the Federal army. "The proclamation [had] granted a pardon unconditionally and without reservation" to every supporter of the Confederacy, and, consequently, it was a "public act of which all courts" were "bound to take notice." Mrs. Armstrong's claim had been preferred within two years, as the law required, and the lower court, therefore, had "erred in not giving the petitioner the benefits of the proclamation" and allowing her claim.[19]

Mrs. Armstrong's victory was a boon to Edward Pargoud when he finally got his case argued before the Supreme Court. The able counsel for the government had insisted that his petition should be dismissed for want of jurisdiction because of an act of Congress of July 12, 1870, providing that neither pardon nor amnesty should be accepted in any court as evidence in allowing a claim for the recovery of funds deposited in the Treasury. Instead, such averment became evidence of the petitioner's support of the rebellion and therefore sufficient ground for denying his right to sue in the Court of Claims for the recovery of his property.[20]

In 1868 Pargoud had offered his special pardon, in lieu of proof of his constant loyalty, in petitioning for the recovery of the proceeds of the sale of his cotton. The Court of Claims had refused to admit the efficacy of such evidence and had denied his petition on the ground that the claimant had not offered proof of his loyalty to the Union. Now, three years later, Chief Justice Chase declared for the Supreme Court that proof of Pargoud's loyalty was not necessary, since that court had "recently decided in the case of Hibernia Armstrong . . . that the President's proclamation of December 25, 1868 . . . relieves claimants of captured and abandoned property from proof of adhesion to the United States during the Civil War. It was unnecessary, therefore, for the petitioner to prove such adhesion or personal pardon for taking part in the rebellion . . ." and consequently he won his suit.[21]

19. *Armstrong* vs. *U. S.*, 13 Wall. 154 (December, 1871).
20. *U. S. Stat. at Large*, XVI, 235.
21. *Pargoud, Appellant* vs. *U. S., Appellees*, 7 Ct. of Cl. 289; also *Pargoud* vs. *U. S.*, 13 Wall. 156 (December, 1871).

FAILURE TO RESTRICT AMNESTY

Mention has been made above of an act of Congress in July, 1870, providing: "That no pardon or amnesty, by proclamation or otherwise, shall be admissible in evidence on the part of any claimant in the Court of Claims" in a suit for the recovery of the proceeds of the sale of his property. Congress was apparently prompted to pass this law by a decision of the Supreme Court in December, 1869. The opinion was rendered in the appealed case of Edward Padelford of Savannah, Georgia, who had won his petition in the Court of Claims for the recovery of the proceeds of the sale of his cotton. The facts of this interesting case have sufficient bearing on the final decision to justify their narration.

In April, 1861, Padelford had subscribed, under duress, to two thousand dollars of a Confederate loan of fifteen million dollars. (The amount reported by the Court of Claims is two thousand dollars; by the Supreme Court, five thousand.) Moreover, his bank, against his will as director and under threat of destruction if it refused, had subscribed to ten thousand dollars of the same loan. He had also gone surety for three friends, who had obtained Confederate quartermaster and commissary offices to avoid actual military service. It was evident, therefore, that Padelford had been an unwilling supporter of the rebellion. He had waited, however, for more than a month (January 25, 1865) after Sherman's capture of Savannah (December 21, 1864) before taking the oath of allegiance provided in Lincoln's proclamation of amnesty. Following his assertion of loyalty the military authorities seized a large quantity of cotton in the city, belonging to him and Randolph Mott. The cotton was transported to New York and sold for $246,277 net, and the money was deposited in the Federal Treasury.

In March, 1866, Padelford and Mott petitioned the Court of Claims for the proceeds of the sale, but the case was on the court's docket for two years before a decision was rendered. Subsequent to the filing of the claim, Congress enacted the law requiring proof of constant loyalty of persons suing in the Court of Claims to recover their property or the proceeds of the sale thereof. Padelford, being permitted to sue independently for half of the claim, proved his loyalty to the satisfaction of the court and won his suit.[22]

22. *Padelford* vs. *U. S.*, 4 Ct. of Cl. 316.

The judges decided this case solely upon its merits without considering the effect of pardon and amnesty. Dissatisfied with the decision, the attorney for the United States appealed the case to the Supreme Court, on the ground that the claimant's personal subscription and the subscription of his bank to the Confederate loan constituted aid to the rebellion. He insisted that the alleged coercion did not relieve the claimant from the consequence of his acts. Furthermore, he contended that the surety bonds made Padelford liable to punishment, since they were voluntarily given. The court held that the subscriptions did not constitute voluntary aid, but that the surety bonds did, notwithstanding the claimant's manifest opposition to the rebellion. Yet Padelford had been loyal as far as it was prudent, and the fact that he was apparently "gratified by the restoration of the National authority" evidently strengthened his case. Moreover, he had taken the amnesty oath before the confiscation of his property, and the Court construed this to mean that he was pardoned, and, as in the case of Augustus H. Garland, "as innocent as if he had never committed the offence." Even if the petitioner's "property had been seized before the oath was taken, the faith of the Government was pledged to its restoration upon the taking of the oath in good faith."

But Padelford's claim was even stronger than the above declaration indicates. The Federal counsel contended that, since the cotton "was captured in fact if not lawfully" and since the proceeds of the sale had "been paid into the Treasury . . . the petitioner" was without remedy in the Court of Claims unless he proved his constant loyalty. The Supreme Court declared this argument "ingenious," or possessing some merit, but nevertheless unsound. "If, in other respects," the decision ran, "the petitioner made the proof which entitled him to a decree for the proceeds of his property, the law makes the proof of pardon a complete substitute for the proof that he gave no aid or comfort to the rebellion." The government, therefore, had merely become the trustee of Padelford's property, and, "having been fully reimbursed for all expenses incurred in that character," it had lost "nothing by the judgment which simply" awarded to the petitioner what was already his own.[23]

It can readily be seen that the decision in Padelford's case in-

23. *U. S. vs. Padelford*, 9 Wall. 531.

sured the restoration of property of any claimant who was the recipient of presidential clemency, provided he had filed his claim within two years after the close of the war, which was declared to be on August 20, 1866. As might be expected, the Radicals sought to obviate this assurance by contrary legislation. Consequently, when Congress, on July 12, 1870, appropriated $100,000 "for the payment of judgments in the Court of Claims," members put into the measure a proviso that no pardon or amnesty should "be admissible in evidence in support of any claim in said court" or in any superior court on appeal, notwithstanding "the effect of any executive proclamation, pardon, or other condition of oblivion."[24] As has been stated above, evidence of the written acceptance of such clemency was to be regarded by the Court of Claims as proof of the claimant's participation in the rebellion and sufficient cause for the dismissal of his suit.

Congress had already passed a joint resolution (approved March 2, 1867) of similar import. This measure forbade the payment of any claim against the United States prior to April 30, 1861, to any person who had "in any manner sustained the late rebellion," or who had not been "distinctly in favor of its suppression. . . ." The act further provided that "no pardon heretofore granted, or hereafter to be granted, shall authorize the payment of such account, claim, or demand, until this resolution is modified or repealed. . . ." Apparently there never was any modification or repeal of the resolution; but it is the proviso denying the benefit of pardon in the appropriation act of July 12, 1870, that requires attention.[25]

This proviso was not to stand the test of the Supreme Court. In May, 1869, the Court of Claims allowed John A. Klein's petition for the recovery of the proceeds of the sale of a considerable quantity of cotton that had belonged to V. F. Wilson, deceased. The Federal counsel, however, appealed the case for further consideration to the higher court, where it remained until December, 1871, when that tribunal also decided against the United States. Klein, as administrator for Wilson, had brought suit to recover the proceeds of the sale of 560 bales of upland cotton. The deceased, a Northerner, who had come to Vicksburg in 1849 to engage in business,

24. *U. S. Stat. at Large*, XVI, 235; also *Cong. Globe*, 41 Cong., 1 Sess.
25. *U. S. Stat. at Large*, XIV, 571.

had purchased the cotton in the autumn of 1862 and had stored it with the intention of shipping it later to Pittsburgh to cancel certain debts there. The Confederates, however, had sequestered the cotton and placed it in the fortifications of the city, where the Federals found it after the fall of Vicksburg. It was then shipped to St. Louis and sold for $125,300 net, and the money was deposited in the Treasury.

Wilson, before his death in 1865, had taken Lincoln's amnesty oath in February, 1864, and, although he had voluntarily become surety on the bonds of certain Confederate officeholders, was proved to have been loyal to the Union throughout the war. The loyalty, however, of those from whom he had purchased the cotton was doubtful, and it was even conceded that Klein himself might not always have been as loyal as was desirable. Moreover, the use of the cotton in the defense of Vicksburg was urged by the Federal counsel as sufficient cause alone for denying the petition. Nevertheless, the objections were overruled and the claim was allowed.[26]

The counsel for the United States appealed this case to the Supreme Court, largely on the ground that Congress had repealed (January 7, 1867) the section of the Confiscation Act of July 17, 1862, giving the President the power to extend pardon and amnesty by proclamation. The appeal was filed in December, 1869, but the decision was not rendered for more than a year (December, 1871) after the passage of the law disallowing the benefit of pardon and amnesty in suits for the restoration of captured and abandoned property. The Federal attorney still insisted that Wilson's loyalty could not be established and, furthermore, that no proclamation of amnesty after January 7, 1867, could be offered in support of Klein's claim. Thus, when the case was finally argued, the counsel for the government not only contended that Johnson's second, third, and fourth proclamations of amnesty were of no effect in such cases, but he also affirmed that the legislation of July 12, 1870, was sufficient cause for the dismissal of suits supported by evidence of pardon or amnesty.

Nevertheless, the argument against allowing Klein's claim was of no avail. The Court took the position that the action of Congress in repealing the clement section of the Confiscation Act "was after

26. *John A. Klein, Admin. of V. F. Wilson, vs. U. S., 4 Ct. of Cl. 559.*

the close of the war, when the act had ceased to be important as an expression of the" disposition of Congress "to carry into effect the clemency of the Executive. . . ." The repeal was also after the Supreme Court, in the case of *Ex parte Garland,* had declared that "Congress can neither limit the effect" of the President's pardon, "nor exclude from its exercise any class of offenders." Moreover, the tribunal further affirmed that there could be no doubt of the obligation of the Federal authorities to allow Klein's claim before the repeal of Section 13 of the Confiscation Act, which repeal "in no respect" changed that obligation, since it did "not alter at all the operation of the pardon, or reduce in any degree the obligation of Congress . . . to give full effect to it, if necessary, by legislation."[27]

This meant, of course, that Klein's suit was not affected by the repeal of the mitigating section of the Confiscation Act; but what about the effect of the proviso denying evidence of pardon in the appropriation act of July 12, 1870? This restriction was intended to prevent the Supreme Court from reviewing such cases on appeal from the Court of Claims when evidence of pardon or amnesty was offered in support of claims. After stating clearly the purpose of this legislation, the Court declared that Congress had "inadvertently passed the limit which separates the legislative from the judicial" power when it presumed to deny the jurisdiction of the Supreme Court in appeals from the Court of Claims in cases where judgments had been founded on evidence of pardons. The proviso, therefore, was declared unconstitutional, and the lower court's decision in allowing Klein's claim was confirmed.[28]

Probably the ablest member of the Supreme Court at the time this decision was rendered was Samuel Freeman Miller. It is interesting to note that he prepared a dissenting opinion, in which he held that only when property remained in the possession of the owner did pardon or amnesty remit "all right in the government to . . . confiscate it." "But where the property," he asserted, "had already been seized and sold, and the proceeds paid into the treasury . . . the pardon does not and cannot restore that which had completely passed away." In other words, Miller insisted that title to the pro-

27. *U. S.* vs. *Klein,* 13 Wall. 128 (1871).
28. See confirmation in the case of *Abram Barker* vs. *U. S.,* 7 Ct. of Cl. 551 (December, 1871).

ceeds of a sale became vested in the United States once the money had been deposited in the Treasury, even though he agreed with the other judges that the denying clause of the law of July 12, 1870, was unconstitutional. He believed, therefore, that the provision in the Captured and Abandoned Property Act of March 12, 1863, allowing persons to sue in the Court of Claims for the recovery of the proceeds of the sale of their property, was intended to benefit only those who had remained loyal to the Union.[29]

In December, 1871, the Court of Claims passed on the efficacy of two faulty oaths taken by a testator, whose executor was suing for the proceeds of the sale of ninety-two bales of cotton. The deceased, John F. Hamilton of Savannah, had taken Lincoln's and Johnson's oaths, with some modifications, in March and July, 1865, respectively. The first was too unlike Lincoln's to support the standing of the claimant. In the second oath the word "protect" had been omitted from the phrase "faithfully support, protect and defend the Constitution," and the term "late rebellion" had been used instead of "existing rebellion." The second oath, however, was admitted as evidence; and the Court declared that, since "the meaning of protect" was "included in *defend*" and the use of "existing" for "late" was "merely a matter of description" which was "immaterial," the validity of the oath was not impaired.[30] Consequently, Hamilton's taint of disloyalty was removed by his amnesty oath, and the claim was allowed.[31]

THE EFFECT OF JOHNSON'S LAST AMNESTY

The sweeping efficacy of Johnson's last proclamation of amnesty was recognized in two other cases by the Court of Claims in December, 1871. These decisions also indicate the effect of the Supreme Court's recent opinion in the case of *Klein* vs. *United States*. In one case the claimant, Harry Haym, who was suing to recover $72,353.98 from the sale of his cotton, had taken, in July, 1865, the

29. 13 Wall. 148.
30. The phrase "existing rebellion" was used in the oath of May 29, 1865; but in the amnesty of September 7, 1867, the word "late" was substituted for "existing."
31. *John F. Hamilton's Ex.* vs. *U. S.*, 7 Ct. of Cl. 144. In winning this case, the claimant recovered $16,295.79, the total net proceeds of eighty-five bales at $175.33 a bale and six bales at $231.79 a bale.

oath provided in the proclamation of May 29, 1865; but the President had not pardoned him until March, 1867. He had accepted the pardon a month later, but did not consider it necessary to renew his allegiance. The attorney for the United States argued that this should have been done after the pardon if Haym was to benefit therefrom. Such repetition appeared necessary since the precedent oath might have been violated before the pardon was granted and accepted. This contention of the counsel for the government appears to have influenced the court to declare: "If, therefore, the claimant's standing here rested on that pardon alone, he could not maintain this action. But under the decision in Klein's case the President's proclamation of December 25, 1868, entitles all who gave aid to the rebellion to prosecute claims in this court."[32] Consequently, since no oath or other condition was required in this act of clemency, Haym's petition was granted.

The other case concerned the claim of James J. Waring, who had accepted a pardon in November, 1865, that had been granted the previous July. Waring, however, had never taken the oath of allegiance. Consequently, his pardon had no vitality, since it was "to begin and take effect [only] from the day on which" he took the oath in Johnson's first proclamation. Thus, had it not been for the proclamation of December 25, 1868, the claimant's failure to renew his allegiance would have caused the court to deny his petition.[33] As it was, the universal, unconditional amnesty without oath obviated the condition specified in the special pardon; and consequently the court allowed Waring's claim of $2,629.95.

Evidently it was partly for the benefit of such persons as Waring that the Christmas amnesty had been proclaimed. In the opinion of the Court of Claims, Johnson surely supposed "that thousands of guilty persons to whom special pardons had been granted, or amnesty offered under previous proclamations, had not complied with the conditions of either, and were still exposed to all the penalties and disabilities due to their respective offences. In view of this class of persons, as well as to those to whom amnesty had never been offered, the proclamation of the 25th of December, 1868, was made

32. *Harry Haym* vs. *U. S.*, 7 Ct. of Cl. 443.
33. *James J. Waring* v. *U. S.*, 7 Ct. of Cl. 501.

Pardon and Amnesty in the Courts 409

universal and unconditional. . . . No conditions, not even an oath,"
the court continued, "were required in this proclamation. . . ."

The Christmas amnesty, however, did not benefit every petitioner
in the Court of Claims. This was evident in the case of *Ralph Meldrim et al* vs. *U. S.*[34] Meldrim and James Doyle of Savannah had
been joint owners of thirty-one bales of cotton, which the government had confiscated and sold after Sherman's conquests in Georgia.
Doyle had died in October, 1865, unpardoned and without having
taken the amnesty oath. In due time his wife and Meldrim brought
suit to recover the proceeds of the sale of the cotton. Meldrim
proved his loyalty and, since he and Doyle had not been strictly
partners in the ownership, received his part of the proceeds. Mrs.
Doyle, however, could not prove her husband's loyalty and consequently lost her claim, the court stating: ". . . We cannot by any
sort of legal imputation hold that the President's proclamation of
the 25th of December, 1868 . . . can in any way affect the legal
status of Doyle while he lived." To have held otherwise, the court
would have revived "the right to action" in Mrs. Doyle, a privilege
which she "lost by the default and neglect of her intestate [hus-
band]." Moreover, the court would have wholely disregarded "the
plain provisions of the third section of the *Act of March 12, 1863*,"
requiring proof of one's constant loyalty before allowing his suit
in the Court of Claims.

In December, 1871, the Court of Claims raised the question of
the effect of amnesty on an alien suing to recover the proceeds of
the sale of his property. The particular case that prompted the inquiry involved the claim of Mrs. Lucy Carroll, whose husband had
died in the autumn of 1863. Cotton belonging to the deceased alien
had been found by the Federals in the fortifications of Little Rock
and sold for $93,353 net. The widow and her husband were proven
loyal to the Union, so the effect of amnesty was not involved in
determining the rights of the claimant. The court, however, in
granting the petition, stated that it had not yet been "determined
whether the doctrine [benefit] of pardon and amnesty extends to
resident aliens, to foreigners, or to those persons who died after
the seizure of their property, but before they availed themselves of

34. 7 Ct. of Cl. 595 (December, 1871).

the proferred clemency and before the general [universal amnesty] proclamation of December 25, 1868."[35]

A year later the Supreme Court reviewed a case, on appeal, in which the appellants were aliens claiming benefit of presidential amnesty. The petitioners, Hugh Carlisle and his partner, were Britishers, who, early in the war, had manufactured saltpeter for the Confederates to use in making gunpowder. In May, 1863, the Englishmen sold their plant near Huntsville, Alabama, to the Confederacy for $34,600 and invested the money in cotton. Sometime in 1864 the Federals seized the cotton and sold it for $42,232 net.

Although Americans were allowed to prosecute claims in the British courts, the Court of Claims dismissed the case on the ground that there was no doubt of the guilt of the claimants, who had aided the Confederacy in making ammunition that was used in the rebellion.[36] The Supreme Court, however, while admitting "the aid and comfort thus given," recognized the right of the claimants to recover the proceeds of the sale of their cotton after the President's proclamation of December 25, 1868, "unless their character as aliens excludes them from the benefit of that proclamation. . . ." The higher court noted earlier decisions (Padelford's, Klein's, Mrs. Armstrong's, and Pargoud's) in which Johnson's last amnesty had benefited petitioners in similar cases, and then raised the question of whether the proclamation embraced aliens. The answer was in the affirmative. "The alien, while domiciled in this country," the decision ran, "owes a local and temporary allegiance, which continues during the period of his residence. This obligation . . . is everywhere recognized by publicists and statesmen. . . ." Such being the case, the claimants were declared amenable to the laws of the United States. They had cast their lot with the Confederates and like them were subject to punishment under the existing laws. And they were also, like the Confederates, benefited by the amnesty proclamation of December 25, 1868, which, the Court declared, "included them and all others in like situations."[37]

This decision of the Supreme Court was indeed timely. A Britisher named Charles Green, domiciled in Savannah, was at that time

35. *Lucy H. Carroll Admin.* vs. *U. S.*, 7 Ct. of Cl. 589 (1871).
36. 6 Ct. of Cl. 398 (December, 1870).
37. *Hugh Carlisle et al. Appel.* vs. *U. S.*, 8 Ct. of Cl. 153.

claiming benefit of the Christmas amnesty in a suit before the Court of Claims to recover the proceeds of the sale of his cotton, amounting to $155,554.89. The lower court, on receiving notice of the decision in the Carlisle case, perforce granted Green's claim. In doing so, it significantly noted that thereafter the opinion of the Supreme Court was "fortunately broad enough to cover" the case "of every domiciled alien likely to come before" the Court of Claims.[38]

THE PERSONAL ASPECT OF PARDON AND AMNESTY

In March, 1872, the Supreme Court declared that the amnesty of December 25, 1868, applied to persons and not to the obliteration of treasonable offenses. The decision was rendered in what is commonly called the "Gold Case." In March, 1864, the Federals seized five thousand dollars in gold on board a steamer in the harbor of New Orleans, on the ground that the money was being taken into enemy territory to buy cotton in violation of certain nonintercourse laws and of trade regulations of the Treasury Department.[39]

The libel suit was entered in the United States district court for Louisiana, which dismissed the action and ordered the money restored to its owner, Edward L. Gay. The Federal circuit court of that area reversed this decision and condemned the property. Thereupon the case was appealed to the Supreme Court, on the ground that the President's universal amnesty obliterated the alleged offense. That tribunal, however, denied the application of the proclamation to Gay, whom the Court regarded as a nonparticipant in the rebellion. Instead, the benefits of amnesty were declared to be "limited to persons who [had] participated in the . . . rebellion and to the offense of treason . . . during the late civil war." In other words, Johnson's last act of clemency in behalf of the Confederates did not restore to a person who had not actually "engaged in the insurrection [any] property forfeited under the non-intercourse laws. . . ." The gold, therefore, remained in the possession of the government.[40]

38. 8 Ct. of Cl. 412.
39. The nonintercourse laws were enacted on July 13, 1861, and May 20, 1862. *U. S. Stat. at Large*, XII, 255-58.
40. *Edward L. Gay et al. vs. U. S.*, 13 Wall. 358.

The following December the Court of Claims applied the Supreme Court's decision in the "Gold Case" in a suit to recover the proceeds of the sale of cotton which had belonged to Isaac Scott of Savannah. At the same time, the lower court cited its own opinion in denying Mrs. Doyle's claim referred to above. An interesting feature of the Scott case, however, was the tribunal's assertion that the proclamation of May 29, 1865, abrogated that of December 8, 1863. The following facts were involved.

Scott, a loyal citizen of Georgia, who came within the twenty-thousand-dollar exception of Johnson's first amnesty, accepted a special pardon in October, 1865. He failed, however, to take the oath required in that proclamation, although he had previously (June 7, 1865) taken the one prescribed in Lincoln's amnesty. The mistake appears to have been due to an error in the Attorney-General's office, from which he had received the blank required in the earlier proclamation instead of the form prescribed in the later measure. Scott died in December, 1867, and his executor brought suit to recover the proceeds of the sale of the cotton. The court admitted the slight "difference between the two oaths," but declared "it an inflexible rule that he who seeks to avail himself of a pardon, granted conditionally, must show a rigid compliance with the conditions which it implies." The operation of the special pardon, therefore, could hardly be allowed.

The court then "inquired whether the deceased claimant was absolved by any proclamation [of amnesty]." He had taken the oath required by the amnesty of December 8, 1863; but that did not gain him anything. On the contrary, the court declared this proclamation abrogated by that of May 29, 1865, "certainly so far as the excepted classes were concerned." Scott's condition, therefore, was not affected by Lincoln's amnesty. Moreover, the deceased could not receive any benefit from Johnson's proclamation of December 25, 1868, since his death had occurred previously. The Supreme Court had held in the "Gold Case" that the amnesty applied only to persons and not to the "general obliteration of treasonable offenses. . . ." This meant that amnesty affected living persons but not wrongful acts engaged in before death, and Scott had died unpardoned. Furthermore, the Court of Claims had held earlier in

Mrs. Doyle's case that the Christmas amnesty did not extend to anyone who had died before its announcement. Consequently, Scott's estate could receive no benefit from that measure.

Notwithstanding the above adverse rulings, the executor of the deceased claimant did win his suit. The judges finally asserted that Scott's acceptance of a pardon from the President did not preclude them "from passing upon the other evidence of his loyalty" in the case. Therefore, on finding that the deceased had not given "aid or comfort to the rebellion," the court ruled "that the claimant recover the proceeds in the Treasury of fifty-one and a half bales of cotton captured at Savannah" and sold for $9,029.49 net.[41] Nor was that all Scott's estate gained by this decision, for there were two other similar claims pending amounting to $80,476 from the sale of 459 bales of cotton belonging to the deceased.

FAILURES OF PARDON TO RESTORE PROPERTY

As time passed, claimants before the courts became fewer, and judgments, less favorable to their interests. It should be remembered that claimants for the recovery of abandoned or captured property, or the proceeds of the sale thereof, were required to file their petitions in the Court of Claims not later than two years after the close of the rebellion. When then did the war end? In December, 1869, the Supreme Court declared the close of the rebellion "as having taken place on the 20th of August, 1866, on which day the President by proclamation declared it suppressed in Texas. . . ."[42] The work of the Court of Claims, therefore, ended early in the 1870's, as far as cases involving the recovery of abandoned or captured property were concerned. There were, of course, many other claims filed before August 20, 1868, where pardon and amnesty did not enter into the litigation. Claims under the Confiscation Act involving pardon and amnesty, however, remained in other Federal courts for many years later, and are yet to be considered.

41. *Isaac Scott's Ex.* vs. *U. S.*, 8 Ct. of Cl. 457. Scott's cotton in this case was one-fourth of 296 bales jointly owned by him and others, one of whom was Edward Padelford, who appears in a case earlier in this chapter.

42. *U. S.* vs. *Anderson*, 9 Wall. 56. On April 2, 1866, the President had declared the "insurrection . . . at an end" in the other states of the Confederacy. Cf. Randall, *Constitutional Problems under Lincoln*, 48-50.

Mention was made above of Justice Miller's dissenting opinion in John A. Klein's case. In the light of decisions in cases that follow, this opinion might well be partially repeated. Miller asserted that "where the property had already been seized and sold, and the proceeds paid into the treasury . . . the pardon does not and cannot restore that which has already passed away." This was in December, 1871; but as early as May, 1868, the United States circuit court for Kansas had held in *Brown* vs. *United States* that a pardon restored to a recipient all rights to property lost by the offense, unless ownership had become vested in another person. In the case before the circuit court, the money from the sale was still in possession of the Federal district court from which the case had been appealed. The higher tribunal, therefore, ruled "that no vested right" to these proceeds had "accrued so as to prevent the pardon from restoring them to the petitioners."[43] Consequently, the lower court was instructed to allow the claim. The inference was, however, that there could have been no recovery if the money had been deposited in the Treasury.

In November, 1871, the Federal circuit court for Louisiana rendered an opinion that confirmed the inference above. The decision was given in refusing General Braxton Bragg's claim to the proceeds of the sale of his "Greenwood Plantation" in Parish Lafourche. The ex-Confederate had been pardoned by the general proclamation of July 4, 1868. His plantation, of course, had been condemned and sold much earlier, and the proceeds deposited in the Treasury. Bragg claimed the recovery on the strength of alleged faulty confiscation proceedings and on the ground that the proclamation of amnesty warranted the restoration. The court, however, denied the operation of such faults and declared the amnesty of no effect in his case. The title to the plantation had vested in the government by court decree "long before the date of the proclamation," which expressly excepted "from its effects any property of which any person may have been legally divested under the laws of the United States."[44] This ruling, therefore, was in keeping with the condition stipulated in the proclamation of amnesty. In fact, as early as December, 1867,

43. *Federal Cases*, IV, No. 2032.
44. *Ibid.*, No. 1800 (*Bragg* vs. *Lorio et al.*, 1871).

the Supreme Court had ruled, in the case of Armstrong's Foundry, that all conditions specified in a pardon must be complied with before its benefits would be allowed.[45]

Soon after the President's universal amnesty another distinguished Southerner, John Slidell, claimed the restoration of certain property in Louisiana that had been sold under the Confiscation Act. At first he appeared to be successful, for the circuit court in which he brought suit set aside the action of the district court in allowing the sale. The case then went to the Supreme Court for final adjudication. The counsel for Slidell insisted that the Christmas amnesty "amounted in effect to a repeal of the Confiscation Act" under which the property had been condemned and sold; but his contention was not admitted. Instead, the court asserted (October, 1873) that "no power was ever invested in the President to repeal an act of Congress. Moreover, the property condemned . . . became vested in the United States by the judgment of forfeiture, and the sale . . . merely converted into money that which was already the property of the Government. . . ."[46] Here again Justice Miller's opinion was confirmed, though not in a case coming from the Court of Claims.

In October, 1875, the Supreme Court rendered a similar decision, with an added important interpretation. The petitioner was Raphael Semmes, the commander of the famous cruiser "Alabama," who claimed the recovery of property condemned and sold through the operation of the general amnesty of July 4, 1868.[47] Such confiscation proceedings as had been instituted against Semmes's property were declared "justified as an exercise of belligerent rights against a public enemy," and were "not in their nature a punishment for treason. Consequently," the court ruled, "confiscation being a proceeding distinct from, and independent of, the treasonable guilt of the owner of the property confiscated, pardon for treason will not restore rights to property previously condemned and sold as the exercise of belligerent rights, as against a purchaser in good faith

45. 6 Wall. 766.
46. 20 Wall. 21. Slidell had been United States Senator and Confederate minister to France.
47. 91 U. S. 21 (*Semmes* vs. *U. S.*).

and for value."[48] Thus the potency of pardon and amnesty was interpreted as operating in releasing persons from the guilt of treason, and not as benefiting persons claiming the restoration of property confiscated as a belligerent right against an enemy.

It should be noted that when the proceeds from a sale remained in the custody of the court, a pardon allowed their restoration to the owner of the property sold. In *Brown* vs. *United States*, above, the Federal circuit court for Kansas rendered an opinion to that effect as early as May, 1868. Seven years later the Supreme Court confirmed this decision in the case of *Osborne* vs. *United States*.[49] The suit involved funds from the sale of real estate that had been mortgaged to secure certain bonds which had been forfeited to the government as belonging to persons supporting the rebellion. When some of the debtors on the bonds failed to pay the amounts due on them, the Federal district court of Kansas ordered the mortgaged lands sold to secure the bonds. The money thus received remained mixed indiscriminately with other funds in the custody of the court, whose officials used it as needs for funds arose. Actually, therefore, the money was not in the custody of the court as it should have been. Furthermore, the personnel of the tribunal had changed since the expenditures, and that condition complicated the case.

At any rate, in April, 1866, the claimant, Osborne, filed suit to gain the proceeds of the sale of his land. He offered proof of a pardon in supporting his claim, but the district court "held . . . that conditions attached to the pardon precluded the petitioner from seeking to obtain the proceeds" of the sale. The case then went to the circuit court of that region, which decided the question as it had in the similar case of *Brown* vs. *United States*, cited above. In due time, the petition was reviewed by the Supreme Court, which declared that, until the proceeds had been lawfully distributed or "actually paid into the hands of the party entitled as informer to receive them, or into the Treasury . . . they were within the con-

48. In *Miller* vs. *U. S.*, 11 Wall. 268, the Supreme Court declared in December, 1870, that the confiscation acts of 1861 and 1862 were "an exercise of the war powers of the government. . . ."
49. 91 U. S. 474 (1875).

trol of the court, and that no vested right to the proceeds had accrued so as to prevent the pardon from restoring them to the petitioner." Hence the money could be restored, but not the bonds or the land, since the title to both had become vested in a third person. Consequently, "Osborne could claim only the proceeds . . . collected by the government." The former judges of the district court, therefore, were informed that they must restore the money to the registry of the court, so that Osborne could be paid what was due him, even though they had "long since ceased to be" officials of the court.[50]

Two years later (1877) the opinion above was further greatly elaborated in the case of *Knote* vs. *United States*.[51] The facts of this interesting suit to recover the proceeds of property confiscated in West Virginia need not be given. It is sufficient to state that the tribunal declared again that neither pardon nor amnesty would permit a restoration if the proceeds had "been paid to a party to whom the law has assigned them," or if they had been deposited in the Treasury. The court also emphasized the fact that: "However large . . . may be the power of pardon possessed by the President, and however extended may be its application . . . it cannot touch moneys in the Treasury . . . except [when] authorized by act of Congress." This limitation, of course, applied to any claim granted against the United States. It should also be stated that the court asserted in this case that both Webster and Worcester defined the words pardon and amnesty as having the same meaning, thereby confirming an earlier opinion of Nevada's highest court.[52]

Perhaps the above denial of restoration where the moneys had "been paid to a party to whom the law has assigned them" needs some explanation. From the proceeds the costs of condemnation proceedings and sales were paid. Moreover, informers and other agents who had been instrumental in causing Federal officers to sequester the properties were paid for their services out of such funds. Especially was this true under the administration of the Captured Property Act, where cotton was the chief item obtained.

50. 91 U. S. 474 (1875).
51. 95 U. S. 149.
52. *Ibid.*; also *Davies* vs. *McKeeby*, 5 Nev. 369 (January, 1870).

Sometimes these agents were allowed to keep more than half of the proceeds of the sales.[53] Money paid out in this manner, therefore, was declared by the Supreme Court to be vested in a third person and consequently beyond restoration.

EFFECT OF PARDON ON CLAIMS TO REALTY

During the session in which the Semmes petition was denied (October, 1875), the Supreme Court rendered a decision in an unusual case where the benefit of amnesty was offered in support of argument to prevent the restoration of property. No proceeds of the sale were claimed; instead, the plaintiffs sought to recover the property itself. The following facts indicate the nature of the case. The children and heirs of Charles S. Wallach claimed real estate in Washington, D. C., that had belonged to their father, who had been a Confederate army officer. The realty had been bought at a confiscation sale in 1863 by one Van Riswick, who held a mortgage note on it for five thousand dollars, part of which had been paid. In February, 1866, Wallach and his wife signed a warranty deed conveying the property to Van Riswick, who now believed his title to be entirely secure.

Six years later Wallach died, and forthwith his children sued for the restoration, claiming the property on the ground that the joint resolution denying bill of attainder appended to the Confiscation Act of July 17, 1862, guaranteed their ownership after the father's death. Of course, they expected to pay the balance due on the note after recovering the property. Van Riswick, on the other hand, insisted that Wallach had a vested right in the real estate when he signed the warranty deed. This condition, he affirmed, existed because the joint resolution in question permitted the United States to hold only an estate in the property during Wallach's life. The title, or fee, therefore, remained vested where it was (in Wallach) before the confiscation and sale. Hence the transfer by the parents was valid. Moreover, Van Riswick claimed that the amnesty of December 25, 1868, restored Wallach's property as far as any interest which the government had in it was concerned, and that this

53. See Randall, "Captured and Abandoned Property during the Civil War," *American Historical Review*, XIX (October, 1913), 65-79.

condition further legalized the previous transfer to him by warranty.

The intricate details of the argument and the decision need not be given. In fact, the main question was not the application of amnesty, but "whether after an adjudicated forfeiture and sale of an enemy's land under the Confiscation Act . . . and the joint resolution of even date therewith," there was left in Wallach any interest which he might convey by deed. In the opinion of the Supreme Court, Congress intended that the condemnation and sale of the property should leave in the owner no interest whatever that he could transfer. Such reservation would have defeated the real purpose of the law; but the Confiscation Act was "not to be construed exclusively by itself." The joint resolution supplementary thereto was passed to comply with the section of the Constitution which provided that "no attainder of treason shall work corruption of blood or forfeiture except during the life of the person attainted."

The intent of the resolution, therefore, had to be respected. No doubt existed "that Congress might provide for foreitures effective during the life of an offender"; and it was to meet this doubt "that the resolution was adopted." Consequently, the Court ruled that to hold that Wallach retained any interest in the property after its confiscation and sale "would defeat the avowed purpose of the Confiscation Act; . . . and [that] to hold that the joint resolution was not intended for the benefit of his heirs exclusively, to enable them to take the inheritance after his death, would give preference to the guilty [father] over the innocent [children]." This, the court could not do. Furthermore, the tribunal declared that Van Riswick's contention that the amnesty restored to Wallach any title to the property was untenable, since at the time of the proclamation the United States had ceased to hold the property or any expectancy of interest in it.[54] Therefore, the decree of the Supreme Court of the District of Columbia which had denied the children's petition was reversed, and the restoration was allowed.

Fifteen years later (1890) the Supreme Court denied a claim similar to that of the Wallach heirs. In this case, however, the father received a special pardon before giving the purchaser of the confiscated property a deed thereto to insure his title against any

54. *Wallach et al.* vs. *Van Riswick*, 92 U. S. 202.

future eventuality. In fact, this transfer did not occur until September, 1871. The children, Charles H. and Mildred Bosworth, claimed the recovery on the ground that the joint resolution mentioned above insured their inheritance after their parent's death. The question before the court, therefore, was whether clemency restored to the father, A. H. Bosworth, the control and power of disposition over the title of his "property in reversion expectant." The judges stated that this question had "never been settled in this court." In arriving at an opinion, the tribunal asserted that, since the "property in question had never vested in any person" and since "nothing but the life interest had been forfeited," the father's "power to enjoy or dispose of it was simply suspended by his disability as an offender against the government. . . ." Consequently, pardon restored to Bosworth "the control of so much of his property . . . as had not become vested in the government or in any other person." His and his wife's transfer in 1871, therefore, was valid, and the children failed in their suit to obtain the realty after the father's death.[55]

The court's ruling in the Bosworth case was somewhat inconsistent with that in the Wallach case, and this inconsistency became still greater a year later (1891) in the case of *Jenkins* vs. *Collard*. In *Wallach* vs. *Van Riswick* the court had held that a fee could not remain in abeyance; that after the confiscation it had become vested in the United States, and, after the sale, in Van Riswick. Moreover, restoration was allowed on the strength of the joint resolution supplementing the Confiscation Act. In the Bosworth case the tribunal affirmed that "the property in question had never vested in any person," and that "nothing but the life interest had been forfeited." Pardon, therefore, allowed the original owner to transfer title, and the heirs could not recover. Now, in the Jenkins case, the court decreed that the warranty deed which the owner and his wife had given the purchaser "stopped him [Jenkins] and all persons claiming under him from asserting title to the premises," even though the deed had been executed before pardon was

55. *Ill. Cent. R. R. Co.* vs. *Bosworth*, 133 U. S. 92. The property involved was in New Orleans and had passed through several purchasers after its confiscation and sale in May, 1865. The father's death was in 1885. Evidently the real estate was worth a considerable amount at the time (1890) of the court's decision, for Bosworth and his wife received nearly twelve thousand dollars for their interest in it in 1871.

granted. Consequently, the original owner might transfer his vested interest in property that the purchaser held only during the life of the confiscatee by guaranteeing the title, and such guarantee might be made before receiving a pardon. Jenkins's heirs, therefore, were denied any interest in the property after their father's death, since the warranty deed precluded any claim which the subsequent amnesty might otherwise have given them.[56]

CONCLUSION

The foregoing covers practically every phase of litigation involving the operation of pardon and amnesty during the Civil War and the years following. On the whole, the courts were very liberal in their interpretations. Acts of presidential clemency were given "the force of public law," as though they had been sanctioned by Congress; and legislation, both state and national, affecting clemency was interpreted in the spirit of leniency toward offenders. Efforts of Congress to limit the benefits of pardon and amnesty were set aside, the disabilities imposed in the reconstruction acts and the Fourteenth Amendment being exceptions. In fact, no cases involving such disabilities ever came before the courts for adjudication. Even claimants under the Captured Property Act were given until August 20, 1868, to file their claims, surely time enough for the most tardy. Moreover, a person's guilt and the infliction of "forfeiture as a penalty" therefor were determined by whether or not he had consented to the use of his property in supporting the rebellion.[57] Aliens were accorded the benefits of amnesty, and women were allowed every advantage given men where clemency affected the restoration of property. Yet the courts respected the laws, and, where the title had become vested in a third person or the money had been deposited in the Treasury, the claimant had difficulty in winning his suit. Even when a claimant won, Congress had to appropriate money to pay the judgment if the proceeds of the sale had been deposited in the Treasury.

Nevertheless, the entire value of the property recovered—money

56. *Jenkins* vs. *Collard*, 145 U. S. 546. Jenkins and his wife had executed the warranty deed in August, 1865, and claimed benefit of the amnesty of December, 1868.

57. *Armstrong's Foundry*, 6 Wall. 769 (December, 1867).

and real estate—was not very great. The larger return consisted of money from the proceeds of cotton sales. Dr. Randall gives $9,-864,300 as having been paid through judgments allowed by the Court of Claims; but pardon and amnesty were not involved in many suits for the recovery of property before that court. Moreover, restorations of land were sometimes made to recipients of pardon without recourse to litigation. Unfortunately, the Supreme Court's decision in Klein's case came (1871) after the time limit set for filing petitions under the Captured Property Act. Had it come three and a half years earlier, other claims would doubtless have been filed. Serious efforts have been made to revive the right to sue for recoveries under that law, but apparently Congress has been unwilling to enact the necessary legislation.[58] It is not likely, therefore, that benefits of pardon and amnesty will ever be offered again before any court in support of any claim growing out of the Civil War.

58. Randall, *Constitutional Problems under Lincoln,* 338-40.

BIBLIOGRAPHY

BIBLIOGRAPHY

ONLY those sources used in preparing the volume are intended to be found in the bibliography. There may be some omissions, however, and some inclusions that should not have been made. The many revisions and deletions necessary in order to shorten the study to publishable length make this likely, and brevity has been advised in preparing the bibliography.

Apparently the Amnesty Papers and some other related material have never been used before except in articles by the author, who began the study of the subject in 1925 on the suggestion of the late Dr. James G. Randall. At that time and for some years later the most important manuscripts bearing on pardon and amnesty under Lincoln and Johnson were in the custody of the Departments of State, War, and Justice. This material has since been placed in the National Archives. Other closely related sources have remained in the Library of Congress. Fortunately the Department of Archives and History of North Carolina obtained photocopies of that state's Amnesty Papers in 1929, and these photostats, which may now be found in Raleigh, reveal the qualities of all the papers in Washington.

I

UNPUBLISHED MATERIAL

In the National Archives: "Acceptance of Pardons, Amnesty, Department of Justice" under President Johnson; Amnesty Oaths under President Johnson's Proclamation of Amnesty of May 29, 1865 (12 vols., Vol. 8 missing); Amnesty Papers, being applications to President Johnson for special pardon with oaths of allegiance and recommendations for pardon (see the first two paragraphs of Chapter VIII for a description); Amnesty Papers for Jefferson Davis (classified separately); Attorneys-General's Office, Letter Books C, E, and F (Department of Justice); "Deserters Who Have Taken the Oath of Allegiance at Little Rock, Arkansas," 1864 (3 vols.,); Index to volumes of Pardon Records; "Amnesty Oaths under Proclamation, Dec. 8, 1863" (4 vols. of names of persons); Pardon Duplicates, 25 vols., duplicates of some 13,500 special pardons granted by President Johnson; Pardon Record Books A, B, daily pardons to persons in various states, 1865-67 (Department of Justice); Pardon Records of Lincoln's Administration, Vol. VII; Requisitions for Pardons, Books A, B, 1865-66 (Department of Justice); Miscellaneous Letters (State Department).

In the Division of Manuscripts of the Library of Congress: Attorneys-General's Papers, 1866; Lincoln Papers (sundry manuscripts, not Robert Todd Lincoln Collection); Papers of John Cabell Breckin ridge (Vol. 263); Papers of Benjamin F. Butler; Papers of William Pitt Fessenden; Papers of Joseph Holt; Papers of Andrew Johnson (171 vols.); Papers of Reverdy Johnson; Papers of John Sherman (Vols. CXVIII, CXXI); Papers of Edwin M. Stanton; Papers of Gideon Welles; Pardon Records: "Endorsements and Memoranda," 1865-66 (2 vols.); General Pardon Records of Johnson Administration, 1865-67 (3 vols., A, B, C); Photostats of some Lincoln Papers (Brown University Collection); MSS Bureau of Refugees, Freedmen, Special Orders, No. 4, Commissioner's Office, Sept. 8, 1865, Gen. Howard's Order, Sept. 14, 1865.

North Carolina Manuscripts: The Amnesty Papers for North Carolina (photocopies of the original in the National Archives), the Governor's Papers for 1865-66, some papers of W. W. Holden (1865), the Zebulon B. Vance Papers, and the Executive Papers of Jonathan Worth, in the Department of Archives and History, Raleigh; papers of Richard S. Ewell and E. Kirby Smith, in the Library of the University of North Carolina; Ruth Anna Ketring, "The Clays of Alabama: Two Generations in Politics," doctoral dissertation, Duke University (1934); in the Library of Duke University, MS Duke University, Wheeler to Halleck, May 20, 1865.

Miscellaneous: "Bonds and Custody for Good Behavior," United States Circuit Court, 1862-65 (5 vols.), Federal Building, Louisville, Ky.; Pres. David G. Burnett to Capt. W. H. Patton (letter concerning the treatment of Gen. Santa Anna, Oct. 8, 1836), Museum of San Jacinto Battlefield; William A. Russ, Jr., "Congressional Disfranchisement, 1866-1898," doctoral dissertation, University of Chicago (1936); Executive Letter Book, 1866-67, Archives, Atlanta, Ga.; Fee Book, Law Firm of Curtis F. Burnam and James W. Caperton, 1863-1869, in possession of Mrs. Paul Burnam, Richmond, Ky.; Edgar E. Folk, "W. W. Holden, Political Journalist," doctoral dissertation, George Peabody College (1934); Lincoln Papers, Robert Todd Lincoln Collection (original in the Library of Congress), microfilm, reels 70-71, nos. 31645-9, Library, University of Illinois; Robert E. Lee's Oath on becoming President of Washington College, Archives of Washington and Lee University, Lexington, Va.; Order Books A, B, Disposition of Cases, 1862-64, United States Circuit Court, Federal Building, Louisville, Ky.; Order Book B, United States Circuit Court Records, 1862-64, Frankfort, Ky.;

Charles Sumner's Papers, Vols. LXXXII, CLIV, CLV, CLVI, Widener Library, Harvard University.

II

GOVERNMENT PUBLICATIONS AND RELATED MATERIAL

American Law Register. Vols. VI, VIII (new series, 1869).
Appendix to the Cong. Globe, 30 Cong., 1 sess.
Congressional Globe, 37-42 Cong. (1861-73).
Congressional Record, 43-55 Cong. (1873-98).
Executive Document, 39 Cong. 1 sess. (1865).
Federal Cases (U. S. Federal Courts). Vols. IV, XXVI.
Messages and Papers of the Presidents, 1789-1897, ed. J. D. Richardson. 10 vols. Washington, D. C., 1896-99.
Messages and Papers of the Presidents, 1789-1913, ed. J. D. Richardson. 11 vols. Washington, D. C., 1913.
Opinions of the Attorneys-General, X, XI, XII, and *House Exec. Doc.*, No. 99, 39 Cong., 1 sess. (1865).
The Political History of the United States of America during the Great Rebellion . . . , ed. Edward McPherson. Washington, D. C., 1865.
The Political History of the United States of America during the Period of Reconstruction . . . , ed. Edward McPherson. Washington, D. C., 1875.
Mississippi Reports. Vol. 5, *Jefferson Davis* vs. *J. H. D. Bowmar, Executor et al.*, Department of Archives and History, Jackson, Miss.
Report of the Joint Committee on Reconstruction, 39 Cong., 1 sess. (a separate volume).
Report of the Select Committee on the New Orleans Riots (1867).
Revised Regulations for the Army of the United States (1861).
House Exec. Reports, 39-55 Cong.
Senate Exec. Reports, 39-55 Cong.
Trial of John Y. Beall as a Spy and Guerilla by Military Commission. New York, 1865.
U. S. Court of Claims Reports. Vols. 4, 6, 7, 8 (1868-71).
U. S. Supreme Court Reports, through reports by Black, Wallace, *et al.*
United States Statutes at Large. Vols. XI-XVIII, XXI, XXIII, XXX.
War of the Rebellion: . . . *Official Records of the Union and Confederate Armies.* 128 vols.; 1880-1901.

III

BIOGRAPHIES AND AUTOBIOGRAPHIES: DIARIES, LETTERS, REMINISCENCES, ETC.

American Historical Association. *Annual Reports.* Vol. II. Washington, D. C., 1911.

Appleton's Cyclopaedia of American Biography, ed. James Grant Wilson and John Fiske. 6 vols. New York, 1894-1900.

Badeau, Adam. *Military History of Ulysses S. Grant from April, 1861, to April, 1865*. 3 vols. New York, 1868-81.

Baker, George E., ed. *The Works of William H. Seward*. New York, 1853-84.

Bancroft, Frederic. *The Life of William H. Seward*. 2 vols. New York, 1900.

———, ed. *Speeches, Correspondence and Political Papers of Carl Schurz*. 6 vols. New York, 1913.

Barton, William E., *The Life of Abraham Lincoln*. 2 vols. Indianapolis, 1925.

Blaine, James G. *Twenty Years of Congress: From Lincoln to Garfield*. 2 vols. Norwich, Conn., 1884-86.

Bradford, Gamaliel. *Confederate Portraits*. Boston and New York, 1923.

Brooks, Noah. *Abraham Lincoln, a Biography for Young People*. New York, 1888.

Butler, Benjamin F. *Private and Official Correspondence of Gen. Benjamin F. Butler, during the Period of the Civil War*, ed. Jessie Ames Marshall. 5 vols. Norwood, Mass., 1917.

Capers, Henry D. *The Life and Times of C. G. Memminger*. Richmond, Va., 1893.

Castleman, John B. *Active Service*. Louisville, Ky., 1917.

Chittenden, L. E. *Recollections of President Lincoln and His Administration*. New York, 1896.

Clay, Cassius M. *The Life of Cassius Marcellus Clay, Memoirs, Writings, and Speeches*. Cincinnati, Philadelphia, Chicago, 1886.

Cleveland, Henry. *Alexander H. Stephens, in Public and Private*. Philadelphia, Chicago, 1866.

Connor, Henry G. *John Archibald Campbell, Associate Justice of the United States Supreme Court, 1853-1861*. Boston and New York, 1920.

Coulter, E. Merton. *William G. Brownlow, Fighting Parson of the Southern Highlands*. Chapel Hill, N. C., 1937.

Craig, Hugh. *The Biography and Public Services of Hon. James G. Blaine*. New York and Chicago, 1884.

Craven, John J. *Prison Life of Jefferson Davis*, New York, 1866.

Davis, Varina Howell. *Jefferson Davis, Ex-President of the Confederate States of America; A Memoir by His Wife*. 2 vols. New York, 1890.

Dennett, Tyler, ed. *Lincoln and the Civil War in the Diaries and Letters of John Hay*. New York, 1939.

Dictionary of American Biography, ed. Allen Johnson. 20 vols. New York, 1928.

Dowd, Clement. *Life of Zebulon B. Vance.* Charlotte, N. C., 1897.

Dowdey, Clifford. *Experiment in Rebellion.* Garden City, N. Y., 1946.

DuBose, John W. *The Life and Times of William Lowndes Yancy.* Birmingham, Ala., 1892.

Dyer, John P. *"Fightin' Joe" Wheeler.* University, La., 1941.

Fairman, Charles. *Mr. Justice Miller and the Supreme Court, 1862-1890.* Cambridge, Mass., 1939.

Foulke, William D. *Life of Oliver P. Morton, Including His Important Speeches.* 2 vols. Indianapolis-Kansas City, 1899.

Freeman, Douglas Southall. *R. E. Lee: A Biography.* 4 vols. New York, 1934-35.

Gordon, John B. *Reminiscences of the Civil War.* New York, 1903.

Grant, Ulysses S. *Personal Memoirs of U. S. Grant.* 2 vols. New York, 1885-86.

Hall, Clifton R. *Andrew Johnson, Military Governor of Tennessee.* Princeton, N. J., 1916.

Hamilton, J. G. de Roulhac, ed. *The Correspondence of Jonathan Worth.* 2 vols. Raleigh, N. C., 1909.

———, ed. *The Papers of Thomas Ruffin.* 4 vols. Raleigh, N. C., 1918-20.

Hapgood, Norman. *Abraham Lincoln, the Man of the People.* New York, 1899.

Harrison, Fairfax, ed. *The Harrisons of Skimino; a Memoir of an American Family. . . .* 1910.

Hill, Louise Biles. *Joseph E. Brown and the Confederacy.* Chapel Hill, N. C., 1939.

Holden, W. W. *Memoirs of W. W. Holden.* (The John Lawson Monographs of the Trinity College Society, Vol. II.) Durham, N. C., 1911.

Howard, Oliver Otis. *Autobiography of Oliver Otis Howard, Major General, United States Army.* 2 vols. New York, 1907.

Jones, James S. *Life of Andrew Johnson.* Greenville, Tenn., 1901.

Jones, John B. *A Rebel War Clerk's Diary at the Confederate States Capital.* 2 vols. Philadelphia, 1866.

Lee, Robert E. *Recollections and Letters of General Robert E. Lee, by his son Captain Robert E. Lee.* Garden City, N. Y., 1924.

Lewis, Lloyd. *Sherman, Fighting Prophet.* New York, 1932.

Long, A. L. *Memoirs of Robert E. Lee; His Military and Personal History.* New York, Philadelphia, 1887.

Longstreet, James. *From Manassas to Appomattox: Memoirs of the Civil War in America.* Philadelphia, 1896; rev. ed., 1903.

McCall, Samuel W. *Thaddeus Stevens.* Boston and New York, 1909.

McClure, A. K. *Abraham Lincoln and Men of War-Times.* Philadelphia, 1892.

McElroy, Robert M. *Jefferson Davis; the Unreal and the Real.* New York, 1937.

Meade, George. *The Life and Letters of George Gordon Meade, Major-General United States Army.* 2 vols. New York, 1913.

Merriam, George S. *The Life and Times of Samuel Bowles.* 2 vols. New York, 1885.

Moore, Frank, ed. *The Rebellion Record: A Diary of American Events, with Documents, Narratives, Illustrative Incidents, Poetry, etc.* . . . 12 vols. New York, 1861-68.

Morse, John T., Jr. *Abraham Lincoln.* Boston and New York, 1893.

Muzzey, David S. *James G. Blaine, a Political Idol of Other Days.* New York, 1934.

Nicolay, John G. *A Short Life of Abraham Lincoln.* New York, 1921.

——, and Hay, John. *Abraham Lincoln; a History.* 10 vols. New York, 1890.

——, eds. *Abraham Lincoln; Complete Works, Comprising His Speeches, Letters, State Papers, and Miscellaneous Writings.* 2 vols. New York, 1920.

Pease, T. C., and Randall, J. G., eds. *The Diary of Orville Hickman Browning.* (Collections of the Illinois State Historical Library, Vols. XX, XXII. Lincoln Series, Vols. II-III.) Springfield, Ill., 1925-33.

Perry, Benjamin Franklin. *Reminiscences of Public Men.* Philadelphia, 1883.

Phillips, Ulrich B. *The Life of Robert Toombs.* New York, 1913.

Pierce, Edward L. *Memoir and Letters of Charles Sumner.* 4 vols. Boston, 1877-93.

Pollard, Edward A. *Life of Jefferson Davis, with a Secret History of the Southern Confederacy, Gathered "Behind the Scenes in Richmond."* Philadelphia, Chicago, etc., 1869.

Reagan, John H. *Memoirs of John H. Reagan with Special Reference to Secession and the Civil War.* New York and Washington, D. C., 1906.

Rowland, Dunbar, ed. *Jefferson Davis, Constitutionalist, His Letters, Papers and Speeches.* 10 vols. Jackson, Miss., 1923.

Rowland, Eron. *Varina Howell, Wife of Jefferson Davis.* 2 vols. New York, 1927-31.

Russell, Charles E. *Blaine of Maine; His Life and Times.* New York, 1931.

Sandburg, Carl. *Abraham Lincoln; the War Years.* 4 vols. New York, 1939.

Savage, John. *The Life and Public Services of Andrew Johnson.* New York, 1866.

Schurz, Carl. *The Reminiscences of Carl Schurz.* 3 vols. New York, 1907-8.
Semmes, Raphael. *Memoirs of Service Afloat, during the War between the States.* Baltimore, 1869.
Sherman, William T. *Memoirs of General William T. Sherman.* 2 vols. 2nd ed. rev. and cor.; New York, 1886.
Stephens, Alexander H. *The Recollections of Alexander H. Stephens; His Diary, Kept When a Prisoner at Fort Warren, Boston Harbour, 1865.* New York, 1910.
Sterling, Ada, ed. *A Belle of the Fifties; Memoirs of Mrs. Clay, of Alabama, Covering Social and Political Life in Washington and the South, 1853-66.* New York, 1905.
Stillwell, Lucille. *John Cabell Breckinridge.* Caldwell, Idaho, 1936.
Tarbell, Ida M. *The Life of Abraham Lincoln.* New York, 1909.
Thayer, William R. *The Life and Letters of John Hay.* Boston and New York, 1929.
Townsend, William H. *Lincoln and His Wife's Home Town.* Indianapolis, Ind., 1929.
Warden, Robert B. *Account of the Private Life and Public Services of Salmon Portland Chase.* Cincinnati, Ohio, 1874.
Welles, Gideon. *Diary of Gideon Welles,* ed. John T. Morse, Jr. 3 vols. Boston and New York, 1911.
Woodburn, James Albert. *The Life of Thaddeus Stevens; a Study in American Political History.* Indianapolis, Ind., 1913.
Young, James C. *Marse Robert, Knight of the Confederacy.* New York, 1929.
Young, John R. *Around the World with General Grant.* 2 vols. New York, 1879.

IV

Newspapers

Atlanta *Daily Intelligencer* (April 15, 1865; April 10, July 3, 6, September 18, 26, 1867).
Augusta *Constitutionalist* (September 26, 1867).
Boston *Christian Science Monitor* (February 16, 1935; February 12, 1937).
Central Christian Advocate (May 3, 10, 17, June 21, November 24, 1865).
Charleston *Courier* (July 3, 8, September 10, 11, 1867).
Charleston *Mercury* (March 23, May 31, 1867).
Chicago *Journal* (September 9, 1867).

Chicago *Times* (January 5, 1864; August 30, September 5, 11, October 20, 1867).
Chicago *Tribune* (September 13, 27, 1867).
Cincinnati *Daily Commercial* (December 10, 11, 21, 1863; November 9, 1865; September 21, 1867).
Cincinnati *Enquirer* (September 10, 1867).
Columbia, S. C., *Daily Phoenix* (July 3, 1865).
Columbus, Ga., *Enquirer* (September 12, 1867).
Fredericksburg, Va., *News* (July 2, 1867).
Huntsville, Ala., *Advocate* (July 19, November 30, December 14, 1865).
Louisville *Courier-Journal* (October 3, 1867; February 14, 1937).
Milledgeville, Ga., *Southern Recorder* (July 25, 1865; September 11, 1867).
Nashville *Daily Press* (December 24, 25, 1863; January 9, 1864).
Nashville *Dispatch* (January 8, February 5, 23, March 2, 1864; June 7, 20, 1865).
Nashville *Press and Times* (September 10, October 3, 5, 1867).
Nashville *Union* (January 2, 31, July 10, 12, 1864; March 1, April 3, 1865).
New Orleans *Republican* (September 10, 11, 21, 22, 1867).
New Orleans *Times* (September 10, 1867).
New York *Herald* (April, 1865, through March, 1868).
New York *Observer* (June 1, 1865).
New York *Times* (April 10, 1866; June 29, September 9, 13, 27, 30, 1867).
New York *Tribune* (December, 1863, through November, 1866).
Philadelphia *Enquirer* (December 10, 1863).
Philadelphia *Press* (September 7, 1867).
Raleigh, N. C., *Daily Sentinel* (December 14, 1864; September 1, 1865).
Raleigh *Daily Standard* (December, 1863, through November, 1865).
Richmond, Ky., *Daily Register* (March issues, 1938).
Richmond, Va., *Dispatch* (March 19, 1864).
Richmond, Va., *Enquirer* (January 25, March 23, 1867).
Savannah *Republican* (December 16, 29, 1863; January 19, 1864; August 31, September 1, 15, 19, 21, 30, 1865; July 15, 1867).
Southern Historical Society Papers, Vols. 24, 37.
Springfield, Illinois, *State Journal* (December 11, 1863; February 10, 1864; July 5, 12, 1865).
Vicksburg, Miss., *Herald* (September 11, 22, 29, 1867).
Washington *Evening Star* (July 10, 1865).
Washington *National Intelligencer* (July 14, August 5, December 10, 31, 1863; January 4, 1864; September 11, 12, 1867).
Western Christian Advocate (July 19, 1865).

V

ARTICLES IN PERIODICALS

Bolles, John A. "Why Semmes of the Alabama Was Never Tried," *Atlantic Monthly*, XXX (July, August, 1872), 88-97, 148-56.

The Century Magazine, XXXVIII (1899) and LXXXV (1913).

Deatherage, Nathan B. Quoted in "Comrades of War Days," *Confederate Veteran*, XXXVI (August, 1928), 305.

Dorris, J. T. "Pardon Seekers and Brokers: A Sequel of Appomattox," *Journal of Southern History*, I (August, 1935), 276-92.

———. "Pardoning the Leaders of the Confederacy," *Mississippi Valley Historical Review*, XV (June, 1928), 3-21.

———. "Pardoning North Carolinians," *North Carolina Historical Review*, XXIII (July, 1946), 360-401.

———. "President Lincoln's Clemency," *Journal of the Illinois State Historical Society*, XX (January, 1928), 547-68.

Ebell, Adrian J. "The Indian Massacres and the War of 1862," *Harper's New Monthly Magazine*, XXVII (June, 1863), 1-24.

Folk, Edgar E. "W. W. Holden and the Election of 1858," *North Carolina Historical Review*, XXI (October, 1944), 294-318.

———. "W. W. Holden and the North Carolina Standard, 1843-1848: A Study in Political Journalism," *North Carolina Historical Review*, XIX (January, 1942), 22-47.

Harper's Weekly, VIII (May 13, 1864), IX (April 8, May 6, June 24, 30, 1865), X (April 21, June 30, July 7, October 27, 1866), XVI (January 20, 1872).

Hill, Lawrence F. "Confederate Exiles to Brazil," *Hispanic American Historic Review*, VII (May, 1927), 192-210.

L. C. K. "The Power of the President to Grant General Pardon or Amnesty for Offences against the United States," *American Law Register*, VIII (September and October, 1869), 513-32, 577-89.

McClelland, Stewart W. "Two Whigs and the Whirligig," *Exchangite* (National Exchange Club), XXIV (February, 1945).

The Nation, I (1865), II (May 17, 1866), III (May 16, 1867).

The New Englander, XXIV (1865).

Nichols, Roy F. "1461-1861: The American Civil War in Its True Perspective," *Journal of Southern History*, XVI (May, 1950), 143-60.

———. "United States *vs* Jefferson Davis, 1865-1869," *American Historical Review*, XXXI (January, 1926), 266-84.

Randall, James G. "Captured and Abandoned Property during the Civil War," *American Historical Review*, XIX (October, 1913), 65-79.

Russ, William A., Jr. "Disfranchisement in Louisiana, 1862-1870," *Louisiana Historical Quarterly*, XVIII, No. 3 (July, 1935), 557-80.

———. "Radical Disfranchisement in Georgia, 1867-1871," *Georgia Historical Quarterly*, XIX (September, 1935), 176-209.

———. "Radical Disfranchisement in North Carolina, 1867-1868," *North Carolina Historical Review*, XI (October, 1934), 271-83.

———. "Radical Disfranchisement in South Carolina (1867-1868)," *Susquehanna University Studies*, I (January, 1939), 148-60.

———. "Was There Danger of a Second Civil War during Reconstruction?" *Mississippi Valley Historical Review*, XXV (June 1938), 39-58.

Sellers, James L. "The Economic Incidence of the Civil War in the South," *Mississippi Valley Historical Review*, XIV (September, 1927), 179-91.

Stampp, Kenneth M. "The Milligan Case and the Election of 1864 in Indiana," *Mississippi Valley Historical Review*, XXXI (June, 1944), 41-58.

Stephens, Robert. "An Incident of Friendship," *Lincoln Herald*, XLV (June, 1943).

Weaver, Blanche Henry Clark. "Confederate Immigrants and Evangelical Churches in Brazil," *Journal of Southern History*, XVIII, No. 4 (November, 1952), 446-68.

Yates, Richard E. "Governor Vance and the Peace Movement," *North Carolina Historical Review*, XVII (January, April, 1940), 1-25, 89-113.

VI

GENERAL WORKS

Abel, Annie Heloise. *The American Indian as Slaveholder and Secessionist*. Cleveland, 1915.

Andrews, Sidney. *The South since the War; as Shown by Fourteen Weeks of Travel and Observation in Georgia and the Carolinas*. Boston, 1866.

Annual Cyclopedia, 1864, 1865, 1869.

Annual Register, 1902.

Arnold, Isaac N. *The History of Abraham Lincoln, and the Overthrow of Slavery*. Chicago, 1866.

Avary, Myrta Lockett. *Dixie after the War; an Exposition of Social Conditions Existing in the South, during the Twelve Years Succeeding the Fall of Richmond*. New York, 1906.

Avery, I. W. *The History of the State of Georgia from 1850 to 1881*. New York, 1881.

Baker, L. C. *History of the United States Secret Service*. Philadelphia, 1867.

Battle, Kemp P. *History of the University of North Carolina*. 2 vols. Raleigh, N. C., 1907-12.

Beale, Howard K. *The Critical Year; a Study of Andrew Johnson and Reconstruction*. New York, 1930.

Bettersworth, John K. *Confederate Mississippi, the People and Policies of a Cotton State in Wartime*. University Station, Baton Rouge, La., 1943.

Blackford, Charles M. *The Trials and Trial of Jefferson Davis*. Lynchburg, Va., 1901.

Bledsoe, Albert Taylor. *Is Davis a Traitor; or, Was Secession a Constitutional Right Previous to the War of 1861?* 2nd ed.; Baltimore, Md., 1879.

Burgess, John W. *Reconstruction and the Constitution, 1866-1876*. New York, 1902.

Coulter, E. Merton. *The Civil War and Readjustment in Kentucky*. Chapel Hill, N. C., 1926.

Cox, Samuel S. *Three Decades of Federal Legislation, 1855 to 1885*. Providence, R. I., 1885.

Davis, Jefferson. *The Rise and Fall of the Confederate Government*. 2 vols. New York, 1881.

Davis, William Watson. *The Civil War and Reconstruction in Florida*. (Columbia University Studies in History, Economics, and Public Law, Vol. LIII, no. 131.) New York, 1913.

Dawson, Henry B., ed. *The Federalist*. New York, 1865.

DeWitt, David Miller. *The Impeachment and Trial of Andrew Johnson, Seventeenth President of the United States*. New York, 1903.

Dorris, Jonathan Truman. *Old Cane Springs; a Story of the War between the States in Madison County, Kentucky*. Rev. and suppl., from the original by John Cabell Chenault; Louisville, Ky., 1936.

Dunn, Ballard S. *Brazil, the Home for Southerners*. New York, 1866.

Dunning, William A. *Reconstruction, Political and Economic, 1865-1877*. (American Nation Series, XXII.) New York, 1907.

Eckenrode, Hamilton J. *The Political History of Virginia during the Reconstruction*. (Johns Hopkins University Studies in Historical and Political Science, Series XXII, nos. 6, 7, 8.) Baltimore, Md., 1904.

Evans, Clement A., ed. *Confederate Military History; a Library of Confederate States History.* . . . 12 vols. Vol. X, *Arkansas*, by J. M. Harrell. Atlanta, Ga., 1899.

Fertig, James W. *The Secession and Reconstruction of Tennessee*. Chicago, 1898.

Fleming, Walter L. *Civil War and Reconstruction in Alabama.* New York, 1911.

———, ed. *Documentary History of Reconstruction, Political, Military, Social, Religious, Educational and Industrial, 1865 to the Present Time.* 2 vols. Cleveland, Ohio, 1906-7.

Garner, James W. *Reconstruction in Mississippi.* New York, 1901.

Greeley, Horace. *The American Conflict: A History of the Great Rebellion in the United States of America, 1860-'65.* 2 vols. Hartford, Conn., and Chicago, 1864-66.

Hafen, LeRoy R., and Rister, Carl Coke. *Western America; the Exploration, Settlement, and Development of the Region beyond the Mississippi.* New York, 1941.

Hamilton, J. G. de Roulhac. *Reconstruction in North Carolina.* Raleigh, N. C., 1906.

Hanna, A. J. *Flight into Oblivion.* Richmond, Va., 1938.

Hendrick, Burton J. *Statesmen of the Lost Cause; Jefferson Davis and His Cabinet.* Boston, 1939.

Henry, Robert Selph. *The Story of Reconstruction.* New York, 1938.

Herbert, Hilary A., *et al. Why the Solid South? or, Reconstruction and Its Results.* Baltimore, Md., 1890.

Hesseltine, William B. *Civil War Prisons; a Study in War Psychology.* Columbus, Ohio, 1930.

Hill, Lawrence F. *The Confederate Exodus to Latin America.* Austin, Tex., 1936.

Hollis, John P. *The Early Period of Reconstruction in South Carolina.* (Johns Hopkins University Studies, Series XXIII, nos. 1-2.) Baltimore, Md., 1905.

Jefferson, Thomas. *Notes on the State of Virginia.* Baltimore, Md., 1801.

Kettell, Thomas P. *History of the Great Rebellion, from Its Commencement to Its Close. . . .* Hartford, Conn., and Cincinnati, Ohio, 1865.

Lonn, Ella. *Desertion during the Civil War.* New York, 1928.

Markens, Isaac. *President Lincoln and the Case of John Y. Beall.* Privately printed; New York, 1911.

Marshall, John A. *American Bastile: A History of the Illegal Arrests and Imprisonment of American Citizens during the Late Civil War.* Philadelphia, 1869.

McCarthy, Charles H. *Lincoln's Plan of Reconstruction.* New York, 1901.

McCulloch, Hugh. *Men and Measures of Half a Century; Sketches and Comments.* New York, 1888.

McKee, Thomas H. *The National Conventions and Platforms of All Political Parties, 1789-1900.* 3rd ed.; Baltimore, Md., 1900.

Bibliography 437

Milton, George F. *The Age of Hate: Andrew Johnson and the Radicals.* New York, 1930.

New Learned History for Ready Reference. Vol. X, 1924.

Oberholtzer, E. Paxson. *A History of the United States since the Civil War.* Vols. I-III. New York, 1926.

Oppenheim, Lassa F. L. *International Law, a Treatise.* 2 vols. 3rd ed.; New York, 1920-21.

Pollard, Edward A. *The Lost Cause; a New Southern History of the War of the Confederates.* . . . New York and Baltimore, Md., 1866.

Ramsdell, Charles W. *Reconstruction in Texas.* (Columbia University Studies in History, Economics and Public Law, Vol. XXXVI, no. 1; whole no. 95.) New York, 1910.

Randall, James G. *The Civil War and Reconstruction.* Boston and New York, 1937.

———. *Constitutional Problems under Lincoln.* New York, 1926.

———. *Lincoln and the South.* Baton Rouge, La., 1946.

Rhodes, James F. *History of the United States from the Compromise of 1850.* 7 vols. New York, 1904.

Robinson, William M., Jr. *The Confederate Privateers.* New Haven, Conn., 1928.

Simkins, F. B., and Woody, R. H. *South Carolina during Reconstruction.* Chapel Hill, N. C., 1932.

Stanwood, Edward. *A History of the Presidency from 1788 to 1916.* 2 vols. Boston and New York, 1916.

Staples, Thomas S. *Reconstruction in Arkansas, 1862-1874.* (Columbia University Studies in History, Economics and Public Law, Vol. CIX, whole no. 245.) New York, 1923.

Stephens, Alexander H. *A Constitutional View of the Late War between the States.* . . . 2 vols. Philadelphia and Chicago, 1868-70.

Sweet, Charles. *A Trip to British Honduras and to San Pedro in the Republic of Honduras.* Pamphlet, 1868.

Thomas, David Y. *Arkansas in War and Reconstruction 1861-1874.* Little Rock, Ark., 1926.

Thompson, C. Mildred. *Reconstruction in Georgia, Economic, Social, Political, 1865-1872.* (Columbia University Studies in History, Economics and Public Law, Vol. LXIV, no. 1; whole no. 154.) New York, 1915.

Vattel, Emmerich de. *The Law of Nations; or, the Principles of Natural Law* (1758). 3 vols. Trans. by Charles G. Fenwick. Washington, D. C., 1916.

Wesley, Charles H. *The Collapse of the Confederacy.* Washington, D. C., 1937.

Wilson, Samuel M. *The History of Kentucky.* Vol. II, *From 1803 to 1928.* Chicago, Louisville, Ky., 1928.

INDEX

INDEX

Abandoned Property Act, provisions of, 8, 243

Acts of Congress: test oath for jurors, 383, repealed, 385; test oath for military service, 385, repealed, 386; test oath for attorneys in United States courts, 396, declared unconstitutional, 397; threat to hamper Supreme Court, 397-98; offer of pardon to be evidence of disloyalty, 401, 404, declared unconstitutional, 406; joint resolution requiring loyalty as proof for claims, 404; repeal of Section 13 of the Confiscation Act, 328, 405, of no effect, 405-6

Adams, President John, granted an amnesty, 328 n. 27

Adams Express Company, distribution of pardon warrants, 152 and n. 28

"Adelso," vessel seized according to public law of war, 394-95, 399

Aiken, S. C., petitioners for Davis, 285

Alexander, Thomas W., asked to be re-enfranchised, 363

Alexander's (Mrs.) cotton, property captured on inland waters not maritime prize, 395-96

Allen, ex-Governor Henry Watkins, 277

Allison, Abraham, compared with Mallory and Yulee, 261-62; petitioned from Fort Pulaski, 262; paroled and pardoned, 263

Alston, Lieutenant W., believed to have been in plot to abduct Lincoln, 252-53

American Bastile, 17

American Law Register, The, discussed amnesty and pardon, 360

Amnesty, defined, xvii, 29, 417; problems arising under, xvi-xvii; advised by Attorney-General, 109-10; Preston King's counsel, 110; Seward's influence, 110-11; Johnson's first proclamation, 111-13; a basis for restoration of the states, 110-13; the amnesty oath, 111-12; rules for application of, 114-15, 190-91; scope of, 153-54. *See also under* Johnson, Andrew, and Lincoln, Abraham.

Amnesty, congressional, in Fourteenth Amendment, and suggested in repeal of Section 13 of Confiscation Act, 320-21, 327, 330, 369; early petitions for, 362-65; special individual relief measures, 367ff.; new oath for beneficiaries, 368; desire for general or universal amnesty, 370ff.; amnesty law of 1872, 378; individual reliefs continued, 379-80; bills for universal amnesty defeated, 380-82; universal amnesty law, 389-91

Amnesty, general, Lincoln's plan of, xvi; early suggestions of, 29; encouraged by victories at Gettysburg and Vicksburg, 31; encouraged by Rosecrans, 32; as basis for restoration of states, 32; proclamation of, 34-36; Southern opposition to proclamation, 38-42; Northern opposition, 42-46; diversity of opinion in the North, 43-44; London papers divided, 44; fear of unfavorable Supreme Court decision, 44-45; supplementary proclamation necessary, 54-57; rules for administering, 55-57; appealed to prisoners of war, 63; evaluation of effect, 73

Amnesty, universal, in the offing, 301; effects of, 311. *See also* Amnesty bill of 1876

Amnesty bill of 1872, time ripe for passage, 376; and civil rights for Negroes, 376-77; becomes law without civil rights, 377-78; number remaining disabled, 378, 387

Amnesty bill of 1876, universal, Blaine's "bloody shirt" speech, 380-81; and news of Johnson's death, 382; bill defeated, 382

Amnesty oath, difficulty in administering, 48-53; omitted from Johnson's fourth amnesty, 127

Amnesty Papers, located and described, 135; estimate of number, 135

Amnesty proclamations, Lincoln's first, 34-35; his explanatory, 56-57; Johnson's first, 111-12; second, 343-44; third, 354-55; last, 357-58, mentioned,

xxi. *See also under* Johnson, Andrew, Lincoln, Abraham, *and* Thirteenth exception from amnesty

Anderson, General John J., recommended by Governor Marvin and pardoned year later, 173-74; related to M. F. Pleasants, 174

Anderson, General Joseph R., deserving of punishment, 222; pardoned, 226

Andersonville Prison, 282, 301, 381

Andrews, Sidney, account of proceedings in Georgia conventions, 289

Antietam, Battle of, encouraged Emancipation Proclamation, 31

"Arlington," question of title to, xx, 123-24

Armstrong, Mrs. Hibernia, claim denied by Court of Claims but allowed by Supreme Court, 400-1

Arrington, A. H., original secessionist, 194; pardon mentioned, 216

Atlanta *Daily Intelligencer,* concerning Georgia's pardon agent, 151; pardoned citizens wanting to vote, 333

Bagley, Paul, missionary, assistance in obtaining Vance's pardon, 218; urged Davis to petition, 302, 305; quoted on Judge Underwood, 309 n. 63

Baker, General Alpheus, petitioned for pardon, 173; recommended by Provisional Governors Parsons and Patton, 173; pardoned, 173

Baker, General L. C., Chief of National Detective Police, observation on pardoning business, 139-40; controversy with Johnson over activities of pardon brokeress, 147-50; observation on Mrs. Washington, 148-49; clash with Johnson, 148-49; resigned commission and stood trial, 149, 151; Lincoln and Stanton appreciated his service, 150-51; President's secretary charged him with falsehoods, 149-50; evidences of his integrity, 151 n. 26; reported on fees for pardons, 151-52 and n. 28

Ballard, Judge Bland, 12, 14

Bank, Aaron, editor, predicted clemency for Davis, 293-94

Bankhead, General Smith P., deserted to Union, 66-67

Banks, General Nathaniel P., on power to restore political privileges, 322

Baringer, Dr. William, on Chase's threat while Governor of Ohio, 307 n. 58

Bates, Attorney-General Edward, opinion that pardon benefits were not allowed in prize court cases, 394

Battle, Kemp P., on integrity of Vance, 202

Beall, Captain John Y., sentenced and executed, xvii, 77-78; attempt to liberate prisoners of war, 76; employed by Confederate commission in Canada, 76; raids on Lake Erie, 76-77; captured, 77; efforts to cause Lincoln to commute sentence, 77-78; no connection between Beall's execution and Lincoln's assassination, 78-79

Beck, James B., interviewed Johnson, 275-76; defeated an amnesty bill, 372

Belle of the Fifties, A, by Mrs. Clement C. Clay, 265

Benjamin, Judah P., in exile, 244

Berry, Captain Michael, captured, 14; refused to take oath, 14-15; declared loyalty to U. S., 15; took oath and was paroled, 15-16

Biggs, Judge Asa, petition deferred, 214-15

Bingham, John A., offered relief bill for several, 366

Black, Jeremiah S., sought Howell Cobb's pardon, 170; counsel for Clay, 266

Blackburn, Dr. Luke P., communication with Davis, 383

Blackburn, Lieutenant Colonel Joseph H., threatened with court martial, 177

Blaine, James G., on effect of third section of Fourteenth Amendment, 321, 373; estimate of number disabled, 372-73; opposition to Amnesty Bill of 1876, 381-82; nomination for President, 382

Blair, Francis P., favored return of Breckinridge, 276; favored segregation, 375

"Blair House," 276

Bolles, Naval Solicitor Major John A., prosecuted Captain Beall, 77-78; on the Semmes case, 183-84

"Bonds and Custody for Good Behavior," federal court records, 13

Boston *Advertiser,* described Georgia convention, 289

Bosworth, A. H., children of, denied

restoration of property under bill of attainder clause of Constitution, 419-20 and n. 55

Bosworth, Charles H., 420. *See also* Bosworth, A. H.

Bosworth, Mildred, 420. *See also* Bosworth, A. H.

Botts, John Minor, opposed secession, xix; bond for Davis, 312

Boutwell, George S., urged legislation in the House to make Supreme Court more submissive, 332

Bowles, William A., treason case, 101-2

Bowling Green, Ky., 273

Bowmar, J. H. D., purchased property from Joseph E. Davis, 238

Brady, John G., counsel for Captain Beall, 77; for Davis, 295

Bragg, General Braxton, invasion of Kentucky, 18; lost claim for proceeds of the sale of his property, 414-15. *See also Brown* vs. *United States*

Bramlette, Governor Thomas E., recommended Vance's pardon, 218

Breckinridge, John Cabell, political experiences, 272-73; abandoned neutral position, 273; in exile, 244, 274; a unique case, 275; effort to encourage his return, 275-76; finally induced to return, 276; telegram to Davis, 281

Bridgers, John L., original secessionist, 194; pardon mentioned, 216

"Brierfield," Joseph Davis's plantation, 238

Brougham, Henry, on the American Union, 290-91

Brown, B. Gratz, Liberal Governor of Missouri, 370; candidate for Vice-President, 379

Brown, Major Campbell, son of Mrs. Ewell, in Fort Warren, 162; efforts of mother to secure his release, 162-66

Brown, John, 282

Brown, Justice John W., 14

Brown, Governor Joseph, pardoned, 217; urged clemency for Stephens, 249; relief desired, 363

Brown, William Murray, case of, 12

Browning, Senator Orville Hickman, advised clemency for Captain Beall, 77; speculated on Beall's execution as cause of Lincoln's assassination, 78; related two other instances of Lincoln's refusal to grant clemency, 79-

80; greeted committee from Virginia, 223; disagreed with Evarts on Davis, 310; on nomination of Johnson, 355

Brownlow, Governor William Ganneway, 163

Brown vs. *United States*, property restored by pardon unless ownership had become vested in a third person, 414; proceeds of sale restored when remaining in custody of court, 414, 416

Bunting, John N., recommended Holden, 364

Bureau of Military Justice investigation of Lincoln assassination, 266, 268, 279-80

Bureau of Refugees, Freedmen and Abandoned Lands, instructions from Johnson, 227-28, 230-31; General Howard, Commissioner, 228; rules for, 228-29; refused restoration to merely pardoned owners, 229; new instructions for restorations, 230-31; Senators Pomeroy and Sumner believed freedmen deserved land, 232; acreage restored, 233; problem on Edisto Island, 233-34; wise policy of Bureau, 234; restored plantations to Joseph Davis, 238

Burke, Edmund, quoted, xiii-xiv

Burnam, Curtis F., friend of Lincoln, 18

Burnam, Curtis F. and Caperton, James W., law firm of, secured release of prisoners from Camp Douglas, 60-61; friends of Lincoln, 60

Burnam, Mrs. Paul, 60 n. 33

Burnett, David G., petitioned Johnson for Davis, 286-89

Burnside, General Ambrose E., instructions concerning oath of allegiance, 26

Burr, Aaron, Davis likened to, 296

Burton, General Henry S., in command of Fortress Monroe, 299

Butler, General B. F., suggested general amnesty, 29; announced general amnesty at New Orleans, 30; registered citizens on taking oath, 30 and n. 3; reported prisoners at Point Lookout, 57-58; thought Johnson pardoned prisoners for political reasons, 351; sponsor of bills, 371, 375-76

Butler, R. R., first to be relieved by Congress, 367

Caldwell, Tod R., avoided military service, 192
Caldwell and Caldwell, law firm of, 11
Calhoun, John C., advocate of states' rights, 290
Cammack, Judge J. W., statement concerning Breckinridge, 275 n. 65
Campbell, John Archibald, high position in government before war, 250; active for peace, 251; petitions important, 251 and n. 13; criticized Davis, 252; offered to resign as Assistant Secretary of War, 252; commended Judge Nelson for effort at conciliation, 252; denied knowledge of any plot to assassinate Lincoln, 252-53 and n. 16; petition endorsed by many, 253-54; wife and daughter sought his release from prison, 254; released with Reagan and Stephens, 255
Camp Chase, 13
Camp Douglas, desertions at, 59
Canby, General Edward R. S., received instructions regarding amnesty, 67
Canby-Smith surrender agreement, 156
Caperton, ex-Confederate Senator Allen T., said Campbell believed Confederacy would fail, 253
Caperton, W. H., and son, James W., voted for Lincoln, 61 n. 34
Captured and Abandoned Property Act, 8; administration of, 417-18
Carlisle, Hugh, Britisher and alien, amnesty of December 25, 1868, benefited aliens, 409-10
Carman, Joseph S., editor of Raleigh *Standard*, 189 n. 7
Carroll, Mrs. Lucy, and question of the status of aliens, 409-10
"Carroll Hall," annex to Fortress Monroe, 265
Cartel for exchange of prisoners, 23; policy of exchange by August, 1862, 24; guerrillas denied, 24; disregarded, 76; broke down, 154 n. 1
Castleman, Captain John Breckinridge, published *Active Service*, 82; captured while spying and imprisoned at Indianapolis, 82-83; visited by mother with a loaded Bible, 83; danger of suffering fate of John Y. Beall, 83; Judge Samuel Breckinridge interceded with Lincoln, 83-84; exchange as prisoner of war arranged,

84; Lincoln's death caused preparations to try him as a spy, 84; finally paroled and banished, 84; allowed to return and take oath of allegiance, 84
Caton, Justice John, 255 n. 20
Central Christian Advocate, likened acts of seceders to assassins of Lincoln, 293
Centralia, Ill., petition to punish Davis, 283
Chandler, Senator Zachariah, favored repeal of Section 13 of Confiscation Act, 325; charged that pardons were being sold in Washington, 326
Charleston *Courier*, believed Johnson's second amnesty would enlarge white electorate, 345
Chase, Salmon P., to preside at trial of Davis, xxi, 295; required at impeachment, 307-8; believed Confederates not traitors, 358
Chenault, Colonel David Waller, organized regiment for C. S. A., 18
Chestney, James, offered teachings of early statesmen as argument for clemency, 290
Chicago, instructions to commander of prison camp at, 23
Chicago *Journal*, believed Johnson's second amnesty a Southern victory, 345
Chicago *Times*, opposed to Lincoln's amnesty, 42-43; favored freeing and arming slaves, 43; counseled leniency, 294; advised universal amnesty, 341; urged registration, 345
Chicago *Tribune*, described Georgia convention, 289
Choctaw and Chickasaw Indians, liberal treaty with, 99-101; treatment of Indians compared with that of whites, 100-1
Christmas Amnesty, intended to have wide application, 408-9; not every petitioner benefited, 409
Churchill, General T. J., his reason for desiring pardon, 176
Cincinnati *Enquirer*, expected Johnson's second amnesty to increase white electorate, 345
Civil rights, Lincoln's belief in, xiv
Civil Rights Bill, 324
Clark, Henry T., Governor of North

Carolina, 205; action on petition delayed, 218-19

Clay, Brutus J., 19 n. 19

Clay, Mrs. Brutus J., 19 n. 19

Clay, Cassius M., minister to Russia and general in Union army, 18

Clay, Clement C., member of Canadian Commission, 76; in Fortress Monroe, 263-64; compared with Davis, 264; transferred to better quarters, 265; Mrs. Clay's work for liberation, 265-70; his informative letter to Mrs. Clay, 265-66; able legal talent secured, 266; proof that he had no part in the assassination, 266; visited by Mrs. Clay, 267-68; took oath of allegiance and was paroled, 270; Holt believed evidence warranted trial for part in the assassination, 270-71; petition granted, 387-88

Clay, Mrs. Clement C., work for liberation of husband, 265-70; appealed to Holt in behalf of husband, 266; obtained legal talent for Clay, 266; interview with Johnson, 266-67; took copy of Holt's report to Clay, 267-68; second visit to Johnson, 269; obtained other support for her cause and freedom of the prison for her husband, 270; obtained Clay's parole, 270

Clay, Clement C., Sr., pardoned, 267

Clay, Henry, Lincoln's support of, xiv

Clayton, General Henry D., pardon delayed, 173

Clemency, desired in 1862-63, 22; purposes of, 25; not recognized by C. S. A., 26. *See also* Lincoln, Abraham, clemency of

Cleveland, President Grover, 386

"Clyde," vessel that took Clay and Davis to Norfolk, 264

Cobb, General Howell, official positions and war record, 167; order for arrest not executed, 167-68; applied for pardon and desired to aid in reconstruction, 167-68; activity of General Henry Jackson in his behalf, 168-69; disposition in Washington to punish, 169; appealed for liberation of Jefferson Davis, 169-70; informed Mrs. Cobb of legal prosperity, 169; visited Washington, 170; Jeremiah S. Black sought his pardon, 170; relieved by Johnson's third amnesty, 171

Cobb, Mrs. L. L., pardon brokeress, methods disapproved by Chief of Detectives Baker, 147-51; clash with General Baker, 148-51; integrity defended by husband, 148 n. 19

Colfax, Schuyler, editor, 345; cast vote in the Senate to amend House bill, 374

"Colored Orphans' Home," District of Columbia, property restored to pardoned owner, 235-36

Colquitt, General A. H., petition highly endorsed, 172-73

Columbia *Daily Phoenix*, complained of thirteenth exception, 226

Commissioner-General of Prisoners, instructions to, 27-28

Committee on the Judiciary, House, received impeachment charges, 332; considered Johnson's universal amnesty, 358-60; opposed unconditional amnesty, 373-74; favorable to universal amnesty, 389-90

Compact theory of Federal government, belief in, an argument for clemency, 290-91

Confederate Canadian commission, 76

Confederate generals, many not pardoned, had to wait until Johnson's third amnesty, 171

Confederate military authorities, attitude toward deserters, 22

Confederates, Unionism among, xix-xx; plight of, 244-45, 313, 315; necessity of asking for clemency, 245; opportunity to plead the cause of the South, 245

Confederate States, population supporting the rebellion, 4 n. 1; attitude toward policy of clemency at Washington, 26; evaluation of objectives, 132-33

Confiscation Act of July 17, 1862, suggested amnesty, 6-7, 30; effect of Fourteenth Amendment on Section 13, 321; debate on repeal of Section 13, 322, 325-29; Section 13 repealed, 329, 339-40

Congress, United States, enacted punitive laws, 5-8; disapproved of Lincoln's amnesty, 45; investigated amnesty policy, 318-19; Radicals denounced Johnson, 320; proposed Fourteenth Amendment, 320-21; debate on powers to grant pardons and amnesties, 321-24; Fourteenth Amendment made less restrictive by Senate, 322-23; repealed mitigating clause of the Confiscation Act, 325-29; resolved to prevent other amnesties and annul partial benefits of past amnesties and pardons, 330; passed four reconstruction measures, 330-31, 336, 337; made civil officers subject to military commanders, 336-37

Congressional Globe, 371

Conover (or Dunham), Sanford, imprisoned for conspiracy, 294-95; pardoned, 295

Cooper, General Douglas H., Indian agent, pardoned, 101 n. 14

Cooper, Dr. George, successor to Dr. Craven, 299

Cooper, General Samuel, 253

Cooper Union, Lincoln's speech at, xiv

Corwin, Governor Thomas, letter from Gilmer to, 196

Council Bluffs, petition to punish Davis, 284

Court of Claims, hesitation to allow pardon in lieu of proof of loyalty, 399-400

Covode, John, favored relieving Gilmer, 366

Cox, General Jacob Dolson, recommended Gilmer's pardon, 197; and relief for Robert P. Dick, 364

Cox, Major Richard L., pardoned and property restored, 235-36

Cox, Samuel S., author, *Three Decades of Federal Legislation*, 17

Crabb, Dr. A. L., author, *Supper at the Maxwell House*, 237 n. 26

Craige, Burton, original secessionist, 194

Craven, Dr. John J., removed from Fortress Monroe, 299

Custis, G. W., estate of, 123

Dana, Charles A., letter to Stanton, 129-30; on trial of Davis and Underwood's presiding, 309

Danbury, Conn., petition to punish Davis, 282-84

Davis, Henry Winter, disapproval of Lincoln's amnesty and plan of reconstruction, 46

Davis, Jefferson, as exceptional case, xx-xxi, 303-5; considered Lincoln's amnesty unacceptable, 40; petitions for clemency and effort to escape,
202; arrest of, 269, 279; bail bond, 270; dislike of Johnson, 279-81; demands for punishment, 281-84; pleas for clemency, 284-89; compared to Napoleon, 291-92; conspiracy against, 294-95; abandonment of trial before a military commission, 295; indictments for treason, 295 and n. 35, 358; excuse for treatment in Fortress Monroe, 297; poor health, 298-99; given apartment in Fortress Monroe, 299; increase of favorable sentiment, 299-301; refused to ask for clemency, 302-5; plea for the Union, 304; brought to court and liberated on bail, 306; trial deferred again, 308; effect of third amnesty on case, 309; effect of Fourteenth Amendment, 310; effect of universal amnesty, 311; pardoned, 311-12, 358; excepted from Johnson's third amnesty, 354-55; deferment of trial, 357; partial restoration of privileges, 369; declined to apply for amnesty, 382-83; death, 387

Davis, Joseph E., pardoned, 237; restoration of property, 238

Davis, Mrs. Varina Howell, mentioned, 269; compared to Mrs. Ewell and Mrs. Clay, 296; defiant attitude, 296-97; denied permission to see Davis, 297-98; allowed to visit husband, 298; anxiety over Davis's health, 298; visited Johnson, 298-99; attitude toward asking for pardon, 303-4; honored at death, 304

Davis, General W. G. M., petition endorsed, 174

Davison, Virginia and Bessie, and "Ladies of the Valley of the Shenandoah," petitioned for Davis, 286

Deatherage, Nathan, complained of desertions at Camp Douglas, 59; exchanged, 156-57 and n. 5

"Deerhound," English yacht that rescued Admiral Semmes, 179, 183

Dennis, O. W., opposed to re-enfranchising Magrath, 364

Deserters Who Have Taken the Oath of Allegiance at Little Rock, Arkansas, 62-63

Desertions, from the Confederate army, number of, 62-63, 69-72; problem within Union lines, 63-64; effect of amnesty on, 69; reports from Nashville, Chattanooga, and Little Rock, 70-71

Dick, Robert P., petition of, 363-64

Dix, General John A., appointed to a commission dealing with state prisoners, 16; in command of Fortress Monroe, 16; arranged cartel for exchange of prisoners, 23

Dixon, Senator James, denied pardons were for sale, 326

Dockery, General Alfred, defeated for Governor of North Carolina, 216

Dockery, General Thomas P., recommended for pardon, 176

Doolittle, Senator James R., on Fourteenth Amendment, 323

Dortch, William, delay in pardoning, 215-16

Douglas, Mrs. Stephen A., companion of Mrs. Clement C. Clay, 266-67

Dowd, Clement, on arrest of Vance, 201

Doyle, James and Mrs. James. *See Ralph Meldrim et al. vs. U. S.*

Dunn, Rev. Ballard S., author, *Brazil, the Home for Southerners,* 116

East Baptist Association of New Jersey, against releasing Davis, 306

Echols, General John, 75

Eleventh Kentucky Cavalry, C. S. A., 18

Eliot, Thomas D., on restoring the suffrage, 322

Ellis, John W., defeated Holden for Governor of North Carolina, 205

Ellsworth, Representative Charles C., 383-84

Emancipation, compensated, recommended by Lincoln, 90-91. *See also* Slavery

Emancipation Proclamation, 32-33, 223

Embry, County Judge James N., 13-14

English Chartists, clemency shown to, 287-88

Evarts, Attorney-General William M., deferment of trial of Davis, 306; disapproved of trying Davis, 309-10

Ewell, Mrs. Lizinka Campbell Brown, attempt to regain property by taking Lincoln's oath, 162; indiscretion and imprisonment, 162-63; efforts to obtain release of husband and son from prison, 162-66; applied for pardon, 164; Lincoln's pardon recognized, 164-65

Ewell, General Richard S., imprisoned in Fort Warren, 161; applied for pardon, 161-62; efforts of Mrs. Ewell to secure his release, 162-66; complained of restrictions on his liberty, 166; pardoned under Johnson's third amnesty, 166

Ewing, E. H., advised acceptance of Lincoln's amnesty, 38 and n. 21

Ewing, Thomas, testified for John A. Campbell, 253-54

Ex parte Garland, mentioned by General Lee, 123; President's power not subject to legislative control, 331-32; pardon restored all privileges, 396-98; Magruder not benefited, 398

Ex parte Milligan, bearing on Semmes case, 184

Farnsworth, John F., advised relief measures, 366-67

Finegan, General Joseph, advised to oppose Union forces, 260

Fitz, Mrs. of Mississippi, denied clemency, 79

Fleming, Walter L., on exceptions in Johnson's first amnesty, 136

Floyd, John, Secretary of War, refused request for troops to defend Washington, 253-54

Forney, John, concerning Breckinridge, 273

Fort Delaware, Confederate prisoners in, 23; oath to be administered in 1863, 26

Fort Lafayette, Confederate prisoners in, 257

Fort Pulaski, Confederate prisoners in, 257, 258, 262

Fortress Monroe, Davis imprisoned in, xx, 297; prisoners in, 264, 265, 270, 279; described by Clay, 265

Foster, General John G., reply to criticism by General Longstreet, 39

Fourteenth Amendment, probable effect on persons pardoned, 321; defeat of ratification, 323; opposition to disability clause, 370; Republicans aid Democrats in removals of disabilities, 370; relation to rise of Ku Klux Klan, 370-71; number disabled, 373; relation to disorder in South, 374

Freedmen's Bureau. *See* Bureau of Refugees, Freedmen and Abandoned Lands

Freeman, Douglas Southall, on Lee, 131, 133; letter to author, 134 n. 29

Freeman, M. J., engineer of "Alabama," pardoned, 186

French, T. Scott, confidence in Johnson, 97

Gaither, Burton S., recommended for pardon, 217

Gantt, Colonel E. W., comments on pardon, 36; advised submission to Union, 67-68

Garland, Augustus H., Governor of Arkansas and Attorney-General, 397; court victory a boon to other lawyers, 397-98. *See also Ex parte Garland*

Gay, Edward L., denied claim to money seized from person not a beligerent, 411. *See also* "Gold Case"

Georgia, legislature of, petitioned for Davis, 289

Gettysburg, victory encouraged amnesty, 31

Gilmer, John A., a late secessionist, 194; recommended for pardon, 195-97; early activities for the Union, 196; work for Vance's pardon, 197; controversy over removing disability, 366

"Gold Case," decision that amnesty applied to persons and not to the voiding of treasonable offenses, 411

Good, Representative John, 383-84

Gordon, General John B., on certainty of Lincoln's leniency, 93

Graham, G. Mason, requested relief, 363

Graham, William A., a late secessionist, 194; political positions, 199; contents of petition, 199-200; long delay in delivery of pardon, 200-1, 216; and requests to pardon Vance, 202; supported Campbell's plea, 253

Grant, General U. S., announcement to deserters, 63; recommended Lee be pardoned, 120; threatened resignation, 120-21; recommended Longstreet be pardoned, 171-72; spoke highly of Pickett, 176-77; disposed to leniency, 177; concerning paroles, 185; objected to eighth and thirteenth exceptions, 221; recommended clemency for Clay, 269; advice on Seddon's petition, 272; on prison status of Davis, 297 n. 38; report on reconstruction, 317-18, 342; directed that

proceedings against office holders be dropped, 378; recommended universal amnesty, 372-73; *Memoirs*, quoted, 391

Grant, Mrs. U. S., appreciated Mrs. Davis, 304

"Gray Jacket," no benefit of amnesty because seizure was according to public law of war, 395

Greathouse, Ridgely. *See In re Greathouse*

Greeley, Horace, recommended Vance's pardon, 218; advised Mrs. Clay, 267; opinion on return of Breckinridge, 294; implored clemency for Davis, 300 and n. 44; on Davis's bond, 306; candidate for President, 379

Green, Charles, Britisher and alien, claim determined by decision in case of Hugh Carlisle, 410-11

"Greenwood Plantation," Braxton Bragg's, 414

Grimes, Senator James W., opposed repeal of Section 13 of Confiscation Act, 326

Guerrillas. *See* Cartel for exchange of prisoners

Hale, Eugene, sponsored amnesty bill, 372

Hall, C. W., United States District Attorney, Knoxville, 242

Halleck, General Henry W., wanted to try Captain John B. Castleman as a spy, 84

Hamilton, Governor A. J., recommended release of Reagan, 247

Hamilton, Alexander, believed President should proclaim amnesties, 328

Hamilton, John F., faulty wording of his two amnesty oaths of no consequence, 407 and n. 31

Hampton, General Wade, petitioned for pardon, 176

Hampton Roads peace conference, xvii, 90

Hanes, Lewis, Holden's secretary, 194; recommended Gilmer's pardon, 197

Harlan, Justice John Marshall, 388

Harper's Weekly, reasons for slow sale of cotton, 223; for punishing Davis, 292-93; attitude toward liberating Davis, 300-1

Harrison, Burton N., 306 and n. 54

Harrison, William Henry, Lincoln's support of, xiv

Haxall and Crenshaw, milling company, 222

Hay, John, claimed Lincoln pleased with Senators' attitude toward his amnesty, 45-46; report on amnesty in Virginia and Florida, 48-49

Hayes, President Rutherford B., 384

Hayes-Tilden campaign, effects of, 384

Haym, Harry, decision in Klein's case favorable to, 407-8

Haynes, Landon C., petition sent without recommendation, 195-96

Hedrick, Benjamin S., succeeded Powell as pardon agent, 212; reported on petitions, 213-14

Henderson, Senator John B., on repeal of Section 13 of Confiscation Act, 326

Henderson, Governor Thomas Jefferson, recommended Gilmer's pardon, 197

Hendricks, Senator Thomas A., on repeal of Section 13 of Confiscation Act, 329

Hill, Benjamin H., expressed Southern view in debate on bill of 1876, 381-82

Hill, Senator David B., 386

Hill, General D. H., arranged cartel for exchange of prisoners, 23

Hillyer, George, reported status of Cobb in Washington, 168-69

Hines, Thomas H., plotted to liberate Captain Castleman, 83

Hoar, Senator George F., 388

Hoffman, Mayor John T., endorsed Vance's petition, 218

Hoffman, William, Commissioner-General of Exchange, for relief of prisoners of war, 154-55; ordered releases after oath of allegiance, 158

Holden, Joseph W., assistant editor of Raleigh *Standard*, 189 n. 7

Holden, W. W., appointed Provisional Governor of North Carolina, 188; announced amnesty and rules for restoration, 189-90; received instruction from the President, 190-91; consideration of petitions for pardon, 138, 191-92; reasons for recommending pardons, 194, 195; left three hundred petitions in his office, 196; recommended Vance's parole, 202; attitude toward secession, 204, 205; denounced policies of Confederates,

205; relations with Vance, 205-6; advocate of peace, 206-7; special instructions for election, 208-9; desired election as Governor, 209; defeated, 211; Johnson refused to set aside the election, 211; blamed for delays in obtaining pardons, 216-17; elected Governor and impeached, 216; edited Washington *National Republican*, 216; recommended for relief, 364, 366

Holt, Judge-Advocate-General Joseph, instructions concerning oaths, 27-28; advice against paroling Major Prentice, 82; desire to try Castleman, 84; aid appreciated in obtaining pardons, 239; revealed secession activities of Mallory and others, 259-61, 263; prosecuted assassins, 266, 268, 291; approved Conover's evidence against Davis, 294

Horsey, Stephen, treason case of, 101-2

Hough, W. H., request for relief, 363

Houston, General Sam, 287

Hovey, General Alvin P., regarded Castleman as a spy, 84

Howard, Senator Jacob M., on repeal of Section 13 of Confiscation Act, 325

Howard, General Oliver O., Commissioner Freedmen's Bureau, restored Mrs. Ewell's property, 164-65; *Autobiography* quoted, 228; circular concerning Bureau, 228-29; instructed by Johnson, 229; other instructions for the restoration of property, 230-31; purpose of Congress thwarted, 231; sought advantages for freedmen, 231-33; solved problem on Edisto Island, 233-34; approved policy followed, 234

Howlett, Provost Marshal, 12

Hughes, Edward L., pardoned, 393-94

Hull, Representative John A. T., quoted on removal of last disability, 386

Humphreys, Andrew, treason case of, 101-2

Huntsville *Advocate*, announced boat for emigrants, 116

"Hurricane," Joseph Davis's plantation, 238

Illinois *State Journal*, on pardon of Colonel Gantt, 36

Impeachment of Johnson, charge of abuse of pardoning power, 329-30; charges preferred, 332

Ingersoll, Colonel Robert G., endorsed Colquitt's petition, 173; nominated Blaine, 382

In re Greathouse, pardon allowed contrary to Lincoln's intentions, 53-54, 56, 393-94

Is Davis a Traitor; or, Was Secession a Constitutional Right Previous to the War of 1861?, argument for clemency, 290-91

"Island Queen," overpowered by Captain Beall, 76-77

Jackson, General Henry R., sought pardon for Howell Cobb, 168-69

Jacksonville, Fla., plight of Union prisoners at, 157

Jefferson, Thomas, advocated states' rights, 290

Jefferson County, Ky., peace bonds in, 14

Jenkins, John J., quoted Blaine on number disabled by the Fourteenth Amendment, 373; quoted Grant on era of harmony, 391

Jenkins vs. *Collard*, heirs were denied interest in property after father's death, 419-21 and n. 56

Johnson, Andrew, early policies of, xviii, 95-98; and case of Jefferson Davis, xviii, 279-81, 298, 301-3 and n. 4, 311; program a continuation of Lincoln's, xviii; general policy of, xxi; Military Governor of Tennessee, 21; opinion on clemency in 1862, 21; restrained by Lincoln, 22; instructions concerning prisoners, 24; announced stricter amnesty oath, 50-51; proclaimed second oath, 52; not interfered with by Lincoln, 53; favored over Lincoln for reconstruction, 94-97; disallowed Sherman-Johnston agreement, 98-100; and Milligan-Bowles treason case, 101-2; yielded to Grant on question of indictments, 120-21; concerning interview between Grant and Lee, 130; pardoning policy of, 143; and Mrs. Ewell, 162-64; on pardon of Davis, Longstreet, and Lee, 172; greater leniency to civil than to military leaders, 178; interest in Semmes case, 179-85; began restoration in North Carolina, 187; appointed Holden Provisional Governor of North Carolina, 188; instruc-

tions to Holden, 190; insisted on Quakers' taking amnesty oath, 193-94; concern with defeat of Holden, 211; delay of advertised pardons, 212-14; extended Vance's parole, 217-18; illness, 223; on thirteenth exception, 221-22, 226, 227; policy on Freedmen's Bureau, 230-31; appealed to in Major Cox's case, 235; proclamation for arrest of assassins, 270, 278-79, 281; on return of Breckinridge, 275; conspiracy against, 284-95; baneful influence on, 305-6; second amnesty, 308, 340-44; fourth (universal) amnesty, 310-11, 357-58; causes of increasing leniency, 314-16; sent Schurz to report on reconstruction, 316-18; sent Grant to report on reconstruction, 317-18; sent Truman to report on reconstruction, 319; reported on number pardoned in thirteenth exception, 319; denounced Radicals, 319-20; continued pardon policy despite congressional opposition, 323-24; congressional efforts to curtail pardoning power of, 324-29; loss of influence in reconstruction, 337; and effect of repeal of Section 13, 339-40; press reaction to second amnesty, 344-49; impeachment charges against, 351-52; freed of impeachment charges, 352; influence of Cabinet on third amnesty, 352-54; third amnesty and nomination of 1868, 354-55; continued pardoning policy during congressional reconstruction, 369; death while member of Senate, 382

Johnson, Andrew, Esq., pardoned, 226 n. 10

Johnson, Mrs. Andrew, 162

Johnson, Bradley T., discriminated between waging war and levying war, 106-7; account of Davis's case, 311

Johnson, Judge George W., 14

Johnson, Provisional Governor James, endorsed Cobb's petition, 168

Johnson, Senator Reverdy, letters from Lee, 123; opposed repeal of Section 13 of the Confiscation Act, 325-26; upheld power of President to proclaim amnesties, 327-28

Johnson County, Ind., petition to punish Davis, 284

Joint Committee on Reconstruction, on Lincoln's assassination, 270-71; appointed, 318; investigation of reconstruction and amnesty, 318-19; full report, 323-24

Jones, General Sam, urged General Vogdes at Jacksonville to accept Union soldiers, 157

Jones, Thomas L., for universal amnesty, 356

Juries, removal of disabilities to serve on, 383-85

Keifer, Representative J. Warren, 387

Kenan, Owen T., recommended for pardon, 217

Kentuckians, favored by Lincoln, 84-85

King, Paul, gave bond, 12

Kittrell Springs, 192

Klein, John A. *See Klein* vs. *United States*

Klein vs. *United States,* claim for proceeds of sale of cotton allowed, 414-16

Klingberg, Frank Wysor, xx

Knights of the Golden Circle, 253

Knote vs. *United States,* limitation of recovery of confiscated property, 417

Ku Klux Klan, efforts to suppress, 216; blamed on Republican illiberality, 370-71

Lacey, John Fletcher, 390

Lafayette, Ohio, proposition from, 283

La Forge, Mr., interceded for Dr. Shiff, 80

Lancaster, John, owner of "Deerhound," 183

Lander, William, original secessionist, 194

Langley, Edward, favored special clemency, 225-26

Latham, R. W., advocate of clemency, 293

Lathrop, Colonel L. B., letter to Davis, 280

Lawrence, Mass., petition to punish Davis, 283

Lay, Colonel George A., 253 n. 16

Lay, Mrs. Henrietta, worked for her father's liberation, 254

Leake, B. B., property restored, 229

Lee, General Custis, copied father's petition for pardon, 121-22; in Fort Warren, 161

Lee, General Fitzhugh, 390

Lee, Captain Robert E., message from Custis Lee, 121-22

Lee, General Robert E., clement treatment of, xx; on desertions from C. S. A., 22, 63; proclamation, 37; presidency of Washington College, 117, 127; sentiment for his pardon, 119; appealed to Grant to prevent arrest, 120; applied for pardon through Grant, 120-21; concern for Davis's welfare, 122; reasons for not taking amnesty oath, 122-27; desire to be able to administer Arlington, 123-24; advised by General Meade to take oath, 125; on reconstruction, 125-26; opposition in the North, 128; disapproved emigration, 128-29; protected by military parole, 129; probable desire for interview with Grant, 129-30; compared with Generals Scott and Thomas, 131-34; evaluation of, 131ff.; sought to have parole privileges at Appomattox extended, 161

Leland, Ill., petition to punish Davis, 283-84

Lellyet, John, disapproved taking of Lincoln's amnesty oath by loyal Tennesseans, 49; opposed Johnson's oath, 51

Letcher, Governor John, in Old Capitol Prison, 201; opinion of Vance, 204; pardoned, 217

Lewis, Joshua, United States District Attorney for Kentucky, 242

Libby Prison, 282

Liberty City, Iowa, petition to punish Davis, 283

Lincoln, Abraham, attitude toward South, xiv-xv, 86-93; plan of amnesty and reconstruction, xvi, xx, 87-88, 92; clemency of, xvii, 314-15; leniency at last Cabinet meeting, xvii-xviii, 92; reliance on Unionism in South, xix; favored paroling McCreary, 19-20; restrained Johnson, 21-22; reply to Fernando Wood, 30-31; reasons for deferring amnesty, 31-33; influence of Seward, 33; excepted Confederate leaders from benefits of amnesty, 35-36; pardoned Colonel Gantt, 36; abused by Confederates for amnesty, 39-40; criticized by Southern press, 40-41; pocket-vetoed Wade-Davis bill, 46-47; no objection to Johnson's amnesty oath, 51; on who must take oath, 51; policy of no interference in

Tennessee, 53; interpretation of scope of amnesty denied, 53-54; issued supplementary amnesty, 54-55; effect of amnesty, 58, 63; distressed by Union desertions, 64; evaluation of amnesty, 72-73; three aspects of his clemency, 76; paroled Clarence J. Prentice, 82; arranged for exchange of John B. Castleman, 84; favored Kentuckians, 82-85; approved Sherman's liberal terms to Johnston, 89-90; effect of his death on fate of South, 93-94; Davis on, 281; on secession in speech of 1848, 288; influence on Seward, 315

Little, Bishop, claimed to have counseled Lincoln, 300

Little Rock, Ark., report of desertions, 71

Logan, Senator John A., 385

Long, Colonel A. K., secretary to Johnson, reported unfavorably about General Baker, 149-50

Longstreet, General James, criticism of distribution of amnesty, 39; recommended for pardon by Grant, 171-72; petition denied by Johnson, 172

Longyear, John W., on power to pardon, 322

Lonn, Dr. Ella, classified prisoners of war, 61-62

Louisville, Ky., court records, 13

Louisville *Journal,* probable political influence on Lincoln, 80-81

Lowe, Representative William M., 387

Lozier, Major John Hogarth, poetic petition against pardon of Davis, 284

Lyons, James, on Davis's bail-bond, 306; proposed evidence if Davis were tried, 307 and n. 58

Madison, James, advocate of states' rights, 290

Madison County, Ky., defeat of Union troops in, 18

Magrath, A. G., paroled from Pulaski, 271; re-enfranchisement opposed, 364

Magruder, Allan B., denied petition to practice in District courts, 398

Mallory, Stephen R., self-defense of, 257-58; recommended by Marvin, 259; evidence against, 260-68; paroled and pardoned, 263

Marshall, Chief Justice John, quoted on pardon, 359-60

Marshall, John A., author, *American Bastile,* 17

Marvin, Provisional Governor William, recommended clemency for Mallory, Yulee, and Allison, 259, 261, 262

Masonic Order, members inquire for terms offered deserters, 69

Massachusetts, petition to punish Davis, 282

"Maxwell House," built by John Overton, 237 n. 26

Maynard, Horace, opposed relieving Gilmer, 366

McClellan, General George B., communication from General Lee, 22

McClernand, General J. A., petitioned for Colquitt's pardon, 172-73

McCreary, James Bennett, early vacillation, 18-20; officer in Chenault regiment of C. S. A., 18; captured with General Morgan, 19; aided Morgan to escape, 19; refusal of parole, 19-20; denied applying for position on General Clay's staff, 19 n. 19; in Fort Delaware, 19, 388

McCullough, Treasurer Hugh M., recommended Vance's pardon, 218, 395

McElroy, Dr. Robert M., on Johnson and Davis, 278-80

McFarland, Samuel, on Johnson and Lincoln, 96-97

McHenry, General James W., pardon of, 68-69

McLain, James R., petition rejected, 195

Meade, General Gordon, visited and advised Lee, 125

Meadville, Pa., petition to punish Davis, 284

Meagher, Timothy. See "Gray Jacket"

Means, J. S., duplicate of pardon desired, 220

Meldrim, Ralph. See *Ralph Meldrim et al. vs. U. S.*

Memminger, Christopher G., why not arrested and imprisoned, 255; petitioned for pardon to regain privileges and property, 255-56; pardon granted, 256-57

Memphis, Tenn., destitute Confederate soldiers at, 156

"Merrimac," commanded by Captain Josiah Tattnall, 122 n. 9, 124

Miles, General Nelson, in command at Fortress Monroe, 264, 299

Military parole, 129

Milledgeville *Recorder*, favored deferring elections after Johnson's second amnesty, 345

Miller, Justice Samuel Freeman, dissenting opinion in case of John A. Klein, 406-7, 414, 415

Miller, William P., pardon warrant of, 143

Miller vs. *United States*, Civil War characterized by Supreme Court, xv

Milligan, Lamdin P., treason case of, 101-2

Milton, Governor John, suicide of, 262, 277

Mississippi, legislature petitioned for Davis, 289

Mitchell, John, of Richmond *Examiner*, liberated from Fortress Monroe, 264-65

Moore, Colonel W. G., secretary to Johnson, 220

Morehead, John M., a late secessionist, 194

Morgan, Senator John T., 384, 387

Morton, Governor Oliver P., against trial by military commission of Milligan *et al.*, 101-2; proposed relief bill, 366

Mott, Randolph, partner of Edward Padelford, 402

Mt. Zion, Ill., petition to punish Davis, 283

Murrah, ex-Governor Pendleton H., 277

Muzzey, David Saville, 338 n. 50.

Napoleon, compared to Davis, 291-92

Nashville, Tenn., report of desertions, 70

Nashville *Daily Press*, urged acceptance of Lincoln's amnesty, 38

Nashville *Union*, revealed fraudulent taker of amnesty oath, 65-66

Nation, differed with English correspondent in likening Davis to Napoleon, 291-92; increasing sympathy for Davis, 301-2; view of release of Davis, 306-7

National Archives, for amnesty oaths of persons not in excepted classes, 141-42

Negroes, civil rights for, 374ff. *See also* Emancipation, Slavery

Nelson, General William, defeat of, 18

Nevada, highest court declares pardon and amnesty synonomous, 417

Newell, Isaac, pardoned, 144

Newlin, Joseph, spokesman of Quakers, 193

New Orleans, petition on responsibility for the war, 285

New Orleans *Republican*, said Johnson would not resort to violence, 346

New Orleans *Times*, elated over Johnson's second amnesty, 345

New York *Daily News*, editor appealed to, 266

New York Harbor, prisoners confined in, 20

New York *Herald*, prediction of ill effect of Lincoln's death, 94; on first West Pointer to apply for pardon, 136; on number of pardon applicants, 141; on illness of Johnson, 142; on pardoning, 142-43; on activities of Mrs. Cobb, 149; letter concerning General Ewell, 165; exultation over Wade Hampton's petition, 176; on pardoning activities in North Carolina, 192; on purpose of thirteenth exception, 223-24; on effect of universal amnesty, 312; advised second amnesty, 341; on Johnson's universal amnesty, 358

New York *Times*, deplored rumors that Johnson would use force, 346

New York *Tribune*, estimate of numbers of pardon seekers in Washington, 140-41; on pardon policy, 142; on activities of pardon attorneys, 144-45; counseled leniency, 294

Nichols, Dr. Roy F., on "The American Civil War in Its True Perspective," 182 n. 44; quoted O'Connor on Davis's release, 307

North Carolinians, effect of Johnson's second amnesty on, 220; granted universal amnesty by legislature, 340; relief asked by convention, 364

Oaths, of allegiance to U. S., 11; of parole, 15-16, 20; clemency allowed for 20-21; of an officer, 20; administered in 1863, 26-27; special rules for, 27; applications denied, 27; controversy in Tennessee, 51-53; fraudulently taken, 64-66 and n. 44; in North Carolina, 189 and n. 9; modified for reliefs under Fourteenth Amendment, 368; for Federal jurors, 383-85; for United States officials, 385

O'Conor, Charles, counsel for Clay, 266, 267; counsel for Davis, 295; moved to release Davis, 306; advised Davis to flee, 308

Old Capitol Prison, D. C., prisoners in, 14

Olden, Governor Charles S., recommended Memminger's pardon, 256

Olney, Richard, Secretary of State, 386

Oppenheim, Lassa F. L., definition of civil war, 105-6

Ord, General Edward O. C., 120

Orr, Governor James L., advised Vance's pardon, 218

Orr, Dr. John, case of, 13

Osborne vs. *United States,* no benefit of amnesty, 416-17

Overton, John, took Lincoln's oath and claimed property, 236-37

Owens, Representative William C., 388

Owsley, Dr. Frank L., letter to author on Lee, 134 n. 29

Padelford, Edward, claim allowed as benefit of pardon, 402-4

Palmer, General John M., endorsed Colquitt's petition, 173

Palmetto flag, of South Carolina, 15

Paradise, Pa., petition to punish Davis, 282

Pardon, defined, xvii, 417

Pardon attorneys, need for and activities of, 144-47

Pardons, Lincoln form for, 68-69; character of petitions, 137; approved by governors, 138; number overestimated, 139-43; President overworked by, 142-43; pardon board recommended, 142-43; second form by Johnson, 143-44; charges for, 151-52; delays in granting, 239 and n. 28; appreciated by recipients, 239; revoked, 239-40; recipients in particular exceptions, 240; number specially issued by Johnson, 227, 240-41, 340

Pargoud, John F., claim allowed as benefit of pardon, 400-1

Parker, Governor Joel, recommended Memminger's pardon, 256

Parole, defined, xvii

Patterson, Mrs. David Trotter, daughter of Andrew Johnson, 162, 163

Patton, Governor Robert M., opposition to re-enfranchisement of, 363, 365

Patton, Captain W. H., 287 n. 18

Pease, former Governor E. M., recommended release of Reagan, 247

Pemberton, General John C., re-enfranchised, 387

Perry, Benjamin F., Provisional Governor of South Carolina, account of pardoning duties, 138; recommended Memminger's pardon, 256

Perry, Governor Madison S., urged to prevent Federal occupation of Pensacola, 260

Pettus, ex-Confederate Governor John J., 277

Phelps, Justice Peter T., 14

Phillips, Wendell, doubted constitutionality of Lincoln's amnesty, 44-45; on Confiscation Act, 45; criticized by Johnson, 320

"Philo Parsons," overpowered by Captain Beall, 76

Pickett, General George E., petition denied, 176-77

Pierce County, Wis., petition to punish Davis, 282

Pierpont, Governor Francis H., on number in Virginia relieved by Lincoln's amnesty, 225-26

Pierrepont, Judge Edward, 16

Pillow, General Gideon J., request for restoration of mules denied, 176

Pleasants, M. F., assisted Attorney-General in pardon cases, 139-40

Pollard, Edward A., on Lincoln's amnesty, 42

Pomeroy, Senator Samuel Clark, on freedmen's obtaining land, 232

Pope, General John, dispatch to Mrs. Ewell, 163

Porter, Admiral David D., believed Lincoln approved Sherman-Johnston agreement, 90

Porter and McDonald, law firm engaged to defend Captain Castleman, 83 and n. 16

Powell, Dr. Robert J., pardon agent for North Carolina, 151, 191; received list of petitions, 195; requested relief for nine persons, 364

Pratt, Senator Daniel D., believed disfranchisement a source of evil in the South, 374

Prentice, Major Clarence J., Lincoln's clemency to, 80-82

Prentice, George D., appealed to Lincoln for clemency to son, 80-82

Prison camps, instructions to commander at Chicago, 23; location of, 28 n. 33, 158 n. 8; evacuations after war, 154; General Orders No. 109 for releases, 155-56; releases after taking the oath of allegiance, 158; releases especially beneficial to prisoners in the South ordered, 159; ill prisoners in, 159; total number of prisoners, 159, 161; details of releases, 160-61; generals last to be released, 163

Prisoners of war, problem of, 16-17; paroled on oath, 17-21; cartel of exchange, 23; policy at Washington, 24-25; three classes of, 57-58; questions asked, 58; policy of releasing suspended, 59; special consideration for deserters, 59-60; liberated from Camp Douglas, 60-61; classified by Lonn, 61-62; numbers and releases after end of war, 153-61

Prison funds, 160 n. 11

Pritchard, Colonel B. D., report on capture of Davis, 283 n. 11

Prize Cases, Civil War characterized by Supreme Court, xv

Quakers, not excused from taking amnesty oath, 193-94

Quincy, Ill., ropemaker of, 282

Quinn, Captain Morton E., threatened with court-martial, 177

Radicals, refused to seat Southerners in Congress, 126; angered by Johnson's second amnesty, 344-45; estimated armed strength, 347-48; desire to impeach Johnson increased, 350-51; thought British practice warranted amnesty in the United States, 350-51; displeased with Johnson's third amnesty, 356; opposition to Johnson's universal amnesty, 358-60; told to move slowly in re-enfranchising, 364; opposed to re-enfranchising Patton, 365; and civil rights for Negroes, 374ff., 377-78; had passed on, 389

Rainey, Joseph H., asked civil rights for Negroes, 376-77

Raleigh *Sentinel*, promoted Graham's pardon, 200; opposed Holden and supported Worth, 209

Raleigh *Standard*, attacked Lincoln's plan of reconstruction, 41, 189 and n. 7; attacked by mob, 207; supported Holden, 209-11; on defeat of Holden, 211

Raleigh *State Journal*, attacked by Holden's friends, 207

Ralph Meldrim et al vs. U. S., widow of unpardoned deceased denied claim to proceeds of sale of cotton, 409

Ramsey, Dr. James G., pardoned, 195

Randall, James G., on relationship between C. S. A. and U. S. A., 103-4, 422

Reagan, John H., imprisonment and release, xx, 247; on Lincoln at Hampton Roads, 90; petitioned from Fort Warren, 245-47; urged Texans to submit to reconstruction, 247

Rebellion, punishment for, 5-8

Restoration of the Confederate States, Lincoln's plan, 36-37; Johnson's plan foreshadowed by Lincoln, 112-13; North Carolina plan applied to other states, 113-14; congressional plan, 330-31, 336, 337; interpretation of laws favorable to Southerners not applied, 335-36

Revised Statutes of the United States, repeal of section excluding former rebels from armed services, 385-86

Rice, General B. F., delivered pardon to General Bankhead, 68

Richmond, Ky., home of Burnam and Caperton families, 60-61

Richmond, Va., petition to release Davis, 285

Richmond *Dispatch*, denounced Lincoln's amnesty, 40-41

Richmond *Enquirer*, attributed Lincoln's amnesty to smallpox, 41 n. 27

Richmond *Republic*, advocated clemency for Davis, 293

Richmond *Sentinel*, disapproved of Lincoln's amnesty, 41

Riddle, George R., opposed pardoning Pillow, 176

Rise and Fall of the Confederate Government, The, by Jefferson Davis, ending quoted, 304

Rock Island, prison post, 60

Rogers, Zion H., benefited by amnesty law, 378

Rosecrans, General William S., suggested amnesty, 32

Ross, Senator Lewis W., desired Vance's pardon, 218

Sailor's Creek, battle at, 161

Santa Anna, treatment of compared to that of Davis, 286-87 and n. 18

Saulsbury, Senator Eli, on removing disability in Fourteenth Amendment, 323; recommended repeal of Confiscation Act, 328-29

Savannah *Republican*, on pardon of Colonel E. W. Gantt, 36; scorned Lincoln's amnesty, 41-42; on Lee's feelings when applying for pardon, 128; on the pardoning problem, 143; on pardon of Anderson, 226-27

Schenck, General Robert C., on restoring political privileges, 322

Schofield, General John M., relations with Vance, 201, 203

Schurz, Carl, reported on reconstruction, 316-17; champion of liberalism, 370; on examples of amnesty in Europe, 375

Scott, Isaac, claim not granted to deceased, 412-13. *See also* "Gold Case" *and Ralph Meldrim et al* vs. *U. S.*

Scott, General Winfield, sent General Baker to Richmond, Va., 151 n. 26; compared with Lee, 131-34; defended Washington, 253-54

Scott County, Ky., petition to release Davis, 285

Section 13, Confiscation Act. *See* Confiscation Act of July 17, 1862

Seddon, John A., in Libby Prison and Fort Pulaski, 271; petition discussed by Cabinet, 271-72; petition granted, 272

Semmes, Admiral Raphael, escaped from sinking "Alabama," 178-79; later service, surrender, parole, and arrest, 179-80; denial of charges, 180-81; controversy over character of offense, 181-83; justified secession, 182 n. 44; Gamaliel Bradford on, 183-84; uncertainty of trial, 184-85; released, 184-85, 301; tirade against Johnson, 185-86; lost suit for claim, 415-16

Semmes, Mrs. Raphael, pleaded for husband's release, 185

Settle, Evan E., quoted on Union, 390-91

Seward, William H., letter from Michael Berry, 15; refusal to recommend Shiff's pardon, 80; and Howell Cobb's petition, 168; advice on Seddon's petition, 272; influence of Lincoln on, 315; blamed for Johnson's leniency, 333; contribution to Johnson's second amnesty, 342-43

Seymour, Horatio, nominated for President, 355

Shea, George, counsel for Clay, 266; counsel for Davis, 295

Sherman, General William T., on Lincoln's clemency, 89; terms to Johnston, 99; relations with Vance, 203-4, 218

Sherman-Johnston agreement, terms of, 98-99; anathema to Johnson, the Cabinet, and Grant, 99; disappointment of Sherman, 99

Shiff, Doctor, petition denied, 79-80

Sickles, General Daniel E., concerning operation of Lincoln's amnesty, 72; plea for release of Davis, 169-170; Military Governor of Carolina district, 219; recommended universal amnesty, 334

Simms, Colonel William E., last individual relief, 338

Slavery, question of emancipation, 32-33; not restored by amnesty, 34, 111; effect of abolition on Southern economy, 115; as cause of Civil War, 137; recognized as extinct, 172, 204; hope that secession would preserve, 173; fear that prolonging war would endanger, 206; hope for compensation for loss of slaves, 239; emancipation seen as calamity, 265

Slidell, John, denied proceeds of sale, 414. *See also* Bragg, General Braxton, and *Brown* vs. *United States*

Smith, General E. Kirby, invasion of Kentucky, 18; relieved, 387

Smith, Gerrit, 312

South Bend *Register*, opposed Johnson's second amnesty, 345

South Carolina, Palmetto flag of, 15; desertions in, 66; memorialized Johnson for Davis, 289

Southern Claims Commission, evidence in archives of, xx

Southerners, Unionism among, xix-xx; fears and plight, 115, 136; emigration and return, 115-16, 128-29; regarded as traitors, 115-16; hope in amnesty, 117; anxiousness for relief, 136; distaste for treason, 357-58; uncertainty concerning Johnson's second amnesty, 349; Davis a hero to, 374

Speed, Attorney-General James, advised Johnson to proclaim amnesty, 109-10; announced rules for operation of amnesty, 114-15; spoke to committee to see Johnson, 223-24; opinion on trying Davis, 295 n. 34; discrimination between prize and municipal courts, 394-95; ruling on seizures under Confiscation Act, 399

Speed, Joshua F., Lincoln's friendship for, xiv

Spence, Thomas, on American Union, 290-91

Stanbery, Attorney-General Henry, recommended Anderson's pardon, 174; advised Vance's pardon, 218; interpretation of reconstruction laws, 335; instructions voided by Congress, 336-37; ruling on benefits of pardon, 399

Stanley, Henry M., dual allegiance of, 17-18

Stanton, Edwin M., directed release of prisoners, 10-11; ordered Cobb released, 168; displeased with reliefs under thirteenth exception, 231; advised second general amnesty, 340

States' rights, a waning principle, 132, 133; origin in colonial times, 182 n. 44; question of coercing states, 198; devotion to, 203; Jefferson and Madison as authors of, 246, 248, 290; assertions of, 256; still believed in, 265; Lincoln on, 288; famous advocates of, 290-91; early manifestation of, 291

Steedman, General James B., advised pardoning property owners quickly, 229-30

Stephens, Alexander H., Lincoln's friendship for, xiv; opposed secession, xix-xx; imprisonment and release, xx, 250; nephew received favor from Lincoln, 74-75; on Lincoln at Hampton Roads, 90; motives in petitioning for pardon, 245; pleadings from Fort Warren, 247-49; influences in behalf of, 249-50

Stephens, Lieutenant John A., recipient of Lincoln's clemency, 74-75 and n. 2

Stephens, Linton, interviewed Johnson on behalf of brother, 249

Stephens, Dr. Robert, account of Lincoln's clemency, 74-75

Stephens, William N., oath of, 11

Stevens, Thaddeus, approved clemency for Clay, 269; criticized by Johnson, 320; promoted Fourteenth Amendment, 321; on effect of pardon, 322; proposed radical reconstruction law, 332-33; prevented relief for Patton, 365

Stewart, Senator William Morris, quoted on universal amnesty, 389

Stuart, Alexander H. H., worked for reunion, xix

Summit Hill, Pa., petition to punish Davis, 283

Sumner, Senator Charles, on freedmen's obtaining land, 232; criticized by Johnson, 320; for civil rights for Negroes as condition of amnesty, 377

Supreme Court, defined nature of Civil War, xv; declared against military commission in conviction of Milligan *et al.*, 102; declared pardon and amnesty synonymous, 311; on power of President's pardon, 331-32; threatened in Congress, 332; fixed date of end of Civil War, 413 and n. 42. *See also under individual cases*

Surratt, Mrs. Mary, 312, 314

Swain, Governor David L., opposed appointment of Holden, 188; pardoned to become president of University of North Carolina, 195; and requests to pardon Vance, 202

Swann, Thomas, Governor of Maryland, 347

Tattnall, Captain Josiah, letter from General Lee, 124. *See also* "Merrimac"

Taylor, General Zachary, Lincoln's support for, xiv; Davis's resolution of thanks to, 279-80

Tevis, Joshua, attorney, 12

Texas, pioneers of, petitioned for Davis, 286-89

Thirteenth exception from amnesty, nature of, 112; affected more than all other exceptions, 221 and n. 1; pleased Johnson, 221-22; Grant and Seward objected, 221-22; Blaine's opinion, 222; a serious disability, 222-

24; committee asked President for relief, 223-24; probable effect of, 225; objection to numerous reliefs from, 227; number reported relieved, 227, 319, 340; omitted from Johnson's second amnesty, 343

Thomas, General George N., released Howell Cobb, 168

Thomas, General Lorenzo, inquired concerning exchange of prisoners, 23-24

Thompson, Jacob, member of Confederate Canadian commission, 76; arrested, 270

Tocqueville, Alexis de, on America Union, 290-91

Toombs, Robert, escape to Cuba, 174-75; exile and return, 175; interview with Johnson, 175-76; exile referred to, 244, 381

Tourgee, A. W., advised caution in re-enfranchising, 364

Treason, definition of and punishment for, 4; Davis's opinion, 102-3; opinion of the Supreme Court, 103-4; Randall's double-status theory, 103-4; Vattel on, 104-5; Oppenheim on, 105; Bradley T. Johnson on, 106-7; municipal rather than international law applied, 108-9; indictments continued, 241-43

Tredegar Iron Works, 222, 226

Trenholm, George A., petition and parole, 257

Trimble, Judge L. D., interviewed Johnson, 275-76

Truman, Benjamin C., report on condition in South, 319

Trumbull, Senator Lyman, opinion on punishment for treason, 5; believed only Congress could authorize amnesties, 327; letter from Sickles recommending universal amnesty and suffrage, 334

Turner, Josiah, Jr., late secessionist, 194; petition a criticism of the Democratic Party, 197-99; pardon delayed, 217, 219-20

Underwood, Judge John C., on treatment of South, 5; and indictments at Norfolk, 120; delayed action on Major Cox, 235; not desired in trial of Davis, 309 and n. 63

United States Circuit Court for Kentucky, records, 12

United States Court of Claims, evidences of Unionism presented to, xx. *See also under individual cases*

United States Supreme Court. *See* Supreme Court

Vallandigham, Clement L., xiv

Vance, Zebulon B., late secessionist, 194; commendable attitude in 1865, 201-4; reason for arrest and imprisonment, 201; reason for parole from prison, 202; need for pardon, 202; petitioned for pardon, 202-3; numerous requests for pardon, 202, 204; elected Governor of North Carolina, 205-6, 208; break with Holden, 206-8; no approval of pardon expected, 208; feared imprisonment again, 211; blamed Holden and Stanton for Johnson's delay, 217; aided by missionary Bagley, 218; finally pardoned, 218

Vanderbilt, Cornelius, signed Davis's bail-bond, 306

Van Riswick, 418-19

Vattel, Emmerich de, on treason and civil war, 104-5

Venable, Abram, original secessionist, 194; pardoned, 215-16

Vicksburg, victory at, encouraged amnesty, 31

Vicksburg *Herald*, favored another registration, 345-46

Virginia House of Burgesses, spurned Lincoln's amnesty, 40

Vogdes, General Israel, hesitated to receive Union soldiers, 157

Voorhees, Senator Daniel W., 386

Vroom, Governor Peter D., recommended clemency for Memminger, 256

Wade, Senator Benjamin, expressed confidence in Johnson, 95-96

Walker, Robert J., financier, 270

Wallach, Charles S., property restored to children, 418-20

Warden, W. W., 355

Wardlaw, Judge David L., in defense of Mrs. Davis, 296-97

War Department, transfer of state prisoners to custody of, 16

Waring, James J., claim and pardon of, 408

Washington, D. C., prisoners confined in, 20

Washington, George, loyalty of, 134; granted amnesty, 327 and n. 27

Washington College, Lee became president of, 127

Washington *Daily Chronicle,* 273

Washington *National Intelligencer,* on Johnson's second amnesty, 349

Washington *National Republican,* edited by Holden, 216

Wayne, Justice John M., 255 n. 20

Webster, Daniel, passenger of Michael Berry, 15

Welles, Gideon, on disintegration of the Confederacy, 31-32; on Lincoln's sagacity and wisdom, 33; on Lincoln's attitude toward Confederates, 92-93; in Semmes case, 179-85; on Grant's attitude toward Confederates, 272; not favorable to dropping Davis case, 310; part in formulating Johnson's second amnesty, 342-43; on pardoning power, 350-51; on Johnson and the Democratic nomination for President, 355

Wheeler, General Joseph, assaulted, 177; defended Republican administration, 387, 390, 391

Whig party, Lincoln's support of, xiv

White, Representative Harry, 387

Willey, Senator William T., desired Vance's pardon, 218

Wilson, Bryce, oath questioned, 243

Wilson, Clay. *See* Castleman, Captain John B.

Wilson, Henry, candidate for Vice-President, 379

Wilson, James F., on removing disabilities, 366

Wilson, General James H., Davis's conversation with, 281

Winslow, John A., Captain of "Kearsage," sank "Alabama," 178-81; recommended engineer of "Alabama," 186; on Semmes, 186 n. 51

Wirz, Henry, 312

Women, provisions for applicants for pardon, 136-37; as agents for pardon seekers, 146ff.; seeking pardon, 164; seeking clemency for relatives, 83, 162ff., 185, 254-55, 265ff., 269, 296-99; seeking clemency for Davis, 285-86; seeking benefit of amnesty, 79, 396, 400-1, 409, 412, 413, 420

Wood, Benjamin, editor, 266

Wood, Mayor Fernando, recommendation to Lincoln, 30-31

Wood, John Taylor, relieved, 388

Woodruff, William E., insincere oath-taker, 65-66

Worth, Jonathan, provisional treasurer of North Carolina, 195; candidate for Governor, 209; assumed office and recognized by Johnson, 211-12; delay in receiving Holden's advertised pardons, 212-13; petitioners to, 213; petitions forwarded by, 214-15; delay in recommending Vance's petition, 216-17; urged lifting ban on Graham and Turner, 217

Wright, Crafts J., Davis to, 281

Yulee, David Levy, defense of, 258-59; evidence against, 260-63; paroled and pardoned, 263